FIFTY

GREAT MIGRATION COLONISTS

TO NEW ENGLAND

&

THEIR ORIGINS

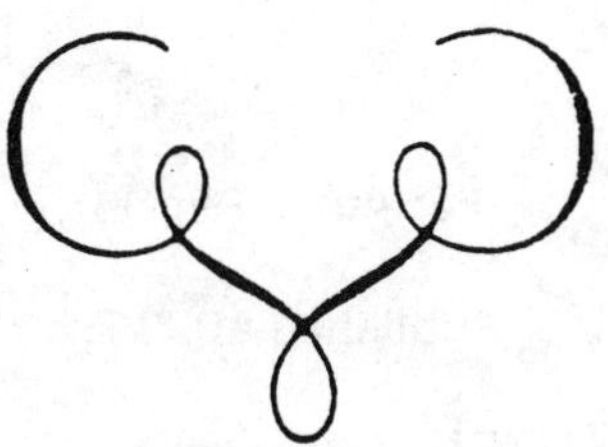

by

JOHN BROOKS THRELFALL

Madison, Wisconsin

1990

Other Books by the Author

Heads of Families at the Second Census of the United States in the Year 1800, New Hampshire

Facsimile Reprint

Published 1992 By

HERITAGE BOOKS, INC.

1540E Pointer Ridge Place, Bowie, Maryland 20716
(301) 390-7708

ISBN 1-55613-685-4

The South part of New-England, as it is Planted this yeare, 1634.

INTRODUCTION

This collection of biographical-genealogical monographs is intended to present everything of any consequence that is presently known about the fifty colonists herein presented. It is hoped that this work will inspire others to publish the same sort of material as it is discovered or expanded for other colonists who settled in New England during the great seventeenth century migration. Perhaps in time, a series of such books might be published so that together they would constitute an encyclopedia of the first generation to New England.

It is always a great satisfaction to discover just where these colonists come from. Generally, we know from the history of the great migration that these people came almost entirely from England or Scotland. Determining just what parish they came from has been difficult, and only a fraction of the total has thus far been located.

As each year goes by, more parish registers get transcribed or searched, more wills are read, other obscure records are examined, and the origins of a few more settlers are discovered. With more material being put into computers and the search process thus being automated, discoveries should increase. Still, there are some colonists whose origins will surely forever remain a mystery, particularly the many Smiths, and others with common names. I have provided monographs for several such settlers, in particular, for four Smiths. These sketches tell just about all that is presently known of these men. For some colonists, I present several generations of their recently discovered ancestors in England. For a number of others, their ancestral roots have long been known, but I have been able to extend back several more generations or otherwise contribute more information which ought to be of interest.

While I have searched diligently for material on these various families, rest assured that there is still some more material to be found. No one should assume that the well of records is yet completely dry. Every year sees more primary material published or otherwise made available. Now and then, someone stumbles on a bit of pertinent information while searching for something else.

These sketches have been written in a format that hopefully will be readable and pleasing to the average family historian. Some specific references are given within the body of the texts, such as the references to wills. At the end of each monograph is a list of the general sources. I do not choose to clutter the material with superfluous details, explanatory notes and references that make reading tedious. A baptismal record obviously comes from a parish record and one certainly doesn't need a page number when the entries are in chronological order. The reader is expected to be competent enough to locate any of this material from the information given, should verification ever be desired. Any unusual sources certainly are explained.

Some material already long in print has been transcribed more or less verbatum. There is no intention to claim otherwise. The only reason for repeating such material is to provide continuity of the several generations for the reader and to provide a complete account of a colonist or his ancestor. For example, the Peck genealogy has been thoroughly done by Mr. Peck and others. The account of Nicholas Babbs, a Peck ancestor, has not been previously published. The Babbs line would be unclear to the reader without the inclusion of the several generations of Pecks that show the connection. Due credits are rendered to all those earlier genealogists who discovered so much upon which these articles are built. Most genealogy is built on earlier work by others, and so this work is also.

So, let this volume be the first with more to come. I hope that others will more or less approve the format and follow it.

Family historians are free to copy this material at will. I hope that the format and the material will be attractive enough that parts may be photocopied and used in family histories without the need to rewrite them and reset type. Permission to copy from this work is hereby granted.

John B. Threlfall
Madison, Wisconsin

TABLE OF CONTENTS

JOHN ANDREWS, called Lieutenant John Andrews or John Andrews, Sr., to distinguish him from Corporal John Andrews who lived at the same time in Ipswich, Massachusetts, was born in England, it is supposed, about 1620, and died at Chebacco Parish in Ipswich on 20 April 1708. The names of his parents or his origin in England have not been found. He married about 1645, Jane Jordan, the daughter of Stephen Jordan of Ipswich and later of Newbury, Massachusetts. She was living in 1705 when her husband made his will. In a deposition of 1701, he was stated as being aged 80 and she one year younger, which would place their births about 1621 and 1622.*

He first appears in Ipswich records about 1637 when he served in the Pequot War, for which service he was granted an eight acre lot. It being unlikely that he would serve in the war if younger than 17, he was probably born about 1620, even though several depositions make his birth as late as 1621. It has been thought that he may have been a nephew of Captain Robert Andrews, master of the ship *Angel Gabriel* (wrecked off Pemaquid in 1635) and later keeper of the *Whitehorse Inn* at Ipswich, but no evidence has been found.

Lieutenant John Andrews was a house carpenter and farmer and lived in that part of Ipswich which, in 1679, was organized as Chebacco Parish and in 1819 was incorporated as the town of Essex, Massachusetts. His name is frequently found in the land and court records of Ipswich, where he accumulated considerable property and was a man of some distinction.

He appears first in the court records in December 1641 versus Mr. Samuel Symonds, the subject of the suit not known. In November 1645 he was in court as plaintiff against Mr. John Clark regarding a debt on bond.

In 1646 he and others gave a day's work carting binds in lieu of the rate (tax) toward the cart bridge then just built. The same year, on 30 November 1646, John Andrews of Ipswich, husbandman, sold to widow Mary Webster of the same town:

*In November 1659, he deposed at about 40, in November 1668 at about 48, in March 1678 at about 57; he died on 20 April 1708 "aged 90".

all ye island lately in possession of George Carr, twenty acres more or less, bounded by the Labour-in-Vain Creek, west, Thomas Emerson's farm southeast, Thomas Boreman's farm on the northeast, which said Island lyeth in the town of Ipswich.

As John Andrews, Senior, he subscribed to the allowance of Major Denison for his military service in 1648.

On 26 March 1652, the ship *Eagle* of London was cast away on the northeast side of the Isle of Sable, but most of the cargo was saved and transferred to another ship. John Andrews of Ipswich was the commander of this vessel which carried copper bars, casks of wine, brass kettles, iron, guns, powder, etc. This could have been Corporal John Andrews, who was then about 24, but it would seem more likely to have been Lieutenant John, who was then about 33, a more likely age for the command of a ship.

He and his wife, Jane, of Ipswich, sold land there to John Choate on 27 September 1660.

In September 1662, he deposed in a court case. This could only be Lieutenant John, because Corporal John Andrews had died the preceding March and their sons were yet underage.

In September 1663, 5, and 6, he was a trial juror. In 1666, he was called a carpenter of Ipswich. In 1669, he served on the Grand Jury.

... 25 October 1673, - John Andrews Senr of Ipswich - in consideration of a small parcell of marsh & £8, deeded to Henry Bennett, of the same towne, all that my Division lott, being a middle lott granted to me by the towne of Ipswich aforsd, No: 52 ... at Castle Neck ... upon Wiggwam Hill...

The same day Henry Bennet deeded to John Andrews the marsh which was a part of my ffarme lyeing neare to the foote bridge over the creeke being cumpassed by a creeke & ditched out to part it from the farme, containing one acre 7 a halfe ...

20 November 1673 - John Andrews Senr. of Chebacco, carpenter, bought of Richard Lee, planter, all that six acres of marsh, more or less, scituate, lyeing and being on the ffar syde of that creek that bounds Proctor's Land & bounded by that creeke, buting down to a cove toward Goodman Dane's Island to the great creeke and so upon a straight line up to that creeke to Proctor's ground ... for nyne pounds in corn.

19 March 1673/4 - John Andrews, Senior, and wife Jane, of Ipswich, sold land there to Sergt. Thomas Burnham.

16 June 1674 - John Andrews of Ipswich, carpenter, bought of Samuel Symonds of Ipswich All that pcell of his land or lott ... which Killigresse Rosse now holdeth ... containing three acres, etc.

29 October 1675 - John Andrews of Ipswich, bought of Robert Cross, Jr. of Ipswich, two parcels of marsh and land in Ipswich at an Iland ... in Chebacho River, one parcell conteineing six acres ... the other parcelle of six acres of marsh & one acre of upland being upon the same Iland.

In 1675, he was on a committee to lay out land near Ipswich.

On 13 July 1676, he bought of Nathaniel Emerson a three acre lot on Hogg Island.

Lieutenant John Andrews entered, in the town book, according to law:

One Iron gray Horse
One White mare with a long tayle

21 November 1676 - John Andrews, Senr. of Ipswich bought from Robert Cross, Jr. of Ipswich 10 acres of marsh in Chebacco by the river.

30 June 1677 - John Andrews, Senr. of Ipswich ... for and in consideration of that natural affection I doe beare to James Gidding and Elizabeth, his wife, my daughter ... conferme ... one moyaty and halfe part of that land at Averill's Hill, the upland as it is already parted where the said James and my son John Andrews now dwell, and also halfe the meadow belonging thereunto...

16 June 1678 - John Andrews, Senr. of Ipswich, carpenter, bought of John Cogswell and his wife Margaret, a parcel of upland and marsh about 40 acres, also, an island of marsh & thatch of about 2 acres, which lyeth by Goodman's old saw mill, bounded by land of Goodman Coleman's fence, by Clark's Brook, by Gloster line & by Chebacco River, &c, Andrews to pay yearly to Cogswell 20 in pork during the term of the said lease.

In 1687, John Andrews, chairman of the selectmen of Ipswich, was confronted with a decree by Governor Edmund Andros which ordered them to make up a list of property owners and estates on which a new tax of 1 penny per pound value and 20 pence per head was to be levied.

Mr. Wise, the minister, reported to Governor Andros what they had done, or more exactly, what they had refused to do. The consequence was that he, John Andrews, William Goodhue, John Appleton, Robert Kinsman and Thomas French were arrested and carted off to jail in Boston. Here they were denied bond for their appearance in court. Finally tried, they were found guilty of contempt and high misdemeanor, and held in prison another twenty-one days before being sentenced. Mr. Wise left the following account of their mistreatment.

> We, John Wise, John Andrews, Sen., Robert Kinsman, William Goodhue, Jr., all of Ipswich, about the 22nd of August, 1687, were, with several principal inhabitants of Ipswich, met at Mr. John Appleton's and there discoursed and concluded, that it was not the town's duty in any way to assist that ill method of raising money without a general assembly, which was generally intended by above said Sir Edmund, and his Council, as witness a late act issued out by them for that purpose. The next day in a general town meeting of the inhabitants of Ipswich, we the above named J. Wise, J. Andrews, R. Kinsman, W. Goodhue with the rest of the town, there met, (none contradicting) and gave our assent to the vote then made. The ground of our trouble, our crime, was the copy transmitted to the Council, viz: 'At a legal town-meeting, August 23, assembled by virtue of an order from John Usher, Esq. for choosing a commissioner to join with the Selectmen to assess the inhabitants according to an act of His Excellency the Governor, and Council, for laying of rates. The town then considering that this act doth infringe their liberty, as free English subjects of His Majesty, by interfering with the Statute Laws of the land, by which it was enacted, that no taxes should be levied upon the subjects without the consent of an Assembly, chosen by the freeholders for assessing of the same, they do therefore vote that they are not willing to choose a commissioner for such end, without said privilege, and, moreover, consent not, that the Selectmen do proceed to lay any such rate, until it be appointed by a General Assembly, concurring with Governor and Council.'
>
> We, the complainants, with Mr. John Appleton and Thomas French, all of Ipswich, were brought to answer for the said vote out of our own county thirty or forty miles into Suffolk and in Boston, kept in jail for contempt and high misdemeanor, as our mittimus specifies, and upon demand, denied the privilege of *habeas corpus*, and from prison overruled to answer at a Court of Oyer and Terminer in Boston. Our Judges were Joseph Dudley of Roxbury, Stoughton of Dor-

chester, John Usher of Boston, and Edward Randolph. He that officiates as Clerk and Attorney in the case, is George Farwell. The Jurors only twelve, and most of them (as is said) non-freeholders of any land in the colony, some of them strangers and foreigners, gathered up (as we suppose) to serve the present turn. In our defense was pleaded the repeal of the Law of assessment upon the place; also the Magna Charta of England, and the Statute Laws, that secure the subject's properties and estates, &c. To which was replied by one of the judges, the rest by silence assenting, that we must not think the Laws of England follow us to the ends of the earth, or whither we went. And the same person (J. Wise abovesaid testifies) declared in open council, upon examination of said Wise, 'Mr. Wise, you have no more privileges left you, than not to be sold as slaves,' and no man in Council contradicted. By such Laws our trial and trouble began and ended. Mr. Dudley, aforesaid Chief Judge, to close up a debate and trial, trims up a speech that pleased himself (as we suppose) more than the people. Among many other remarkable passages to this purpose, he bespeaks the jury's obedience, who (we suppose) were very well preinclined, viz: 'I am glad,' says he, 'there be so many worthy gentlemen of the jury so capable to do the king's service, and we expect a good verdict from you, seeing the matter hath been so sufficiently proved against the criminals.'

NOTE: The evidence in the case, as to the substance of it, was, that we too boldly endeavored to persuade ourselves we were Englishmen and under privileges, and that we were, all six of us aforesaid, at a town-meeting of Ipswich aforesaid, and, as the witness supposed, we assented to the aforesaid vote, and, also, that John Wise made a speech at the same time, and said that we had a good God and a good King, and should do well to stand to our privileges.

The jury returned us all six guilty, being all involved in the same information. We were remanded from verdict to prison, and there kept one and twenty days for judgement. There, with Mr. Dudley's approbation, as Judge Stoughton said, this sentance was passed, viz: John Wise suspended from the ministerial function, fine £50, pay cost, £1000 bond; John Appleton, not to bear office, fine £50, pay cost, £1,000 bond; John Andrews, not to bear office, fine £30, pay cost, £500 bond; Robert Kinsman, not to bear office, fine £20, pay cost, £500 bond; William Goodhue, the same; Thomas French, not to bear office, fine £15, pay cost, £500 bond. These bonds were for good behavior for one year. We judge the total charges for one case and trial under one single information, involving us six men, above said, in expense of time and moneys to us and our relations for our necessary succor and support, to amount to more, but no less, than £400, money. Too tedious to illustrate more at this time, and so we conclude.**

**The Revolution in New England, justified: as quoted by Felt

This narration was drawn up at the request of the government, which succeeded that of Andros, so that it might be sent to England among the charges against him. Two years afterwards, the town made up the loss which the narrators incurred.

On 21 September 1687 Reverend John Wise, Thomas French, constable, John Appleton, clerk, John Andrews, Robert Kinsman, Nathaniel Treadwell, Thomas Hart and John Whipple, selectmen, realizing the power and arrogance of their oppressors, apologized, begged forgiveness, pled ignorance and promised to make up the tax list and assessment of persons and estates in the town.

On 4 October, John Andrews, "being aged, and suffering in person and property", petitioned to be bailed from prison. His plea was denied.

Thus, for having asserted their English rights, they were severely handled, imprisoned for several weeks, fined and placed under bond for their future behavior. This act of resistance has been called the foundation of American Democracy, and was the beginning of those events which eighty years later culminated in the American Revolution. It is commemorated in the seal of the town of Ipswich, which bears the motto, "The Birthplace of American Independence 1687."

After the expulsion of James from England and the introduction of William and Mary to the throne, Andros was put down by the people of Boston and sent to England. Before a new governor arrived, Mr. Wise and Nehemiah Jewett were chosen by Ipswich to meet in Boston with the representatives of the other towns to consult with the council about the public affairs of the colony. Sometime after, Mr. Wise brought an action against Chief Justice Dudley for denying him the privileges of *habeas corpus* and he recovered some damages.

During the unhappy days of the witchcraft delusion, John Andrews and his four sons were among those who signed the petition to save John Proctor and his wife, who had lived at Chebacco and had been tried and convicted of witchcraft at Salem. Although they could not save the husband, they put themselves on record as among the more tolerant ones.

On 8 October 1703, Lieutenant John Andrews gave to his "Eldest sonne John Andrews, house carpenter of ye same town", his homestead with eight acres of land, and confirmed to him other pieces of land, subject to certain conditions.

John Andrews made his will on 13 March 1705/6, bequeathing to his four sons and one daughter. He died two years later on 20 April 1708. He left 5 shillings to his son John, who had moved to Connecticut; the rest of his estate equally to his other four children who were to share equally in the cost of maintaining his wife who was to live with the daughter, Elizabeth.

Children, probably all born at Ipswich:

JOHN, b about 1646; m Judith Belcher, dau. of Jeremiah & Mary (Lockwood) Belcher, b 19 Aug. 1658; 8 ch.; in 1704 bought 550 acres in Norwich, Conn. (that part now in Preston) and sold his Ipswich property at the same time. He d at Norwich 19 May 1717 (T.R. 1:68). In his youth, he and his brother William and a cousin Stephen Cross were convicted of ripping up a bridge, digging up the bones of an Indian Sagamore and other pranks. In 1667, a house carpenter.

WILLIAM, b about 1649; m 20 Oct. 1672, Margaret Woodward; 12 ch.; d 7 Feb. 1716/17 - g.s. at. Essex

ELIZABETH, b 1652; m prior to 1677, James Giddings, son of George & Jane (Tuttle) Giddings of Ipswich; she was alive in 1709

THOMAS, b about 1654; m 9 Feb. 1681/2, Mary Belcher, sister of Judith, b 12 July 1660; 2 ch. per his will; he d 22 March 1718/19 ae 64 - g.s. at Essex; his wife d 31 March 1731; he d testate

JOSEPH, b 1657; m 16 Feb. 1680/81, Sarah Ring, who was b 17 Aug. 1659, dau. of Daniel & Mary (Kinsman) Ring; 9 ch.; he made his will 13 Feb. 1724/5, pr. 5 March, naming his ch.; she was alive in 1714

Ref.: History of the Andrews Family, by H.F. Andrews, 1890; N.E.H.G.S. - 70; Maine Hist. & Gen. Recorder - 3,4; Hammatt; Quarterly Court Files; Essex Antiquarian, Vol. 3, pages 97-103

HERE LYES INTARRED
WHAT WAS MORTALL
OF JNSIGN WILLIAM
ANDREWS WHO
DIED FEBRUARY Ye 7
1716 AGED 67
YEARS

WILLIAM BARNES was born probably in England about 1610. Just when he came to New England is not known. His wife was named Rachel. They must have been married about the time he came to America, but whether in England or in New England is unknown.

William Barnes settled first in Salisbury, where he received land in the first division in 1640 and 1643. He was made freeman on 2 June 1641. He was among the first settlers of Amesbury about 1654, receiving land there at various times. In 1659, he was granted some of the "children's land" for a daughter. With his wife, he was presented at Court on 15 December 1642 for holding that the baptism of infants was not an ordinance of God. He served on the Trial Jury in 1648, 50, 51, 52, 63, and 66, and on the Grand Jury in 1653, 69, 72, 75, and 78. He was made a Commissioner-to-End-Small-Causes, that is, Justice of the Peace, in 1669. He was a selectman of the town in 1682 and served as the constable in 1673. He was a "house-carpenter".

In 1654, with others, he sued Richard Currier and William Osgood for felling and carrying away lumber.

He owned a one fourth share in a sawmill on the Powwow River in Salisbury. This mill was put into operation about 1652 and ran for ten to fifteen years, more or less without interruption. It had a capacity, when there was a sufficient flow of water, of about 1,000 feet of boards in a 24 hour run. The partners had an agreement regarding the mill and it was copied into the court records in 1679 when the town started an action to collect its due for the mill and timber rights. The gist of the partnership agreement follows:

4 November 1658 - whereas there is a saw mill in possession of Wm. Osgood, Phil. Challis, Wm. Barnes, Anthony Colby and Samuel Worcester, copartners with said Colby in one-fourth part of the mill in Salisbury upon Pawwaus river near the corn mill, they should keep it in good working order, and agreed to make good to Wm. Osgood the grant of the town; the timber to be equally divided among them and each partner to have the privilege of using the mill for sawing his own timber into boards or planks to be used only on the land where said Osgood now

dwells for building or repairing, provided they bring the timber to the mill already cut; if any one of them makes a new way to any parcel of timber, the others were to pay part of the cost if they used said way; if any one of them cleared the river for floating down logs to the saw mill, the others should bear part of the charge if they used the river for this purpose, etc.; each partner was to be allowed 3s. per day for what time he gave to repairs on the mill, if he be a good workman, and 4s. per day for making the head block and 3s. per day for a hinder head block and 2s. 6d. for a wallower or sweep; each partner was to provide saws for himself and the saws now at the mill to be equally divided, except those for oak; each partner was to take the mill to run for a week and so in order through the year, Willi. Osgood beginning, followed by Colby, Worcester, Barnes and Challis in order; each was to lay his boards and logs at the mill where they had formerly. Witnesses: Tho. Bradbury, Humphrey Verney, Rodger Easman and Jno Hoyt

William Barnes frequently bought and sold land. There are at least sixteen conveyances on record between 1650 and 1669. The last two were to his sons-in-law.

1668 - William Barnes of Salisbury, house-carpenter, for love, conveyed to his son-in-law John Hoyt, jr., of Salisbury, planter, 4 acres of marsh in Salisbury which I bought of Mr. Samuell Hall, bounded by George Martyn, Samuel Felloes, John Eaton, John Ilsley and Tho: Barnard. Witnesses: Tho: Bradbury and William Screven. Ack. 25 March 1672 before Samuel Dalton, commissioner.
(Old Norfolk Deeds)

22 October 1669 - William Barnes of Amesbury, house carpenter, for love, conveyed to my son in law Thomas Sargent of Amesbury, planter, meadow in Salisbury near *Barnes Island,* being parts of two lots, one of which I bought of Luke Heard, and the other of Josiah Cobham, bounded by a little creek, Roger Eastman, Barnes' Island, the main creek and Tho:Bradbury. Witnesses: Rebecka Maverick, Jean True and Tho: Bradbury, scr. Ack. by grantor, his wife Rachell yielding up her dower, 11 November 1669 before Robert Pike, commissioner. (Old Norfolk Deeds)

All his deeds were signed by mark, so it is apparent that he was illiterate.

William Barnes deposed in court in 1680 at age 70 years. His wife, Rachel, deposed the same year, aged 60 years. She died at Amesbury 9 February 1685/6, and he died there on 14 March 1697/8. He left the following will, dated 7 April 1696:

I William Barns of ye town of Almsbury in ye County of Essex in their Majests province of ye Massashusets Bay in New Engld: Being weake & infirme in body but through ye goodness of God of perfect memory & understanding Do make this my last will & testament ...

Imprimis I do .... Ratifie .... ye agreement about a drift way through my great Lott or farme adjoyning to ye Country pond in Almsbury unto Mr Thomas Wells now minister of Almsbury according to ... ye ... Agreemt made ... betwixt my Son in law John Hoyt Senr & sd Wells about ye same as it is now extant in a Script under both their hands Datd May ye twenty third day, An: Dom: one thousand six hundred eighty & eight

It: I give & Bequeath unto my daughter Mary Hoyt ....to keep or dispose of without controlle at her own pleasure after the death of her now husband John Hoyt of Almsbury all ye rest of my sd Great farme .... and yt ye sd John Hoyt her husband shall have ye use .... of it during ye terme of his naturall life onely.

It: I give .... unto my son-in-law John Prowse .... forever ye one half of my great swamp lott in Almsbury And one fourth part of my salt marsh .... wanting one third part thereof which I gave to Abigail Diamond her heirs or assigns forever

It: I give .... unto my Daughter Deborah wife to Samuel Davis of Almsbury.... all my land at a place.... called ye peek in Almsbury .... And also one half of my lott of land in Almsbury called ye childrens Land ....

It: I give .... unto my daughter Rachel wife unto Thomas Sargent of Almsbury .... my sixty acre lott .... at a place .... called ye Champion Green in Almsbury .... & one half.... my lot.... in Almsbury .... ye childrens land ....

It: I give ... unto my daughter Sarah wife to John Harvee of Almsbury my fourty acre lott of upland .... to be disposed of by her .... to ye children wch she hath had or may have by her former or now present husband ....

It: I give .... unto my daughter Rebecca wife unto Moses Morrel of Almsbury .....my dwelling house & homestead .....one half my great swamp lott ...." etc.

It: I give .... unto my Grandson William Barns Morrel son to sd Moses & Rebecca Morrel my Lott of Land in Almsbury which I purchased of Will: Huntington deceased ....

It: I give .... unto my Grand Daughter Sarah, Daughter to John & Mary Hoyt abovesd now wife to ffaun Clements of Newbury my Lott of Land in Almsbury at a place commonly called Briggsmore ....

It: I give .. unto James George Senr of Almsbury .. A piece of Land near his dwelling house in Almsbury which he now hath in possession

It: my will is yt my other Estate .... Be equally divided amongst all my Daughters ....

Finally I make .....my Sonns-in-law Thomas Sargent & Moses Morrel of Almsbury Joynt executors unto this my last will and testiment: April ye seventh day .... one thousand six hunded ninety & six.

William his mark Barnes

An Inventory of the Estate of William Barns of Almsbury, Dec'd Given in by the Executors, Thomas Serjantt & Moses Morrel of Almsbury and Apprized by Thomas Barnard Senr and Thomas Currier Senr and John Barnard of Almsbury according as in ye opinion of the Apprizers it is worth in pay March ye 25th 1698

Item	£
Homsteed, Houseing wth fences, privilidges & appertenances	140.
his grate lott adjoyning to ye country Pond . . .	50.
his lott in ye Champion Ground	50.
a Champion lott purchased of Wm Huntington . .	25.
a Childrens land lott £25, a bare hill lott £30 . .	55.
a Buggsmore lott	10.
his Right in ye Peek land upland and meadow . .	5.
a lott in ye Lyens mouth £8, a Grate Swamp lott £10	18.
his Goats meadow at ye Back River	3.
a lott of Meadow at ye beach Bars	60.
a peice of Meadow at Landers Cove	18.
a peice of Meadow adjoyning to John Prowse & an acre and halfe	10.
a peice of land out of Winslies lott given to Jeams George	.10
his Wareing apparel: Cloths, bible & other books .	8.
beds, bedsteads, bedding and curtains . . .	12.
all other household stufe, utensels, tools & Appertenances to Housekeeping and husbandry .	8.
two oxen & two Cows viz (one ox sparked £6 ye oth^r £5.15) (one Red cow £5 ye other £4.18)	21. 13
2 Swine 30/ , one ewe 12/	2. 2
Due to ye Estate from Mary Hoyt £9, Tho: Sergant £6, Moses Moret £4. 15s	19. 15
Totall	£ 516.

Children, born is Salisbury, except the last two:

MARY, b about 1639; m 23 June 1659, John Hoyt, jr.; 10 ch.; he was killed by Indians in Andover 13 Aug. 1696; she was living 1704

WILLIAM, b about 1641; d 11 June 1648

HANNAH, b 25 Jan. 1643/4; m John Prowse; 4 ch.; she d 27 May 1688; his estate admin. 2 Sept. 1706

DEBORAH, b 1 April 1646; m 19 Dec. 1663, Samuel Davis, son of Thomas & Cicely; 10 ch.; res. Haverhill; he d 10 Sept. 1696; she d 14 Jan. 1718/19

JONATHAN, b 1 April 1648; d.y.

RACHEL, b 30 April 1649; m 2 March 1667/8 at Salisbury, Thomas Sargent, son of William & Judith or Elizabeth (Perkins Sargent); he d 27 Feb. 1705/6 testate; she d 1717 testate; 12 ch.

SARAH, b about 1651, prob. at Amesbury; m 1, 8 Sept. 1670, Thomas Rowell, son of Valentine & Joanna (Pinder) Rowell, b 7 Sept. 1644; 5 ch.; he d 1684 testate; she m 2, about 1685, John Harvey of Boston; settled in Amesbury; he d 8 March 1705/6; she d 17 April 1720

REBECCA, b about 1653, prob. at Amesbury; m Moses Morrill; she received her father's homestead

Ref.: Essex County Quarterly Court Files; V.R.; Essex County Probate Files; Old Families of Salisbury and Amesbury, by David W. Hoyt, 1897-1919

WILLIAM BEAMSLEY, with his wife Anne, crossed the ocean as early as 1630 in one of the eleven vessels of the Winthrop Fleet. The first five ships sailed April 8th from Yarmouth, Isle of Wight, and arrived at Salem on 13 June and following days. The other half of the fleet sailed in May and arrived in July at various dates. About 700 colonists were in the group.

The surname Beamsley is a place name, having its origins in the village of Beamsley which lies within the bounds of the parishes of Addingham and Skipton in Yorkshire. Just where William Beamsley came from has not been discovered. There was, in the 16th and 17th centuries, a clan of Beamsleys living in Whitgift, Yorkshire. This parish is just 50 miles southeast by east from Beamsley. There is no record of a William Beamsley among them.

William Beamsley settled in Boston, where he first appears on record in 1632. The term *yeoman* was invariably applied to him in deeds, but when he became a member of the First Church of Boston on 2 August 1635, he was recorded as *Labourer.* On 25 May 1636, he was made a freeman. In 1637 he was granted 16 acres at Muddy River and in January 1637/8, it was surveyed or bounded. In 1641, he was paid by the town for about 10 rods of causeway built by him at Rumney Marsh, now Chelsea.

His wife Anne died, probably in December 1643 with the birth of Hannah or soon after. By 1645 he had remarried to Martha (Hallor) Bushnell, a widow with three children. He evidentally became a good step-father to these children, for he treated them equally with his own children in his will.

His home lot contained about one half acre near Merry's Point, later North Battery, and ran from Hanover Street thru to the bay. It lay between Salutation Alley (adjoining the widow Ann Tuttle's famous Salutation Inn) and what became Methodist Alley or Hanover Avenue. This Salutation Alley was originally only five and one half feet wide, and was created as a passageway between the Beamsley home and a piece of land sold by William to Henry Kemble. William and his family appear to have lived there at least until 1645 and probably until his death.

In 1644, he bought a shore lot near Merry's Point, probably an addition to his home lot. In March 1648/9, he was elected as one of four constables of Boston.

The following Boston records apply to him:

27 August 1649 - It is ordered that William Beamsley shall remove away his oyster shells from of the towne's hye way before his dore by the 1 of the 11th mo., on the penalty of 20s fine.

11 March 1650 - Mr Adam Winthrop, Wm Phillips, Wm Beamsley were chosen to joyne with the selectmen of the towne, to lay out the high wayes bye the new meeting howse.

12 April 1650 - the same three were chosen to lay out High Wayes at the North end of Towne.

24 February 1650/51 - William Beamsley hath Libertie granted to Warfe or peare before his propertie to low water marke, provided he goe no Broader there than his ground is at hie water mark.

28 July 1651 - William Beamsley and Jarratt Borne are chosen to see the Generall Fence at Muddy River to be put into repayre according to order.

26 April 1652 - Same appointments and order.

26 May 1656 - William Beamsley is fined 10s for receiving an inhabitant without license.

9 March 1656/7 - William Beamsley appointed Surveyor of Hyhway at Rumney Marsh. (He owned land at the north end of town as he was assessed highway taxes against it)

25 January 1657/8 - Elizabeth Blesdale was permitted to reside in Boston and William Beamsley was bound in a bond of £20 to save the town from any charge arising from her residence.

26 January 1662/3 - His widow asked the selectmen for permission for "stilling strong watters and retailing of the same, considering it hath been a former imploymt", etc.

In 1656 William Beamsley joined the Ancient and Honorable Artillery Company. He was designated as Ensign. He frequently witnessed documents and made various land purchases, including some of Hog Island in 1651, which he sold in 1657. On 14 September 1658 (the date of his will) he confirmed by deed the land, house and orchard adjoining his own on which his daughter Anne and her husband, Ezekiel Woodward, had lived for about seven years.

On 14 September 1658 William Beamsley made his will. He died two weeks later on the 29th of September. In his will he named his own four children and the three children of his wife. His widow Martha signed a deposition on 28 October 1658. From 1659 to 1668, a number of deeds were made by heirs to clear the title to the land he had owned.

THE WILL OF WILLIAM BEAMSLEY
14 September 1658

In the name of God Amen, I William Beamsley, being sick in body, but of a perfect memory, praised be God, do make and ordain this my last will and testament, in manner and form following. First I committ my body unto the earth and bequeath my spirit to God that gave it. First In general I make my wife full executrix and administratrix of all my houses, lands, orchards, goods and chattels whatsoever, that she shall enjoy and possess the same, unto her own proper use, as long as she shall live, provided she shall let Mercy have that chamber wherein she now lies for her own, and that there shall be with all conveniency made therein a chimney, and she to enjoy it during her widowhood. And I desire that my wife may take the care and charge of her and see that she wants neither meat, drink nor clothing during the time of her widowhood. And further my will is that after my wife's decease, my whole estate shall be then prized and set to sale, the whole estate that is then left to be equally distributed amongst all my children, namely Anne Woodward, Grace Graves, mercy Wilborne, Hannah Beamsley, Edward Bushnell, Elizabeth Page, Mary Robison. And in case any of these die unpossessed, then it shall return to the next heirs. And my desire is that these three Bretheren, Thomas Clarke, Richard Gridley and Alexander Adams see this my will be fulfilled, according to their best endeavor. In witness whereof I have set to my hand and seal this fourteenth of September.

Sealed in the presence of us:
Thomas Clarke
Alex. Adams, sen.
The mark R G of
Richard Gridley

William Beamsley

Proved 28 October 1658

Inventory of the Estate of the Late Ensigne William Beamesly (who departed this life the 29th September last) taken this 15th October 1658 & Apprized per Thomas Clarke, Alexander Addames & John Richards

	£ s d
Imp's in Sylver	1.04.06
one cloth suite	3.00.00
one Serge suite	1.10.00
more wearing apparell	7.12.00
more wearing cloakes	2.00.00
haberdashery & broad cloth	6.01.06
Amunition	3.00.00
In ye parlor	
Bed, Drawers, Table	5.05.00
Linnen, Sheets, Napkins	3.02.07
Chest, Stooles & Looking glasse	.12.00
In Kitchin	
potts, Skillett, pewter	2.10.00
In the Hall	
One presse, wth Cushions	1.00.00
One Table wth Carpett, forms & joynt Stooles	1.02.00
Chaires, Buffett Stooles & Cushions	1.10.00
Handirons, Tongs, Spitt &c	1.00.00
Bookes	1.08.00

In hall chamber	
one standing bed, one trundle bed & furniture -	7.00.00
one Table, Side cubberd wth Carpetts, 2 stooles -	2.00.00
one Scarfe 5^{s}, pr Buttons & Silke 40^{s} - - -	2.05.00
8 small dressed skins 6^{s}, 17 yds linnen 32^{s}, 2 yds kersy 10^{s} } - -	2.08.00
In ye Shop	
16 gallons liquors - - - - - - - - -	4.00.00
5^{lb} wooll; & 11^{lb} hopps - - - - - - -	.16.00
In ye Sellar	
One still 10^{lb} - - - - - - - - - -	10.00.00
One hogshead molosses - - - - - - -	4.00.00
One still for herbes - - - - - - - -	.10.00
One Steele mill, one old grapmill, wth other Lumber	2.00.00
A loome, & tackling - - - - - - - -	1.15.06
2 Quintalls fish - - - - - - - - -	1.02.00
House & Land at Boston - - - - - - -	140.00.00
Land att Muddy River - - - - - - -	24.00.00
One Cow & Calfe - - - - - - - -	4.00.00
2 hoggs & 3 piggs - - - - - - - -	3.00.00
2 hives bees - - - - - - - - -	1.00.00
Thomas Clark Alex. Adames	251.14.01

Martha Beamsly deposed y^{s} to be A true Inventory of Wm Beamsly hir late husband's Estate to the best of hir knowledg, y^{t} when she knows more she will discover it.

Debts	
to m^{r} William Paine is due - - - - - -	4.00.00
to Capt. Walden " " - - - - - -	3.00.00

Children, born in Boston, baptized at First Church of Boston:

ANN, b 13 Feb. 1632/3; m Ezekiel Woodward; 9 ch.; she d 1670-72; he d 29 Jan. 1698/9

GRACE, b 10 Sept. 1635, bapt. 20th; m Samuel Graves of Ipswich; 5 ch.; she d 26 Nov. 1730

MERCIE, b 9 Dec. 1637, bapt. 10th; m 1, 17 Oct. 1656, Michael Willborne who d before her father's will (?26 Sept. 1658); 1 ch.; she m 2, 1658-9, Andrew Peters of Boston, Ipswich, Andover; 7 ch.; d 5 Nov. 1726

SAMUEL, b 31 Dec. 1640, bapt. 7 Feb. 1640/41; d April 1641

HABAKUK, twin to Samuel, also d April 1641

HANNAH, b Dec. 1643, bapt. 17 Dec. "at about 4 days old"; m 16 Oct. 1661 at Ipswich, Abraham Perkins, son of John; 5 ch.; d 16 Oct. 1732; he d 1722

----- by wife Martha -----

ABIGAIL, b 6 Feb. 1645/6, bapt. 8 Feb. "age about 2 days"; not named in father's will, so prob. d.y.

Ref.: Savage; Suffolk County Deeds; Suffolk County Probate 198; Boston Records; Ipswich V.R.; Pope; Dawes and Allied Families, by Mary Walton Ferris

The Ancestry of
ABRAHAM BELKNAP & MARY STALLON
Compiled By
John Brooks Threlfall

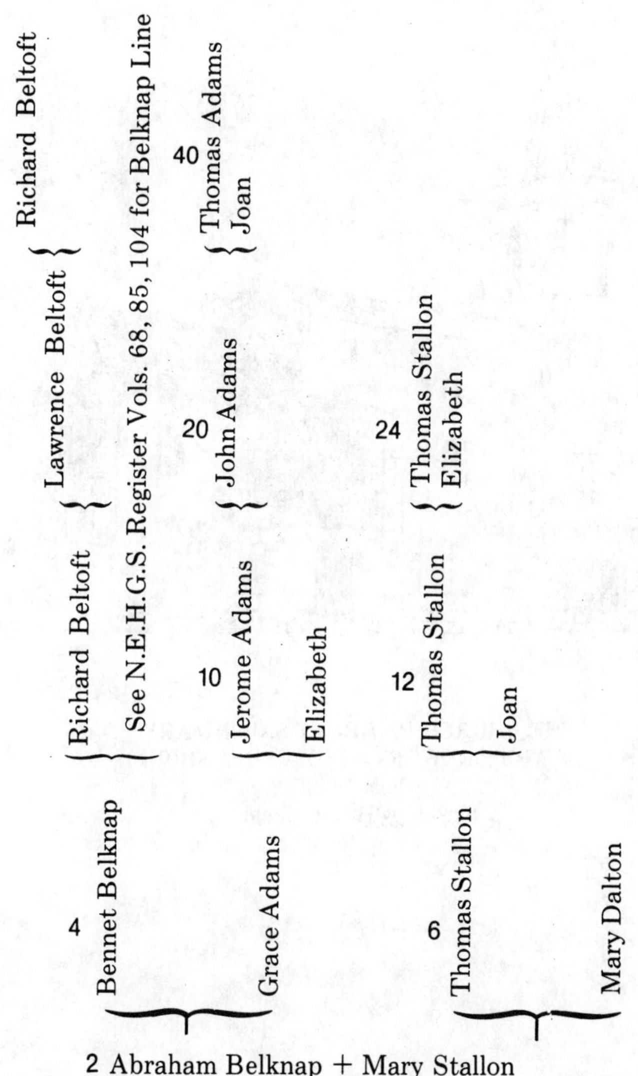

2 Abraham Belknap + Mary Stallon

THE CHURCH OF GREAT SAINT MARY
SAWBRIDGEWORTH, HERTFORDSHIRE
Circa 1800
Sketch by H.G. Oldfield

2

ABRAHAM BELKNAP *alias* **BELTOFT** (*Bennet, Richard, ?Lawrence, Richard*) was baptized at Sawbridgeworth, Hertfordshire, England, on 10 March 1589/90. The names of his parents are not given in the record, but his grandfather, Richard Beltoft, in his will of 20 August 1594, bequeathed 10 shillings to "Abraham Beltofte sonne to Bennett Beltoft my Godchilde", and he is also mentioned in his father's will of 14 April 1623. On 28 October 1617 at Latton, Essex, he married Mary Stallon, daughter of Thomas and Mary (Dalton) Stallon. She was baptized at Latton on 24 December 1595. They lived at Latton, Nettleswell and Northweald in Essex. The first indication of his residence in England is in the parish register of Nettleswell: *Abra Bel ... f.s. Abra et Mara*, buried 6 December 1620, which seems to refer to an infant, probably born and baptized in some other parish. Altho baptized as Beltoft, he resumed the original ancestral name of Belknap sometime before 1624 when the trial of Emmanuel Norrington of Loughton for stealing 7 white sheep worth 5 shillings each from "Abraham Belknap of Latton" confirms the use of the name.

About 1635, Abraham Belknap emigrated to New England. In 1638, he received a grant of 40 acres at Lynn. He moved to Salem and died in early September 1643, leaving a will which has been lost. However, the inventory of his estate has survived.

Children:

ABRAHAM, buried 6 Dec. 1620 at Nettleswell
ABRAHAM, b about 1622; alive 14 April 1623; d.y.
DAVID, b about 1624; buried 2 March 1624/5 at North Weald, Essex
SAMUEL, (recorded as Immanuel - evidently a clerical error for Samuel); bapt. 16 March 1627/8; m before 1653, Sarah Jones, dau. of Robert & Elizabeth Jones of Hingham, Mass.; 8 ch.; she d 18 April 1689 at Haverhill, Mass.
DORCAS, bapt. 7 Feb. 1629/30 at N. Weald.; d.y.

JOSEPH, bapt. 12 May 1633; m before 1657/8, Ruth Williams, dau. of Nathaniel & Mary, b 1638, bapt. 2 June 1639 ae 1 year; 4 ch.; m 2, before 1668, Lydia Ingalls; 1 ch.; m 3, before 1670, Hannah Meakins, dau. of Thomas of Hatfield, bapt. 13 March 1646/7; 6 ch.; she d 26 Dec. 1688; res. Hatfield 1682-96; returned to Boston & d there 14 Nov. 1712; buried in King's Chapel, Boston; a glover by trade

JOHN, bapt. 10 May 1635; only rec. of him in N. E. is a deposition made 27 March 1655 & filed at Ipswich a year later (Quarterly Ct. I:417)

HANNAH, b about 1639-40; m 6 Dec. 1663, Christopher Osgood, b 1643; 6 ch.; she d 21 Nov. 1679; he m 2, 3, 4 & d 9 May 1723 in his 80th year at Andover

ESTATE OF ABRAHAM BELKNAP OF LYNN

Will of Abram belknap sworn to 20: 12: 1643

Inventory of estate of Abraham Belknap of Lynn, who deceased the beginning of the 7 mo. 1643, taken by William (his mark) Tilton and Edward Tomlins, 16: 12: 1643:

Item	£	s	d
Sheep, 4 yewes	£5	00	00
2 wethers	1	06	08
7 yerlinge calfes	3	00	10
2 cowes and calfes	8	10	00
2 yerlinge calfes	3	15	00
4 yow gotes	1	06	08
1 kidd		04	00
1 sow and piggs	1	00	00
4 shottes	1	10	00
the houses and 5 akres of land	7	00	00
2 akers of planting Land	1	10	00
2 akers salt marsh	1	00	00
6 akers salt marsh at fox hill	2	00	00
30 akers at the village	2	00	00
1 braspitt		10	00
1 iron cettle		06	08
1 brascettle		03	04
3 ould skillets		03	00
1 friing pan		01	00
pot hookes and pot hangers		02	06
1 spitt		01	06
7 pewter platters		14	00
1 bras pestill & Morter		02	06

Item	£	s	d
1 candle stick and dripping pan		02	00
1 ould warming pan		03	04
1 payre of tongs		01	00
1 payre andirons		02	00
1 table		03	00
1 Chyer		02	06
1 chest, 1 box		04	00
1 chest		01	00
2 flock beds			
1 boulster		13	04
1 fether bed & boulster	1	00	00
3 coverlettes	1	06	08
4 blankits		13	04
3 pillowes		06	00
3 prs. sheetes	1	00	00
1 sheete		02	06
2 payre pillow beres		06	00
2 table clothes		04	00
1 doos. of napkins		03	00
ould iron, 4 wedges		04	00
1 ould ax		01	00
1 ould hatchett			08
1 mattock,		01	06
Total	£ 53	10	03

Mary (her mark) Belknap

The estate owed Joseph Armytage, Francis Ingalls, Goodman Phillipes, Rich. Rowton, Tho. Laighton, Ed. Farington, Jerard Spencer, Mr. Kinge and John Person, amounting to £5. 13s. 3d.

Ref.: N.E.H.G.S. - 68, 85, 104; Quarterly Court Files as published; Heritage With Honor, by W. Dean Belnap, M.D., 1974

6

THOMAS STALLON (*Thomas, Thomas*) *alias* Butler, was baptized on 21 August 1567 at Latton, Essex. On 14 April 1592 at Great Parndon, which is about 2 miles west of Latton, he married Mary Dalton. She was buried at Latton 14 August 1610. He married secondly, 5 October 1612 at Latton, Elizabeth Benbowe, probably a widow.

23 October, 36 Elizabeth (1594) - It was found by the Homage (manor jury) that Thomas Stallon out of court and after the last court had surrendered the east part of a tenement late of Thomas Stallon his father called *Harlowe*, in which Robert Weylet late dwelt (which said Thomas took to himself and his heirs at the court on 15 June, 32 Elizabeth), to the use of John Stallon and his heirs; and John being present at court was admitted. Afterwards, at the same court, the said John surrendered the same to the use of George Wright and his heirs; and George was admitted. It was found that Emmanuel Stallon out of court and since the last court had surrendered the middle part of a tenement called *Harlowe*, in which Joan Planche alias Joyner widow dwells, to the use of Nicholas Sibley and his heirs; and Nicholas was admitted. (Ref.: Manor Court Rolls in Essex Record Office)

Thomas Stallon was on an Inquest Jury held at Latton 5 February 1602 regarding the death of Thomas Warde, a one year old child, who was killed by the accidental discharge of a fowling piece.

He was on a Trial Jury to decide on an indictment against John Cornell of Borley, a joiner, and Robert Parker of Toppesfield, gentleman, for murder by witchcraft, they allegedly having bewitched Thomas Browne, junior, who died on 25 July 1612. (Calendar of Assize Records - Essex Indictments, James I, H.M.S.O., 1982)

Thomas was a carpenter according to his will. No doubt sick at the time, he made his will on 13 June 1619 and died a few days later. He was buried at Latton on 18 June. Elizabeth survived him. His children were all by his first wife. His homestead, called Bromley's, was inherited from his father. An abstract of his will follows.

13 June 1619 - the will of Thomas Stallion alias Butler of Latton in county of Essex, carpenter, to wife Elizabeth all my lease and term of years yet to come in the house wherein I now dwell & the land belonging thereto called Bromleis ... to her all my five leases ... to daughter Parnell the settle in the parlor with the featherbed in the chamber above, one pair of sheets at day of her marriage ... to daughter Elizabeth my joined bedstead in

the parlor, the malt quern and a pair of sheets immediately after the death of my wife ...to daughter Susan one pair of sheets... to daughter Margaret one chest standing in the parlor with the joined chair there, and one pair of sheets ...to each of four said daughters Parnell, Elizabeth, Susan & Margaret three table napkins each, all the corn of wheat & barley growing in the common field at Mets Cross upon my ground there, to be equally divided among them, except wife to have one quarter of barley and two quarters of wheat ...to daughter Dorcas a sheep, a lamb and one young bullock ... Executrix shall pay unto my son in law Abraham Beltoft £6 of lawful money of England within 3 years next after my decease, which said sum I owe him as part of his wife's portion ...to son Emanuel the joined press in the parlor ... to daughter Katherine the joined cupboard there. Residue to wife Elizabeth whom I make sole executrix.... In consideration - - - - - (damaged part of will) - - - - Joane Walet my mother with all things necessary for her estate during her natural life. Thomas (his mark) Stallion. Witnesses: Thomas Denne, Seth Hagger, John Wood, George Harrison. Proved Tuesday 22 June 1619. (Reference: D/ABW 36/341)

Children:

EMMANUEL, prob. b late 1592 or 1593; alive in 1619
KATHERINE, prob. b 1594; alive in 1619
3 MARY, bapt. at Latton 24 Dec. 1595; m 28 Oct. 1617 at Latton, Abraham Belknap, alias Beltoft, son of Bennet Beltoft; they went to N.E. about 1635, settled in Lynn where he d in Sept. 1643; 8 ch.
PARNELL, bapt. 3 Dec. 1598 at Latton; alive in 1619
ELIZABETH, bapt. 31 Aug. 1600 at Latton; alive in 1619; perhaps she was the Elizabeth Stallon who m Anthony Griffin at St. Antholin, London
SUSAN, bapt. 1 May 1603 at Latton
MARGARET, bapt. 10 March 1604/5
DORCAS, bapt. 8 Feb. 1606/7; alive in 1619

Saint Mary-at-Latton, a Norman Church Built on Saxon Foundations using Early Roman Tiles

Ref.: Parish Registers; Essex County Probates

JEROME ADAMS (*John, Thomas*) was born probably about 1525-35. He married Elizabeth ——, who may have been a widow Perry at the time. He died before late 1598. She made an oral will on 29 November 1598 and probably died within a few days, although the will was not proved until June, 1606.

Adam, Elizabeth, widow of Sawbridgeworth

In the name of God Amen. Item, I bequeath my soul unto almighty God and my body to be buried in the churchyard of Sawbridgeworth. Item, I bequeath and give unto Grace, being the wife of Benet Balcoft, a bed with all belonging to it, also an anvil and a barrel, a brass pot. Item, I give unto John Pery a bed with all belonging to it and a little brass pot and one kettle and a quern, also a salting trough. Item, I give unto Anyes the wife of Thomas Adam one kettle and two pewter platters, also my best coat. Item, I give unto Grace my old gown and a red petticoat and my best hat. Item, I give unto Ralph Pery one kettle and two pewter platters. Item, I give unto Jerome Adam one kettle and also a bed with all belonging to it. Item, I give unto Thomas Adam the cow which he hath of his mother, also one kettle and two pewter platters and a pair of sheets. Item, I give unto Tabitha Luce one hutch and a pair of sheets and a table cloth and 20s. of money. Item, I give unto John Adam the cupboard in the parlor, also the cauldron and the trivet, also one spit and the best candlestick and one joined stool. Item, I give unto Thomas Pery the old cupboard in the hall and one joined stool and also a tub. Item, I give unto my children my corn and cattle the which is spare of those charges which is they shall be at after my decease to be equally divided among them by even portions and thus in name of the lord friend, being the last will and testament of mother Adam made, she being in perfect memory, God be thanked, being delivered as her own act and deed in the 29 day of November in the 41 year of our gracious queen Elizabeth 1598.

Thomas Pery and John Adam
Executors to their mother's will

Witnesseth
John Poole
John Wall

Proved 18 June 1606
(Reference: D/ABW 2/187)

Children:

5 GRACE, prob. b about 1561; m Bennet Beltoft who d 1624; res. Sawbridgeworth; d 1630

JOHN, alive in 1598; made a will 17 April 1591, proved 25 May 1593

THOMAS, of Sawbridgeworth; m Agnes ——; he was a Harlow draper; he d 1632

JEROME, alive in 1598 per his mother's will

TABITHA, m —— Luce before 1598

DAUGHTER, who m Thomas Perry & had sons John & Ralph or, she may have had 3 sons by an earlier m:

THOMAS PERRY, named by her as her son, but may actually have been a son-in-law

JOHN PERRY, named in her will, relation not stated

RALPH PERRY, named in her will, relation not stated

Ref.: Essex County Probates; Parish Registers

12

THOMAS STALLON *alias* Butler, (*Thomas*) was born about 1540, probably at Harlow, Essex. He married about 1564 Joan ——, who was born about 1543. They lived at Latton which is about 2 miles from Harlow. From his will, it appears that he was a prosperous businessman with rental property who also did some farming. He had a brother-in-law, Nicholas Sybley, who was a linen draper of Harlow and who died in 1618. He had another brother-in-law named William Wytham and a son-in-law named William Lewter. Since he named no daughter in his will, this last is a puzzle. Possibly Lewter was a step-son by an earlier marriage of his wife's.

Thomas received from his brother John in 1560 a cottage in the Wood of Harlow which had been left to John by their mother. John was then living in Clavering. Thomas was presented for having two tenants in one house, against manor court orders given at the last court. In 1566, he was again presented and fined 20 shillings for not evicting one of the tenants. In 1568, he still had two tenants and was fined another 20 shillings and the bailiff was ordered to distrain the fine.

> Thomas Tagell of Harlow, glover, was indicted for grand larceny. On 2 November 1565 he broke into the close of Thomas Stalland *alias* Butler at Latton and stole a black horse worth 46s.8d. Not guilty. (Calendar of Assize Records, Essex Indictments, pub. by H.M.S.O., 1978)

On 28 November 1582, Thomas Stallon was named on the list of manor jurymen.

At the manor court of 15 June 1590, it was reported that Thomas Stallon "now deceased" had surrendered the west part of a tenement called Harlowes in which the widow Newman dwells, to the use of John, son of the same Thomas, to enter immediately after his death, according to his will dated ... and John being present at court was admitted. Fine [i.e. ordinary fee] 20d.

A similar entry that Thomas had surrendered the middle part of the same tenement in which widow Planche *alias* Joyner dwells, to the use of Emmanuel Stallon, his son. Fine 20d.

Similar entries treat on Thomas's surrender of the east part of the same tenement in which Robert Waylett dwells to the use of son Thomas, surrender of two tenements called *le Highowse* in which Richard Morrice and John Cooke dwell, to the use of his wife Joan until his sons Robert and William attain age 21.

Thomas Stallon made his will 13 September 1587, being sick at the time. He apparently recovered for a while and did not die until about two years later, for the will was proved 25 May 1590. His wife survived him and remarried to (Robert?) Walet. She was living in 1619 according to their son Thomas's will. An abstract of his will follows.

13 September 1587 - the will of THOMAS STALLON of Latton, county of Essex, sick in body, to be buried in the churchyard of Latton ...wife Johan to have the lease house wherein I now dwell, with all lands, meadows, pastures, yards, orchards, gardens, ponds, the 2 acres & a half of ground lying against the highway leading from Harlow to Roydon already let to Nicholas Sybley my brother in law excepted for the term let to him, for term of her life, on condition that she bring up my two youngest children in honest & decent manner, reversion to all my sons upon her death or immediately if she marry, they to then pay her 20 marks within 3 years of her marriage. If wife becomes delinquent in rent for 6 weeks, then any or all his sons may make payment and take over premises.. to wife Joan two joined hutches, one covering of carpet work red & green, one pair of blankets, two bolsters, two pillows, four pillowbiers, the curtains of the foresaid bed, two pairs of fine sheets, two pairs of coarse sheets, one flaxen table cloth, half a dozen diaper napkins, four brass kettles one of them bigger than the other, one skillet, one scummer, one pewter basin, six pewter platters, four pewter dishes, one great candlestick of pewter, three latten candlesticks of the biggest sort, four pewter pots, one a thirdendeale, another half a thirdendeale, the third a quart pot, the fourth a flower pot, my branded cow, my two hogs, all my hens & other poultry, half the painted cloths in all my house, a trivet, a pair of pot trammels, a spit, a pair of brandirons, a fire shovel, the brass pot that I last bought, my pails, milk vessels & brewing tubs.. the following to Joan for life as long as she does not remarry: my cupboard in the hall, my best table frame & form in the hall, the bedsteadle in the chamber over the parlor where I lie, my malt quern & featherbed, a bolster, a covering, a blanket & a mat to the same belonging.. to Emanuel my son all my black apparel, viz. a coat, a doublet, a pair of hose & a Spanish jerkin of leather, my largest cloak, my long sword at my cousin Archers at Epping, my largest clock with that belonging to the same, my back sword & dagger, my privy coat made with eyelet holes with a breast plate to the same, all these immediately after my death ....to said Emanuel my son my joined frame, table and form standing in the

hall & one of my shorter settles standing in the hall, he to have them immediately after the decease of my wife Joan or on the day of her marriage.. to Thomas my son my long whip saw, my iron crow, my black bearing bill, my table in the barn & frame at Fords & all my boards, trestles & poles & other things being at Harlow in the house that Robert Jenings now holdeth of me... to son Thomas one of my blue coats, a doublet & a pair of hose, my malt quern & the joined work with the bench in the hall & joined chair in the hall, all to him immediately after the marriage or death of Joan my wife ....to John my son my lesser clock, my joined trundle bed, my brasen mortar with iron pestle which be at my brother Sybley's, my great scales with an iron beam and all the leaden weights, a hanging candle stick of latten, my black halberd, two hutches great, with all the rest of the stuff in the chamber over the hall house where the widow Plancke alias Joyner my tenant now dwelleth, except one joined cupboard with four locks the which shall there remain to the use of my executors to keep my will & testament, with the lease also of Brumleas with other writings therein lying... to son John one of my blue coats, a doublet, a pair of hose ...after the death of my wife to son John my joined press in the parlor ... to Robert my son a joined frame, a table, a joined form to the same being at my brother Sybley's, a laver of pewter standing in a frame of wood to wash hands with, one basin of latten to the same & my three footed kettle of brass, all to be delivered at age 21 ...to Robert my son a coat cloth of rat's color, a doublet & a pair of hose to be delivered immediately after my decease, to Robert my son my great joined settle standing in the hall & one of my shorter joined settles in the hall immediately after the death or marriage of wife Joan ..to William my son one of the best joined frames & a table to the same with a joined form & a pair of pot hangers being at the house where one John Cooke now dwelleth, & my great brass pot, at age 21 ...to said William a coat, doublet & a pair of hosen immediately after my decease...to said William my joined cupboard standing in the hall after death or marriage of wife Johan ... residue, debts paid, legacies fulfilled, my body honestly buried to be equally divided among my five sons ... rents & letting of my tenement called the High House wherein Richard Morris & John Cooke dwell, with yards & garden thereto, to son John for three years, he to pay the Lord's rent and repairs. I surrender to the Lord of the manor of Harlow Bury by the hands of Nicholas Sibley & John Jenyngs two of the tenants customary of the same manor, the west end of my tenement called Harlowes wherein widow Newman now dwelleth with the yard or garden, to the use of my son John immediately after my decease. If I live until the next Court Baron of the manor of Harlow Bury, then it shall be lawful for me to call in again this my surrender, etc... I do surrender the middle part of the same tenement wherein the widow Plancke alias Joyner now dwelleth, to the use of Emanuel my son immediately after my decease.. I surrender the east end of same tenement where Robert Waylett now dwelleth to the use of Thomas my son immediately after my decease. I surrender my two tenements called the High House wherein Richard Morris & John Cooke now dwell to the use of Joan my wife until sons Robert & William are 21 except son John to have it for first three years, he to pay the Lord's rent ... I do surrender the north end of High House wherein John Cooke dwelleth to use of son Robert when he is 21, same conditions as before, south end where Richard Morrice dwelleth to the use of son William at age 21, same conditions. Executors to be Nicholas Sibley my brother in law, William Lewter my son in law, Thomas & John my sons, each to have 2s. 6d. Overseers: William Wyttam of Gyngrave Hall my brother in law and he to have 3s. 4d. for his pains. Witnesses: Richard Harrison, Richard Shelley et al. Signed Thomas Stallon. Proved at Stortford 25 May 1590 by the executors. (Reference: D/ABW 35/67)

Children:

EMMANUEL, prob. b about 1565; apparently eldest son. He became a a haberdasher in London

22 December 1607 - Manor of Harlow Court Rolls: Homage found that Emmanuel Stallon of London haberdasher on 8 November had surrendered a messuage lying on the south side of High Street [in Harlow] to the use of George Kilner of London tallowchandler and his heirs for ever.

6 THOMAS, bapt. 21 Aug. 1567 at Latton; m 14 April 1592 at Great Parndon, Mary Dalton who was b about 1573. She was buried at Latton, 14 Aug. 1610; he m 2, 5 Oct. 1612 at Latton, Elizabeth Benbowe who survived him; he d testate & was buried 18 June 1619

JOHN, bapt. 26 Aug. 1568; alive 1587 and 1590

JOAN, bapt. 20 March 1574/5; prob. d.y.

ALICE, bapt. 20 March 1574/5; prob. d.y.

ROBERT, bapt. 12 Nov. 1574; alive in 1587 and 1590

WILLIAM, bapt. 31 Aug. 1580; alive in 1604

17 October 1604 - Manor of Harlow Court Rolls: Homage found that William Stallon held the south part of a customary tenement called *le Highe Howse* in which Joan Morris widow now dwells and that Emmanuel Stallon of London haberdasher is his brother and next heir, who being present is admitted; he paid the fine [i. e. entry fee] 6s. 8d.

Ref.: Parish Registers; Essex County Probates; Manor of Harlow Court Rolls; Calendar of Assize Records, Essex Indictments

20

JOHN ADAMS (*Thomas*) was born probably in the first decade of the sixteenth century. He lived in Sawbridgeworth on Newnes Farm where he died. He was buried in the churchyard of Sawbridgeworth, if his wishes were carried out. He made his will on 22 March 1577/8 and died shortly thereafter. His will was proved in June. Since he mentioned no wife, she must have died earlier. An abstract of his will follows.

In the name of God the 22nd day of March in the 20th year of the reign of our sovereign Lady Elizabeth, etc. I John Adam of Newnes farm in the parish of Sawbridgeworth in the county of Hartford, husbandman, being of sound mind & good memory albeit in body acrased do ordain, constitute & make this my last will & testament in manner & form following. First, I give & bequeath my soul to almighty God, my body to be buried in the parish church yard of Sawbridgeworth aforesaid. And I give to the most needy poor people of the parish of Sawbridgeworth 6s. 8d. of good & lawful money of England within one month next after my decease. Also, I give to my son Jerome Adam & to his assigns 20s. of lawful money of England to be paid to him or his assigns immediately after one year following my decease. Also, I give to Agnes Flayle my daughter 40s. of lawful money of England & to Alice Burle my other daughter 40s. of lawful money of England to be paid to them & either of them or their assigns within one year next following after my decease. Also, I give to John Herde my servant the sum of £5 of lawful money of England to be paid unto him or to his assigns within one year next following after my decease. Also, I give to William Adam my son & to his assigns one lease of the land called Whittengers bearing date the 16th day of September in the 10th year of the reign of our sovereign Lady the queen's majesty Elizabeth. Also, I give to Joan Kinge my servant 3s. 4d. of good & lawful money and I give to every one of my godchildren 12d. of lawful money. The residue of all my goods and cattle & moveables I give to Thomas Adam & William Adam my sons whom I make mine executors of this my last will & testament, charging them & either of them to see the same will & testament truly fulfilled & kept & to occupy together all these my lands as I have done & do until Michaelmas next coming & then to divide their goods & to pay the rents between them as heretofore they have done by equal portions and further to see my debts justly paid, my body honestly brought to the earth and my funeral charges discharged. And I appoint & assign Peter Lyndsell of Sawbridgeworth & Richard Fanne of Sawbridgeworth, yeomen, supervisors of this my last will & testament and for their charges I will them to be allowed & recompensed. In witness whereof I the said John Adam have set to my mark with my own hand in the presence of the said Peter Lyndsell, Richard Fanne & Nicholas Compton, clerk, the writer hereof and others. Proved at Stortford 23 June 1578. (Reference: D/AMR 3/277)

Children:

10 JEROME, m Elizabeth ____; he d before 1598; at least 5 ch.
AGNES, m ____ Flayle before 1578
ALICE, m ____ Burle before 1578
WILLIAM, b before 1650; he made his will 1616; pr. 1619; 2 sons & 1 dau.

16 July 1616 - the will of William Addams of Sawbridgeworth, county of Hartford, husbandman, in perfect health ... to be buried in the churchyard there .. to eldest son John 4½ acre field called Halestock ... if it have a crop of corn at time of my decease, the crop to son William; if fallow, they to share next crop & William to pay John 3s. 4d... to son William my mansion house called Nakes ... to Clemence the wife of son William my cupboard standing in the hall and 20s... to Elizabeth my daughter, wife of George Prentice, 5s. & to her 3 children 12d. each... to Edward Whorlicane 2s. .. to Thomas Addams the son of my brother Thomas 10s... to the poor of Sawbridgeworth 6s. 8d. worth of bread... residue to sons John & William ... 20d. each to son William's 3 children... John Dane to be overseer and he to receive 3s. 4d. for his pains. Signed by mark. Witnesses: Ralph Brown the elder, John Dane. Proved 22 June 1619. (Reference: D/ABW 2/290)

THOMAS, b before 1560; m Agnes ____; he d 1608; 5 ch. per his will

1 May 1608 - the will of Thomas Adam of Sawbridgeworth.. sick of body ... to Henry Sawman and his wife my daughter one quarter of malt and my screen ... to son Thomas Adam one quarter of malt, a bedsteadle, a flock bed, a coverlet, a bolster, a blanket ... to John Adam my son one brass pot and 20s. at end of his apprenticeship ... to daughters Lydia Adam and Sara Adam each a bedsteadle, a flock bed, a coverlet, a blanket and a bolster ... residue to wife Annys who is to be executrix. Signed by mark. Witnesses: Richard Barker, Thomas Thackgure... n.p.. (Ref.: D/ABW 2/202)

Ref.: Parish Registers; Essex Probates

24

THOMAS STALLON (*alias* Butler) was born about 1509. He married Elizabeth ______. They lived in Harlow, Essex, where they had a shop of some sort, according to their wills. That he bequeathed a quadrant, an astrolabe and an ?a[ne]m-omter suggests that in his prime he was perhaps a sea captain, or at least a mariner of some rank, or possibly an amateur astronomer.

He made his will on 5 August 1556 and died soon afterwards. Elizabeth made her will on 16 September 1557. She died shortly thereafter but the will was not proved until 26 April 1559. He had a brother John who survived him.

According to the Manor Court Rolls, Elizabeth left to her son, John Stallon *alias* Butler, a cottage in the Wood of Harlow. This bequest does not specifically appear in her will, so perhaps she gave it to him before she made her will and died. John, who lived in Clavering, surrendered the cottage to his brother, Thomas Stallon, in 1560.

The name Stallon is a corruption of the place name Stalham, a parish in Norfolk. It derives from *ham by a stall* or *pool,* there being quite a few shallow ponds in the area. There was an Alfwin Stalun and his wife Goda mentioned on 4 July 1202 at Norwich in a Feet of Fines which involved 9 acres in Swinethorp, Lincolnshire, and the payment of 4 shillings sterling by Alfwin and Goda. In 1273 there was a Nicholas de Stalham, a Ralph, and a Herbert Stalum in Norfolk. In 1336, Jeffrey de Stalham was bailiff of Yarmouth. William de Stallon was bailiff of Norwich in 1367. John de Stalham was living in Norfolk in 1370.

John Stalonn of Mildenhall, Suffolk died about February 1452/3, leaving a wife Joan and a daughter Christian. He mentioned his late wife Etheldrada and a John Stalonn of *Ham'le* (or Gazeley?) barker and a John Stalonn, son of John Stalonn of Kentford. All these towns are nearby. A John Stalham of Mildenhall died in 1461 and in his will mentioned his late brother John and wife Joan. This must have been the John who died eight years earlier. Thus there were two brothers, both named John. Further, he named his wife, Katherine, and his late wives Margaret, Katherine and Alice, two married daughters, a son John, and William Stalham of London. The son John was probably the father of John Stallon who married Benet Howe.

The origins of Thomas Stallon are unproved, but not far from the Harlow area is Foxearth, Essex, where some Stallons also lived. One John Stallon and his wife, Benet, daughter of William Howe (or de Hoo) held lands there, lands which Benet apparently inherited from her father. John was probably the father of Thomas, and also of a John Stallon whose wife Joan, apparently a second wife, had a daughter Katherine by an earlier marriage. In later years there were Stallons in Foxearth, so we can deduce that John left at least one son, but Thomas moved on to Harlow.

William Howe, who had the land in Foxearth, lived in Melford, Suffolk, and died testate in 1516. He left a wife, Agnes, apparently a second wife. He was apparently the son of Robert de Hoo of Foxearth, who died testate in 1497 and left, beside a son William, a daughter who was married to —— Matthews.

The Robert mentioned above had two brothers: John and Roger of Melford who died testate in 1482, left a wife Emma. This Robert and Roger were sons of Thomas de Hoo and his wife Isabell of Melford. Thomas died in 1470/71. He was probably a grandson of John de Hoo and great grandson of Nicholas of Bury Saint Edmunds who died in 1361.

In the name of God, Amen, the fifth day of August in the year of our lord God 1556, I Thomas Stallon alias Butler of Harlow in the county of Essex & Diocese of London, whole of mind & of perfect memory, thanks be unto almighty God, I do ordain and make this my testament & last will in manner & form following. First, I bequeath my soul unto almighty God my creator & to our Blessed Lady Saint Mary the Virgin & to all the blessed company of heaven and my body to be buried within the church yard of Harlow aforesaid. Item, I bequeath unto John my eldest son my chest standing at London and that which is in it, my little clock called A[ne]mometer, my great written book with a boarded cover that Isaac wrote, my quadrant & a great astrolabe that was wont to hang over the sphere in the hall & twenty marks in ready money to be delivered unto him by the hands of mine executrix within one year next after my decease. Also, I bequeath unto my said son, his executors & assigns the lease of the moor and the Park Land lying in the parish of

Latton, he to enjoy it immediately after the decease of Elizabeth my wife. Moreover, I bequeath unto my said son [and] his heirs a house in Harlow aforesaid called Harlowes with all & singular the appurtenances, he to enjoy it immediately after the decease of my said wife. Item, I bequeath unto my son Thomas my press, my jack, my shears, my cutting board, my clock, my joined chest in the shop and a box of iron & twenty marks in money to be delivered unto him by the hands of my executrix within one year next after my decease. Also, I bequeath unto my said son Thomas, his executors & assigns immediately after the decease of Elizabeth my said wife, the lease of Brome Lees in the said parish of Latton. Item, I give & bequeath to Alice my daughter a great chest in the chamber, a little coffer with two bottoms, a brazen mortar & twenty marks in money or money's worth, a feather bed with that which belongeth thereto and also honest apparel for a chamber at her mother's appointment, to be delivered unto her by the hands of mine executrix within two years next after my decease or else at the day of her marriage. And if it fortune any of my said children to die before the time appointed that they should receive their portion, I will then that his or their part or parts shall be equally distributed among the rest of my children being alive. Item, I bequeath unto John Awnewell of Cobowne (Cobham?) in Kent for that I owe unto him 40s. Item, I bequeath to the amending of the highway between Harlow church and Latton church 20s. to be bestowed by mine executrix within one year next after my decease. Item, I bequeath unto the poor people of Harlow & to the maintenance of the song books & other necessaries in the said church, over & besides the charges which heretofore I have been at in the said church, £3 to be delivered by my executors unto the church wardens within one year next after my decease, to be distributed and disposed according to their discretions. Item, I bequeath unto the poor folk within the parish of Latton & to the maintenance of the song books & other necessaries in the said church 40s. to be delivered by my executrix unto the church wardens of that parish within one year next after my decease. Item, I bequeath unto Alice Stallon my son's daughter five marks to be delivered unto her at 18 years of age. Item, I bequeath unto my brother John Stallon a coat, a doublet & a pair of hosen of the best. Item, I bequeath unto Elizabeth my wife the lease of Bromelees, the moor and park land aforesaid, to occupy and enjoy during her life time, provided always if it fortune the said Elizabeth my wife to marry with any man, I will then that the said leases shall remain unto my sons as is above appointed immediately after her marriage, anything therein to the contrary notwithstanding. All the rest of my goods, moveable and immovable, unbequeathed over and besides, my debts paid and my said bequests performed, I give & bequeath unto Elizabeth my wife whom I ordain & make my sole executrix to see this my will performed, my debts paid and my funerals discharged. And also I ordain & make William Somner of Harlow the elder & Thomas Genyns of Harlow aforesaid the overseers of this my last will and testament & I give to either of them for their pains 6s. 8d. These being witnesses: Sir William Howe, vicar of Harlow aforesaid, Robert Gladwin, William Somner the elder, Thomas Genyns, Robert Steven & others. (Ref.: D/A MR 1/55)

16 September 1557 - the will of Elizabeth Stallon of Harlow, widow, late the wife of Thomas Stallon alias Butler of same, to be buried in the churchyard of Harlow... to John Stallon my son my lease of the moor & parkland in the parish of Latton ....to the church of Harlow 2s... to the said John all the goods and stuff in my parlor, one cow, one quarter of rye, one quarter of malt & one quarter of oats, the third part of all the wares in my shop or else the value thereof in money... to Agnes Stallon my daughter-in-law my best frock, my red kyrtle and 2 pair of sheets... to Alice Stallon daughter of my said son John two pair of sheets, a table cloth, three table napkins, a pewter platter, a pewter dish, two saucers, the least brass pot and a trundle bed with the least featherbed thereto belonging, and a chest standing in the chamber over the woolen shop at the bed's feet next the door and also a table, a pair of trestles, a form and five marks of money to be delivered unto the said Alice at age 18 or the day of her marriage if she marry before age 18...to the three sons of my said son John, viz. Zachary, Samuel and Christopher, to every one of them a pewter platter...to Thomas Stallon my son my lease of the house wherein I now dwell, all the goods and stuff in my hall, my greatest brass pot, my least chafer, my least posnet, a chafing dish, four pewter platters, two pewter dishes, all the remainder of my corn not bequeathed, to said Thomas all the goods and stuff in my great chamber except one chest already given, also two kine and he to deliver to Alice Stallon aforesaid one milk cow at age 18 or day of marriage... to said Thomas the third part of the wares in my shop..to Alice Knyght my daughter a quarter of rye and a quarter of malt and a quarter of oats, my best gown, my best kyrtle, with a pair of sleeves belonging thereto, my best petticoat, a great kettle, a great pan, the greatest posnet, the biggest brass pot saving one, the biggest chafer, a new chafing dish, one cow, and the third part of the wares in my shop ...to Thomas Knyght my son in law four cushions embroidered... I have already delivered with my own hands to my daughter Alice one silver spoon which I will her to deliver to the child that she now goeth with at age 16. Residue of estate equally to sons John and Thomas Stallon whom I make my executors. William Sumner the elder & Thomas Jenyngs of Harlow to be overseers, they each to have 2s. 6d. for their pains. Witnesses: William Sumner, John Godsave, Thomas Harrys, Thomas Jenyngs et al. Proved 26 April 1559. Administration granted to Thomas Stallon, the other exec. renouncing admin. (Ref.: Essex County Probate D/AMR2)

Children:

JOHN, eldest son, prob. b about 1532; res. Clavering; 4 known ch.: Alice prob. b about 1555-6, Zachery, Samuel, Christopher, of whom no further rec. can be found

12 THOMAS, b about 1541; m about 1561, Joan ——— ; his will proved 25 May 1590; res. Harlow

ALICE, m Thomas Knyght, prob. son of Thomas & Joan of Great Parndon

Ref.: Parish Registers; Essex Probates

40

THOMAS ADAMS of Harlow in Essex was born probably about 1470. He married Joan ____. He asked to be buried in the churchyard at Harlow, but left bequests to the church of Northweald Basset, which suggests that perhaps he was born and grew up there. He had land in Little Parndon. Thomas Adams died in 1542. Joan survived him.

5 June 1542 - the will of Thomas Adam of Harlow, county of Essex ... to be buried in the churchyard of Harlow .. to the high altar 20d... to Sir William, the chantry priest of Harlow, to pray for me 20d... to the church of Harlow 20s... to the church of Northweald Basset 6s. 8d....to Johan my wife my house and lands in Roydon called Rossers with all the free and copy lands for life, then to son John Adam; to son William the house and lands called Deneuels in parish of Little Parndon, conditional that he pay to wife Johan 40s. per year for her life, payable quarterly, Johan to see that I have sung for me every quarter of the year a trental of masses and that Sir William How, clerk of Northweald, shall sing the four yearly trentals until such time as he be beneficed, he to sing it in the church of Northweald aforesaid or else where he shall after serve, and after he shall be beneficed, I will that he shall find some other honest priest to sing for me quarterly as he did before during the term and life of Johan my wife, and after her decease, the said house and lands to son William and his heirs male, in tail to son Robert and his heirs male, in tail to son John and his heirs male, in tail to heirs general of son William ....to wife Johan for life the house and lands called Pollard's lying in Epping, then to Robert and his heirs male, in tail to son William and his heirs male, in tail to son John and his heirs male, in tail to heirs general of Robert ... to Johan Adam my daughter 5 marks sterling, to Agnes my daughter 5 marks sterling, to Richard Chelly my servant 40s., to Agnes Swaston 3s. 4d..... godsons 4d. apiece, to children's children 3s. 4d. each. Executors shall keep a yearly obit for me for which they shall have the profits and rents of my house and lands in Magdalenlaver. Residue to wife Johan. Sons William and Robert to be executors. Witnesses: Sir William Howe, priest, Thomas Lacy, William Westood et al. Proved 22 September 1542. (49EW2)

Children:

20 JOHN, prob. eldest; 5 ch.; d 1578 testate

WILLIAM, prob. 2nd son; d 1573; his will:

> 8 July 1573 - the will of William Adam of Little Parndon, Essex, yeoman .. sick in body .. to be buried in churchyard of Little Parndon .... for the poor of Little Parndon, Much Parndon & Epping, 12d. to each parish .. to my son William Adam my house and land called Daniulls in Little Parndon & lands I bought of Richard Adam in Much Parndon & Epping, his mother to occupy half until Michaelmas 1575, she to have a chamber and meat & drink for life and William to provide her with a nag or mare for life as long as unmarried ... if

William d.s.p., to his wife Joan for her life or until remarraige, then to be divided among my four daughters ..to wife Elizabeth house and land called Dunches which Hawknett holdeth in Much Parndon for life ...after her decease to Katherine 20 marks, also £6.13.4. at 21 or marriage, to other 3 daughters Annis, Martha & Alice £6.13.4. within a year after decease of wife. Son William to pay these legacies, in consideration he to have Dunches after wife's decease ...to William my dun horse, to Alice my long coat, 2 geldings & 2 harnesses, 6 thongs, 2 rackropes, 2 beasts ...to Alice a standing bed, a feather bed, 3 pair of sheets, a bolster, 2 pillows, a coverlet, 2 blankets & a cupboard, 3 pewter platters, 3 pewter dishes, the whole stock of boards lying in my sheapon, the salt trays in the milk house, the best spit, 2 quarters of oats, a quarter of wheat, the best witchin table in the kitchen, a sow, a hog ...to daughter Katherine a standing bed, a feather bed, a bolster, 2 pillows, 3 pairs of sheets, a coverlet, 2 blankets, my cupboard in the hall, the long chest with 2 lids, my white bullock & a calf, 3 pewter platters & 3 pewter dishes...to Matthew Ryme the other calf to daughter Martha my black mare ..... to godson Edward Graygoose my ambling colt ...to godson Edward Ryme the other colt ...other son in law Richard Marion & his wife to continue in my house with wife until Michaelmas 1574 .... Residue to Elizabeth, she & son William executors. Cousin John Yngold overseer. Wit.: John Ingold, William Stracy, Silvester Assheby. Pr. 28 October 1573 (Ref.: D/AM R3)

AGNES, living in 1542 (one of these girls perhaps m
JOAN, living in 1542 John Spranger of Northweald)

ROBERT, prob. youngest son; m Joan Thoroughgood, dau. of Robert of Magdalen Laver; res. Harlow; 5 ch.; he d 1565

25 April 1565 - the will of Robert Adam of Harlow, county of Essex, yeoman, to be buried in the churchyard of Harlow; to the poor people of Harlow 40s.. to Marcas my eldest son my tenement called Pollard's and all the land thereto belonging in Epping, in tail to my son Robert, possession to son Marcas at age 21, and in the meantime after the decease of my mother, my wife Johan shall receive the rent of the said tenement for the benefit of son Marcas until he reaches 21.. to son Robert my tenement called Fannes at Waterman's End in the parish of Little Laver, in tail to son Barnaby, possession to Robert at age 20 and his grandfather Robert Thoroughgood of Magdalen Laver shall take the rents for the benefit of Robert until he comes to age 20...to son Barnaby four score pounds money at age 20, but if he die before age 20, then the £80 to be divided among his other brothers and sisters ...to each of my daughters Ellenor and Sara £20 apiece at age 21 or at day of marriage but if one should die before, then her £20 to the other also ... residue and lease of my farm to wife Johan whom I make sole executrix ... my father Robert Thurgood of Magdalen Laver and my brother John Spranger of Northweald to be my overseers. Witnesses: Richard Harryson, Clerk, Thomas Lyndsell, John Cramphorne, with others. Proved 7 July 1565 (91BR3)

Ref.: Parish Registers; Probates

The Ancestry of

JOHN BIGGE & RACHEL MARTIN

Compiled By

John Brooks Threlfall

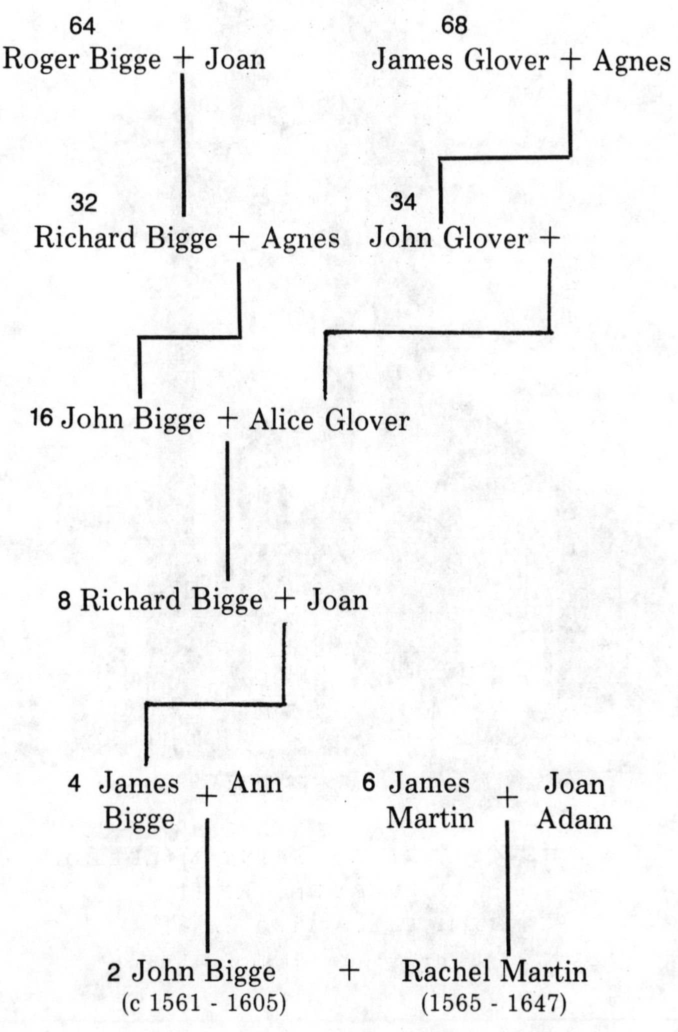

THE CHURCH OF SAINT MILDRED
TENTERDEN, KENT
Built Circa 1180 on site
of a previous Saxon Church

2

JOHN BIGGE (*James, Richard, John, Richard, Roger*) of Cranbrook, Kent, was born about 1561. He was a cloth merchant as were many other members of his family. He married at Tenterden, Kent, 14 September 1583, Rachel Martin, the daughter of James and Joan (Adam) Martin of Lydd. She was baptized there 17 June 1565.

John Bigge seems to have been the brother of John Scotchford's wife, Elizabeth, of Brenchley, who bequeathed to the children of John Bigge. John Bett's wife, Mary, was probably also a sister of John Bigge. John Bigge was buried at Cranbrook on 13 August 1605 and his infant son the next day. An abstract of his will follows.

> 11 August 1605 - the will of JOHN BIGGE, clothier, of Cranbrook, Kent ... to my daughters Patience, Elizabeth, Rachel, Mary and Thankful, 100 marks each to be paid to them at age 20 or on day of marriage ... to my wife 100 marks and all my household stuff ... my executors shall pay such money as is due the executors of my brother Scotchford ... to my wife £10 per year out of my lands for her dower ... my house and land at Linton and Maidstone to my son Smallhope ... if my son John, at full age of 21, shall release his right to the house & land where I now dwell, then he shall have instead the house and land at Linton and Maidstone, and my bequest of it to Smallhope is void ... Executors to be my wife Rachel and my son Smallhope. Witnesses: Wm. Plummer, Thomas Stone, Richard Maitham. Proved 20 October 1605. (Consistory Court of Canterbury Wills 39:196)

Mrs. Rachel Bigge, aged 66, with her widowed daughter, Mrs. Patience Foster, aged 40, and grandson Hopestill Foster, aged 14, embarked on 17 April 1635 on the ship *Elizabeth* for New England. They arrived at Boston in mid-summer and settled in Dorchester, where she was a member of the church and a proprietor in 1637. Her daughter, Elizabeth Stowe, and family had been in Roxbury for a year. Many other relatives of the Bigge family also joined in the migration, including James and Clement Bate, William Batchelor and wife, John Compton, Edward White and wife Martha, Marie Terrie, John Moore, Thomas Bridgdon, Thomas Betts and Goodman Beale.

Rachel Bigge made her will 17 November 1646 and it was proved 30 June 1647. In it she mentioned most of her relatives. Hers was the will of a woman of property and some education. The Bigge family appears to have been one of the wealthier clothier families of Kent. Why they emigrated will probably never be known, altho religious freedom must have been a consideration.

Smallhope Bigge was called "loving kinsman" and appointed executor of his will by Edmond Sheafe, a member of another noted family of cloth merchants from which several other emigrants to New England originated. An abstract of her will follows.

17 November 1646 - I Rachell Bigg of Dorchester ... widdow being aged and weake .. make this my last will & Testament .. I haveing sould my house and land wherein now Idwell unto my Nephew [grandson] Hopestill Foster for £120 to be payed.... he shall paie unto Thankfull Stowe Three score pounds within half a yeare next after my decease and ..... £20 which is due unto me from the said Hopestill ffoster ... to be paid unto her w^th^in three months after my decease And if the said Hopestill ffoster doe not pay the said threescore pounds .... then I give the said house and land unto her the said Thankful Stowe ..... he shall give £3 unto his daughter Thankfull to bee layed out upon a silver Pott for her marked with R. B. and 20s to his sonne Hopestill to buy for him three silver spoones And also 40s to his daughter Patience to be layed out upon sixe silver spoones for her all the spoones to be marked R. B. and also I give unto him the said Hopestill ffoster a ffeather Bedd and a boulster. And whereas my sonn in law John Stow oweth unto me one hundred and fforty pounds which he prmisseth to pay out of his house and lands in Roxbury if not otherwise as god shall inable him out of wch I give unto his Eldest sonn Thomas Stowe Thirty pounds he paying out of it 40s to be layed out uppon sixe silver spoones to be marked with R. B. of wch I give three of them to his daughter Marie & the other three to his sonn Samuell And I give unto his Eldest sonn John a silver Cup wch I bought of his father Itm I give unto Elizabeth Stow the wife of Henery Archer Thirty Pounds paying out of it £5 to be layed out in ffifteene spoones marked with R. B. of wch I give sixe unto her daughter Rachell & three to John & three to Isaac and three to Theophilus their three sonnes moreover I give unto Elizabeth Stow the wife of the said Henery Archer my silver Pott and my Booke of Dockter Preston to be delivered unto her by mine executo^r^ Itm I give unto Nathaniell Stow haveing given him formerly a smale Tenement & land I give him now £20 Item I give unto Samuell Stow £30 All which legacies so given and bequeathed unto them shall be paid unto them by their father .. w^th^in one yeare after my decease Itm I give unto Peter Masters my sonn in law now living in England 20s & to his daughter Elizebeth 10s and to his wife Katherin my silke

Kirtle to be payd ... by mine executo or his assignes Itm I give unto mr Richard Mather 40s and to the poore in Dorchester 20s to be distributed to them by the Deacons where they see most need. Itm I give unto mr Newman & to mr John Miller 10s apeece Itm I give unto James Batte seino 5s & to his sonne James 5s. Itm I give the now wife of Thomas Lyne 5s and to Clement Batte 20s and [to] his Daughter Rachell 10s And to the residue of his Children 5s apeece. Also the now wife of Will Batcheller 20s & to every of her children 5s apeece and to Thomas Batts 20s Itm I give unto Thomas Beal, John Compton, Goodwife Turner the wife of Richard Brittanine Goodman Meade, Old Margery & to Goodwife Place to every one of them 5s. Itm I give unto poore _____ Goodwife Hill and to goodwife Patching 10s apeece these Legacies soe given and beqathed to be paied wthin one yeare after my decease Itm some considerations Moveing me theire unto I further give unto Thankfull Stow all my household stuffe & plate ungiven and bequeathed to be unto her and her heires forever ...

Residue to son in law John Stow, he to be sole executor

Witnessed by: Richard Peacock — signed by mark
Gabriel Meede — (Rachell Bigg & a seal)

Children, all baptized at Cranbrook, Kent:

ANNA, bapt. 16 Aug. 1584; buried 27 Aug. 1584

SMALLHOPE, bapt. 29 Aug. 1585; m Ellen _____. In a deposition of 1611, he stated that he was a clothier, had lived in Cranbrook all his life, was age 26 (PRC 39/31, f. 71); no ch.; he was buried 6 Sept. 1638, she 26 Dec. 1638; their wills:

3 March 1637/8 - Will of Smallhope Bigg of Cranbrook, Kent, proved 9 Oct. 1638 ... brother John Bigg, executor; to aunt Mary Bridger of West Peckham & her 2 sons, Robert & Thomas Betts; to kinswoman, the wife of Wm. Hunt, of Brenchley, widow; to the wife of John Saxby of Leeds; to Judith, wife of Thomas Tadnall, late of Dover; to Godfrey Martin of Old Romney & his sisters; to the children of Robert Pell of New Romney, jurat, deceased; to kinsfolk Thomas Bate of Lydd, James Bate, Clement Bate, the wife of Wm. Batchelor, John Compton, Edward White & Martha, his wife, all now in N. E., 20s each. £20 to them or to others in N. E. to be distributed by my mother and my brother John Stow. To Peter Master of Cranbrook who married my sister; to my mother Rachel Bigg £100. Land etc. at Rye, Sussex, to my wife Ellen. To my sisters Patience Foster & Elizabeth Stow in N. E. To Hopestill Foster, son of my sister, £300. To Thomas & John Stow, sons of my sister Stow £200 each; to Elizabeth Stow & the other 3 children (under age) of my said sister Stow. Lands in Horsmonden to my brother John Bigg. Lands at Wittersham, Lidd and Cranbrook to Samuel Bigg, my brother's son at age 23. Friends John Nowell of Rye, James Holden & Thomas Bigg the elder, of Cranbrook, clothiers, to be overseers. To my cousin Hunt's children & John Saxbey's children; to the two sons of my aunt Betts; to my cousin Bottenn's children; to my cousin Pell's children: Joan, Elizabeth, Richard, Thomas Baytope's wife. *(Waters' Gleanings)*

After a hearing of the case between John Bigg, brother and executor of the one part, and Hellen alias Ellen Bigg (the relict), Patience Bigg alias Foster, wife of Richard Foster, and Elizabeth Bigg alias Stow, wife of Richard [sic] Stow, testator's sisters, of the other part, sentence was pronounced to confirm the will 4 April 1639 (the widow having previously died) (*Consistory Court, Canterbury, 51: 115.*)

Ellen Bigg of Cranbrook, widow of Smalehope Bigg of Cranbrook, clothier, made her will 24 Nov. 1638, proved 12 Feb. 1638/9. She directed that she be buried in Cranbrook Cemetery, "near my husband". To Samuel Bigge, son of my brother John Bigge, of Maidstone; to my sister-in-law Katherine Master. James Holden of Cranbrook and brother-in-law Peter Master, mercer, to be overseers. (*Archdeaconry Canterbury, 70: 482.*)

PATIENCE, bapt. 5 May 1588; m Richard Foster of Biddenden who d about 1630; she & her son Hopestill came to N.E. in 1635; he m Mary Bates, dau. of James, had 6 ch. b in Dorchester

ELIZABETH, bapt. 1 Nov. 1590; m 13 Sept. 1608, John Stowe, son of John & Joan (Baker) Stowe, bapt. 14 Jan. 1581/2 at Biddenden; 9 ch.; she was buried 21 Aug. 1638; he d about 1653-4

JAMES, bapt. 28 Jan. 1592/3; buried 12 Jan. 1593/4

RACHEL, bapt. 20 Oct. 1594; m 1617, Moregift Starr (1592-1617); m 2, 1619, Peter Masters, a mercer, of Tunbridge, later of Cranbrook; had ch.; she was buried 16 Dec. 1625 & he m 2, 16 Aug. 1626, Katherine Rogers

ANNA, bapt. 30 Jan. 1596/7; buried 16 May 1597

JOHN, bapt. 25 June 1598; buried 18 Dec. 1598

MARY, bapt. 18 May 1600; d.y.

JOHN, bapt. 19 Dec. 1602; m 1, lic. 12 May 1626, Mary, dau. of Edward & Dorothy (Curtis) Maplesden; she wa buried 10 Nov. 1632; he m 3, lic. 16 Sept. 1634 at Otham, widow Sybylla Beacon; he d about 1642/3; his only son Samuel d after 1638 but before him; she m 2, Kent Clark; his will:

Will of John Bigg of Maidstone, Kent, jurat, begun 17 Aug. 1640, finished 27 March 1641, proved 7 Feb. 1642/3. Bequeathed to servants, ministers, many friends, relatives. To Hopestill Foster, to Thomas, John, Nathaniel & Samuel Stowe, and my brother Stowe's 2 daughters Elizabeth and Thankful; my wife Sibella Bigg; Marie Terrie in N. E.; my cousin Godfrey Martyne; my brother Peter Masters of Cranbrooke and his 4 children; my cousin James Bate in N. E.; my cousin Lyne of N. E.; my mother Mrs. Dorothy Maplisden; my brother Smallhope Bigg. (*Crane, 11*) (*Waters' Gleanings*)

THANKFUL, bapt. 17 Feb. 1604/5; buried 14 Aug. 1605, the day after her father. What illness took away father and infant at same time?

Ref.: Cranbrook Parish Register; Ancestry of E.W. Blake; Stevens-Miller Ancestry, by W.L. Holman; The American Genealogist 19:135; N.E.H.G.S. 5:300, 29:256, 38:60, 66:54, 92:397; The Genealogist 5:23

4

JAMES BIGGE (*Richard, John, Richard, Roger*) was born probably about 1530 at Cranbrook, Kent. He himself settled in Capell which is about ten miles northwest of Cranbrook. James, like many of the rest of his family, seems to have been in the cloth trade, which at that time was flourishing in Cranbrook and nearby towns. He died at an early age, leaving three small children. His wife was named Anne

He made his will 31 May 1562. It was proved a year later on 27 May 1563. Altho the will does not say he was sick, he must have been expecting to die soon. He entrusted most of his estate to his brother Gervase of Cranbrook. An abstract of his will follows.

31 May 1562 - the will of JAMES BIGG of Capell in the Diocese of Rochester. . to wife Annes three score pounds of good and lawful money of England, all the household that she brought and 2 kyne. unto John Bigg my son £240 and one maser of silver and gilt and my best presse and my best bed stedle and a bed and all things belonging to the bed, and my best table cloth and all the brass and pewter and two kettles of iron work that I brought at Maidstone 23 pieces in all, also a chest that Edward the joiner made for me, and my best chair, and all my weights and scales, and the iron ponder in the work house, and a pair of brand irons and a great spit, and a great dripping pan, and a pan that my mother did give me, and the greater trivet, and a pair of tongs, all this to be paid to him at age 22. To Mary Bigg my daughter three score pounds of money, a bed stedle and a bed, etc. at age 20 or day of marriage. To Susan Bigg my daughter, same as to Mary. To sister Love £5, to Jane Love my sister's daughter 40s. and a two yearling budd; unto Annes Berry 24s.; unto Annes Walrar 20s. and a two yearling. Unto my three boys William Markey, John Reve and Walter Love 20s. each. If son John die before age 22, then £140 of John's inheritance to be divided between daughters Mary and Susan and my brother Richard Bigg to have £40 of John's inheritance. To Walter Bigg the son of my brother John £20 and £40 to the discretion of my brother Jarvys Bigg. If any of my daughters die before age 20 and unmarried, then her part shall remain to her sister or to her sisters. If son John outlives the daughters, then all their inheritance to him. If wife be with a man child, then there shall be taken from son John's money 4 score pounds and from the money of my two daughters £20 and given to said son. If it shall be a woman child, then from John's money £30 and from my two daughter's money £12, and given to the said daughter. If such posthumous child live to age 22 but son John die before age 22, then John's share to that child. Executor may sell lands to the extent required to pay John's inheritance. Profits of lands to wife until son John

is age 14, then profits to John. II Richard Cortopp of Cranbrook will give unto Margery Love my sister one house for her to dwell in well worth 20s. a year for term of her life and 2 loads of wood every year for her life, then Richard shall have all my rights in the land bought of the heirs of Franklyn in fee simple for ever, provided Richard make sure unto my sister Love within 13 weeks after my decease. Debts paid, residue of household goods to wife Annes. Residue of other goods to brother Jarvis whom I make sole executor, Edward Bisshopp the elder to be my supervisor. Witnessed by Edmund Tomson. Attested at Cranbrook by me John Awcoke, by me Robert Kyppynge. Proved 27 May 1563 at London by Jervase Bigg the executor. (Ref.: P.C.C. 22 Chayre)

Children:

MARY, perhaps b about 1557; prob. m John Betts (or Bates), had ch.

SUSAN, perhaps b about 1559; living 1568

2 JOHN, perhaps b about 1561. "...of Cranbrook," he m 14 Sept. 1583 at Tenterden, Kent, Rachel Martin, dau. of James & Joan (Adams) Martin. She was bapt. at Lydd, Kent 17 June 1565; 11 ch.; he was buried at Cranbrook 13 Aug. 1605. She went to N.E. as an old woman with 3 of her ch. & d about 1647 at Dorchester, Mass

ELIZABETH, b about 1562/3, posthumous; m John Scotchford; prob. her grandson John who d at Concord, Mass. 1696. However, John Scotchford m Elizabeth Blackamore 28 Jan. 1576/7 at which time Elizabeth Bigge was only 14. So, his m to Elizabeth Bigge must have been a 2nd m, or some other explanation.

THE PARISH CHURCH OF ALL SAINTS, LYDD, KENT

Ref.: Probates at Maidstone, Kent; N.E.H.G.S. 5:300, 29:256, 38:60, 92:397; Cranbrook Parish Register

6

JAMES MARTIN lived at Lydd, Kent, where he was probably some sort of a merchant or trader. Lydd is in the extreme southeast of Kent in a low, sandy area better suited for commerce than agriculture. All that is known of him is derived from his will and the parish register of Lydd. James Martin married at Lydd on 27 July 1562, Joan Adam. She was baptized there on 10 April 1544 and was the daughter of William and Alice (Baker) Adam of Lydd. She died there in 1582. William Adam and Alice Baker were married in 1542 at Lydd. Administration of the estate of William Adam was granted to Mildred, his widow, in 1571, hence Alice must have died earlier and he remarried. James Martin died in 1583. An abstract of his will follows.

> 8 August 1583 - the will of JAMES MARTIN of the town of Lydd in the parish of All Saints, county of Kent .. to my daughter Rachel £10 in ready money, one silver goblet next the best one pot covered with silver, 6 silver spoons of those that be 7 marked, one feather with silver, 6 silver spoons of those that be 7 marked, one feather bed next the best that lyeth in the chamber over the parlor, that bolster that lyeth upon the bed, the coverlet, that blanket, two pillows, two pillow coats, 4 pair of sheets neither of the finest nor of the coarsest, 3 table cloths, one dozen of table napkins, her mother's best coat with her kyrtle, and all such things as her mother did give her ... unto my daughter Batt [Bates] 10s... Adryen Wood my servant shall have that little chamber he now lyeth in for life, one feather bed, one bolster, 2 pair of sheets, one blanket, one coverlet, £3.6s.8d. ... to son in law James Batt 2 seames* of wheat, and 3 seames* of malt. Godfrey Martin my son to be sole executor, he to have all the rest of moveable goods, houses, lands not willed. Witnesses: Alexander Weston, writer, Richard Glover. Proved 26 November 1583 at Canterbury and Godfrey Martin, executor, and Maria Martin alias Batt, also Rachell Martin natural daughters of the deceased, all came into court, etc. (Reference: 35:60)
>
> * Seame = one horse load, or usually 8 bushels of grain

Children:

GODFREY, he had a son Godfrey and other ch.

MARY, b about 1560; m 1, 6 June 1580, James Bate, son of John & Mildred (Ward) Bate of Lydd; he d 2 March 1613/14; 13 ch. of whom Clement & James went to N.E. & founded the numerous Bates family of America; she m 2, —— Bridger of West Peckham, Kent

3 RACHEL, bapt. 17 June 1565 at Lydd; m 14 Sept. 1583 at Tenterden, Kent, John Bigge of Cranbrook; 11 ch.; he was buried 13 Aug. 1605; she went to N.E. in her old age with some of her ch. and d about 1647 at Dorchester

SAINT DUNSTAN'S CHURCH, CRANBROOK, KENT

Ref.: Kent County Probates; Parish Registers

8

RICHARD BIGGE (*John, Richard, Roger*) was a wealthy cloth merchant of Cranbrook, Kent. He was born probably about 1475-8 in Benenden. He was certainly related to the many others of the same name who lived in Benenden, a smaller village about 3 miles southeast of Cranbrook. He was probably one of the sons of John (and Alice) Bigge who died in 1479 leaving at least two sons unnamed under age 18. This John Bigge was the son of Richard (and Agnes) Bigge who died in 1474 and in his will named sons Robert, Thomas and John and a daughter, Katherine. Of these three sons, Robert died in 1500, naming in his will sons Thomas and Edward, but no Richard. Thus, Robert probably was not the father of Richard. Thomas left no will, so we know little about him. Since Richard, the subject of this monograph, named children Alice, Richard and John, but no son Thomas, it seems more likely that Thomas is eliminated and John was the father of this Richard Bigge.

Richard Bigge made his will on 4 November 1532 and it was proved 5 August 1533. He named 9 children and a wife, Joan, who survived him. She was sued in Chancery Court between 1538 and 1544 by Robert Bigge regarding detention of deeds for land on the "denne" of Walkhurst in Benenden. (Chancery File 949:69-70). This must have been Robert, the son of William Bigge, who, in his will of 1542, left such property to his son Robert, the land then in the possession of Richard Bigge who, according to an agreement they had made, was to transfer the property to Robert when he reached age 24. Upon Richard's death in 1550, the contractual responsibilities would have fallen to Joan as executrix of Richard's will. Her failure to perform the obligations was apparently the reason for the suit. In the suit, she is referred to as Joan, late wife of Richard Bigge.

Joan Bigge, widow of Benenden, made her will and died in 1550, naming 10 children, 5 of which were not named by Richard, and omitting 4 that he did name. It would almost seem that this Joan was not the widow of Richard, but the cross references to these children made in the wills of sons James and Gervase indicate otherwise. Did they both omit some children? Did Joan marry again to another named Bigge? Her son John was still under the age of 22 in 1550, but John son of Richard was his eldest son with five younger brothers in 1532, so there must have been two Johns. But, she had an elder son, Walter. Perhaps Richard had an earlier marriage and Joan also, hers to another Bigge. Also, perhaps some of these children were adopted children of another Bigge. Thomas Bigge of Benenden died in 1531 leaving a wife, Katherine, and children Joan, Juliane, John and William, who have not been traced thereafter. But this possibility does not explain son Walter, nor why Joan omitted James from her will. The conflicts seem impossible to satisfactorily resolve, unless one assumes some errors and omissions. In any event, it seems clear that James was a son of Richard who died in 1533. Joan may or may not have been his mother.

4 November 1532 - the will of Richard Bigge of Cranbrook, Kent, clothier. To be buried in the churchyard of Cranbrook as near where my children lie as may be convenient. To the high altar 6s. 8d., to the light of our lady 12d., to the friars in Canterbury 7s. 6d... to the friars of ? o ynden 12s. 4d.... to son John all my household stuff...and moveables which I have in my messuage at Benynden, my best gown, 2 little kettles, 2 brass pots, one gilt cup with cover, £20, also £6. 13. 4 out of money Robert Moore of Benynden oweth me, one of my looms ... to my son Robert my second gown, my salt of silver with a cover piece gilt, another loom... to son Gervase 4 silver spoons ... to each of my sons William, Richard and James one of my little silver pots to be delivered after decease of wife Joan .. to sons Robert and Gervase the residue of the money owed by Robert Moore over and above the said £6. 13. 4., to be paid them at age 24.... to sons William, Richard and James each £20 at age 24 in tail, executrix may invest the money in land ....to daughters Alice, Katherine and Annes Bigge £20 each at marriage if by advice of friends: £10 at day of marriage, £10 half year later. Residue of goods and cattle to wife Joan, she to be executrix..... Gervase Hendle the elder and his son Walter Hendle to be supervisors. Concerning lands, etc. in Cranbrook and Benynden, to eldest son John Bigge my messuage, workhouse and all lands in Benynden. If John d. s. p. before age 30, then to son William, then to son Richard, then to son James, then to my next heirs. Wife Joan to have £4 per annum for life out of income from these properties unless she remarry, then only 30s. per year unless 2nd husband die, then the £4 reinstated. Joan to have my messuage, workhouse with implements, gardens and lands that I dwell in purchased of Richard Brikenden until son Robert is 24, then to him,

except Joan to have, during widowhood, the old parlour and the buttery to it, the chamber over the same and two little chambers next adjoining, half the   at her pleasure, free occupying in the kitchen and brewhouse there, liberty to fetch water at the well, and a cow kept for her summer and winter at charge of Robert or his heirs. If Robert d.s.p. before 30, then in tail to Richard, to James, to next heirs. Wife Joan to have income from messuage, workhouse with implements, gardens and lands in Nether Willesley in Cranbrook which John Luffe now occupyeth and farmeth, until son Gervase Bigge is 24, then to him. If Gervase d.s.p. before age 30, then to son James, to son William, to son Richard, then to my right heirs. Feoffees to deed to wife Joan as soon as Gervase is 24, a yearly rent of 40s. out of the estate in Nether Willesley at 4 usual feasts of the year as long as she is a widow, then 20s. per year at two terms as long as married, etc. Joan to have profits of lands and lodge I purchased of Richard Harman at Goldeford which I have to farm of William Lussher, gent., until son William is 24, then to him, also the lands called Fermours. If William d.s.p. before 30, then to son Richard, to son James, then to right heirs, and further William shall suffer the heirs of John Brykenden to have the water course from the water mill pond called Brikenden's pond, etc. Joan to have issues and profits of the messuage in which Richard Erley dwells, the garden adjoining and the meadow I purchased of John Carkerage the elder, until Richard is 24, then to Richard. If Richard d.s.p. before 30, then to James, then to William, then to next heirs.... unto Richard Courtopp a piece of land I bought of Steven Draner at Nether Willesley, on condition that he deed unto my feoffees a piece of land now held by Peter Courtopp and next to my lands to the use of wife Joan until son Gervase is 24, then to him. Executors to pay James at age 24, £20 in recompense of the land willed to Richard Courtopp. Witnessed by Gervase Hendley sen., Richard Courtopp, Gervase Hendley, Richard Scheff, John Bigge, Henry Manaring [Manning] jurat, Walter Hendley, William Brikenden, Thomas Chistopp.

Proved 5 August 1533 by Joan the relict and executrix. (Reference: P.C.C. 4 Hogen)

10 May 1550 - the will of Joane Bigge of Benenden, widow ... to be buried in the churchyard of Benenden ... to Alice, Margery and Anne my daughters one cow each ... to daughter Julian and to son Richard a twelvemonth heifer, to son John a 3 year old heifer .... all household and moveable goods shall be divided between Alice, Margery and Anne, except that daughter Joane to have my best table cloth. As for lands and tenements, to my son Walter Bigge my messuage Gardyne Lane and 30 acres of land and wood in Benenden on condition that Walter pay to Robert Barnes of Rye £10 which he lent unto me and if Walter does not pay the said £10 and discharge my son Robert of one obligation unto the said Robert Barnes, then the said Robert to have two pieces of land called the Fredde and the Croft at the Cross containing $3\frac{1}{2}$ acres ... Walter to pay my son Robert £6, half within half a year, the other half at end of the year ... Walter to pay £8 each to sons John, Richard and Gervice at age 22 and to my daughters Alice, Margery, Anne and Juliane 40s. at marriage

or at age 30 . . . Walter to pay to Joane Lede my daughter 40s. within 2 years . . . . Walter to pay all debts, to be sole executor and to prove will and pay bequests within half a year, otherwise other sons to have equally the said messuage Gardyne Lane and lands . . . Richard Lede my son in law shall have the room and easement that I have here, that is to say the parlour and chamber over the parlour with fire and flete(?) as I have used the same room, and one cow kept there also unto the feast of Saint Michael the Archangel next coming, freely without any payment. To the poor men's box at Benenden 12d. Witnesses: Robert Aynyston, Edward Bigge and Richard Lede. Pr. 26 January 1550/51 (27:325)

Children, probably all born at Benenden, Kent:

JOHN, apparently eldest son; under 30 in 1532, hence b after 1503; he had a son Walter who was an adult in 1568 as he was named executor to the will of his uncle Gervase Bigge. He may have been the John Bigge who m Rose Courthope 21 May 1565 at Cranbrook, but if so it would certainly have been a 2nd m.

ROBERT, b perhaps about 1520; he was of age in 1550; Agnes dau. of Robert Big bapt. 21 Oct. 1560 at Benenden; Benett wife of Robert Bygg buried 1 Nov. 1560 at Benenden (B.T.s)-these may apply to Robert son of William. Perhaps the Robert of Tenterden who d testate 1600, leaving wife Katherine, sons Thomas, William, & 3 daus., the 5 ch. bapt. there 1572-80

ALICE, unm. 1550

GERVASE, b prob. about 1530 as he was under 22 in 1550; prob. ch. Gervisse, jr. bapt. 13 March 1565/6, buried 4 June 1566 at Cranbrook. Joan Bigg *ux,* i.e. a wife, who was buried 30 May 1566 was prob. his wife. Gervase was buried there 10 Sept. 1568, s.p.

8 September 1568 - the will of Gervase Bigge of Cranbrook, Kent. . . to be buried in the churchyard at Cranbrook . . . . to the mending of the highways between Cranbrook and Lynton 6s. 8d. . . to Walter Love my sister's son 20s. given to him by the last will of my brother James Bigge . . . to my sister Margery Love 20s. . . . to Agnes Love my sister's daughter 5s. . . to Elizabeth Love my sister's daughter as I owe her 6s. 8d. . . to the 4 daughters of my brother Richard Bigg, that is to say Dorothy, Joan, Martha and Mary Bigg all such goods as was their father's standing in my mother's chamber as it appeareth by a bill of myne own hand . . to Lettice Bigg my servant the best flockbed in the chamber over the kitchen, the best coverlet, a pair of the best blankets, the bed stedle and a pair of sheets . . I give to Kinge of Buckestede the warp spinner my second best coat . . . to Robert Scarborough 2s. at 4d. per week until paid if he so long live . . . To John Bigg my brother all money he doth owe me. To Richard Bigg my god son the son of John Bigg of Wallingford 40s. . to William Bigg his brother 20s. . to my cousin John Bigg of Hawkhurst my black cow. Residue of movable goods and cattle, the implements of the workhouse excepted, to Robert Bigge my brother and to Walter Bigge my brother's son equally to be

divided, they to be executors. Richard Brikkenden and Edward Jordenn to be overseers. Re lands and tenements in Cranbrook and Lynton, Thomas Sheffe of Cranbrook, clothier, shall receive the income of all my lands and tenements until John Bigge the son of my brother James Bigg is 22, out of which income the said Thomas Sheffe at the marriage of Mary Bigge daughter of my brother James shall pay to my executors such money as I stand charged to pay to Mary at her marriage by the last will of her father and also such income as said Thomas shall have received from the day of Mary's marriage to the day of marriage of Susan Bigge toward the payment of such money as I stand charged to the said Susan towards her marriage by the said will of said James Bigge her father and such income received after Susan's marriage to be paid to son John when he reaches 22 as part of recompense of such money as I stand charged to the same John by the last will of his father. .... to the said John all my lands and tenements in Cranbrook and Lynton at age 22 in full recompense of what is due him by the will of his father. If John die before age 22, then executor to sell the house and lands thereto appertaining in Cranbrook sometimes of Richard Bigge my brother now in the occupation of William Barrett and all my lands in Linton, proceeds to be paid to Mary and Susanne Bigge all and every such sums of money as I stand charged to the said Mary and Susanne by the last will of the said James Bigg their father ... to Richard Bigge my brother £40 according to the last will of the said James.. the £40 to be paid out at my discretion according to the will of James, I will the said £40 to Robert Bigge and Walter Bigge my executors equally to be divided. If John died before 22, then the messuage I now dwell in and the dye house and implements thereunto belonging in Cranbrook, sometime Richard Bigge's my father deceased and which the said Richard Bigge by his will gave and willed to me the said Gervase Bigge to Walter Bigge my executor forever. If said Thomas Sheff die before John comes to 22, then Robert Amoore and Robert Brykkenden to replace him. Witnesses: Edward Jorden, Robert Raynte, John Fuller, William Barrett, Gyles Gybson, Thomas Berry, Richard Brickenden, Henry Allard. Proved 19 February 1578/9. (Reference: P.C.C. - 4 Sheffeld)

WILLIAM, under age 24 in 1532; apparently d between 1532 & 1550 as not in Joan's will; on the other hand, Joan Bygge, infant dau. of William Bygge of Benenden, husbandman, was supposedly murdered by witchcraft 3 July 1566 by Margery Kancham late of Rownden alias late of Benenden, Kent, widow, for which she was pardoned in 1570 (Patent Rolls c. 66/1062); this was prob. Joan bapt. 22 Aug. 1563 at Benenden (B.T.)

KATHERINE, living in 1532, but not named in Joan's will of 1550, so perhaps she d in the interim

RICHARD, had ch.: Dorothy b about 1556, Joan b about 1558, Martha bapt. 27 Oct. 1560 at Cranbrook, Mary bapt. 2 May 1563, prob. Richard buried there 24 May 1566. He was alive in 1568 per his brother Gervase's will

4 JAMES, m Anne——; lived in Capell, where he was a cloth merchant; 4 ch.; d 1563. He was named in his father's will, in his brother Gervase's will, but NOT in the 1550 will of Joan Bigge his putative mother; his will named several brothers and sisters

ANNE, named in wills of both parents; she was unm. in 1550

MARGERY, perhaps b 1525; she was unm. in 1550; m perhaps about 1551, ——Love, had ch.: Jane, Walter who was buried 23 Sept. 1570, Agnes & Elizabeth by 1568 & was a widow by June 1558 per will of Richard Courthope the elder. She was NOT named in the 1532 will of her putative father Richard, but was named as their sister in the wills of James & Gervase.

JOAN, m Richard Lede before 1550; NOT named in Richard Bigge's will of 1532, but clearly a dau. of Joan per her will; Richard Lede/Leed may be the one who d intestate 1558-9

JULIANE, named only in the will of her mother Joan in 1550

WALTER, called eldest son in will of his mother Joan Bigge in 1550; perhaps he was the Walter Bygge who m 28 Nov. 1560 at Benenden, Alice Wat' of High Halden (B.T.)

JOHN, was named in will of his mother Joan Bigge in 1550 at which time he was under 22. So, he could not have been the same John named as eldest son of Richard in 1532.

Ref.: Parish Registers; Bishop's Transcripts; Probate records at Maidstone, Kent; Prerogative Court of Canterbury Wills; Chancery Court Records

16

JOHN BIGGE (*Richard, Roger*) of Benenden, Kent, was born probably between 1445 and 1455 at the latest. He married Alice Glover, daughter of John Glover of Benenden. This we learn from the wills of her father and of her brother, Thomas. John Bigge died at an early age, probably at about 30. He must have been ailing, for he had time to make his will. Altho he named no children, he did bequeath to his sons. So, he had at least two when he died. Of these, Richard apparently was the only one to survive for long, for only Richard was named in the will of his grandfather Glover in 1489. Since Alice was not among the legatees of John Glover, she too probably died between 1479 and 1489. An abstract of John Bigge's will follows.

> 27 October 1479 - the will of John Bygg junior of Benynden. to be buried in the parish church there ... to the high altar there 3s.4d., to the high altar of Tenterden 20d. To Agnes Bygg my mother whom I make executrix, all the residue... Regarding my lands in Benynden willed to me by Richard Bygg my father, lately deceased, to my mother for life, then to be divided among my sons at age 18...if they all die s.p. then to my brothers Robert and Thomas Bygg who shall pay £10 for prayers for my father, my mother and Alice my wife, 5 marks to my sister Katherine, etc. Proved 17 May 1480 by the executrix. (Reference: A 3:294)

Children, all born at Benenden:

8 RICHARD, b prob. 1475-79; m Joan ____ ; he d 1533; Joan d 1550; he had at least 9 ch. which 9 he named in his will; some of them may have been by an unk. earlier wife; Joan may have m again to another Bigge, had more ch., as she named 5 other ch. & omitted 4 that he had named

SON, another, referred to in his father's 1479 will; he prob. d before 1489 as his grandfather Glover named only Richard as a legatee

Ref.: Probate Records at Maidstone; P.C.C. Wills

SAINT GEORGE'S CHURCH, BENENDEN, KENT

RICHARD BIGGE (*Roger*, probably) was born about 1420 perhaps, most likely at Benenden in Kent where the Bigge family lived for many generations. Richard Bigge died in May or June 1474, survived by his wife, Agnes, and their four children. Agnes and one Thomas Henley were named as executors. Perhaps she was a Henley and Thomas was her brother. She was living in 1479 according to her son John's will.

12 May 1474 - the will of Richard Bygge of Benynden ...to be buried in parish church there ..executors to be my wife Agnes and Thomas Henley...witnesses: John Bygge senior, Richard Daye, John Willard senior et al.. to Robert my son my tenement called Bowmannys of 7 acres, also all lands and woods between Everyndens Cross & Hallynden on north side of street, a piece of land called Strodes of 5 acres, Pettefield of 5 acres, Southlands of 8 acres, etc., Robert to pay my wife Agnes yearly for life 26s.8d., to pay my son Thomas Bygge 20 marks...son John to have all other lands not bequeathed, he to pay to son Thomas £20, and to wife Agnes £20, she to have west end of the hall of my principal tenement, maintenance for life ...a piece of land next to Thomas Freynch to be sold and of money received to Agnes the daughter of Robert 26s.8d. and to Joan his daughter 6s.8d. and residue for repair of the church way from the church to Walkhurst gate. Proved 14 June 1474. (A 2:302)

Children:

ROBERT, prob. eldest son; he d in third quarter of 1500, survived by 6 ch. of whom his dau. Elizabeth d a few days later, both leaving wills, abstracts of which follow.

1 July 1500 - the will of Robert Bigge of Benynden....to be buried in the churchyard of Saint George at Benynden...to Agnes Watt and to Johane Lellysden my daughters a cow, to William Day, Harry Bigge, Harry Asten and John Watt my feoffees deliver after my decease to Elizabeth my daughter 2 pieces of land at Benynden in the parish of Rollynden... Residue to Thomas Bigge and Edward Bigge my sons, they to be executors. Witnesses: Robert Marden, Richard Astyn, William Watt, Thomas Lellysden. Pr. 15 Sept. 1500 (8:31)

17 July 1500 - the will of Elizabeth Bigge of Benynden...to be buried in the churchyard..to Elizabeth Lellisden my god daughter 10s., to Johane Watt my goddaughter an heifer, to Anne Benneman 12d., to Johane Bigge the daughter of Stevyn Bigge 12d., to Anne Mannyng 12d., to Elizabeth Willard 4d., to Richard Hamond and Alcon his wife 3s. 4d., and to the said Alson my petticoat, to each of the sons of

Richard Asten 12d., to John Watt, James Watt and to Alice Watt 12d. each, to each of the sons of Thomas Lellysden 12d., to Robert Bigge the son of Edward Bigge 12d., to Parnell Asten my sister my best gown, to Alice the wife of the said Edward Bigge my gown next the best, to Johane Lellysden my best kirtle, to Johane Anoke my next best kirtle and 2 pewter dishes, to 2 unmarried daughters of William Hart each a pewter platter, to Johane Marden a platter and a dish, to Mildred Yonge a platter and my best necklace, to Johane Raynold a pewter dish and a candlestick, to the wife of Richard Motard my harnessed girdle. Thomas Bigge and Edward Bigge my brothers to be executors. Pr. 15 Sept. 1500 (8:31)

THOMAS, named in his father's will of 1474 and brother John's will of 1479; perhaps he was the Thomas Bigge who d in 1509, intestate

16 JOHN, m Alice Glover, dau. of John; he d 1479-80, leaving wife, mother & several underage ch. One of his sons was Richard Bigge who d testate in 1533. An abstract of his will follows

27 October 1479 - the will of John Bygg junior of Benynden. to be buried in the parish church there ... to the high altar there 3s.4d., to the high altar of Tenterden 20d. To Agnes Bygg my mother whom I make executrix, all the residue... Regarding my lands in Benynden willed to me by Richard Bygg my father, lately deceased, to my mother for life, then to be divided among my sons at age 18...if they all die s.p. then to my brothers Robert and Thomas Bygg who shall pay £10 for prayers for my father, my mother and Alice my wife, 5 marks to my sister Katherine, etc. Proved 17 May 1480 by the executrix. (Reference: A 3:294)

KATHERINE, mentioned in brother John's will, but not his father's will. Perhaps she was an in-law, rather than a blood sister

Ref.: Wills In Archives of Maidstone, Kent

34

JOHN GLOVER (*James*) of Benenden, Kent, was probably born between 1439 and 1446. He was a prosperous land holder of Benenden and nearby. His first wife was the mother of his children. His second wife was Joan, apparently the widow of John Locas. John died in 1489. Joan died in 1502. Both left wills.

6 June 1489 - the testament of John Glover of Benynden...to be buried in the church of Saint George of Benynden..to the high altar for tithes forgotten 10s. ..for a light at the altar 12d., to Saint John the Baptist 12d., to the image of the Blessed Virgin Mary 12d. ..to my wife Joan my two best cows...wife Joan to enjoy for the term of her widowhood one ten gallon cooking pot, 2 boards, one pair of trestles and the hangings in the hall, but if she remarry, then to my son Thomas...to Joan my wife one silver bowl while she remains a widow, then at age 24 to Richard Bigge son of John Bigge, but if she remarry before Richard comes to age 24, then the silver bowl to be in the custody of Thomas Glover my son...if Richard dies before age 24, then to my son Thomas...to Thomas Watt son of Thomas Watt one of my cattle to the value of 6s.8d...residue of my utensils to wife Joan...to each of my feoffees 3s.4d...Residue to my son Thomas Glover whom I make executor.

The will of John Glover...wife Joan to occupy the place that I dwell in at Benyndennys forstall and a house with a garden at that other side of the street as long as she is a widow, with sufficient fuel each year... if Joan will release 13s.4d. every year of the sum that she hath to her jointure in way of her marriage, then she shall have 2 pieces of land of which one is called Bermfield and the other lying in Benynden on the denne of Benynden, for the time of her widowhood...Joan to have 2 acres called Kynton..the heirs of the said Joan to have 8 days of remedy after her decease to have out of the abovesaid place all the stuff and goods of the said Joan my wife...to Richard Bigg son of John Bigge and of Alice my daughter all my lands and tenements lying in Old Romney at his age of 24, but if he die without issue before that age, then to my next heirs...the profits from the said lands to be spent for my soul until the age of 24 of the said Richard Bigge...to John Glover my godson, son of Thomas Glover aforesaid all my lands and tenements in Sandhurst at his age of 24, except a parcel of land late purchased of Reynold A broke, which I will to Thomas my son...if son John Glover die before age 24 without issue, then lands in Sandhurst to Thomas my son. Proved 14 October. (Ref.: Prerogative Court of Canterbury, 19 Milles)

4 September 1499 - the will of Joan Glover of Benynden, widow... to be buried in the churchyard of Saint George of Benenden...to the high altar for tythes forgotten 6s.8d... a taper of a pound of wax to burn in the church...another to burn before the image of our lady...to William Locas a little chest with a cracked hasp...to the marriage of Joan

Locas £3.6.8...if she dies, then to the marriage of Benett Locas, then to Alice Locas...to John Locas the younger 6s.8d...to Richard Locas 6s.8d...a piece of land called the heath to the said John and Richard when they come to age 18...to the marriage of Joan Hogge 20s. to be paid by John Locas the elder....to the marriage of Agnes Hogge 6s.8d...to John Locas the elder the said land called Heath ...residue to said John Locas the elder, he to be executor. Witnesses: Stephen Philpott and John Crothole. Proved 14 July 1502. (Reference: Archdeaconry Register 8:212)

Children:

17 ALICE, b prob. 1460-66; m John Bigge; a son Richard

THOMAS, b prob. 1460-65; m Agnes (poss. nee Tilden); 5 ch. per 1511 will; son John b by 1489

30 May 1511 - the will of Thomas Glover of Benynden...to be buried in the church of Saint George of Benynden before the images of Saint Sithe and Saint Anthony..to the churches of Benynden, Sandhurst and Cranbrook...6s.8d. toward the repair of the footway between my mansion and Teldene mill .. there be made a door to the utter porch door at the north side of the church of Benynden with 2 windows of wood to the side windows being in the said porch, etc...to Richard my son my second featherbed, a mattress, 2 bolsters, 2 pillows, a white tester, 2 pair of sheets which were James Glover my uncle's, 2 pair of canvas sheets, 4 blankets, a coverlet which was the said James Glover's, another coverlet, a red chest and a black chest which was his mother's, 6 silver spoons, my mazer, a russett harness girdle gilt, a table cloth of diaper, my bed, my great brass pot, another little brass pot, a stolid pan, a bread pan, 6 plates, 6 dishes and 6 saucers...Residue to be divided between Agnes my wife and my 2 young sons. Also, to Richard my cupboard.. to Joan my daughter 5 sheep and to Agnes my daughter 2 sheep... residue unto the disposition of Edmund Roberth, John Rumylden the elder and James Ennyndon the younger, whom I make my executors. To Agnes my wife £6.13.4. within one year after my decease and £5 per year until John and Stephen my sons are 24..Agnes to have 16 loads of fuel wood per year during her widowhood..Agnes to have 6 kine, my best mare...to Richard my son when he...24 years my principal mansion that I dwell in and all lands in Cranbrook except Appulbyes...Richard to have 12 marks a year until age 24...to son Stephen at 24 all my lands in Tenterden and Halden...for the yearly finding of Stephen my son until age 24, 53s.4d. ..to John my son at age 24 all my lands in Rolvenden, Hawkhurst, Lydd and Stone and all the lands my said wife Agnes occupyeth for her widowhood, lands called Appulbye in Benynden, etc...53s.4d. per year for son John until age 24...toward the marriage of each of my daughters £20...if sons die, then to daughters the lands in Benynden and Cranbrook...lands in Sandhurst to Richard Bygge my nephew...lands which descended to me after the death of John Glover my father...Proved 13 November 1511. (Ref.: Prerogative Court of Canterbury, 4 Fetiplace)

Ref.: Wills at Maidstone, Kent; P.C.C. Wills

ROGER BYGGE of Benenden, Kent, died before 1471/2 leaving a widow, Joan, who was almost certainly a second wife and not the mother of his son John whose will identifies them. She perhaps was the mother of William who seems to have been several years younger than the others.

John, Alice and William were certainly the children of Roger. Richard was of the right age and was probably also a son of Roger. There was a John Bygge senior who witnessed Richard's will in 1474, and he was still around in 1479 when John, son of Richard, called himself junior in his own will. How this John senior fits in is unknown.

Of these three sons, we are interested mostly in the one who was the ancestor of Richard Bigge, who died in 1533. William was apparently not that ancestor, as when he died in 1488, he left all minor children, none named Richard, and all probably too young to have been Richard's father.

Probably Richard of 1533 was a grandson of John or Richard below.

Children:

32 RICHARD, prob. b 1420-25; m Agnes ____ who survived him; 4 ch.; he d 1474

12 May 1474 - the will of Richard Bygge of Benynden ...to be buried in parish church there ..executors to be my wife Agnes and Thomas Henley...witnesses: John Bygge senior, Richard Daye, John Willard senior et al.. to Robert my son my tenement called Bowmannys of 7 acres, also all lands and woods between Everyndens Cross & Hallynden on north side of street, a piece of land called Strodes of 5 acres, Pettefield of 5 acres, Southlands of 8 acres, etc., Robert to pay my wife Agnes yearly for life 26s.8d., to pay my son Thomas Bygge 20 marks...son John to have all other lands not bequeathed, he to pay to son Thomas £20, and to wife Agnes £20, she to have west end of the hall of my principal tenement, maintenance for life ...a piece of land next to Thomas Freynch to be sold and of money received to Agnes the daughter of Robert 26s.8d. and to Joan his daughter 6s.8d. and residue for repair of the church way from the church to Walkhurst gate. Proved 14 June 1474. (A 2:302)

ALICE, m William Wayte who d 1488 testate & s.p.

JOHN, m Eleanor ____; had ch.; d 1471-2

27 January 1471/2 - the will of John Bygge the son of Roger Bygge of Benynden ...to be buried in the churchyard of St. George of Nenynden...to each of my sons and daughters 4d. .. executors to be Richard Day, Alain Marden & John Wolff sexton.... all things assigned to Joan the widow of my said father by his will to be carried out.. 3 pieces of land called Bromefields of about 15 acres in Cranbrook to be sold.... wife Eleanor to have £10, provided she release all her rights in 2 pieces of land called the Toote and Welfield of about 4 acres in Benynden in which William Asden, Richard Asden, John Watt & Robert Holstok stand feoffed ...any daughters living to 18 or marriage to have 5 marks ...if no daughters but a son be living then that son to receive the same, and if no son or daughter lives so long, then to wife Eleanor the 5 marks..residue from sale of the land to Joan my father's widow ....in tail half to my brother William and half to my sister Alice Wayte. Household goods to wife Eleanor. Proved 7 September 1472. (Reference: A 2:71)

WILLIAM, m Margery ____; 6 ch.; d 1488

20 May 1488 - the will of William Bygge of Benynden ...to be buried in the churchyard of Benynden...to the high altar 12d...to each godchild 4d...for prayers 33s.4d...for the making of a new rood loft 13s.4d...to Margery my wife 2 oxen, to Stephen my son 2 oxen..Margery to have the home in Benynden as long as she remains a widow, but if she remarry and will release a piece of land called Highfield, then she to receive an annual rent of 13s.4d. for life. Son Stephen to have land called Upperhighfield, a croft of 3 acres beside the house of Thomas Bighe, etc. he to pay 5 marks to daughter Benet at marriage or of age. After decease or remarriage of wife Margery to sons John, Roger, Robert and Thomas when youngest comes to age 21, in tail to each other, then to son Stephen...after decease of Alice Wayte my sister all such lands as were assigned to me by the last will of William Wayte for my son Stephen to be delivered to him, in tail to sons John, Roger, Robert and Thomas, if they all die the land to be sold and £20 to daughter Benet, 10 marks to church work, to the children of John Bygge yeoman 10 marks, to the children of Robert Bygge 10 marks. Residue to wife Margery & Richard Astyn, they to be executors. Proved 10 July 1488. (Ref.: A 5:62)

Ref.: Probate Records at Maidstone, Kent

68

JAMES GLOVER of Wittersham, Kent, had a first wife named Agnes, who apparently was the mother of his children, or at least some of them. His second wife, Joan, was a widow with children by her first marriage when James Glover married her. He had a brother, Thomas Glover, and a sister, Alston Gylden of Halden, according to his will. James Glover made his will 15 February 1456/7 and presumably died shortly thereafter. An abstract of his will follows.

15 February 1456/7 - the testament of James Glover of Wittersham...to be buried in the churchyard of Saint John the Baptist of Wittersham...several bequests to the church ...to each godchild 6d...to each godchild of my wife Agnes 4d...residue to Thomas Potyn, James Maplesden, Stephen Boyden of Wittersham to dispense for good of my soul. Executor William Martyn, Rector of the church of Wittersham

16 February 1456/7 - my will...my executor to sell my woods at Knolle and at Pandyng, my oxen, steers, etc..... Joan my daughter to have one of my best coverlets...servant Joan Pyper 3s.4d..to son John my best bed and he and one of his brethren 2 of my best gowns...remnant of blue cloth & the green cloth for clothing my sons..to John Jaliff my man my best medley gown...to John Piper my other medley gown, to Thomas Bond my green gown, to Browning my fryzzled gown, to George my man my best coat, to Henry Hikoth my other coat, to Harry Downe my nephew hose, to Stephen Germayn my doublet...residue to be divided, part for myself to executors, part to wife, the third part to my children, of which I will that my three eldest sons be supervisors..John my eldest son..2 sons William and Lawrence to go to school 'til they can read and write...then to be put to a worldly occupation...Joan my daughter to have household goods from my part as her share...executor to bestow on works of alms for the soul of John Pen 5s...for the soul of John Potyn sometime my man 3s.4d...for the soul of Po?emanny 6s.8d..my executor to drape a cross at Wittersham beside the place of John Glover for the soul of Agnes Southwyn...Thomas Glover my brother...to William Harlakynden, William Clerk, Thomas Potyn, James Maplesden, Stephen Boyden and Harry Goldynn my feoffees of and in all lands and tenements, etc. in Wittersham, in the isle of Oxena...to deliver such lands...my children come of age.. wife Joan to have yearly 46s.8d...residue of profits from lands 'til my sons come to age 18...when sons come to 24 then lands to them..John my eldest son to have first choice. James my youngest son...if all sons die without issue, then to Thomas Glover my brother and Alston Gylden of Halden my sister and her heirs...Joan my daughter to have toward her marriage 20 marks...John my son to have 3s.4d. of the bequest of Joan Odyerne...Julian Glover the daughter of Joan Odyerne to have 13s.4d...each of my wife's sons

to have 6s.8d. ..each of her daughters to have 3s.4d... each feoffee for his labors 6s.8d...to John Borlin 3s.4d., to Harry Hikott a noble. Witnesses: Stephen Jeffe, Thomas Godfray, William Brownyng. (Ref.: Consistory Court of Canterbury, Book 2:100)

The Parish Church of Saint John the Baptist, Wittersham, Kent. Wittersham was the home of James Glover, grandfather of John Bigge.

Children, probably all born at Wittersham:

34 JOHN, eldest son, b prob. 1439-1446; under age in 1456
SONS, 2 more, referred to in their father's will
JOAN
WILLIAM, of preschool age in 1456
LAWRENCE, of preschool age in 1456; prob. d.s.p.
JAMES, youngest son, prob. b 1450-1456

Ref.: Wills at Maidstone, Kent; P.C.C. Wills

THE BRACKETT – BLOWER – FROST ANCESTRY

Compiled by
John Brooks Threlfall
Except Ancestors Nos.
30, 56, 58, 62, 124 & 248
which are the work of
Harold F. Porter, Jr.

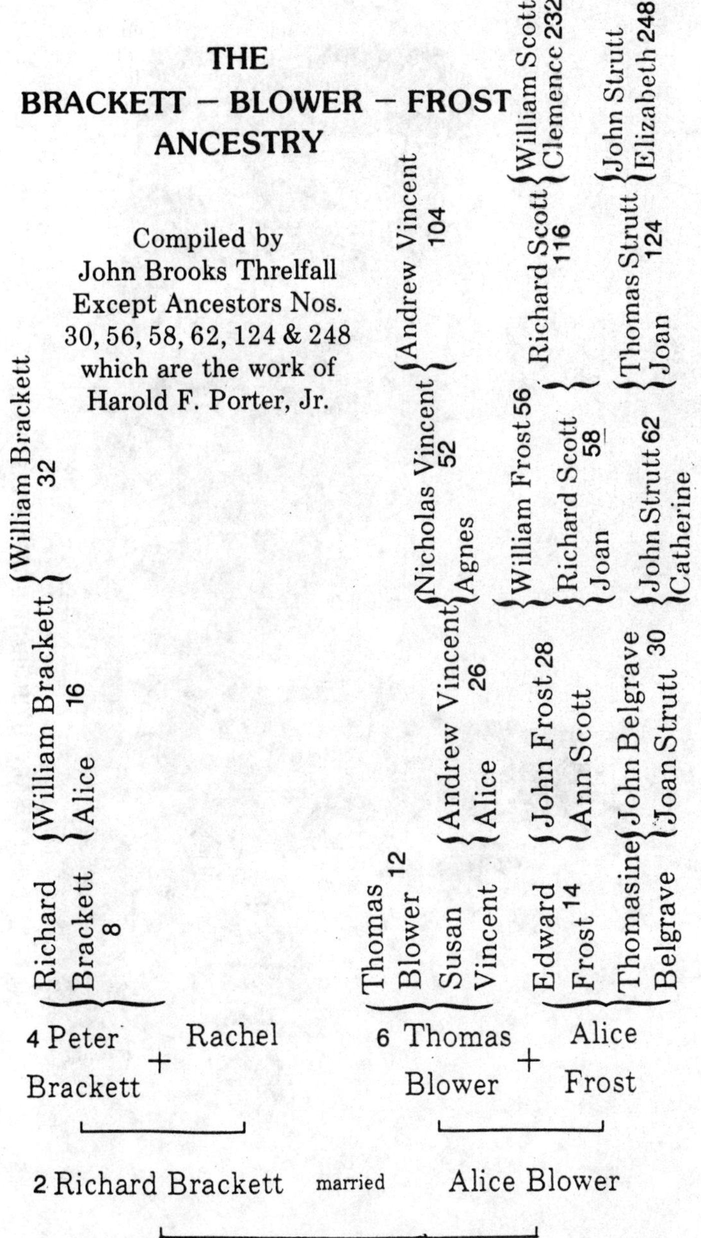

ALL SAINTS CHURCH, SUDBURY, SUFFOLK

2

RICHARD BRACKETT (*Peter, Richard, William*) was baptized 16 September 1610 at Saint Gregory's in Sudbury, Suffolk, England. At the age of six, he was left fatherless, but his mother soon remarried to Martin Saunders. At the age of about 20, he sailed off to New England with the Winthrop Fleet, for he was in Massachusetts as early as 27 August 1630, when he was among the organizers of the First Church of Boston, being 144th on the list of members.

He returned to England, perhaps in 1633, for in the register of Saint Katherine by the Tower, London, is the 16 January 1633/4 marriage of Richard Brackett and Alice Blower. Alice, like Richard, grew up in Sudbury, but her parents had moved to London about this time. They surely knew each other in Sudbury. A year later they were in Boston where their daughter, Hannah, was baptized on 4 January 1634/5. Presumably they sailed for America shortly after their marriage. On 8 November 1635, "Alice, wife of our brother Richard Brackett signed the covenant", thus joining the church in Boston. He was admitted freeman in Boston on 25 May 1636 and on 23 November 1636 he joined the Ancient and Honorable Artillery Company.

On 21 March 1636, he was granted a lot on which to build. He chose a lot now on Washington Street, nearly midway between the present West and Boyalston Streets. He lived there until about 20 November 1637 when he was appointed by the General Court to keep the prison. His salary was £13.6s.8d. (increased 6 June 1639 to £20) and the use of a house. The next year, he sold his Washington Street property, permission to sell being granted 11 June 1638.

About 1637-8, his older brother Peter joined him in New England at Boston, his mother and step-father having crossed over in 1635. They all later settled in Braintree.

On 12 February 1639, leave was granted "to our Bro. Rich. Brackett to mowe the Marsh lying in the Newfield which he hath usually mowen, for the next summer time". The marsh was at Mount Wollaston in Braintree, at that time a part of the town of Boston. Braintree was incorporated in 1640. Richard Brackett moved there about 1641 or 1642, for the records of the First Church of Boston under 26 June 1641 read:

"Richard Brackett was with wife Alice and his sister dismissed from the First Church in Boston with letter to church connected therewith at the Mount."

His sister referred to above was Rachel Newcomb.

Under 8 May 1642:

"Our Bro. Richard Brackett was granted by the church to be dismissed to ye church at Braintree at theer desire with ye Office of Deacon amongst you."

He was ordained a deacon on 21 July 1642 at Braintree and held the office until he died.

A Suffolk, Massachusetts Deed of 25 October 1660 reads:

Richard Brackett of Braintree, husbandman, sells 30 acres of woodland in township of Braintree but belonging to Boston, and about 25 years past by sd town of Boston g'td and laid out to other men as by record of said town appeareth - (Deed 6:237)

There were tracts of land in Braintree that were claimed by the town of Boston. It appointed Captain Richard to oversee these tracts as its agent, as:

"Agreed with Captain Richard Brackett of Braintree that he should, in the town's behalf, take care that noe wast or strip of woods or timber be in the land belonginge to this town lying neere their towne, but do his utmost to prevent it, or give information to the Selectmen. In consideration whereof he hath libertie to cutt out of the wood already fallen to the value of 40 cord. - 25 December 1676".

Richard was granted by the town of Boston:

"Libertie to cut soe much Tymber upon the Common land of Braintree as may serve for ye buildinge of a ¼ pte of a vessel of 25 tun, in consideration of his care of the timber lands".

Clearly, Richard was a trusted agent of the town of Boston.

There was another tract of considerable extent in Braintree, which the town of Boston claimed. Quite all, or a large part of the tract, the town of Braintree purchased from an Indian chief. It was the desire of a great portion of the people to commence action for the recovery of the tract from Boston. This was opposed by a few of the town, notably by Richard Brackett and Edmund Quincy.

In March 1682, they were appointed to a committee to deal with the town of Boston. Ultimately, the committee secured for Braintree what is known as the six hundred acre lot.

He became the first town clerk of Braintree. In 1652, he was chosen selectman, and again in 1670 and 1672. The highest office his townsmen could bestow on him was deputy to the General Court. He was first elected to this position in 1643, next in 1655 and again in 1665 and 1667. In 1671, he was elected again and continued for four years until there was a greater need for his services in another capacity. In 1675, King Philip's War commenced. No lasting peace was secured until 1679. In 1680, he again returned to his seat in the General Court for the last time.

He was chosen sergeant on the organization of the train band in Braintree. In a few years he rose to Lieutenant. About 1654, he was appointed Captain.

The raids by the Indians induced the colony to establish a garrison near the line between Braintree and Bridgewater. The military committee of the General Court appointed Mr. Richard Thayer to take charge thereof. He raised an alarm on the most meager of rumors and stalked every phantom of the forest. Night and day, the people of Braintree lived in terror of being attacked by King Philip and his braves.

One day, one of King Philip's men, John George, a poor half starved wretch, came through the snow on his hands and knees to the garrison house to surrender. He was too weak to walk. He was the only Indian seen by Thayer and his garrison during their campaign. The capture of John George was loudly proclaimed as an instance of Thayer's vigilance and as evidence that real Indians were in the country. Thayer kept John George in the garrison house for five weeks at the expense of the town, apparently wanting to get the Indian in good physical condition as an exhibit. What with being constantly on the alert for weeks, marching at all seasons, night and day, with one false alarm but passing away before another was raised, Richard Brackett's patience was sorely strained. He had to put up with it because Thayer was the General Court's man. However, when Thayer got a live Indian whom he kept in the garrison house at the expense of the town, an opportunity was presented to do something. The old jailer thought the jail was a good enough place for John George. He went with a detail of men to where Thayer was boarding John George, took the Indian away from his keeper and carried him forthwith to Boston. Thayer protested and petitioned. He said that he had a grievance and that all his bills were not paid by the town. Richard had ready the evidence of his men in support of the course he had taken, which was approved by those in authority.

The General Court, in its might, took upon itself to banish the poor Indian from the country. That is, he was sold into slavery. It is indeed sad that Richard did not free the poor fellow.

There is evidence that Captain Richard Brackett taught the school in Braintree.

On 15 October 1679, he was appointed to take oaths in civil cases and perform marriages.

As he grew older, he sought release from the burdens of public office. On 15 October 1684, the General Court recorded the following:

> On request of Captain Richard Brackett being 73 years of age and the infirmities of age upon him: having formerly desired, and now again to-day, to lay down his place as chief military commander of Braintree, the court granted the request and appointed Lieut. Edmund Quincy to succeed him.

At that time, he had been connected with the company for about 43 years and for 30 years had been its Captain.

In Braintree he was a farmer and was described as a husbandman. He acquired a considerable estate in Braintree and when the town of Billerica was formed, he became a proprietor there. Two sons and two daughters settled there.

He died 5 March 1689/90 and Alice Brackett died eight months later on 3 November 1690, aged 76. No stone marks her burial place but he is buried in the old North precinct of Braintree, now the city of Quincy. His grave is marked by a stone cut about 150 years after his death. However, the inscription seems to be a duplicate of what had been on the original stone.

Here lyeth buried
ye body of
Captain Richard Brackett
Deacon
Aged 80 years
Deceased March 5
1690

The town record says he died 3 March.

A silver cup inscribed B over R & A and used in the Unitarian Church in Braintree (which in early days was Congregational) at communion service, is the gift of Richard Brackett and his wife, Alice, to the church.

His will follows:

January 29, 1689 In the name of God, amen

I, Richard Brackett of Braintree in New England, being mindful of my mortallyty and being of memory and a disposing mind a trusting in God through Jesus Christ, my only savior for eternal life salvation, revoking and making null all former wills by me made, do make and ordain this my last will and testament as followeth.

My will is that all my just debts, if any, be first paid, and funeral charges be defrayed.

Item. I give and bequeath unto my beloved wife, Allice Brackett, all my estate in housing, orchards, lands, and meadows in Braintry for her comfortable subsistence during her natural life, as also the income of my estate at Billerica.

Item. I give to the children of my son John Brackett one-fourth part of all my land and meadows and housing in Billerica, as it shall fall by equal division, to be equally divided to them and their heirs. My meaning is the children that he had by his wife, Hannah Brackett.

Item. I give and bequeath the remaining three parts of my housing, and lands, and meadows in Billerica to my son Peter Brackett and son in law, Simon Crosby, and son in law, Joseph Thompson, and to their heirs, to be equally divided between them.

Item. I give to my son Peter Brackett five pounds in current pay, to be paid by my executors.

Item. My will is that the division of my lands in Billerica, as above disposed, shall be made by indifferent men, the persons concerned in each part to choose one man.

Item. My will is that the children of my son John, and Peter Brackett, Simon Crosby and Joseph Thompson, shall pay unto the two daughters of my son Josiah, deceased, Elizabeth and Sarah, twenty pounds a piece in good pay when they shall attain the age of twenty years respectively: and in want of the payment of said forty pounds, they the said Elizabeth and Sarah shall have one half of the land above mentioned, to them and to their heirs, to be equally divided to them. And in case either of said Elizabeth or Sarah shall die without issue, the legacies to her given shall be to the survivor. I give to the said Sarah, the daughter of my son Josiah, five pounds in current pay and the feather bed her mother carryed away.

Item. I give to my son James all of my now dwelling house, barn, orchard, land and meadows, lying and being in Braintry aforesaid, next and immediately after my wife's decease (excepting what may be necessarily expended for her maintenance during her life) to him and to his heirs forever.

Item. I give to my son in law, Joseph Crosby ten pounds in good pay which ten pounds with the five pounds given to my son Peter Brackett as above, is to be paid within two years after myne and my wifes decease.

Item. I give unto my daughter Hannah Brackett twenty shillings in good pay. I give my great Bible to my daughter Rachel Crosby for her use during her life, and at her decease to be to my grandchild Abigail Thompson.

Item. I give to Hannah Brackett, daughter of my son John, the feather bed which she lyeth on, and bolster what belonged to it and my bedsted in Billerica, with as much movable goods as shall amount to twenty pounds.

Item. I give and bequeath to my beloved wife, Allice Brackett, all the rest of my movables for her comfortable sustenance while she lives, and to be disposed of by her to whom she please at her death.

Item. I appoint and nominate my son James Brackett to be sole executor to this my last will and testament. I have hereunto set my hand and seal the day and year above written.

Signed sealed and published
in presence of us
John Ruggles, Senr.
John Ruggles, Jr.
John Parmenter

Whereas I have given to my grandchild Sarah Brackett, the daughter of my son Josiah Brackett, deceased, five pounds, my will is that it shall be null and void and of none effect; as also the ten pounds given to Joseph Crosby, I give to his daughter Anna Crosby. (seal)

Christopher Webb
Boston, December 19, 1690
Approved John Ruggles, Sen.
John Ruggles, Jr., both at Braintree appearing at Probate

Children:

HANNAH, bapt. 4 Jan. 1634/5 in Boston; m 1, Samuel Kingsley who d 21 May 1662 in Billerica; 3 ch.; m 2, John Blanchard who d 1693 in Dunstable (now Nashua, N.H.). She was killed by Indians in Dunstable 3 July 1706; 11 ch.

JOHN, bapt. 7 May 1637 in Boston; m 1, at Braintree 6 Sept. 1661, Hannah French, by Peter Brackett who was his uncle; 9 ch.; she d 9 May 1674; he m 2, at Billerica, 31 March 1675 widow Ruth Ellis, nee Morse; 4 ch.; he d 18 March 1686/7

PETER, bapt. 7 May 1637, twin to John; m 1, 7 Aug. 1661 Elizabeth Bosworth; she d 30 Nov. 1686; m 2, 30 March 1687 Sarah Foster of Cambridge, nee Parker; 5 ch.; she d 18 April 1718 at Billerica

RACHEL, bapt. 3 Nov. 1639 in Boston; m 15 July 1659 at Braintree, Simon Crosby of Billerica, son of Simon & Ann, b Aug. 1637; 9 ch.; he d 22 Jan. 1725 ae 87 - g.s. at Billerica

MARY, b 12 May 1641; m at Braintree 22 July 1662 Joseph Thompson; 5 ch.; she d 23 March 1671; he d 13 Oct. 1732; res. Billerica

JAMES, b about 1645 at Braintree; m about 1674 Sarah Marsh; he was a cooper; d April 1718 in "ye 73rd year of his age"; she d 6 Oct. 1727 aged 77; 6 or more ch.; res. Braintree

SARAH, m 1 June 1675 at Braintree, Joseph Crosby, b in Feb. 1638/9, brother of Simon; sev. ch.; he d 26 Nov. 1695; she m 2, at Billerica, 26 Oct. 1700, William Rawson of Braintree; he d there 20 Sept. 1726

JOSIAH, b 8 May 1652 at Braintree; m at Billerica 4 Feb. 1672/3 Elizabeth Waldo, dau. of Cornelius of Chelmsford; 2 daus: Sarah b 1674 Billerica, and Elizabeth b 1678/9 at Braintree; he d before 1689

Ref.: Brackett Genealogy; Published Braintree Town Records; Savage; Pope's Pioneers; Suffolk County Probate File #1775; Parish Registers; Bishop's Transcripts

S.W. View of St. Katharine's Church; drawn by Hollar, 1660.

Church was 69' long, 60' wide, choir 63', breadth 32', height of roof 49'. Correctly 5, not 6, windows on the south side - Gentleman's Magazine 1825

4

PETER BRACKETT (*Richard, William, William*) of Sudbury, Suffolk, England was born about 1580-85. His wife's name was Rachel. Taken ill in the prime of his life, he made his will 18 August 1616 and died a week later. He was buried on 25 August 1616 at All Saints, Sudbury. One must wonder what fatal malady it was, which gave him so little hope of recovery that he prepared for death. Three days after his burial, the 28th, his widow proved his will. Except for the religious preamble, it is given in full below. From it, one learns that he left three small children and his wife was expecting a fourth within a few weeks.

Peter Brackett was apparently a substantial citizen, for he owned a house in another parish which was rented out, and the rent from this he left to his father for life.

8 August 1616 - I PETER BRACKET of Sudbury in the countie of Suff and diocesse of Norwich being sicke in bodie but whole in minde ..... Rachell my wiffe shall have all my goods chattells and implemts of householde in consideration that she shall bringe up my children and pay unto every one of my children twentye shillings apeece as namely Peter Richard and Rachell and my will is that that childe wch my wiffe is wth childe wth shall have twentye shillings to be paid unto them at their severall ages of Twenty and one yeares and if any of them doe dye before their portion to be divided among them that shalbe liveing. Item I will and my mynde is that my ffather Richard Bracket shall have the rente of my house in the pishe of St. Peters in Sudburye wherein one Martyn London now dwelleth during his naturall liffe and after his deceasse I will and my minde is that my said house shalbe solde by my wiffe and the money thereof to be devided amonge my children that shalbe then liveing and my will is that my eldest sonne Peter Bracket shall have ffive pounds more then the residue. Item I ordaine and make Rachell my Loving wiffe tobe executrix of this my last will and testament

Witnesses:	------- Ruggle	Peter Bracket
Rychard Bracket	Thomas Grigges	(Proved 28 August 1616)
Edward Strachie	William Strutt	(Reference: Legate 122)

After being left a widow, Rachel doesn't appear in any other English records yet found for two years. Then, however, she remarried to Martin Saunders, a currier of Sudbury.

On or about 10 April 1635, Martin Saunders, Rachel, and their seven minor children, and also her daughter Rachel (Brackett) Newcomb and her husband Francis and two children, all set sail from London aboard the *Planter,* Nicholas Trerice, Master. They arrived in Boston 7 June following. On the passenger list, Martin and Rachel are listed as aged 40 and from Sudbury. With them also were three servants: Mary Fuller age 15, Richard Smith age 14, and Richard Ridley age 16. No more is known of the three young servants. Now the ages given on the passenger list for the Saunders family members were mere estimates on the part of the clerk, as can be shown in the case of the children. Martin and Rachel were apparently nearer 45, or born around 1590, which would make her about 18 at the birth of her first child and 42 at the birth of the last one.

The Bracketts, Newcombs and Saunders, all from Sudbury, all settled in that part of Boston which was soon set off as the town of Braintree. Rachel Saunders was of course the mother of Richard and Peter Brackett, of Rachel Newcomb, and the Saunders children.

Rachel Saunders was admitted to the Boston church on 8 November 1635, the same time as was Richard Brackett's wife, Alice. On 16 April 1639 she was dismissed to the new Braintree church.

Rachel died at Braintree 15 September 1651. Martin Saunders remarried 23 May 1654 to Elizabeth Bancroft, widow of Roger. When his son John was about to marry Mary Munjoy, he deeded him some of his land.

Martin Saunders died 4 August 1658, having made his will 5 July preceding.

THE ESTATE OF MARTIN SAUNDERS

Inventory of the estate of Martine Saunders, senior, of Brantrey, deceased, 4th: 6 ^{mo}.: (58) ....Amount £321.17 ....Appraisers: William Allis, Moses Paine, Edmund Quinsey

For a full, fynall & Amicable Conclusion & Agreement betweene John Saund^{r}s, Martine Saund^{r}s, Francis Elliott & Robert Parmenter, all of Brantrie, sonnes & Sonnes in Law to ye Late Martine Saund^{r}s, of Braintrie. It is agreed upon ye 10th8^{mo}. 1658.

That John Saund^{r}s, Eldest sonne to the Late Martine Saund^{r}s, (the will of ye said Martine, the father, notwithstanding) shall have the house, barne, Cowhouse, together with ye yards, Orchards, Gardens & a Little piece of meadow lyeing to ye house, all wch ye said Martine Saund^{r}s died possessed of, with all ye liberties, &c.

2. It is agreed upon, yt Francis Elliott in right of his wife, shall have yt piece of meadow Lying on ye neck, 6 acres, more or less, to him & to his heirs, &c. And also, with ye £7 he hath had, have it made up out of ye estate of Martine Saundrs ye father, an equall portion with Martine Saundrs & Robert Parmenter.

3. It is further agreed upon, yt Martine Saundrs, youngest sonne, to ye late Martine Saundrs, shall have a piece of upland & meadow, formrly his fathers, in pumpkin hill, Running from his brothr John Saundrs Lyne of 25 Rodds brooad, till it come to the sea, & shall also have it made up an equall prportion with ye rest of his sisters, with what he hath had, at his marriage.

4. It is Lastly concluded & agreed, yt Robert Parmenter, in right of his wife, shall have all ye Lands Lying in Pumpkin hill, together with ye meadow thereunto belonging, excepting 4 acres, yt is John Saundrs, as above, & ye upland & meadow yt is Martine Saundrs, wch Lyeth at ye end of John Saundrs, for his dau. in Law Rachell's use, & shall also have it made up out of ye Estate Left by ye said Martine Saundrs, ye father, an equall p'portion, with his sister Elliott, accounting what his wife had at marriage. Ye parties above mentioned bind ymselves in ye penall sum of £100. This Octr. 1658.

Whereas Francis Elliott, sonne In Law to the Late Martine Saundrs, prsenting a will signed by the Late Martine Saundrs, bearing date 5th 5mo. 1658, about wch yr was some difference & discontent between ye sonnes of ye said Saundrs, wch ye Court Considering of, advised ye Children to Come to a Loveing Agreemt amongst ymselves, yr being severall objections made against ye said will. [All things being amicably settled, an inventory was made, and allowed by the court 2 February 1659]

Children, all born at Sudbury:

PETER, prob. b late 1608, "eldest son"; m 4 Oct. 1632 at Cavendish, Martha Raye; 3 ch. bapt. at All Saints, Sudbury: Peter 7 Sept. 1633, Rachel 22 Feb. 1634/5, Martha 5 May 1636. Martha Brackett was buried 14 Dec. 1637 at All Saints. he m 2, Faith ——, for James son of Peter & Faith was bapt. 6 Oct. 1644 at All Saints. He m 3, Priscilla —— & had 1 more ch., at least 9 total. He m 4, Mary, widow of Nathaniel Williams of Boston who d in 1661. He deposed 19 May 1673 as aged 64

2 RICHARD, bapt. 16 Sept. 1610 at St. Gregory's Sudbury; m 16 Jan. 1633/4 at St. Katherine by the Tower, London, Alice Blower, dau. of Thomas & Alice (Frost) Blower of Stanstead; went to N.E.; 8 ch.; he d 5 March 1689/90 ae 80-g.s. at Quincy, Mass.; she d 3 Nov. 1690 ae 76

RACHEL, bapt. 28 April 1614 at All Saints, Sudbury; m 27 May 1630 at All Saints, Francis Newcomb who was b about 1605; ch.: Rachel bapt. 13 Nov. 1631, John bapt. 8 Aug. 1634, 8 more ch. b in N.E. They sailed for N.E. in 1635 in the *Planter* with her mother, etc., settled in the part of Boston which was soon set off as the town of Braintree. He d 27 May 1692

JONATHAN, bapt. 4 Oct. 1616 at All Saints, a posthumous ch.; prob. d.y.

----Saunders Children----

MARY, bapt. 26 Aug. 1619 at All Saints, Sudbury; m about 1640 in N.E. Francis Eliot, younger brother of the Apostle; 6 ch.; he d 1677

MARTIN, bapt. 4 March 1621/2; buried 25 Nov. 1622 at All Saints

LEAH, bapt. 10 Oct. 1623 at All Saints; m 1, about 1643 at Braintree, John Wheatley who d about 1646; 1 ch. Rachel b about 1644; m 2, 3 April 1648 at Braintree, Robert Parmenter, b about 1622, prob. son of Joseph; 4 ch.; he d 27 June 1696 "ae 74" at Braintree; she d at Braintree 24 March 1706/7

JUDITH, bapt. 27 Dec. 1625; d unm. at Braintree 5 Sept. 1651

JOHN, bapt. 10 March 1627/8; m 9 Oct. 1650 at Braintree, Mary Munjoy, dau. of John of Abbotsham, Devon, England; 6 ch.; she d before 10 Jan. 1683/4 when he made his will naming dau. Mary, wife of Wm. Veazy, sons John & Josiah, both minors; 1 Oct. 1684, prob. contemplating m, he deeded land to sons John & Josiah; he m 2, Hannah —— & had 3 more ch.: Rachel, Daniel, Patience; his will pr. 28 March 1689

MARTIN, bapt. 29 Aug. 1630; m 1 April 1651 at Braintree, Lydia, dau. of Richard & Elizabeth Hardier; of 4 ch. recorded, only Eliz. surv.; he d 4 Sept. 1706 "ae 78" at Braintree; she d 9 March 1712/13

DANIEL, bapt. 25 March 1631/2; buried at All Saints 1 Aug. 1634

CHURCH OF SAINT PETER, SUDBURY, SUFFOLK

Ref.: Probate Records at Bury Saint Edmunds; Parish Registers; Bishop's Transcripts; N.E.H.G.S.-10, 66, 70

6

THOMAS BLOWER (*Thomas*) was baptized 23 April 1587 at Stanstead, England. At the age of ten, his father died. What became of his mother or who cared for the family is unknown. On 19 November 1612 at Stanstead, he married Alice, the daughter of Edward and Thomasine (Belgrave) Frost. She was baptized 1 December 1594 at Stanstead. They probably both grew up in Stanstead which is 5 miles north of Sudbury.

Within two or three years after their marriage, they moved to Sudbury where their children were baptized. Here they must have lived for at least fifteen years. In 1633, Alice got into some sort of dispute with the church authorities, for on 18 February 1633/4, Alice Blower was charged with Contempt of Ecclesiastical Laws before the Court of High Commission. She was fined £100 which was certainly a ruinous amount, which neither she or her husband could raise. This must have been cause for a hasty move to London and an appeal against the fine, for on 26 June 1634, Alice Blower of London, defendant, "having long since removed from Sudbury where the offense was given, to London, whereby the scandal was taken away, she was dismissed". (Calendar of Domestic Papers, Charles I)

It was this sort of religious harassment that prompted so many to leave England for the New World between 1620 and 1640. Whatever the reason, in September 1635 Thomas Blower, set sail in the *Truelove,* John Gibbs, Master. The ship arrived in Boston in late November. He was listed as aged 50 on the passenger list and alone. Ages were often mere estimates and in this case he seems to have been actually aged 48. There is no record of a family with him. His daughter Alice had preceeded him to Boston two years earlier as the young bride of Richard Brackett. Three years later, his sister-in-law and her husband, Edmund Rice, also came to New England to join him.

Nothing can be found of him in New England records except in the Winthrop Papers there is extant a letter written by one Nathaniel Lufkin to Mr. John Winthrop the elder of Boston from Hitcham, Suffolk, dated 1 April 1640, by which Lufkin was owed £24 by Thomas Blower, the debt having been incurred in England, and Lufkin wished it collected in New England where Blower was then living. Lufkin wrote, "...there is one Edmond Rice and Henry Bruning who the bearer knows well who can tell of the debt as well as myself..."

Edmund Rice was married to Thomasine (Frost), sister of Thomas Blower's wife, Alice.

In the Colonial Records is the following:

9 September 1639 - Capt. Keayne was ordered to pay the 12.10s which he rec'd of Mr Saltonstall for pt of Mrs Blowers N [necessaries ?] to the treasurer - Rec. of the Mass. Bay 1:273

Thus, Thomas Blower must have died about 1639, which explains the dearth of record of him. Other Blowers, including John, his son, also appear in the New England records. The others were probably all related to him. When his wife Alice died is not known.

Children (only the father named in the records):

HANNAH, prob. b 1613, 1617 or 1619; buried 7 May 1630 at All Saints, Sudbury

3 ALICE, bapt. 30 June 1615, "daughter of Thomas Blower", at St. Gregory, Sudbury; m 16 Jan. 1633/4 at St. Katherine by the Tower, London, Richard Brackett, son of Peter & Rachel of Sudbury, bapt. 16 Sept. 1610 at St. Gregory; went to N.E.; 8 ch.; she d 3 Nov. 1690 "ae 76" - town of Braintree rec.; he d 5 March 1689/90

HANNAH, prob. b 1617; buried 7 May 1630 at All Saints

THOMAS, prob. b 1619-20; buried 22 Aug. 1623 at All Saints

JOSHUA, bapt. 15 Dec. 1621 at All Saints; buried 22 March 1623/4

THOMAS, bapt. 29 Feb. 1623/4 at All Saints; buried 25 April 1625 at All Saints

MARY, bapt. 13 Feb. 1625/6; buried 7 Feb. 1639/40 at All Saints

JOHN, bapt. 23 March 1627/8; he was in Boston, N.E. in 1650; m Tabitha ——— ; 5 ch.: Tabitha b 12 Feb. 1654/5, Mary b 25 April 1657, John b 19 Oct. 1659, Sarah b 1 July 1662 - d 22 June 1664, Thomas b 19 May 1665. His will of 9 Sept. 1675 named his wife & 4 ch. was pr. 11 Nov. 1675. He was a cooper, had slaves; in 1663 he was recorded as age 36 when he leased an island in Boston Harbor for 7 years. She was alive on 6 June 1684 when she was referred to in a deed as the widow of John Blower.

THOMAS, bapt. 16 May 1630 at All Saints, Sudbury

Ref.: Probate Records at Bury Saint Edmunds; Parish Registers; Bishop's Transcripts; Suffolk County, Mass. Probate Files; Savage; Records of the Mass. Colony, Vol. I; T.A.G. - 21:238

8

RICHARD BRACKETT (*William, William*) was probably born about 1550-1554 at Sudbury, Suffolk, England, where his family had lived for several generations. On 25 September, 1589, at All Saints Church, Sudbury, he married Alice Harper. This must have been a second marriage for him, for it was too late for the births of Richard, Rose, Peter and Tobias, who must have been his children, and certainly for Margerie, whose baptism is recorded. By Alice he had one or two children. Then she died and was buried on 17 May 1595 at Saint Peter's in Sudbury. He then married for a third time, on 4 February 1601/2 at Long Melford, the widow Greengrasse. He apparently moved to Long Melford about this time. Long Melford is the next town to the north of Sudbury.

He and his son, Richard, junior, were on a jury in Long Melford in 1609 and again on 8 June 1612. On 16 June 1617, Richard Brackett surrendered a tenement, which he had taken on 20 June 1614, so that it might be regranted to himself and his wife, Elizabeth. This amounted to a renewal of a farm lease. It would imply that Elizabeth was the former widow Greengrasse. Richard Bracket, senior, was buried on 26 May 1626 at Long Melford.

Children:

RICHARD, presumably a son, b about 1580-85; m 30 May 1607 at Long Melford, Margaret Weeden; ch. bapt. there: Agnes 26 April 1608, Abraham 31 May 1609 (he m Ann Mabson 1633 & had ch.), Isaack 14 March 1610/11, Alice 1 April 1613 - d.y., Richard 13 Dec. 1614 (he m Joan —— & had ch.), Margaret 11 Jan. 1617/18, Eden 10 Oct. 1619 - prob. d.y., Anne [dau.] "of Richard" buried 12 Oct. 1620. Margaret, wife of Richard, was buried 19 July 1620. He m 2, Mary; ch.: Abigail 22 Aug. 1621, Alice 16 Feb. 1622/3; Mary, wife of Richard, buried 21 Sept. 1626; he m 3, ?; ch.: William 1 July 1627, Thomas 26 Sept. 1630, Dorothy 26 Jan. 1633/4. A ch. of Richard Brackett's was buried 24 March 1638/9.

ROSE, prob., a dau.; she m 28 Aug. 1603 at St. Peter's in Sudbury, William Chapman

TOBIAS, was prob. a son b about 1585-90; he m 1, 1 Sept. 1613 at Long Melford, Joan Fleete; had a dau. Katherine bapt. 20 Aug. 1614 - buried 5 Sept. 1624. Tobias was buried 23 June 1634; the widow Joan was buried 18 Jan. 1635/6 at Long Melford

4 PETER, b about 1580-85; m Rachel ———; 4 ch.: Peter b about 1608, Richard bapt. 16 Sept. 1610, Rachel bapt. 28 April 1614, Jonathan bapt. 4 Oct. 1616 (all at Sudbury). He was buried 25 Aug. 1616 at All Saints, Sudbury

MARGERIE, bapt. 17 Feb. 1582/3 at St. Peter's

----by wife Alice Harper----

ROBERT, bapt. 30 Sept. 1593 at St. Peter's; buried there 6 Dec. 1598

ELLEN, perhaps, who m 14 Nov. 1615 at All Saints, Sudbury, Stephen Wood

----by his last wife, the widow Greengrasse----

EDWARD, bapt. 24 Dec. 1603 at St. Peter's Sudbury; m 5 Feb. 1628/9 at All Saints, Frances Landsall; ch.: Edward bapt. 12 Dec. 1630 at Long Melford, Mary bapt. 13 Oct. 1633 - buried 23 Feb. 1633/4 at St. Gregory's in Sudbury, Mary bapt. 13 Oct. 1633, George bapt. 23 Oct. 1639 at St. Gregory's

HOLY TRINITY CHURCH, LONG MELFORD, SUFFOLK

Ref.: Parish Registers; Bishop's Transcripts; Probate Records at Bury Saint Edmunds

12

THOMAS BLOWER (*Thomas?*) a tanner of Lavenham, Suffolk, England, came from a family that had lived nearby for many generations. In 1464, Thomas Blower of Bildeston made his will and bequeathed to his son John Blower, his son [in-law?] John Cowper of Boxford, and to Thomas Blower who was another son. The will was proved on 23 September of that year. On 7 September 1503, Peter Blower of Melford made his will. No children were mentioned. On 8 October 1481, Mawte [i.e. presumably Maud] Blower of Lavenham made her will and bequeathed her estate to several church and charitable entities, but named no relatives. These were surely relatives of Thomas, perhaps ancestors.

Nicholas Blower of Lavenham was probably Thomas's brother. Nicholas had the following children recorded there.

NICHOLAS, bapt. 8 Jan. 1575/6; buried 6 Oct. 1577
RACHEL, bapt. 27 April 1578; buried 6 Aug. 1580
RACHEL, bapt. 18 Oct. 1580; buried 26 Oct. 1581
WILLIAM, prob. a twin; buried 25 Oct. 1581
ANNE, bapt. 23 Sept. 1582
SAMUEL, bapt. 2 May 1585
ISAAC, bapt. 26 Nov. 1587
ELIZABETH, bapt. 1 Feb. 1589/90; buried 23 Oct. 1590

Another probable brother to Thomas was Robert Blower of Lavenham whose first wife, Joan, was buried there on 2 March 1563/4. He married secondly, on 12 June 1567/8, Joan Hareknop. Robert Blower was buried 4 June 1585. A Joan Blower, probably his widow, married on 7 April 1591, Edmund Yates. Joan Blower, who was baptized 18 June 1559, was probably the youngest sister of these three Blower men. There is no more record of her. Who were their parents? Rose Blower, wife of Thomas Blower of Lavenham, was buried there on 2 April 1568. She was probably their mother and Thomas, her husband, their father.

Thomas Blower married first, on 10 August 1574 at Long Melford, Suffolk, Alice Sparpointe. She died in 1581, and he married secondly, on 27 February 1581/2 at Bildeston, Susan Vincent, daughter of Andrew and Alice Vincent of Bildeston. Alice was born about 1560.

On 28 September 1597, sick and knowing that death was near, he made his will and died, probably the next day. He was buried at Lavenham on 1 October 1597. Except for the religious preamble, his will is given in full below. No further record of Susan can be found.

28 September 1597 - I Thomas Blowere of Lavhame in the countie of Suff tannere Beinge sycke in bodye But holl in mynd ... Item I will that Sussana my wyfe paye unto John Blower my eldest sonne when he shalbe of the age of xxiiij yers the sume of thyrtie pounds of good & lawfull monye of England & xx£ when he shalbe of the age of xxv years & yf ye said John soo longe shall lyve But yf the forsayd John doo dye befor eyther of ye payments growe dewe then I wyll his porcione to be equalye devyded amongst my sonnes & daughters then shalbe lyvinge Item I will that my land lyinge in Melforde holdene of the parsones of Melford ase these landes be equallye devided Betwene my ii sonnes John & Thomas Blowere eyther of them payinge out of it unto ye childe that now Sussan my wyfe is wthall yf it happene to be a sonne & lyve to ye age of xxiiij yers at ye age of xxiiij yers xv£ apece & yf it hapene to be a daughter then eyther of them to paye unto yt fyftye shyllynge in good & lawfull monye of England and soo then further to pay unto there other fower systers Sussana Alice Rachell & Mary Blowere fyftie shillynge apece of lyke Englyshe monye when they shalbe of the age of xxi yers & yf eyther of my sayd daughters dye before then there porcione to be devd then I will that those of them that lyve untill it be dewe shall equallye Injoye there partes Item I will that Susana my wyfe shall have to here & here heyres forevere all that my tenment wth ye lande & pasture thereunto belonging syttuate lying & being in Stanstede wythe all my debtes & other my movabell goods what soo ever yeldynge & payinge to that chylde that now she is wthall yf it be adaughter at the age of xxi yers the sum of v£ of lawfull English monye & allsoo to my other fower daughters Susana Alice Rachell & Mary lyke sums of v£ apece to bee payd unto eyther of theme at ye lyke age of xxj yers And to this my last will I apoynte and ordayne for my executors Susana Blower my wyfe & Nicholas Vincent Brother unto ye for named Susana and in testymonye that this is my wyll & testament I the forsayd Thomas have setto my hand thes beinge witnesses

John Day — by me Tomas blower
John Wright — (Proved 27 October 1597)

(Reference: Blomfield 313)

Children, all baptized at Stanstead:

THOMAS, bapt. 10 Oct. 1576; buried 20 Oct. 1576
MARGARET, bapt. 17 Nov. 1577; buried 16 Dec. 1577
JOHN, bapt. 14 June 1579; eldest son alive in 1597.

The will abstracted below is probably his.

10 May 1642 - the will of JOHN BLOWER, clerk, of Mildenhall, Suffolk ... to undutiful daughter Emily whom I beseech God to forgive & make her his servant £5 ... daughter Mary already given unto ... to son John now in St. Christopher £10 one month after his arrival in England ... to Thomas my son £25 within 3 months after the expiration of his apprenticeship ... to my son William £20 when he has served his apprenticeship ... all the rest of my goods to my wife Audry, she to be executrix ... signed John Blower. Proved 5 September 1642. (Ref. R2/58/372)

SUSANNA, prob. b 1581; m 20 May 1602 at Lavenham, George Rugle [Ruggles?]

---- by his second wife ----

JOSHUA, bapt. 16 Dec. 1582; d.y.

THOMAS, bapt. 15 Dec. 1585; d.y.

6 THOMAS, bapt. 23 April 1587; m 19 Nov. 1612 at Stanstead, Alice Frost, dau. of Edward & Thomasine (Belgrave) Frost, bapt. 1 Dec. 1594; he came to N.E. in 1635 in the *Truelove*, aged about 50

CALEB, bapt. 7 July 1588; buried 16 July

ALICE, bapt. 15 March 1589/90; alive in 1597

RACHEL, bapt. 12 Oct. 1591; buried 13 Dec. 1595

MARY, bapt. 25 Feb. 1592/3; alive in 1597

RACHEL, bapt. 13 Dec. 1595 at Lavenham; m 22 Oct. 1615 at St. Gregory's, Sudbury, Mark Salter; ch.: John bapt. 24 May 1618 - buried 2 Nov. 1618, Samuel bapt. 8 Sept. 1633, Matthew bapt. 1 March 1625/6 at All Saints, Rachel buried 11 Sept. 1626

CHILD, posthumous, b 1597-8

CHURCH OF SAINT JAMES, STANSTEAD, SUFFOLK

Ref.: Parish Registers & Bishop's Transcripts of same; Suffolk County, England Probate Records

THE CHURCH OF SAINT PETER & SAINT PAUL,
LAVENHAM, SUFFOLK

14

EDWARD FROST *(John)* was baptized 13 March 1560/61 at Glemsford, Suffolk, England. On 26 September 1585 at Glemsford he married Thomasine Belgrave, daughter of John and Joanna (Strutt) Belgrave. She was baptized 1 February 1561/2 at Leverington in Cambridgeshire. Edward Frost was a clothier. About 1588-9 they moved to Stanstead, the next town to the northeast, for there their children born thereafter were baptized. Edward was buried at Stanstead on 3 August 1616, his wife surviving him. An abstract of his will follows.

> 26 July 1616 - the will of Edward Frost of Stanstead, county of Suffolk, clothier...bequests to Thomasine my wife, to William my son, to my five daughters: Elizabeth, now the wife of Henry Rice; Anne, now the wife of Lawrence Collen; Alice, wife of Thomas Blower, Mary Frost and Thomasine Frost...and to Edward Rice, son of my daughter Elizabeth Rice. Executrix to be my wife Thomasine. Witnesses: Ambrose Bigges, senior & Ambrose Bigges, junior. Proved 4 October 1616. (Prerogative Court of Canterbury 129 Cope)

Children:

ANNE, bapt. 28 Nov. 1586 at Glemsford; buried 27 Dec. 1586

ELIZABETH, bapt. 24 March 1587/8 at Glemsford; m at Stanstead 12 Nov. 1605, Henry Rice, prob. elder brother of Edmund (#532), possibly his father - a 2nd wife in that case; 6 ch.; he d in Nov. 1621 at Stanstead; she m 2, at St. Mary's, Bury St.Edmunds, 24 Jan. 1621/2 Philemon Whale; they moved to N.E., settled in Sudbury, Mass.

WILLIAM, bapt. 19 Sept. 1589 at Stanstead; m 29 Nov. 1610 at Stanstead, Abigail Bowser who was bapt. 25 April 1592, the dau. of Henry Bowser, clerk; he was buried 3 Feb. 1624/5. he had ch.

ANN, bapt. 3 Dec. 1592 at Stanstead; m 25 Oct. 1613 at St. Mary's in Bury St. Edmunds, Laurence Collin

7 ALICE, bapt. 1 Dec. 1594 at Stanstead; m 19 Nov. 1612 at Stanstead, Thomas Blower son of Thomas & Susan (Vincent) Blower, bapt. 23 April 1587; prob. 9 ch.; he d about 1639 in Massachusetts.

MARY, bapt. 20 Sept. 1596 at Stanstead; buried there 13 Nov. 1596.

MARY, prob. b 1597 or 1598; living & unm. 1616; she was prob. the Mary Frost who m 11 Sept. 1617 at Stanstead, Edmund Salloman, or 18 Sept. 1622, John Scott

THOMASINE, bapt. 10 Aug. 1600 at Std.; m 15 Aug. 1618 at St. Mary's, Bury St. Edmunds, Edmund Rice; 10 ch.; went to N.E.; she d 13 June 1654; he m 2, 1 March 1654/5, widow Mercy Brigham, had 2 more ch.

Ref.: American Genealogist, Jan. 1950; Parish Registers; Bishop's Transcripts

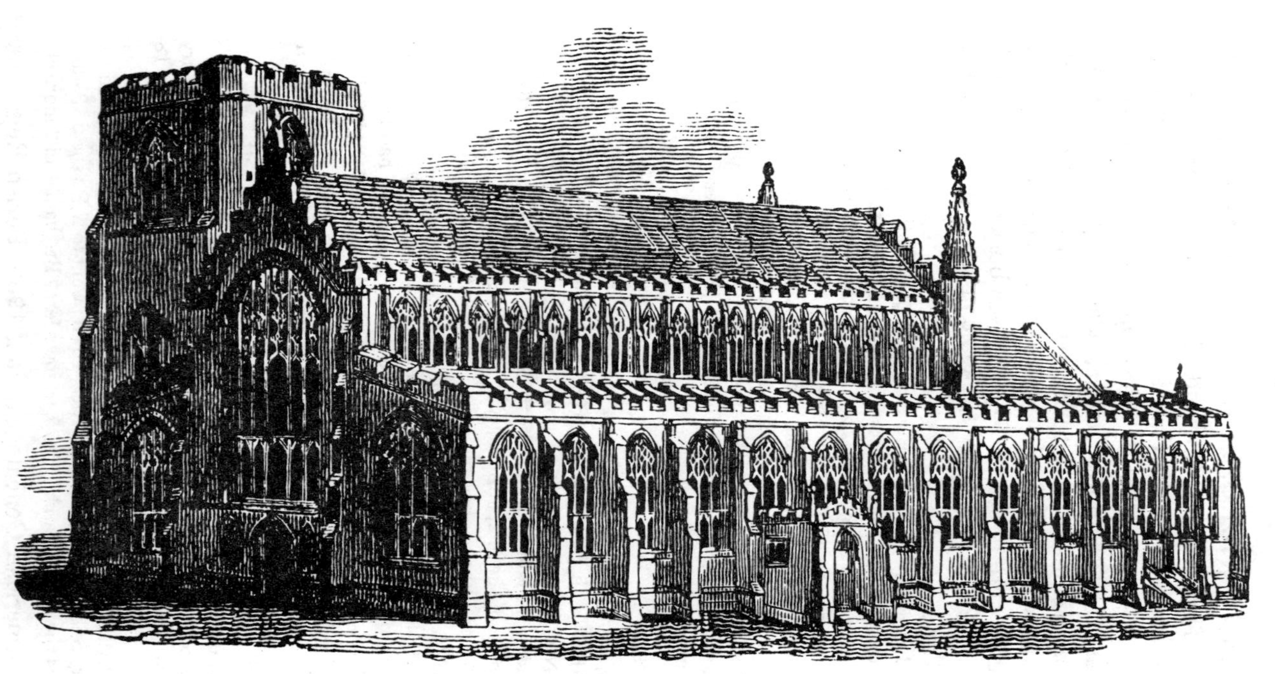

Saint Mary's Church, Bury Saint Edmunds, where Thomasine Frost was married. Built about 1433, the fifth church on this site, the first one built about 633 A.D.

16

WILLIAM BRACKETT (*William*), like his brothers George and Thomas, and his father before him, lived in Sudbury, Suffolk. He was born about 1515-1520. He was a butcher by trade and had a shop, or stall as it was called, in Sudbury. This he left to his son William.

However, it appears that he lived for a few years in Bury Saint Edmunds, for here we find the baptismal records of several children. Of the six entries, only the last one for the baptism of a daughter gives the father's name. Presumably all the others were also William's children. Also, there was no other known William Brackett and there is no record otherwise of him in Bury Saint Edmunds, so he must have returned to his native Sudbury where he died. Sudbury and Bury Saint Edmunds are about 14 miles apart.

In the 1568 Subsidy Return, he is listed in the parish of Saint Peter, and was taxed 14 shillings on £5 worth of goods.

On 4 May 1575, he made his will and was buried two days later on the 6th at Saint Peter's, not Saint Gregory's as he had requested in his will.

On 11 September 1575, four months later, at Saint Gregory's Church, Alice Brackett remarried to Richard Morells (or Merrells).

4 May 1575 - The will of WILLIAM BRACKETT of Sudbury, Suffolk, Botcher, being at this time in perfect memory ... my body to be buried in the churchyard of St. Gregoryes ... all my houses with the appurtenances in Sudbury which I have shalbe sold by Richard Brackett my son & Peter Haliwell of little Cornard within two years next & immediately ensuing my decease to the most advantage ... the money to be disburst in manner & form following ... to Alyce Brackett my wife £40 presently after the sale is made. In consideration of it she shall keep Willm Brackett & Maud Brackett my children & if she chance to die or sale be made then I will and give the same £40 to Willm Brackett my son & Maud Brackett my daughter to be equally divided between them ... to Edmond Brackett my son £30 to be paid after my houses be sold ... if he die, to his children at 21 .... to Maud Brackett my daughter £10 which Alice my wife is to receive and give bond to my executor to pay to Maud at age 18, but if Maud die before age 18, the £10 to go to William Brackett my son ... to Richard Brackett my son the residue of the proceeds of the sale .....if the said Richard be able to bind the said houses then I will that he shall have the p'forment thereof giving for the same as another man will ... Alice my wife to have the occupation of all my said houses rent free until they be sold ... to George Brackett my

brother my maser tipped with silver & all my apparrell .... to Willm Brackett my son & to his heirs my staule in the m'kytte ... Alice my wife to receive the profit thereof until he reaches 21 but if he die before 21, then the same staule unto Maud my daughter ... to Alice my wife all the movable goods within the houses, one cow & all the swine, except one feather bed & one boulster which lyeth on the bed next the entry which I do give unto Richard my son ....to Richard Brackett my son all my leases of all those grounds, lands & meadows which I now hold & occupy..., all my corn now growing, and all my goods, chattels & movables unbequeathed. Richard to be the executor, Thomas Smyth to be overseer. Witnesses: Lawrence Newman Clarke, George Brackytte, Willm Curd, Nicholas Ruggell, John Brackytte & Thomas Smythe with others.
Proved 5 July 1575 (Ref.: Wroo 88)

Children:

EDMUND, apparently eldest surv. son; ch.: William buried 23 Jan. 1564/5, Faythe bapt. 2 Dec. 1665 (both at St. Gregory's), prob. 4 more ch. b 1667-73, Elizabeth bapt. 10 July 1575 at St. Peter's, Judith bapt. 8 Sept. 1577 & buried 9 July 1580, Edith bapt. 5 June 1580 (last 2 at All Saints)

MARGARET, prob. his dau., was bapt. 30 June 1544 at St. Mary's, Bury St. Edmunds, buried there 1 July 1545, parents not named

SUSAN, bapt. 14 June 1545 at St. James, Bury St. Edmunds, parents not named; she must have d.y. as no further record of her

(ILLEGIBLE), bapt. 22 Feb. 1546/7 at St.James, parents not named.

MARGARET, perhaps another dau. b about 1548; on 10 Oct. 1566 at Belchamp, Margaret Brekett of Sudbury, spinster, was murdered by Thomas Curley of Bures St. Mary, cook, who attacked her and cut her throat as she was walking along the road to Sudbury. For this murder he was indicted by an Inquisition held at Belchamp St. Paul on 12 Dec. 1566 (Calendar of Assize Records - Indictments, Essex, Elizabeth - H.M.S.O. 1578)

8 RICHARD, prob. b 1550-54; m 1, -?-; 3 or more ch.; m 2, 25 Sept. 1589 at All Saints, Alice Harper; 2 ch.; Alice was buried 17 May 1595 at St. Peter's; m 3, 4 Feb. 1601/2 at Long Melford, the widow Greenglass; 1 ch. He was living in 1616 for he witnessed his son Peter's will

WILLIAM, prob. b 1555; m 21 July 1582 at St. Peter's, Alice Bull; he prob. d about 1583-5, for an Alice Brackett m John Goslin, 29 Aug. 1585; ch.: William bapt. 27 Jan. 1582/3 at St. Peter's. However, this may be the marriage & child of his cousin William who was son of Thomas

MAUD, was prob. "the dau. of William Brackett" bapt. 20 Nov. 1560 at Bury St. Edmunds. Maud was under 18 in 1575 which makes this identification likely. She m 2 Feb. 1585/6 at St. Gregory's, Sudbury, George Goldyng

Ref.: Probate Records at Bury Saint Edmunds; Parish Registers; Bishop's Transcripts; Suffolk Green Book

26

ANDREW VINCENT (*Nicholas*) of Bildeston, Suffolk, England was probably born 1520-1530 at Bildeston. He married Alice ______ and had eight known children. He made his will on 3 December 1580, being sick and knowing that death was near. He probably died the next day for he was buried on the 5th in the churchyard at Bildeston. An abstract of his will follows. From this will it can be seen that he owned a fair amount of property and was a substantial man of his day. Some of this property, if not all, had been inherited from his father. His home was on Newbery Street in Bildeston.

3 December 1580 - The will of ANDREW VINSENT of Bildeston, Suffolk, yeoman... being sick in body... to Alice my wife all my messuages, houses, lands and tenements in the parishes of Naughton, Whatfield and Offton for her life, then to my four daughters, viz. Alice, Susanne, Brigett and Marie for a term of 9 years after the death of my said wife. At the end of the 9 years to my son Nicholas Vinsent for ever...... To my said wife my capital messuage where I dwell in, sometime Willm Kookes, with all the houses, lands, tenements, meadows, feedings and pastures now in my occupation, and the meadow called the brook, for her natural life, and after her decease to my son Nicholas.... To Alice my daughter all my messuage or tenement called Gatinolds lying in Newbery street... To Marie my daughter my messuage or tenement called Bennys late partings lying in Newbery street.... To Brigett my daughter my messuage or tenement called Bulls tenement lying in Newbery street.. To Alice my daughter £10 to be paid on the feast day of Saint Michael the Archangel 1582. To Susanne my daughter £10 to be paid same day 1584. To Brigett my daughter £10 to be paid same day 1586. To my daughter Marie £10 to be paid her at her age of 24.... £15 owed against the tenement called Bulls, payable at 20s per year, my executrix shall fully discharge and pay.... All moveables unbequeathed to Alice my wife whom I make sole executrix. Witnesses: John Barker, Thomas Grymwade, Thomas Bantofte and Willm Grymwade (Proved 19 June 1581 at Bury St. Edmunds) (Browne 274)

Children, probably all born at Bildeston:

ANDREW, named in his grandfather Vincent's will of 1553; apparently d.y., as not mentioned in his father's will of 1581

NICHOLAS, perhaps b about 1556; m 1, Susan ______; had: a son b and buried 20 Sept. 1581, Joshua bapt. 18 Aug. 1583; his wife Susan was buried 26 Aug. 1583; he m 2, Agnes/Ann ______; ch.: Susan bapt. 2 Feb. 1584/5, Caleb bapt. 4 Sept. 1586 - buried 22 Dec. 1588, Andrew bapt. 18 Dec. 1588 - also buried 22 Dec. 1588, Phebe bapt. 5 April 1590, Samuel bapt. 3 Dec. 1592 - buried 1 April 1593 [P.R. reads *bapt.*], Nathaniel bapt. 9 Jan. 1593/4

ALICE, prob. b about 1558; m 1, 16 Feb. 1580/81 at Bildeston, Edmund Reicroft; ch.: Samuel bapt. 16 Sept. 1582, Joshua bapt. 18 Oct. 1584, Susan bapt. 2 Oct. 1586 - buried 19 Aug. 1587, Mary bapt. 10 Nov. 1588, Elizabeth bapt. 14 Feb. 1590/91, Sara buried 22 Jan. 1603/4; his will pr. 1603; she m 2, 2 Feb. 1604/5, Erasmus Coree (or Corre)

13 SUSANNE, prob. b about 1560; m 27 Feb. 1581/2 at Bildeston, Thomas Blower, a tanner of Lavenham, his 2nd wife; 8 ch.; he d 1597

BRIGETT, prob. b 1561-2; living 1581

JOAN, bapt. in Oct. 1563 at Bildeston; buried there 26 Nov. 1579

MARY, bapt. 13 Jan. 1565/6; m 21 Sept. 1587 at Bildeston, Henry Coe; 6 ch.; he was buried 28 Jan. 1630/31, she on 20 Oct. 1631 at Boxford; a son Robert founded the Coe family of U.S.A.

ELIZABETH, bapt. 13 June 1568; buried 6 Aug. 1569

THE CHURCH OF SAINT MARY MAGDALENE
BILDESTON, SUFFOLK

Reproduced from *Ecclesiastical Antiquities of the County of Suffolk*, 1818, by Isaac Johnson — courtesy of the County Record Office, Suffolk, England

Ref.: Suffolk County Probate Records; Parish Registers

28

JOHN FROST of Glemsford and Hartest, Suffolk, England, was born about 1530-1535. He was a clothier as we can infer from his will. On 29 January 1558/9 at Glemsford, he married Ann Scott. She was the daughter of Richard Scott of Glemsford, also a clothier. Sometime after the birth of their last child, they moved to Hartest, the next village. There, on 30 July 1588, Anne, wife of John Frost, was buried. John Frost remarried, for when he died, he left a widow named Ellen. He died and was buried at Hartest 6 February 1609/10. His will, apparently a nuncupative one, was dated the same day he was buried, so we can assume he also died that day. An abstract of his will follows.

> 6 February 1609/10 - the will of John Frost of Hartest, senior... to Ellin my wife all household stuff and £10 out of two broad cloths now at the weavers whereof one cloth is in the custody of John Cawston of Stanstead, weaver, and the other cloth is now in the custody of one Permefy of Hartest, weaver ... to my son John Frost one russett broad cloth & one dozen & a half of twill now lying at the house of Thomas Hardy, shearman, in Glemsford ... to Alice my daughter the wife of John Hayward £8 which is now in the hands of my son Edward Frost of Stanstead ... to Elizabeth my daughter the wife of William Pratt 50s. out of the £3 which Ambrose Graygoose owes me ... to Francis my son 50s. of which 10s. is in the hands of the said Ambrose Graygoose and 40s. in the hands of Bartholomew Woolward ... residue as follows: 50s. to Elizabeth my daughter the wife of said William Pratt, rest to Ellin my wife, John Frost my son, Alice my daughter the wife of John Hayward, to be divided equally among them ... son Edward Frost executor. Memorandum that the testator did give 20s. to the children of William Boram who was the son of William Boram late of Glemsford & 6s.8d. unto D-- Andrews his now man servant. Witnesses: Robert Galt, Rychard Holwell, Thomas Cronshaye.
>
> (Ref.: R2/47/95; W1/66/112; A5/3/78)

Children, baptized in Glemsford:

JOHN, prob. b 1559; living in 1610

14 EDWARD, bapt. 13 March 1560/61, "son of John"; m 26 Sept. 1585 at Glemsford, Thomasine Belgrave, dau. of John & Joan (Strutt) Belgrave; 8 ch.; he was buried 3 Aug. 1616

ERASMUS, bapt. 10 June 1564, "son of *Thomas* & Anne Frost", but this may be a mistake as there is no other record of a Thomas Frost at that time; if so, Erasmus died before 1610 as he was not named in John's will

HENRY, bapt. 27 March 1568, "son of John Frost junior"; apparently d.y.

ELIZABETH, bapt. 8 Oct. 1570, "dau. of John Frost junior"; buried 21 Sept. 1579, "dau. of John & Ann"

ANNE, bapt. 7 June 1572, "dau. of John Frost junior"; apparently d.y.

AMBROSE, bapt. 6 March 1574/5, "son of John Frost junior & Ann"; m 17 Nov. 1601 at Glemsford, Margaret Hayward; he was buried 1 May 1604

ALICE, bapt. 13 Oct. 1577, "dau. of John Frost junior"; m 30 July 1596 at Glemsford, John Hayward

FRANCIS, bapt. 6 Nov. 1580, "son of John Frost junior"; living 1610

ELIZABETH, bapt. 24 Jan. 1584/5, "dau. of John Frost"; m 10 Nov. 1607 at Stanstead, William Pratt; ch: Ann bapt. 1 May 1608, Elizabeth bapt. 7 Jan. 1609/10 - d.y., William bapt. 18 March 1610/11

SAINT MARY'S CHURCH, GLEMSFORD, SUFFOLK

Reproduced from *Ecclesiastical Antiquities of the County of Suffolk*, 1818, by Isaac Johnson –

Ref.: Parish Registers; Probate Records at Bury Saint Edmunds

30

JOHN BELGRAVE of Leverington, Cambridgeshire, England, married Joanna Strutt, daughter of John and Catherine Strutt of Glemsford, Suffolk, 22 September 1560 at Glemsford. Joanna was buried at Leverington 14 August 1577. John Belgrave married secondly at Saint James parish, Bury Saint Edmunds, 25 August 1578, Elizabeth Fayerfoxe (or Fairfax) of Bury Saint Edmunds. John Belgrave was buried at Leverington 12 February 1590/91. His will, bearing his signature, is abstracted below.

Leverington is fifty miles northwest of Glemsford.

3 February 1590/91 - the will of JOHN BELGRAVE of Leverington, Isle of Ely, county Cambridge, yeoman, sick in body ... to be buried in the churchyard of Leverington ... to son Abraham Belgrave my house and lands in Leverington where I dwell ... to son George Belgrave land in Seafield, Long Meadow and Catfield, all in Leverington ... to son Jacob Belgrave land in Hylcrofte and Mayes Lane ... to son Thomas Belgrave land in Long Meadow in Leverington and my house and buildings in Glemsford in Suffolk ... my three daughters Tomyzin, Elizabeth and Catheren Belgrave, to have 10s. each from the estate, and £10 from my sons Abraham, George and Jacob respectively ... to Elizabeth and William Froste, children unto my son Edward Froste, a ewe and a lamb ... to Mr. Bowler our parson two of my best wethers ... residue to wife Elizabeth Belgrave, she to be executrix ... son in law Edward Froste supervisor. Witnesses: Mr. Richard Bowler the writer of this will, Henry Johnson, Richard Coxen, Thomas Fricewell with others. Proved 11 March 1590/91.

(Ref.: Consistory Court of Ely, 5:39)

Children, baptized at Leverington:

15 THOMASINE, bapt. 1 Feb. 1561/2; m 26 July 1585 at Glemsford, Edward Frost, son of John. Edward was bapt. there 13 March 1560/61, was buried at Stanstead, Suffolk, 3 Aug. 1616

ELIZABETH, bapt. 16 Feb. 1563/4; alive in 1591

CATHERINE, bapt. 31 March 1566; alive in 1591

THOMAS, bapt. 13 Dec. 1567; m 8 April 1602 at Glemsford, Suffolk, Susanna Fosbrook; ch.: Susanna bapt. 14 Nov. 1602, Anna buried 20 Feb. 1611/12. He was alive 1638 per will of George Osborne of Sudbury

ABRAHAM, bapt. 27 Dec. 1569; alive in 1591

GEORGE, bapt. 31 Aug. 1571; alive in 1591

JACOB, b prob. 1573; m 1,—— ; ch.: Susan bapt. 14 Sept. 1607 at Stanstead, Ann bapt. 20 Jan. 1610/11, John bapt. 5 March 1613/14, Thomas bapt. 17 May 1618; he m 2, 23 Jan. 1631/2 at Stanstead, Susan Watlock(?), a widow; ch.: Jacob bapt. 27 Dec. 1632, Richard bapt. 24 Aug. 1634, Susan bapt. 16 Sept. 1636 at St. Peter's, Sudbury. He d intestate & his widow was granted admin. of his estate on 3 April 1638.

BARBARA, bapt. 12 June 1575; buried 4 May 1576 at Leverington

BARBARA, bapt. 27 June 1577; buried 17 Sept. 1589 at Leverington

----

JOSEPH, bapt. 20 March 1579/80; buried 26 March 1580

DORCAS, bapt. 9 May 1584; buried 1 May 1585 at Leverington

ISAAC, bapt. 8 Oct. 1589 at Leverington; apparently d.y., as not in father's will of 1591

SAINT LEONARD'S CHURCH, LEVERINGTON
(From a photograph of 1853)

Ref.: The American Genealogist 61:161-166; Parish Registers; Wills at Bury St. Edmunds Record Office

32

WILLIAM BRACKETT was a resident of Sudbury, Suffolk. Also living there at the same time was Edward Brackett, presumably his brother. Both these men appear on the Sudbury list of the Military Survey of 1522, William as an able archer, Edward as an able billman, both listed as butchers, each assessed 12 pence on goods valued at £2. One can reasonably assume that they grew up in the trade and learned it from their father who also must have lived in Sudbury. Two years later, they both appear again on record as taxpayers in the 1524 Subsidy return, each down for 4 pence tax on wages of 20 shillings.

No earlier record of the name in Sudbury has been found, but it does occur somewhat earlier in other parts of England, or at least possible variations of the name such as Brokett.

Edward Brackett died in 1540.

20 June 1540 - The will of EDWARD BRACKETT, balie of the town of Sudbury, Suffolk, hale of mind and in good and perfect remembrance ... my body to be buried within the churchyard of St. Gregory in Sudbury... to every of my children John, James, Edward, George and Faythe 5 marks at age 20 and if Faythe marry before age 20, then on day of marriage ..... to Maud my wife all those my copyhold lease, interest and term of years which I have and hold of the right worshipful Lady Dame Jane Corbett of and in certain lands and pastures lying in Assington, Suffolk, called by the name of Perefield...... Richard Barker of Sudbury to hold and occupy these leases during the nonage of son George Brackett, paying £4 13s 7d sterling yearly to Maud my wife and 6^{c} of fresh wood with the felling making and carrying of the same toward the keeping and bringing up of the same George and Edward my sons.. Also, to wife Maud a certain lease in lands called Chyllton wente and Duckslade...The residue of all my goods and cattle, money, plate, debts and implements of household not assigned or bequeathed to Maud my wife whom I make sole executrix. John Oxburghe of Sudbury, gentleman, and the said Richard Barker to be aydors and comforters to my said wife and for their pains 6s 8d sterling. Witnesses: John Bannasted, Raulff Feosdike, John Blanche, John Beele, Ronert Cooke, Willm Hayward. Proved 19 March 1540/41 (Ref.: Coole 364)

William Brackett had at least three sons who referred to each other in their wills.

Children, born in Sudbury:

16 WILLIAM, prob. b about 1515; m Alice____ ; ch.: Edmond, Richard, William, Maud, others who d.y.; buried 6 May 1575 at St.Peter's; she m 2, 11 Sept. 1575, Richard Morrell (or Merrill)

GEORGE, named in wills of his brothers William & Thomas; sev. ch.: Robert who had Barbara 1593 and Robert 1594/5, George bapt. 2 Dec. 1565 at St. Gregory's who m Elizabeth & had Elizabeth 1603 & Anne 1608, Grace & Christian bapt. 29 March 1581 at St. Peter's, prob. also John who witnessed the will of William Brackett in 1575 & may be the John B. bapt. 22 Aug. 1557 at St. Mary in Bury St. Edmunds

THOMAS, m Emma____ ; he d 1573, naming in his will his wife & sons Edward & William. His son Edward was slain by Anthony Burr on 15 June 1591 & was buried the next day at St. Peter's. An abstract of his will follows.

> 10 September 1573 - The nuncupative will of THOMAS BRACKETT of St. Gregory, Sudbury, Suffolk ... sick in body ... to Robert Brackett son of George Brackett his brother one pewter platter ... to Edward Brackett his son one brass pot, one pewter platter, one pewter porringer, one saucer of pewter ... to Willm Brackett his other son one candlestick. .all these to be delivered unto his brother George Brackett to keep for his children until they come to lawful age... the residue of his goods to my wife Emma Brackett freely, she seeing his body honestly buried & brought to the ground, his debts paid & his little children brought up in the fear of god. Witnesses: Thomas Byknell, Willm Smyth, Thomas Collins, with others. Proved 13 January 1573/4 (Ref. Large 214)

CHURCH OF SAINT GREGORY, SUDBURY, SUFFOLK

Ref.: Suffolk Green Book X; Probate Records at Bury Saint Edmunds; Parish Registers; Bishop's Transcripts

52

NICHOLAS VINCENT (*Andrew*) of Bildeston, Suffolk, England was probably born about 1494-7 in or near Bildeston, where he apparently spent his life and where he owned considerable property, being a substantial yeoman farmer of his day. In the 1524 Subsidy return, he was listed at Bildeston for a tax of 9 shillings on £6 worth of goods.

On 13 November 1553, he made his will. Altho he did not state in the preamble of the will that he was sick, he probably was and anticipated death. He died shortly thereafter and the will was proved 12 March following. He is undoubtedly buried in the churchyard at Bildeston, as he requested in his will.

He married Agnes, who survived him. His home was on Newbery Street in Bildeston.

12 November 1553 - The will of NICHOLAS VYNCENT the elder of Byldstonne, Suffolk, yeoman, being in whole mind and good & perfect remembrance....my body to be buried in the churchyard of Byldston....to the relief of the poor people of Bildestonne 20s..to Agnes my wife 20 marks and my tenement which Thomas Lawrence now dwelleth in in Byldstonne with the close and pasture thereto adjoining & called the brooke for term of her life, then to Nicholas my son and the heirs male of his body lawfully begotten, and for want of such male heirs to remain to the heirs of Agnes my daughter forever and for default of issue of Agnes lawfully begotten, to remain to Elizabeth my daughter and her heirs lawfully begotten and for default of issue of her body lawfully begotten to remain to Alice my daughter... Agnes my wife to have the house that I now dwell in in Newbery street with their appurtenances as long as she is widow and if she marie and take a husband during the term of Thomas Lawrence years having no habitation or dwelling, then Nicholas my son find her a competent habitation and dwelling in Byldstonne during the term of the said Thomas Lawrence without any rent payment....and after the marriage of the said Agnes the said house I now dwell in in Newbery street with all land, meadows, feedings & pastures with their appurtenances which were sometimes Willm Cooks and other land called Melfield with the meadow belonging, to Nicholas my son....to Nicholas all my lands, pastures and meadows in Chellesworth free, and lands and all my tenements lying in Muncks Ellie, to Nicholas a piece of land called Brymlye field, to Nicholas my tenement in Newbery street in Bildeston late John Harries and one acre of meadow in Bradmeadow which I had late of the lords grant ... Andrew my son shall have my tenement that he dwelleth in late John Merchants with a garden & an acre of meadow thereto belonging and the said acre in Bradmeadow for 20 years next after my decease, paying yearly to Nicholas his brother 22s 6d, and for the said

acre in Bradmeadow 7s 6d. And after the said 20 years expired to Andrew Vincent my godson, son of the said Andrew my son. To Nicholas all my other lands, tenements and meadows in Bildeston not before bequeathed. To Andrew my son in money £10 and my two tenements lying in Nawton. To Nicholas my son 7 horses, 6 milche neate and bullocks and parte of swine and pullerie, a shodde carte, a plough with all things belonging, the half of all manner of grain and twenty sheep..... To Agnes my daughter in money 20 marks and to Alice my daughter 20 marks, all which legacies to my daughters to be paid them at age 21. If any be deceased, that part to be divided among the surviving ones. If Nicholas die, then the tenement in Bildeston late John Smiths to go to daughter Agnes and daughter Elizabeth to have another tenement in Bildeston which Robert Jervys now dwelleth in and Alice my daughter to have my tenement in Bildeston called the Dale house hold as it doth appear in the Lords court rolls..... If Nicholas my son die without issue, then my tenement which I now dwelleth in in Newbery street, with all lands, meadows, feedings and pastures to the same belonging.. which were sometime Willm Cooks and other lands called Melfield to be sold for one hundred marks 6s 8d to be paid in 7 years the performance of the sale whereof I will Andrew my son have before any other for the said price if he will and be able to purchase the same and if the said Andrew willnot or be not able to purchase the same, then the husband of Agnes to have like p'ferment before a stranger and £22.6s.8d of the sale of the said tenement ... the first payment of the first year I will shall be equally divided amongst my said 3 daughters Agnes, Elizabeth and Alice and likewise £22 6s 8d the second year and £22 6s 8d the third year resydewe of the said 100 marks 6s 8d.... The remainder of my movable goods before not bequeathed to be appraised by 4 indifferent honest men in 3 parts whereof Agnes my wife shall have one part, the second part to be equally divided amongst my daughters then living and the other 2 parts to Nicholas my son, provided that if Nicholas any time alienate, sell or by any defraud or craft defeat or dispose his heir or heirs of any of the said lands and tenements in Bildeston aforesaid by me to him before bequeathed, then Andrew my son enter into the said lands to hold and enjoy to him and to his heirs for ever. Nicholas my son and Willm Blomefylde of Appall Stomham to be executors and Henry Osmonde of Bildeston to be supervisor. To the latter two 6s 8d each for their pains and labor. Witnessed by Steven Chapley and John Gage. Proved 12 March 1553/4. (Wood 169)

Children, probably all born at Bildeston:

26 ANDREW, prob. b 1520-30; m Alice —— & had a ch. Andrew jr., by 1553, then 5 other known ch.; buried 5 Dec. 1581; res. Bildeston

NICHOLAS, prob. b 1520-30; alive in 1553

AGNES, b after 1532 (under 21 in 1553)

ELIZABETH, b after 1532

ALICE, b after 1532

Ref.: Probate Records at Bury Saint Edmunds; Parish Registers; Suffolk Green Book X

WILLIAM FROST of Glemsford, county Suffolk, England, was probably born about 1495-1500. His wife was named Philippa. William died in the summer of 1549, testate. After his death, his widow remarried on 15 September 1552 at Glemsford, John Webb of Lidgate, which is about eight miles from Glemsford. He was a widower, his wife Rose having been buried at Lidgate on 11 February 1551/2. John and Philippa (-------) (Frost) Webb had a daughter, Anna, baptized in 1553, so it is apparent that Philippa was probably born after 1508. Philippa was buried at Lidgate on 20 January 1577/8 and John Webb on 25 July 1558.

A William Frost appears in the Glemsford Subsidy list for 1524 when he was taxed two shillings on £4. An abstract of his will follows.

5 July 1549 - the will of WILLIAM FROST of Glemsford. county Suffolk ... sick in body ... to be buried in the churchyard of Glemsford ... for tithes forgotten 11s ... to wife Phyllip £5 a year for life ... Roger my eldest son shall pay every year for 4 years this sum ... to wife Phillip her dwelling in "these howss of my hed house", including use of parlor, parlor chamber and buttery. Son Roger to keep for my wife 2 beasts during her life and firewood during the 4 years ... Son Roger to have profits and usage of hall lands for 4 years on condition that he see Henry my son relieved with meat, drink and apparell at school or to see him set to a good service. Son Roger to keep house in repair during 4 years. Roger to have plow, cart, 15 head of beasts and bullocks and 40 sheep ... to John my middle son my tenement and lands that were Strutt's except one pightell called Rawlyns, and one piece of land lying in Melfed and a piece of pasture called Rogylles pasture, to him for 4 years ... to him at his entrance, 2 horses, 5 head of cattle, 15 sheep ... and after the entrance of the said John my middle son into his tenement and land to him given, he shall pay to my wife Phyllip 40s. a year of the said £5, he also to find his mother fire wood ... to my younger son John at the age of 26 my tenement called Rogille's with Rogille's pasture, Rawlings pightell, and a meadow of an acre. And that young John shall have his ease always to carry and drive to his grounds over old John's lands, said brother to pay his brother old John rent of 10s. a year ... to son young John a bullock and 5 sheep ... to son Henry when he reaches age of 26, 2 meadows at Sedmell and Newcroft. If son Roger pays 40 marks within 1 year after Henry reaches 26, then Roger shall have it. To son Roger after the death of his mother, 6 silver spoons. To Jonas Woode my acre of land in

Melfyld that I bought of Stynte, at age 26, or £4 which son Roger shall pay him for it. If Jonas die before he reaches 26, son Roger shall pay my 3 daughters' children the said £4. To John Wood the new house at Strut's where he dwells now, for 3 years, paying for reparations 3s.4d. yearly ... To Roger Rysbye my tenement called Rogell with the yard except Rawlins, he to pay 22d. a year for reparations for 3 years ... to my 3 daughters the debt due me by Stephen Tonye and William Merchall. To daughters Audrye and Jane each a seam of barley ... to my sister Jurdon a quarter of barley and a combe of wheat ... If wife remarries, she is not to have her dwelling or beasts but shall have yearly £6 to be paid to her by 2 eldest sons Roger and John, Roger to pay her £3.13s. and John my eldest son 46s. 8d. Executors: sons Roger and Henry, Wife Phullip to have half my household stuff ... to wife Phullip 2 of my best beds. Witnesses: Robert Stansbye, Giles Fyrman. Proved 15 September 1549. (Ref.: R2/21/536 & W1/8/43)

Children, probably all born at Glemsford:

ROGER, "my eldest son", prob. b 1525-30; m 1, Agnes ——— who was bur. at Glemsford 10 Feb. 1558/9; 2 ch.; he m 2, Katherine ———; 7 ch.; he was bur. 4 April 1580. He was on the 1568 Subsidy list for Glemsford as taxed 5s.4d. on £4 in lands. His will calls him husbandman & names his 6 surviving ch.: Anne, John, Katherine, Alice, Edward & Henry

JOHN, called "old John" or "middle John". He was one of his father's 2 eldest sons, but since he was also called "middle John", Roger must have been the elder of the two; prob. b about 1527-32; m Elizabeth ———, who was his wife 7 Dec. 1564 when their twin sons were buried (earlier records do not name the mother); 12 ch. b 1554 - 1576/7

28 JOHN, called "young John" in his father's will & mentioned therein as being under 26. So, he was b perhaps 1530-35. He m 1, 29 Jan. 1558/9 at Glemsford, Ann Scott, dau. of Richard. 9 or 10 ch.; she was bur. 30 July 1588 at Hartest; he m 2, Ellen ———; he was bur. 6 Feb. 1609/10 at Hartest, testate

HENRY, prob b after 1535 as his father in his will made provision for his schooling

AUDREY

JANE

DAUGHTER, referred to, but not named in her father's will

Ref.: The American Genealogist 63:129-135; Probate Records at Bury Saint Edmunds

58

RICHARD SCOTT (*Richard, William*) of Glemsford, Suffolk, was a clothier and was probably born about 1510, presumably in Glemsford, where he lived and died. His first wife, Joanna, was buried 23 August 1556. Seven weeks later, on 8 October 1556, he and Joan Tollington (or Tollerton) were married. She was the widow of Christopher Tollerton of Cavendish, whose will, dated 12 May 1556, was proved 23 September following. She apparently had a still earlier marriage, for she had a son named Andrew James, according to Richard Scott's will. This was, no doubt, the Andrew who was bequeathed 40s. and a cow by Christopher Tollerton, no surname or relationship given. Richard Scott was buried on 5 February 1564/5. He was then designated as "senior" to distinguish him from a younger Richard Scott also living in Glemsford - a first cousin once removed. His widow, Joan, remarried 26 September 1565 to Thomas Hayward, apparently her fourth husband. Richard Scott's will follows.

> 7 February 1564/5 - the will of Richard Skote of Glemsford, clothier...to be buried in the churchyard of Glemsford...to wife Joan all household stuff that she had before her marriage, etc. and £20...to son Edward Scotte £20...to son Richard Scotte £8 at age 21...to son in law Thomas Warren £5 and my mylche beast...to son in law John Froste two leases which I now have of Mr. Polye of Boxsted, and lands at Howldens, and 40s...to son in law William Lellye £5...to two youngest daughters Margaret and Elizabeth £18 which I must have of Robert Carleton, to be paid at age 20 or marriage...to eldest son John £8...to wife's son Andrew Jeames 40s...residue to be divided among my children that are now married. Executors to be George Hixe and Roger Frost. Witnesses: George Collingwood, Robert Carleton. proved 28 May 1565. (R2/32/171 & W1/151/43)

Children, probably all born in Glemsford:

JOHN, eldest son; m 6 Oct. 1560, Ann Strutt; had a dau.. Elizabeth, bapt. 30 Aug. 1562; a John Scott m 10 June 1574 at Glemsford, Margaret Hilles, prob. his 2nd m; John Scott was buried 25 May 1578; Margaret Scott was buried 12 March 1591

29 ANNE, b about 1535?; m 29 Jan. 1558/9, John Frost; he m 2, Ellen _

KATHERINE, b about 1538?; m 7 Nov. 1563 at Whepstead, William Lilly

MARY, b about 1540?; m 27 May 1564, Thomas Warren

EDWARD, perhaps b 1540 - 44; m Elizabeth _____ ; ch.: Mary 1571, Edward 1574, Richard 1576-d 1577, Elizabeth 1578, Richard 1580, Francis 1583, George 1585 - d.y., Faith. An Elizabeth Scott was buried 14 March 1596/7; he d 1627, was a clothier

8 September 1627 - the will of EDWARD SCOTT of Glemsford ... in reasonably good health ... £60 for the poor of Glemsford, to be invested in land, £3 per year in the meantime ... to daughter Mary late wife of Ambrose Brewster deceased £500 ... to Ambrose Brewster & Edward Brewster, two of the sons of the said Mary £500 each ... to Thomas, Matthew, Faith and Alice, children of my said daughter Mary Brewster £50 each at age 21 ... to Elizabeth wife of George Chrispeland, daughter of the said Mary Brewster my daughter £100 ... to Barbara the daughter of my brother John Scott, now wife of Benjamin Roydon £100 ... to Francis Scott the son of Francis Scott my son deceased £250 ... to Faith my daughter, late the wife of William Leader deceased & before the wife of Richard Herrington deceased £270 ... to Mary Herrington daughter of the said Richard & Faith £150 at age 21 ... to Richard Herrington son of the aforesaid Richard Herrington £20 at age 21 ... to all the children of the said William Leader by my said daughter Faith £200 to be equally divided among them at age 21 ... to Thomas Fuller & Elizabeth Fuller children of my daughter Elizabeth deceased who was the wife of Robert Fuller £100, of which £40 to Thomas at age 21, £60 to Elizabeth at age 21 or in one year at choice of my executor ... Whereas Richard Scott my son deceased did in November last year convey to me his capitol messuage called the Place in Glemsford for £406 to be paid, etc. [i.e. mortgaged the property for the £406], I assign it to my son Edward ... to Edward Scott one of the sons of Richard Scott my son £200 at age 21 ... to Elizabeth Scott daughter of the same Richard £50 ... to Mary, Sara, & Frances, 3 other of the daughters of my said son Richard £50 each at age 21 ... to Margaret wife of Thomas Watling, gentleman, & daughter of said son Richard £4 yearly for life and after her decease £50 to be divided among her children at age 21 ... to Faith Scott daughter of said Richard several houses in Glemsford ... to Jane my late servant, wife of Michael Wells, £100 ... to Jane her daughter 40s. at age 21 or day of marriage ... to Susan Brewster my servant 40s. ... to Richard Skingle my servant £3 ... to Philip Towne my servant 20s. ... to Ann my kinswoman, wife of William Turner, weaver, £5 ... to Alice wife of John Hayward my kinswoman £5 ... to Mary wife of John Evered, weaver, my kinswoman, £5 ... to Tabitha wife of Richard Finch £5 ... to Thomas Warren & Edward Warren my kinsmen £5 each ... to Susan wife of Richard Whitmore 40s. ... to Phebe wife of Martyn Briden 40s. ... my loving friend and kinsman Mr. William Gage & my loving friend Thomas Wright of Hartest to be supervisors and to them £10 and £5 respectively ... residue to Edward Scott my eldest son, he to be executor ... to daughters Mary and Faith, one of my least silver cups to each ... Signed ... Witnesses: John Garnons, Anthony Beall, Thomas Wright. Proved 20 December 1627. (P.C.C. 119 Skynner)

JOAN, bapt. 7 June 1550; buried 11 Jan. 1553/4 at Glemsford

SUSANNA, bapt. 11 Feb. 1551/2; buried 21 April 1552

RICHARD, bapt. 26 Sept. 1553; d 1627 testate, (P.C.C.-53, Skynner); a clothier

ELIZABETH, bapt. 30 March 1555; m 1 Nov. 1581 at Glemsford, Ambrose Jeffrey

------ by second wife ------

DOROTHY, bapt. 25 Jan. 1557/8; d by 1564 as not in father's will?

JOAN, twin, bapt. 25 Jan. 1557/8; buried 27 May 1558

Ref.: Parish Registers; Probate records

62

JOHN STRUTT (*Thomas, John*) of Glemsford in Suffolk was married first to Catherine who was buried there on 18 August 1578. He married secondly 21 October 1578, Julian Scott, daughter of Richard Scott, yeoman, of Fynstead which is in the parish of Glemsford.

John Strutt appears on the 1568 Subsidy List as taxed 6s.8d. on £5 worth of land. He was buried at Glemsford on 22 April 1591, having made his will six days before. An abstract follows. Twelve years later, an Inquisition Post Mortem into the property he held was taken. An abstract of the Inquisition also follows.

The will of Richard Scott, dated 13 February 1577/8, named Julyan Scott and two of her brothers, Richard and George Scott, who were named in her husband's will. Julian (Scott) Strutt married secondly at Glemsford, 30 June 1591 widower Ambrose Biggs, senior, and had a daughter who died a year later. Ambrose Biggs was buried 9 May 1621 at Glemsford.

19 April 1591 - the will of JOHN STRUTT of Glemsford, county Suffolk, yeoman ... to the poor of Glemsford ... to wife Juliane all houses and lands until my daughter Anne Strutte is 18, and at Michaelmas following they are to be partitioned, with wife having half for life ... if Anne dies without issue, houses and lands go to my nephew [grandchild] Thomas Belgrave, he paying 20 nobles each to his brothers and sisters, the children of my late daughter Joan Belgrave deceased ... to my sister Ursula Brewster 10s. ... to John Goldinge and his son George Goldinge land in Great Wylwyn ... to Richard Scotte 6s.3d. and to each child of Eustace Strutte 10s. ... my wife and daughter Anne Strutte to be my executors. My brother George Scott supervisor. Witnesses: William Biggs, clerk, Thomas Gardiner, Ambrose Biggs, Thomas Gardener the younger, Richard Symonds and others. On 20 April John Strutt surrendered land bequeathed to John Brewster the elder, mentioned land sometime in the tenure of Thomas Strutt father of the said John Strutt. Proved 12 May 1591.

(Ref.: Archdeaconry of Sudbury, Bacon 24)

INQUISITION POST MORTEM, held at Hadleigh, Suffolk, 21 March 1602/3 on the estate of JOHN STRUTT of Glemsford, yeoman, who died 23 April 1591 seised of the following, in demesne as of fee:

i A chief messuage in which he lived with a garden, orchard, and common pasturage.

ii A piece of land lying in Holbroke, abutting Wilwen Meadow.

iii $1\frac{1}{2}$ acres of land in Mullicrofte, Glemsford.

iv 1 acre on the west of Ridlowe alias Rithe field in Glemsford.

v 1 rood of pasture lately part of Willingham's croft in Glemsford.

All these were held of Richard Eliot, gentleman, as of the manor of Peverells in Glemsford, by fealty and several rents, amounting in all to $21\frac{3}{4}$ pence. And they are worth 20s. per annum clear.

vi Pattys Croft, with a woodland grove adjoining, in all 4 acres.

vii 2 acres of land called Suckenhedge, in Glemsford

viii A piece of land and a grove, now uprooted, in Wilwen field, abutting in part upon the land of the Rectory of Glemsford, and in part upon the piece called Suckenhedge, towards the east.

ix 1 acre in Wilwenfield, abutting on Morgans pightle towards the east.

x 2 acres of meadow in Broad Meadow, in Glemsford

xi Another $\frac{1}{2}$ acre in Broad Meadow

xii 5 roods of pasture in Freedes Field, next to Freed wood, in Glemsford.

xiii Half an acre of land in Melfield

xiv Another $\frac{1}{2}$ acre in Wilwen Field, in Glemsford

xv 1 acre of land in Longland Field, in Glemsford

xvi 3 acres of land called Reedinge, in Glemsford

xvii Another $\frac{1}{2}$ acre in Gravel-pit Field, in Glemsford

xviii An enclosure of land called Rand, in Glemsford

xix $1\frac{1}{2}$ acres with appurtenances, on the east side of Ridlowe Field, in Glemsford.

xx 1 acre called Crowsland in Welwend Field, in Glemsford.

xxi 3 roods of land called Shreves Croft, in Glemsford

Items No. vi to xx inclusive were held of the queen, as of the manor of Glemsford, lately parcel of the possessions of the Bishopric of Ely, then vacant, and now part of the possessions of the queen, by the service of fealty and several rents, amounting in all to 8s.4d. per annum, and suit of court, in free socage and not in chief, for all services. And they are worth in all 20s. per annum, clear.

Item xxi was held of the queen, as of the manor of Glemsford, by fealty and a rent of three pence. It is worth 20s. per annum clear.

John Strutt made a will dated 19 April 1591, the provisions of which, so far as they relate to these properties, are set out in English.

Ann Strutt, daughter and one heir of said John Strutt, had attained the age of 17 years by the 4th of July preceeding the holding of the inquest [1602] and is married to Ambrose Biggs, junior.

Thomas Belgrave, the son of John Belgrave, another daughter of John Strutt deceased, is kinsman and another heir of said John and was over 21 when the latter died.

Julian Strutt [John's widow] subsequently married Ambrose Biggs senior and still lives at Glemsford. This couple has taken charge of the aforesaid tenements and appurtenances, and have received the revenues and profits thereof since the death of John Strutt.

(Chancery Series 285:126)

24 August 1634 - the will of AMBROSE BIGGS of Glemsford, county Suffolk, gentleman ... to daughter Margerie, wife of William Hall, and her lawful heirs, messuage where I now dwell at Tyegreene in Glemsford ... and all lands, etc. which were John Strutt's, deceased grandfather of the said Margerie ... other land to daughter Margerie, if I have no heirs by my present wife Anne ... executor to be William Hall. Proved 12 Jan. 1634/5. (Archdeaconry of Sudbury W1:90:197)

Children, by wife Catherine, baptized at Glemsford:

31 JOANNA, m John Belgrave of Leverington, Cambridgeshire, 22 Sept. 1560 at Glemsford; 9 ch.; she was buried 14 Aug. 1577 at Leverington

THOMAS, buried 17 July 1551 ("Thomas, son of John Strutt")

AMBROSE, buried 22 March 1562/3

----by wife Julian----

JOHN, bapt. 16 Aug. 1579; buried 23 May 1584

ANNE, bapt. 4 July 1585; m Ambrose Biggs, Jr.

----by husband Ambrose Biggs, Sr.----

MARGERY BIGGS, bapt. 19 March 1591/2; buried 7 July 1593

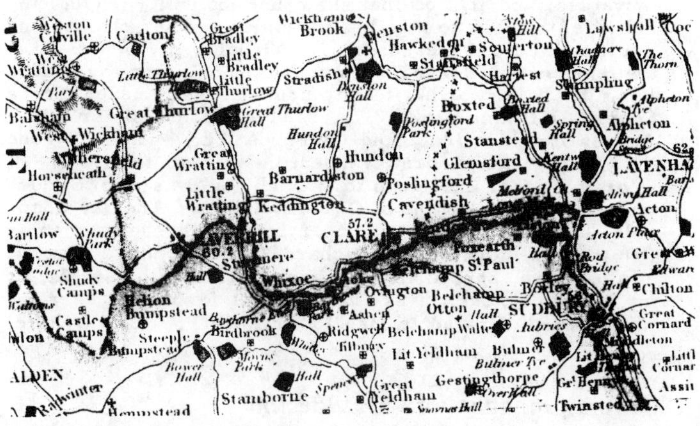

Ref.: The American Genealogist 61:161-166, 63:129-135; Parish Registers; Wills at Bury Saint Edmunds

104

ANDREW VINCENT lived in Bildeston, Suffolk. All that is known of him comes from his will, an abstract of which is given below. His bequests to the churches of Whatfield and Nettlestead suggest that perhaps one of these was the parish of his origins, perhaps the other that of his wife. She survived him. Altho his will names only one son and a son-in-law specifically, the other bequests suggest grandchildren by other daughters.

21 February 1521/2 - the will of Andrewe Wensent of Bylston, diocese of Norwich... to be buried in the church yard of Bildeston..to the church of Bildeston for the painting of the roll 13s.4d....William Byrche my son in law to have my house and land in Whatfield which was William Goodwynnes and he to fynde in the church of Whatfield a lamp burning and every year to bestow for dirge and mass 8d. and this to be done by them that shall have the occupation of the said house and land called Goodwynnes... Thomas Chapleyne of Monks Eleigh to have a certain land called Bentesse and to bestow for dirge and mass every year 12d. and after his death to the son of the said Thomas who was begotten of his first wife, and if the son die, then to remain to the 2 daughters his sisters...to Nettlestead church 6s.8d..My wife to have the house and land in Naughton for life, then to Nicholas my son and to his heirs. Nicholas to have all my houses and lands in Bildeston except I will my wife his mother have her dwelling house for life if she keep her widow, also the movables, and if it be that she cannot be with Nicholas and his wife, then she to take her movables and her chamber or dwelling where it pleases her... Nicholas my son to have the tenement at Monks Eleigh called Shoppis, and my ground lying in Chellesworth.. to Edy Broke 3s.4d., Andrew Broke 6s.8d., William Broke 20d., and Alice his sister 20d., Andrew Hommys 12d., Andrew Bonde 12d., William Byrche the younger 12d., Andrew Vynsent the younger to have 6s.8d. to pray for me. Executors to be Nicholas Vynsent of Bildeston and William Byrche of Chellesworth, and Thomas Chappelen of Monks Eleigh to be supervisor. Witnesses: Nicholas Brownsmyth, John Taillor, Richard Wryth, Edmund Raycroft, et alia. Also, 26s.8d. for my burial, at my 7th day 10s., at my month day 20s., every year an obit for thirty years for which 6s.8d. Proved 16 May 1522. (Ref.: P.C.C. 3 Ayloffe)

Children, probably born in Bildeston:

DAUGHTER, prob. b 1490-95; m Thomas Chaplin; d before 1521/2; had 1 son, 2 daus.; res. Monks Eleigh, Suffolk, which is 2 miles SW of Bildeston

DAUGHTER, perhaps, who m —— Brooke; had 4 ch. by 1521/2, all named in Andrew's will

52 NICHOLAS, b prob. 1494-7; m Agnes ——; 5 ch. of which Andrew was b before 1521/2; his will of 12 Nov. 1553, proved 12 March 1553/4

DAUGHTER, m William Byrche; res. Chellesworth, Suffolk, which is 1 mile SE of Bideston; had a son William jr. by 1521/2

THE CHURCH OF SAINT MARY, NETTLESTEAD, SUFFOLK

Ref.: P.C.C. Wills

ALL SAINTS CHURCH, BOXSTED, SUFFOLK

Reproduced from *Ecclesiastical Antiquities of the County of Suffolk*, 1818, by Isaac Johnson — courtesy of the County Record Office, Suffolk, England

116

RICHARD SCOTT (*William*) of Boxsted, county Suffolk, England, was probably born about 1476, presumably at Glemsford, where his father was living when he died in 1498. Since his father named him executor of his will, he was probably of age, but certainly not far from it. Richard inherited lands in Glemsford, Boxsted, Cavendish, Somerton and Hawkedon, all parishes near Glemsford. He apparently settled on the Boxsted property, for Boxsted was his residence when he made his will, in which he bequeathed his house and lands in Boxsted and Somerton. Richard died probably in April, 1560. There is no burial reord for him in the Boxsted parish register, nor in Glemsford. There was another Richard Scott living in Boxsted at this time. He and his wife, Agnes, were buried there on 12 June 1561. This other Richard Scott was probably quite a bit younger and perhaps a cousin.

> 30 May 1559 - the will of RICHARD SCOTT of Boxsted, county Suffolk, the elder ... sick of body ... to be buried in the parish churchyard ..... to Thomas Scott my eldest son my house & lands with appurtenances in Boxsted and Somerton ... to children Robert, Joan, William, Richard & John £20 to be paid by Thomas my son as follows: to Robert £4 within one year after my decease, to Joan £4 the next year, to William £4 the next year, to Richard £4 the next year, to John £4 the next year ... If son Thomas die without lawful issue, then house and lands in Boxsted and Somerton to son Robert, in tail to William, to Richard, to John, to Joan ... to Joan Scott & Dorothy Scott the daughters of Richard Scott my son 2s. each ... to Joan all my wife's apparel both woolen and linen ... all my household brass & pewter, except a posnet, to daughter Joan ... all bedding, etc. in the house to be equally divided amongst all my children ... corn, cattle, residue to son Thomas, he to be executor. Witnesses: John Hoo of Glemsford, John Petiwatt of the same town, John Farmer of Boxsted and others. Proved 6 May 1560 (R2/29/26)

In his will, there are some errors or contradictions which are explained only with difficulty. He named his grandchildren Joan and Dorothy Scott. These were the youngest children, twins, of his son Richard. Of all the Scotts in the area, this was the only Dorothy on record, so there can be little doubt that these twins were the ones he was naming.

However, Joan died at age 4 months, just a year before the date on his will. Was he unaware of the death of this grandchild? Perhaps he was old and forgetful, and no one had the heart to tell him? Also, he bequeathed to his son William, who had died four months before the date of his will. Was he unaware that his son was gone? Probably the will had been roughed out between February and May 1558, after the birth of the twins and before Joan died and while his son William was still living. Then, just before he died, it was completed and witnessed, no attempt having been made to modify it accordingly. It must be borne in mind that he was probably illiterate, and those helping in the matter knew little about his family. There were two other William Scotts living nearby; first cousins of his son William. Could there be confusion between them? This seems unlikely, for his son William in his will dated 16 January 1558/9 named his brother Richard to be executor. The two cousins had no brother Richard, hence the testator, William, was Richard's son. Also witnessing the will was brother Richard's son, Richard. Indeed, this brother Richard had a son, Richard, which further helps identify the relationships. This son Richard, however, had to have been a minor. At that time, minors did now and then witness documents. Thus, these puzzling things seem to cast a shadow of doubt. Yet, no other relationship can be deduced.

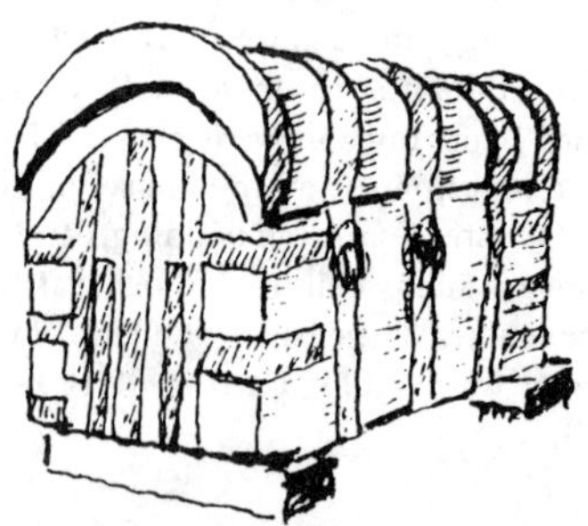

The Glemsford Parish Chest

This huge 14th century iron banded poplar chest was used for the storage of parish documents. It had three padlocks. By tradition, one had to be unlocked by the Rector and the other two in turn by two Churchwardens. The chest has been badly damaged by death-watch beetles.

Children, probably born at Boxsted or Glemsford:

THOMAS, eldest son, perhaps b about 1500; he inherited his father's lands in Boxsted and Somerton

ROBERT, second son, prob. b about 1502

JOAN, apparently the 3rd ch.;

WILLIAM, 4th ch.; m Margaret ——; he was buried 8 Feb. 1558/9 at Glemsford; 6 ch. named in his will; she m 2, 29 Jan. 1559/60 at Glemsford, Jacob Gally; his will:

16 January 1558/9 - the will of WILLIAM SKOTT of Finstead in the parish of Glemsford, ... to be buried in the churchyard of Glemsford ... to Margaret my wife my homestall wherein I now dwell with all my lands pertaining unto the same for term of her life, she to bring up all my children ... after her decease, homestall & lands to Andrew my eldest son, he to pay each of my children 40s., to wit, to Elizabeth my daughter, to John my son, to Maryon my daughter, to Peter my son, to Avyes my daughter, the said 40s. to be paid over a period of five years next after the decease of wife Margaret, 40s. per year starting with Elizabeth and in order of their descending ages ... lands in tail to second son John, then to Peter ... Margaret and Andrew to be executors, Richard Skott my brother supervisor to whom 3s4d. Witnesses: Richard Skott, Richard Skott his son and Robert Skott & others. Proved 18 April 1559. (W1/22/27)

58 RICHARD, 5th ch.; m 1, Joanna —— who was buried 23 Aug. 1556; 10 ch.; he m 2, 8 Oct. 1556, Joan Tollington, a widow, her 3rd m; twins; he was buried 5 Feb. 1564/5; she m 4, 26 Sept. 1565, Thomas Hayward

7 February 1564/5 - the will of Richard Skote of Glemsford, clothier...to be buried in the churchyard of Glemsford...to wife Joan all household stuff that she had before her marriage, etc. and £20...to son Edward Scotte £20...to son Richard Scotte £8 at age 21...to son in law Thomas Warren £5 and my mylche beast...to son in law John Froste two leases which I now have of Mr. Polye of Boxsted, and lands at Howldens, and 40s...to son in law William Lellye £5...to two youngest daughters Margaret and Elizabeth £18 which I must have of Robert Carleton, to be paid at age 20 or marriage...to eldest son John £8...to wife's son Andrew Jeames 40s...residue to be divided among my children that are now married. Executors to be George Hixe and Roger Frost. Witnesses: George Collingwood, Robert Carleton. proved 28 May 1565. (R2/32/171 & W1/151/43)

JOHN, youngest ch.; living in 1559

Ref.: Parish Registers; Probate Records at Bury Saint Edmunds

124

THOMAS STRUTT *(John)* of Glemsford, Suffolk, paid a tax of £2 on £40 in the 1524 subsidy. When he made his will he was living in Long Melford which is adjacent to Glemsford. His wife was named Joan.

20 June 1544 - the will of Thomas Strutt of [Long] Melford, county Suffolk, Doicese of Norwich, yeoman...to be buried in the holy sepulcher of Melford...to the churches of Melford and Glemsford...to my wife Joan my capital place and lands in Glemsford, Melford and Welwynfield for her life, then to sons John and Eustace...to sons Eustace and Erasmus Strutt land in Syldenfield, Longland and Weston Mill...to wife Joan a lease in Foxearth, Essex...£20, a featherbed, a brass pot, kettles, pewter and other movables to daughter Audrey Strutt...shop stuff at Glemsford to be sold...wife Joan and son John to be executors....Thomas Robards of Glemsford to be supervisor. Witnesses: Walter Bright, Mr. James Hyll, baker; Robert Wright, glasser, John Wacye, surgeon, John Bowght, yeoman, Edmund Jeffrey and Thomas Bowght, writer, cum multis aliis. Proved 10 December 1548. (Reference: Prerogative Court of Canterbury 19 Populwell)

Children, born at Glemsford:

62 JOHN, m 1, Catherine ________; she was buried 18 Aug. 1578; He m 2, 21 Oct. 1578, Julian Scott, dau. of Richard Scott; he d testate 23 April 1591; 5 ch.

ERASMUS, prob. b about 1525; m 9 Oct. 1552, Alice Roberdes; ch.: Joanna bp. 15 July 1553, John bp. 12 April 1556 - d.y.; he d 1557-8; she m 2, 13 June 1558 at Glemsford, John White

5 November 1557 - the will of Erasmus Strutt of Glemesforth, diocese of Norwich...to be buried in the churchyard of Glemesforth...to wife Alyce my mansion house called Cowtells for her life, and then to my daughter Joan Strutte and her lawful heirs, and lacking heirs, to be sold and proceeds go to my brothers and sisters and their children....lands in Gleemesforth to be sold and proceeds, after debts, go to my two sisters Ursula Browster, wife of Thomas, and Audria Hatch, and their children... wife Alyce to have four hogs, wheat, barley, bedding with all other implements of household whatsoever...to the parish clerk and poor people of Glemesforth...my brothers John Strutt and Ewstas Strutt to be executors. Witnesses: Sir Alexander Emot priest, Wylliam Crosse, Wylliam Brincleys, Edwarde Gefferayes, and John Stowe with others. Proved 24 May 1558 (Bell 115)

AUDREY; m ________ Hatch between 1544 and 1557

EUSTACE; living 1557; had ch. per br. John's 1591 will.

URSULA; m by 1557 to Thomas Brewster; she was not mentioned in her father's will, but was named as wife of Thomas Brewster in her br. Erasmus's will, as Ursula Brewster in br. John's 1591 will

Ref.: T.A.G. 61:161-166; Suffolk Green Book X:406

WILLIAM SCOTT of Glemsford, county Suffolk, is the earliest Scott ancestor of this family who can be identified. He apparently died at a rather young age, as his son Richard outlived him by sixty two years. William was probably born about 1450. His brief will names only two sons, to whom he bequeathed his lands in seven nearby parishes, i.e. in Glemsford, Boxsted, Cavendish, Somerton, Hawkedon, Wickhambrook and Denston. No wife was mentioned, but that does not prove she was dead, considering the brevity of his will. In the 1524 Subsidy (tax) list, there was a Clemence Skot, widow, who paid 2s.6d. on property worth £5. Clemence was probably his widow. His son Thomas had a daughter named Clemence, which suggests as much. His will was dated 24 April 1498, proved 29 September following, so he died around late summer of 1498.

24 April 1498 - the will of WILLIAM SKOTT of Glemsford in the diocese of Norwich ... to be buried in the churchyard of Glemsford ... to the high altar for tithes forgotten 20d. ... to Richard my son all my chattels & goods, he to be executor. Witnesses: Thomas Brewster alias Aldeby of Glemsford & Thomas Fyrmyn of Hawkedon with others ... Richard my son to have all lands & tenements I hold in the towns of Glemsford, Boxsted, Cavendish, Somerton & Hawkedon ... to Thomas Skott my son lands & tenements I hold in Wickhambrook & Denston. Proved 29 September 1498. (R2/13/79)

Children, probably all born in Glemsford:

116 RICHARD, b prob. about 1476; he inherited the lands in Glemsford, Boxsted, Cavendish, Somerton & Hawkedon; he must have settled on the Boxsted lands as he was a resident of that parish when he made his will in 1559 & d the next year; 6 ch. named

30 May 1559 - the will of RICHARD SCOTT of Boxsted, county Suffolk, the elder ... sick of body ... to be buried in the parish churchyard ..... to Thomas Scott my eldest son my house & lands with appurtenances in Boxsted and Somerton ... to children Robert, Joan, William, Richard & John £20 to be paid by Thomas my son as follows: to Robert £4 within one year after my decease, to Joan £4 the next year, to William £4 the next year, to Richard £4 the next year, to John £4 the next year ... If son Thomas die without lawful issue, then house and lands in Boxsted and Somerton to son Robert, in tail to William,

to Richard, to John, to Joan ... to Joan Scott & Dorothy Scott the daughters of Richard Scott my son 2s. each ... to Joan all my wife's apparel both woolen and linen ... all my household brass & pewter, except a posnet, to daughter Joan ... all bedding, etc. in the house to be equally divided amongst all my children ... corn, cattle, residue to son Thomas, he to be executor. Witnesses: John Hoo of Glemsford, John Petiwatt of the same town, John Farmer of Boxsted and others. Proved 6 May 1560 (R2/29/26)

THOMAS, b perhaps about 1478; he inherited the lands in Wickhambrook & Denston, but remained in Glemsford; m Joan _____; he d about 1529, testate; 6 ch. named in the will; in the 1524 Subsidy, he paid a tax of 2s. on lands worth £2

3 August 1524 - the will of THOMAS SCOT of Glemsford ... to be buried in the parish churchyard of Glemsford ... to William Scot my eldest son & to Isabell now his wife all my land & tenements in the downs & fields of Wickhambrook, Stradishall & Denston, county Suffolk, for their lives, then to Richard Scot son of the said William & Isabell, then in tail to eldest son of the said William & Isabell, etc., then to daughters & to their heirs ... If all children of William & Isabell d.s.p. then to my other sons, then to my daughters ... to said son William my tenement called Clases in Boxsted in which he is living, for life of my wife Joan his mother, he to keep her for life in sickness & in health as it seemeth a woman of her degree to be found ... if William d.s.p. then to son John ... to the said young William & John my sons my tenement wherein I dwell for life of their mother, then to son John ... daughter Clemens to have chamber in my tenement wherein I dwell with the said John for life if she be unmarried ... whoever has tenement called Clases after decease of wife Joan shall pay Clemens 3s.4d. yearly for life ... if son John d.s.p. then tenement to Clemens & to Andrew Scot son of eldest son William ... to Thomas Everard my son in law 40s. payable after decease of wife Joan ... to Clemens my daughter 10s. ... residue to wife Joan to dispose of at her pleasure ... William my eldest son to have tenement called Hokys ... Executors to be said eldest son William & John Segar my farmer at Wickhambrook. Witnesses: John Walis, chaplain, Thomas Brewster, the aforesaid Thomas Everard,John Grome, Robert Ailmer et alia. Proved 12 May 1529. (R2/18/9)

Ref.: Probate Records at Bury Saint Edmunds; Suffolk Green Book, No. X

248

JOHN STRUTT of Glemsford, Suffolk, England, was born about the middle of the fifteenth century in the reign of Henry VI. His wife was named Elizabeth, sometimes called Isabell, since the two were synonymous then, much as Elizabeth and Betty are today.

All that is known of John and Elizabeth comes from their wills, abstracts of which follow. He was apparently a blacksmith. In the 1542 Suffolk Subsidy (tax) Roll for Glemsford, she was taxed on £13.6.8. and paid 6s.8d.

12 September 1516 - the will of JOHN STRUT of Glemsford, county Suffolk ... to be buried in the parish church of Glemsford ... to the priests, clerks and poor people ... to wife Isabell my capital messuage in Glemsford and tenement in Cavendish for her lifetime, then to my son Thomas ... to my wife 100 marks, to my son John 40 marks, to son Robert 20 marks ... to son Thomas my shop and stuff therein belonging to smythescraft ... and to Thomas Elice and my daughter Elizabeth his wife, three tenements purchased of Master William Ailof, one tenement purchased of Sir John Parson, and land purchased of John Roberd, all in Sudbury ... to each of my daughters Katheryn and Margery a bed, a brass pot, a kettle and a steel pan, they receiving yearly from Thomas Elice 26s.8d. equally divided ... to John Bigge and Elizabeth Bigge which were the daughters of Alice Bigge my daughter, 20 shillings each at age 16 ... Executors to be wife Isabell, sons John & Thomas, & John Roberd of Sudbury, mercer. Witnesses: Sir John Waleis, parish priest, the forsaid Thomas Elice, Thomas Browster, John Cobb the elder & many others. Proved 5 February 1516/17. (Ref.: P.C.C. 26 Holder)

22 September 1526 - the will of ELIZABETH STRUTTE of Glemsford, county Suffolk, widow ... to be buried in the church of Our Lady Saint Mary in Glemsford ... to the church ... to daughter Elizabeth Ellice the featherbed with the boulster which I lie upon the day of my death and one salt of silver ... to son Thomas Strutte the residue of goods movable and unmovable, he to be executor. Witnesses: Sir Thomas Dyninge, parish priest of Glemsford, John Disse and others. Proved 13 November 1626. (Ref.: W1/23/25)

Children, probably all born at Glemsford:

124 THOMAS, m Joan

JOHN, living in 1516

ROBERT, listed under Glemsford on the "anticipation" list (1523) for the 1524 subsidy as taxable on £40 (Suffolk Green Books, X:406)

ELIZABETH, m by 1516 to Thomas Ellice; she was living in 1526

ALICE, m ____ Bigg, had John & Elizabeth; d by 1516
KATHERINE, living in 1516
MARGERY, living in 1516

SAINT MARY'S CHURCH, GLEMSFORD, SUFFOLK - c 1900

Ref.: The American genealogist 61:161-166

THOMAS BRADBURY *(Wymond, William, Matthew, William, Robert, William, Robert)* was baptized at Wicken Bonhunt, Essex, England, on 28 February 1610/11. He came to New England as a young single man and there married about 1636 Mary Perkins, daughter of John and Judith (Gater) Perkins. She was baptized 3 September 1615 at Hillmorton, Warwickshire.

Sir Ferdinando Gorges, who was related by marriage to Thomas Bradbury, sent him in 1634 to Maine as his agent. It is known that he was in London on 1 May 1634 and in New England by 5 May 1636 or earlier. Before 1640 he moved to Salisbury, Massachusetts, being made a freeman in that year. He was a constable in 1641. Later he was a schoolmaster, town clerk, clerk of courts, Captain of the military company, a deputy to the General Court for seven years, and an Associate Justice.

As agent for Gorges he made some of the earliest deeds in Maine. One follows.

5 May 1636 - Thomas Bradbury, Gentleman, now agent of Sr. Ferdinando Gorges, Knight, in these parts of New England doe . . . sell . . . unto Edward Johnson, Gentleman, for the proper use of John Treworgy of Dartmouth, merchante & his heirs . . . 500 Accors of Land bordering upon the North East side of Pascataquacke River . . . conditioned to pay annually one hundred of merchantable cod dried and well conditioned (York deed 1:11)

His graceful handwriting appears in many documents in the archives of Essex County, Massachusetts, and the Provincial archives of New Hampshire. He lived to be an old man as he must have been about 85 when he died. In the witchcraft delusion of 1692, his wife was accused of witchcraft and in spite of testimonies to her excellent character, she was convicted but not executed.

During the trial of Mrs. Bradbury on 28 July 1692, her husband gave testimony thus:

Concerning my beloved wife, Mary Bradbury, this is what I have to say: We have been married fifty five years, and she hath been a loving and faithful wife unto me unto this day. She had been wonderful laborious, diligent and industrius in her place and employment about bringing up our family which have been eleven of our own and four grandchildren. She was both prudent and provident, of a cheerful spirit, liberal and charitable. She being now very aged and weak, and grieved under afflictions, may not be able to speak much for herself, not being so free of speech as some others might be. I hope her life and conversation among her neighbors has been such as gives a better or more real testimony than can be expressed by words.

One hundred and eighteen of Mary Bradbury's neighbors signed this statement:

We the subscribers do testify that it [her life] was such as becomes the gospel. She was a lover of the ministry in all appearances, and a diligent attender upon God's holy ordinances, being of a courtesy and peaceable disposition and carriage, neither did any of us (some of whom have lived in the town with her about fifty years) ever hear or know that she had any difference or fálling out with any of her neighbors, man, woman, or child, but was always ready and willing to do for them what lay in her power, night or day, though with hazard of her health and other danger. More might be spoken in her commendation but this for the present.

Mary Bradbury said in defence of herself:

I am wholly innocent of any such wickedness through the goodness of God who has kept me hitherto. I am the servant of Jesus Christ and have given myself up to him as my only Lord and Savior, and to the contempt and defiance of the devil and all his works as horrid and detestable and have accordingly endeavored to frame my life and conversations according to the rules of his holy word, and in that faith and practice, resolve by the help and assistance of God to continue to my life's end. For the truth of what I say, I humbly refer myself to my brethen and neighbors that know me, and unto the searcher of all hearts for the truth and uprightness of my heart therein (human frailties and Unavoidable excepted) of which I bitterly complain every day.

The Salisbury minister, who at the time was the prominent Rev. James Allen testified:

I, having lived nine years at Salisbury in the work of the ministry and now four years in the office of pastor to my best notice and observation of Mrs. Bradbury, she hath lived according to the rules of the gospel amongst us; was a constant attender upon the ministry of the work, and all the ordinances of the gospel; full of works and charity to the sick and poor; neither have I seen or heard anything of her unbecoming the profession of the gospel.

In spite of her social position - she was always spoken of as Mistress Bradbury - or her husband's prominence, the Colony was in the grip of hysteria, and she was convicted. How she escaped execution has never been shown. The foolish testimony against her was in the nature of one case here quoted:

The deposition of William Carr, who testified and saith that, about thirteen years ago, presently after some difference that happened to be between my honored father, Mr. George Carr, and Mrs. Bradbury, the prisoner at the bar, upon a Sabbath at noon, as we were riding home by the house of Capt. Thomas Bradbury, I saw Mrs. Bradbury go into her gate, turn the corner of, and immediately there darted out of her gate a blue boar, and darted at my father's horse's legs which made him stumble; but I saw it no more. And my father said, 'Boys, what did you see?' And we both said, 'A blue boar.'

This venerable woman was about seventy seven when she was arrested for the crime of bewitching John Carr so that he became crazed and prematurely died. The testimony of William Carr at the trial went to show that his brother fell in love with Jemima True, but the proposed match being opposed and broken off by young Carr's father on account of his youth, he became melancholy and at times insane. He further stated that he was with his brother and cared for him in his last sickness, and that his brother died peaceably and quietly, and never spoke anything to the harm of Mrs. Bradbury or anyone else. Mrs. Bradbury was defended by Major Robert Pike, one of the outstanding men of his day and one of the few who stood firmly and outspoken in opposition to the witchcraft mania. Major Pike's daughter was married to Mrs. Bradbury's eldest son. She was convicted with four others who were executed but somehow she escaped execution.

Thomas Bradbury died 16 March 1694/95 and his widow died 20 December 1700. An abstract of his will follows.

14 February 1694 - I Thomas Bradbury of Salisbury, Massachusetts Bay . . . aged, weak of body . . . unto my grandchildren Thomas Bradbury and Jacob Bradbury, all my housing and lands which I have now in Salisbury . . . and said grandchildren to pay unto their Aunt True £ 14 each . . . within one year after they come to . . . 21 . . . Thomas and Jacob shall pay unto their grandmother twenty bushels of corn yearly . . . to find her sufficient wood, winter and summer and cut and fit; as also winter and summer meat for two cows . . . wife to have half the house as she require it . . . to grandchild Thomas Bradbury all my implements of husbandry and also my young colt . . . unto my daughter Mary Stanyan 20s, she having had her portion upon her marriage . . . unto my daughter Jane True £ 10, to my grandchild Elizabeth Buss £ 5 . . . also £ 5 to the selectmen to dispose to such of the poor . . . well beloved wife Mary Bradbury and my well beloved daughter Judith Moody executors . . . Signed

Children, all except eldest born in Salisbury:

i. WYMOND, b 1 April 1637; m 7 May 1661, Sarah Pike, dau. of Robert & Sarah (Saunders) Pike; 3 ch.: he d 7 April 1669 on the island of Nevis, West Indies; she m 2, John Stockman, had 5 more children

ii. JUDITH, b 2 Oct. 1638; m 9 Nov. 1665 Caleb Moody, son of William & Sarah, his 2nd wife; 10 ch.; he d 25 Aug. 1698 age 61; she d 24 Jan. 1699/1700

iii. THOMAS, b 28 Jan. 1640/41; probably died unm.

iv. MARY, b 17 March 1642/43; m 15 Dec. 1663, John Stanyan, son of Anthony & Mary, b 16 July 1642; 8 ch.; he d 27 Sept. 1718; she d 29 May 1724

v. JANE, b 11 May 1645; m 15 March 1667/68, Henry True, son of Henry & Israel (Pike) True, bapt. 8 March 1646/7; 7 ch.

vi. JACOB, b 17 June 1647; d 1669 at Barbados; unm.

vii. WILLIAM, b 15 Sept. 1649; m 12 March 1671/2, Rebecca Maverick, widow of Samuel & dau. of Rev. John & Mary (Hutchinson) Wheelwright; 3 ch.; he d 4 Dec. 1678; she d 20 Dec. 1678

viii. ELIZABETH, b 7 Nov. 1651; m 12 May 1673 at Salisbury, Rev. John Buss; 2 ch.; he m 2, 3; he d in March 1736

xix. JOHN, b 20 April 1654; d 24 Nov. 1678; unm.

x. ANN, b 16 April 1656; d 1659 at Salisbury

xi. JABEZ, b 27 June 1658; d 28 April 1677 at Salisbury

His Signature
from his will

Tho: Bradbury

See THE ANCESTRY OF THOMAS BRADBURY & HIS WIFE MARY PERKINS, by John B. Threlfall, 1988, privately printed, for further information on this family.

Ref.: Bradbury Memorial; Savage; Genealogical Dictionary of Maine and New Hampshire, by Noyes, Libby, Davis

The Ancestry of
ANTHONY COLBY

Compiled By
John Brooks Threlfall

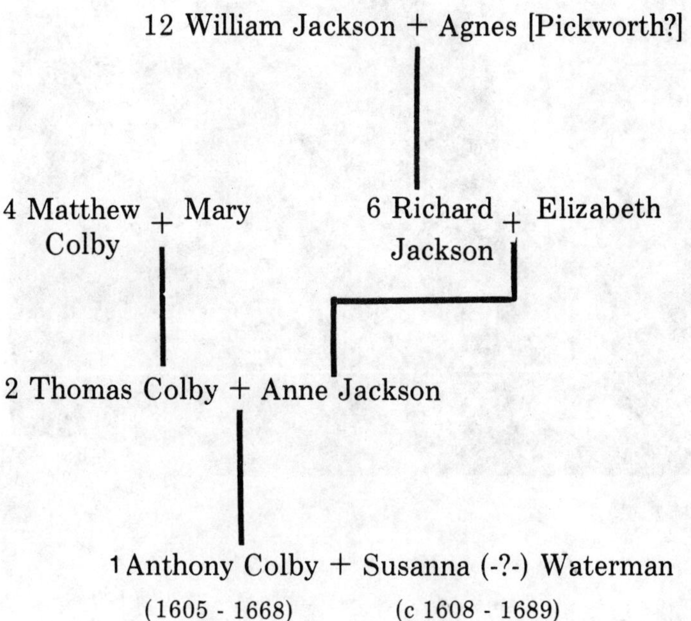

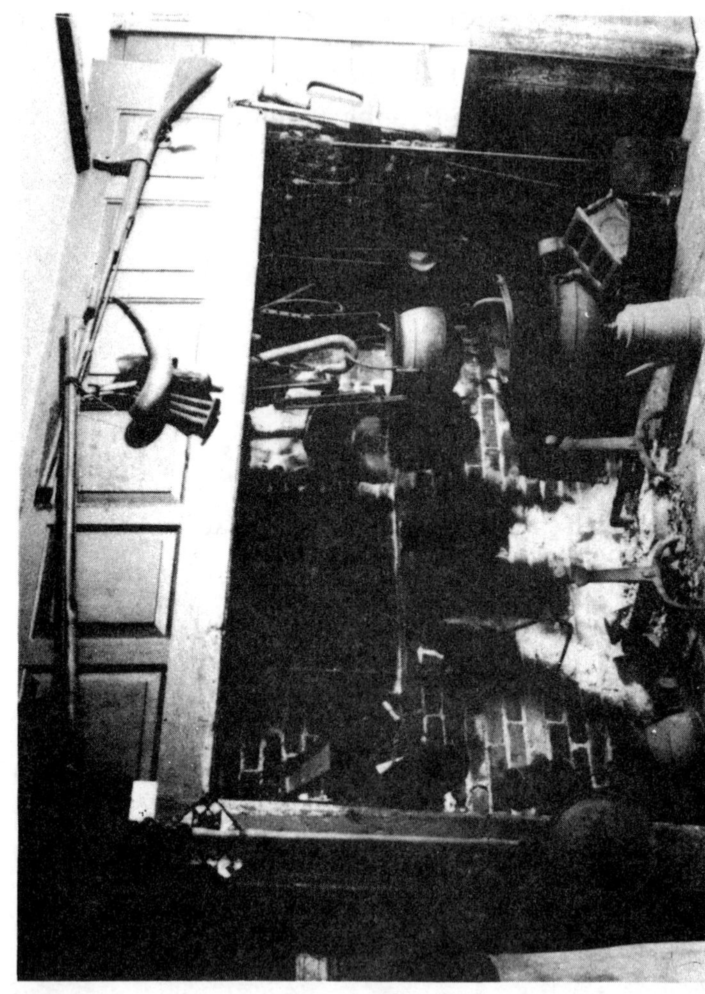

INTERIOR OF MACY-COLBY HOUSE, AMESBURY

1

ANTHONY COLBY (*Thomas, Matthew*) was baptized on 8 September 1605 at Horbling, Lincolnshire. Horbling is next to Sempringham where his Colby ancestors had lived for several generations. He was apparently named for his uncle, Anthony Jackson.

Anthony Colby was the only one of the name to come to America in the 1600s, so most of the name in America are his descendants. He crossed the Atlantic with the Winthrop fleet, landing in Boston in June or July, 1630. With him from Horbling was Simon Bradstreet, who later became governor of the Massachusetts Bay Colony, and several others from nearby villages. Anthony Colby's name is found on the list of original church members at Boston. Cambridge was soon selected as the best place to fortify, but by the fall of 1631, only eight families were known to have gone there. Anthony Colby is believed to have been one of them. In 1632 settlers came in larger numbers and the town was laid out in a compact form from the college grounds to the Charles River and surrounded by a palisade. As early as January 1632, the erection of houses outside the village was prohibited. Anthony's farm was up the Watertown Road beyond Ash Street. He must have built there before the prohibition. He was called on to build 4 rods of a mile long garden fence. He was now surrounded by neighbors, so he built a second house up by Observatory Hill, owning both for several years.

Although a church was built in Cambridge in 1632, he apparently retained his membership in the First Church of Boston. As soon as Reverend Cotton arrived, he took his child to Boston on 8 September 1633 to be baptized. He apparently married about 1632, probably at Cambridge, Susanna Waterman, a widow. He was made a freeman on 14 May 1634 at Boston with some 80 others.

On 21 June 1637 he was apparently an inhabitant of Ipswich where he signed a petition. In 1639, he sold his two houses and the several parcels of land in Cambridge to Simon Crosby and moved to Salisbury, for in that year he is called a planter in Salisbury. He received land there in the first division in 1640, again in 1643, 1654 and 1658, when he received 40 acres in Amesbury. On 13 May 1640 he was appointed by the General Court, with two other men, to value horses, mares, cows, oxen, goats and hogs for the town. On 2 August 1646, he was dismissed by letter from the First Church in Boston to the First Church in Salisbury. In 1647, he sold his house and two acres in Salisbury to William Sargent and moved west of the Powwow River between Salisbury and Amesbury. Amesbury was set apart as a separate town in 1668. He was on the rate list (tax list) for 1650, but not for 1652. In 1653, he was one of a commission to run the line between Haverhill and Salisbury. In 1654, he bought from Thomas Macy his dwelling house. Macy was fined for harboring Quakers and moved to Nantucket, becoming the first white settler there, as related in Whittier's poem *The Exiles*. The house was sold for a mare, boards, corn and other such things as he would most need, with £12 or £14 of money, the whole amounting to over £200 in payment for:

> "the house together with the barns, together with the well and bucket and rope belonging to it, all to be delivered unto y[e] aforesaid Anthony Colby at or before last of May next."

The house is still standing and was occupied by direct descendants for ten generations until taken over by the D.A.R. in recent years.

Anthony Colby and three neighbors owned and operated the first saw mill in Amesbury. It was at the falls of the Powwow River. They were permitted to cut timber on the common lands by paying a percent of boards to the town. The worst that can be found against him is that he was once fined for being disorderly in a town meeting. He died 11 February 1660/61 and was probably buried in the old cemetery called *Golgotha*, on the west bank of the Powwow River, as were some of Amesbury's first dead. The cemetery graveyard has long ago vanished.

His widow, Susanna, remarried in 1663 to William Whitridge of Amesbury. He died 5 December 1668, and she died 8 July 1689 "or thereabouts" ae 81.

Children:

JOHN, prob. b at Cambridge; bapt. 8 Sept. 1633 at Boston First Church; m 14 Jan. 1655/6, Frances Hoyt, dau. of John; 9 ch.; he d 6 Feb. 1673/4

SARAH, b about 1635, prob. at Salisbury; m 6 March 1653/4, Orlando Bagley; 5 ch.; she d 18 May 1663; he d before 1700

SAMUEL, b about 1638, prob. at Salisbury or Ipswich; m about 1667, Elizabeth Sargent, dau. of William & Elizabeth (Perkins) Sargent, b 22 Nov. 1648; 5 ch.; he d 1716 and she d 5 Feb. 1736/7; he was in the Falls Fight of King Phillips's War

ISAAC, b 6 July 1640 at Salisbury; m Martha Parrat, dau. of Francis, b 9 Oct. 1649; 8 ch.; he d in April 1684; she d 13 July 1730; res. in Salisbury, Amesbury, Haverhill, Rowley

REBECCA, b 11 March 1642/3; m 9 Sept. 1661, John Williams jr. of Haverhill; 6 ch.; she d 10 June 1672 at Haverhill; he m 2, 5 May 1675, Esther (Blakeley) Bond; he d 30 April 1698

MARY, b 19 Sept. 1647 at Salisbury; m 23 Sept. 1668, William Sargent, son of William & Elizabeth (Perkins) Sargent, b 2 Jan. 1645/6; 6 ch.

THOMAS, b 8 March 1650/51 at Salisbury; m 16 Sept. 1674, Hannah Rowell, dau. of Valentine & Joanna (Pinder) Rowell, b in Jan. 1653; 5 ch.; he d before 31 March 1691 when his inventory was taken; she m 2, Henry Blaisdel; she d 9 Aug. 1707 at Amesbury

Anthony Colby

Ref.: The Colby Family, by Weis; Old Families of Salisbury & Amesbury, by Hoyt; Essex County Probates; Suffolk County deed 11:176; Savage; Quarterly Court Files; Pope; T.A.G. 51:65-71

MACY - COLBY HOUSE, AMESBURY, MASSACHUSETTS

Inventory of the estate of Anthony Collby, late of Salisbury, deceased, taken Mar. 9, 1660, by Sam. Hall, Tho. Bradbury and Tho. Barnett:

	£	s	d
His waring Apparrell	2.	10.	
1 feather bed & bolster & old Cotten Rugg, a payer of course sheets & a course bed case	4.	15.	
one old warming pan		3.	4
an other feather bed, feather pillow, feather bolster & a payer of sheets & Cotten Rugg	4.	10.	
about 8 li. of sheeps wooll		10.	8
five pound of cotton wooll		5.	
10 li. of Hopps		6.	8
a bed case, feather pillow & bolster case, a payer of sheets & old cotten Rugg	1.		
an Iron pott, pott hooks & Iron skillett		6.	8
a copp. kettle & a payer of tramells	1.		
a little old brass skillett & old morter & pestle		3.	4
trayes & other dary ware		15.	
a landiron, gridiron, frying pan, old cob iron		5.	
in old peuter		3.	4
4 scythes		8.	
2 pillow beers		3.	
table, two joynstooles, 2 chayres	1.		
old swords & 2 old muskets	1.		
one chest & one box		10.	
an old saddle & a pillion		10.	
old lumber		10.	
a grindle stone with an Iron handle		3.	4
a new millsaw & ½ an old one	1.		
a croscutt saw & half a one	1.		
a broad how, 3 forkes, a rake, 2 axes & an Iron Spade		12.	
5 yoakes		10.	
2 Iron cheynes		10.	
halfe a tymber cheine & a new draft sheyne	1.	15.	
an old tumbrill with an old payer of wheeles	1.		
2 sleades	1.		
a long cart & wheels & Spanshakle & pin & 4th pt. of an other cart	2.		
a plough & plough Irons		10.	
2 Canoas & ½ a canoa	3.	15.	
6 oxen	42.		
6 Cowes	27.		
2 3 yeare old steers	7.		
2 Yearlins	3.		
2 calves	1.		
7 swine	5.	5.	
8 sheep	4.		
1 mare & colt	20.		
1 horse		10.	
a dwelling house & barne & 14 acres of upland in tillage	70.		
a pasture of about 30 acres	20.		
2 lotts att yt wch is cald Mr. Hall's Farme	5.	10.	
about eighteen acres of fresh meadow	40.		

Item	Amount
ye accoodacon bought of Mr. Groome . . .	6.
2 lots of sweepage & one higgledee piggildee lott	4.
60 acres of upland towards pentucett bounds with meadow to be laid out	10.
ye 8th pt. of ye old saw mill	30.
40 bushells of wheat	9.
10 bushels of barley & 6 of rie	3. 4.
about 60 bushels of Indian corne	9.
total . . .	£ 359. 19. 4.

Copied from the files of the Norfolk county court records, and sworn to by the widow Colby, Tho. Bradbury, rec.

Anthony Colby, debtor:

Creditor	Amount
To Sam. Worcester	1. 7.
Willi. Osgood	2. 9.
Goodman Tappin	1. 2. 6
Abram Morrill	2. 10. 10
John Tod	10.
Tho. Clarke	9.
Mr. Russell of Charlestown	10.
Mr. Gerish	5. 8. 6.
Mr. Woodman	2. 14.
Jno. Bartlett	2. 2. 1.
Steven Sweat	2. 5. 5.
John Webster	13.
Steven Greenleif	13.
Goodman Peirce	10.
Goodman Cillick	3.
Jno. Lewis	1. 10.
Orlando Bagly	5. 19.
Jno. Blower	6.
Mr. Worcester	1. 13. 6
Mr. Bradbury	16. 9
to the widow Colby	10.
Henry Jaques	2. 10.
Willi. Huntington	11.
John Severans	1. 13. 8
Jno. Clough for grass	6.
for 9 weeks worke	8. 2.
total	£ 68. 14. 7

Debtor p Contra:

Item	Amount
Rodger Eastman	10.
Robert Clements	1. 5.
from ye town	9.
Jno. Maxfield	2.
Leonard Hatherlee	1.
Sam. Worcester	14. 6
Goodman Morrill	1. 10.
Steven Flanders	6.
Goodman Randall	6.
boards at ye saw mill	3. 7. 6
loggs to make 2000 of bord . .	2. 5.
for work done to ye estate . .	1. 2. 6
total	£14. 15. 6

2

THOMAS COLBY (*Matthew*) was baptized on 20 December 1567 at Sempringham, Lincolnshire, England. On 4 May 1596 at Horbling, he and Anne Jackson were married. She was born probably about 1571 the daughter of Richard and Elizabeth Jackson of Horbling. There are no surviving baptismal records for Horbling from 1567 thru 1575. In Thomas's will she is called Agnes, but at that time, Anne and Agnes were often used interchangeably, as Elizabeth and Betty are today. Horbling is about two miles north of Sempringham.

Thomas Colby was usually designated as "junior" to distinguish him from his elder brother, also named Thomas. From his will and the burial record, we learn that he was a tailor. He made his will 10 December 1625 and was buried 11 December 1625 as "Thomas Colby jun., taler". His wife survived him.

> 10 December 1625 - the will of THOMAS COLBIE of Horbling, county of Lincoln, taylor, sick of body ... to my five sons William Colbie, Richard Colbie, Anthony Colbie, Mathew Colbie & Rob't Colbie half of my goods to be equally divided amongst them, but my will is that my son William Colbie shall have my house at Dunnington for part of his portion of goods aforesaid, which cost me eight pound ... if any of these my sons die before age 21 at which time the legacies shall be due unto them, then his or their shares to be divided amongst the overlivers. Residue to wife Agnes Colbie whom I make executrix. Robert Allen supervisor. Witnesses: Rob't Allen, Thomas Baxter. Signed by mark. Proved 21 April 1626.
>
> (Ref.: Lincoln Consistory Court Wills - 1626/292)

In March 1636/7, an assessment was made for expenses of repairing the church at Horbling. Thirty seven names were listed. William Colby, who had a small stock of animals, must have been the older brother. The widow Colby must have been their mother. Robert was mentioned for having been paid for some work. Nowhere is there any mention of Anthony or Matthew after their father's will of 1625. Possibly both of these brothers left for America with the Winthrop Fleet in 1630, but if so, there is no trace of Matthew. His fate will probably remain a mystery. As for Anthony, he is surely the one who went to New England in 1630. All the other known contemporary Anthony Colbys in Old England can be eliminated from consideration for one reason or another.

Assessment agreed upon the fifth of March 1636 for the church-wardens for the repairing of the church [of Horbling] and other duties by us whose names are here under written - Mathias Browne, William Stringer, John Hardie, with others. Every horse 7d., every beast 7d., and every score of sheep 2s.4d.

	horse	beast	sheep	
William Coulbe	1	4	5	3s.6d.
Widow Coulby	1	5	0	3s.6d.

Children:

MARGARET, bapt. 25 Sept. 1597 at Aslackby, "dau. of Thomas"; prob. d.y.

WILLIAM, prob. b 1598; named first in his father's will; m 12 Oct. 1626 at Horbling, Anna Sewell, "widow of Anwick"; ch. bapt. at Horbling: John 2 Sept. 1627, Matthew 4 Jan. 1632/3, Joseph 27 Oct. 1640. He was Surveyor of the Highway 1633, Collector for the Poor 1634, Constable 1634, 1638, 1640, and Surveyor of the Highway in 1642. In 1638 he witnessed a tenancy agreement recorded in the town book. In the list of church expenses for Horbling dated 19 April 1636, there is a payment of 26s.4d. to William Colby for scaring crows and keeping the pea fields, also 16s. for helping the glazer and the plumber five weeks, and 5s. for washing the church linen.

Note: There is a possibility that these records apply to his cousin William who was bapt. 21 Dec. 1600.

ABRAHAM, bapt. 13 Sept. 1600 at Aslackby, "son of Thomas"; buried 2 Sept. 1625 at Horbling, "son of Thomas jun."

RICHARD, bapt. 30 Jan. 1602/3 at Horbling, "son of Thomas Colbye"; m Ann ——; living 1655 in Horbling

1 ANTHONY, bapt. 8 Sept. 1605 at Horbling, "son of Thomas jun."; he apparently was the one who went to N.E. with the Winthrop Fleet in 1630, settled in Boston, then to Cambridge, then to Ipswich, finally to Salisbury & Amesbury; he m the widow Susan Waterman; 7 ch.; he d 11 Feb. 1660/01

MATTHEW, bapt. 13 Dec. 1607 at Horbling, "son of Thomas junior"

ROBERT, b prob. about 1609; named last in his father's will of 1625. There is the possibility that he was actually an adopted nephew & the biological son of Thomas sen. & bapt. 24 Feb. 1614/15 at Horbling, his mother having died when he was about 11 months old. It would have been quite reasonable for his uncle, Thomas the younger, to have adopted him. This suggestion is reinforced by there being no record of a baptism of another Robert. In the list of expenses for repairs of the Horbling church in 1636, Robert Coulbe was paid 5s. for helping the glazer and to wash the old glass.

Ref.: Parish Registers; Bishop's Transcripts; Lincoln Consistory Court Probate Records; Churchwarden's Accounts 7/1 for Horbling, from the Toller Charity

4

MATTHEW COLBY lived in Pointon, a village or chapelry in the parish of Sempringham, Lincolnshire. He was probably born about 1530. He married Mary ——— , probably about 1555. He had at least two brothers and a sister also living in Sempringham. The names of his parents are unknown. Matthew Colby was buried 10 October 1591, his wife Mary on 18 December 1591, followed soon by their two youngest children, four in all dying within a three month period. Both parents left deathbed wills in which they stated that they were sick. One can wonder at what sort of epidemic struck this family. Horbling is just to the north of Sempringham.

8 October 1591 - the will of MATHEW COLBY of Poynton, Sempringham parish, county Lincoln, husbandman ... sick in body ... to be buried in the churchyardof Sempringham ... to John Colbye my son one cow & a quoye+, to Edward Colby one cow & a quoye, to Agnes Colby one cow & a quoye, to William Colby one cow & a quoye, to Elizabeth Colby one cow & a quoye, to Thomas Colby the younger one cow & a quoye, to Thomas Colby the elder half a quarter of barley and half a quarter of pease, to Robert Colby my brother one stricke of barley, to Alise my syster one stricke of barley, to Agnes Colby the daughter of Thomas Colby of Horbling two stricks of barley ... all the rest of my goods & cattells ... to Mary Colby my wyfe ... she to be sole executrix ... Roger Lawrence to be supervisor. Witnesses: Robert Baxter, Roger Lawrence, Thomas Colbye and Francys Barton. Proved 22 October 1591. (Ref.: C.C. of Lincoln, 1591, Book 1:235)

1 December 1591 - the will of MARY COLBY of Poynton, [Sempringham], county Lincoln, widow ... sick in body ... to Thomas Colby the elder one horse mill & the house it standeth in, one bay nag, one red starred cow which was bought of Thomas Dinge & two of my four steers ... to Edward my son the other two steers, one red sorell feelie [vealer?], one calf of this year ... to Thomas Colby the younger one gray mare, one young beast & a calf ... to William my son one bald foal which was in Wright's farm, one burling* & a calf ... to Agnes my daughter three kine, one burling & a calf, one rand bald filly ... to Elizabeth my daughter three kine, two burlings, one calf ... my two bullocks equally to be divided amongst them ... to Thomas Colby the elder one quarter of barley & half a quarter of pease ... to Robert Colby one strike of barley ... all my corn & crop unbequeathed about my yard & barn to be divided amongst them ... to John my son the shod cart & all the cart

+quoye = quey = a heifer (Scot.)

*burling =a yearling heifer

gears thereunto belonging ... to Edward my son one wayne & the wayne gears thereunto belonging ... to John & Edward my two sons the kill house, the vat & the hair ... to Agnes my daughter one feather bed, one cowling & eight pair of sheets, one new chest, one new table with a frame, six table napkins which be at Bullar's, 4 pillows & pillowbears for them, two table cloths, one new press, one chafing dish, one candlestick, the best lead, 12 pieces of pewter, one brass pot & two kettles ... to Elizabeth my daughter 4 pair of sheets, 4 pillows & pillowbears, one great brass pan, one cowling, two napkins, two table cloths, one mattress, one cowling, six pieces of pewter, one Ambry, one square table, one breuing lead & the other table & tressels, one chest & the best chair, one brass pot, two candlesticks & one bed ... to Thomas Colby the younger one pair of sheets ... to William my son one pair of sheets ... to John & Edward my sons either of them two pair if there be so many ... to Thomas Colby his daughter half a quarter of barley ... to John my son one bedstead, to Edward my son one bedstead, to Elizabeth my daughter one bedstead ... the sheep & the field swine shall be equally divided amongst them all ... my sons shall have their parts & portions at age 21, daughters at day of marriage ... to Elizabeth my daughter 20s. that is in the hands of Thomas Colby the elder. I give her two tubs ... to Agnes my daughter 20s. which is in the hands of John Bullar, ... two new tubs ... to Thomas Colbye the elder shall have the use of all their parts till they come of age ... Thomas Colbye the elder and Thomas Colbye the younger my full executors ... Supervisor Roger Lawrence, he to have 3s.4d. for his pains. Witnesses: Robert Colbye, William Thorpe & John Buckminister. Proved 17 December 1591.

(Ref.: C.C. of Lincoln, 1591, Book 1:286)

Children, doubtless all born at Sempringham:

WILLIAM, perhaps b 1556; no record of him except in his parents' wills

AGNES , perhaps b about 1558-9; named in parents' wills in 1591

THOMAS, "senior", b prob. 1561; m 18 May 1590 at Sempringham, Joan Booth, who was bapt. 31 May 1567 at Sempringham, dau. of Thomas & Isabel Booth. Thomas Booth d testate in Jan. 1590/91, left Joan a messuage & 10 acres in nearby Aslackby parish. For a year or two they lived at Horbling, then to Aslackby by 1593, then to Billingborough, which is 1 mile north of Sempringham, then 1606 to Horbling, another mile to the north; 10 ch.: Ann bapt. 9 May 1591 ("Agnes" per her gr.f's will), Elizabeth 1 April 1593 at Aslackby - bur. 25 March 1593/4, William 16 Feb. 1594/5 - bur. 8 Feb. 1595/6, Thomas 14 May 1593 at Billngborough, William 21 Dec. 1600, Edward 19 Jan. 1605/6 at Horbling - bur. 27 Sept. 1606, Richard 30 Aug. 1607, Mary 22 Nov. 1609, Matthew 9 June 1611, Robert 24 Feb. 1614/15. Joan Colby, wife of Thomas Senior, was bur. in Jan. 1615/16 at Horbling. Either Thomas, or their son of the same name, was bur. 9 March 1639/40 at Horbling, a "labourer".

ELIZABETH, bapt. 30 May 1563; apparently d.y.

JOHN, bapt. 26 July 1565; m 23 Oct. 1593 at Sempringham, Elizabeth Davye; ch.: John & Henry bapt. 22 Jan. 1594/5, Anne bur. 15 Feb. 1594/5 (these 3 must have been triplets), Robert son of John bapt. 23 Feb. 1594/5 at Aslackby seems to be a 4th ch., Elizabeth bur. 11 March 1612/13 - "dau. of widow Colby" at Sempringham; therefore, John must have d before 1612/13; widow Colby bur. 31 March 1615 at Sempringham. They lived in Poynton part of Sempringham.

2 THOMAS, bapt. 20 Dec. 1567; m 4 May 1595 at Horbling, Anne Jackson, aka Agnes, dau. of Richard Jackson, b about 1571 or later, prob. at Horbling, of which time there are no surv. rec.; he was bur. 11 Dec. 1625, named 5 sons and wife Agnes in his will.

EDWARD, bapt. 5 Oct. 1570; bur. 31 Dec. 1591 at Sempringham, "son of Matthewe Colbye". His estate, along with his sister's, was admin. in Feb. 1591/2 by his brother Thomas senior

ELIZABETH, bapt. 14 March 1572/3; bur. 10 Jan. 1591/2, "dau. of Matthewe Colbye". The combined inventory of Edward's & her belongings follows. Admin. of her estate granted to Thomas Colby sen., 15 Feb. 1591/2

The two Inventories of all the goods, chattels, debts & credits of Edward Colby & Elizabeth Colby, two of the children of Mathew Colby & Mary his wife late of Poynton, deceased, praysed the sixth day of April A° dm. 1592 by Thomas Baxter, Roger Lawrence, John Buckminster & John Essington, as followeth:

all the housing		.40s.
one covering & a mattress		. 8s.
6 pieces of pewter, 2 candlesticks, a brass pot & a brass pan		.10s.
2 tables		. 3s. 4d.
one chair & a chest, two tubs & one lead		. 6s.
2 bedsteads		. s.12d.
5 kyne, 2 burlings, 2 quyes & 2 steers	£ 9	
12 quarters & a half of corn & other grain	£ 4	
one shodd wayne [a cart with iron shod wheels]		.30s.
one stepefatt [steeping vat] & 2 sheep		.20s.
the third part of a yoke of bullocks		.30s.
the third part of three swine		. 6s. 8d.
in ready money		.20s.
Sum	£ 21.15s.	

Execution was done at Sleford 10 April 1592

Ref.: Parish Registers; Bishop's Transcripts; Probate Records of the Consistory Court of Lincoln, held at the County Archives Office, Lincoln

SAINT ANDREW'S CHURCH, SEMPRINGHAM, LINCOLNSHIRE
(From the Ross Collection)

6

RICHARD JACKSON (*William*) of Horbling, Lincolnshire, England, was born probably about 1537-1542. His wife's name was Elizabeth. He was a churchwarden in 1572-4, 1579, 1584, 1599, and 1600, and Constable of Horbling in 1578. Richard Jackson was buried 25 October 1607 at Horbling. Elizabeth was buried 14 September 1619. An abstract of his will follows.

13 October 1607 - the will of RICHARD JACKSON of Horbling, county Lincoln, yeoman, sick in body ... to be buried in the church or churchyard of Horbling ... to Anne Brinkley 6s.8d., same to Richard Brinkley and Robert Brinkley ... to Thomas Colbie's children 6s.8d. apiece ... same to Richard Segrave's children ... to Horbling church 12d. ... to Anthony Jackson's children 20s. ... to Richard Harreson my man half a seam of barley ... to Edmon Jackson 3s.4d. ... residue to Elizabeth my wife whom I make executor ... to George P'et's two children 6s.8d. apiece ... Richard Segrave and Anthony Jackson my supervisors. Witnesses: John Gauthorn, Anthonie Jackson, Richard Segrave. Proved 6 November 1607.

(Lincolnshire Consistory Court Will/ii/78)

Children, all born at Horbling or Threckingham:

ANTHONY, b perhaps 1567, for which year, and thru 1576, there are no surviving bapt. rec. for Horbling. m 2 June 1590 at Threckingham cum Stow Green, Jane Seagrave; ch.: Ann b perhaps 1591 as she m 1, 3 Oct. 1616 William Tompson, Elizabeth bapt. 6 Sept. 1600 at Threckingham cum Stow Green, Anthony b 1607-1625 as he was a minor in 1626, prob. other ch. who d before their father's will. Jane Jackson of Stow, wife of Anthony, was buried 1 July 1612; he m 2, 6 Oct. 1612 at Threckingham cum Stow Green, Anne Skipp; ch.: Jeffrey bapt. 8 April 1616 - bur. 17 July 1617. Anthony Jackson was churchwarden at Stow Green 1613-14. He was buried 21 March 1626/7, testate. His son Anthony m Anne _____ & had a son Anthony bapt. 2 Aug. 1635 & a dau. Anne bapt. 14 April 1640

19 January (1626/7) - the will of ANTHONY JACKSON of Stowe Green (in Threckingham), yeoman, sick in body ... to Anthony Jackson my son my house in Stowe Green wherein I now dwell and all my freehold there belonging to it and one house in Threckingham now in the tenure of Thomas Kerke and all there belonging to it ... and £20, my horse mill, my iron harrows, and that he shall enter of two parts of my land at age 21, and the £20 to be paid him at same age, my waine and one pair of shod wheels and plow and things belonging to it ... to Ann Linsie my daughter, the wife of Thomas Linsie 10s ... to Ambrose Tompson, Francis Tompson, Thomas Linsie, Jane Linsie my daughter Ann's

children 10s. apiece at age 21, and to Ann Tompson another of them £3 at age 21 or marriage ... to Elizabeth Stubley my daughter the wife of Matthew Stubley £10 ... to Jeffrey Stubley and Ambrose Stubley my daughter Elizabeth's children £3 each at age 21 ... to Ann Watson my niece £3 ... to the poor of Threckingham 3s.4d. To Lincoln minster 12d. Residue to Ann Jackson my wife whom I make executrix ... John Seagrave and Matthew Stubley my supervisors and 12d to each of them. Proved 6 April 1627

(Consistory Court of Lincoln 1627:598)

AGNES, b prob. 1569. On 8 May 1593 at Horbling, Agnes Jackson m Richard Brinkley, a widower, whose wife Joan was buried 20 April 1592, & by whom he had at least 3 ch. whose burials are recorded. Richard & Joan Twell were m 1 June 1576 at Horbling. Richard & Agnes had: Ann (named in gr.f's will), Richard bapt. 18 Nov. 1596 & must have d.y., Robert bapt. 10 June 1599 & must have d.y., Richard again after 1604 & named in his father's will. Richard d 1624-5, Agnes surviving him. His will:

27 December 1624 - the will of RICHARD BRINCKLEY of Swaton, sick in body ... to my son William Grococke ... one ewe hog and all my tools which I use ... to my daughter Elizabeth Enderwell ... to my son Richard Brinckley twenty ... at age 21, also my lease after decease of my wife Agnes Brinckley, and if he die without issue, then unto William Grococke and his heirs ... residue to wife Agnes Brinckley whom I make sole executrix ... Edward Hatfield and John Kirke of Swaton supervisors ... Witnesses: Edward Hatfield minister, Nicholas Wallison, Thomas Tompson. Proved 14 March 1624/5

3 ANNE (a.k.a. Agnes), was prob. b about 1571; m 4 May 1596 at Horbling, Thomas Colby, son of Matthew & Mary Colby, bapt. 20 Dec. 1567 at Sempringham; 6 or 7 ch.; he was buried 11 Dec. 1625 at Horbling; she survived him according to his will, but is called *Agnes* therein

FRANCES, perhaps b 1573; buried 6 March 1576/7

MARY, b prob. about 1575; m 2 Nov. 1598 at St. Michael on the Mount, Lincoln, Richard Seagrave, possibly her 1st cousin; ch. bapt. at Horbling: Anthony 16 Sept. 1599, Richard 7 March 1601/2, John 26 Feb. 1603/4 - buried 26 March 1616, William 2 March 1605/6, Edward 14 Aug. 1608, Mary 10 Feb. 1610/11, Elizabeth 8 June 1612 at Grantham, Thomas 12 Nov. 1615 at Horbling - apparently d.y., John 25 March 1616/17 - buried 26 March 1617, John again prob. b 1618, Thomas 5 Nov. 1620. Mary must have d about 1621 & he m 2, about 1621/2, Elizabeth; ch.: Anna (dau. of "Richard & Elizabeth") bapt. 22 Dec. 1612 at Horbling. Richard Seagrave was a churchwarden in 1603, 4,5,10,11,12,16,17,20,and 21. He died testate in 1637. Richard Seagrave of Horbling who d testate in 1596 was doubtless his father.

18 November 1637 - the will of RICHARD SEAGRAVE of Horbling, yeoman ... to Anthony Seagrave my son 10 sheep or else £4, to Richard Seagrave my son 20 sheep or else £8 ... to William Seagrave my son £50, and 12 sheep ... to Edward Seagrave my son 10 sheep or £4 ...to Mary my daughter the wife of Edward Brightman 10 sheep or £4 ... to Elizabeth my daughter the wife of Thomas Corry 10 sheep or £4 ... to John Seagrave my son £50 at age 21 and 6 sheep ... to Thomas Seagrave my son £50 at age 21 and 6 sheep ... to my daughter Anne Seagrave £50 at age 21 and 6 sheep or else 48s. at age 21 ... to Elizabeth my wife my mault house, my kiln house and kiln and hay ... and ?easterne ... for her natural life in consideration of her thirds of her house and land ... to son Edward the pasture he now occupies likewise the three acres in his tenure ... to my son William the 12 acres which is in the tenure of Mathias Browne ... to Mr. Watson 10s, to Mrs. Watson and their 5 children six sheep or 48s ... to the poor of Swinshead, of Wigtogft, of Donnington, to the town stock of Horbling ... to all my servants 12d apiece ... to William Seagrave my son a brown colt called Robin if he be found again ... residue to wife Elizabeth ... sole executrix ... William Stringer and Thomas Cony supervisors. Witnesses: William Watson, Thomas Conny, William Crosby. Proved 5-?-1637

26 October 1596 - the will of RICHARD SEAGRAVE of Horbling, yeoman ... to Robert Cook son of John Cook ... to the poor of Billingborough and Horbling ... to Richard Buckminster my wife's son ... to Suzanne my daughter ... to wife Katherine 4 cottages in Boston ... to Richard Seagrave my son ... to Elizabeth my daughter ... to William my son ... to my sister Joan Seagrave ... if any of my three children Richard, Adam or Suzanna die before age 21, ... to my wife's mother out of my dovecote one dozen pigeons ... children who are under age to have their portions at age 21, except Adam who is to get his at age 22 ... brother in law Thomas Seagrave and William Seagrave my son and Ralph Hickson my supervisors. Proved 11 February 1596/7.

ELIZABETH, bapt. 16 Nov. 1577 at Horbling. Perhaps she was the dau. who m George Pett & had 2 ch. by 1607: Elizabeth, dau. of George Pett bapt. 12 Dec. 1591, George Pett who d testate 1637 leaving a wife Hester & 2 underage ch. must have been the other ch.

MYLES, perhaps, who was buried 5 April 1598 at Horbling

Ref.: Parish Registers; Bishop's Transcripts; Probate Records of the Consistory Court of Lincoln, held at the County Archives Office, Lincoln

SAINT ANDREW'S CHURCH, HORBLING, LINCOLNSHIRE
(From the Ross Collection)

8

COLBY is a place name deriving, in this case, from the parish of Coleby, which lies seventeen miles northwest of Sempringham and six miles south of Lincoln. There is also a parish of Colby in Norfolk, next to Beccles and it too seems to have been the source of a quite unrelated Colby clan. There are also villages called Colby in Westmoreland, in Yorkshire and one in Denmark.

The place name is of Viking origin and means *coal place.* There are a number of English place names containing the element *cole* (i.e. coal), such as Coleridge, Colclough, and Colebrook. The *-by* suffix is the Viking or Scandinavian word meaning *homestead farm.* Thus, Coleby was probably a farmstead where charcoal was made in ancient times by Viking settlers.

The first record of a Colby in Sempringham is a deed dated 3 February 1421/2 by which William Stanenstone of Pointon conveyed to John Boche and his wife Alice three selions of land in the fields west of Pointon, two of which parcels were bounded by William Colby. This William Colby was undoubtedly an ancestor of the Colbys who lived in the village of Pointon in the parish of Sempringham several generations later.

On 7 May 1505, Robert Rogerson of Pointon granted to John Huchyson of Billingborough and Robert Colby of Pointon, "one messuage and 20 acres of land and meadow with all the appurtenances in the village and the fields of Pointon, which lately was inherited after the decease of William Rogerson his father and Alice his wife." Five days later, on 12 May, John Huchynson and Robert Colby deeded the same property back to Robert Rogerson, his wife Margaret, Katherine (the sister of the late William Rogerson) and a niece, in a somewhat complex deed which was made for the purpose of getting around the laws of primogeniture. Robert Colby was acting as a straw man. This Robert Colby was probably the great grandson of the above William Colby and was probably the grandfather of the four Colbys listed below.

The next generation of the Colby family, that is to say, the father of the four Colbys listed below, surely also lived in the village of Pointon, parish of Sempringham. His name, however, is a mystery. He was probably born about 1500 to 1505. His first wife and mother of his children, name also unknown, died, and he remarried to a widow, Agnes Askew, who had four or five daughters and probably two sons. Then Mr. Colby died and she was a widow for the second time. The widow Agnes Colby was buried on 31 December 1576 at Horbling, which is two miles north of Sempringham. She was undoubtedly living with one of her married daughters who lived there, either Agnes or Elizabeth. Her will names these children and several grandchildren. No Colbys are mentioned or even witnessed her will, all of which suggests that she and her Colby step-children were perhaps somewhat estranged.

There were Colbys in nearby towns, relationship to the Sempringham Colbys unknown. They were probably closely related, surely all descended from, or most of them, from Robert Colby mentioned in the 1421/2 deed. Agnes's Colby husband and his four children were apparently the only descendants of the name still living in Sempringham in the last half of the sixteenth century.

Sempringham is best known as the place where the Gilbertine order was founded. Gilbert was born here in 1083. Being deformed and unfit for the usual knightly duties, his father sent him to France to be educated for clerical life. When he returned to his home, pious and educated, his father's disappointment turned to pride and hope.

Eventually Gilbert founded a religious movement for both men and women which was instituted in 1131. It never took root abroad, but was a success in England and grew to eleven houses thruout England at the time of Gilbert's death, to 26 houses at the time of the dissolution of the monasteries in 1538. At this time, the priory was granted to Lord Clinton who tore it down and built a house with the materials. Close to the site of the priory is a church which is a generation older. It is the parish church of Saint Andrew. It is reached by a path from the village of Pointon, which has some thick walled houses, doubtless built of stone from the priory.

25 December 1576 - the will of AGNES COLBYE of Horbling, widow ... to be buried in the churchyard ... to the repairing of Lincoln minster 2d. ... to Thomas Clipson my son in law my best feather bed & best bolster, one great brass pan, one quye that he hath in his keeping, one ambry, all my wooden vessels, one ark being the best, the best chafing dish, two little pans, one kettle, two spits, one pair of cob irons, two cushions, one pair of mustard --ear--s, one brass mortar & the pestal. Item, I give Agnes Clypson my daughter my best russet gown, two saucers, two bed coverings being the best, one towel of diaper work & a napkin of the same work being the best & one linen sheet beiong the best ... to Joanne Clypson & Elizabeth Clypson daughters of the said Thomas Clypson either of them one larger, one pewter dish and one candlestick ... to John Clypson the younger one brass pot being the best ... to John Clypson the other of them one cushion ... to John Rawlynson's daughter one gallon pan, one gallon pot, one ark, one pair of linen sheets, one pair of semble sheets, one linen towel, one board cloth of semble, one pillow, one candelstick, two pewter chargers, one pewter dish, one board not the best, one coverlet, one blanket being at Thomas Boyle's, one green coverlet that lyeth on my bed & one mattress the best ... to Elizabeth Rawlynson my daughter my violet traynet [?] gown, two gray coats and one red petticoat ... to John Rawlynson one cow that is at Poynton at John [?]-lyscough's ... to Thomas Baxter my son in law's two daughters two chargers, three latten lavers, one chafing dish & one latten basin to be divided betwixt them ... to the younger of the said Thomas Baxter's daughters one ambry and to the elder one kettle that is in his custody ... to the said Thomas Baxter's son 12s.4d. of the money that the said Thomas Baxter doth owe unto me, which sum is in my debt book & likewise I give George Crayne my son in law's children 23s. that he doth owe me as doth appear in my debt book ... to Joanne Baxter my daughter one kirtle of say ... to Mary Spraging's three daughters 4 pieces of pewter being chargers, one pewter dish & two saucers ... to Thomas Askew one featherbed that I lie on with one bolster & my green gallows which he hath in his custody ... to the said Thomas Askew's children one cow color red ... residue to John Askew & Thomas Askew whom I make my executors ... Richard Spraging of Boothby Pagnell my trusty supervisor and for his pains 2s. Witnesses: Thomas [?]-reele, Simond Rolfe & John Burges of the said Horbling. Proved 16 January 1576/7 (Lincoln Consistory Court Wills 1576/215)

Children, probably all born at Pointon in Sempringham:

4 MATTHEW, b perhaps about 1530; m Mary ______; 8 ch.; he was bur. 10 Oct. 1591; she was bur. 18 Dec. 1591, both testate

WILLIAM, prob. b about 1532; m Joan ______; 6 ch.: Richard b about 1556, Alice b about 1558, Adam b about 1560 - d between 1569 & 1577, Margaret b about 1562, Agnes b about 1564, Joan bapt. 31 Aug.

1567 - all at Sempringham; he was bur. 26 Aug. 1569, she 12 Feb. 1577/8, both at Sempringham, both testate. His will refers to his brother Matthew.

24 October 1569 - the will of WILLIAM COLBIE of Pointon in the parish of Sempringham ... to be buried in the churchyard ... to the mother church of Lincoln 4d. ... to my curate for tithes forgotten 2d. ... to the poor in Pointon 6d. ...to Richard my son my house and all my land with appurtenances, a gray horse, a black mare and a red steer of two years old to be paid unto him at age 21 ... to daughters Alice, Margaret, Agnes and Joan 40s. each at age 18 ... to Adam my son 40s. at age 21 and half of the mill that I have with my brother Matthew Colbie, but if he die before age 21, then the value of the mill to be divided between the other children when they come of age ... residue to wife Joanne for bringing up the children, she to be sole executrix ... Edmond Smythe of Pointon to be my supervisor and 20d. for his pains. Witnesses: Edmond Smythe, Phillippe Smythe, Mathia Colbie, Robert Colbie, Robert Horne, et al. Proved 17 November 1569.

(Lincoln Consistory Court Wills 1569/i/43)

4 February 1577/8 - the will of JOAN COLBIE of Sempringham, county Lincoln ... to be buried in the churchyard ... to Alice Colbie my daughter 2 kyne and a mare and a filly ... to Margaret Colbie my daughter 2 kyne and a white mare and one veal calf ... to Agnes Colbie my daughter one red mare and one year[ling] foal and 2 quies ... to Joanne Colbie my daughter one black steer cow, one bullock calf, one gray mare and a black foal ... to Richard Colbie my son rack and rack gears, plow and plow gears and one white horse and one pair of linen sheets, one pillow and bolster, one seam of barley in consideration that he will sow my crop for this time and the crop that is sown for this time shall be divided amongst my five children ... to Alice Colbie my daughter my best table ... to Richard Colbie my son 2 planks to make him a table ... if God doth call any of my children under age, their goods to survivors ... my brother Matthew Colbie shall have Margaret my daughter to bring up and her legacy to paid to her at age 18 ... all children's parts to be delivered at age 18 ... to Margaret Colbie my daughter the table that standeth on the be--- ... to two of my youngest children two planks and all the timber that is in the lathe[?] and in the yard ... my son Richard shall pay 20s. unto all my daughters for the use of the mill that my brother Matthew Colbie hath ... to the poor men's box 12d. ... to my sister Bartill half a strike of peas & half a strike of barley to be delivered at Michaelmas next coming ... to four of my daughters four swine ... Item. There is one red broke steer to pay as rent withall ... all my hovels to be given to all my children ... Richard my son to be my executor and my brother Matthew Colbie and Raffe Bullard to be supervisors and they shall take lands of Richard my son for the performance of my daughter's parts ... children shall keep house together till Michaelmas ... to Robert Colbie one strike of peas ... to John Awger's wife one strike of peas & one strike of barley and to Hedygard a strike of barley ... Alice Atkinson shall have land to sow peas on and half a strike of barley ... husband's legacies to be paid to my aforesaid daughters that my husband their father gave them which was 40s. apiece and also 40s. that was given to one of my sons which is dead & that 40s. must remain to the rest of my children that be alive. Witnesses: George Rodiat curate of Sempringham, Raffe Bullard, Matthew Colbie & Richard Atkinson. Proved 20 February 1577/8. (Consistory Court of Lincoln Wills 1577/i/104)

ALICE, b perhaps 1534-37; named by her brother Matthew in his will of 1591

ROBERT, b perhaps about 1539; m 26 Sept. 1564 at Sempringham, Martha Esington; 5 known ch.: Elizabeth bapt. 4 Aug. 1569 - bur. 11 March 1612/13, Joan bapt. 19 Jan. 1571/2, Philip bapt. 16 Jan. 1574/5 - bur. 17 Jan. 1655, dau. bapt. 18 Jan. 1575/6, Dorothy bapt. 26 Jan. 1577/8 - all at Sempringham. He was buried 3 Sept. 1592, she 3 March 1615/16 at Sempringham. He was named in his brother Matthew's will. His son Philip had 6 more ch. Dorothy m Richard Wright 8 Dec. 1607 & had ch.

An Inventory of the goods of Rob't Colby late of Pointon in the diocese of Lincoln, laborer, deceased, valued the 18 day of September 1592 by John Buckminster, Roger Lawrence, John Esington & Edward Streaker as followeth.

all the neate beasts	£ 8	
all the horse beasts	40s.	
the swyne	10s.	
the piule	s.	12d.
brass & pewter	26s.	8d.
all the tables, stooles, chaires, old ambries in the house	7s.	
all the hey	20s.	
hempe on the land	3s.	4d.
a hovel & wodd in the yarde	10s.	
all the linnen	47s.	
all the beddings	20s.	
all the bedstedds, caffers & pam....clothes about the house	13s.	
butter, cheese & corne redye in the chamber	3s.	4d.
all the milke vessells & bruing vessels	10s.	
all his workinge tooles	3s.	
his purse & apparell	10s.	
Somme totall	£19 4s.	4d.

RICHARD, perhaps. The only record of him is the reference to land in Pointon bought from him by Thomas Booth, according to Booth's will of 1590

Ref.: Parish Registers; Bishop's Transcripts; Probate Records of the Consistory Court of Lincoln, held at the County Archives Office, Lincoln

SOUTH-EAST VIEW OF THE CHURCH AT COLEBY,
LINCOLNSHIRE, 1803

12

WILLIAM JACKSON of Horbling, Lincolnshire, was probably born about 1490-1500. His wife Agnes was probably nee Pickworth, as William Jackson in his will referred to his "brother" [in-law] Richard Pickworth of Sleforth, who was probably dead by 1569 when Agnes made her will. A Richard Pickworth, laborer, of Welburn, made his will 20 November 1568, proved 4 February 1568/9, mentioning his children, William, Elizabeth and Helen, and his wife (but not by name). He was perhaps the brother of Agnes. A William Pykworth was mentioned in the Horbling town records of 1534, and in 1537 he was on a list of the Bretheren of the "plow lathe", a lathe being an Anglo-Saxon land division. William Pykworth was an Alderman in 1539. He was probably the father of Agnes.

William Jackson and one other made a bill (list) of the *harness of Horbling*, which they took to Lincoln in 29 Henry VIII (1537-8). This was the town armoury. Locals were taxed towards its upkeep. William Jackson paid 8 pence.

William Jackson was one of the Aldermen of Horbling in 1538 and also in 1540.

William Jackson died in early May 1549 within a few days of making his will, indicating that it was a deathbed will, and that he was sick. Agnes died probably in late 1571, also leaving a will. William had a brother, Robert, who survived them both, an uncle Richard Jackson, and a sister, Margaret.

In the next parish of Threckingham, there lived a Richard Jackson who had a brother, Adam Jackson. He and Adam, mentioned in William's will, were probably William's brothers. Richard died testate in late 1555, and his wife Elizabeth about March 1557, also testate. They left ten children.

> 6 May 1549 - the will of WILLIAM JACKSON of Horbling, county Lincoln, husbandman ... to be buried in the churchyard of Horbling ... to John my son 2 steers of two year old and two of year old, 2 seams of barley, 2 seams of peas, one cow, two ewes, 2 lambs and two hogs ... to Richard my son 2 steers of 3 years old, the one brown & the other brandy, & 2 ewes, 2 lambs, 2 hogs, 2 weaning calves the one black &

the other red & one seam of barley ... to Alice my daughter one cow, one quye* of two years old, two ewes, two lambs, 2 hogs and one seam of barley ... to Agnes my daughter one brown cow, one black pyed quye of two years old, 2 ewes, two lambs and two hogs ... to Margaret my daughter one pyed young quye, 2 weaning calves, one ewe, one lamb and one hog ... to my daughter Luce one red cow, one flecked calf, one ewe, one lamb and one hog ... to Margerie my daughter one red cow, one weaning calf and one ewe, one lamb and one hog ... to Joan my daughter wife to Thomas Sygryff one ewe & one lamb ... to Margaret Sygryff daughter to the said Thomas one hog and one lamb ... son John to have my house with all the lands and meadow belonging at Threckingham after the decease of Agnes my wife if my said son John will follow the counsel of his mother, Richard Jackson and Richard Pyckworth, but if he will not, then house and lands to remain to Richard my son ... to Robert my brother one leather doublet, one russett jacket, half a seam of barley & half a seam of peas ... to Adam Jackson half a seam of barley, half a seam of peas and one sangwyn** coat ... to my brother Richard Pyckworth one buckskin doublet and one pair of hose ... to my uncle Richard Jackson one worsted doublet ... to my sister Margaret one seam of malt ... to Thomas Andrew one gray russett jacket ... to Richard Crale one ewe and one lamb ... residue to Agnes my wife whom I make sole executrix ... supervisors to be Thomas Mydleton of Horbling & my brother Richard Pyckworth of Sleforth. Thomas Mydleton to have for his pains 3s.4d. ... Witnesses: Richard Jackson of Threckingham, Robert Pole, Richard Crale & Thomas Sygryff of Horbling. Proved 17 May 1549.
(Consistory Court of Lincoln Wills 1547-9/309-310, also 1566 etc./58)

24 August 1569 - the will of AGNES JACKSONNE of Horbling, county Lincoln, widow ... to be buried in the churchyard of Horbling ... to the repairing of Lincoln minster 8d. ... to the vicar of Horbling for tithes forgotten 12d. ... to every cotcher [i.e. a cottar] house in the said Horbling 4d. ... to John Jackson my son one couple steer and one seam of barley and to every one of the said John's children one ewe, and one lamb ... to Thomas Sigriffe my son in law two seams of barley, to Margaret and William his children either of them two ewes and two lambs and to Antonie Sigriffe and Lucy Sigriffe and Elizabeth, the said Thomas's children, either of them one ewe and one lamb and to the said Margaret Sigriffe one linen sheet, one harden|| sheet and best peticoat ... to the said Thomas Sigriffe's wife my daughter my best gown, my best kercher, one veil of mine own clothes and one red cap ... to Agnes Osborne my daughter my red kirtle and to John Osborne her husband one sheet of my best linen ... to Robert Bedall my son in law

*quy=quye=quey=heifer
**sangwyn=sanguine=blood red
||harden=a coarse fabric made from the hards of flax or hemp

one sheet of my best linen, to my daughter Lucy his wife one linen sheet, and to Robert Bedall their son one ewe and one lamb ... to Antonie Langton my son in law one sheet of my best linen, and to Margaret Langton & Jennett Langton and Jane Langton her children, every one of them one linen sheet, one femble** sheet and one canvas, and to every one of the said Margaret, Jennett and Jane one ewe and one lamb, and to the said Jennett Langton the hat and the cap that was her mother's, and to the said Jane Langton one kercher of mine own clothes ... to John Pickworth my cousin a half seam of malt and to Robert Jackson my brother in law two strikes of wheat and two strikes of barley ... to every one of my godchildren unmarried 4d. apiece ... to my son John Jackson's wife one kerchief and one veil ... Residue to Richard Jackson my son whom I make mine executor ... the right worshipful Mr. Vincent Randall my good landlord, Antonie Langton vicar, Thomas Wright and John Jackson my son, my trustee supervisors to do their diligence to see this my last will fulfilled and I give the said Mr. Vincent Randall for his pains taken one colt foal and to Antonie Langton, Thomas Wright and John Jackson, every one of them, 3s.4d. Witnesses: Richard Crale, Thomas Palmer and Bryan Grene. Proved 27 October 1571.

(Consistory Court of Lincoln Will 1571/ii/187)

Children, probably all born in Horbling:

JOAN, b prob. 1520-28; m by 1548 Thomas Sigriffe, i.e. Seagrave; ch.: Margaret b by 1549, Anthony bapt. 9 May 1562, William, Lucy & Elizabeth by 1569, Thomas & Adam. He was buried 26 Jan. 1607/8 at Threckingham. Joan Seagrave, widow, of Stow Green (a part of Threckingham) was buried 4 May 1612. His will:

6 March 1605/6 - the will of THOMAS SEAGRAVE of Threckingham, yeoman ... wife Joan to have for her life all lands in Threckingham, Stowe, Burthrop, Newton, Walcott & Spanby ... to Thomas Seagrave my son one messuage wherein I dwell in Threckingham in northgate next to land of the Earl of Lincoln on the east, etc. ... after death of wife and after his son's death then to *his* son Thomas ... other lands in southgate on same terms ... if it please god to take away my son Thomas and his two sons without issue, then said lands to Edward Seagrave son of my son Adam ... to Peter & Thomas the sons of said Thomas Seagrave each £5 ... to Thomas the son of my son Adam Seagrave my biggest pot, a silver salt & £5 ... to Edward Seagrave son of Adam £5, a silver spoon ... to Elizabeth Seagrave daughter of Adam my son my biggest pot that was my wife's, £5, one silver spoon ... to Joan Seagrave daughter of my son Adam, one pot and £5 & one silver spoon, ... to Elizabeth Seagrave daughter of my brother Richard 40s & a cow ... to Avis Seagrave her sister 5s ... to Margaret Seagrave her sister 5s ... to Mary the daughter of Robert Mudd a cow ... to Thomas Jackson son of Anthony 5s ... to Agnes Buckbury wife of John Buckbury & daughter of John Seagrave 5s ... to Mary daughter of John Seagrave 5s ... to Elizabeth Jackson daughter of John Jackson 5s ... to every

**femble=fimble=light summer hemp that bears no seed

god child 12d ... to every servant 12d ... to son Thomas the lease of my farm in Stow ... residue to wife Joan, she to be executrix ... William Seagrave of Borneby supervisor. Witnesses: William Callis, Richard Sympson, Thomas Mainsfoth. Proved 9 February 1607/8

JOHN, prob. eldest son; he was m with several ch. by 1569; Symon Jackon son of John bapt. 6 April 1576 was possibly his gr. son; John Jackson of Billingborough was granted admin. of the estate of his father John Jackson in Feb. 1576/7, possibly this same person

6 RICHARD, b prob. 1530-40; m Elizabeth ——— ; he was buried 25 Oct. 1607 at Horbling, testate

ALICE, she was unm. in 1549; prob. d by 1569

AGNES, m John Osborne by 1569; ch.: Jennett bapt. 16 May 1561 who must have been his by an earlier wife; Magdalen Osborne who d testate 1576 at Horbling was perhaps his mother

MARGARET, was prob. the dau. who m Anthony Langton; ch. by 1569: Margaret, Agnes bapt. 7 March 1561/2 - buried 11 July 1562, Ann bapt. 29 May 1563 - buried 22 July 1563, Jennett who apparently d before 1582, Joan. He was vicar of Horbling by 1577 to his death in 1583. Margaret was d by 1569

11 January 1582/3 - the will of ANTHONY LANGTON - clerk and vicar of Horbling, county Lincoln ... sick in body ... to be buried in the parish church nigh unto Thomas Wright ... to William Crake's wife one frame of bees ... to John Spenser my first jacket ... to Thomas Grim my worst hat ... to Agnes Burges one ewe & one lamb ... to Margaret Williamson my daughter my best gown ... to the three children of the said Margaret one ewe & one lamb each at age 18 ... to Joan Anthony my daughter my next best garment, my side saddle, 4 of my best kine & the best quye, also my eldest fillie ... to Margaret my daughter one cow & one quye, being the best I have ungiven ... to John Williamson clerk, my riding saddle ... to Joan my daughter four ----hogs & my bed tester with the hangings, three ewes & three lambs, conditionally that if the said Joan have any children then the ewes and lambs to them ... to Katherine Furnam daughter of Hobert Furnam four ewes & four lambs at age 18 and such goods as her father hath of mine & doth withhold from me as appeareth by a bill of memory written with my own hand ... residue to be divided between Joan Anthony and Margaret Williamson my daughters ... Nicholas Anthony my son in law executor ... Sir John White vicar of Billingborough & John Burges of Horbling my supervisors. Witnesses: John Williamson clerk, John Lassels, Anthony Clipson. Proved 3 May 1583. (Consistory Court of Lincoln, wills)

LUCY, m Robert Bedall; ch.: Elizabeth buried 14 Sept. 1562, Agnes bapt. 18 Jan. 1562/3 -buried 23 Jan. 1562/3, Robert by 1569; Alice bapt. 20 May 1586, dau. of Robert, was prob. a gr. dau.

MARGERY, prob. d by 1569

Ref.: Parish Registers; Bishop's Transcripts; Probate Records of the Consistory Court of Lincoln, held at the County Archives Office, Lincoln

RALPH FARNUM (probably *Ralph, Ralph*) was probably the one born on 25 August 1601 and baptized on 30 August at Saint Peter's Church, Cornhill, London, the son of Ralf Varnham, merchant tailor of London "at the sign of the Lute". Ralph, the immigrant, was listed as 32 years old on the ship's passenger list when he set sail from London, England, the latter part of July 1635 in the brig *James*, John May, Master. He arrived in Boston the last week of September. With him was his wife Alice, aged 28, and children: Mary 7, Thomas 4, and Ralph 2. If this age is correct, he was born in 1603 but this could easily be an error, for the ages on the old passenger lists were often only estimates.

The apprenticeship records of the Merchant Taylors' Hall at 30 Threadneedle Street, London, show the following entry:

Radus Varnum fil Radi Varnam de Liverpoole in Con. Lanc. glover defunct-- se Appren Willm Morell de Ould Change pro Septem Annis a die decum et secundo die Augustus 1591

translated, it reads:

Ralph Varnam, son of Ralph Varnam of Liverpool in the county of Lancaster, glover deceased, was apprenticed to William Morell of Old Change for seven years from this day the 12th of August 1591

Seven years later, on 16 October 1598, he was admitted a freeman of the Merchant Taylors' Company.

If this Ralph Varnam was the father of the Ralph who came to New England, then Ralph of Liverpool was his grandfather. The name Varnam or Farnum or other variations does not appear in the index of probate records for Lancashire during that period and so was certainly not a Lancashire name. This would suggest that the deceased Ralph probably moved into Lancashire and originated elsewhere.

Ralph Farnum settled in Ipswich, Massachusetts where he is first mentioned in 1639, but he was probably there earlier. He was called a barber on the ship list but was the first town crier of Ipswich. He probably died there, for his widow, Alice, married on 18 June 1648 Solomon Martin who was listed as 16 years old when he came over on the same ship

James with the Farnums. He had settled in Gloucester where he was a ship carpenter, and the widow Alice was his second wife. They no doubt moved to Andover shortly after their marriage, for he was made freeman there on 26 May 1652. The Farnum children all married and settled in Andover.

Ralph Varnum was agreed with June 11, 1640 for ringing the Bells, keeping clean the Meeting house, and publishing such things as the town shall appoint, shall have for his pains, for every man, for the year past, whose estate is rated under £100, six pense, from £100 to £500, twelve pense, and upward, eighteen pense, the like for the year to come.

Children:

MARY, b in England about 1628; m at Boston 20 Oct. 1650, Daniel Poor who d 1689; 2 sons, 9 daus. per his will (49:32); she d 3 Feb. 1713/14 "aged about 85 years" at Andover, a widow

THOMAS, b in England about 1631-2; m at Andover 8 July 1660, Elizabeth Sibborn, prob. the dau. of John & Mary bapt. at Boston in Aug. 1644; res. Milford; 7 known ch., prob. others who d.y.; she d 26 Aug. 1683; he d 11 Jan. 1685/6 "ae 53"; Sergeant, a tailor

RALPH, b in England about 1633; m 26 Oct. 1658 at Andover, Elizabeth Holt, dau. of Nicholas; she was b 30 March 1636, d 14 Oct. 1710 "ae about 78"; 7 known ch., prob. also Samuel who m Hannah Holt 1697/8; he d 8 Jan. 1691/2 (his son Ralph b 1 June 1662, m Sarah Sterling on 9 Oct. 1685)

SARAH, b prob. at Ipswich about 1638; m at Andover 26 April 1658, George Abbott; 10 ch.; she d 12 May 1728 "in her 90th year"

JOHN, b prob. at Ipswich about 1640; m at Andover 12 Nov. 1667, Rebecca Kent, dau. of Stephen of Newbury; 8 known ch., perhaps more who d.y.; she d 8 Feb. 1728/9 ae about 78; he d 17 June 1723 in his 83rd year

Ref.: Farnum Genealogy; American Genealogist 46:216; Planters of the Commonwealth; Vital Records; Early Inhabitants of Ipswich, by Hammatt; Public Record Office E157/20

1

THOMAS FREAME was born about 1650 in England, most likely in Gloucestershire, where the name is commonly found. On 4 November 1649 at Minsterworth, Gloucestershire, there was baptized Thomas Freame, son of Lawrence and Mary Freame. This was probably the same Thomas Freame who went to New England. On 23 February 1669/70, his name was entered in the enrollment book of the port of Bristol, England, as a servant bound for New England. Grace Smith was named as the person to whom he was bound, that is, indentured as a bond servant. Her name does not appear in New England, so it would seem she was probably sending him off to someone in New England. Most of the persons embarking from Bristol were from Gloucestershire and Somersetshire.

The name Freame, Freme, Frame, Froeme, Frome, derives from the parish of Frome in Somersetshire, 25 miles northeast of Ilchester, and 20 miles southeast of Bristol. There was in 1395 a mayor of Bristol named William Frome.

He next appears on record in Amesbury, Massachusetts where he certainly was by March 1672/3 when his affair with Mary Rowell precipitated a hasty marriage on 18 September 1673. For this morals offense, he was sentenced to be whipped 15 stripes, unless he pay a £4 fine, and she was to be whipped 10 stripes, or pay a fine of 40s. Mary was the daughter of Valentine and Joanna (Pinder) Rowell and was born in Salisbury, Massachusetts on 31 January 1649/50.

On 30 October 1677, he was fined 2s.5d. and was admonished by the court for his part in wagering Samuel Weed, who was drunk, to kiss the minister's wife. On 20 December following, he took the oath of allegiance. In 1680, he was a member of the training band.

On 14 July 1680, he signed a note to deliver to John March of Newbury 4,000 red oak hogshead staves to be delivered to March at some convenient landing place below Holt's Rocks on the Merrimack River side at or before the 25th of September next. He did not deliver and March obtained a judgement against him on 30 November 1680. His signature on the note is reproduced below.

On 23 November 1680, Thomas Freame, aged about thirty, deposed in court, from which age his approximate year of birth is deduced. He served on a coroner's jury 9 January 1684/5 to investigate the accidental death of Nathaniel Griffin, a young lad who was killed while felling a tree, which shot back and killed him. In a 1681 deed, he is called a tailor. He had sufficient education to be the school master in 1693.

On 29 September 1693, in the case of Hugh March, tavernkeeper, versus Thomas Freame, tailor of Almsbury, March got a court writ of execution for his arrest and commitment to jail in Ipswich, for a debt of 45 shillings plus costs. (Essex County Court File 56:62)

Abstracts of all the deeds under his name follow.

2 January 1681/2 - Thomas Fream of ye town of Amesbury, county Essex, on ye north side of Merrimack River, which was formerly Norfolk in ye colony of Massachusetts, taylor, and Phillip Rowell of ye same town, innkeeper ... for £6 sterling and a cow received of Mr Thomas Mudgett of Salisbury, shipwright, sold all of our lot or Division land, viz, 30 acres ... formerly ye land of Valentine Rowell, and lieth in a place commonly called ye Champion Grove, in Amesbury... (Essex County Deed 10:11)

1 June 1683 - Thomas Freame of Almsbury, county of Essex, taylor, & Mary my wife, for £25.10s. sell to Mrs. Anne White of Newbury, widow, all that our mansion or dwelling house in Almsbury together with about seven acres of upland thereto belonging ...
(Ipswich Deed 5:467)

9 August 1692 - Thomas Freame of Almsbury, county of Essex, taylor, bought from William Osgood, senior of Salisbury, millwright, a piece of upland, 10 or 12 acres, more or less, in Almsbury ...
(Essex County Deed 20:151)

3 February 1707/8 - I Thomas Freame of Almsbury, county of Essex, innholder, with the consent of my wife Mary, for £4 received, sell to General John March of Salisbury, gentleman, a lot of land in Almsbury in a division commonly called Bugsmore Division, it being No. 16 and formerly granted to Valentine [Rowell] and containing 30 acres ... signed by Thomas Freame and by mark of Mary Freame.
(Essex County Deed 23:30)

26 May 1708 - Thomas Freame of Almsbury ... taylor ... sells to Joseph Browne of Newbury, land in Amesbury, Mary Freame releasing her dower. (Essex County Deed 20:151)

This is the last mention of Thomas and Mary Freame found in the Essex County records. They were only 58. Possibly they moved elsewhere.

Children, probably all born at Amesbury:

ELIZABETH, b 1 Jan. 1673/4; m 15 Jan. 1693/4, Samuel George who was b 25 Feb. 1665/6, son of James & Sarah; 7 ch.

MARY, b 2 March 1674/5; m 1, 2 Dec. 1702, John Colby; 9 ch.; m 2, 9 Dec. 1725, William Huntington; living in 1740

HANNAH, b 12 Jan. 1676/7; m 16 March 1695/6 at Salisbury, John Hartshorn, Jr. of Haverhill; 6 ch.; he was killed 29 Aug. 1708; she m 2, 1708-10, William Smith; 4 ch.

SARAH, b about 1679; m 26 Jan. 1698/9, John Challis; 12 ch.; she was living 1751

SUSANNAH, b about 1681; m 6 March 1699/1700 at Salisbury, Caleb Norton, son of Joseph & Susanna, b June 1675; 1 ch.; moved to Brunswick, Maine

THOMAS, b prob. about 1683-6, "first son of Thomas & Mary Freame"; d 30 Aug. 1686 at Amesbury

JOHN, prob., who m 13 Oct. 1719 at Boxford, Elizabeth Stiles, prob. dau. of John & Deliverance (Towne) Stiles, b 1 Oct. 1694-6; had ch.: Mercy and Mary (twins) 1720, John 1722/3, Lydia 1726, all at Boxford; no further record of this family has been found so far

2

LAWRENCE FREAME married Mary ——— They lived at Minsterworth, Gloucestershire.

Children, all baptized at Minsterworth:

MARY, bapt. 25 Jan. 1648/9; she perhaps d.y. (A Mary Freame m 8 Oct. 1678 at Radborough, Gloucestershire, Thomas Godsiller, prob. a different person)

1 THOMAS, bapt. 4 Nov. 1649; apparently the Thomas who went to N.E. out of Bristol. However, a Thomas Freame was buried 16 May 1673. If this was the son of Lawrence, then the New England man was of a different family. On the other hand, the Ministerworth records have so many gaps that it is possible that there was another Thomas for whom this burial record applies. Also, the burial record could have been for the old father of Lawrence

LAWRENCE, bapt. 11 Jan. 1651/2; he m 15 Sept. 1677 at Minsterworth, Hannah Wick

DANIEL, bapt. 27 March 1664. Sarah, ch. of Daniel & Katherine Freame was buried 7 March 1694; Daniel Freame of Churcham (the next parish) was buried 29 June 1698 at Ministerworth

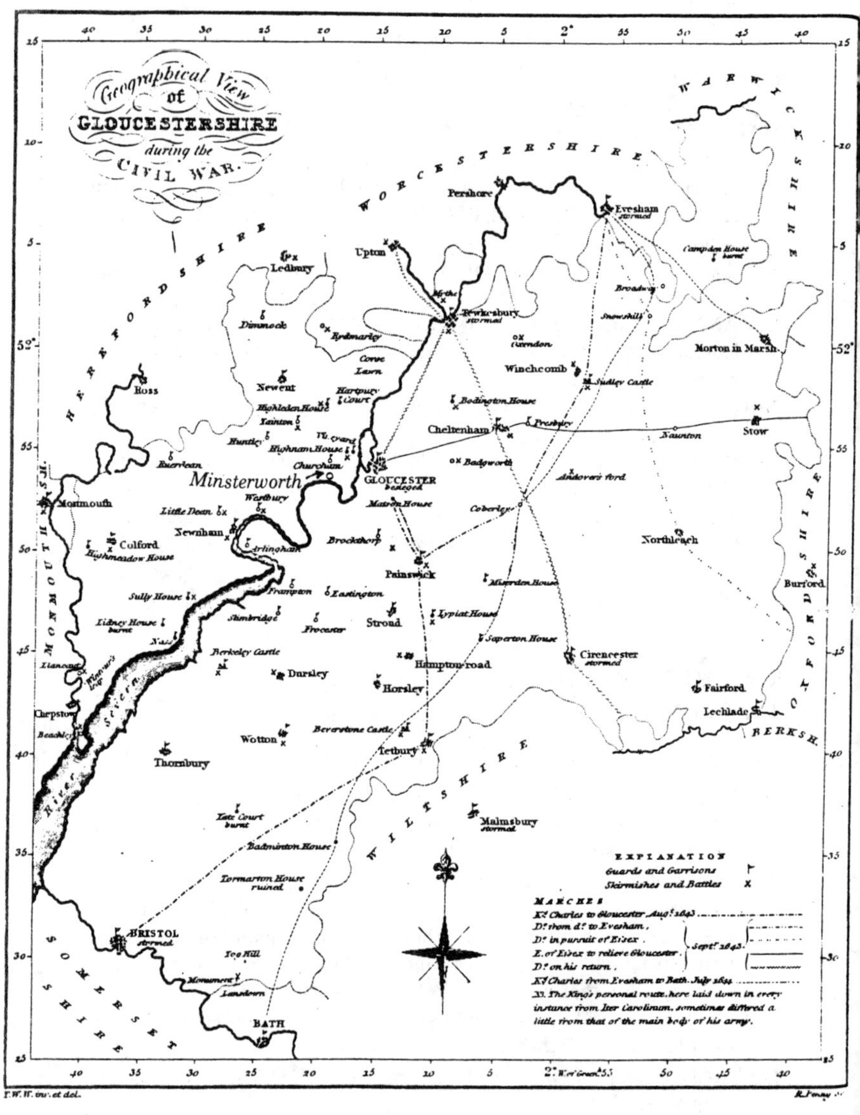

Ref.: The Pillsbury Ancestry; Published V.R.; Deeds; Essex County Court Files; Parish Registers

1

THOMAS FRENCH (*Thomas, Jacob*) was baptized 27 November 1608 at Assington, Suffolk, England. He came to New England with the Winthrop Fleet of eleven ships carrying about 700 colonists, which sailed from Yarmouth, Isle of Wight, in April and May 1630, and which arrived in June and July following. The first of these ships landed at Salem on 13 June. Thomas French first settled in Boston and presumably was married there about the next year, 1631. His wife is identified only as Mary. She may have been the Mary Morton who appears on the list of original members of the First Church of Boston, as was Thomas French, and then is heard of no more.

Thomas French was made a freeman of the colony on 6 November 1632. About 1634, he moved to Ipswich and appears there on record first in 1635 in the following land records.

> 20 April 1635 - There was Granted to Thomas Scott ... Likewise an house lott in Mill Streete havinge Thomas French on the Southeast.
>
> 20 April 1635 - There was Granted to Robert Mussey ... Likewise an house lott in Mill Streete lyinge betweene Thomas French and Richard Jacob.
>
> 20 February 1636/7 - There was Granted to Serjent French ten acres of upland at the hither end of a Neck lying beyond Reedy marsh, to be laid out by the lott layers. Granted to Serjent French, a percell of upland and medow containing about three acres on the South side of the River, adjoyning to his planting lott

From these, we know that his home lot was on Bridge Street just off Mill Street.

About 1637, his parents and his younger brother and sisters joined him at Ipswich. Three sisters had crossed over to New England earlier.

He was formally dismissed from the Boston church to the Ipswich church on 27 January 1638/9.

Thomas French fought in the Pequot War in 1637, for in 1672, he petitioned the colonial government for a grant of land northwest of Salisbury in behalf of himself and eight other Ipswich men who had seen service in that campaign.

His signature to that petition is reproduced below. The inventory of his estate indicated that he owned Pequot lands, that is, lands granted as a bonus to the veterans of that war.

John Bluette, in a letter to Governor Winthrop on 4 March 1632/3, sent his regards to "my scholar Thomas French". Thomas French was also a subscriber to Major Dennison's compensation in 1648. He was called Sergeant French until 1664, Ensign French after that. In 1664, he testified to the mutinous behavior of Samuel Hunt and others during the training of the Ipswich troops on Wolfpen Plain. He served on the trial jury in 1651, 2, 1657-1660, 1662, 4, 9, 1672, 4, 5, and 1678, and on a jury of inquest in 1676. He is listed as a commoner in 1678 and as a voter in town affairs in 1679. A deed of 1 April 1647 calls him *tailor*.

Thomas French died 8 August 1680 at Ipswich and his wife died there 6 May 1681. His will is abstracted as follows:

> 3 August 1680 - The will of Thomas French, senior, of Ipswich, being weak of body ... to Mary my beloved wife the Bed whereon I used to ly ... to my son Thomas French my cloak and closecoat ... to my son John French one Cow, which is to make up the full summe of thirty pounds which I formerly promised him for his portion ... to my daughter Mary Smith one Cow ... to my son Samuel French ... the bed whereon he usually lieth, together with the Bedding and Bed-stead belonging to the same, further, as concrning my lands at the Pequod lots, and my division Lot of marsh at plum-Island my Will is that my sons Thomas and Samuel French for and in consideration of twenty pounds by them engaged according to my order unto my son Ephraim French as ye remaining part of his portion (which summe of twenty pounds is almost all paid, and the remainder due upon demand) ... those my two sonns Thomas and Samuel shall possesse and enjoy the said Pequod lands and division lot of marsh to themselves ... to be equally divided betwixt them. ...to my son Thomas French my dwelling house and homested ... and also my lot lying in Labour-in-vain fields containing 12 acres more or less, with all the rest of my cattell, stocke of all sorts and moveable goods ... and to my son Samuel I give 2 acres of upland joyning to Joseph Quilter's and 2 acres of meadow ground at Reedy marsh, provided that my son Thomas French doe give free libertie to Mary my wife his mother to abide and dwell in the said house and to make use of any room or rooms therof for her convenient accomodation therein, as likewise to make use of all or any such moveables as I doe now leave in the hands of my son

Thomas as may be necessary and convenient for her use ... during the term of her natural life ... after her decease my son Thomas shall deliver to my three children John Sam and Mary three of the biggest pewter dishes which shall then be left and remain, that is to say, to each of them, one ... my two sons Thomas and Samuel to provide for their mother's comfortable maintainance...

Thomas French Sen.

Proved in Ipswich Court 28 September 1680 by Mary French and Samuel French

Inventory of the estate of Ensigne Thomas French taken August 25, 1680, by Jonathan Wade and John Whipple:

	£ s d
his waring apparell, Linon & woolin	4.10.
the grat beed in the parler with what belongs toe it	7.10.
a trundle beed with what belongs toe it	3.
thre chests 20s, 7 cushins 20s	2.
4 payer of sheets 40s, 4 pilowbers 8s	2. 8.
22 nakcines 30s, 3 tablecloths 20s	2.10.
11 yards of hommade cloth	1.13.
warming pann 8s, yd & halfe of serge 6s	14.
a cutlach & belt 6s, 3 small baskits 2s	8.
2 bruches 2s, smal looking glas 1s	3.
6 chayers 6s, table & foorme 7s	13.
one spitt, fire pan, tonges, gridirone, tramell	18.
9 pewter dishes, 2 pint pots & a half pint, two porengers, one beacer cup, 2 poringer	1.17.
two bras Ketls	2.15.
one Irone pott, 3 scilits, a scimer	14.
tine ware 6s, 9 spones 18d	7.6
barels, payels, trayes, kelers	14.
earthen ware	8.
old axe & howe 3s, books 10s	13.
3 loads of haye 30s	1.10.
a bed given to Samuel French with what belongs to it	4.15.
a meane bed with what belongs toe it	2.
doz. halfe of trenchers 18d, sithes 2s	3.6
5 sheep & 3 Lames	2.13.
4 cowes	12.
8 swine	3.11.
his dwelling hous & barne & homestead with the privelidg belonging	70.
12 accers of Lande at Laber in vain	60.
2 accers of Land by Scotes Lane	10.
2 accers of march in the comon feild	10.
debts due by booke	7. 7.6
Total	217.15.6
Debts he oweth	34. 8.5
Making Total	£183. 7.1

Children:

MARY, bapt. 23 Sept. 1632 at Boston; d.y.

MARY, bapt. 2 March 1633/4 at Boston; m Robert Smith of Ipswich; he was b about 1626; 10 ch.; he d 30 Aug. 1693; she d 1719; res. Topsfield

THOMAS, b about 1635-6 at Ipswich; m 29 Feb. 1659/60 at Ipswich, Mary Adams, dau. of Wm. Adams of Cambridge & Ipswich; aged 22 in Dec. 1658, 32 in Feb. 1666/7; 7 ch.: Thomas 1661-d.y., Mary 1662/3, Thomas 1666, Abigail 1668-1703, Hannah 1670, William 1673, Hester 1676/7. He served in the Narragansett campaign 1675/6; being constable, he took part in the tax rebellion against Gov. Andros, for which he was fined £15, put under abond of £500, & to be inelligible to hold office.

JOHN, b about 1637; m about 1660 Phebe Keyes, b 17 June 1639, dau of Robert & Sarah Keyes; 9 ch. b Topsfield: Mary, Sarah 1664/5, Phebe 1667, Martha 1669, John 1671, Lydia 1674, Richard 1676, Phebe 1678/9, Patience 1681, Corporal 1691-4, clerk (prob. of military company) 1696-7, a tailor. He deeded his homestead to his son John in 1701. Phebe d 13 May 1701; he d 25 Jan. 1706. The house he built in 1675-6 still stands.

SARAH, probably, who was brought into court 30 Sept. 1656 by Sgt. French to accuse Hackaliah Bridges of getting her pregnant, but he was discharged; then John Fargison & Sarah, both of Ipswich, were sentenced to be whipped for "uncleanness together"; he was also in trouble for stealing from his master & lying; he was prob. one of the Scot prisoners of Dunbar or Worcester; both appear no more on the rec. She must have d before 1680 as not named in her father's will of that year.

SAMUEL, b prob. 1641; freeman 1663; wid. Eliz. Stacy mentioned her dau. Susanna French in her nuncupative will 1669 at Ipswich. Susanna may have been wife of Samuel or Ephriam. Samuel d 1688 at Ipswich.

EPHRIAM, b about 1643, as aged 15 in 1658 court deposition; he moved to Windsor, then to Enfield, Conn.; had a son Richard b 1674. He d in Sept. 1716 at Enfield, s.p.

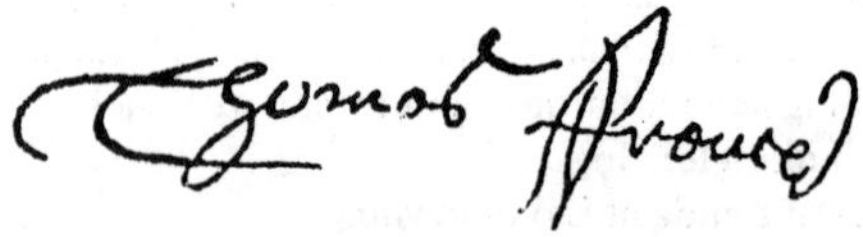

Ref.: Ancestry of Peter Parker, by Linzee, V.R.; Topsfield Historical Collections 13:154; Savage; Ancestry of Lieut. Amos Towne, by A.G. Davis

2

THOMAS FRENCH (*Jacob*) was baptized 11 October 1584 at Bures Saint Mary, the son of Jacob and Susan (Warren) French. On 5 September 1608 at Assington, the next parish, he and Susan Riddlesdale were married. She was baptized on 20 April 1584 at Boxford, the daughter of John and Dorcas. Thomas French occupied a farm located in Assington called *Garlands.* It was owned by John Gurton.

In 1630, his eldest son, then 21, sailed for New England in the Winthrop Fleet of eleven ships and about 700 colonists. In the next few years, three of his sisters, Alice, Dorcas and Susan, also went to New England. In late 1636, Reverend Nathaniel Rogers, the Vicar of Assington, also went to New England, where he became the pastor at Ipswich until his death in 1665. Four other Assington families also came with Rogers. Probably the next year, Thomas French, his wife and remaining children, also crossed the Atlantic to settle in Ipswich, where he first appears on record in New England in 1638 with a grant of land:

25 July 1638 - Granted William Swinden by the company of freemen, Anno 1638, three acres of planting ground lying at the Reedy Marsh, having a planting lott of Thomas French the Elder on the South, and three acres granted to Philip Challis on the north.
27 July 1638 - Memorand, that Richard Lumpkin hath sould unto John Tuttell ... Also pcell of medow ground lying at the Reedy Marsh, lately granted and layd out to the sayd Richard Lumpkin, being about fifteen acres, ... bounded by ten acres of upland of Richard Jacobs on the South, on the North by certaine Lands belonging to Mr. Apleton and Matthew Curren, on the east by medow belonging to Thomas French the elder, on the west by several planting lottes.
22 August 1639 - Granted to Samuel Boreman ... Also six acres of planting ground beyond Mudy River, having a planting lott of Mr. Smith's Southeast, and certaine tenn acre lotts of Thomas French the elder, and others, butting upon the Northwest

Thomas French lived but a couple of years in New England, for on 5 November 1639, administration of his estate was granted to his wife and "the land wheich he left is to be disposed of by sale or otherwise by advice of the Magistrates of Ipswich, for the maintenance of his wife and education of his children which are not yet able to provide for themselves, nor were disposed of in their father's life".

A widow French was a Commoner in Ipswich in 1641. There is no further mention of her until her death in August 1658. Administration of her estate was granted to her son John. Her inventory:

Inventory of the estate of Susan French, widow, of Ipswich, taken 10 March 1658/9 by Robert Lord and Phillip Fowler

	£ s d
a fetherbed old and small, 2 fether pillows, one old coverlet & blankett	2.10.00
her weareing apparell	4 . .
one old chest & box without a lid, an old Hogshead	. 8.
a linen wheele & 2 chaires	. 5.
an old brase pot & a little ould skillet & little Iron pot	10.
2 pewter dishes, poringer & skimmer	8. 6
2 paire of old shires, ould brase & other small things	6. 6
a spitt, tongs, grediron & other small things	12.
an old warmeing pan & frying	6.
2 small trayes, earthen ware & other lumbar	5. 6
a cowe old	3.00.
Total	£12.11. 6

Children, all baptized at Saint Edmund's, Assington:

THOMAS, bapt. 27 Nov. 1608; came to N.E. 1630 with Winthrop Fleet; m ——— about 1631; 6 ch.; he d 8 Aug. 1680; she d 6 May 1681

ALICE, bapt. 9 April 1610; member 1634, dismissed from the Boston church to Ipswich 16 June 1644, "being now the wife of Thomas Howlett", he being among the 1st planters of Ipswich & born about 1606; ch.: Samuel, Sarah, Mary, John, Nathaniel d 1658, Thomas d 1667, William; she d 26 June 1666 at Topsfield; he m 2, Rebecca, widow of Thomas Smith; he d 22 Dec. 1677, testate

DORCAS, bapt. 31 July 1614; came to N.E. 1633 on 3 year service to John Winthrop as maidservant. Admitted to church at Boston 10 Aug. 1634; m 3 Jan. 1636/7, Christopher Peake of Roxbury; ch.: Jonathan 1637, Dorcas 1639/40, Hannah 1642/3, Joseph 1644/5, child d 1647, child d 1648, Ephriam 1651/2, Sarah 1655/6; he d 22 May 1666; he was prob. brother of Thomas Peake of Birmingham, England; she m 2, Griffin Craft of Roxbury, his 3rd wife; she d 14 or 15 Oct. 1694

SUSAN, bapt. 25 April 1616; prob. came over in 1633, to serve Winthrop family for 4 years; no more known

ANNE, bapt. 15 March 1617/18; no more known, but she prob. came to New England in 1637

MARGARET, bapt. 12 March 1619/20; buried 25 Nov. 1635 at Assington

JOHN, bapt. 26 May 1622; m about 1654, Freedom Kingsley, dau. of John & Elizabeth, b about 1630; ch.: Thomas 1657, child b & d 1658/9, Mary 1659/60, Samuel 1661/2, dau. b & d 1664, Hannah 1664/5, Jonathan 1667, John, Elizabeth 1673; she d 26 July 1689 at Northampton, Mass. He d there 1 Feb. 1696/7. He was a tailor

MARY, bapt. 6 Jan. 1624/5; m about 1644, George Smith of Ipswich; ch.: Sarah, Samuel d 1727 ae 80, Thomas, Rebecca, Elizabeth, Joan b 1660; he d testate 15 Dec. 1674 at Ipswich

Ref.: Ancestry of Peter Parker, by Linzee; Topsfield Historical Collections 13:153; Essex Quarterly Court Files; Pope's Pioneers of Mass.; Vital Records

4

JACOB FRENCH first appears on record in the parish of Bures Saint Mary, Suffolk, on 27 September 1578 when he and Susann Warren were married. There being no other records of the French family in Bures Saint Mary prior to his marriage, or for the rest of the sixteenth century, it seems certain that he came from some neighboring village.

About 1585 or 1586, Jacob and Susan French either moved from Bures Saint Mary to Assington, or changed their church affiliations, for subsequent records of the family are found in Assington, either in the parish register which starts in 1598, or in the Bishop's transcripts which cover a few years between 1564 and the advent of the parish register.

Jacob French was buried 11 November 1615 at Assington. Susan's burial is not recorded, unless the burial of Susan French the "daughter" of Jacob French, on 1 August 1613, is an error and was in fact his wife. The record is clear, but such errors are not unknown.

Susan Warren was either the daughter or grand daughter of William and Katherine Warren of Bures Saint Mary. She might have been a posthumous daughter of William, born in 1555, which would make her 45 years old at the birth of her last child in 1600. More likely, Susan was a granddaughter.

William Warren died intestate and administration was granted to Katherine on 26 September 1554. A William Warren was buried at Bures Saint Mary on 12 October 1550. Either Katherine delayed almost four years to settle the estate, or this is the burial record of a still earlier generation, or this was a grandchild. Katherine, in her will of 1567, bequeathed to and specifically named four grandchildren, yet failed to give the names of her four young children. Thus, Susan might have been one of these four young ones, or an unmentioned granddaughter. Of the following children, William and Elizabeth are deduced as such, the others were named in Katherine's will.

31 July 1567 - the will of KATHERINE WARREN of the hamlet of Bures, county of Essex ... sick in body ... to be buried in the churchyard of Bures ... to the poor men's box 3s.4d. ... to Julyan my daughter 2 boulsters & 2 beds with all that [be]longeth to them, both headcloths & ceilings, the one of them in the chamber where I lie & the other in the chamber over it, 2 hutches one in the upper chamber & the other in the nether chamber with all that is in them, a cauldron & the poorest brass pot, 2 kettles & all my woolen apparel, a latten chafing dish, a strainer of latten, a postnet, all my hay and straw, a dripping pan of iron, all my pewter saving 4 platters, a spit, an andiron, all my linen, a frying pan, all the hangings about my house ... I give unto John Awnsell my son in law 20 lbs. cheese, a pair of quernes, a wennel, a black hog, a little brass pot, a little kettle, 3 lb. & a half of wool & 20s. of money and 2 plates. I give to the 2 children of the said Ansell, John & Alice, either of them 3s.4d. To Thomas Waryn my son a young cow, a yellow .....erly, the h...yer, 2 platters, 15s. of money, a kettle, 20 lbs. cheese, a half seam vat & a kneading trough, half the corn of the growing & 3 lb. & a half of wool & the other half I give to Julyan my daughter. I give to John Waryn my son 30s. of money whereof he hath nine of it already in his custody & the great chair & 10 cheeses & all the residue of my cheeses I give Julian Waryn my daughter. I give Thomas Waryn my son a pig, the sow & the shoat I give unto Julyan my daughter. I give unto Robert Waryn my son 40s. of lawful money of England. I give unto William Waryn & John Waryn the sons of Thomas Warren my son 6s.8d. to be equally divided between them, that is to say, 3s.4d. apiece. I give to Julyan Waryn my daughter a cub-board, a table & a form, 2 chairs, a round table, a cheese press & all that belongeth to the milk house, 2 great troughs & a pair of pails, a half seam vat, a f... p... & a laten ladle, a clothe basket, a piece of gold of 15s. I give to Julyan Waryn 20s. All the residue of my goods and chattels ... debts paid, my will fulfilled, my will proved ... I give unto my 4 young children to be equally divided among them share and share alike ... Thomas Waryn my son & Julyan my daughters my executors ... Witnesses: Christopher Raine, William Fisher & John Fisher with others. Proved 15 January 1570/71

Children of William and Katherine Warren:

WILLIAM, prob. an eldest son. He had a son William, "son of William" bapt. 23 Nov. 1561 at Bures Saint Mary; Katherine, dau. of William Warren was bapt. 25 May 1565 at Earls Colne (5 mi. south). Perhaps father & ch. were dead by 1567 as neither were mentioned in Katherine's will. How he relates to the rest of the Warrens is unproved.

THOMAS, prob. 2nd son; ch.: William, John, both b by 1567

KATHERINE, prob. b about 1530-34; on 1 Feb. 1553/4 "John Ansell & his wife Katherine were married"; ch.: John b about 1558-buried 8 Sept. 1588 intestate ("John jr."), Alice bapt. 17 Nov. 1560 - buried 4 Dec. 1560, Alice, "dau. of John", bapt. 22 Nov. 1562. She may have been d by 1567 as her mother bequeathed to John Ansell & the 2 grandchildren, yet made no mention of her. John Ansell m Ellen Hunn(?) 17 Jan. 1573/4. This date suggests another intermediate m for him, or else Katherine was severely incapacitated for a number of years, this the last most likely as there seem to have been no other ch. bapt. at Bures, or was this the son's marriage?

JOHN, perhaps b about 1536; m 10 Nov. 1562 at Bures, Joan H ....

ROBERT, b perhaps 1538-40; apparently an adult in 1567

JULYAN, bapt. 13 Oct. 1542 at Bures; alive and unm. in 1567

ELIZABETH, prob., b about 1544-50; m 10 May 1574 at Bures, William Siday. She must have d early & he m 2, Alice Warren, perhaps a niece to Elizabeth, for Alice was his wife when she was granted admin. of her sister Katherine Warren's estate in 1592/3

THREE OTHER CHILDREN, according to their mother's will

Children of Jacob and Susan (Warren) French:

WILLIAM, bapt. 25 July 1580 at Bures Saint Mary, parents not named. There was a Thomas French, son of William, bapt. 10 Nov. 1606 at Twinstead, Essex, & a Jacob French, son of William, bapt. 17 Jan. 1607/8, also at Twinstead. Twinstead is but 3 miles from Bures Saint Mary.

JACOB, bapt. 12 Aug. 1582 at Bures Saint Mary, parents not named; prob. d.y.

THOMAS, bapt. 11 Oct. 1584 at Bures Saint Mary, "son of Jacob"; m 5 Sept. 1608 at Assington, Susan Riddlesdale, dau. of John & Dorcas, b about 1587; 8 ch.; they went to N.E.; admin of his estate 5 Nov. 1639; she d in Aug. 1658 at Ipswich, Mass.

ELIZABETH, bapt. 27 Feb. 1586/7 at Assington, "dau. of Jacob"

JOHN, prob., bapt 27 March 1596 at Assington, parents not named; he had a dau. Sarah buried 22 Jan. 1620/21

SUSAN, b 1589-98; buried 1 Aug. 1613 at Assington, "dau. of Jacob", unless this record is in error & this is correctly the burial of Jacob's wife, Susan

ROBERT, bapt. 25 June 1600 at Assington, "the son of Jacob & Susan"

OTHER CHILDREN, prob, born 1589, 1591, 1593 & early 1598, for which periods no Assington records survive.

Ref.: Parish Registers; Bishop's Transcripts; Probate Records at Bury St. Edmunds, at Chelmsford

SAINT EDMUND'S CHURCH, ASSINGTON
Reproduced from *Ecclesiastical Antiquities of the County of Suffolk*, 1818, by Isaac Johnson –

HENRY HAGGETT was born about 1594 to 1598 in England. The last of April 1638, the *Confidence,* of London, two hundred tons, John Gibson, Master, sailed from Southampton, England. On the passenger list was Henry *Hangert,* aged 40, servant to John Ludwell. This surely is a record of Henry Haggett, for no other of a similar name appears elsewhere. Ages were often mere guesses. Henry Haggett appears next in Salem, Massachusetts in 1642, when he was granted land there, in what is now Wenham, but then was called Enon. He was the cowkeeper there and received a ten acre lot. During the first four years, he probably worked for Ludwell to work off his debt for passage; otherwise he probably would have been granted land at an earlier date.

At the Salem court held in December 1644, Ann Haggett was presented in some matter concerning a *cockinoven,* i.e. presumably a cooking oven. Whatever the trouble was, she was acquitted.

On 1 March 1647/8 he and Rice Edwards were in court at Salem and were admonished for fighting together, but, "there were no blows given; they only struggled together, and never having been before the court for a similar offence, were to pay only witness fees and costs."

In November 1648, Henry Haggett's wife was fined "for wishing the curse of God on Rice Edwards and that fire might come down from heaven and consume his house, as it did Goodwife Ingersoll's barn."

In September 1649, Ann, wife of Henry Haggett, was fined "for beating her child and calf in a cruel manner with a curtle axe, and challenging Alis Jones on a Lord's day in meeting time, whereby the Sabath was profaned and mischief might have been done."

In June 1651, "Henry Haggett of Wenham was discharged from [military] training on account of poverty and infirmity."

At the Salem court held in July 1657, Francis Ussellton was fined for cursing a swine of Henry Haggett, "a pox of god upon her & the devill take her". At the same court, he was also fined for taking Ann, wife of Henry Haggett, by the shoulders and throwing her down, etc.

There is no record of his ever having particiapted in town or church affairs.

He made his will 17 February 1676/7, "aged 80 three years or there abouts", signed by mark. He died 24 January 1677/8 at Wenham. His wife survived him.

"The last Will and Testament of Henry Haget Aged 80 three years or there abouts made in y[e] year of our Lord one thousand six hundred Seventy & six one 7th of/th/12th Moneth he being Very sick & weak of body but of good Understanding and memorie.
Imp: I bequeth my Bodye to y[e] Dust, & my Spirit to god y[t] gave itt Itm I Bequeth unto my son Henrey all my Estate, namely, my house, Lands, Medow, with all Chatle goods namely all my whol Estate, with all my Rights, Titles, & priviledges, & singular its Appirtainances thereunto belonging To have and To hold to him and his heirs for Ever it is allso my Will, that, my aforesaid Son Henrey, he, Being my heir, & Executor shal Alow his Mother her Reasonable maintaince, Dureing y[e] Terme of her Naturall Life, and, allso, pay unto my fore Children, Namely, to Moses, to Mary, to Deliverence, & to Hannah, I say pay to them y[e] Dowry of Tenn shilling unto each one of them, in Marchantable pay att Currant price within y[e] space of twelve Moneths After my Decease for the Confirmation whereof y[e] aforesaid Henry Haget senr: hath hereunto set his hand & seale.

Henry (his ✓ mark) Haget (seal)

Witness: Charles Gott, John ffiske

Inventory of the estate of Henry Haggett of Wenham taken Mar. 13, 1678 by Thomas Fiske and Charles Gott:

Howseing & Land	£100.	Corne	£ 8.
Neate Catle	22.	plowe tackling & other Utensels	1.15
two Jades	5.	howshold stuff	2.
sheep	12.10	porke	1.10
swine	3.10	Beding & wearing Cloathes	6.
		Total	£162. 5

Debts Due to Severall persons £15

Children:

HENRY, made freeman 11 May 1670; constable of Wenham 1681-3; m Elizabeth who d 7 Aug. 1705; ch.: Susannah who m 1714 Benj. Rogers, prob. Elizabeth who m 1717 James Clerk, prob. Margaret who m 1717 Joseph Killem, Samuel d 27 May 1695. Samuel b 27 March 1700, Abigail b 30 March 1701, prob. Joseph who m 1727 Mary Dodge, prob. Hannah who m 1728 Eliezur Grandy. He m 2, (int. 1 Dec. 1711) Lydia Sachwell of Ipswich who was prob. wid. of John with 2 or more ch.; he d 5 Dec. 1730 at Wenham

18 June 1695 - voted that considering the afflicting hand of God upon Goodman Haggetts familey the Towne see Caus to order that the select men doe allow & pay to Constable Josiah Dodge (in mony) out of the Towne Treashurey: Goodman Haggetts Countrey Rate now due which is six shillings & 4d mony: and also his last Towne Rate being one shilling and 4d mony ---- that so the Constable may suspend the Collecting sd. Haggetts rate till further order.

MARY, b about 1646; m about 1663 John Ross, one of the Scot prisoners taken by Cromwell & exiled to N.E. 1650-51; 13 ch.; res. Ipswich & Windham, Conn. where she d 5 Nov. 1625, "aged about 79 years".

DELIVERENCE, b perhaps about 1638; m 19 Sept. 1662 at Ipswich, Alexander Thompson of Ipswich, one of the Scottish prisoners taken at the Battle of Worcester; 10 ch.; he d 17 Dec. 1693

HANNAH, b perhaps about 1642; m 20 Feb. 1666/7 at Wenham, Philip Welsh of Ipswich, a young Irishman who was kidnapped 1653-4, brought to N.E. & sold for 10 years service to Samuel Symonds; moved to Kingston, N.H.

MOSES, m 23 Oct. 1671 at Andover, Joanna Johnson; ch.: prob. Moses b about 1672, William b about 1675-80, Timothy b 26 Jan. 1681/2, Thomas b 10 Oct. 1684 et al.

ABIGAIL, b prob. about 1646; m 22 Sept. 1668 at Rowley, Thomas Spofford, son of John & Elizabeth (Scott) Spofford; she d.s.p. before her father

Ref.: Essex Quarterly Court Files; Probate Records; V.R.; Wenham Town Records, 1642-1706, pub. by Wenham Hist. Soc., 1930

MAP OF ESSEX COUNTY IN 1643

The Ancestry of

THOMAS HALE & THOMASINE DOUCETT

Compiled By
John Brooks Threlfall

2 Thomas Hale + Thomasine Doucett

- 4 Thomas Hale
  - 8 …
- Joan Kirby
  - 10 John Kirby
    - 20 Thomas Kirby
      - 40 Nicholas Kirby
        - 80 John Kyrkeby
        - Rose
      - Joan
    - Joan Smythe
  - Joan Cranfield
    - 22 William Cranfield
- 6 Gabriel Dowsett
  - 12 George Dowsett
    - 24 John Dowsett
      - 48 Robert Dowsett
        - 96 John Dowsett
    - Alice
  - Joan Gladwyn
    - 26 Robert Gladwyn
      - 52 John Gladwyn?
        - 104 John Gladwyn
      - Joan
    - Joan
- Mercy

HALE HOUSE, NEWBURY NECK
Built before 1682

2

THOMAS HALE (*Thomas*) was baptized in Watton-at-Stone, Hertford, England on 15 June 1606 and died in Newbury, Massachusetts on 21 December 1682, aged 76. He married in London at St. Helen's, Bishopsgate, on 11 December 1632, Thomasine Doucett, daughter of Gabriel and Mercy Doucett. She was born about 1610, and died in Newbury on 30 January 1682/3. He was called a glover in the marriage record.

> 14 December 162_ - the will of Gabriel Doucet of Harlow in the county of Essex, miller. To my son Thomas my copyhold tenement near Harlow Market, in the tenure of George Chapman. To my daughter Tomazen Douset £90. To my son Thomas three roods of freehold land in Harlow Market, on condition that he pay to my daughter Tomazen £10 more. To my grandson Thomas Freeman 10s. at the age of five years. To my daughter Joan 5s. To my wife Mercy and my son Thomas, jointly, the care of the mill and all other chattels, and they are to be executors. Witnesses: Ed. Spranger, John Jocelyn. Proved in January 1627/8. (Archdeaconry of Middlesex for Essex and Herts., Browne - 176)

Administration of the estate of Mercie Dowsett, widow, of Watton-at-Stone was granted to her daughter Thomasine, wife of Thomas Hale, and bond was filed on 25 June 1635.

The parish registers of Harlow were stolen in 1814, so nothing further is obtainable.

It is probable that after his marriage, Thomas Hale returned to Watton, and also that his mother-in-law was living with him and his wife when she died in 1635. He was of Newbury, Massachusetts in 1639. In 1647-8, he was living in Haverhill, but returned to Newbury before 1655. He also was in Salem for some years. The deeds that prove his migrations call him a glover and a leather-dresser.

He came to New England in the *Hector*, apparently in the summer of 1637. His uncle, Francis Kirby, who was a merchant in London and married Susan Downing (whose brother Emanuel Downing had married the sister of Governor Winthrop) wrote a letter to Winthrop about his nephew, giving it to him to deliver to Winthrop on his arrival in New England (Massachusetts Historical Society Series 4,7:19):

To the right worshipful John Winthrop, Esquire, at his house at Boston this dd, in New England.

London, this 10th of May, 1637

Sir. - I wrote you lately per the Hector, wherein I sent a runlet marked with your marke, contayneinge some things your son did write me to send him. John Wood, master's mate, did promise mee & James Downeinge that he would be carefull of it & deliver to you.

These are now to entreat you that you would be assistante to the bearer hereof (Thomas Hale, my neer kinsman) in your counsell & advise to put him in the way how & where to settle himselfe in a hopefull way of subsisteinge with his family. He hath brought with him all his Estate, which he hath heer or can have duringe the life of his mother, my sister. He had almost 200li when he began to make his provision for this voyage. I suppose the greatest halfe is expended in his transportation and in such necessaries as will be spent by him & his family in the first use; the lesser halfe, I suppose, he hath in money, and vendible goods to provide him a cottage to dwell in, and a Milshe cow for his children's sustenance. I suppose his way will be to hire a house or part of a house for the first year untill he can looke out & buy or build him a dwellinge, wherein as in other things I shall intreat you to direct him, and the courtesy that you shall doe him therein I shall acknowledge, as done to myselfe, & I shall be redy (Deo assistante) to endevour to requite it in any service which I can performe for you heer. Thus for this present I commit you all to the protection of the Almighty, & shall ever rest. Your loving frend,

ffra: Kirby

I desire to be remembered to Mrs. Winthrop, to your son Mr. Jo: & his wife, & the rest of yours, also to my cosen Mary & Su: Downeinge. My brother Downeinge will hasten to you, the next spring will be farthest. God Willinge: for he seeth that every year bringeth forth new difficulties: my nephew can tell you how they have met with many interuptions, prohibitions & such like, which Mr. Peirce & others that went since Mr. Peirce were not troubled withall.

Indorsed by Gov. Winthrop, "Mr. Kirby"

He soon went to Newbury, for on 10 August 1638, he was appointed one of the haywards of Newbury and on 7 September, he was made a freeman of the colony. At a town meeting of 5 October 1638, "the town at the acknowledgement of Thomas Hale did confirme the sale of his house and land on Merrimack ridge on both sides to Mr. Dummer". Then, on 27 January 1640/41, he sold to Joseph Carter 52½ acres at the end of Newbury town upon Merrimack Ridge (1:2).

On 23 February 1642/3, he was on a committee to allocate pasturage rights on the town common.

About 1645, he moved to Haverhill where he became one of the selectmen and a commissioner for the trial of small causes. He was appointed in 1648 to keep the ferry across the river and was elected constable in 1649. Until 1650, he was still disposing of Newbury property, selling 4 acres to John Pike, junior, in 1647; 36 acres to James Jackman in 1648; 6 acres to Henry Somerby and 3 acres to Pike in 1650. He returned to Newbury in 1650, for on 12 November 1650 there was granted to him "ten acres of Marsh in the neck over the great river which was formerly Stephen Kents". In 1651, he was granted another 1½ acres adjoining.

On 15 January 1652, Stephen Kent and his wife conveyed house, barn and 70 acres of marsh and upland on the neck on the south side of Newbury River in Newbury, "now in possession of Thomas Hale, and bounded by the river on the north, by creeks on the east and west, and the highway on the south, to the said Thomas Hale of Newbury, late of Haverhill", in exchange for a farm in Haverhill (1:236). On 19 October 1652, he exchanged half acre parcels with the town. He bought another house and 23 acres from John Tillotson in 1655 — possibly the house sold to Joseph Muzzy in 1656/7 (Ipswich Deed 1:330).

In 1652 he was made Sergeant of the military company of Newbury, and later became its Captain.

In 1656 or 1657, he moved to Salem, for on 28 January 1658/9, he bought of John Smith a house and one acre in Salem, selling it in less than two months to Thomas West (Essex Deeds 1:48, 59).

In the Salem deeds, he is called a leather-dresser or glover, and a glover on a list of 1659.

On 12 December 1660, Thomas Hale, senior, of Salem sold to his son Thomas Hale of Newbury, all his houses and lands bought of Stephen Kent on 15 January 1652 (Ipswich Deed 2:215). He also conveyed several other small parcels.

In 1661, he returned to Newbury and lived with his son in the old homestead for the rest of his life, having sold a Salem house, barn and small lot of land to John Knights (2:69).

He served on a number of trial juries and juries of inquest. In 1651, he was sued for slander by Thomas Davis and, although he was acquitted, he was "admonished for reproachful speeches concerning the plaintiff's birth". He dissented from the vote to build a schoolhouse in Newbury in 1652. In the Parker-Woodman controversy, he sided with Mr. Parker while his son, Thomas, was a Woodman adherent. There must have been strong religious arguments in the family circle. For the troops in King Philip's War, he supplied a saddle, a gun, a sword and belt, two pounds of powder and bullets, a pouch and "snapsaicke", oats, provisions, posting and fifty-four pounds of powder and bullets. He took the oath of allegience at Newbury in 1678, "aged 74".

On 11 March 1669, Thomas and Thomasine Hale conveyed to their son, John, a house and 12 acres on Gravel Hill in Newbury. Thomas died in Newbury on 21 December 1682, aged 78, and Thomasine died a month later on 30 January 1682/3.

Children:

THOMAS, bapt. 18 Nov. 1633 at Watton, Herts.; m 26 May 1657, Mary Hutchinson; he d 1688

JOHN, bapt. 19 April 1635; m 5 Dec. 1660, Rebecca Lowell, dau. of Richard; 1 son; she d 1 June 1662; he m 2, 8 Dec. 1663, Sarah, dau. of Henry Somerby; 4 ch.; she d 19 June 1672; he m 3, about 1673, Sarah (Ring) Cottle; 3 ch.; she d 19 Jan. 1698/9; he d 2 June 1707 at Newbury

SAMUEL, b 2 Feb. 1639/40 at Newbury; m 1, 19 March 1669 at Salem, Lydia Musgrove, prob. dau. of Jabez; he m 2, 21 July 1673, Sarah Isley, dau. of Wm.; he moved to Woodbridge N.J.; she d 19 Jan. 1680/81; he d 5 Nov. 1709; some ch.

APPHIA, b 1642 (deposed aged 17 in Sept. 1659); m 3 Nov. 1659, Benjamin Rolfe, son of Henry; 10 ch.; she d 24 Dec. 1708; he d 10 Aug. 1710

Ref.: N.E.H.G.S. - 31:83-99, 35:272-3, 367-376, 64:186, 76:75-76; The Pillsbury Ancestry, by Holman; Parish Registers

THOMAS HALE was born about 1575-1580, probably in Hertfordshire. No baptismal record for him has so far been found. He first appears on record in the parish of Watton-at-Stone where he and Joan Kirby were married on 19 October 1601. She was born about 1582, and was the daughter of John and Joan (Cranfield) Kirby of Watton-at-Stone.

Also living in that parish at the same time was a John Hale and his wife, Martha. John Hale was probably the younger brother of Thomas. The "Goodwife Hale" who was buried 20 April 1628 was probably John's wife, Martha. John Hale was buried at Watton-at-Stone on 29 January 1637/8. They had the following children baptized there:

JOHN, baptized 15 May 1608
THOMAS, baptized 24 June 1610
ABRAHAM, baptized 27 September 1612
SAMUEL, baptized 2 July 1615
MARTHA, baptized 25 December 1618

Thomas Hale died at Watton-at-Stone and was buried there on 19 October 1630. He left a will, an abstract of which follows.

> 11 October 1630 - Thomas Hale of ye parish of Watton-at-Stone in the county of Hartford ... bequeathed certain real estate to wife Joane and son Thomas, to daughter Mary Hale, to daughter Dorothy Hale, to daughter Elizabeth Hale, to daughter Dionis Beane or to her son Henry Beane which shall then be living. Son Thomas to be executor, brother Francis Kirby an overseer. Witnesses: Francis Kirby, John Hale. Proved 9 December 1630
>
> (Ref.: Archdeaconry Court of Hitchin, Herts.)

Apparently shortly after Thomas's death, his son Thomas junior, went to London, for there we find his marriage and the remarriage of his mother. His uncle, Francis Kirby, was a merchant in London, so possibly the family went there to be with him. Joan remarried 17 October 1633 at Saint Helen's Bishopgate, London, to John Bydes of Little Munden, Hertfordshire, yeoman. She was listed as of Watton-at-Stone. After her second marriage, she went back to Hertfordshire to live in Little Munden, her second husband's home. She died probably at Little Munden after 1640 and before 1660.

Children, baptized at Watton-at-Stone:

DIONIS, bapt. 15 Aug. 160[2]; m 29 Sept. 1624 at Watton, Henry Beane; a ch. Henry b 1624 - 30

2 THOMAS, bapt. 15 June 1606; m 11 Dec. 1632 in London at St. Helen's Bishopgate, Thomasine Doucett, dau. of Gabriel & Mercy Doucett; 4 ch.; went to N.E. in 1637 in the *Hector*; he d 21 Dec. 1682; she d 30 Jan. 1682/3

MARY, bapt. 8 Oct. 1609; unm. in 1630; m possibly ——— Whale

DOROTHY, bapt. 28 March 1613; living in 1637

ELIZABETH, bapt. 31 Aug. 1617; living in 1637

SOUTHEAST VIEW OF WATTON CHURCH, HERTFORDSHIRE
A sketch by Buckler, 1832

6

GABRIEL DOWSETT (*George, John, Robert? John*) was the miller of Harlow, Essex. He was born about 1568, undoubtedly at Harlow, eldest son of George and Joan (Gladwin) Dowsett. He married Mercy ____. He was on a jury of inquisition into the death of the illegitimate baby of Alice Pike. The baby had been born on 8 June 1597, and she had suffocated it two days later. She was indicted, and after conviction, was sentenced to be hung.

> Midsummer Quarter Sessions, 1616 - Presentment of the Hundred Jury: Gabriel Dowset the miller of Harlow mill, for that his peck weight and toll dish are not according to the statute. Note added: 'Too much toll, all too big'.

Harlow mill was on the River Stort. The remnant of the last mill structure – perhaps late 18th century – is now a restaurant.

Gabriel Dowsett died in late 1627; his wife survived him. An abstract of his will follows.

> 14 December 162_ - the will of GABRIEL DOWSET of Harlow in the county of Essex, miller. To my son Thomas my copyhold tenement near Harlow Market, in the tenure of George Chapman. To my daughter Tomazen Douset £90. To my son Thomas three roods of freehold land in Harlow Market, on condition that he pay to my daughter Tomazen £10 more. To my grandson Thomas Freeman 10s. at the age of five years. To my daughter Joan 5s. To my wife Mercy and my son Thomas, jointly, the care of the mill and all other chattels, and they are to be executors. Witnesses: Ed. Spranger, John Jocelyn. Proved in January 1627/8. (Archdeaconry of Middlesex for Essex and Herts., Browne - 176)

Mercy went to live with her daughter Thomazine at Watton-at-Stone. Administration on her estate was granted to Thomazine on 25 June 1635.

Children, probably all born at Harlow:

THOMAS, prob. the eldest son

3 THOMAZINE, m 11 Dec. 1632 in London at Saint Helen's, Bishopsgate, Thomas Hale, jr., of Watton-at-Stone, Hertfordshire. He was bapt. there 15 June 1606; 4 ch.; he d 21 Dec. 1682 ae 76, she 30 Jan. 1682/3, at Newbury, Mass.

JOAN, prob. the dau. who m ______ Freeman

Ref.: N.E.H.G.S.-76:75; Wills; The Pillsbury Ancestry, by M.L. Holman; Parish Registers

10

JOHN KIRBY (*Thomas, Nicholas, John*) was baptized on 18 October 1558 at Thundridge, Hertfordshire. On 23 December 1576 at Watton-at-Stone, he and Joan Cranfield were married. She was the daughter of William Cranfield of Watton-at-Stone and was born about 1552-5. John Kirby died before his wife. She was living in the neighboring parish of Little Munden when she made her oral will 29 October 1640 and died shortly thereafter. Her will follows.

Her nephew, William Cranfield of Watton, in his will made in 1630, mentions her as his aunt, Joan Kirby, widow, and also calls Thomas Hale the elder and Francis Kirby of London, his cousins, they being John Kirby's son-in-law and son respectively.

ALL SAINTS CHURCH,
LITTLE MUNDEN, HERTFORDSHIRE

The will of JOANE KIRBY of Little Monden in the County of Hartford, widow, as it was spoken to her in her p'fect memory in the p'sence of her three children Francis Kirby, Joane Bides & Ruth Browne, also in the presence of John Bides, the 29th of October 1640.

First, I comit my soule to Almighty god, my body to the earth, to be decently buried at the discretion of my executor, and for my goods I dispose them as followeth: I give and bequeath unto the poore of the p'ishe of Watton where I was borne twenty shillings, to the poor of Little Monden where I live twenty shillings, to Ruth Cowly my grandchild all the goods which I have in the hands of her father in law Edward Browne, to my grandchild Richard Kirby fortie shillings, to my grandchild Joseph Whale ten shillings, to my cosen Elizabeth Isham ten shillings, to my cosen Mary Newton ten Shillings, to my daughter Joane Bides ten shillings. all the rest of my goods when my debts are paid & burial discharged I leave to my son Francis Kirby to be disposed of as he shall see cause, which said Francis Kirby I do appoint to be sole executor of this my last will.

the mark + of Jone Bides
Ruth Broune } witnesses
the mark of
John J Bides

Proved 2 December 1640

An Inventory of the goods & chattels of Joan Kirby late of Little Munden in the County of Hartfor[d], widow, deceased, as they were seen, valued & aprized the first day of December 1640 by John Bides, Edward Browne, Henry Marson

In the house of Martha Kirby

an old Cupboard, 2 old kettles, a skillet and other lumber ... 0.13.4
a little table & an old chaire ... 0. 3.4

In the house of Mary Newton

one small featherbed & bolster, 3 blankets, 1 Coverlet, all old & 3 Curtains all at ... 1.15.0
an old bedsted, a Chair & other implements ... 0.10.0
1 hive of bees ... 0. 5.0

Linen

1 holland sheet, 1 paire of flaxen sheets, 2 pair of old linen sheets & napkins, 1 pillowber & 2 table Clothes 1.18.8
2 old Chists, a potshelf & lumber ... 0. 6.8
the testator's wearing apparrel ... 3.10.0

At the house of Edward Browne
given in kind to Ruth Cowly

6 pewter dishes with other small trifles ... 1.00.0

10.02.0

In redy mony ... 08.06.9½

Some is .... £ 18. 8.9½

the mark of John Bides
Edward Browne
Henry Marson

Submitted at Wheathampstead 2 December 1640
by Francis Kirbye, son and executor
(74 NW 78)

Children:

FRANCIS, a skinner, or dealer in hides, leather and furs, of London, living in the parish of St. Helen's Bishopsgate, churchwarden 1638,9. His first wife was widow Susan (Downing) Carter, sister of Emanuel Downing, who m. the sister of Gov. Winthrop. She was buried at St. Helen's 22 Jan. 1634. He m 2, widow Elizabeth ——. To his first wife's son Joseph Carter, Kirby gave a letter dated 11 April 1639, introducing him to Gov. Winthrop as "my love-deserving son and faithful servant." Kirby did a large business with the colonies, exporting general supplies and importing principally beaver skins. In the latter years of his life, he was the bridge-master of London Bridge. He d 12 Oct. 1661 in the parish of St. Olave; 2 ch.: Rev. Joshua who was b about 1617 & d 1676, Sarah. His will:

24 July 1660 - the will of FRANCIS KIRBY of Saint Olave parish, London, skinner ... to Mary, wife of my son Joshua Kirby, and to their children Godsgift, Susan, Elizabeth, Phebe, Camdena & Welcome ... to my sister Ruth Browne ... to the poor of Litle Munden ... to the poor of Saint Olave ... to Elizabeth Turfatt, daughter of George Turfatt, grandchild of my late wife Elizabeth ... to Mary Nash, widow, late wife of John Nash ... to my cousin Joseph Alport, scrivener ... to my cousins John & William Kirby, children of my late brother John Kirby ... to my cousin Elizabeth Goad ... to Eunice, Rachel & Sarah Carter, daughters of Joseph Carter, deceased ... to my servant Mary Bradbury.

5 JOAN, m 1, Thomas Hale of Watton-at-Stone; m 2, 17 Oct. 1633, at St. Helen's Bishopsgate, London, John Bydes of Little Munden

JOHN, of Little Munden, yeoman, made his will 23 April, proved 7 July 1628. To Richard and William Ward, brothers of his wife Martha, as trustees for her, his 4 sons: John the elder, younger son John, William and Richard, and his dau. Elizabeth, Executors: his brother Francis Kirby of London and his brother-in-law Thomas Hale

WILLIAM, d before 1600 leaving son William and dau. Ruth Macham

RUTH, b about 1598; m 1, Richard Cowley of St. Botolph's without Bishopsgate, brazier, about 24, she being described as Ruth Kirby, about 23, dau. of John Kirby deceased, license granted 21 Nov. 1621, the marriage to take place at St. Olave's, Old Jewry. William Langton of St. Giles Cripplegate, tailor, testified that Joane Kirby, mother of the said Ruth, was willing and consenting. She m 2, at St. Helen's Bishopsgate, 1 Feb. 1637, Edward Brown of Great Munden, Hertford, yeoman. Her dau., Ruth Cowley, was mentioned in the will of her grandmother Joan Kirby in 1640

Ref.: The Ancestry of Phebe Tilton, by Walter G. Davis, 1947; Parish Registers; Probate Records at Hertford-

12

GEORGE DOWSETT (*John, Robert? John*) was born probably about 1527 at Stanford Rivers, Essex. There, on 23 June 1560, he married Joan Gladwyn, the daughter of Robert Gladwyn. She seems to have been the mother of all his children. They appear to have lived for a few years at Stanford Rivers where two children were baptized, then moved to Harlow, which is about 7 miles northwest of Stanford Rivers. Unfortunately, the Harlow parish register is extant only from 1629 on, in the form of the Bishop's transcripts, so there is no record of the baptisms of the later children.

Joan died before 1578, at which time George had remarried to Anne (or Agnes), the widow of Robert Dickley of Manningtree, Essex, gentleman, who died about 1573. Administration of the estate of Robert Dickley was granted on 20 June 1578 to George Doucett, then Anne's husband.

In the Court Rolls of the manor of Harlow Bury under 25 May 1586 is found the following:

> It is ordered that George Dowzett should scour his ditch towards Symons Mead under penalty of 6d. a rod and that John Gladwyne [George's brother-in-law] should scour his ditch towards Giles Croft under penalty of 6d. a rod.

George Dowsett died in 1594, and was supposedly buried in the churchyard at Harlow as he requested in his will. He seems to have been a bit confused in his references to the several bequests to his children by their grandfather Gladwyn. He named sons Gabriel and William as among those legatees, but they were not yet born when the grandfather made his will. His daughter Alice had a legacy but he forget about that, or else he had already paid it to her. More than 26 years had passed since Robert Gladwyn made these bequests and now George Dowsett was himself an aged man, so the lapse of memory is understandable. An abstract of his will follows.

> 7 March 1593/4 - the will of GEORGE DOWSETT of the parish of Harlow & diocese of London, being sick in body... to be buried in the parish church yard of Harlow... to Agnes my wife a cow and 40s. besides £8 which I am bound to leave her after my decease...to Gabriel Dowsett my son a brown cow

which I bought at Harlow fair & 40s. besides 8s.4d. which his grandfather Gladwin gave him, also my great caldron.. to William Dowsett my son my white pied cow which I bought at Sapesford fair & 40s. besides his grandfather Gladwin's legacy... to George Dowsett my son my brown cow which now hath a calf & 40s...to Avice Dowsett my daughter 40s. besides her grandfather's legacy.... to Alice Clarke my daughter 20s..to the children of the said Alice my daughter now already born 20s. to be equally divided among them... to Elizabeth my daughter my red bullock & 20s. besides her grandfather Gladwin's legacy... to Katherine Dowsett my daughter my western cow & 40s... to the same Katherine my daughter my biggest kettle & a bearing sheet which was her mothers & a face kerchief which also was her mothers. Gabriel & George my sons shall have all the profits that shall arise of my mill & grounds belonging to the same betwixt the day of my death & the feast of St. Michael the Archangel next...to Agnes my wife all her apparell both linen & woollen & all such chests as she brought... residue to be divided equally between Agnes my wife and these my children Gabriel, George, William, Elizabeth & Katherine... son Gabriel to be executor, my landlord William Sumpner the elder overseer. Witnessed by Nicholas Wright & Richard Harrison. Signed by mark. Pr. 16 December 1594 (239 BW12)

Children:

AVICE, bapt. 28 Sept. 1651 at Stanford Rivers; m after 1593, before 1606, John Archer

ALICE, bapt. 26 March 1564 at Stanford Rivers; m ______ Clark, had several ch. by 1594

ELIZABETH, b about 1566, prob. at Harlow; prob. unm. in 1593

6 GABRIEL, prob. eldest son & b about 1568 at Harlow; m Mercy ______; he d 1627/8, testate

14 December 162_ - the will of GABRIEL DOWSET of Harlow in the county of Essex, miller. To my son Thomas my copyhold tenement near Harlow Market, in the tenure of George Chapman. To my daughter Tomazen Douset £90. To my son Thomas three roods of freehold land in Harlow Market, on condition that he pay to my daughter Tomazen £10 more. To my grandson Thomas Freeman 10s. at the age of five years. To my daughter Joan 5s. To my wife Mercy and my son Thomas, jointly, the care of the mill and all other chattels, and they are to be executors. Witnesses: Ed. Spranger, John Jocelyn. Proved in January 1627/8. (Archdeaconry of Middlesex for Essex and Herts., Browne - 176)

WILLIAM, perhaps one who d 1616 testate, wife Sarah & 2 ch.
GEORGE, living in 1593
KATHERINE, unm. in 1593

Ref.: Wills at Chelmsford, Essex; Parish Registers

20

THOMAS KIRBY (*Nicholas, John*) was born probably 1520-25 at Standon, Hertfordshire. His home, called Fabdens, he inherited from his father who had inherited it from his father. On 22 July 1548 at Therfield, he married Joan Smythe. Therfield is a small parish about ten miles north of Standon. In this parish the Kirbys held some property which apparently came into the family thru Thomas Kirby's mother who probably came from there. Thomas's brother, George, was married and lived in Therfield, and five of Thomas's children were baptized there. Thomas's brother John, however, was the one who inherited the Therfield property. This John may have been the John Kirby of London, a grocer. Perhaps he sold the Therfield property to his brother. Altho his children were baptized in Therfield and Thundridge, Thomas apparently lived in Standon. Thundridge is the next parish south of Standon, so this suggests that the family lived in the south part of Standon but attended church in Thundridge.

Thomas Kirby made his will on 14 November 1573 and died a short time later. His wife survived him.

14 November 1573 - the will of THOMAS KYRBYE of Fabdens in the parish of Standon, county Hertford...to the poor of Standon 3s.4d. wife Joan provided for for life, household stuff, a cow, feed for it, 6 sheep, 2 hogs, orchard, chambers in the house.. to son John £30 at age 21, to John a 2 year old bullock, 6 sheep, to be delivered to him one month after my decease...to my daughters Alice, Agnes and Rose, £10 each, to be paid within 2 years to Alice and Agnes, to Rose at age 21 or day of marriage; to each daughter 6 sheep and a bullock ...wife Joan to have one acre tilled for life by son Thomas Kyrbye, and one acre of oats; remainder to son Thomas, he to be executor ...overseers to be loving friend, my loving brother Robert Smyth & Christopher Hodge. Witnesses: Thomas Granger, Thomas Lambin, Richard Barber et al. Proved at Braughing 15 February 1573/4. (Essex County Probate DIAMR-3/174 at Chelmsford)

Children:

THOMAS, bapt. 9 Feb. 1548/9 at Therfield; m 25 May 1575 at Watton-at-Stone, Katherine Shakerley; several ch.; she was buried 23 March 1594/5 at Thundridge

ALICE, bapt. 28 Oct. 1550 at Therfield; prob. the Alice Kirbie who m 15 June 1573 at St. Albans Abbey, John Shipton; in any event, living in 1573

JOHN, bapt. 21 Jan. 1551/2 at Therfield; buried 12 Feb. 1551/2
KATHERINE, bapt. 31 Jan. 1552/3 at Therfield; d.y.
ELIZABETH, bapt. 4 Jan. 1554/5 at Therfield; buried there 2 April 1555
AGNES, b prob. 1556; living in 1573
10 JOHN, bapt. 18 Oct. 1558 at Thundridge (B.T.); m 23 Dec. 1576 at Watton-at-Stone, Joan Cranfield, b about 1552-5, dau. of William; 5 ch.; Joan Kirby, a widow of Little Munden, made her will 29 Oct. 1640 & d soon after
HENRY, bapt. 10 Aug. 1561 at Thundridge; buried there 13 Nov. 1570
ROSE, bapt. 25 Jan. 1564/5; living in 1573
MARGARET, bapt. 4 July, buried 4 Sept. 1568 at Thundridge
NICHOLAS, bapt. 28 Aug., buried 22 Oct. 1569 at Thundridge

SAINT MARY'S CHURCH, THERFIELD, HERTFORDSHIRE

*John Kyrbie was bapt. 18 Oct. 1558 at Thundridge, according to the transcript. This may be an error for Agnes.

Ref.: Wills at Chelmsford; P.C.C. Wills; Parish Registers

22

WILLIAM CRANFIELD of Watton-at-Stone, Hertfordshire, was born about 1530. He was a glover. He lived to a ripe old age, for when he made his will in 1611, he had a daughter who had been married for 35 years, and a grandson old enough to serve as executor of his estate. He had a brother, John Cranfield, who was living at the time he wrote his will, but of him no other record has been found. William Cranfield was buried 5 November 1614 at Watton-at-Stone.

There were other Cranfields living in London and in Hertfordshire at that time. They were probably closely related. One of them, William Cranfield of Hertford, was probably twenty-five to thirty years younger that William of Watton-at-Stone. He was probably a nephew. He died testate in 1592, leaving two minor daughters and a pregnant wife named Dorothy. He mentioned his father, Richard Cranfield, who was then living. This Richard was thus probably a brother of our William Cranfield. Richard had children baptized at Hertford: Agnes in 1560, Cicely in 1562, Richard in 1565, and George in 1568. A Thomas Cranfield of Therfield, which is 12 miles north of Watton-at-Stone, had two children baptized there: Elena in 1562, and Joan in 1565. Thomas was probably also a brother of our William.

The name Cranfield is a place name derived from Cranfield in Bedfordshire, which is about 26 miles northwest of Watton-at-Stone. The name means literally "crane field", that is, a field on which cranes congregated during their annual migrations.

11 December 1611 - the will of WILLIAM CRANFIELD the elder of Watton at Stone, Hertford, glover ... sick in body ... to the poor of Watton 10s. ... to reparation of the church of Watton 3s.4d. ... to Thomas Cranfield of London my grandchild £10 which he doth owe unto me to be cancelled, also my first coverlet ... to William Cranfield my grandchild son of John Cranfield my son deceased £6 to be held by the said Thomas Cranfield of the parish of Saint Thomas the Appostle in London, to be paid by him one month next after the end of the year of the apprenticeship of the said William Cranfield, Jun ... to Diones Cranfield my grandchild, sister of the said William Cranfield the younger £5 ... to Diones Plumer & Elizabeth Haywood ----s to my son in law William Chamber to either of them one pair of towen sheets ... to

Robert Chamber my grandchild my feather bed, etc. ... to Joan Krybye my daughter wife of John Kyrbye the elder of Dane End my seamed flaxen sheet, one flaxen pillowbeere, 4 platters and 3 servers ... to every one of the children of the said Joan Kyrbye my daughter 3s.4d. ... to William Cranfield the elder of London my grandchild my tenement or barn with the orchard situate in the town of Watton aforesaid which I lately purchased of John Cranfield late of Hartford my brother deceased, conditional that he pay to Dyones Chamber my daughter wife of William Chamber of Watton £15, which sum I do give to the said Diones my daughter in consideration of the great kindness which I have found at the hands of my said daughter and her husband in my old age and in part of a recompense of the charges that they have been at with me by the space of divers years past, also that the said William Cranfield my grandchild shall pay to Joan Kirby my eldest daughter out of the price of the said tenement 40s. ... in case of default of William Cranfield my grandchild, then the tenement to the said Diones my daughter for the next 21 years ... residue to the said William Cranfield the elder my grandchild whom I make my executor. Signed. Witnesses: William Chamber, Sen., Wm Chamber, Jun., Edward Attkins, Thomas Hedd, Thomas Humfrey. Proved 16 April 1615. (Hertfordshire Wills 21 NW 29)

Children:

11 JOAN, eldest dau., prob. b about 1552-55; m 23 Dec. 1576, John Kirby, son of Thomas & Joan, bapt. 18 Oct. 1558; 5 or more ch.; she d 1640

THOMAS, b prob. about 1555-59; m Joan ____; ch.: William bapt. 27 March 1583 - buried 13 Sept. 1630 - testate, Thomas bapt. 20 Dec. 1584 (no parents named), John bapt. 17 Sept. 1587 (no parents named), Joan bapt. 22 Dec. 1589 - buried 10 March 1603/4. Thomas was buried 16 Jan. 1590/91, testate. Joan m 2, 21 Aug. 1592 at Watton-at-Stone, John Dichfield; no further record of them at Watton, so prob. moved to another parish

On 20 September 1586, Anthony Browne of Watton-at-Stone, a glover, stole 9 sheepskins worth 11 pence from Thomas Cranfield, for which petty larceny he was indicted and found guilty 10 March 1586/7 at the Hertford Assizes. He was sentenced to be whipped.

[Date torn off] - the will of THOMAS CRANFIELD of the parish of Watton ... to be buried in the churchyard ... to son William Cranfield my best cow, two ewes and my best hutch that standeth in the parlor ... to son Thomas Cranfield my second cow, two ewes and the feather bed that my grandfather Cranfield gave me ... to son John Cranfield my third cow, two ewes and my cubberd that stands in the hall ... to daughter Joanne Cranfield my fourth cow, two ewes, my bedstead in the parlor and a matress ... all unbequeathed goods to my wife ... all children's bequests to be received at age 18 or marriage ... if wife takes another husband, she must give surety to my father, William Cranfield, or to my brother in law, William Chamber, or to another friend of the children that they shall receive upkeep and bequests ... wife to be executrix. Witnesses: William Cranfield & William Chambers. Proved 1590. (Hertfordshire Wills 1 HW 203)

23 August 1630 - the will of WILLIAM CRANFIELD of Watton at Stone, Herts. (formerly City of London) ... to wife Rebecca, bequests to Elizabeth Cranfield my eldest daughter & Francis Kirby of London my cousin ... to my daughters Hester Cranfield & Rebecca Cranfield ... to my aunt Joan Kirby, widow ... my tenement in Watlyn St., London ... my 2 servants Lodwicke Bowyer and Margaret Rogers ... overseers my cousins Francis Stuke & Thomas Hale sen. ... witnesses Thomas Hale sen., & Thomas Kent, all of this parish, & Francis Pecke of Aldermary, London, woollendraper, Christopher Boteler esq., Hugh North. Proved 3 September 1630. (P.C.C. Scroope 80)

DENNISE, bapt. 14 July 1561, "dau. of William"; m 25 Aug. 1583, William Chambers; ch.:Ann bapt. 13 Aug. 1584, William bapt. 20 Feb. 1587/8, Robert bapt. 4 Feb. 1592/3, Jane bapt. 15 June 1598 - buried 19 June; "old Mr. Chambers" buried 23 July 1622

WILLIAM, bapt. 24 Dec. 1564, "son of William"; ch.: William; he d before 1611; an Elizabeth Cranfield buried 16 Aug. 1627 may have been his widow

JOHN, bapt. 24 Oct. 1568 (parents not named); m 4 May 1595, Dorothy Woodlie; ch.: William bapt. 15 Aug. 1596, Nicholas bapt. 17 April 1598 (parents not named) - buried 14 March 1598/9, Dennise bapt. 16 Nov. 1600 (parents not named) was apparently a posthumous child. John was buried 17 May 1600; she m 2, 2 Nov. 1601, George Semer, & had more children

THE CHURCH OF WATTON-AT-STONE, c 1806, by H.G. Oldfield

Ref.: Parish Registers; Probate Records at Hertford and at Chelmsford; P.C.C. Wills

24

JOHN DOWSETT (*Robert?, John*) of Stanford Rivers, Essex, was born about 1485-95, probably in the parish of Kelvedon Hatch, which is two miles southeast of Stanford Rivers. What is known of him comes from his will, an abstract of which follows. He had two wives who predeceased him, and was survived by his third wife, Alice, who probably was the mother of his last four named children. He died about February 1529/30.

> 23 January 1529/30 - the will of John Dowsset of Stanford Rivers in Essex...being sick...to be buried in the church yard of Stanford...to the high altar for tythes forgotten 3s. 4d...for a priest to sing a trental of masses for my soul 10s...for 5 masses for my 2 wives now dead 20s...Robert my son to have a cow and 3s. 4d...to sons Thomas and John each a cow to be delivered at Michaelmas next... to Agnes my daughter a cow and 20s. at day of marriage..to Thomas, William, George and Nathaniel each a cow at day of their marriage.......Residue to wife Alice whom I ordain my executrix, and Henry Dowsset my brother to be overseer, he to have 3s. 4d. for his pains. Proved 15 March 1529/30. (Reference D/AER 4/57)

Children, born at Stanford Rivers, probably:

ROBERT, prob. b about 1515-20; living in 1530
THOMAS, living in 1530
JOHN, living in 1530
AGNES, living unm. in 1530
WILLIAM, living in 1530; prob. testator of 25 March 1572, of Northweald
12 GEORGE, b prob. 1527-29; m 1, 23 June 1560 at Stanford Rivers, Joan Gladwyn, dau. of Robert; 7 known ch.; m 2, before 1578, Anne (or Agnes), widow of Robert Dickley. He d 1594
NATHANIEL, prob. b about 1528-9; prob. d.y.

Ref.: Probate Records at Chelmsford

26

ROBERT GLADWYN lived at Harlow Market in Essex, England. He was perhaps the son of John Gladwyn of Latton who died testate about the first of September 1558, naming a wife Joan and a son Robert. He was probably the grandson of John Gladwyn who, in 1468, sold some land in High Laver and Harlow, according to a deed, an abstract of which follows. These last two villages are adjacent to Harlow.

1468 - John Hierd of High Laver and John Cressy, plaintiffs vs. John Gladewyn the elder, defendant - 1 messuage, 30 acres of land and 10 acres of pasture in High Laver and Harlow, which Alice late the wife of John Kentyssh holds for life. Plaintiffs and the heirs of John Hierd to hold the reversion of the chief lords. Consideration 40 marks. (Feet of Fines for Essex, 8 Edward IV, Trinity term)

From Robert's will, the source of most of the information on him, one can deduce that he was a fairly prosperous farmer. He died in late 1567. An abstract of his will follows.

5 September 1567 - the will of Robert Gladwyn of Harlow Market, Essex.... To the poor people of Harlow 20s. to be delivered to the collectors [for the poor]. To the reparations of the church 10s. To John my eldest son my house and lands free and copy in Harlow and Latton. To Thomas my son a silver spoon, a mattress, a coverlet, and a pair of sheets. To Robert my son 10 quarters of barley, 2 beasts, a mattress, a covering, 2 pair of sheets, a tablecloth, a pillowbere, a candlestick, a silver spoon, 4 platters, 2 kettles (a great and a little), and 40s. To John my youngest son 4 quarters of wheat, 10 quarters of barley, 4 beasts, a flockbed, a mattress, a covering, 4 pairs of sheets, a pillowbere, a tablecloth, a candlestick, a silver spoon, 4 pewter platters, a kettle, a brass pot, a dripping pan, and £13.6.8. To Alice my daughter 2 bullocks, a featherbed in the parlour, a covering, a mattress, a silver spoon, 4 pewter platters, 2 kettles, a chafer, a brass posnet, a dripping pan, 4 pairs of sheets, 6 table napkins, 2 pillowberes, a tablecloth, a candlestick and £10. To Joan my daughter 5 marks, a silver spoon, 4 pairs of sheets, a covering, 6 table napkins, and a little kettle. To Avice my daughter's daughter a bullock and a pair of sheets. To my daughter Joan's three children, Avice, Alice and Elizabeth, each a saucer and a pair of sheets. The residue to John my eldest son, whom I make executor. I ordain John Reede my overseer, and for his pains 6s. 8d. Witnesses: Nicholas Sybley, John Reade, Richard Harrison clerk. Proved 16 December 1567. (61MR3)

Children, probably all born at Harlow:

JOHN, eldest son, b 1520; m 1, ______; m 2, Anne ______; apparently no ch.; res. Manewden, Essex; he persevered in lawsuits against the lord of the manor of Harlow to maintain the customary rents on copyhold lands, for which he was memorialized with a brass in the church of Harlow. He and his younger brother John also sued in behalf of the poor re. a tenement left in a trust for charity. He d 17 April 1615 ae 95. An abstract of his will:

6 May 1606 - the will of John Gladwyn of Manewden in the county of Essex ... in good health ... my soul into the hands of almighty God my creator and redeemer and my body to be coffined and decently buried in the parish church of Harlow... to the poor of Farnham, Thorley and Sawbridgeworth to each town 6d. 8d... to the poor of Stortford 10s... to the poor of Manewden where I now dwell 40s... to the poor of Harlow 2 barrels of white herrings yearly for 10 years to be distributed at Lent... to Anne my well beloved wife 4 of my best kyne and all the household stuff that she brought with her... to Thomas Gladwyn my brother Robert's son £40, one table cloth, a brass pot and a horse or gelding if it fortune that I have one at time of my death... to the 3 daughters of my said brother Robert 20s. each... to Avis Dowset now wife of John Archer, being daughter of my sister Joan £5...to each of my brother John's children 40s... to six of my sister Dowset's children 10s. each... to each of my godchildren 12d...... to John Gladwyn my brother Robert's son all my messuage or tenement situate in Harlow or Latton... his failing of male heirs, then to his brother Thomas, then back to my brother John and his heirs male, then to _____ Gladwyn of Wyld-Gullet... to William Tomson of Harlow his children 6s. 8d. each... residue to John Gladwyn my brother Robert's son whom I make executor and my friends Thomas Hurst of Sheering, gentleman, and Nicholas Sybley of Harlow to be supervisors, and to each of them for their pains 6s. 8d. Signed by mark. Witnesses: Thomas Hurst, William Sawen, Thomas Gladwyn, Roger Hurst and Nicholas Syble. Proved 2 May 1615 by John Gladwyn, sr. and John Gladwyn, jr. (Reference: P.C.C. - 49 Rudd)

THOMAS, prob. not living in 1606

ROBERT, had sons John & Thomas, and 3 daus. in 1606

ALICE, prob. not living in 1606

13 JOAN, m George Dowsett, son of John, 23 June 1660 at Stanford Rivers, Essex; 7 ch. of whom 6 were living in 1606; she d & he m 2, Agnes; he d 1594 test.

JOHN, youngest son; m Barbara ______; had ch.; d in 1623

14 August 1620 - the will of John Gladwin the elder of Harlow in the county of Essex, yeoman... ill in body... to be buried within the churchyard of Harlow... to the poor £4. . to my son John all my lands & tenements in the parishes of Gilstone & Sawbridgeworth, county of Hertford, and £20... to my son George £20... to James Ruff my grandchild £10

at age 21..., to grandchild George Ruff £10 at 21... to my son in law Austen Parker £20 within three years for the use of his two daughters Barbara & Katherine at 21 or marriage ... to my grandchild John Whale £20 at age 21... to Ellen the wife of Edward Ramsey of Parndon £5 and one gold ring of 20s... to Bridget Campion sister of the said Ellen £5 at age 21 or marriage... to my son Nicholas £100 within one year... to my daughter Thomizen one gold ring of 20s... to William my son one gold ring of the same price... to my daughter Katherine one gold ring of like value.... to my friend Edward Brigge of Chigwell, gentleman, one gold ring of like worth... unto Prudence the wife of George Harrison one gold ring of same price... to William Gladwin of Latton 5s... to my cousin William Thompson the elder £5. Residue unto Barbara my wife whom I make my executrix and my son John Gladwin and my son in law Austen Parker to be overseers, they to have 20s. each for their pains. Signed by mark. Witnesses: George Harrison, writer hereof and Nicholas Scott. Pr. 13 October 1623. (P.C.C.-103 Swann)

HERE LYETH BVRIED Y^{E} BODY OF IOHN GLADWIN Y^{E} ELDER WHO
DEPTED THIS LYFE Y^{E} 17 DAY OF APRILL A^{O} DNI 1615 · BEING
OF Y^{E} AGE OF 95 YERES · WHO IN HIS LYFE TYME W^{TH} LONGE
AND TEDIOVS SVTES IN LAWE, W^{TH} Y^{E} LORD OF Y^{E} MANNOR OF
HARLOWE, DID PROVE THE CVSTOME FOR THE COPIE HOLDS
TO Y^{E} GREATE BENIFITT OF POSTERITIE FOR EVER ·

Ref.: Probate Records at Chelmsford

THE CHURCH OF SAINT MARY & SAINT HUGH
HARLOW, ESSEX
From the Rear Path

40

NICHOLAS KIRBY (*John*) was born probably about 1490 - 1500 at Standon, Hertfordshire, and there grew up and lived out his life. His home, which he inherited from his father, was called *Fabdens.* All that is known of him is derived from his will and that of his father. In his will, he bequeathed to his son a house in the parish of Therfield which is about ten miles north northwest of Standon. This property is not mentioned in his father's will, so John must have acquired it in his own lifetime, probably thru his wife or some inheritance. It seems odd, otherwise, that he would hold a house so far from his own home place. He died in July or August of 1555 and was probably buried in the churchyard of Saint Mary's Church, as were his parents. Joan, his wife, survived him almost ten years and was buried 19 January 1564/5 in the next parish of Thundridge, to which the family seems to have shifted its attendance, altho still living in Standon.

1 July 1555 - the will of Nicholas Kyrbye of Standon ... to the high altar 8d.. house called Fabdens in which I now dwell, with all lands, meadows, pastures, feedings, woods and underwoods to Thomas my eldest son ... notwithstanding, Joan my wife to have her dwelling in my chamber in said house for life, and five kyne with pasture .. to Joan all moveables lying within my hall, parlor, chambers and kitchen and in other houses together under that one roof; unto my son George my house lying in a field called Culvers field nigh unto the fulling mill by Standon Street; unto my son John the house lying in the parish of Therfeld, with all the lands, meadows, pastures, feedings, woods and underwoods, after the decease of Jane my wife ... son John to pay 20 marks as follows: 5 marks to son George, 5 marks to Isabell Raynold my daughter, 5 marks to Rose my daughter and the other 5 marks to Ellen my daughter, to be paid within 9 years next after the decease of me and my wife. Residue to be equally divided among children. Sons Thomas & George to be executors, John Parnell to be overseer and he to have 3s.4d. Witnesses: William Dowsing, John Almond, George Skyngle. Proved 17 September 1555. (Essex County Probate DIABR-1/45)

Children, probably all born at Standon:

20 THOMAS, eldest son, b prob. about 1520 - 25; he inherited *Fabdens* & d there late 1573; m Joan Smyth 22 July 1548 at Therfield; 5 ch. per will of 14 Nov. 1573, pr. 15 Feb. 1573/4

GEORGE, prob. b about 1530; m 27 Sept. 1556 at Therfield, Elizabeth Lucke; 11 ch. bapt. there: Ralph 1557-1601, Robert d 1561, William 1561-1562, Mary 1563, Agnes 1565, John 1566/7, Edward 1568, George b & d 1570, Joan 1571, Margaret 1573, Martha 1574/5, Anne 1576.

JOHN, prob. b 1532-35; he inherited the house & lands in Therfield; the grocer of London?

ISABELL, m _____ Raynold before 1 July 1555

ROSE

ELLEN

St. Mary's Church, Standon

Ref.: Probate Records at Chelmsford, Essex

48

ROBERT DOWSETT (*John*) eldest son of John, was born probably between 1460 and 1465 at Kelvedon Hatch, Essex. He perhaps lived at Navestock in the house his father bequeathed to him. It was called Cokeby's. There is no known probate record of his estate or other records of him. He probably died at a rather early age. It is presumed that he was the father of John who provided the heirs for the next generation.

Children:

24 JOHN, b prob. about 1485-95, perhaps at Kelvedon Hatch, perhaps at Navestock; m 1, ... ; m 2, ... ; m 3, Alice ...... ; 7 ch. named in his will of 1529/30

HENRY, named in the will of his brother John, otherwise no further record of him has been found

ROBERT, possibly a son; m Joan ....; res. Northweald Bassett, where he d testate in 1534, naming his wife and leaving to 'every child at age 18 one bullock of 4 years'

THE PARISH CHURCH OF SAINT THOMAS THE APOSTLE
NAVESTOCK, ESSEX

Ref.: Probate Records at Chelmsford, Essex

80

JOHN KYRKEBY was probably born about 1470-1480 in or near Standon, Hertfordshire, where he lived and died. What little is known of him and his family is derived from his will, an abstract of which is given below. From this, we know that he was buried in the churchyard of Saint Mary's Church, Standon. Standon is a small village about six miles west of Bishop Stortford. His wife, named Rose, survived him. He held a sizable amount of property in and about Standon, including a place called *Fabydons*, which was where he lived. He bequeathed a tanhouse and also some leather, indicating that he was a tanner.

He died between 22 November 1522 and 22 January following. The godchildren mentioned were probably really grandchildren, the term being often so used at that time, but not always.

Kyrkeby is a place name, deriving from the Vikings. It means "place by the church". His sons contracted the name to the more common Kirby.

St. Mary's Church, Standon

20 November 1522 - the will of JOHN KYRKEBY the elder in the parish of Standon in the diocese of London in the county of Hartford ... to be buried in the churchyard of our Lady Saint Mary in Standon ... to the high altar for tythes forgotten 3s.4d. ... unto Rose my wife the place that I dwell in Standon Strete with all the lands, meadows, woods and pastures, free and copy, with a close called the lye, to her for life, then to Elyne my daughter, except 2 acres in Stapell folde ... if Elyne die without issue, then to my daughter Kateryn ... also to Kateryn my daughter my tenement called Johnsons with 2 crofts lying at Bromley green ... to Nicholas my son my place called Fabydons as my son and heir to the said place, also to Nicholas my meadow called Longmeed, conditionally that he pay unto John my son 40s. within one year after my death ... also to Rose my wife 2 acres in Stapell folde for life, then to Nicholas my son ... also to Rose one croft called Longe croft, for life, then to Nicholas ... to son John my tanhouse in Mylstrete that I bargained with Lorkyn or else the house that Lorkyn should have for that bargain ... to son John land and tenements called Martyne, conditionally that he pay 3s.4d. every year unto Alice Martyn and her dwelling for life in the said house and 4 loads of wood every year for life ... unto Margaret Orgar my daughter 40s. ... unto Elizabeth Hawnteler 20s. ... unto the repairs of the leading of the church in Standon 40s. ... unto the mending of the highway between Colyers rude and high Crosse 20s. ... to each godchild 4d. ... unto Rose my wife 4 Dyker of leather backs ... unto Michael my son 2 Dyker of leather backs and one of other leather ... unto John my son 3 dyker of leather backs and 2 of other leather ... to Elyne my daughter a leather back and a dyker of other leather ... unto Kateryn my daughter one dyker of leather backs and a dyker of other leather ... unto Edward Woode one back of leather. Executors to be wife Rose and son Nicholas. Overseers to be Thomas Master and Richard Green. Witnesses: Thomas Kent, Sir John Astell, priest, John Lamkyn, Edward Wood et al. Proved 22 January 1522/3.

(Ref.: Prerogative Court of Canterbury - 1 Bodfelde)

Children, probably all born at Standon:

ELYNE, (Ellen), prob. the eldest daughter

40 NICHOLAS, prob. b about 1500-1510; prob. eldest surviving son; m Joan ____ ; 6 ch. per will; he d 1555 at Standon; he lived at Fabdens

KATHERINE, living in 1522 per her father's will

JOHN

MARGARET, m ____ Orgar before 1522 will of her father

MICHAEL

Ref.: Probate Records at Chelmsford, Essex

96

JOHN DOWSETT of Kelvedon Hatch, Essex was born perhaps about 1435-40, presumably in Kelvedon Hatch or Navestock which is 2 miles southwest. He died in August or September 1486, and was survived by his wife Joan and six children named in his will. It seems likely that Joan was a second wife and perhaps the mother of only his two youngest children. John Bishop and John Radley, named in his will, were probably grandchildren. An abstract of his will follows.

> 6 August 1486 - the will of John Dowcet...to be buried in the churchyard of Saint Nicholas in Kelvedon... to the high altar 10s. which is in the hands of Richard Smert, to Robert Dowcet my eldest son my house in Navestock called Cokebyes after the decease of Joan my wife, to John Dowcet my youngest son my house in Navestock called Wyllemotts after the decease of Joan my wife...to the same John my son my ground lying in Kelvedon called Beredens after the decease of Joan my wife, paying therefor after her decease the sum of 40s., that is to say, to Margaret Radley my daughter 5s. ..to Alsbn' Mors 5s...to Joan Salkyns my daughter 5s...to Kateryn Lukyns my daughter 5s...to Elyanore my youngest daughter 20s...to Isabell Cokes my sister 3s.4d...to John Bysthopp 12d...to John Radley a lamb or 12d...to each of my godchildren 4d...to the church of Navestock 10s...to Joan my wife all my goods and household except corn and cattle the which I will that it be divided between my wife and John my son whom I make executors. And Robert Dowcet my overseer. Witnesses: Henry Salkyn, John Mors, Thomas Sabyn and others. Proved 18 September 1486. (Ref.: 79ER1)

Children, probably all born at Kelvedon Hatch:

48 ROBERT, eldest son, prob. b 1460-65
MARGARET, m _ __Radley before 1486
ALSBN, (*sic?*, prob. Elizabeth); m ____ Morse, prob. the John Mors who witnessed her father's will
JOAN, m Henry Salkyns (i.e. Sawkin) who d 1518 at Kelvedon Hatch, test.
KATHERINE, m ____ Lukyns, possibly Geoffrey who d 1552 at Kelvedon Hatch, test., or was he her son?
ELEANOR, youngest dau., apparently unm. in 1486
JOHN, youngest son, prob. b 1475-85

Ref.: Wills at Chelmsford Record Office

JOHN HEALD was of Concord, Massachusetts, about 1637. In the parish register of Alderley, Cheshire, is recorded the marriage of one John Heald and Dorothy Royle, on 3 December1636, and also the baptism of John Heald, son of John and Dorothy Heald, 26 march 1637. This surely must be the same as John of Concord.

He was made a freeman 2 June 1641. He lived in Concord, apparently in the north quarter of town. He wrote his own will, signed it on 19 April 1662, and died five weeks later on 24 May 1662. The will was proved 16 June following. The will commences: "I John Heald of Concord in the County of Middlesex in Massachusetts Collony being sick in body butt of perfect mind and memory, doe make this my Last Will and Testament...". He names his three eldest children only, John being "my eldest son". Hannah was named only by her given name altho she was then married. These three had already received their portion of the estate. To each of his five younger children, he bequeathed the sum of thirteen pounds, six shillings and eight pence to be paid to them by "my loving wife Dorothy" when they reached twenty one or at their marriage. He left one suit of clothes to John, his great coat to Timothy, and a waist coat to Hannah. The rest of the estate was to go to his wife. The net value of the estate was £140.1s. His will is unusual for that time in that the handwriting, his own, is clear and graceful and the spelling and punctuation are that of an extremely literate man. In light of the lack of specific evidence that he was from Alderley, it is interesting to note that at Alderley, a few yards from the parish church, is an ancient school house which was built around 1628. This would explain how John Heald learned to read and write with skill as great as any university trained clergyman. This school house was used until 1908.

Dorothy, "the widow Heald", was listed as a land holder in 1665 with 6 lots of about 161 acres total in the north quarter of Concord. She died 29 October 1694 at Dedham. How she happened to die in Dedham is hard to explain. None of her children are known to have lived there. The record would seem to apply to her, as no other person of similar name has been identified. Usually deaths were recorded where the person lived so it would seem she must have been living there during her last days.

31 of May 1662

A prisall of the goods and estat of John helld sen. lat desesed, by us hose names are under writen as foloweth,

	£
in housing upland & medow and orcherd with the Crope upon the ground	80-00-00
3 Cowes, 2 two year olds & two yearlings	23-10-00
in 3 swine with 3 peiges	03-10-00
in Inden Corne 16 bushells	02-08-00
1 bushell of peese	00-03-06
in bedding	02-10-00
two sheetes & 2 bedhelings	02-18-00
1 peece of Linsywolsy & wolen yearne, & tow yearne	03-14-00
in shipes wole, & 3 bages & on bage of flaxse tiare	02-13-00
on bushill of salte, & two sives & on saa	00-08-06
on muskit & soord, & 3 bushells of rie mele a cradell & bedstedd	01-09-00
in linnan & wearing apparill, hose & shoose & hat	07-14-00
4 Coushings, 1 Iron pot, 3 skilits, 1 warming pan, 2 kettelles	04-00-00
1 paier of tongs, & 1 paier of bellowes, 3 old exxes, 3 wedges	00-09-00
in peauter & tinne, & Cooppry weare, & bookes	02-15-00
in Chaiers Stooles, 1 Cheese pres & wolen Coards, 1 lanthorne	01-04-00
in linsinol -----------n	01-10-00
1 Iron Crow & on spad	00-05-00
	141-01-00
and in debts to be paied out of this	1-00-00

so the hole estate is on hundred and forty pounds and on shilling

Robert Meriam
Thomas T Brooke
his mark
Georg Wheeler

Children:

JOHN, bapt. 26 March 1637 at Alderley, Cheshire, Eng.; m at Concord 10 June 1661, Sarah Dane (or Dean), dau. of Thomas & Elizabeth; 7 ch.; He was a sergeant in King Philip's War; he d 17 June 1689; she d 22 July 1689 at Concord

HANNAH, prob. b about 1639 at Concord; m at Chelmsford 18 May 1658, John Spalding; 8 ch.; d 14 Aug. 1689; he d 3 Oct. 1721 ae 88

TIMOTHY, prob. b about 1641 at Concord; m 26 Nov. 1663, Sarah, dau. of Thomas & Jane Barber, bapt. 19 July 1646; settled first at Windsor, then to Suffield, Conn.; 5 sons, 3 daus.; he d 26 July 1689 at Suffield (1:6)

DORCAS, b 22 May 1645 at Concord; d 1 May 1650

GERSHOM, b 23 March 1646/7; m 6 May 1673, Ann Vinton, dau. of John & Ann, b 4 April 1656 at Lynn; 9 ch.; last 5 ch. bapt. at Concord; he d 13 May 1717 at Springfield; she d there in 1698 from childbirth

DOROTHY, b 16 Oct. 1649 at Concord; m at Lancaster 3 Aug. 1670, Jonathan Prescott; 3 ch.; d 8 Oct. 1674; he m 2, Elizabeth Hoare; m 3, widow Rebecca (Wheeler) Bulkeley; m 4, Ruth Brown

THOMAS, b 19 Jan. 1651/2; m 1, 18 Nov. 1675 at Enfield, Priscilla Markham, dau. of William of Hadley; 8 ch.; she d 15 April 1712 ae about 58; m 2, 17 Dec. 1713 at Enfield, widow Sarah Osborn, dau. of John Patch of Salem; he d 22 April 1725 at Enfield; she was prob. living 1742/3

ISAAC, m Elizabeth ____; moved to Stow; 3 ch. recorded there; d testate 1 June 1717 at Stow

CHILDREN, prob. more, who d before 1662

ISRAEL, b 30 July 1660; m Martha Wright, dau. of Edward & Elizabeth (Mellows)(Barrett) Wright, b 18 June 1659 at Concord; 1 ch. rec. at Concord; moved to Stow; 4 sons & 2 daus. grew up; wounded in 1690 expedition to Canada; she d 14 June 1746 ae 87 - g.s.; he was a blacksmith, farmer; d 8 Sept. 1738 ae 78 - g.s.

Ref.: Amer. Gen. 10:15; Middlesex County Probate 11053; N.E.H.G.R. 5, 29, 32; V.R.

THE PARISH CHURCH OF SAINT MARY, ALDERLEY, CHESHIRE

THE OLD SCHOOL HOUSE AT ALDERLEY, BUILT ABOUT 1628

DANIEL HENDRICK first appears on record in Hampton, New Hampshire, where he was one of the young men who received lots of land in 1638 or 1639 shortly after the settlement of the town.

Hendrick would seem to be a Dutch name. There were many of them in New Amsterdam and Long Island at this time. Since New England was settled primarily by people from England, perhaps Daniel Hendrick's ancestors were among those Protestants who fled from Holland during the persecutions under the Duke of Alva in 1567 and on.

Daniel Hendrich remained a resident of Hampton for no more than two or three years. He married as early as 1642, Dorothy Pike, who was born about 1617 in England, and was the daughter of John and Dorothy (Day) Pike. He moved to Newbury, Massachusetts, where her parents lived. He was there in 1644-5, when he bought a house and lot in Haverhill. He was made a freeman on 31 March 1646. On 8 October 1649, he sold his Hampton property, 6 acres of marsh, and his wife Dorothy signed. He was apparently living in Haverhill by this time and his property there was valued at £120. He was constable at Haverhill 1651-54, and was on the grand jury several times. In the fall of 1651, he and George Brown were appointed to lay out the highway between Haverhill and Salisbury. In February 1658, he, Thomas Davis and John Hutchins were granted the privilege to build a saw mill, but for some reason did not. On 20 January 1653, Daniel Hendrick, Henry Palmer, Theophilus Satchwell and Thomas Whittier were chosen to lay out some meadow lots. He had the same duties again on 14 October 1659 when he drew Lot No. 8, which was located in that part of Haverhill that became Salem, New Hampshire. This piece of land descended thru several generations of his descendants.

His wife Dorothy died 5 June 1659 at Haverhill and he remarried 8 April 1660 in Boston, to Mary Stockbridge, widow of John who died 13 October 1657, the ceremony performed by Governor John Endicott.

Daniel Hendrick was selectman in 1675, representative to the General Court in 1681. From 1692 on, he gave and sold his land to his children and others. His wife, Mary, was living as late as 1695 when she signed a deed. He signed his last known deed in 1700. Just when he died is unrecorded, but his son Jotham and Ephraim Robards were bonded for £200 on 27 February 1718/19 for the settlement of his estate, he apparently having died intestate. He would have been over 100 at this time, so it appears that this was a belated settlement of his estate. The inventory consisted only of land and this list was made 16 September 1720.

A true Inventory of all & Singular the goods, Lands, Chattles &c of Daniel Hendrick Late of Haverhill, Deceased, Apprized at Haverhill the Sixteenth Day of September Anno Dom: 1720 By the Subscribers &c. as followeth. Viz

A Second Division of meadow containing 8 acres	6-00-00
A 3rd Division of Upland containing 125 acres	80-00-00
An addition to the third Division being 25 acres	15-00-00
part of a 3d Division of meadow being 2 acres	4-00-00
4 Acres of accomodation bought of Jn Robinson anno 1695 to be added to his house Lott	100-00-00
3 Acres of accomodations by a Town Vote	45-00-00
4 Comings in ye Cow Comen	21-00-00

Septr 20, 1720 Sworn p Jotha' Hend.

Joseph Peaslee
Nathaniel Peaslee

Children, all born at Haverhill except Daniel:

DANIEL, b about 1643, perhaps in Newbury; moved to Piscataway, N.J.; no other record

HANNAH, b 4 June 1645; worked 1662 as servant to family of Rev. Wm. Worcester of Salisbury

JOHN, b 22 May 1648; m about 1677, Abigail Morse; 5 ch.; d about 1692; she m 2, Moses Pengry, went to Carolinas; her mother was condemned to hang as a witch, reprieved

JOTHAM, b 21 March 1649/50; m 21 Oct. 1722, widow Hannah (Foster) Austin; no ch.; d 9 Oct. 1727 at Haverhill. He & br. Israel were convicted of taking about 2600 cedar clapboards belonging to Wm. Neff, 1680

JABEZ, b 3 Dec. 1651; m 20 Dec. 1677, Hannnah More of Elizaabethtown, N.J., where he moved to, early 1677, aged 16, with his brother Daniel; 7 ch.; d 28 Oct. 1694, she a month after at Piscataway, N.J., leaving 4 ch. 2 to 10 years old. He was convicted of "night walking and other miscarriages", admonished Oct. 1674

ISRAEL, b 11 Nov. 1653; m 8 Nov. 1688 Sarah Gutterson; 5ch.; soldier Narragansett Fight

DOROTHY, b 31 May 1659; m 28 Aug. 1684, Ephraim Roberts; d 9 Jan. 1701/2, prob. at b of 8th child

-------Children by 2nd Wife, Mary-------

SARAH, b 8 Aug. 1661; m 4 June 1682, Samuel Ingalls; 11 ch.

ABRAHAM, b 2 Aug. 1663; d 1 Dec. 1690, smallpox

DEBORAH, b 25 Nov. 1666; m 2 July 1696, Jeremiah Page; 7 ch.; living in 1742 per his will

Ref.: Daniel Hendrick of Haverhill; V.R.; Probates

1

ROBERT JONES (*Robert*) was born about 1596 at Caversham, Oxfordshire (now, in 1990, a part of greater Reading and in Berkshire). He was almost certainly the son of Robert Jones of that parish who had other children recorded there a few years later. The existing parish register of Caversham starts in October, 1597 and has some gaps after that date, and there are no Bishop's Transcripts of an earlier date.

Robert Jones married 30 April 1621 at Caversham, Margaret "Garnebord" (i.e. Garnford). She was presumably the younger sister of Jane Garnford, who two years earlier had married his brother John. There are no other instances of this name in the Caversham parish register, nor are there probate records listed under this name. It is indeed a rare name, which may explain the crude spelling in the marriage record.

During the next seven and a half years, four children were born to them and baptized at Caversham. There is no further record of them. They also had daughter, Sarah, perhaps born about 1630. Margaret perhaps died about this time, possibly much later, but in any event, he later had a wife who had two daughters by an earlier husband named Curtis. There were quite a few Curtis families in Caversham at that time.

Jones is a patronymic, meaning literally son of John, and is the Welch equivalent of Johnson. Garford is a place name deriving from the chapelry by that name in Marcham, Berkshire, which is 23 miles northwest of Caversham. Garnford is probably derived from Garford.

About 1636, Robert Jones left for America and settled in Hingham, Massachusetts, where he was granted land in 1637. With him was his wife and four children, also possibly two step-daughters. Also coming to Hingham were Thomas and Richard Jones. Thomas was the son of Roger Jones and was baptized 25 January 1602/3 at Caversham. Richard was baptized there 14 May 1604, the son of Richard Jones. These three Jonses were perhaps first cousins. Both Thomas and Richard also received land in Hingham in 1638, but soon moved on, Richard to Dorchester, Thomas to Hull.

His next wife was the widow Curtis, perhaps nee Alexander. She had two daughters by her earlier marriage, Elizabeth and Jane. On 4 December 1646, these two girls gave their step-father power of attorney to handle matters relating to a legacy from their grandmother, Jane Alexander, late of Reading, *Oxford*, England. Reading is actually in Berkshire, near the county line.

4 December 1646 - Elizabeth Curtes & Jane Curtes granted unto Robert Jones of Hingham theire father in lawe a p'r of Attur[r] to aske &c. of the executors of the last will &c. of Jane Alexand[r] late of Reading in Oxfordshire deceased theire severall & respective Legacies given them by the last will & testament of the said Jane Alexand[r] theire grandmother & the Receipt &c. also to compound &c. & to appeare &c. there to required &c. & generally to doe all things. witnes theire hands & seales.

These two step-daughters, Elizabeth and Jane Curtis, married respectively, Moses Collier, son of Thomas, on 29 March 1655 at Hingham, and Thomas Collier, jr., brother of Moses, on 30 December 1647. Elizabeth died on 10 April 1657, five days after the birth of her son, Benoni.

Robert's second wife must have died about 1660 after which he married for a third time. This last wife was named Elizabeth, and she must have been at least twenty years younger than Robert.

Robert Jones died testate at Hingham between 20 April 1688, when he made his will, and 27 January 1691/2, when it was proved. Elizabeth died at Hingham 25 September 1712.

Robert Jones lived in Hingham Center, "over the river". In 1680-81, at the time the new meeting house in Hingham was built (now known as the Old Ship Church, the oldest extant wooden church in the United States), there were but three persons named Jones on the tax lists of Hingham, viz: Robert, Joseph, Sr., and Joseph Jr., that is, father, son, and grandson. An abstract of his will follows.

20 April 1688 - I Robert Jones of Hingham in ... New England, Planter, being weake in Body but yet of perfect minde and memory .... unto my sonne Joseph Jones 3s. .... to my sonne John Jones 1s. 6d.,... unto my sonne Benjamin Jones the elder 1s. 6d.,... unto my daughter Sarah Belknap 1s. 6d....unto Jane Collier my daughter 1s. 6d... unto my grandchildren which are the children of my sonne Robert Jones deceased to every one of them 12d. apeece ..... to be paid by my executor within two

months after my decease at my now dwelling house in said Hingham.. to my welbeloved wife Elizabeth Jones all my whole estate of houses & lands orchards and gardens and all my meadows & shares of Commons & Commonage which I now have & am possessed off in said Hingham either by gift or purchase or by exchange....during the term of her naturall life for her Comfortable livelyhood and maintainance... unto the said Elizabeth all my personal estate ... unto my sonne Benjamin Jones the younger which the said Elizabeth my wife Bore unto me, all my said estate of houses lands .. at the death of the said Elizabeth. Wife Elizabeth Jones to be sole executrix. Witnesses:
James Hanks
Theophilus Cushing
Daniel Cushing, senior   Proved at Boston 27 January 1691/2

When the will was proved, it was stated that Elizabeth, the executrix, was unable to come to court but desired that the will be presented for probate.

Children, first four baptized a Caversham, Oxfordshire:

ROBERT, bapt. 6 Oct. 1622; m, prob. at Hull in late 1651 or 1652, Anne Bibble, dau. of John & Sybil (Tincknell) Bibble of Hull and Malden, Mass.; he spent a few years in Rehobeth, returned to Hingham, moved to Hull about the time of his m'. On 28 Oct. 1651 she was of age & single. They cared for her parents until her father d at Hull 21 July 1653 when they & their son John inherited from him. They moved back to Rehobeth in 1654; in 1666 at Swansea, which was formerly part of Rehobeth. On 24 June 1675, there was a skirmish at Swansea. Robert Jones, his son John, & his son-in-law Joseph Lewis were all killed and scalped by Indians; 9 ch.

SARAH, b in England about 1630. In the Caversham parish register is recorded, "Sarah Joans, daughter of ----as", bapt. 28 Jan. 1630/31. This record would fit very well, yet the ----as suggests that it was a child of Thomas Jones who indeed did have a dau. Sarah also. Sarah, dau. of Robert, m before 1653, Samuel Belknap, son of Abraham & Mary (Stallon) Belknap, bapt. 16 March 1627/8; res. Salem, then Haverhill; 8 ch.; she d 18 April 1689 at Haverhill

JOHN, bapt. 9 Jan. 1624/5; named in his father's will; res. of Marshfield; his will of 21 May 1720 named, among others, ch. of his brother Joseph. Living to age 95 is not impossible, but could this John have d.y. & a later son John been the one who d in 1720 at a somewhat younger age? There are no records to support this possibility

BENJAMIN, prob., bapt. 15 July 1627, "son of Robert" - the surname missing in the parish register. Benjamin, "son of Robert Jones", was buried 24 Sept. 1627

JOSEPH, bapt. 30 Nov. 1628; m 11 Nov. 1657 at Weymouth, Patience Little, dau. of Thomas & Anna (Warren) Little of Cambridge. She was b about 1639, d at Hingham 25 Oct. 1723, ae 84; 9 ch.; he was a selectman; his house was burned by Indians in 1676 in King Philip's War. He lived "over the river"; he d 18 July 1714

BENJAMIN, bapt. at Hingham in March 1638; m, perhaps 2nd, before 1684, Bathsheba Bosworth, dau of Jonathan, b about 1654; he may be the B.J. who moved to Exeter, N.H. with other Hingham families, but by 1679 he was in Hull, for on 4 Feb. 1679 Thomas Collier of Hull, husbandman, & wife Jane (Benjamin's step-sister) sold to Benjamin Jones of Hull, mariner, for £5, a 20 rod parcel (Suffolk Deeds 14:71-72). The deed was acknowledged 25 Oct. 1686, along with another dated 10 Dec. 1684, whereby Benjamin Jones of New Bristol in the Colony of Plymouth, husbandman, & Bathsheba, his wife, sold to Luke Squire of Hull their dwelling house and land in Hull. He should not be confused with another B.J., son of Abraham & b about 1668. They lived across the street from one another in Hull. He d at Bristol 12 Jan. 1717/18; she d there 17 Sept. 1740

Children, by last wife Elizabeth, both bapt. in Hingham
by the Rev. Peter Hobart

ELIZABETH, bapt. in Aug. 1662; prob. d.y.

BENJAMIN, b 27 Oct. 1666; m prob. about 1692, Patience ——; he d 29 Jan. 1703/4 ae 37, & she rem. twice; 2 ch.; she d 1747 ae 80

THE OLDEST MEETING-HOUSE IN THE UNITED STATES, AT HINGHAM, MASSACHUSETTS

Ref.: History of Hingham, by Lincoln; N.E.H.G.S.-68; 143; Diary of Rev. Peter Hobart of Hingham; 1852 Issue of Gleason's Pictorial Drawing Room Companion, p 112; Suffolk County Probates; V.R.; T.A.G.-31

2

ROBERT JONES was probably born about 1565-1570 in Caversham, Oxfordshire. There lived in Caversham several contemporary Joneses who were probably his brothers, certainly kinsmen. The Caversham parish register starts in October 1597, long after these several Joneses would have been born. The following records pertain to these brothers or kinsmen.

ROGER JONES who had a son Thomas, baptized 23 January 1602/3. This son Thomas and his wife Anne had three children baptized at Caversham, probably more, but part of the register has gaps, They emigrated to Hingham, Mass. about 1636 with Robert's son Robert.

RICHARD JONES who had a son Richard baptized 14 May 1604. This son Richard also emigrated to Hingham, Mass. about 1636. He also had a son Symon who was buried 28 August 1624, if the same one.

LEWIS JONES who was buried 16 November 1604 might have been another brother, or perhaps a child of one of the above.

WILLIAM JONES who married Elizabeth Courteyes 24 September 1604. There is no further record of this couple in Caversham.

Children, probably all born at Caversham, Oxfordshire:

JOHN, prob., b about 1594; m 15 Aug. 1619 at Caversham, Jane Garnford who was prob. the sister of Robert's wife. The name is prob. more conventionally Garford, deriving from the chapelry of that name in Marcham, Berkshire, and about 23 miles northwest of Caversham

1 ROBERT, prob., b about 1596; m 1, 30 April 1621 at Caversham, Margaret Garnford*; 5 known ch.; m 2, widow Curtis; m 3, Elizabeth ____ , by whom 2 ch.; he d testate at Hingham, Mass. between 20 April 1688 & 27 Jan. 1691/2; Elizabeth d 25 Sept. 1712

SYMON, bapt. 18 May 1606, "son of Robert"; he prob. d.y. 1606-1610, for which period the burial records are lacking

SILVANUS, bapt. 1 April 1610, "son of Robert"; buried 26 Feb. 1611/12, "son of Robert"

*The Parish Register seems to read Garnebord or Gamebord, neither of which are known surnames. The correct interpretation is probably Garnford or Garford.

Ref.: Parish Registers; Bishop's Transcripts; Probate Records at Oxford and Reading; P.C.C. Wills

SAINT PETER'S CHURCH, CAVERSHAM, 1794

The Ancestry of
WILLIAM MOULTON & MARGARET PAGE
Compiled by
William Haslet Jones

Vincent
John
William

104 William
Margery

32 Robert Moulton
Margaret

16 John Moulton
Thomasine

18 William Taylor

8 John Moulton
Ann Taylor

52 John Goodwin
Alice

56 Roger Ward
Katherine

24 Robert Page
Martha

26 Francis Goodwin
Katherine

28 Robert Ward
Alice Pixton

12 Robert Page
Margaret Goodwin

14 Francis Ward
Sussanna Brown

4 Robert Moulton + Mary   6 Robert Page + Lucy Ward

2 William Moulton + Margaret Page

2

WILLIAM MOULTON (*Robert, John, John, Robert*) was born probably in 1615 at Martham, which is next to Ormsby and near Great Yarmouth, England. On 11 April 1637, he was listed as a servant to Robert Page of Ormsby, husbandman, who, with his wife and three children, was about to sail to New England in either the *John and Dorothy* of Ipswich, William Andrews, master, or the *Rose,* of Yarmouth, William Andrews, his son, master. He was listed as age 20, which is probably an estimate, whereas he seems to have been almost 22. These two ships sailed from Ipswich and arrived at Boston on 8 June following. Also with them was Ruth Moulton of Ormsby, a single woman, aged 20, relation to William unknown.

William Moulton and the Pages first went to Newbury, Massachusetts, where they remained a little over a year before joining the new settlement to the north at Winnacunnett, now Hampton, New Hampshire, in 1639. There they settled near Thomas and John Moulton who were distant cousins. William Moulton undoubtedly worked for several years for Robert Page.

A few years later, perhaps as early as 1646, he married Margaret Page, daughter of his employer, who had been his fellow passenger years before when she was only eight.

William Moulton made his will on 8 March 1663/4, "being sick and weak of body...". He died 18 April following, being about 48 years old. He named his wife, each of his children, and referred to his child yet unborn. He named his father-in-law, Robert Page, and his brother-in-law, Henry Dow, to be executors, thus indicating the identity of his wife's family.

His widow Margaret remarried on 2 August 1671 to John Sanborn, whose first wife had died on 30 December 1668. They had one son by this second marriage. She died 13 July 1699, aged 70.

Their seven children, Mary having died, were named in her father's will of 1679.

8 March 1663/4 - the will of WILLIAM MOULTON of Hampton, county Norfolk ... sick & weak in body ... to Margaret my loving wife my new house being west part of my dwelling house, use of the leanto, half the orchard, all furniture, my warming pan & smoothing iron, fire shovel & tongs ... the rest of the iron, brass and pewter to be divided between wife and two eldest sons ... wife Margaret to have neat cattle, horse & swine toward bring up my children except those already accounted theirs, viz: my son Joseph three cattle, son Benjamin two, Hannah one & Mary one ... to son Joseph Moulton my dwelling house & barn, out housing, ten acre house lot, ten acre planting land in the north plain, 5 acres in the East field, 9 acres of fresh meadow near to the Great bores Head, 2 acres of salt marsh in a place called Severalls, 5 acres of salt marsh on the other side of the falls, 3 shares of *commonedy,* 2 shares of cow common & one share of the ox common ... to son Benjamin Moulton 10 acres of planting land adjoining my house lot, 10 acrs of planting land in the north plain, 4 acres of meadow in the Great Meadow, 3 acres in the Great Bores Head meadow, 5 acres of Salt marsh, one share of cow common, one of ox common ... to son Robert Moulton 6 acres of planting land in the east field ... when son Joseph reaches 21 he is to receive his inheritance and then lay in for his mother four loads of hay and every year 15 bushels of Indian corn, 8 of wheat and 5 of malt ... son Benjamin to provide her with 3 loads of hay yearly, 10 bushels of Indian corn & 6 of wheat yearly ... to daughter Hannah Moulton £10 at age 20 or marriage ... to daugter Mary £10 of which £5 at age 16, £5 the next year ... to daughter Sarah the same, to daughter Ruth the same ... to child unborn £5 when it comes of age to be paid by my sons Joseph and Benjamin ... when sons Joseph and Benjamin come to age my plows, carts, yokes, chains, etc. to be divided between them ... Joseph to bring home for his mother 13 loads of wood per annum, Benjamin 7 loads ... father in law Robert Page, yeoman, and my loving brother in law Henry Dow to be executors. Witnesses: Robert Page, Samuel Dalton, Thomas Page. Proved 11 October 1664 (Essex County Wills 19049)

Children:

JOSEPH, b prob. about 1647; m 24 May 1677, Bethia Swayne, dau. of William & Prudence (Marston) Swayne, b 22 Nov. 1652; 5 ch.; she d 19 Dec. 1723 ae 71 per g.s.; in 1726 he deeded his estate to 4 daus. & a grandson

BENJAMIN, b about 1649; m Hannah Wall, dau. of James & Mary (Philbrick)(Tuck) Wall, b 17 March 1658/9; 6 ch.; he d 28 March 1728, testate

HANNAH, b 15 Feb. 1651/2; m 25 Aug. 1681 to Josiah Sanborn, son of Wm. & Mary (Moulton) Sanborn; 3 ch.; she d 6 Nov. 1687; he m 2, widow Sarah Perkins

MARY, b about 1654; d 27 July 1664 (erroneous Newbury m register says she m Jonathan Haynes, whereas it was Sarah who m him)

SARAH, b 17 Dec. 1656; m 1, 30 Dec. 1674 at Hampton, Jonathan Haynes of Newbury; 12 ch.; m 2, 19 Jan. 1702/3, Thomas Kingsbury

RUTH, b 7 May 1659; m 5 Dec. 1678, Richard Sanborn, her step-br.; 3 ch.; she d 3 May 1685; he m 2, widow Mary Boulter

ROBERT, b 8 Nov. 1661; m 29 May 1689, Lucy Smith; 4 ch.; d 11 Oct. 1732

WILLIAM, b 25 May 1664; m 1, 27 May 1685, Abigail, dau. of John Webster, jr.; she d 24 July 1723; he m 2, Sarah ——; 9 ch.; weaver, innholder, merchant; he d Oct. 1732, leaving estate of £1433

--------Sanborn Child--------

JONATHAN, b 25 May 1672; m Elizabeth Sherburne; 12 ch.; he d 20 June 1741

SAINT MARY THE VIRGIN, MARTHAM

Ref.: Moulton Annals; Pope's Pioneers; Savage; Maine Historical & Genealogical Recorder; V.R.; Genealogical Dictionary of Maine & New Hampshire, by Noyes, Libby & Davis

4

ROBERT MOULTON (*John, John, Robert*), eldest son of John and Ann (Taylor) Moulton, was born about 1585-90, presumably at Ormsby, Norfolk, England, where he grew up. About 1612, he and his wife Mary were married. About this time they must have settled in Martham, which is next to Ormsby on the north. Robert Moulton's name appears in the 1619 Court Rolls at Martham (SC2-193/7). He was buried there 21 August 1622. No will of his has been found.

The widow, Mary, married secondly, 15 July 1623 at Ormsby Saint Margaret, William Eastow (or Estow), son of George of Ormsby. The Eastows emigrated to New England about 1637 or 1638 and settled in Hampton, New Hampshire, where he was one of the grantees and first settlers. he was made freeman on 13 December 1638. He had ten acres for a house lot, lying between William Palmer's on the east and William Moulton's (sometimes Thomas Jones's) on the west, and the meeting house green on the south. He was representative for three years.

Possibly the Eastows followed her oldest son William, who sailed from Ipswich, England, in April 1637. In any event, Mary ( )(Moulton) Eastow left behind her second son, John, and her two daughters. If they had any plans to eventually follow, there is no evidence of it.

William Eastow died 23 November 1655. His will mentions no wife, so Mary must have died earlier. He left bequests of 10 shillings each to William Moulton's four children, which seems to be rather clear circumstantial evidence that William Moulton was his step-son, though there is no baptismal record to prove William Moulton's parentage. Both families lived as neighbors in Hampton. He was not named in the will of his grandfather, John Moulton, dated 20 August 1637, because he, William, had left for New England the previous April.

16 October 1655 - the will of WILLIAM ESTOW of the town of Hampton, county Norfolk ... to my son in law Morris Hobbs & my daughter Sarah my house wherein he dwelleth, the lot tenement belonging with two shares of the cow commons, one share of the ox common, an acre of salt marsh at the sevenells ... ten acres to my two daughters to be equally divided, Sarah to have the southside towards Christopher Palmer ... one share of the cow common to daughter Mary ... twelve acres in the mill field to be divided betwixt my two daughters ... to daughter Mary eight acres of salt marsh, to daughter Sarah nine acres ... twelve acres of fresh meadow to be divided between them ... to daughter Sarah Hobbs 4 oxen and 2 cows and one yearling heifer ... to my grandson John Hobbs one heifer of 2 years old, he to give his sister Sarah the second calf this heifer shall bring and I give unto him my gun ... to daughter Mary Marston all the rest of my cattle which is three cows, one two year old heifer, one bull and three calves, seven bushels of wheat ... to the children of William Moulton 40 shillings which is 10s. to each of them, the eldest first, the others yearly according to their ages ... residue to daughter Sarah Hobbs ... to son in law Thomas Marston the furthermost stack of salt marsh hay and two good loads of fresh hay ... son in law Morris Hobbs to pay my debts. Witnesses: Abraham Perkins, William Moulton. Proved 8 April 1656.

(Essex County Wills 9110)

Children, baptized at Martham:

ABIGAIL, b prob. 1613; she m ___Swallows before 1637 when she was named in her grandfather's will

2 WILLIAM, b prob. before 1615; he emigrated to N.E. in April 1637 as a servant to Robert Page whose dau. Margaret he eventually m; he d 18 April 1664; 8 ch.; she m 2, 1671, Lt. John Sanborn, had 1 more ch.; she d 13 July 1699.

JOHN, bapt. 5 Jan. 1616/17; buried 4 April 1617

JOHN, bapt. 20 June 1619; as the only son remaining in England, he inherited his father's rights in his grandfather's estate; he may be the John Moulton who m Susan Emms 6 June 1641 at Thurne, which is 6 mi. west of Ormsby

ANNE, bapt. 21 June 1621; d 21 May 1640 at Martham

--------Eastow children, by 2nd marriage--------

SARAH, b about 1624; m about 1643, Morris Hobbs who was b about 1615. They lived with or near her father; 10 ch.; he d 4 Jan. 1706

MARY, bapt. 8 June 1628 at Ormsby; m about 1648, Thomas Marston, son of Capt. William; 8 ch.; he d 28 Sept. 1690; she was living 1700

Ref.: Parish Registers; Probate Records at Norwich; History of Hampton, N.H. by Joseph Dow, 1894

6

ROBERT PAGE (*Robert, Robert*), son of Robert and Margaret (Goodwyn) Page, was born in Ormsby, Norfolk, England, about 1604. He married Lucy Ward on 8 October 1629 in Saint Mary's, the parish church of South Walsham. In 1637 he and his family received permission to leave for America, as is recorded in the following entry:

> April the 11th 1637. The examination of Robertt Page of Ormsby in Norff. husbandman, ageed 33 yeares and Lucea his wife, aged 30 yeares, with 3 children, Frances, Margrett, and Susanna, and 2 Sarvants, William Moulton and Anne Wadd; the one aged 20 yeares the other 15 yeares, and are all desirous to passe for New England to inhabitt and Remaine.

They sailed in either the *John and Dorothy* of Ipswich, William Andrews, Master, or the *Rose* of Yarmouth, William Andrews, Jr., Master. These ships sailed from Ipswich and arrived in Boston on 8 June 1637. The Pages first went to Salem, where Lucy was admitted to membership in the church in 1639. The same year they moved on to Hampton, having received a grant of 10 acres for a house lot lying between the lots of William Marston on the west and Robert Marston on the east, abutting on the meeting house green on the south, and other land of his on the north. This home property remained in the Page family for six generations.

Robert Page became a freeman of the Massachusetts Bay Colony on 18 May 1642 and was a Selectman of the town of Hampton eight times in the period 1644-1671. He was a Deputy to the General Court in 1657 and 1668. He was also a Marshall of the old county of Norfolk in which Hampton was then included. He was granted the privilege of building the first sawmill, which he was required to do within one year, but because he was busy constructing a parsonage the time was extended to two years. The sawmill was built at Taylor's River in 1656. In 1660 he was a church deacon and continued to be so until his death when his son succeeded him.

In 1659 when 76 persons were taxed, Robert Page's tax was the highest and amounted to one twentieth of the taxes levied. He and his wife were assigned front seats in the meeting house, the seating being assigned according to one's standing in the community. Notwithstanding the many offices he held and the extent of his business affairs, he was unable to write his name and always used a mark for his signature.

Concerning Ann Wadd, aged 15, who accompanied the Pages to New England, there is some evidence that the name Wadd, as published, was correctly Ward, and that Ann was his wife's sister and later the wife of Edward Colcord of Hampton. On 24 June 1673 Robert Page of Hampton conveyed land by a deed in which he called Edward Colcord of Hampton his brother and Colcord's wife Ann his sister. There was no Ann Page for Colcord to have married. Also, Ann Colcord bore ten children between 1641 and 1667, so she must have been born between 1621 and 1625. Ann Wadd (or Ward) was born about 1622. So, Ann and Lucy were probably sisters.

Lucy Page died on 12 November 1665, aged 58, and Robert Page made his will on 9 September 1679, and died on 22 September following, aged 75. He bequeathed to sons Francis and Thomas, to daughters Mary Gogg, Margaret Sanborne, and Hannah, wife of Henry Dow. He named his son-in-law, William Marston, and bequeathed to many of his grandchildren, including the children of his daughter Margaret and her first husband William Moulton: Joseph, Benjamin, Hannah, Sarah "now Sarah Haines", Ruth and William. The list of Moulton children is the same as in their father's will of 15 years earlier, except for Mary who died on 27 July 1664, shortly after her father died, and with the addition of William who was born after his father's death. His inventory:

Church of Saint Margaret
Great Ormsby, Norfolk

The Enventory of the Estate of Deacon Robertt Page of Hampton decessed taken this 10th of October 1679

Impm. his House lott 14 Acres £3 p acre - -	£ 42- 0
the Houses ye widow Fog lives in - - - -	30- 0
the two Barns ye Stable and malt house - -	30- 0
4 Acres of land bought of John Smith - - -	12- 0
16 Acres of medow £8 p Acre - - - -	128- 0
60 Acres of pasture land £3 - - - - -	180- 0
one forth pt of ye old mill - 20 Acres land - -	15- 0
19 Acres of Land in the north plaine 2 pcells -	19- 0
ye little medow of 4 Acres & 6 acres of pasture there	32- 0
4 Acres next ye beach fresh medow - - -	20- 0
13 Acres of Salt marsh att £4 p Acre - - -	52- 0
3 Acres of marsh bought of James Philbrick -	12- 0
3 a and halfe of pasture by Ensign Sanborns -	06- 0
100 Acres of outt land westward - - - -	05- 0
a Grant of Land of north Division - - - -	10- 0
5 shares of the Cows Comon £10 p share - -	50- 0
2 shares of the ox Comon £5 p share - - -	10- 0
	653
His Cattle	
ye 2 Greatt oxen £18, the 2 younger £12 - -	30- 0
3 Cowes £11, 5 two yerolds £10, 6 Calves 3:3s -	24- 0
one bull £2. 10s, ye mare £3 - - - - -	05-10
4 swine £4 & 7 shots 8s a peece - - - -	06-16
4 load of Indian Corne £3, in barly & pease £3 -	06-00
18 Load of hay £9 - - - - - - -	09- 0
a malt mill att - - - - - - - - -	01- 0
one p wheeles, turnbariel 3 shaves, 1 yoak & caps	03- 0
one plow & plow Irons, 2 axes, 3 wedges - -	00-15
two Collars & one bridle - - - - - - -	- 5
(sic)	76- 6
Houshold Stuff	
one feterbed & furniture & new bedsted - -	06- 0
one small fetherbed given to Robert Moulton with whatt belongs to itt - - - - - -	03- 0
one Joyne Cubbord - - - - - - - -	01- 0
one Greatt kittle bras 20s, two old pots 4s - -	1- 4
4 puter dishes, 3 basons & other dishes & things on the shelf - - - - - - - - -	0-15
one bras warming pan 4s Chamber pot 2s - -	0- 6
4 Chairs 2 stooles speel Andirons & tonges -	1-15
& two stakes two Chests 25s 2 shets 4 napkins 10s	1-15
1 bibell a carpet & other things - - - -	2-10
a payer of sheres 1 smothing Ioran - - -	0- 3
a table & a kittell & other small things - -	1-10
Sum totall	£ 759- 4

Tho: Page gave oath to the truth of this Inventory before ye Court held att Salisbury November ye 11th 1769 And if more shall appear he is to add it to ye Inventory

Apprized by us
Thomas Marston
Nath[l] Weare

this 1 Septem 1679

Children, probably all born at Ormsby:

3 MARGARET, b about 1630 in England; m William Moulton; 8 ch.; he d 18 April 1664; she m 2, John Sanborne; 1 ch.; she d 13 July 1699 ae 70

FRANCIS, b about 1630 in England; m 2 Dec. 1669 Meribah Smith, dau. of Robert & Susanna of Exeter, then Hampton; 8 ch.; he d at Hampton 15 Nov. 1706 ae 76

SUSANNA, b about 1630-35 in England; prob. d.y. as not in father's will

REBECCA, b about 1637, prob. at Salem; bapt. there 1 Sept. 1639; m 15 Oct. 1652, William Marston, Jr.; 9 ch.; she d 27 June 1673 ae 37 per g.s.; he m 2, 5 July 1675, Ann, widow of James Philbrick

THOMAS, b 1639 at Salem, bapt. there 1 Sept. 1639; m 2 Feb. 1663/4, Mary Hussey, dau. of Christopher & Theodate (Batchiler) Hussey, bapt. at Newbury 2 April 1637; 7 ch.; d 8 Sept. 1686 per g.s.; she m 2, Henry Green, m 3, Capt. Henry Dow; she d 21 Jan. 1732/3 ae 94

HANNAH, b 1641 in Hampton; m 17 June 1659, Henry Dow, Jr.; 4 ch.; d 6 Aug. 1704 ae 63 per g.s.; he m 2, 10 Nov. 1704, the widow Mary (Hussey) Green, also widow of Thomas Page

MARY, b 1644 at Hampton; m 28 Dec. 1665, Samuel Fogg, his 2nd wife; 3 ch.; he d 16 April 1672; she d 8 May 1700

THE OLD VILLAGE CHURCH AT FILBY,
Ancestral home of the Ward family

Ref.: The Page Family, by William Prescott; N.E.H.G.S.-66; History of Hampton, by Dow; Savage; N.H. Probates; New England Ancestry of Dana Converse Backus

8

JOHN MOULTON (*John, Robert*) of Ormsby in the county of Norfolk, England, was under 21 when his father died in 1573. He was probably born about 1560, as he married Anne Taylor on 14 June 1584 at Hemsby. She was the daughter of William Taylor. John Moulton and William Taylor held adjacent land in the southeast fields of Ormsby. John's name appears on several Subsidy (tax) and Rental Rolls from 1597 to 1627. He held two messuages (enclosed farm yards) in Ormsby. They were called Miller's and Cordiner's. Miller's was at the east end of Ormsby. He had a total of about 26 acres of farmland in Ormsby and Caister, divided into nine plots. John Moulton died in late 1637 having made his will on 20 September. It was proved on 7 February following at Norwich. From this will we can deduce that he was a fairly wealthy man. He had acquired the land bequeathed by his father to his younger brother Robert in 1573. Robert apparently died without issue.

20 September 1637 - the will of John Moulton of Ormsby Saint Margaret, the elder, county Norfolk, yeoman...to be buried in the church of Ormsby... to the reparations of the church 10s..to the poor 20s..to Mr. Snailwell the minister 10s.....to John Moulton my grandchild my tithing called Miller's at the east end of Ormsby and 11 acres of arable land & pasture being in 6 pieces (long descriptions) on condition that said John release $5\frac{1}{2}$ acres of land which he hath by right of Robert Moulton my son his father, otherwise the messuage & 11 acres to my son Joseph Moulton.. John also to pay to Abigail Swallow & Anne Moulton his two sisters £5 each....to Joseph my son my messuage called Cordiner's lying within Ormsby & Castor..to the said John (sic) Moulton my son...to Anne my wife the use of the parlor chamber with the buttery adjoining, one posted bedstead in the parlor, one framed table & the forms thereto belonging, the featherbed, bolster, blankets, sheets, one pillow & one covering, one truckle bedstead, for life, then to son Joseph. ... to Anne my wife all household stuff within the house, brass, pewter, linen & woollen, except two chairs in the hall & my two chests & the great brass pot which are to son Joseph..to Anne £10 to be paid by Joseph, 5 combs of wheat, 5 combs of malt yearly for life, and half a chalder of sea coal, one hundred five faggots & half a thousand billets yearly for life..to wife Anne half the fruit of the orchard, one milk cow, two young swine..son Joseph to keep her with summer meat & winter meat...if wife make any claim of dowery or

thirds against lands which I have given in this my will, then the bequests to her are voided... to Sarah Bee my daughter £40..to Esther my daughter £40...to Rebecca Larwood my daughter £40..to Martha Ilberd my daughter £30..to Sarah Bee my daughter £20 more within five years... to Esther Dawkin my daughter £20 more in six years...to Rebecca Larwood my daughter £20 in seven years & also £15 more to Martha Ilberd within eight years...if son Joseph refuse to pay these legacies to his sisters or their children, then they shall enter into the messuage called Cordiner's to distrain until satisfied...to Lidia Ilberd my grandchild £5 in 2 years...to Abigail Moulton my grandchild £5 in one year.. to Robert Greene my grandchild £5 within three years...to Hannah Moulton my grandchild the daughter of Benjamin Moulton my son £5 within 5 years...unto Mary Estoe my apprentice 10s. at age 24...to every grandchild unnamed in this will 20s. at age 22...to Lidia Ilberd my grandchild one truckle bedstead & a covering...residue of goods, cattle & all implements of husbandry, carts, plows, harrows & barrows whatsoever belonging to husbandry I give to Joseph Moulton my son, he to be sole executor...Edmond Larwood my son in law to be supervisor. Witnesses: Robert Watson, John Smith, Rob't Watson. Proved 17 February 1637/8. (Ref.: Archdeaconry of Norwich Wills, 1637 - 260 Bankes)

Children, probably born at Ormsby:

4 ROBERT, b about 1585-90, eldest son; m about 1614, Mary ____ ; 5 ch.; he was buried 21 Aug. 1622 at Martham; she m 2, 15 July 1623 at Ormsby St. Margaret, William Estow, had at least 2 more ch. She, Estow & ch. went to N.E. in 1637

JOSEPH, m Susan ____ ; living in Ormsby in 1623 when he witnessed the will of Margaret Marston; his will dated 21 Aug. 165?, pr. 3 Jan. 1658/9 at London (P.C.C. Pell 31); Susan survived him; 6 ch. of which son John apparently d.s.p. by 1637, & son Eleazer d in Nov. 1679 leaving 4 daus.

BENJAMIN, m & had a dau. Hannah by 1637

SARAH, bapt. 12 April 1600 at Ormsby St. Margaret; m George Bee of Runham before 1637

ESTHER, m ____ Dawkin, before 1637

REBECCA, m Edmond Larwood; had Edmond bapt. 12 Aug. 1626, Thomas bapt. 20 Sept. 1629, both at Runham

MARTHA, m Thomas Ilberd; by 1637 she had a dau. Lydia

DAUGHTER, m ____ Green, had a son Robert by 1637

Ref.: Parish Registers; Probate Records at Norwich

ROBERT PAGE (*Robert*) of Acle and of Ormsby Saint Margaret, Norfolk, England, husbandman, was born probably about 1575-77. He married on 16 July 1598 at Hemblington, Margaret Goodwynge (Goodwin). She was the daughter of Francis and Katherine Goodwyn, and was born about 1574 at Blofield. Hemblington is 4 miles west of Acle and Ormsby Saint Margaret is 7 miles east of Acle and on the coast of the North Sea.

The parish register of Ormsby Saint Margaret begins in 1675 and the register of Acle starts in 1664.

Robert Page died in July 1617 and was probably buried in the churchyard of Saint Margaret as requested. He was obviously ill and knew that death was imminent. Margaret was listed on the Subsidy Rolls of Ormsby in 1622 and 1627. There is then no more mention of her.

1 July 1617 - Will of ROBERT PAGE of Ormesby, County of Norfolk, husbandman... in body weak & sick... to be buried in the churchyard of the parish of Ormesby St. Margaret's. To the church of St. Margaret's 12d. To Margaret Page my wife my house and land with all appurtenances thereto belonging, situate and being in Acle in the county of Norfolk for the term of her life. And after her decease the s[d] house and land and all appurtenances thereto belonging to Robert Page my son, he paying all such legacies in such manner as is hereafter mentioned. To Thomas Page my son £ 5, to be paid by the said Robert Page two years after the decease of Margaret my wife. To Rebecca my daughter £ 5, to be paid by the s[d] Robert Page four years after the decease of Margaret my wife. To Henry Page my son £ 5, to be paid by the s[d] Robert Page six years after the decease of Margaret my wife. If it happen the said Robert Page my son does not pay the aforesaid legacies in manner and form aforesaid my will and mind is that he or she who shall be unpaid their legacy shall reenter and possess the aforesaid house and land with all belonging until the fearme of the aforesaid house and land in Acle shall satisfy and pay their aforesaid legacy of £ 5. To Francis my son £ 7, Margaret my wife to pay it in manner following, viz. 40s. when the s[d] Francis attain the age of 21 years, and £ 5 when he shall attain the age of 24 years. My will is that my wife Margaret shall enter into two several bonds unto the s[d] Francis for the payment of the said seven pounds within five days after my death. The rest of my goods and chattels, movables and immovables, unbequeathed, I give to Margaret my wife whom I make sole executrix, to pay my debts and funeral charges and prove my will within one month of my death. If she shall refuse, then I ordain Francis my son to be sole executor and Margaret my wife to be void. Any of my children departing this life before

their legacy is due, their legacy shall be divided among the survivors. If Robert my son depart this life before Margaret my wife, then I will my son Thomas have the house and land in Acle and pay the aforesaid legacies that Robert should have paid. Witnesses: Ralph Smith, William Larwood, Edward Boughton. Proved 23 July 1617 by the Executrix. (Archdeaconry Court of Norwich, 1617)

Children:

6 ROBERT, b about 1604; m 8 Oct. 1629 at S. Walsham, Lucy Ward; 7 ch.; went to N.E.; she d 12 Nov. 1665 ae 58, he d 22 Sept. 1679 ae 75 at Hampton, N.H.

THOMAS, bapt. 1 May 1605 at Hemsby; living 1617

REBECCA, bapt. at Ormsby Saint Michael 16 May 1608; m ——— Rix; living in 1667, prob. near Ormsby

HENRY, living in 1617 per his father's will

FRANCIS, husbandman; d at Ormsby 1666-7, s.p., test.

4 February 1666/7 - the will of FRANCIS PAGE **of Ormsby St. Margaret in Norfolk, husbandman..to Rebecca Rix my sister my piece of ground in Ormsby on the north of the tenement where I now dwell... which I purchased of Clement Harcocke, deceased, estimated to be about 5 roods...to my said sister all my goods whatsoever, and I appoint her sole executrix. Witnesses: William Worde, William Bryspoole. Proved 5 April 1667. (Archdeaconry Court of Norwich 1667)**

SAINT EDMUND'S CHURCH, ACLE, NORFOLK

Ref.: N.E.H.G.S.-68; Norfolk Wills at Norwich; Norfolk Parish Register Marriages 1:22, Public Record Office -E-179-153/594, 606

14

FRANCIS WARD (*Robert, Roger, ?William*) was baptized on 25 October 1579 at Filby, Norfolk, England. There in June 1603, he married Susanna Browne who was possibly the daughter of Edmund and Elleyne Browne of Filby. Francis and his family appeared to have left the parish of Filby shortly after the death of his mother in February 1609, and settled in the parish of Saint Mary in South Walsham about 8 miles to the west. Susanna died and Francis remarried on 23 August 1627 to Margaret (Denton) Holle. She was the widow of Robert Holle of North Walsham. Eventually they moved to Great Yarmouth which is 5 miles southeast of Filby and on the coast of the North Sea. Here Francis died in late 1647. His will names only those children who were then living in England. Two daughters and possibly a son had gone to New England and these were not mentioned. An abstract of his will follows.

> 6 September 1645 - the will of Francis Ward of Great Yarmouth, county Norfolk, yeoman, being weak & sick in body. .to Francis Ward of South Walsham my son, all my houses, messuages, lands & tenements in Great Yarmouth after the decease of Margaret my wife, conditional that he pay unto Susan my daughter £15, unto William Ward my son £10... Margaret my wife shall have all such goods & household stuff as were hers before marriage... residue to Margaret my wife for life, then to daughter Susan...other goods & chattels & money owing unto Francis Ward my son, he to be sole executor...Nicholas Lackington of Great Yarmouth, gentleman, to be supervisor... Witnesses: John Willcock. Thomas Jollir. Proved 29 January 1647/8. (ANW - 345 Disney)

Children:

7 LUCY, bapt. 13 March 1604/5 at Filby; m Robert Page 8 Oct. 1629 at S.Walsham, St. Mary's. He was of Ormsby, St. Margaret's where their first 3 ch. were prob. b. They went to N.E., settled in Salem, Mass., then Hampton, N.H.; 4 more ch.; she d 12 Nov. 1665 at Hampton; he d 26 Sept. 1679 ae 75

SUSANNA, bapt. 20 Sept. 1606; alive in 1645

MARIE, bapt. 4 Sept. 1608; d.y.

FRANCIS, b about 1610; m Rachel_____ ; 7 ch. bapt. at S. Walsham. Living in 1656

WILLIAM, alive in 1645

THOMAS, possibly a son b about 1620; an original settler of Hampton in 1639; m Margaret Shaw, dau. of Roger & Anne of Hampton; 4 ch. per his will of 18 June 1678, inv. 27 July 1680; she d 15 April 1704. In 1651 & 1652, he was taken into court & ordered to bring his wife home from England. Why she had gone there & when she returned in unknown. Samuel Fogg named Thomas Ward his "loving brother" in his 1672 will. His 1st wife was sister of Thomas Ward's wife, making him a brother-in-law, but Samuel's wife at the time he d was Mary, dau. of Lucy (Ward) Page. Was "loving brother" the relationship from his 1st or 2nd m? Thus, the evidence that Thomas was a brother of Lucy is uncertain.

ANNE, b about 1622; emigrated in April 1637 as a servant of her brother-in-law Robert Page. At Hampton, N.H. she m Edward Colcord about 1640; he was b about 1615; he bought the James Hall mill in Exeter, then moved to Dover 1640, to Hampton in 1644, to Saco in 1668, back to Hampton in 1673. He d 10 Feb. 1681/2; 11 ch.; she d 24 Jan. 1688 at Hampton

St. Mary's Church, South Walsham, Norfolk.

Ref.: Parish Registers; Probate Records

JOHN MOULTON (*Robert*) of Ormsby, Norfolk, England, was born probably about 1525-1530. He married, probably about 1555-65, Thomasine, who was perhaps nee Green, as John referred to his brother-in-law, William Green. John Moulton died testate in 1573, naming his mother, Margaret, who was then dead, and his brother, Thomas who was then living. An abstract of John's will follows.

> 22 June 1573 - the will of John Moulton of Ormsby Saint Margaret, county Norfolk, yeoman....to be buried in the parish church of Ormsby in the middle aisle.. to my curate William Ballard for tithes forgotten 3s.4d...for the reparations of the church 6s.8d., to the poor men's box 12d... to John Moulton my son the house and land that I dwell in at age 21...to Robert Moulton my son the house and land that was Margaret Moulton's my late mother being in Ormsby and same of the land in Caster, excepting 4 acres in Ormsby which I have sold unto William Green my brother in law, and I make my brother Thomas Moulton my attorney to deliver the said 4 acres to the said William Green at age 21 (a lengthy description of the 4 acres and who the neighbors were)...to said son John two geldings valued at £3 each or else £6, my shallow cart with harness to the same, my bed in the solar room, featherbed, bolster, sheets, a downbed, a pillow with the bier, a milk cow, 10 ewes and 10 lambs, 5 combs of seed wheat, 5 of food barley, 3 of fetches, my best and biggest brass pot, 2 pewter platters and a latten candle stick, unto him the table in the house, form and bench...to Robert my son a mare of value 40s. and a milk cow, 5 ewes, 5 lambs and my tumbrell or work cart, a pair of sheets, a flock bed with a transom and a coverlet, a brass pot, two platters or dishes of pewter, 5 combs of food wheat, 5 of food barley, one of fetches.... to Margaret my daughter £5 at day of marriage or age 20.. to Grace my daughter £5 at day of marriage or age 20.. all other goods unbequeathed to wife Thomasine Moulton, she and William Battololy of Caster to be executors, he to have 40s. and my brother Thomas to be supervisor and he to have 40s. Witnesses: William Burywey, Scriptor, William Green, Robert Green and others. Proved 1 October 1573. (Reference: Archdeaconry of Norwich Wills, 1573, folio 201)

Children, probably all born at Ormsby:

8 JOHN, prob. eldest son, b after 1553 as he was under age in 1573 when his father made his will; m 14 June 1584 at Hemsby, Anne Taylor, dau. of William. Hemsby is east of Ormsby and on the coast. 8 ch.; he d late 1637; she survived him.

ROBERT, under 21 in 1573

MARGARET, under 21 in 1573

GRACE, under 21 in 1573

Ref.: Parish Registers; Probate Records at Norwich

ROBERT PAGE of Acle, Norfolk, England, is the earliest Page ancestor that can be positively identified as such. He was born before 1550 and died between 20 April 1587, the date of his will, and 15 May following when it was probated. His wife, named in the will and living at the time, was Martha. He also named four children, the only ones known.

20 April 1587 - The will of ROBERT PAGE of Acle in Norfolk, husbandman. My body shall be buried in the church-yard at Acle. I bequeath to Edmund Page my son my houses, tenements and lands in Acle with all pertaining thereto, to him and his heirs forever. To Robert Page my son £10, to be paid 20s yearly for ten years. To Cicely Page my daughter £5. 20s. to be paid each year until £5 is paid. To Margaret Page my daughter £5 to be paid in like manner. I will that Martha my wife shall have for life the house where John Taylor now dwelleth, and 10s. yearly, to be paid 5s. half yearly or as she may need. Also the hole furniture, one table now in the house where Gosling dwelleth, etc. All the rest of my goods, cattells, implements and stuff of household I bequeath to the disposition of my executor, and I appoint Edmund Page my son my sole executor. Witnesses: Peter Downhill, Ralph Cootes, John Plum, William Smith, William Johnson, and John Downing. Proved in Acle 15 May 1587 by the executor.
(Archdeaconry Court of Norwich, Barnes 1587)

Below are abstracts of two early wills of Pages of Acle who were no doubt closely related to Robert.

2 December 1534 - Will of JAMES PAGE of Acle. To be buried in the churchyard of St. Edmund King and Martyr in Acle. To the Church of St. Mary burgh within Flegge [Fleggborough] 6s. 8d. To the reparation of the Church at Ridlington a quarter of malt. The residue of my goods and chattells whatsoever, I bequeath to my executors and I ordain Henry Page of Acle and James Hall, mariner, of Burgh in Flegge executors. Witnesses: William Corbet, Thomas Calne, with others. Proved at Acle 16 January 1535 by the executors.
(Archdeaconry Court of Norwich, 1529-1536, folio 152)

8 May 1450 - Will of ROBERT PAGE of Acle... I Robert Page desire my body to be buried in the churchyard of St. Edmund King and Martyr at Acle. To the high altar 12 pence. To the emendation of the sd church 8s. To the light of the Blessed Virgin Mary in sd church 6d. To the brotherhood of St. Edmund King and Martyr 2s. The residue of my goods I give to my executors. I appoint Nicholas Hardy and Margaret my wife my executors. Proved at Norwich 16 May 1450 by Nicholas Hardy with powers reserved to Margaret wife of the deceased.
(Consistory Court of Norwich, 1448-1455, Alleyn 41.)

Children, named in their father's will:

EDMUND, inherited the homestead in Acle and was appointed executor 15 May 1587.

12 ROBERT, m Margaret Goodwin 16 July 1598; 5 ch. per his will; he d in July 1617.

CICELY

MARGARET

Ref.: N.E.H.G.S.-66

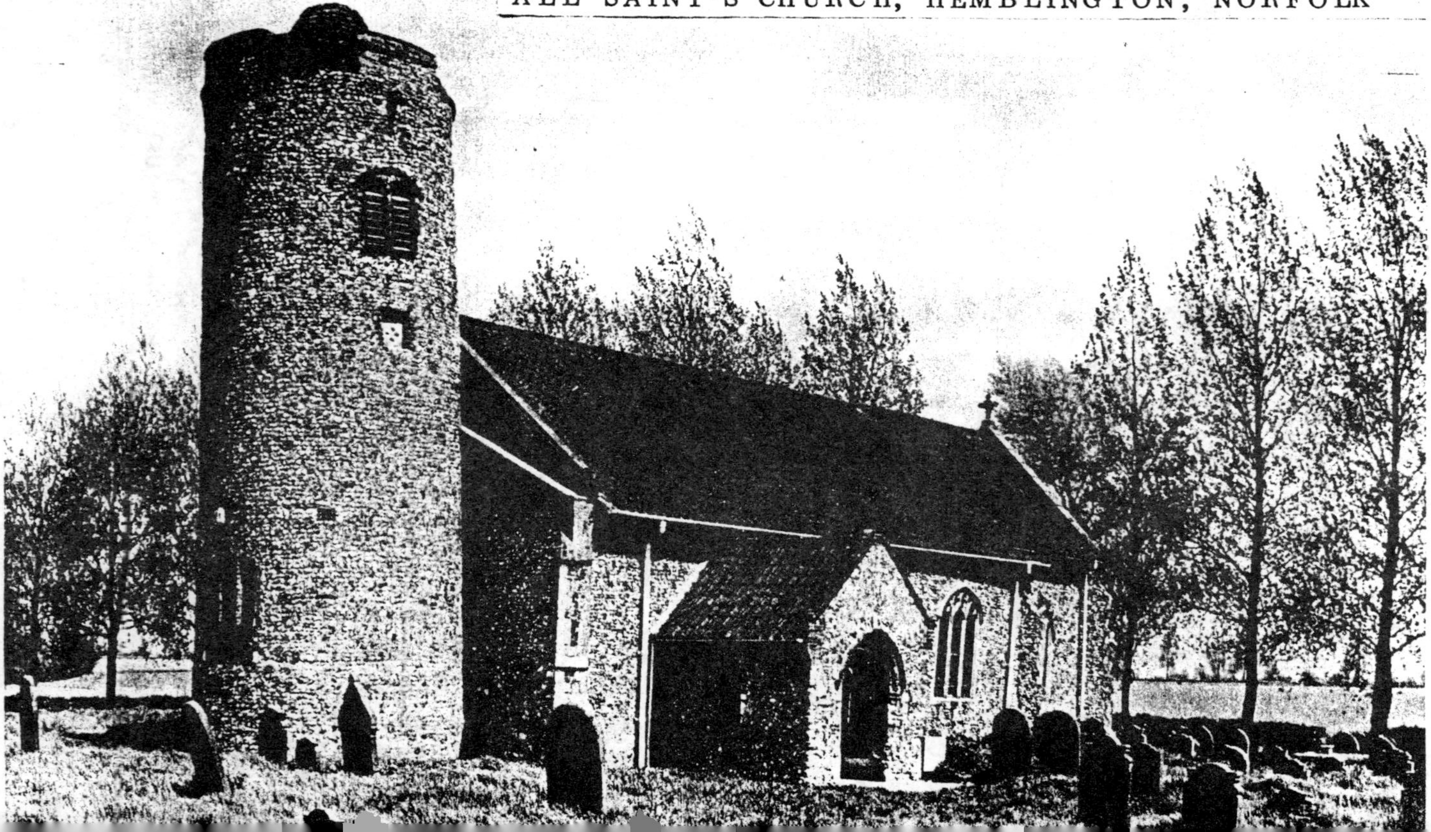

ALL SAINT'S CHURCH, HEMBLINGTON, NORFOLK

26

FRANCIS GOODWYN (*John, William, William? John? Vincent*) of Blofield and later of Hemblington, Norfolk, England, was a moderately wealthy farmer with extensive land holdings, many cattle and other livestock, servants, and children. All this is deduced from his will. His first wife was the Katherine Goodwyn who was buried at Hemblington on 25 September 1584. On 12 October 1585 at Hemblington, he married the widow Joan Lynes. She brought with her several children and property from her first marriage, all of which is evident from their wills. Francis was buried 25 June 1602 at Hemblington. Joan was buried on 17 March 1610/11 at Ranworth. These villages are all within a two mile radius.

21 June 1602 - the will of FRANCIS GOODWYN of Hemlyngton in the county of Norfolk, husbandman... sick in body... to my wife Joan two of my best milk cows, and one young heifer, my sorrel ambling mare colt, my red ambling gelt colt, ten wethers and five ewes, one of my best skeps with bees, one shock cart with steel wheels, one good plow with the irons thereto belonging with sufficient furniture and trace belonging to a plow, one pair of cart trace appertaining to a pynn or hand hoist, one chillers trace and furniture, one pair of harrows and harrowing trace and collars to them, five combs of good wheat and three combs of good barley or malt, to be taken out of my crop of corn now growing and to be delivered by my son John out of that crop, one half of all my wool, and one half the cloth that is or shall be made of this year's wool, the other half to son John.. in default of their consent, to be divided at discretion of my neighbor Henry Black and William Goodwyn of Burlingham... milk neats shall remain as now they be, to be pastured.... until the feast of St. Michael Archangel next... profits and produce towards maintenance of my wife, children, rest of my household and workmen, wife to have the government thereof..to wife two of my best hogs, two of my best young shoats, 10 geese and a gander, six hens and a cock, six ducks and one drake, all to be kept with the rest of my swine and fouls at said farm till the feast of St. Margaret... to said wife all such stuff of household as were her own before her marriage to me, my best featherbed, my best pair of sheets, and a blanket and bolster, my best covering, etc...said Henry and William and my cousin Thomas Goodwyn of Ranworth.... remainder to son John except my brew and dye vessels which are to be divided betwixt them..to son John the farm now in my occupation in Hemblington and Burlyngham, and all such plows, carts, harrows and other implements not heretofore given or hereafter, also all the rest of my bees and bee skeps, four of my best work mares and geldings, my bay horse foal, three weanling

calves and five milk neat.... children and servants shall have such sheep and lambs which are among my sheep but are known to be their own, rest to son John...wife to have one weanling calf, son John to have one steer and one heifer now at market paying the toll due for their feed... to Peter Goodwyn my son £5 to be paid by son John in Hemblington church porch within two years...to Elias Goodwyn my son £5 within 4 years...to Frances Goodwyn my daughter £3 within five years...to Susan my daughter 20s. after age of 21...to Mary my daughter £3 at age 21...to said Susan my daughter my little brindle cow...to Margaret my daughter the wife of Robert Page my black cow known by the name of the marsh cow...to Sampson my son my young bay colt and to Elias my son my bay mare colt...to Peter my son my young gray colt...John upon reasonable request to be made at my now mansion house in Hemblington within 21 days next after my decease shall become bound by obligation formal......John to pay Robert Lynes all such debts as I do owe him...to the maintenance of the parish church of Hemblington 40d., to the poor 40d. ..to wife all crops upon any of my lands in Ranworth and Panxforth which I now hold in the right of my wife...rest of my goods and movables unbequeathed except armour and weapons which I give to my son John, to executors whom I ordain and make: John --------, and Sampson Goodwyn my son. Witnesses: William Goodwyn, John Robinson, clerk, Thomas Goodwyn and Henry Black. Proved 21 July 1602. (Norwich Archdeaconry Court 1602-3, #62)

9 February 1610/11 - the will of JOAN GOODWYN of Raynworth in county Norfolk, widow..... to be buried in Raynworth churchyard...to son Robert Lynes lands in Raynworth and Panxforth.. to my son Sampson Goodwyn £20, etc...to daughter Elizabeth Lynes £3, a red cow, ewe sheep, etc...to daughter Susan Goodwyn £5, a calf, son Robert Lyne to keep till a young cow, etc...to daughter Mary Goodwyn £5 and one weaned black calf......ewe sheep, etc...to daughter Elizabeth Sadd £20...to Thomas Downing 20s. after Elizabeth Sadd be paid...to Francis Downing 20s...to Sampson Goodwyn flock transom bed, blanket, sheets, cushion pillow, pillow bere, table cloth and napkins and three pieces of pewter...to Elizabeth Lyns a featherbed, etc...to Susan Goodwyn a bedstead, etc..and down covering, latten candlestick.. to Mary Goodwyn featherbed, feather transom, flock etc. and a white coffer and all in it to be parted with her sister Susan except to daughter Elizabeth Lynes one sheet. Residue to son Robert Lynes, he to be executor. Witnesses: Robert Benshyn, Thomas Redditch the younger, Thomas Wright. Proved 27 April 1611

(Consistory Court of Norwich, Stywarde:73)

Children:

THOMAS, bapt. 5 April 1568 at Blofield, "son of Francis"; he was not named in his father's will, so must have d.y.

JOHN, b prob. 1570; m 1, 18 Jan. 1601/2 at Hemblington, Elizabeth Kypping, if this is the same John; if so, she d, as he m 2, 28 Oct. 1602 at Hemblington, Bridget Beckyt; had ch.: Francis bapt. 10 July 1603, John bapt. 7 Oct. 1604, Faith bapt. 14 Sept. 1606, prob. William bapt. 4 Dec. 1608 (no parents named), Richard bapt. 22 Sept. 1611; 4 ch. living in 1614. John Goodwyn of S. Walsham was buried at Hemblington 5 July 1617 - him????

JAMES, bapt. 21 March 1571/2; buried 21 Sept. 1574

13 MARGARET, b prob. 1574 at Blofield; m 16 July 1598 at Hemblington, Robert Page, son of Robert & Martha of Acle; m rec. at Acle also

FRANCES, bapt. 5 Aug. 1576 at Blofield; m 9 Oct. 1605 at Hemsby, John Younger, *if* same one

PETER, bapt. 23 May 1578 at Blofield; m 10 Oct. 1614 at Billockby, Mary English; he prob. d before 1624

ELIAS, bapt. 30 March 1581 at Blofield; reputed the father of an illeg. son Peter bapt. 22 June 1608 at Ranworth; m 1, ______ ; m 2, 1 Feb. 1616/17 at Norwich, Saint Mary in the Marsh, Dorothy Austin; he was living in 1624

----children by 2nd wife, Joan----

SUSAN, bapt. 9 Sept. 1586 at Hemblington; she d 1614-15 unm.; her will:

21 May 1614 -the will of SUSAN GOODWYN of Ranworth, county Norfolk...to the four children of my brother in law Robert Page of Ormesbye 10s. each...to sister Page 5s...to Peter Gooding 20s..to the four children of my brother John Goodwyn of Hemblingham 5s. each...to the two children of my sister Sadde 20s. each...to Elizabeth Lynes 10s...to my sister Mary Trywell £5....to the eldest daughter of Elias Goodwyn 5s...to the wife of Robert Lynes 20s...to the poor of Ranworth 5s...residue of goods to brother Robert Lyns, he to be executor. Witnesses: Nicholas Brechbye, Thomas Wright, scriptor. (Ref.: Arch. Norf. Book 1614-15, p. 302)

SAMPSON, bapt. 17 Feb. 1588/9 at Hemblington; he was living in 1610, but no further record of him

MARY, bapt. 27 March 1592 at Hemblington; m 11 Oct. 1613 at Ranworth, Robert Trevet

Ref.: Parish Registers; Wills proved in the several courts of Norwich; English Goodwin Family Papers, compiled by Frank Farnsworth Starr, 1921; P.R.O. SC12-12/52; E179-152/448, -153/509

It was in Great Yarmouth that Francis Ward, son of Robert, died and was buried in 1647.

ROBERT WARD (*Roger, ?William*) married on 18 November 1566 at Stokesly-with-Herringby, Alyce Pixton, a widow with at least two children. She was perhaps the widow of Thomas Pixton of Tattersett who died in 1562. Robert Ward's name is on the Ormsby Rental Roll of circa 1570 and on the 1593 and 1597 Subsidy Rolls for Filby. Robert Ward was buried 2 January 1598/9 at Filby. Alyce Ward, widow, was buried on 23 March 1608/9, also at Filby. Abstracts of their wills follow.

30 December 1598 - the will of ROBERT WARD of Filby, county Norfolk, yeoman.. sick of body... to be buried in the church of Filby in consideration of which I give 6s. 8d. towards the reparation of the church..to Alice my wife all my household goods except the bed wherein I now lie and one brass pot sometime Elizabeth Isabelle's which I give to my youngest son Francis Ward... to wife Alice two milk neat, one red, the other black with a white face, three combs of barley wheat, three combs of malt, all my butter and cheese... to Anne Filby my daughter £10 of which £5 payable one half year after my decease, the other £5 two years after the decease of wife Alice.. to Katherine Arnolde my daughter £10 payable £5 within one year and a half after my decease, and £5 within three years after decease of wife Alice..to Francis Ward my youngest son £5 within 4 years after decease of wife and one milk cow or 40s. at day of his marriage, also three acres, three rods of copy hold held of the manor of Filby late [held by] John Pyxton son of Thomas Pyxton, one horse or 40s... Joan Filby the daughter of Thomas Filby shall have 20s. at age 5... 20s. to the child my said daughter Katherine Arnolde is now with at age 5, but if either of these children die before age 5, then the legacy to Elizabeth and Joan Larwood the daughters of William Larwood of Ormsby ... to Katherine Harbacke my servant 6s. 8d... to William Anthony my servant 3s. 4d. at age 21... to Roger Ward my eldest son one tenement called Cettwood's being copyhold of the manor of Holmehalle in Filby and 2 acres and one rod held of the manor of Filby Cleares in Filby.. residue to my eldest son Roger Ward, he to be sole executor.... Thomas Ward my brother to be supervisor. Witnesses: Thomas Sturrye, William Prior, John Mathewes and John Thornill, clerk. Proved 23 January 1598 (Ref.: Norwich Archdeaconry Wills - 272 Lynidre)

12 February 1603/4 - the will of ALICE WARD of Filby, county Norfolk, widow, the relict of Robert Ward of the same town, deceased, being aged, feeble and weak in body..to be buried in the church or churchyard of Filby..executor my youngest son Francis Ward...to the reparation of the parish church of Filby 3s. 4d...to Roger Ward my son all household implements which I left where my said son Roger now dwelleth at my departure from the house at the feast of Saint Michael the Archangel 1600, viz. a cheese press, two cowles, a great chair, two trundle bedsteads, a pair of malt querns, a hair cloth for the kiln, a mynging* trough, a form, certain ale tubs, a long chest, a bed bolster, one pillow, one stand together with the rest of all such implements as I left in his custody at my removing.. to said son Roger the best spote# of the three, for life, then to William Ward my grandchild, unto whom also a brass posnet at age 21...to my son John Pixstoane a cow and a cupboard standing in the parlor where I now dwell, for life, then to William Pixstoan his son my grandchild, in tail to Alice Pixstone his daughter my grandchild...to daughter Margaret now the wife of William Larwood a little featherbed that was her father Pixstons, for life, then to Thomas Larwood my grandchild, in tail to Edmund Larwood my grandchild, then to Elizabeth Larwood, then to Joan Larwood...to said daughter Margaret my best petticoat and my best cloak.. to daughter Ann or Agnes now the wife of Thomas Filby my best gown, the best pillow of the three, a pair of sheets, for life, then to Joan Filby her daughter my grandchild, in tail to the rest of the children of the said Thomas and Agnes...jointly to my two daughters Agnes, wife of Thomas Filby, and Katherine, wife of John Arnold, all my best linen...to Katherine a cow, then to her children......to grandchild Joan Filby my bible, posted bedstead, at age 21...to grandchild Suzan Filby 2s. 6d. and my damask chest at 21...to youngest daughter of son John Pixstoan born in or about September 1603, 2s. 6d. at age 21 ..to grandchild William Ward a brass posnet at 21...to my daughter Agnes the wife of Thomas Filby a bearing sheet and a spreading sheet upon condition that the said Agnes and her husband shall lend the said two sheets unto my other daughters or daughters in law for their affairs and business of childbirth only...to my four grandchildren the children of John Pixston my eldest son, that is to William, Alice, John and Nicholas Pixston each 2s. 6d. at age 21...to my four grandchildren the children of William Larwood and Margaret my daughter, that is, to Elizabeth, Joan, Thomas and Edmund Larwood, to each 2s. 6d. at age 21...to Joan Filby daughter of Thomas and Agnes Filby my daughter 2s. 6d. at age 21...to my grandchild Elizabeth Arnold the daughter of John Arnold and Katherine his wife my daughter 2s. 6d. at age 21...to my grandchild William Ward son of Roger Ward my son, 2s. 6d. at age 21...to Alice Malliatt my goddaughter a new sheet and a pewter platter.... to Katherine Harbert my servant...residue to my younger son Francis Ward.... published 18 March 1608. Witnesses: Godfrey Pendleton, clerk & writer, Robert Clark, Thomas Pixstoan, Richard Malliott, William Malliott. Proved 28 March 1609. (Ref.: Norwich Archdeaconry, 162 Remare)

Children, by first husband ______ Pixton:

JOHN (Pixton), b prob. about 1560; he was m with 4 ch.: William, Alice, John, Nicholas, per will of 1604 of his mother

MARGARET, (Pixton), b prob. 1562; m William Larwood; by 1604, she had: Elizabeth, Thomas, Edmond, William bapt.21 Feb. 1591, Joan bapt. 8 Dec. 1594, Dorothy 13 Jan. 1597/8; the 3 bapt. were at N. Elmham if same family. Joan & 1st 3 only ch. living in 1604

Children by Robert Ward, baptized at Filby:

ROGER, bapt. 27 Dec. 1567; m Elizabeth ______ ; a son William bapt. 2 Feb. 1600/01; in 1611 Subsidy Roll; he was buried 26 Feb. 1618/19. His will:

> 24 July 1618 - the will of ROGER WARD, yeoman, of Filby, county Norfolk ... to be buried in the churchyard at Filby ... to wife Elizabeth ... to son William ... to Elizabeth Arnold 30s. (Norfolk Archdeaconry Court Wills)

ANNE/AGNES, bapt. 20 March 1569/70; she m Thomas Filby; ch.: Joan bapt. 20 Feb. 1597/8 at Beeston (if same Joan), Susan

KATHERINE, bapt. 30 April 1573; m John Arnold; had a dau. Elizabeth by 1604

RICHARD, bapt. 8 Sept. 1575; d.y.

DOROTHY, bapt. 8 Feb. 1576/7; d same day per B.T. (twin?)

CYCELYE, bapt. 18 Feb. 1576/7; buried same day per P.R.

ELIZABETH, bapt. 23 March 1577/8; buried 8 April 1578

14 FRANCIS, bapt. 25 Oct. 1579; m Susanna Brown in June 1603 at Filby

* myngging = minging = mixing
# spote = spout?

Ref.: Parish Registers; Probate Records

32

ROBERT MOULTON of Ormsby, Norfolk, England, was probably born about 1485. He died testate in 1535, his wife Margaret surviving him. She was dead by 1573, according to their son John's will. She probably died soon after 1549 when the last record of her is found. His will in full follows.

The surname Moulton is a place name deriving from the parish of Moulton, which is 8 miles southwest of Ormsby and 9 miles east southeast of Norwich. There are at least ten towns in England so named, but this one in Norfolk surely must be the source of this family's name.

> In the name of god amen the 4th day of June the year of our lord god Mcccccxxxv [1535], I Rob't multon of Ormysby being in good mynd & memory makyng this my last will & testament in this manner following. First I bequeath my sowell to all myghty god, our lady seynte Mary & to all the holy company of heaven, and my body to be buried in the churchyard of Saint Margaret in Ormysby aforesaid. Also, I bequeath to the high altar for my tythes negligently forgotten 16d. Also, to the reparation of the church aforesaid 3s. & 4d. Also, to the gyld of Saint Margaret 3s. & 4d. Also, to the gyld of our lady 3s. & 4d. Also, to the place of sick men in yer-----g 4d. Also, I bequeath to my daughter Margaret 20s. Also, to Isabel my daughter 40s. Also, to Thomas my son 4 marks starling. Also, I will that John my son shall have my house & my land after the decease of his mother getting from him 16 pounds of good lawful money of England to be paid in the space of 7 years to the performance of his father's will. The residue of my goods not bequeathed by me, I give them to my executors whom I ordain & make Thomas Watts & Margaret my wife, to do for me & bring me honestly to the earth as they think best for to do.
> In witness hereof: Thomas Stodratt, Vicar of Ormysby, & Thomas Watts ---? --- of the same town, as with many others. (Reference: Norwich Consistory Court, N.P.-30)

Children, probably all born at Ormsby:

16 JOHN, eldest son; m Thomasine (?Green perhaps); he d testate 1573; 2 sons, 2 daus. per his will

MARGARET, prob. m by 1535 as she received only half as much as Isabel and Thomas, suggesting she had already received something. Usually this was at a child's marriage. She prob. m William Green who was buried 18 July 1573 at Filby. She m 2, 9 Jan. 1576, Thomas Morley at Filby.

ROBERT, perhaps; if so, he d.y. before 1535

ISABEL, possibly; she or Margaret m ______ Green

THOMAS, b about 1513 in Ormsby as aged 74 in 1587 per deposition; m Joan Green, dau. of Richard; 4 known ch.; d in Sept. 1587

Ref.: Parish Registers; Probate Records at Norwich

52

JOHN GOODWYN (*William, ?William, ?John, Vincent*) of Blofield, Norfolk, England, was born probably between 1505 and 1515. He was perhaps the grandson of William, son of John Goodwyn who died testate in 1465, and which John was perhaps the son or grandson of Vincent, who died testate in 1433. Vincent is the earliest known Goodwyn living in Blofield and was probably the ancestor of all the later ones. An abstract of the brief will of Vincent Goodwyn follows.

> 6 December 1433 - the will of Vincent Goodwyn of Blofield. to be buried in the churchyard of Saint Andrew, Blofield... to son William...to wife Asilia. Proved 26 November 1433. (Ref.: Consistory Court of Norwich, Surflete 129)

John Goodwyn and his wife Alice, her surname unknown, were married about 1537. She was surely the widow Agnes Goodwyn who was buried at Blofield on 24 February 1565/6. Alice and Agnes were synonymous at that time. John died before 1563 as is implied by the will of his son Thomas.

Roger Goodwyn of Blofield, who had children baptized in 1546, '48, '50, and '54, was a brother to John. He probably had other children born before 1546, as did John, but the parish register for baptisms starts in 1546, so we have no exact record of such children's births or baptisms.

Children, baptized at Blofield:

THOMAS, b prob. about 1538; buried 7 Jan. 1562/3 at Blofield; unm.; his will, made the day he died:

> 6 February 1562/3 - the will of Thomas Goodwin of Blowfield in the county of Norfolk, husbandman... to be buried in the churchyard of Blowfield Saint Andrew..to John Goodwin my brother all my lands and tenements within the township of Blowfield or elsewhere in Norfolk on condition that he make bond with Elys Bodyphant of Blowfield to perform the following: to pay to Cycelie Goodwin my sister 20s. within one year...to my brother Francis Goodwin 40s. within the next year after payment to Cycelie, then another 40s. the next year...to Myles Goodwyn my brother at age 24, 20s... to Elizabeth Goodwyn my sister at day of marriage 20s.. to James Goodwyn my brother at age 21, 20s..if brother John refuse to lay in bond, then lands to brother Francis on same terms... residue to Alice Goodwin my mother whom I make my sole executrix, she to have her dwelling
> my sole executrix, she to have her dwelling in my house for life...I have surrendered my copyhold lands according

to the use of this my will unto the hands of Ellys Bodyphant bond tenant of this manor in the presence of John Bussye, John Churche the younger, & Edmund Bodyphant. Thomas Edon scriptor. Proved 29 January 1563/4. (Ref.: Norwich Consistory Court 211 Knightes)

JOHN, b about 1540; m about 1564, Elizabeth ——; 7 ch.; buried 29 April 1593 "at ye pit"; widow Elizabeth Goodwin was buried 11 Dec. 1616. His will:

25 April 1593 - the will of John Goodwyne of Blowfield...to be buried in the churchyard... to eldest son Thomas Goodwyn both my tenements with 8 acres, one called Nicholas at Gran, the other called Gybbes, said Thomas to pay my three daughters 5 marks each as follows: to daughter Grace 33s. 4d. within one year, same a year later, then to Joan, then to Agnes in same manner... son Thomas to pay son Robert £5 at age 21; if he die to son John...to son William my tenement called Dirabs with close of 2 acres, he to pay my son John £5 at age 21...residue to wife Elizabeth, she to be executrix. Witnesses: Robert Bussye, Robert Corpe, Edmund Bodyvant, William Woodcock, the writer, and others. Proved 20 August 1593. (Ref.: Archdeaconry of Norwich, Holmes 86)

CICELEY, b about 1542; m 22 Jan. 1560/61 at Blofield, William Cook

26 FRANCIS, b about 1544; m 1, Katherine ——; 7 ch.; she was buried 25 Sept. 1584 at Hemblington; m 2, 12 Oct. 1585, widow Joan Lynes; 3 ch.; he was buried 25 June 1602 at Hemblington; she was buried 17 March 1610/11 at Ranworth; both d testate

MYLES, bapt. 8 Sept. 1546, "son of John"; m 16 June 1574, Sisley Barnard; 5 ch. bapt. at Blofield: Elias bapt. 3 Oct. 1575, Elizabeth bapt. 23 May 1578, Cicilie bapt. 16 Feb. 1579/80, Robert bapt. 26 Dec. 1583, Myles bapt. 30 Oct. 1586; he d April 1624 at S. Walsham; the wife who survived him was Margaret; his will:

24 April 1624 - the will of Miles Goodwine of South Walsham. to be buried in the church of our Lady of South Walsham... to wife Margaret...to poor of Walsham, Ranworth, Pauxford, Hemblington, Upton, Acle, Woodbastwick ...to Mary Betts, wife of Robert Betts of Ranworth a house and cottage called Tygate Green.. to wife Margaret the tenement where I now dwell called Pilson Green for life, then to Miles son of Roger Goodwine my nephew; if he die then to William son of John Goodwin of Hamblington, deceased. If Miles come to it he to pay £10 to his brother John, otherwise William to pay the £10...to each of the children of James Goodwine of Strumpshaw, blacksmith 40s...to each child of the wife of Humfrey Warren of Blofield which she had by John Goodwin her deceased husband 40s..to Bryant Estoke of Blofield corner 40s..to John Hewke of South Walsham and Elizabeth his wife £4....to each child of Thomas Galt of Blofield, thackster, 40s...to Myles Goodwin of Hempstead, my godson, £5...to each child of Ales Tetford which she had by

her husband Sponer, deceased, 40s.... to Ellyce Goodwin son of Francis Goodwyn of Hemblington 40s....to Swanie daughter of Ellen Cooper my niece £5...to each child of Andrew Beare of Ranworth by Margaret Goodwin my niece 40s...to child of Peter Goodwin late of Oby deceased, 40s. to John Younger of Acle 20s..to each child of John Goodwin son of Francis Goodwin late of Hemblington deceased £4... to each child of William Guchen of Ranworth 40s... to each child of John Jolly which he had by Barbary his wife deceased, 40s...to each child of Robert Beettes of Ranworth 40s...to Ales Chamberlayne my apprentice 40s. in 6 years. to Bennett Hornor, daughter of John Hornor my late servant 20s....to Nicholas Reman of Norwich, currier, £5....to William Reaman of Salthouse £-... to Robert Goodwin of Blofield sole executor..... forgives Roger Ingle of Great Yarmouth, his kinsman, what he owes him... Edward Goodwin of Ranworth, his nephew, to be supervisor, or if he will not be so bound, then Myles Goodwin of Hempstead, his godson, to be executor. Witnesses: William Cobb, Robert Fann and John Hewke. Proved 19 May 1624. (Ref.: Archdeaconry of Norwich, Book 1624, folio 23)

ELIZABETH, bapt. 12 Jan. 1548/9, "dau. of John"; d.y.
EDMUND, bapt. 8 Jan. 1550/51, "son of John"; prob. d.y.
JAMES, bapt. 8 Jan. 1550/51, "son of John", (twin?); m Cicely Rising 27 April 1578 at Blofield
JOAN, bapt. 29 Jan. 1557/8, "dau. of John"; buried 8 Feb. 1557/8

Ref.: Parish Registers; Probate Records at Norwich

CDR.

SAINT ANDREW'S CHURCH,
BLOFIELD, NORFOLK

56

ROGER WARD was possibly a son of William and Margaret Ward, which William was named in a 1524 Court Roll (SC2-193/36). Roger married Katherine, who was buried on 30 January 1572/3 at Filby, Norfolk. On 28 October 1573 at Great Yarmouth, he remarried to Cycely Baldry, the widow of Edmund Baldry. She had children by this first marriage. Roger Ward is named in the 1546 Subsidy Roll at Filby (E179-151/348) and later Rolls there. A 1563 Rental Roll for Ormsby lists his name, confirming his holdings there (SC12-22/24). Roger Ward the elder was buried 4 July 1579 at Filby. On 28 January 1598/9 Cycely Huggen, "sometyme ye wyef of Roger Warde" was buried. His will follows.

8 May 1579 - the will of Roger Ward of Filby, county of Norfolk, yeoman...to be buried within the parish church of Filby and in consideration of which 20s. for the reparation of the church... to Sir Robert Stele, parson of Filby, for tithes forgotten 3s.4d...to Thomas Ward my son my head messuage wherein I dwell in Filby sometimes Symon Garrard's which I purchased of Henry Marsham, my bond tenement called Bykerton's, my dovehouse with the barn and the yard and a building commonly called Makin's yard which I purchased of Thomas Whyte of Marsham, and all other lands, tenements, pastures, feedings and breweries.... in Filby, Ormesby and Mautby, etc. except my messuage and tenement in Thrykby which I purchased of John Skott... and except others hereinafter bequeathed to John Ward my son...to my son John Ward my said messuage in Thrykby ... if either Thomas or John wish to sell their property the other to have right of first refusal......to Margaret Norwich my daughter £20...I do forgive unto Henry Church of Runham, my son in law, all he oweth me.... to Lucy Church my daughter the wife of the said Henry Church 40s. and to each of her children 20s.... except Roger Church their son to whom 40s...at their ages of 21...to each of my godchildren 12d... to each of the children of my son Robert Ward 20s. at age 21...to the township of Filby two milk neat to the use of the poor...son Thomas to have his legacy immediately after my decease... Cecilye now my wife shall have her dwelling in the south parlor of my said head messuage with free and peaceful egress and regress at all times, sufficient meat and drink, for one month after my decease, then she to have five combs of wheat and five combs of malt and one of my milk neat at the said months end when she shall depart, conditional that my executors shall quietly and peacefully receive to dispose of as they see fit all such household things as I have at Yarmouth... Sons Thomas and John to be executors, they to pay that

£100 which is to be paid to my wife Cycilye after my decease.....residue of household goods to her and her children in performance of the last will of her late husband Edmund Baldrye. Witnesses: Thomas Skurrye, John Speede, William Maryote, John Watson, clerk, and William Thirkill. Proved 26 August 1579. (Ref.: N.C.C.-Woodstock 276)

Children, presumably all born at Filby:

28 ROBERT, m 18 Nov. 1566 at Stokesly-with-Herringby, Alice Pixton, a widow with ch.; he had 8 ch.; he was buried 2 Jan. 1598/9 at Filby, she 23 March 1608/9, both testate

THOMAS, m 27 Jan. 1572/3, Dynoise Corpe; 7 ch. bapt. at Philby; he was buried 21 May 1616, testate; she was buried 22 April 1628, testate. His name is on the Subsidy Rolls of 1597 & 1611 (E179-153/509 & E179-253/36)

JOHN, m 1, Anne __ __ ; 3 ch. bapt. at Filby; m 2, Agnes Larwood; 4 ch. bapt. at Filby; there may have been but 1 wife, Anne & Agnes being synonymous at times; he was buried 25 April 1600, testate; Agnes d 1616/17.

2 April 1600 - the will of John Ward of Filby...house and lands thereto belonging to wife for life, then to three daughters...daughter Barbara to have a 3 year old heifer at age 16...daughter Katherine to have 26s. 8d. in two years... wife to be executrix...Thomas Ward to be supervisor... daughter Margery to have a 2 year old heifer at age 16. Witnesses: Thomas Ward, John Richman, Roger Ward. Pr. 6 May 1600. (Ref.: Norwich Consistory Court, 36 Force)

LUCY, m 18 June 1564, Henry Church of Runham

MARGARET, m 24 Nov. 1575, Henry Norwich, at Filby

WILLIAM, buried 6 Feb. 1561/2

GRACE, buried 11 July 1566

ROGER, buried 4 July 1599 (not named in father's will, so perhaps a posthumous child

WILLIAM, named in his brother Thomas's will; in Subsidy Roll of 1623 (PRO: E179-153/603); m Anne ____ ; ch.: Rose

Ref.: Parish Registers; Probate Records at Norwich

WILLIAM GOODWYN (*?William, ?John, Vincent*) lived at Blofield, Norfolk. He was probably the son of William, the son of John and Alice, which son died in 1465 and Alice in 1480, both of them testate. John was probably the son of Vincent Goodwyn who died testate in 1433, naming only a son, William, and a wife, Asilia.

22 September 1465 - the will of John Goodwin of Blofield... to be buried in the cemetery of Saint Andrew of Blofield... to the high altar 12d...to the light of Saint Andrew...to the repair of the mother church of Norwich...to leper houses at Norwich... to wife Alice and son William, they to be executors. Witnesses: William Deed, clerk. Proved 13 November 1465. (Consistory Court of Norwich - Cobald 42)

2 January [14]79/80 - the will of Alice Goodwyn of Blofield. to be buried in the churchyard of Saint Andrew of Blofield.. to the high altar 8d...for a light at the crucifix in the same church one pound of wax...for Saint Andrew two pounds of wax...to Saint John the Baptist a half pound of wax...to the Blessed Mary a half pound of wax... for the restoration of the church of Plumstead a half coomb of pork..to my executors to arrange a celebration for my soul.. after my death a trental of 30 masses.... 8d. for a suitable celebration & prayers for my soul & which prayers to be held yearly for three years next following death...to the brothers of the convent at Norwich 2s.6d. ..to Edmond my son 10s... to William my son 10s...to Thomas my son all my common domestic utensils, all the stuff of my husbands...residue, debts paid, to my executors to dispose of for the good of my soul and those who have gone before me...my executors to be John Gyles & Thomas Goodwyn my son to whom for their labors I give 3s.4d...Proved at Blofield 18 October [14]80. (Consistory Court of Norwich - 85 Hubert)

William made his will in March 1528/9 and it was proved two years later, suggesting that he died early in 1531. Altho the will names no places, it is obvious that he was of Blofield, because he referred to the parish church of Saint Andrew which is in Blofield, but more, he bequeathed to his son John the tenement called Gibb's. This tenement was in Blofield and was later bequeathed by John's son, John junior, in his will of 1593. Thus, these two items in his will establish William as being of Blofield and that he was the father of John thru whom this line of descent runs.

William's wife was named Margery.

16 March 1528/9 - the will of William Goodwin the elder of (no place names given)...to be buried in the churchyard of Saint Andrew...to the high altar there 12d. ..to each house of friars in Norwich 12d...to John my son the elder the tenements called Gibbys and Graves and Doraunts in fee simple, and he to be executor, he to keep Margery my wife, his mother...to Little John my son the tenements called Harts... to Roger my son... Proved 20 May 1531. (Ref.: Archdeaconry of Norwich 1529-36, folio 118)

Children:

52 JOHN, the elder, m Alice _____ about 1537; he d before 1563, but Alice was then alive per the will of their son Thomas; 9 ch.

WILLIAM, m _____ ; had Edmond bapt. 1558

ROGER, had 4 ch. bapt. at Blofield: Ellyne 5 May 1546, Adam 24 Dec. 1548, John 11 Feb. 1550, Roger 30 Nov. 1554. A Roger Goodwyn was buried 2 June 1579

JOHN, ("Little John"), named in his father's 1528/9 will

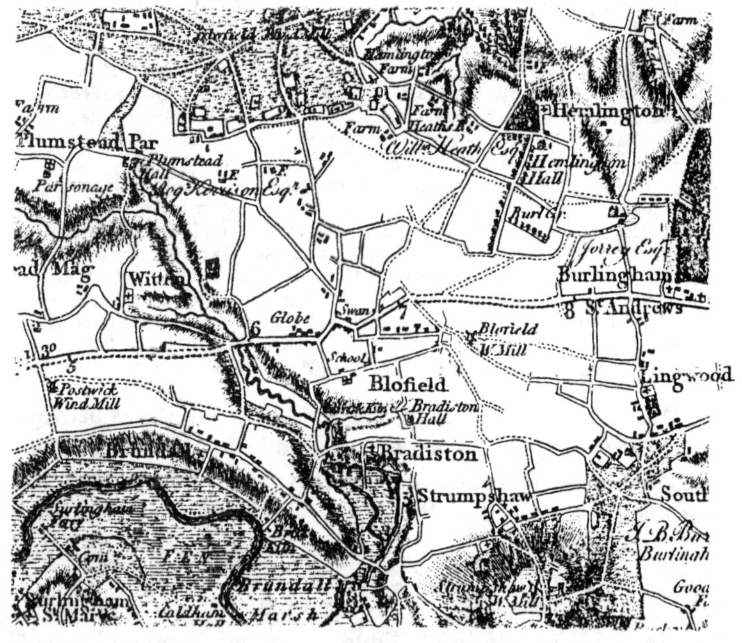

Ref.: Probate Records from the several courts, filed at the Norwich Record Office

2

MILES NUTT (*Michael*) was baptized 7 May 1598 at Barking, Suffolk, England. He married there 16 July 1623, Sarah Branson. They and their one daughter, Sarah, came to New England by 1636 in which year he was a proprietor of Watertown and received a grant in the first distribution and each successive one. He had a 51 acre farm and several other smaller parcels. On 17 May 1637 he was admitted freeman. He then moved to Woburn where he became a proprietor in 1645. He was a selectman in 1647 and during seven of the next nine years. He next moved to Charlestown where he was one of the petitioners in favor of the freedom of the church. His wife died and he married secondly, presumably at Malden about January 1658/9, Sybil, the widow of John Bible and the daughter of John and Margery (Rodford) Tincknell. She was born at Wedmore, Somerset, England, and baptized there on 2 August 1607. She had a daughter, Anne, wife of Robert Jones. At the time of their marriage, Miles Nutt and Sybil made a contract in which he agreed that she should have his house in Malden for the rest of her life and half his estate in the event he died first, or to her daughter Anne if she died first.

A mutual Agreement made the 4th day of Januarie 1658 Betweene Miles Nutt and Sibell his Wife Concerning the Settling of his Estate upon his said wife for her future. Imp. it is my will and reall Intention that my wife Sibell that now is shall have and enjoy hir Life in the house I now live in in Charlestowne after my decease And that she hold and possess it with all things thereunto belonging or in any wise appertaining for terme of her Life. Moreover it is my will & desire that my aforesaid wife Sibell shall have the one halfe part of my whole Estate as well reall as personall of all and whatsoever I may die possessd of at the time of my death Excepting the house above mentioned which she shall Enjoy only for terme of Life, with all appertaining thereunto. Furthermore it is my will and desire that if God take first away by death my wife Sibell before me that in such Case my will is that the sd halfe part of my Estate as above mentioned (at the time of my death and decease) shallbe given and fall unto ye daughter of my Wife Sibell by name Anna the wife of Robert Jones and unto his Children of hir Bodie. And further it is my desire that if after my decease my wife Sibell survives, and that then shee shall desire to live & dwell in my house and land at Maulden in such case my will & desire is that she shall have libertie to have and Enjoy that house & land conditionally that the Estate being equally divided shee give a full Allowance for such hir Libertie as Indifferent men shall Judge meete in that case. And further I doe fully & really make over unto my wife Sibell that tenne pounds which I lately received of William Morris the which he is to receive by exchange of his friends in England. I doe hereby make it safe unto her to be at hir dispose After my death and decease. In witness of truth I have hereunto sett my hand and seals.

Witnesses hereunto
James Cary
Solomon Phipps
Thomas Carter

The mark of
Miles Nutt

Sworne in Court by James Cary & Thomas Carter 15.10.74

Miles Nutt made his will 1 February 1660/61 and in it confirmed his marriage contract with his wife and then left the remainder of his estate to his daughter Sarah, wife of John Wyman, for life, then to her children. He signed by mark. He died at Malden on 2 July 1671, "aged about 73".

The Last Will and Testament of Miles Nutt made the first day of ffebruarie in the yeare 1660 being with sensible and in good understanding - - - I do ffirstly comit my soule unto God who gave it me and my Bodie to be laid in the grave - - - Nextly I doe bequeath unto my wife Sibell all and what so ever I have by deeds under hand and seal of a first date. I say I doe hereby fully ratifie and confirme what is therein exprest & mentioned And no more - - - Nextly whatsoever Estate I shall leave or die seased of ~~I doe bequeath all such Estate~~ more and besides what is by deade given to my wife Sibell, I doe bequeath all such Estate be it more or lesse unto my daughter Sarah the now wife of John Wyman to have and poses whatsoever may appear to be mine shee to enjoy for terme of life And after her decease the said Estate to fall unto her children that are or may bee divided equally between them only the eldest son John to have a double portion. And farther my will is that John Wyman the eldest be Executer unto this my Last will and testament and I doe farther desire and heere nominate my trusted friends Solomon Phipps and John Catler to be my overseers in trust to see this my will performed

Witnesses hereunto James Cary
Solomon Phipps
Thomas Carter

The mark of
Miles Nutt

She remained a widow for three years, then she married thirdly at Malden in 1674, John Doolittle, his second wife. She died 23 September 1690, "aged about 82 years", at Malden.

Children, baptized at Barking, Suffolk:

SARAH, bapt. 19 Sept. 1624; m 5 Nov. 1644, John Wyman of Charlestown; m 2, 25 Aug. 1684, Thomas Fuller; 10 ch.; she d 24 May 1688

CHILD, stillborn, buried 19 Sept. 1627

Ref.: Parish Registers; Genealogies and Estates of Charlestown, Mass., by Wyman; Vital Records

4

MICHAEL NUTT probably grew up in or near Barking, Suffolk, England, for in that parish on 23 May 1586, he married Elizabeth Jackaman. On 5 February 1617/18, she was buried in the same parish. They apparently lived there during the thirty two years they were married, for here their several children were baptized. He married again in 1619 at Old Newton, Suffolk, Christian Godard. Michael Nutt was buried on 24 November 1630 at Barking, Suffolk, "an oulde man of Needham", and she, "a poor widow of Needham" was buried on 29 June 1631, also at Barking. Barking is about one mile southwest of Needham and Old Newton, where he married his second wife, is about five miles north of Needham.

Children, baptized at Barking:

WILLIAM, who had a wife Susan and had the following ch. bapt. at Barking was perhaps also a son of Michael, altho he would have been by an earlier marriage. At least he was certainly a relative. "old William Nutt of Needham" was buried 26 Jan. 1630/31.

1609 July 2, Mary, dau. of William & Susan Nutt bapt.
1611 Oct. 6 Ambrose son of William Nutt bapt.
1614 June 5 Jane (?), dau. of William Nutt bapt.
1617 Sept. 21 William, son of William Nutt bapt.
1623 April 27 John, son of William & Susan Nutt bapt.
1623 May 11 John, son of William & Susan Nutt buried
1625 April 4 Margett, dau. of William Nutt of Needham buried

MICHAEL, bapt. 17 April 1587; buried 29 Oct. 1596
ANNE, bapt. 22 Feb. 1589/90
AMBROSE, bapt. 14 Nov. 1591; buried 27 Sept. 1594
2 MYLES, bapt. 7 May 1598; m 16 July 1623 at Barking, Sarah Branson; 2 ch.; went to N.E.; she d & he m 2, about Jan. 1658/9, Sybil, wid. of John Bible; he d 2 July 1671, "aged about 73"; she m 3, & d 23 Sept. 1690
AMBROSE, bapt. 24 May 1601
MARY, bapt. 17 May 1604; buried 23 Oct. 1605
FRANCIS, bapt. 27 March 1607

Ref.: Parish Registers; Bishop's Transcripts; Suffolk County Probate Records

THE PARISH CHURCH OF SAINT MARY, BARKING, SUFFOLK

Reproduced from *Ecclesiastical Antiquities of the County of Suffolk*, 1818, by Isaac Johnson — courtesy of the County Record Office, Suffolk, England

10

AMBROSE JACKAMAN (*John*) was born about 1540-44, presumably at Mendlesham where he must have grown up. His wife's name was Rose. During the first few years of their marriage, they lived in Mendlesham and here their first three children were baptized. They then moved to Barking, which is nine miles south of Mendlesham. There Rose was buried 3 April 1594. A little over a year later, on 17 August 1595 at Barking, he remarried to Rose Hart, a widow, whose first husband, William Hart, was buried 10 February 1594/5 at Barking.

In the manorial court rolls of Barking, for the court held 2 October 1604, it was presented that Ambrose Jackaman had received from John Woods the surrender of a cottage in Needham in the occupation of Michael Nutt, with a small yard adjoining, which Woods had received by the surrender of Roger Colchester in 43 Elizabeth (1600). Michael Nutt was his son-in-law. Thus, Ambrose Jackaman was living as late as 1604.

Rose Jackaman of Needham, widow, was buried on 30 December 1625. At this time, Needham Market was within the parish of Barking.

Children:

5 ELIZABETH, bapt. 29 Sept. 1567 at Mendlesham; m 23 May 1586 at Barking, Michael Nutt; 7 ch.; she was buried 5 Feb. 1617/18; he m 2, 1619 at Old Newton, Christian Godard; he was buried 24 Nov. 1630 at Barking; she, "a poor widow of Needham" was buried 29 June 1631, also at Barking

JOAN, bapt. 18 Oct. 1569; buried 29 Aug. 1597 at Barking, "a mayd"

JOHN, bapt. 13 Jan. 1571/2 at Mendlesham; m Alice Folkes, 28 Aug. 1597 at Barking

MATTHEW, prob. a son b 1574; buried 8 Sept. 1599 at Barking, tho the rec. reads "of Balam," i.e. Baylham which is the next parish on the southeast

EUNICKIA, bapt. 29 April 1576 at Barking (the entry is quite unclear, only the E & a are certain); Unica buried 17 Oct. 1576

Ref.: Parish Registers; Probate Records at Bury Saint Edmunds; Manorial Records (HA1/BD1/4-6)

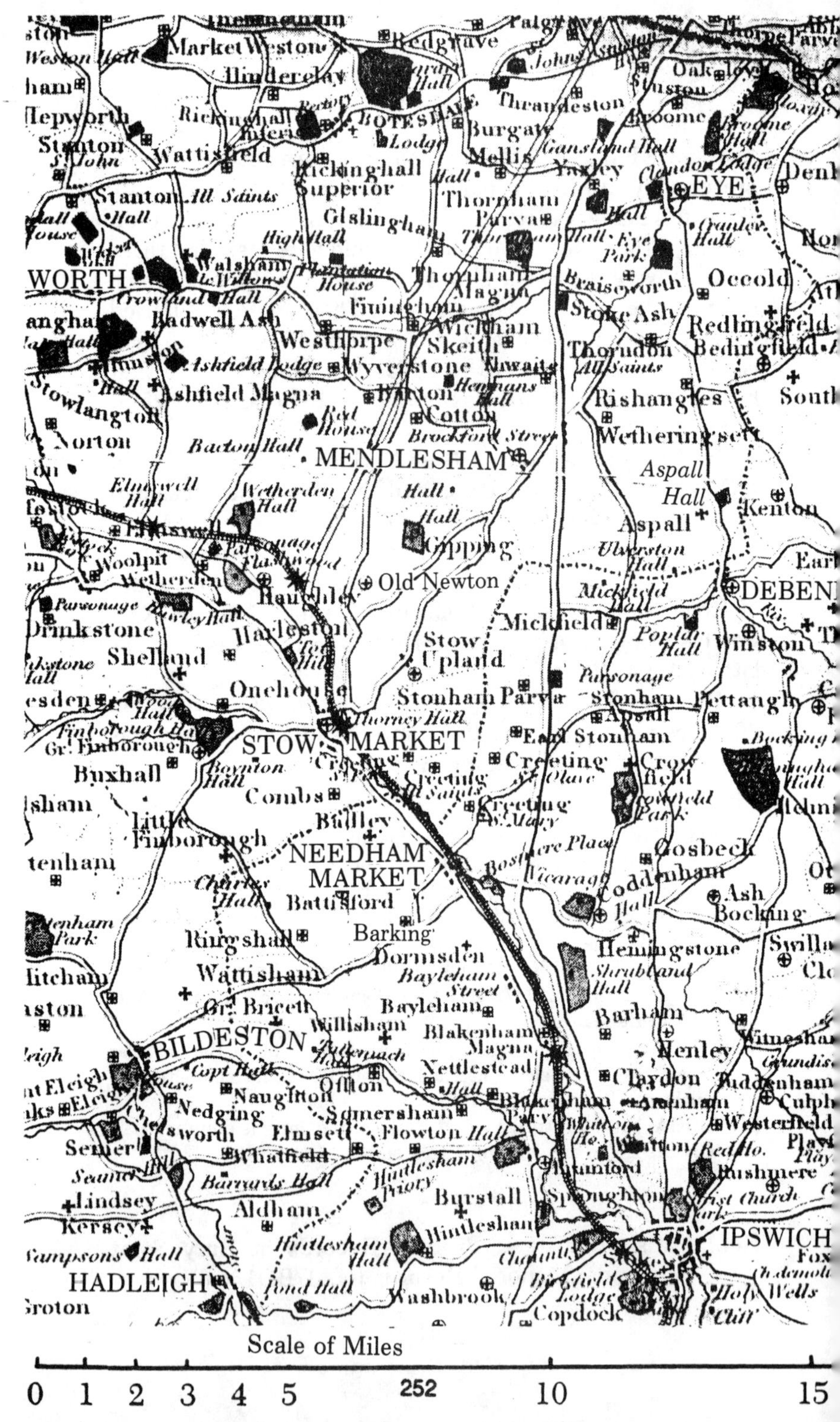

Market Weston
Weston Hall
Redgrave
Hinderclay
Hepworth
Stanton
Wattisfield
Rickinghall Inferior
BOTESDALE
Burgate
Thrandeston
Mellis
Yaxley
EYE
Rickinghall Superior
Stanton All Saints
Thornham Parva
Gislingham
Oakley
Broome
Occold
Redlingfield
Bedingfield
WORTH
Walsham le Willows
Crowland Hall
Badwell Ash
Thornham Magna
Braiseworth
Stoke Ash
Finingham
Westhorpe
Wickham Skeith
Thorndon All Saints
Wyverstone
Thwaite
Ashfield Lodge
Ashfield Magna
Stowlangtoft
Norton
Bacton
Cotton
Rishangles
Wetheringsett
MENDLESHAM
Brockford Street
Aspall Hall
Aspall
Kenton
Bacton Hall
Elmswell Hall
Wetherden Hall
Gipping
Woolpit
Wetherden
Haughley
Old Newton
Mickfield
DEBEN
Drinkstone
Harleston
Stow Upland
Winston
Shelland
Onehouse
Stonham Parva
Stonham Aspall
Pettaugh
Finborough Hall
Gr. Finborough
STOW MARKET
Thorney Hall
Earl Stonham
Creeting
Crowfield
Buxhall
Combs
Creeting All Saints
Creeting St. Mary
Little Finborough
Battisford
NEEDHAM MARKET
Gosbeck
Coddenham
Ash Bocking
Ringshall
Barking
Dormsden
Hemingstone
Shrubland Hall
Wattisham
Baylenham
Barham
Gr. Bricett
Willisham
BILDESTON
Blakenham Magna
Henley
Nettlestead
Offton
Naughton
Nedging
Somersham
Claydon
Tuddenham
Westerfield
Semer
Elmsett
Flowton
Whatfield
Bramford
Rushmere
Lindsey
Kersey
Aldham
Burstall
Sproughton
Hintlesham
Hintlesham Hall
IPSWICH
HADLEIGH
Washbrook
Copdock
Groton
Scale of Miles
0
1
2
3
4
5
10
15

20

JOHN JACKAMAN of Mendlesham, Suffolk, England was probably born about 1510-1515. He married Katherine ——, probably about 1538. He was buried in Mendlesham on 12 January 1566/7. In his brief will he named only his wife and son John. However, there is no reason to doubt that there were other children, that is, Ambrose and Margaret, who appear in the parish records of Mendlesham.

Katherine Jacoman, widow, was married 10 November 1567 to Thomas Sprage.

> 9 January 1567/8 the will of JOHN JAKEMAN ... being sick in body ... to be buried in the churchyard of Mendlesham ... unto Katherine my wife my mansion house in Mendlesham, with the appurtenances, both free and copy, during her natural life, then to son John, provided he shall not claim no *(sic)* debt or duty of my wife, and if that John my son do refuse this my gift, then I will that Katheryn my wife shall sell it and pay my son that debt that is between my son and me. Also, I give unto Katheryn my wife all my moveable goods both within the house and without the house and she to pay my debts and take my debts. Katheryn to be mine executrix. Witnesses: William Doone, Robert Collane, Thomas Alldows & others. Proved 5 July 1567
>
> (Norwich Consistory Court Wills: 19 Bun)

Children, probably all born at Mendlesham:

JOHN, b about 1540; m 1, 14 Oct. 1565 at Mendlesham, Margaret Bumstead; ch.: Faith bapt. 23 Dec. 1571, Joan buried 23 Aug. 1573. Margaret was buried 2 April 1574; he m 2, 20 Oct. 1579 at Mendlesham, Agnes Collman; ch.: Alice bapt. 16 Feb. 1580/81, Margaret bapt. 6 April 1584 (posthumous). His will dated 11 April 1583, pr. 25 March 1584, mentions unborn ch. Agnes m 2, 5 Feb. 1587/8, George Baldwin *alias* Smith, a widower with grown ch. He was buried 28 May 1589. Agnes Jaceman, widow, was buried last day of Oct. 1604, surely her. Having been m not quite 16 months to Baldwin & her ch. bearing the name Jackaman, she undoubtedly resumed that name. There were no other Jackamans in the area. An abstract of his will:

> 11 April 1583 - the will of JOHN JACKEMAN of Mendlesham, county Suffolk, husbandman ... to be buried at Mendlesham ... to Agnes my wife my houses which I now dwell in, for life, she to maintain them in good repair and bring up my children Alice Jackeman and the child she is now with ... to my two daughters and to the child she is now with, my aforesaid house and tenement after the death of their mother Agnes my wife, equally divided ... residue to wife Agnes, she and William Colman to be executors and to each of them 3s.4d. for their pains ... testator has surrendered his copyhold lands to the use of his will ... Witnesses: George Baldwin *alias* Smyth, Henry Dyxon, Robert Culham. Proved 25 March 1584 (R2/39/115; W1/42/46)

10 AMBROSE, b about 1542; m 1, Rose ——— ; she was buried 3 April 1574; he m 2, 17 Aug. 1595 at Barking, Rose Hart, widow of William Hart; 5 ch.; he d after 1604; she, "Rose Jackaman of Needham, widow" was buried 30 Dec. 1625

MARGARET, b about 1545; m 30 July 1570, at Mendlesham, Richard Wills

THE PARISH CHURCH OF SAINT MARY,
MENDLESHAM, SUFFOLK

Reproduced from *Ecclesiastical Antiquities of the County of Suffolk*, 1818, by Isaac Johnson — courtesy of the County Record Office, Suffolk, England

Ref.: Parish Registers; Probate Records at Bury Saint Edmunds, at Norwich, etc.

The Ancestry of

GEORGE PARKHURST & PHEBE LEETE

Compiled by

John Plummer

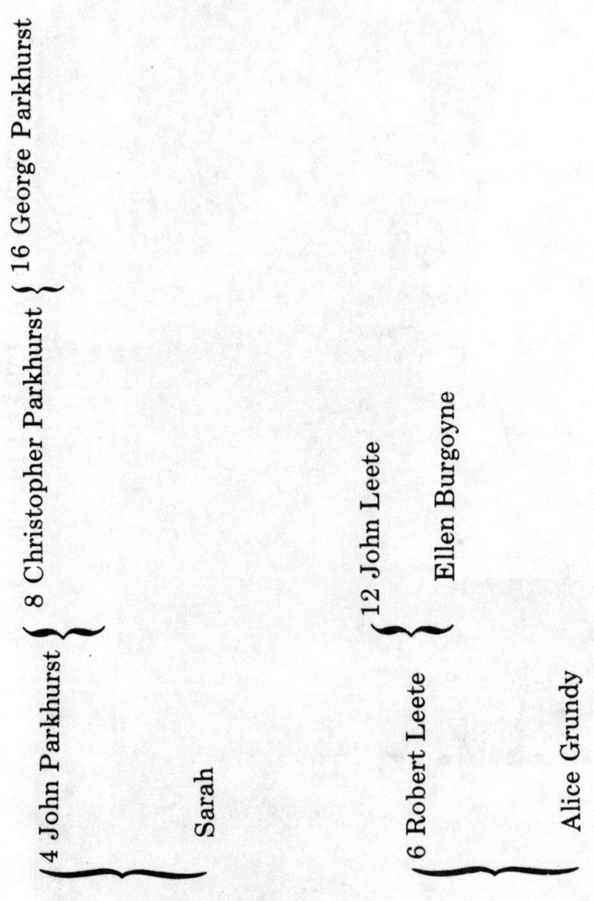

2 George Parkhurst + 3 Phebe Leete

SAINT MARGARET'S CHURCH, IPSWICH, ENGLAND

2

GEORGE PARKHURST (*John, Christopher, George*) was born abut 1588, probably in Ipswich, England. About 1611-12, he married Phebe Leete, the daughter of Robert and Alice (Grundy) Leete of Eversden, Cambridgeshire. Phebe was baptized at Little Eversden on 20 December 1585, the youngest of seven children. They lived in Ipswich where their children were baptized, but after the last one until their departure for England, there is no record of them and they may have lived elsewhere.

George Parkhurst first appears in New England on record at Watertown in 1642 when it was ordered that a highway should be laid out by his house. He is not mentioned in the four grants of land between 25 July 1636 and 9 April 1638. When he arrived and whether he brought with him his wife Phebe is unknown. If he brought her, she died shortly, for about 1644, he remarried to Susanna Simson, the widow of John Simson, who was buried at Watertown on 10 June 1643, leaving two sons and three daughters. By this marriage, George Parkhurst acquired most of the real estate of the deceased. She deeded some of it 9 November 1643 and George Parkhurst sold two acres of it on 16 November 1644, indicating that they married between these dates. He soon left Watertown for Boston where he made the following deed:

> 4 October 1645 - George Parkhurst of Boston sold to John Cooledge and Thomas Hastings of Watertown 6 acres bought of Hue Mason of Watertown for a valuable summe of corne
>
> (1:31)

On 13 June 1655, he sold the last twelve acres of what had been John Simson's land for £21. This last conveyance was made by permission of the General Court, granted 23 May 1655 in response to his petition in which he asserts that he was then "near 67 years old", that he and his wife and most of her children were in destitute condition, that she had had ten children during her twenty years residence in America - seven sons and three daughters (five sons by Parkhurst therefore), that she had gone to London, England with six of her children but found her mother, brothers and sisters unable to do what she had expected, that four of her children had remained in America, and that the petitioner desired to sell the land (apparently all that remained) in order that he might go to the aid of his wife. He probably returned to England as soon as possible after the deed of 13 June 1655, his last act on record in New England. He was probably the "Old George Parkhurst" buried 18 June 1675 at Saint Lawrence, Ipswich, England. He may have been living with his cousin Nathanial Parkhurst, who had six hearths in the Suffolk Hearth Tax of 1674.

The children she took back to England probably remained and grew up there, never returning to America, except Benjamin who, if he was taken back, apparently returned as a young man to his American brothers and sisters and then migrated to New Jersey. A letter of 25 June 1669 from George Jr. to his cousin requesting payment to his brother Benjamin of £5 of the £20, which would be due him from his Aunt Dalton (his legacy), shows that Benjamin lived to maturity, had dealings with his brother, and was probably then in New England, further support to the identity of the Benjamin Parkhurst in New Jersey the next year. The letter follows:

> Loveing Cous^{n} Bashelder: after my kynde love remembered to you and all the rest of my frinds, these fue lines are to desire you if you plese to paye unto my brother Benjamen, fife pounds of that twenty which will bee due to me from my ant Dolton, which I understand you are to paye; and if you will plese so to doue, this shall be your discharge for that fife pounds. as witnese my hand. George Parkis haveing nothing alrd. att present of, rest your loveing frind. Endorsed: My unkell Gorg. Parkes his letter: sent by benjeiman Parkes

Phebe, George's first wife, had a sister Ruth, wife of Reverend Timothy Dalton, Rector of Woolverstone, which is five miles from Ipswich, England. She died without surviving children and left legacies to six of the children of her sister Phebe, suggesting that Samuel, John and Abigail had died young. Timothy Dalton and Ruth Leete were married on 13 June 1615 at Gislingham, Suffolk, where Ruth had cousins. Thus, Phebe was nee Leete.

Children,by first wife Phebe, all born at Ipswich, England:

PHEBE, bapt. 29 Nov. 1612 at St. Stephen; m 1, at Wolverstone, Suffolk, home of her Aunt Ruth, 27 March 1635, Daniel Dan, "both single"; m 2, (his 2nd wife) Thomas Arnold; res. Watertown, Mass;, then Providence R.I.; at least 4 ch.

MARY, bapt. 28 Aug. 1614 at St. Lawrence, parish of St. Mary-at-the Quay; m 1638, Rev. Thomas Carter, 1st minister, of Woburn; 8 ch.; she d 1687

SAMUEL, bapt. 2 Feb. 1616/17 at St. Margaret; prob. d.y.

DEBORAH, bapt. 1 Aug. 1619 at St. Margaret; m John Smith of Watertown; moved to Hampton, N.H. 1644, Edgartown 1653; 5 ch.

GEORGE, bapt. 5 June 1621 at St. Margaret; m 1, 16 Dec. 1643, Sarah Brown, dau. of Abraham; 2 ch.; m 2, 24 Sept. 1650, widow Mary Veazie (or Pheza); he d 16 March1698/9 "ae 81" at Watertown; she d 9 March 1680/81

JOHN, bapt. 19 Oct. 1623 at St. Margaret; prob. d.y.

ABIGAIL, bapt. 1 Jan. 1625/6 at St. Margaret; prob. d.y.

ELIZABETH, b in parish of St. Margaret, bapt. in parish of St. Mary-le-Tower 18 May 1628; m 1, Emanuel Hilliard who was lost in a boat 20 Oct. 1659; m 2, 14 Dec. 1659, widower Joseph Merry & moved to Edgartown 1678; he d there in April 1710

JOSEPH, bapt. 21 Dec. 1629 at St. Margaret; m at Concord 26 June 1656, Rebecca Reed, dau. of Esdras Reed, bapt. 27 Sept. 1627; 5 ch.; res. Chelmsford; he d 30 Nov. 1709

------Children by second wife, Susanna------

BENJAMIN, prob. born at Watertown or Boston about 1645 or 7; if taken back to England by his mother, he returned, for he settled in Woodbridge, N.J. about 1670; m 1, Martha who was prob. sister of Benjamin Homan (or Oman) who d a bachelor 1684, leaving bulk of his estate to her; Inventory of B.P.'s estate was taken 16 Feb. 1683/4 at Elizabethtown, N.J.

SON, prob. b at Watertown or Boston about 1645 or 7; taken back to England

DANIEL, bapt. at Boston 1st Church 10 June 1649 ae about 11 days old; taken back to England

JOSHUA, bapt. at Boston 1st Church 7 March 1651/2; taken back to England

CALEB, bapt. at Boston 1st Church 26 Feb. 1653/4; taken back to England; prob. the Caleb Parkhurst with wife Sarah of St. Giles, Cripplegate, London with 5 ch. bapt. there

Ref.: N.E.H.G.R. - 27:364; 68; Bond's Watertown; New Jersey Index of Wills - III, V. VI; The Family of Leete, by Joseph Leete & John C. Anderson, London, 1906; Parish Registers

JOHN PARKHURST (*Christopher, George*) was baptized 29 October 1554 at Saint Mary's Guildford, Surrey. He married, probably about 1582, Sarah, who was probably the Sarah Parkhurst who married at Saint Stephen, Ipswich, 7 January 1611/12 Benjamin Cole. He was a clothier.

John Parkhurst made his will 29 March 1610 and died about a year later, for it was proved 7 June 1611.

> 29 March 1610 - the will of John Parkhurst of the parish of Saynte Marye Keye, in the town of Ipswich, Suffolk, Clothier ... to wife Sara all household stuff, as bedding, brass, pewter, linen and woolen, and the annual rent of £8 to be paid half yearly for life ... to son George Parkhurst all shopstuff, all implements of trade as a shearman, all my books of what title and print, and all the rest of my goods and stock, movables and immovables ... to son John Parkhurst 100 marks at age of 21 ... to daughter Thamar Parkhurst the annual rent of £5 to be paid her half yearly for life ... to daughter Hellen Parkhurst £50 at the age of 21 or marriage .. to daughter Sara Parkhurst £40 at the age of 21 or marriage ... my executor to put forth to best profit the portions of said John and Hellen for their further education and bringing up ...son George to be sole executor ... Cousin Nicholas Babbe of Nedeham Markett, supervisor, and he is to receive 20s. for his pains. My executor is to give to the supervisor a bond of £300 for the faithful performance of my will. Witnesses: Nicholas Babbe, scriptore, Jno Parkhurst, Samuel Pecke, Edward Catherall. Proved 7 June 1611. (Ref.: Prerogative Court of Canterbury, Wood-50)

Children:

ROBERT, bapt. 22 ____ 1583 at St. Lawrence, Ipswich, "son of John", He may be the one mentioned in a Star Chamber Court case, in the time of James I. Not mentioned in John Parkhurst's will

THAMAR, b prob. about 1586; living, unm. in 1610

2 GEORGE, b about 1588; m 1, Phebe Leete, dau. of Robert & Alice (Grundy) Leete of Eversden, Cambridgeshire; 9 ch.; went to N.E.; m 2, Susanna, widow of John Simson; 5 ch.; they returned to England; he was buried 18 June 1675 at St. Lawrence, Ipswich

JOHN, b perhaps about 1595; prob. the one who m at Kersey, Suffolk, in 1618, Margaret Ambrose; ch.: bapt. at St. Mary-on-the-Quay, Ipswich - Margaret 1619, Mary 24 Feb. 1621, John 28 Nov. 1624, Samuel 16 Dec. 1627; at St. Margaret's - Thomas 17 Feb. 1632, Benjamin 24 June 1636

HELEN, bapt. at St. Mary's at the Quay, Ipswich 7 [Januar?] y 1598/9

MARY, bapt. at St. Mary at the Quay, 12 ____ 1601

SARAH, b perhaps about 1603

Ref.: N.E.H.G.R. 68:373-4; Parish Registers

6

ROBERT LEETE (*John*) of Eversden, Cambridgeshire, was probably born about 1525, for he was granted a degree of Bachelor of Arts (first in the ordo) 1544-5, Master of Arts in 1548. He was a Fellow of Saint John's College about 1545, and was so designated in a deed of 1551.

> 24 September 1551 - Deed of sale by Christopher Roger of Little Eversden, husbandman, to **Robert Leete**, Fellow of Saint John's College, of ½ acre in Little Eversden.
>
> (Queen's College Archives, Eversden Deed 664)

This transfer was for property which Robert's brother Edmund had bought from Christopher Rogers by a deed of 10 August 1550 (Deed 663) and which Edmund bequeathed to Robert in his will dated 12 July 1551. The bequest was apparently implemented by reconveying it to Robert.

On 4 May 1558, Mary Lete, widow, and Robert Lete, gentleman, quitclaimed to the College of Saint John certain lands in Great and Little Eversden, which lands had been deeded four days earlier by his brother Thomas Lete of Little Eversden, gentleman, for £60. (Deeds 672, 673). A performance bond of £100 was also executed. These must have been inherited lands in which Robert could have had some vague claim; otherwise there would have been no need for him to execute a quitclaim deed. As for the widow Mary, she was perhaps the widow of Brother Henry of whom little is known.

On 6 April 1573, "Mr. Robert Leete" and Alice Grundy were married at Great Eversden. He must have been about 48 years old at the time of this marriage. Perhaps he had an earlier wife of whom there is no record. There seem to have been no other children except by his marriage to Alice Grundy. Their first child was baptized a mere 2½ months after their marriage. Apparently he resisted marriage as long as possible!

Robert Leete died about 1597-8 intestate, and administration was granted to his widow Alice on 17 February 1597/8. Alice must have been about 20 years younger than her husband.

Alice Grundy's parents are so far unknown. They apparently were from Lancashire and moved south to Cambridge or nearby. She had a brother John, who entered Pembroke College at Cambridge University 1557-8, received his B.A. in 1560-61, his M.A. from Saint John's in 1564, a B.D. in 1570, was a Fellow of Saint John's in 1561, a University Preacher in 1567, a Rector of Great Livermore, Suffolk, in 1571, of GreatCressingham, Norfolk, 1582-98, Vicar of Little Fakenham 1582-1608, and of Great Barton until 1583. He was of Gislingham when he died in 1608. He and his second wife, the widow Frideswide Smith, were married 21 January 1601/2 at Heigham, Norfolk. She died 1609/10. Both of their wills name many relatives. Alice also had a sister Margaret, who married Hugh Wood, had children and died probably by 1606. A brother James had a wife Margaret, children, and died testate at Saint Andrew's Parish, Norwich.

Children, baptized at Eversden, Cambridgeshire:

SYMEON, bapt. 23 June 1573; 2 ch. bapt. at Therfield, Herts.: John 4 Jan. 1600/01 - buried 21 Jan., Samuel 28 Jan. 1601/2, then 8 ch. bapt. at Little Eversden: Elizabeth 18 Dec. 1603, John 15 Dec. 1605, William 27 Dec. 1607, Israel 11 Dec. 1610, Anne 11 Oct. 1612 - buried 21 May 1616, Robert 13 March 1614/15, Edmund 16 Dec. 1617 - buried 4 Jan. 1617/18, Giles 7 Dec. 1618, Anne 5 March 1620/21. Simeon Lete signed as churchwarden in 1606

JUDETH, bapt. 11 July 1574; m 2 Aug. 1601 at Eversden, William Scotte, prob. son of William; ch.: Thomas bp. 12 Jan.1601/2, Edward bp. 17 Jan. 1604/5, Margaret bp. 20 Sept. 1607, Katherine bp. 7 Oct. 1610, Henry bp. 7 March 1612/13-buried 14 Jan. 1613/14

DEBORAH, bapt. 22 July 1576

RUTH, bapt. 8 May 1579; m at Gislingham, Suff. 13 June 1615, Timothy Dalton. What was apparently their last ch. was buried 28 Aug. 1624-5 when she would have been 45 or 46. She d 12 May 1666 "aged 88", which would have had her b 1577-8. Her husband who was a minister was suspended by the Bishop in April 1636. Her 1st cousin m a son of John Rogers the Martyr. On 22 March 1663/4 Ruth made legacies to various heirs of her sister Phebe Parkhurst, also to Abigail Ambrose, dau. of the wife (Susanna) of John Severence, Walter Roper, (H)anna(h) Willix, formerly servant of Rev. Timothy Dalton, & Mary, wife of William Fifield (prob. the one m at Hampton, N.H.)

MORDOCHIAS, bapt. 23 July 1581; living in 1606

SUSANNA, bapt. 10 Nov. 1583. Perhaps she was the mother of Susanna who m Henry Ambrose of Sudbury, Suffolk. She may also have been mother or aunt of Walter Roper. The Ambroses and Ropers both lived in Hampton, N.H., as did the Fifields, sev. Parkhurst ch. and the Daltons.

3 PHEBE, bapt. 20 Dec. 1585 at Little Eversden; m about 1611 George Parkhurst of Ipswich, Suffolk

GREAT EVERSDEN CHURCH

LITTLE EVERSDEN CHURCH

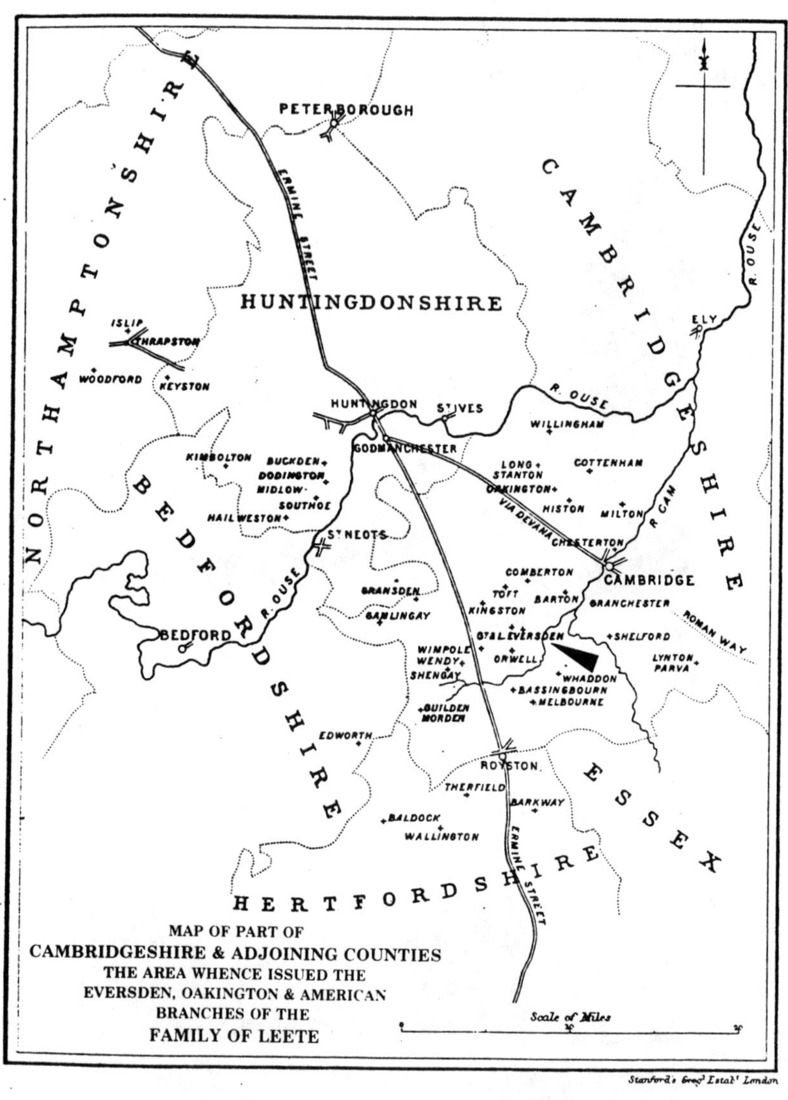

Ref.: The Family of Leete, by Joseph Leete & John C. Anderson, London, 1906; Cambridge University Archives; Parish Registers; Visitation Pedigrees

CHRISTOPHER PARKHURST (*George*) is first on record on 2 May 1546 on a tax list of Saint Mary's parish, Guildford, Surrey. He was assessed 4 pence for goods and 20 pence for lands and tenements. By a 1550 Feet of Fine, he and his sister sold land to his brother-in-law, probably property which he had inherited from his father. Probably his mother had died at that time and this was the final settlement of the estate.

> Octave of Hilary 1550 - Nicholas Babbe, plaintiff, vs. Henry Alby, gentleman, and Elizabeth his wife, and Christopher Parkeherste, son and heir of George Parkeherste, deforciants, re a messauge, 42 acres of land and 8 acres of pasture in Guldeford, Stoke next Guldeford, and Merrowe. Consideration £40.

Christopher Parkhurst was probably born in the period of 1520-24, married about 1546, and had five known children by this marriage. His wife must have died about 1567 and he remarried, perhaps about 1568-9, and he then had several more children almost a generation younger than the first ones. This is apparent as there seems to have been a gap in the sequence of children. His son Christopher was too young to have been the father of these younger children. This is apparent from the will of Bishop John Parkhurst, in which he expressed concern about the education of his nephew Christopher, son of his brother Christopher. The nephew was thus surely underage at the time (1573/4), and was perhaps born about 1572.

In 1561, Christopher Parkhurst was named Keeper of the Bishop's Palace in Ipswich, county Suffolk, by his brother, who had been appointed Bishop the year before. He was probably the one of that name buried at Saint Lawrence, Ipswich, 10 August 1595.

Children:

HELEN, bapt. 25 June 1547 at St. Mary's, Guildford; m 1574 in St. Peter's, Creeting, Suffolk, William Crosse

ELIZABETH, bapt. 2 April 1549 at St. Mary's, Guildford

GEORGE, bapt. 13 March 1550/51 at St. Mary's, Guildford; m 1, Joan ——— ; she was buried 8 June 1619 at St. Lawrence, Ipswich; m 2, Thomasine Allen, 1 Aug. 1624 at St. Lawrence; he was buried 18 Dec. 1631 at St. Lawrence; Thomasine was buried "out the gaile" (jail) 15

Sept. 1636. He was a grocer. He had a son John bapt. 5 Nov. 1581, who m 7 Jan. 1603/4, Rose, dau. of Thomas Sicklemore who in his 1619 will mentioned his "bro. George Parkhurst". George's will dated 12 Sept. 1631, names wife Thomasine, dau.-in-law Rose Parkhurst, & gr. ch. George Parkhurst & Robert Parkhurst, both under 21 (George bp. 10 Aug. 1606, d before 1634/5; Robert bp. 23 June 1611, prob. buried 1666 at St. Clement's, Ipswich); son John had 5 or 6 other ch. who d.y.

JOHN, bapt. 29 Oct. 1554 at St. Mary's, Guildford (parents not named); m Sarah _____ who was prob. the Sarah Parkhurst who m 7 Jan. 1611/12 at St. Stephen's, Ipswich, Benjamin Cole; 7 ch.; he d 1611, testate

JAMES, apparently m at Stonham Aspall, Suffolk, 12 July 1584, Joan Saunders alias Hewe, under age. The m record which says John (sic) Parkhurst is evidently in error. James is mentioned as an overseer in the Stonham Aspall P.R. for 1584. Joan Parkhurst was buried at Stonham Aspall 25 May 1629; 6 ch. bp. at Stonham Aspall: Mary 6 July 1585-bur. 8 July 1585, Sarah 4 Dec. 1586-m 1616 Wm. Sheppard, Agnes 28 Sept. 1589, Joan 19 Aug. 1593, John 26 July 1597-bur. 10 Dec. 1597, John 11 March 1598/9

ANN, bapt. 1 Nov. 1569 at St. Nicholas, Ipswich, "dau. of Christopher Parkhurst"

CHRISTOPHER, b perhaps c. 1572; surely a child at time of his uncle's will 1573/4; possible the burial in 1595 refers to him rather than his father.

SAMUEL, perhaps a son born c. 1574; dead by 31 July 1619 as will of Benjamin Osmond of Ipswich mentions Benjamin Parkhurst son of Samuel deceased (P.C.C. Somes 776). His wife was prob. Margaret of Ipswich whose estate was admin. by her son Henry 1616 (Ipswich Rec. Office IC/AAG/2); 7 ch.

JOSEPH, perhaps a son born c. 1576; m 1 Jan. 1598 at St. Lawrence, Ipswich, Joan Shibdum; m 2, Elizabeth _____; his will of 28 Feb. 1634, pr. 2 Oct. 1635 (P.C.C. Sadler 101) left everything to widow Elizabeth; widow Elizabeth P. of Ipswich m 12 May 1640 at St. Clement's, Ipswich, Edmund Morgan, widower.

Ref.: Guildford Borough Records 1514-1546, edited by Enid M. Dance, pub. by The Surrey Record Society, 1958, Vol. XXIV; Surrey Feet of Fines; Parish Registers; Probate records; Encyclopedia Heraldica, by William Berry, London, 1828-1840, Vol. II

12

JOHN LEETE of Eversden, Cambridgeshire, was apparently born about 1500. In the Lay Subsidy (tax) of 1522, a John Leete was assessed at £6 for goods on the Kingston roll. It is possible that this was actually his father of the same name, for John was quite young then; probably not yet married. On the other hand, if his father was then dead, then he, even tho a young man, might well have come into his estate and been subject to the tax.

John Leete was taxed in the Subsidies of 1540 against Little Eversden, and in 1542 at Great Eversden. He was buried at Little Eversden on 25 December 1551.

In 1594, his grandson, Giles Leete of Shelland, sued for recovery of the title deeds of his (the grandson's) father's estate in Kingston, Eversden and Tofts. These three parishes are adjacent to each other.

By about 1526, John Leete married Helen (or Ellen) Burgoyne. On 10 October 1539, Ellen was described as a "gentlewoman" when she was named as godmother in the baptismal record of Alice Sutton at Toft.

Administration on the estate of Helen Leete, widow, of Eversden, was granted to her son Thomas Leete on 2 May 1564.

10 November 1549 - Deed of sale by Walter Barnarde of East Hatley, husbandman, of £40 worth of lands, etc. in Great and Little Eversden inherited from his father Thomas Barnarde, to **John Lete**.

(Queen's College, Cambridge University Archives, Eversden Deed 661)

20 December 1549 - Grant by William son of Oliver Taunte, deceased, late of Little Eversden, to **John Lete**, gentleman, Thomas Hinde, clerk, Alex. Graunden, Edmund Lete, John Reynolde, Robert Harwarde, Cuthbert Lindsey, Christopher Rogers, and other parishoners of Little Eversden of a tenement in Little Eversden and 8 acres, 1 rood in Great and Little Eversden, formerly Henry Taunte's. (Deed 662)

10 August 1550 - Deed of sale by Christopher Rogers of Little Eversden, husbandman, to **Edmund Leete** of Great Eversden, yeoman, of ½ acre in Little Eversden. (Deed 663)

1 December 1557 - Lease by the College of Saint John to **Thomas Leete** of Little Eversden, yeoman, of the manor place called the Lordship Place in Little Eversden, together with other lands for 40 years at annual rent of £13.10s. and also *one able and sufficient bore for brawne* or 10s. at Christmas annually. (Deed 670)

1 December 1557 - Bond in £20 in regard to above (Deed 671)

26 April 1558 - Deed of sale by **Thomas Lete** of Little Eversden, gentleman, to the College of Saint John for £60 of certain lands in Great and Little Eversden. Full terrier attached; also bond of £100. (Deed 672)

30 April 1558 - Grant of above land to college and livery of seisin. (Deed 673)

20 April 1561 - Deed of sale. **Thomas Lete** of Little Eversden, gentleman, to Harry Scotte of Great Eversden, of 1½ acres of pasture in Great Eversden. (Deed 676)

The name Leete seems to derive from or have the meaning of light. This is evident from the family coat of arms which includes three lighted matches (fuses) and a lamp in the crest.

The Leete family is an ancient one that can be traced back to before the Norman conquest of England. According to the Domesday Survey, Leit was a thane of Edward the Confessor, King of England from 1042 until his death 5 January 1065/6. The manor of Foxcote in Buckinghamshire, worth £3 annually, is mentioned as being formerly held by Leit.

Gloucestershire. Land of the King

In Chenemertone tenuit. Let. viii. hid. 7 un maner erat. Modo
ten Girard. 7 ibi ht .iii. car. 7 xiiii. uill cu .vi. car. Ibi. viii.
serui. 7 iii. molini de .xv. solid. Valuit. viii. lib. modo. vi. lib.

Translation

In Kemerton Let held 8 hides; it was a manor. Now Girard holds it; there he has 3 ploughs, 14villagers with 6 ploughs, 8 serfs. 3 mills there at 15 shillings. The value was £8, now is £6.

Buckinghamshire. Land of the Bishop of Bayeux. In Stodfald Hundred)

Turstin' ten' de epo Foxescote. p' vi. hid' se defd. Tra. e. iiij. car. In dnio. ii. sunt. 7 un' uills cu. ii. bord' hnt. ii. car. Ibi. i. seru. 7 pra. iiii. car. Silua. xxx. porc. Val' 7 ualuit sep. iii. lib. Hoc m tenuit Leit teign' r. e. 7 uendere potuit.

Translation

Thurstan holds Foxescote from the Bishop. It answers for 6 hides. Land for 4 ploughs, in lordship there are 2. 1 villager with 2 smallholders have 2 ploughs there, 1 serf. Meadow for 4 ploughs, woodland sufficient for 30 pigs. The value is and always was £3. Leit, a thane of King Edward's, held this manor; he could sell it.

In the 10th year of the reign of King John (1208), four actions-at-law relating to lands at Morden in Cambridgeshire were brought before the Justices Itinerant, then sitting in the King's Court at Cambridge. The plaintiff in all these actions was Gerard, the son of Lete or Letie, and Sama, the daughter of Wulfric. The defendants were William de Fonte, Roger, son of Robert, Reiner, son of Roger, and Julia, the wife or widow of Robert de Gatewell, respectively. The settlement of these suits, recorded as *Final Concords*, otherwise known as *Pedes Finium* or Feet of Fines, are preserved in the Public Record Office of London. Morden is about 37 miles from Foxcote. He was probably related to the four brothers, Radmund, Walter, Nicholas and Peter de Lete, who were Knights Crusaders 1213-1230.

The following documents from the Close Rolls, translated and abstracted from the original contracted Latin, pertain to these brothers.

26 June 1213 - The King to Peter de Malo Lacu, and Brian de Insula, etc. we command you that your come to us, with Hugh de Boves, and other our lieges who are with you, and with our ships as quickly as you can. And you, Peter, give assistance to the companions of Hugh de Boves, namely, Peter de Delette and Nicholas and William de Haia towards furnishing their ships, and acquit Thomas de Galway of the wages, viz. of four knights and 15 squires for 15 days but not by name of wages. Witness I myself at Beram.

PETER de LETES and his brothers, Knights

19 September 1213 - The King to the Sheriff of Norfolk greeting. We command you that the manor of Wyhton which belonged to William de Kau you divide into two equal halves, and likewise the corn, and one half, with the capital messuage, you cause to go to our beloved Geoffrey de Lucy, and the other half to Peter de Delete and his two brothers, Knights, which we give to them to maintain themselves in our service. But if there shall be so many houses on the capital messuage that the said Geoffrey can spare one, you shall cause the said Peter and his brothers to have one, for storing their harness (or arms). Witness, I myself, at Pontefract.

Of the following documents, the first one is transcribed, the Latin contracted as in the document, and then a translation follows.

Rex Philippo Marc̃ t̃c. Mittim⁹ ad vos Wiłłm Roillard, Petr̃ de Letes, Radm de Letes, Radm de Wyme, Ernald de Waṽans, Oliṽum de Punchard Milites, mandantes qd eor corꝑa jaceant de nocte in castro nr̃o de Notingeh̃, t̃ equi illor t̃ h̃nesia jaceant infª baillum, t̃ cũ ad nos miseritis ꝑ denar̃ ad op⁹ illor qⁱ nũc penes vos sũt, mittem⁹ voƀ denar̃ ad op⁹ illor ꝑut eos ꝯtinget. Videatis aut̃ bñ qd h̃ant arma t̃ h̃nesia sic̃ milites hr̃e deƀnt. T. me ip̃o ap̃d Selveston̄, xvij. die Febr̃."

17 February 1214/15 - The King to Philip Marc, etc. We send to you William Roillard, Peter de Letes, Radmund de Letes, Radmund de Wyme, Ernald de Waverans, Oliver de Punchard, Knights, commanding that their bodies may lie by night in our Castle of Nottingham, and their horses and harnes lie within the bailiwick, and when you shall send to us for the cost of those who are now in your keeping, we will send you money for their necessity. And observe well that they have arms and harness as knights ought to have. Witness, I myself, at Selveston.

24 October 1215 - The King, etc. to the Sheriff of Nottingham, greeting. Know that we grant to Peter de Elettes twenty marks of land, and to Nicholas de Elettes fifteen librates, and to Walter de

Elettes fifteen librates of land, which belonged to Henry de Bayllot, and therefore we command you, that you cause these lands to be assigned to them of that land in your bailiwick, without delay. Witnessed by the lord Peter, Bishop of Winchester, at Feismantell.

4 April 1216 - the King to the Sheriff of Nottingham, etc. Know that we have committed during our pleasure to our dear and faithful Peter de Delettis and his brothers the manor of Skermiton with appurtenances which belonged to William de Albiniac, and therefore we command you that you cause the manor to be held by the same Peter and his brothers without delay; and the mandate to the Constable of Beuveir is that he releases it to him in peace. Witness, I myself, at Windsor.

8 August 1216 - It is ordered to Peter, Nicholas and Walter de Lettres that they render to Agatha wife of William de Albiniac the manor of Skerinton which the lord king committed to them in the soke of Oskinton. Witness the King at White Minster.

8 August 1216 - It is ordered to Philip Marc that of the lands of the enemies of the lord king in his bailiwick he provides for Peter, Nicholas & Walter de Lettres, the value of the Manor of Skerinton which the lord king committed to them in the soke of Oskinton. Witness the King at White Minster.

3 September 1216 - The King to Philip Marcus, etc. Know that we concede to Peter de Lettres and his brothers all the land which was William de St. Michael's in place of the land of William de Albiniac which we had previously assigned to them. And therefore we command you that without delay you cause them to have full seizin thereof in your bailiwick. And that you also convey to Ernulph de Waverans the land which belonged to Robert de Hareston, ec. Witness, myself at Oxford.

13 September 1216 - It is ordered to the Sheriff of Nottingham that Peter de Lettres and his brothers have the residue of that land which is in the hand of the lord King in the town which was William de St. Michael's which the lord King previously gave them. Witness the King at Sunington.

1217 - The lord King gave to Nicholas and Peter de Lettes the land which was Ralph Teissun's with its appurtenances in Wattelee without letters.

The next few documents tell us more of these Leete brothers and their affairs. The first one following, which indicates that they were Crusaders and can be dated at 1220, is given in the original contracted Latin, followed by a translation. The dates indicate the Sixth Crusade.

Rex ven̄abili p̄ri in Xp̄o W. eadē gr̄a Ebor Archiep̄s ɫ Angl Prim̄ sal̄ɫ. Consiliū nr̄m recolit ɫ memoriɫ̄ tenet qđ villā de Wetelegh̄ cū ptiñ q̄ Joh̄s Malherƀ optinuit in vita sua de dono dñi J. Reḡ pr̄is nr̄i, de dono ejusdē postea obtinuit dilc̄us ɫ fidel nr̄ Roger̄ de Monte Begonis tota vita sua possidendā ɫ ejusdē ville balliū cōmisit idē Rex pr̄ nr̄ tēpe guerre **Petro ɫ Nicho de Delettres crucesignatis,** pacē V° reformata idē Roger̄ saisinā q̄ prius habuit de p̄dc̄a villa ingssus est scđm cōmunē formā pacis. Quoniā v° dicta villa debet ip̄i Roḡo cedere tota vita sua ex cōcessione dñi J. Reḡ pr̄is nr̄i p̄dc̄a, ɫ p̄dc̄i **Petr̄ ɫ Nicholaus** nich̄ in ea habuerñt nisi balliū qđ fc̄a pace evanuit ɫ ex hoc nich̄ juris sibi possunt vendicare, voƀ mandam̄ ne occ̄one huj⁹ mod ballii habiti a p̄dc̄is **crucesignatis** u ip̄m Rogerū excomunic̄ois ferre sentenciā attēptetis."

The King to the venerable father in christ by the same grace Archbishop of York and Primate of England greeting.

Our Council recollects and holds in remembrance that the town of Wetelegh with its appurtenances which John Malherb obtained in his life by gift of the lord the King John, our father; of the gift of the same afterwards our beloved and faithful Roger de Monte Begonis obtained it to be held for his life and the King our father committed the office of bailiff of the said town in the time of war to **Peter** and **Nicholas de delettres**, crusaders. On the restoration of peace the said Roger had seizin as before of the said town and entered upon it according to the common form of the peace. Since therefore the said town ought to yield to the said Roger for his whole life on the grant of the lord King John our father, and the aforesaid **Peter** and **Nicholas** had nothing in it except the office of bailiff which terminated at the peace, and from this can claim no right to themselves, we order you not to attempt to carry out a sentance of excommunication on the said Roger by any occasion of an office of bailiff of this kind exercised by the said crusaders.

27 January 1220/21 - The King to the Sheriff of Nottingham, greeting. We command you that without delay you cause **Nicholas de Lettres** to have full seizin of the manor of Wattelee as the same **Nicholas** and his brothers formerly left it. Tested at Westminster.

1226 - The King to the Justices of his Bench greeting. We command you that the Assize of novel desseisin that Roger de Monte Begonis arraigned against **Nicholas de Lettres** for holding of Wetleya you place in delay until the eighth after Easter. Witness, etc.

1228 - **Nicholas de Lettres** attorned Walter de Claworth against Nicholas and Galfrid le Macun "*de placito nativitatis,*" etc.

21 July 1228 - Augi, Countess. Manor of Watel, which **Nich. de Lettres** holds.

Among the Charter Rolls are found the following documents.

16 November 1228 - Westminster. Grant to **Nicholas de Lettres**, and his heirs of the Manor of Bingeham, late of Fulk Paynel, which the said **Nicholas** previously had of the King's bail, until the King shall restore it to the heirs of the said Fulk of his free will or by a peace, rendering therefor the service thereto pertaining; and if the King restore the said manor, he will make to the said **Nicholas** a reasonable exchange in wards or escheats; saving to the King the advowson of the Church of the same manor.

14 August 1231 - Painscastle. Gift to **Nicholas de Lettres**, and his heirs, of the Manor of Ippelepen, late of Ralph de Meudlent, to hold by the service of the fee of half a Knight, until the King restore it to the right heirs of his free will or by a peace, whereupon he shall make to the said **Nicholas** a reasonable exchange in wards or escheats.

1235 - Grant to Amaury de Sancto Amando, and his heirs, saving to any man his right, of the manor of Iplepenn, which **Nicholas de Letteres** previously held of the King's bail, to hold until the King restore it to the heirs of the said **Nicholas** of his free will or by a peace

Of the many Inquisitions of various sorts held during the reigns of Henry III and Edward I, that is, between 1216 and 1307, these are recorded. The original documents are of course in Latin; the following are but brief abstracts.

Nottingham	The Vill of Wetele is an escheat of the lord King and is worth thirty pounds a year. **Nicholas de Lettres** holds the same for the lord King John.
Nottingham and Derbyshire	The vill of Lindeby is an escheat of the lord King of the honor of Peverell of Notingham and William de St. Michael of London has half of that vill by gift of King John rendering thence yearly into the King's exchequer one skin of a gris [a kind of weasel, or little beast of bluish color] and that half is worth £7.6s. annually. And **Peter de Lettris** and his brothers have the other half by similar gift of the lord the King because they had long pleased the lord King and that half was worth £7.6s.

Devonshire Hundred of Haytorr	The lord Ralph de Meulent holds the manor of Ippolepenn from the lord King in chief since the coronation of the lord King. And because Ralph de Meulent did not come to the army of the lord King when the lord King was in Brittany the lord King gave the said manor to **Nicholas de Lettres** who held that manor during the rest of his life.
Lincolnshire Wapentake of Boby	Inquisition made in the wapentake of Boby by the oaths of subscribers namely **John de Lettres**, (and other Jurors).

The Patent Rolls are the formal enrollments of a wide variety of documents of a public nature. The following ones pertain to the Leetes.

7 January 1216/17 - The King to all who these letters shall inspect, greeting. Know that **Peter de Letres**, **Nicholas**, and **Walter**, his brothers, have served us well and faithfully, and their services we very much commend. We give, moreover, to them licence to go their journey abroad into the land of Jerusalem, at the general movement of the Crusaders. And in testimony of this, etc., Witness (I myself), at Notingham.

16 January 1216/17 - The King to all who shall inspect these letters, greeting. Know that we have given licence to **Peter de Lettes**, **Nicholas** & **Walter**, his brothers, that they may pledge their lands until the term fixed for the Crusaders. So, nevertheless that, laying hand on the Holy Gospels, they make us sure that they will not depart from England without our licence, before the movement previously fixed and appointed for the Crusaders. And in testimony of this, these our letters patent, etc., to the same **Peter**, **Nicholas** and **Walter**, we have caused to be made. Witness: the Earl (of Pembroke), at Oxford.

29 July 1224 - Notingham. Adam of New Market, John de Birkin, John de Daivill, & William de Cressi are appointed Justices at the Assize of *Morte d' Ancestor* (death of Ancestor) holden at Notingham in the Octave of the Assumption of the Blessed Mary; & summons is before the Justices of the first Assize, when into these parts they shall come, between Eudo de Lungvilers, plaintiff, & **Nicholas de Lettres**, holder of the vill of Wetele with its appurtenances. Witness by the King, at Bedford.

19 October 1229 - **Nicholas de Lettres** is mentioned third on a list of forty-two Knights, in a safe-conduct granted by Henry the Third, and witnessed by the King himself, at Portsmouth. The expedition was ordered abroad by the King.

1230 - The King to all whom this present letter shall come before, greeting. Know that we grant to **Nicholas de Lettres** that we will not give up to Fulk Paynel the Manor of Bingham, which the same **Nicholas** holds of our bailiwick, nor shall he himself be otherwise removed from that place until for the value of that Manor an equivalent shall have been made to him in escheats, or wardships. In this, etc., Witness: the King.

1230 - **Nicholas de Lettres** is granted similar letters for the Manor of Ippelepenn, which Ralph de Meulent held, to have & to hold during his lifetime, etc.

The records known as *Rotuli Hundredorum*, The Hundred Rolls, contain the Inquisitions taken by two special commissions issued in the second and seventh years of Edward I, by which certain commissioners were empowered to summon juries to enquire as to the King's preogatives and royalties, and into the frauds and abuses connected therewith.

Rolls of the Hundreds: County of Devon Time of Edw. I. 1272-1307

Ippelapenne. And for a certain transgression which (Ralph de Mullond) committed against our lord King John the same King took from him that manor and gave it to the lord **Nicholas de Lettres** who lived long and held it for his whole life and died without heir of his body in the time of Henry father of the present King, etc.

Compare the above with the preceding entry relating to Ippolepenn.

Rolls, etc. Cambridgeshire, 1272-1307

We say that the Prior of Bernewell has in free tenants in the vill of Fendr'yto seven virgates of land of the fee of Robert Furniwas and of **John Delet** rendering to the same freely fifteen shillings and fourpence annually in pure alms.

Stachedene. In the same town...**Nicholas** son of **Lete** [holds] half a virgate.

Rolls, etc. Bedfordshire, 1272-1307

La Leye. Richard de la Leye holds in the same town half a hide of the honour of Beauchamp of Bedford...he has in demesne a hundred acres of land...Of which **Geoffrey Lete** [holds] one quarter, etc.

Rolls, etc. Suffolk County, 1272-1307

Walter Lete occurs under the Hundred of Waynesford, in the hundred-rolls of the County of Suffolk, in the reign of Edward the First.

Rolls, etc. Oxfordshire, 1272-1307	**Roger Lete** (Rogs Lete) is named among the "Servi" of Aston, in the Hundred of Bampton, Co. Oxford, temp. Edw I.

Among the Inquisitions Post Mortem in the time of Edward I (1272-1307) is found one regarding Henry de Letters and the manor of Boby in Lincolnshire, held of the King for half a Knight's fee.

In 1303, Richard le Lyte and the Monks of Swafham held a half a Knight's fee in Toft and Cumberton of the Bishop of Ely. There was a Priory in Swafham Bolebeck, Cambridgeshire.

Richard Lete was probably a descendant of one of the above Crusaders.

Robert, son of Lete of Toft, listed in the Subsidy of 1326-7, was surely a close relation, if not an ancestor, of the later Leetes of Cambridgeshire. He was probably the son of Richard, above.

In 1341-2, the Parliament of England granted to King Edward III a tax amounting to a 1/9th levy to be paid over two years, to pay for the cost of waging war. Among the jurors selected to levy the tax were Robert Lete of Arrington in Cambridgeshire, Hugh Lete of Henlow in Bedfordshire, William Leyt of Aston in Northamptonshire, John Lety of Hertfordshire, and William atte Lete of Haverhill in Suffolk.

In the Heralds' Visitation of Cambridge in 1575, the Leete family arms were recorded and then confirmed in the Visitation of 1619. John Leete and his wife, Ellen Burgoyne, were then recorded as the progenitors of the family. The arms were described as follows.

The parentage of Ellen Burgoyne is unknown. There were in the sixteenth century and before, a number of Burgoynes living in Cambridgeshire and nearby Bedfordshire. According to the Visitation of Cambridgeshire and some supporting evidence, the earliest known Burgoyne was Bartholomew of Boxworth, who was living 8 Edward III (1334). He was followed by his son Bartholomew who married Anne, daughter and heir of John Freville of Caxton. This second Bartholomew also lived in Boxworth. He had a son John, who married a daughter of Roger Harleston of Essex, and who was Escheater of Cambridgeshire in 1398/9, 1401, 14, and 16. His son John married a daughter of Thomas Payton and they lived in Dry Drayton. He had several children, including a son Thomas of Impington whose first wife was Isabell and second wife Alice Tay. He had a son Thomas, who married Alice Booth and lived in Long Stanton, Cambridgeshire.

If Ellen descended from Thomas Payton, then she had royal ancestors through that family. The Freville family also had royal ancestry and it seems certain that she at least descended from them. The Burgoyne arms and crest are shown below.

LEETE

ARMS: Argent, on a fess gules between two matches kindled proper, a martlet or.

CREST: On a ducal coronet an antique lamp or

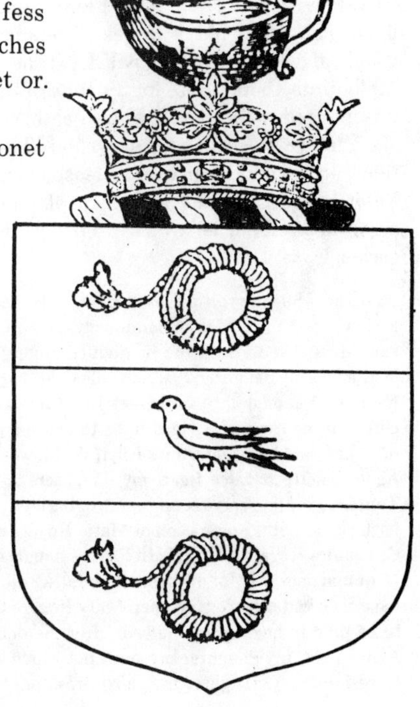

BURGOYNE

ARMS: Azure, a talbot passant argent
CREST: A tiger sejant argent, attired tufted, and maned sable

Children:

WILLIAM, perhaps b 1520-30; m Flower (or Flora) Browne of Yorkshire; 6 ch. named in her will; res. Eversden, Melbourne & Kingston, Cambridgeshire; Dr. of Civil Law; he appears to have died at Melbourne about 1560, for 29 June of that year admin. of his estate was granted to Flower. After his death, she settled in Kingston where she died in the end of April 1580. The year after his death, she renewed for a 21 year term, a lease from the Master and Fellows of Peter-House College, Cambridge, of a house called *Sparrows* and 40 acres in Melbourne, which property they had occupied under an earlier lease.

25 April 1580 - the will of Flower Leete of Kyngston, county Cambridge, widow ... sick in body ... to Marsie Seddon my daughter £20 ... to all the children of the said Marsie Seddon £10 to be divided among them ... to every child of Ellyn Widdowes my daughter 20s. ... to Giles Leett my son my table, etc. [a long list of household goods] ... to said Giles Leett my son all lands and tenements and closes in the town of Kyngston, he to prove and execute this will ... if he does not, then said lands, etc. unto Ellyn Widdowes, Marie Rogers, M^rsie Seddon, Agnes Leette & Luce Leett my daughters ... to the poor 20s. ... to William Tompson my late servant one comb of barley ... to Robert Johnson one comb of barley ... to John Rogers son of Marie Rogers my daughter £20 at age 21 ... to Cassandra Rogers & Elizabeth Rogers daughters of the said Marie £10 at age 15 or marriage ... if John Rogers their father die before any of the children shall have received their legacy, then Mary Rogers their mother shall have the £30 to be paid to her within one year after the decease of her said husband ... to Agnes Leett my daughter my great pot which was her grandmothers, etc. .. to Luce Leett my daughter my third brass pot, etc. ... to Ellyn Widdowes my

daughter my four silver spoons ... to Dorothy Widdowes one yearling calf ... to Flower War'ener one ewe & one lamb ... to Marrian Wysse my sister one gold ring which was my mothers ... to Damyan Peck one ewe & one lamb ...to George my servant one bushell of wheat ... to Margarett Awfeld one bushel of barley ... to John Greystock the son of Richard Greystock one bushell of barley .. to John Widdowes my son in law £12.12s. which I owe unto him .. to Giles Leete my son and John Widdowes my son in law £13.6.8. to be divided between them, they to be executors ... residue to daughters. Witnesses: John Peck, Aline Greystocke & Radulph Atwell, chirurgian. Proved 18 May 1580.

(Archdeaconry Court of Ely Wills)

John Rogers, husband of daughter Marie, was the son of John Rogers, the proto-Martyr in the reign of Queen Mary.

EDMUND, of Eversden; his will pr. Aug. 1580; apparently unm.

12 July 1551 - the will of Edmund Leete of Eversden, diocese of Ely ... to my father 12 royals & all that he hath in his custody, to my mother 4 oxen & 2 milk beasts, to my brother William 4 milk beasts, 4 young bullocks and 20s. in money and to every one of his children 10s. ... to my brother Thomas 20 quarters of barley, £3 in money & 2 draught steers ... to Oliver Warner 40s. & to his sister 40s ... to my aunt Madew 40s. to distribute among her children ... to every one of my servants 10s & to every one of my father's 5s. apiece ... to 5 priests which my brother Robert knoweth 10s. apiece ... all my malt to the poor ... to the poor scholars & other townsmen £8 whereof 40s. shall be given at Ashwell ... residue to my brother Robert & his heirs, with all my free land that I bought of Mr. Saint George ... & one acre of land that I bought of Robert Harwarde & one selion that I bought off Christopher Roger lying in the quarry, & also one selion of John Greystocke the elder ... my father and mother to have all the free lands unbequeathed, & all my copyhold lands in Eversden to them jointly, except the new house I dwell in, which I heartily desire my father & mother to surrender to my brother Robert ... brother Robert to be executor. Witnesses: William Huet, Robert Lane, Thomas Chapman. Proved 22 August 1551 in the Archdeaconry Court of Ely.

HENRY, known only by Visitation report; he must have m Mary ______, for a widow Mary signed a quitclaim deed with Robert Leete 4 May 1558 re property deeded by Thomas Leete. This must have been inherited property. Thus, Henry died before 1558

THOMAS, moved to Bury St. Edmunds; m Dorothy, dau. of Richard Warde of Barton, Cambridgeshire; named in br. Edmund's will; 2 known ch.: John of Bury St. Edmunds, Elizabeth who m Thomas Winde of Warwickshire

6 ROBERT, b about 1525; m 6 April 1573 at Great Eversden, Alice Grundy, possibly a 2nd m for him; he died 1597-8 intestate, Alice surviving him; 7 ch. bapt. 1573-1585

Ref.: The Family of Leete, by Joseph Leete and John C. Anderson, London, 1906; Cambridge University Archives; Parish Registers; Visitation Pedigrees; Probate Records at Cambridge

KNIGHT CRUSADER
From the Temple Church, London

16

GEORGE PARKHURST of Guildford, Surrey, is first found on record on the first page of the Guildford Borough records on 3 April 1514, apparently receiving a license to sell in the local market. Later that year he was chosen as a Hallwarden. This office had the responsibility of the actual fabric of the Guild Hall as well as the collection of sums due to the Guild Merchant for Admissions, and so on. Two men usually served together. A century later, they were Borough Treasurers in general. The office of Hallwarden dates back at least to 1361. The medieval Guildhall is now gone, the present building on the site in High Street having been built in the 17th century.

On 6 October 1515, George Parkhurst was named Bailiff. On 18 January 1517/18, he was again sworn in as a Hallwarden. He is on the first list of Approved Men on 3 October 1519. Approved men were associates of the Mayor, entry being restricted to those who had served as Bailiff. There are many more entries in the Borough records for his appointment as Hallwarden and he was on the list of Approved Men year after year for the rest of his life.

On 15 January 1514/15, he and Henry Cowper were sworn in as Flesh and Fish Tasters.

In 1522, George Parkhurst was elected Mayor and Coroner of Guildford, being sworn in 6 October. He was re-elected Mayor in 1529 and 1533. In 1533 he was one of two men elected a warden of the *scole* house (school house).

In a list of "harnes appoynted within the Towne of Guldeford" in 1539, the third entry is: "George Parkehurst the Elder A harnes with...a Byll in his owne handes". This meant that he was a member of the local militia with a suit of armor and a weapon, the bill being a form of pike used by the English militia then, harness being an archaic word for a suit of armor.

On 27 April 1545, fines were levied against William Hamonde senior (2d.), Thomas Stoughton (4d.), George Parkhurst (6d.) and several others for "permit[ting] their taverns in the High Street to be inclosed to the common nuisance". A year later he was fined 4 pence for the same offence. This may well be one of the old taverns mentioned in

Colonial Homes (Vol. 9, pp. 40-41) as still standing on High Street.

George Parkhurst probably died between 27 April 1545 and 2 May 1546 as he is mentioned in the Guildford Borough records on the earlier date, but is not on the tax list of the latter date. Christopher Parkhurst is called "son and Heir of George Parkhurst" in 1550 in a Surrey Feet of Fines.

The earliest mention so far found of the name Parkhurst is of a place of that name in the parish of Abinger Hammer, county Surrey, on a record of 1464. Parkhurst is about 9 miles SEE of Guildford. It was from this wooded park, so named, that the family took its name. By the early 1500's, Parkhursts were living in Shere, Guildford, Shalford and nearby. All were certainly closely related, the same given names being repeatedly used.

Children, no doubt all born at Guildford:

JOHN, b 1510-1512; m Margaret, dau. of Thomas & Margaret (Fraunceys) Garneys of Kenton, Suffolk. At an early age he entered Magdalen College School at Oxford, and subsequently joined Merton College, where he was admitted to a fellowship in 1529 after graduating B.A. (24 July 1528). He was a good classical scholar and was adept in the composition of Latin epigrams. He took holy orders in 1532, and proceeded M.A. 19 Feb. 1532/3. While he was acting as tutor at Merton, John Jewel, afterwards Bishop of Salisbury, was his pupil; he deeply interested himself in Jewel's progress, and they remained through life the most intimate of friends (Strype, *Annals*, II. i. 149-50). A thoroughgoing supporter of the Reformation, Parkhurst imbued Jewel with his rigidly protestant opinions. When, in 1543, Henry VIII and Queen Catherine Parr visited Oxford, Parkhurst wrote Latin verses in their honor and became chaplain to the queen. He was already chaplain to Charles Brandon, Duke of Suffolk, and to his wife Katherine, and his friends included Miles Coverdale and John Aylmer. Soon afterwards, he was appointed Rector of Pimperne, Dorset, and in 1549 was presented by Thomas, Lord Seymour, to the rich living at Cleeve Episcopi, Gloucestershire. Jewel and other Oxford scholars often visited him there, and he rarely sent them back to Oxford without gifts of money. When Jewel gave humanity lectures at Corpus Christi College, Oxford, Parkhurst went over to hear him, and declared in a Latin epigram that he was metamorphosed from a tutor to a pupil. On the accession of Queen Mary, he left the country and settled at Zurich, where he was hospitably received by Rudolph Gaulter and other Calvanistic divines. Returning on the accession of

Elizabeth, he was robbed on the journey, which he made alone, of all of his money and of "the fair copy of his epigrams". On 13 April 1560, he was elected Bishop of Norwich, and was consecrated and installed in September following. He was created D.D. at Oxford in 1566.

The see of Norwich was thoroughly disorganised at the time of Parkhurst's appointment; many of the livings were without incumbants. Parkhurst did not prove himself equal to the situation. His Calvanistic leanings led him to encourage nonconformist practices; he declined to stay "prophesying" in his diocese, and, although he drew up a careful report of its condition in 1563, and prosecuted papists with some vigour, he took no steps to remedy the disorders with which the diocese abounded. He was hospitable, genial and extravagant in private life. In 1572, shortly before his death, he lost much money by the dishonesty of a servant, who had converted to his own use the "tenths" due to the exchequer from the diocese. In order that he might be able to refund the amount, Parkhurst moved from the bishop's palace, which he had elaborately repaired, to a small house at Ludham. To prevent the recurrence of such frauds as those which had crippled his resources, Parkhurst introduced a bill into parliament which was accepted by the government.

Parkhurst published in the year before his death a collection of Latin epigrams which he had composed in his youth, and which were prepared for publication, as the preface states, at Zurich in 1558 (cf. Strype, *Annals*, II.i. 344 sq.). They have been unjustly described as matching Martial in obscenity. Though a few of them deal with topics which bishops usually deem unfitting to notice, the majority are eulogies or epitaphs on friends, and offend only by their tameness. Verses by Thomas Wilson, Alexander Nowell, Bartholomew Traheron, Lawrence Humphrey, and others, are prefixed. The title of the volume runs: *Ioannis Parkhursti Ludicra sive Epigrammata Juvenilia, Londini apud Johannem Dayum Typographum, 1573.* A few are translated in Timothy Kendall's *Flowres of Epigrammes,* 1577. Parkhurst is commonly credited with another volume, *Epigrammata Seria,* London, 1560, of which no copy is known. The theory of its existence seems to rest on a confused interpretation of the preface to the extant book of epigrams which is dated 1558. He contributed to the collection of *Epigrammata in mortem duorum fratrum Suffolcensium Caroli et Henrici Brandon*, London, 1552, and to John Sheepreeve's *Summa...Novi Testamenti disticis ducentis sexaginta comprehensa*, Strasburg, 1558. The translation of the *Apocrypha* in the bible of 1572 is also ascribed to him (Strype, *Parker*, ii. 222). Bale dedicated to him, in a eulogistic address, his *Reliques of Rome* in 1563.

Some of his papers dealing with the regulation of his diocese are in the Cambridge University Library (E.e. ii. 34).

He died on 2 Feb. 1574/5, aged 63, and was buried in the nave of his cathedral on the south side, between the eighth and ninth pillars. A monument marks the spot. Elegies by Rudolph Gaulter and his son were published at Zurich in 1576, in a rare tract which was dedicated to Edwin Sandys, Bishop of London (Brit. Mus.). The title runs *In D. Ioannis Parkhvrsti Episcopi Nordouicensis in Anglia dignissimi obitum Epicedia Rodolphi Gvalteri Tigurini, Patris et Filii. Excvdebat Christoph. Frosch. Anno M.D.LXXVI* . No children. On 24 Sept. 1559, he was granted these arms: *Argent, a cross ermines between 4 bucks trippant proper, on a chief argent, 3 crescents gule.* These were his paternal arms varied by the addition of the chief and crescents. An abstract of his will follows.

> 1 February 1573/4 - the will of John Parkhurst, Bishop of Norwich... to Marton College in Oxford where I was a Fellow the less Maudlin cup with the cover having a naked man in the top as it were Hercules and a bat in his right hand and a man's head in the left... to the town of Guildford where I was born a great bowl of silver and gilt with a man's head in the bottom being polled and having a long beard with the cover having at the top a naked man with a spear in his left hand and a shield in his right... to the library of the same town most of my Latin books... all my English books to my two brothers Christopher Parkhurst and Nicholas Parkhurst ... to the student *Stove* in the city of Zurich a standing cup of silver and gilt called the great Maudlin Cup with three liberty heads about it having holes through them and a cover to that with a naked woman in the top as it were *Pallas* with a *siverdo* in the right hand and a rod in the left hand... to Mr. Rodolphe Gualter, a preacher there, another high Maudlin cup with the brim bowed inward and the cover to the same for him and his son Rodolphe... also my best coverlet made at Norwich by the Strangers... to the Mayor of Norwich my great salt... to Guildford my common salt and my basin and ewer... to the five hospitals in Norwich to each 20s. ... to Mr. Peregrine Bertie as a token of my love to him and all his stock a standing piece with the figure of a woman hid in it and the cover thereof which hath on the top a man harnessed having a helmet on his head, a spear in the left hand and the shield broken from the right... I will that a new shield be made and joined to it with my arms graved in the same... to Mr. Thomas Roberts my steward the gilded cup which he used to drink, one white silver cup, one bowl of silver and gilt with a man's head in the bottom, having a monster's upperbend and a great helmet with three or four faces on it... my sister Helene to have a summer gown, a winter gown and two peticoats ready made to her back and then delivered to her with cloth for smocks kerchiefs sufficient... to my youngest sister Elizabeth 40s. ... to my sisters Agnes and Alice each of them a new Soverign bowed for a token only, for I here say they be wealthy enough... I give to my brother Christopher Parkhurst one goblet of silver and gilt and to my brother Nicholas Parkhurst a goblet of silver and gilt... to my foresaid two brothers all my gowns, cassocks, clothes, doublets and all my other apparel... to my brother Beckingham one of the little bowls of silver and gilt... to my cousin Margaret Crampton a cup of silver and gilt and to Richard Crampton her husband one of the little bowls... to Walter Baispole of Higham, potter, a bowl... also a silver cup... to Dr. Walker the

preacher a salt of silver and gilt..to Dr. Gardner the preacher one of the little bowls of silver and gilt and a silver cup..to Mr. Bird of Norwich a goblet of Silver... to Robert Phillips my servant one of my little bowls... to Robert Woodcock's wife two spoons having on the top J and P... to Dorothie Crabbe for her great pains taken with my wife in sickness £6.13.4. ...to little Margarett, being fatherless and motherless a good featherbed, a bolster and two pillows of feathers, a good coverlet, two blankets, a quilt, three pairs of good sheets and £20 in money to paid on the day of her marriage... to every of my servants a whole year's reckonings... to the poor of Guildford £5... to the poor men's box in Ludham £3.13.4., at Horinge £3, at Saint Martin's in Norwich £3... residue to executors desiring them to be mindful of Christopher Parkhurst son to my brother Christopher, John Parkhurst son to my brother Nicholas being my godson and others of my brother's children whom I would have fain brought up in learning that they may be profitable members in Christ's church hereafter... also consideration of John Chalhurst, And I ordain William Blen'haisett, Esquire, Walter Baispole, Henry Bird, and Robert Phillips to be my executors..Overseers to be Dr. Maister my chancelor, Mr. Thomas Roberts of late my steward, Richard Crampton, Notarie, Thomas Hopkins, D. Gardner, Houghe Spendloue, John More, preacher, and Robert Phillips, and to each 26s.8d. for their pains.

1 February 1574/5 - Codicil... Debts owing unto me by George Thimelthorp my bailiff farmer tenant, and any others, to be divided into four parts... one part to my two brothers Christopher and Nicholas, second part to students of Oxford, Cambridge and Zurich, third part to my servants, the poor of Norwich, Guildford, Ludham and other villages about Ludham. The fourth part to William Blen'haisett, Esquire, Walter Baispole and Robert Phillips. Witnesses: William Maister, Thomas Broke, John Moore, Christopher Parkhurst, Richard Crampton, Richard Hill, George Parker, John Holand. Proved at London 4 March 1475/6.
(Reference: P.C.C. 10 Daughtry)

GEORGE, perhaps b about 1514. He is first mentioned in a list of "harnes appoynted within the Towne of Guldeford" in 1539 as "George Parkehurst the yonger". Wife Agnes & an unnamed child mentioned in his will of 6 Aug. 1540, pr. 25 Sept. 1540; he asked to be buried in the porch of the parish church of the Trinity in Guildford. John P. buried at St. Mary's 16 Sept. 1550 was perhaps the unnamed son. George P. bur. 9 June 1541 at St. Mary's was perhaps a posthumous son born a few days earlier.

HELEN, m 1, Nicholas Babbs (Bab, Babb, Babbe, etc.) who was buried 4 Oct. 1550 at St. Mary's in Guildford; m 2, 18 April 1551, Thomas Beckingham. Nicholas Babbs is first heard of in 1539 when he appears on the list of "Harnes appoynted within the towne of Guldeford"; Constable in 1541, Flesh & Fish Taster in 1542, along with another man, 1544 on the jury, 1545 on the list of approved men indicating he had been a Bailiff, same year named as an Affeerer (an official who assesses fines and fees not already standardly fixed), 1545 Bailiff again, and same year listed as a fishmonger for the whole of Lent for which privilege he was assessed 6d. His burial record says he had been Mayor of Guildford. The family attended the church of Saint Mary, Guildford's oldest church, still standing on Quarry St.; 6 ch. by _abbs: Richard, Henry, Margaret, Helen, Nicholas, Edward (posthumous)

1550 - Nicholas Babbs bought from Henry Alby, gentleman, and Elizabeth his wife and Christopher Parkhurst, son & heir of George Parkhurst, a messuage, 42 acres of land and 3 acres of pasture in Guildford, Stoke next Guildford and Merrowe; consideration £40. (Surrey Feet of Fines, No. 620)

AGNES, mentioned in the will of her uncle, the bishop

ALICE, mentioned in the will of her uncle, the bishop

ELIZABETH, "youngest sister"; prob. m Henry Alby, gentleman, who was named in the Feet of Fines, No. 620, above

8 CHRISTOPHER, first on record 2 May 1546 on a tax list under St. Mary's parish, Guildford; moved to Ipswich, county Suffolk; 6 ch.

NICHOLAS, first mentioned in two feet of Fines:

1557 - John Austen and Nicholas Parkhurst bought from John A Stret, a barn, 20 acres of land, 6 acres of pasture and a 6 acre heath and furze in Wonershe; consideration £40. (Surrey Feet of Fines, No. 904)

1556 - Nicholas Parkhurst and John Austen bought from Robert Atlee and Margery his wife, a messuage, a garden, a barn, an orchard, 20 acres of land, 4 acres of meadow, 6 acres of pasture, 5 acres of wood and 2s. in rent in Effyngham, consideration £40. (Surrey Feet of Fines, No. 835)

He was probably the clerk of Flowton, Suffolk, who was buried there 4 April 1598; wife was apparently Margaret who was buried there 24 March 1596/7; 9 ch. b at Guildford: Ann 1547/8, Elizabeth 1549, Agnes 1550, Elizabeth 1553/4, Alice-bur. 1565/6, Joan 1560, Joan 1562/3 (possibly this is the burial rec. of the earlier Joan), John 1565

Ref.: Guildford Borough records, edited by Enid M. Dance, pub. by The Surrey Record Society, 1958, Vol. XXIV; Surrey Feet of Fines; Colonial Homes, Vol. 9; N.E.H.G.S. - 68; Dictionary of National Biography; Encyclopedia Heraldica, by William Berry, London, 1828-40; Research of John Plummer

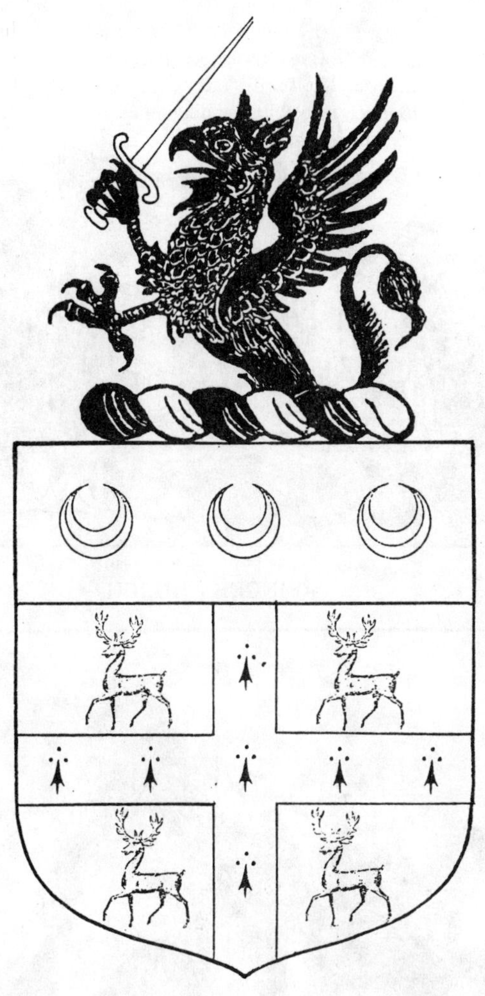

ARMS: Argent, a cross ermines between 4 bucks trippant proper, on a chief gules charged with 3 crescents or
CREST: A demi griffin with wings endorsed sable, holding in the dexter paw a cutlass argent, hilt and pomel or

Engd. for Brayley's History of Surrey.

ABINGER CHURCH

Drawn by J.R. Thompson. Engd. for Brayley's History of Surrey

SAINT MARY'S CHURCH, GUILDFORD

1a

ROBERT PECK (*Robert, Robert*), was born about 1580, probably in Beccles, Suffolk, England. The Parish Registers for Beccles do not begin until 1586. He attended Magdalen College, Cambridge University, where he received his B.A. in 1599 and his M.A. in 1603. On 8 January 1605, he was inducted over Saint Andrew's Church, Hingham, Norfolk, England. Probably that year or the next, Robert Peck married his first wife, Ann Lawrence, the daughter of John and (Agnes?)(Herne) Lawrence of Saint James, South Elmham, Suffolk.

Reverend Peck served at Hingham, England for 30 years, until he was deprived of his living in 1636. He was excommunicated for nonconformity and then threatened with citation to the High Commission Court. But he had obviously become very popular with his parishioners in those 30 years, for when he escaped to New England in 1638, 132 others from Hingham and vicinty joined him. They arrived at Boston, Massachusetts on 10 August 1638 on the *Diligent* from Ipswich, Suffolk, England. Robert Peck had his wife, 2 children, and 2 servants in his household. The entire company apparently settled in Hingham, Massachusetts.

On 28 November 1638, Robert Peck was ordained a teacher in the Hingham church. His difficulties with the church authorities in England would have barred him from officially being the minister. He was admitted a freeman on 13 March 1638/9.

Winthrop records under 2 June 1641 that Parliament was engaged upon a general reformation of both church and state. Robert Peck no loger needed to stay in America. He embarked for England on 27 October 1641 with his wife, son Joseph, and a maid. He never returned to New England and was reinstated in his former parish, serving from 1646-56.

Ann (Lawrence) Peck died in Hingham, England, being buried there on 30 August 1648. Reverend Peck married second Martha Bacon, widow of James Bacon, rector of Burgate, Suffolk.

Reverend Peck is said to have died in 1656, being buried in his churchyard at Hingham, England. His funeral sermon by Nathaniel Joslin was published. (See the several articles in the N.E.H.G.S. Register per reference below for a more extensive treatment of the Peck family.)

24 July 1651 - I ROBERT PECKE Minister of the word of God at Hingham in the countye of Norff beinge in bodilye health and perfect memory ... Imprimus I give and bequeath unto Thomas my Sonne and Samuel my Sonne and their heirs forever All that my messuage wherein I now dwell situate and lyenge in Hingham ... unto Robert Pecke sonne of my sonne Robert deceased the sume of £20 at his age of 23 years ... unto John Pecke sonne of the said Robert deceased £10 To be paid to him at his age of 22 years ... unto Benjamin Pecke the youngest sonne of the said Robert deceased at his age of 22 years £20 ... to the children of Anne Mason my daughter wife of captain John Mason of Seabrooke on the river Connecticut in New England the sume of Forty pounds to be devided equally unto them and to be sent to my sonne John Mason to dispose of it for their use within 2 years after my death ... to my sonne Joseph during his natural life the sume of 141s. yearlie to be in the hands of my sonnes Thomas and Samuel ... for his maintenance ... duringe the terme of his naturall life ... to the children of Thomas and Samuell my sonnes which shall be liveinge at my decease the sume of Five pounds apiece at their several ages of 21 years ... to my now wife Martha Peck £40 ... to the poore of Hingham 51s. ... Executors Thomas Pecke and Samuel Pecke ... my body to buriall which I desire if I depart this life in Hingham may be entered in the church yard near unto Anne my wife deceased ... proved at London 10 April 1658.

Children, baptized at Hingham, England:

ROBERT, bapt. 23 July 1607
THOMAS, bapt. 6 Sept. 1608
JOSEPH, bapt. April 1610
BENJAMIN, bapt. 29 Sept. 1611
SAMUEL, bapt. 14 March 1612
NATHANIEL, bapt. 13 Sept. 1614
DANIEL, buried 8 June 1616
ANNE, bapt. 18 Nov. 1619; m Hingham, Mass. July 1639, Maj. John Mason

Ref.: N.E.H.G.S. 89:327-8; 138:80; TAG 23:83-4,217-20; Peck Genealogy, by Ira B. Peck, 1868

1b

JOSEPH PECK (*Robert, Robert*) was baptized in Beccles, Suffolk, England on 30 April 1587. He died in Rehoboth, Massachusetts on 23 December 1663.

Joseph Peck married first, at Hingham, Norfolk, England, on 21 May 1617, Rebecca Clark, buried there on 24 October 1637. Evidence exists indicating that Rebecca was the sister of Mary Clark, who married Edward Gilman at Hingham on 3 June 1614. It is thought that Jane Clark, who married Robert Kirby at Hingham 25 July 1616 and Margaret Clark, who married Anthony Cooper there on 25 July 1609 were also sisters; all thought to be daughters of John Clark, who was buried at Hingham on 6 June 1615, and Elizabeth Clark, wife of John, buried there on 11 April 1602. Anthony Cooper, Edward Gilman, and Joseph Peck were all early settlers of Hingham, Massachusetts. The parish registers for Hingham begin in 1601, but there is a record in the Genealogical Society of Utah's International Genealogical Index of a Rebecca Clark, baptized there on 21 May 1585, the daughter of Samuel and Martha (Lincoln) Clark. The ultimate source of this record is apparently a "Peck Family Bible," no further information given. The submitter of the record is now deceased. Suspicion is aroused, however, by the fact that family bibles usually give birth, not baptismal records. Also the baptism happens to be exactly 32 years prior to the marriage.

John Clark, buried in 1615, was probably the son of Thomas Clark of Hingham, husbandman, whose 1593 will mentions a wife Elizabeth and children Valentine, Stephen, John, Elizabeth and Margaret. He was probably the grandson of Richard Clark of Hingham, whose will dated 20 August 1557 mentions a wife Margaret and children John, Thomas (relationship not specified but assumed to be son), Margery and Joan. He was probably the great grandson of Richard Clark, as Thomas Clark's will mentions a tenement which was formerly his grandfather Richard Clark's.

Joseph Peck's second wife, who he married in 1637 or 1638 in England, was apparently the sister of Thomas Cooper or his wife Rachel.

Children, baptized in Hingham, England:

ANNE, bapt. 12 March 1617/18; buried 27 July 1636
REBECCA, bapt. 25 May 1620; m about June 1646, Rev. Peter Hobart
JOSEPH, bapt. 23 Aug. 1623; d Rehoboth, Mass. 1702?
JOHN, b about 1626/7; d Rehoboth, Mass. 1713; m 1st Elizabeth Hunt-ting; m 2, 30 Dec. 1668, Elizabeth Preston; m 3, Rebecca____;
NICHOLAS, bapt. 9 April 1630; d Rehoboth, Mass. 27 May 1710; m 1st Mary Winchester; m 2, Rebecca Bosworth

Children by his second wife, born in Hingham, Mass.:

SAMUEL, bapt. 3 Feb. 1638/9; d Rehoboth, Mass. 1708; m 1st, Sarah ____ ; m 2, 21 Nov. 1677, Rebecca (Paine) Hunt
NATHANIEL, bapt. 31 Oct. 1641; buried Rehoboth, Mass. 12 Aug. 1676; m about 1669, Deliverance Bosworth
ISRAEL, bapt. 4 March 1643/4; d Rehoboth, Mass., 2 Sept. 1723; m 15 July 1670, Bethiah Bosworth

SAINT MICHAEL'S CHURCH, BECCLES, SUFFOLK

Ref.: Ackley Bosworth Ancestry; TAG, 12:132-4, 13-151-4; LDS Microfilms 94,917 & 94,894

2

ROBERT PECK (*Robert*) was probably born about 1544. He married, probably about 1572, Helen Babbs, who was baptized at Saint Mary's, Guildford, Surrey, on 15 September 1546. She was buried at Beccles, Suffolk on 31 October 1614. A Visitation of Suffolk some 50 years after her death gives her as the daughter of Nicholas Babbs of Guildford. This is supported by other evidence.

In 1582 Robert Peck was the register and collector for the Archdeacon of Suffolk. (See the several articles in the N.E.H.G.S. Register per references below for a more extensive treatment of the Peck family.

22 March 1592/3 - the will of ROBERT PECK - of Beccles, co. Suffolk, whole of mind and perfect of remembrance, although sick and weak of body at Chelmsford, co. Essex ... of ... pleurisy ... My body to be buried where it shall please God to call me. To Helen, my well-loved wife ... all my houses, lands, tenements ... leases, plate, goods, and chattels within the towns of Beccles, Barsham, Ingate, or elsewhere ... my very good friends, Mr. Bartholomew Stiles and Mr. John Talbot, to aid my wife with their good counsel ... To Richard Peck, my son, all my houses wherein I dwell in Blibergate [?Balligate) Street, my close at Ingate church, and my "pightill" in the same field ... Whereas Thomas Peck, my brother, deceased, by his last will gave unto the said Richard, my son, two tenements in Balligate Street, lately burnt, one of which has been built again on the same ground and the other on part of the same ground and on part of other free ground which I purchased of my uncle, William Waters, I will that the said Richard, my son, within one month after he shall become twenty-one years of age, shall make over ... To Nicholas Peck, my son, ... [and] To Samuel Peck, my son, ... my son Robert at Cambridge ... my two daughters and my son Joseph ... Helen, my wife, ... sole executrix, desiring her to have care of those my children whose legacies I have left to her consideration, and also of Joane Babb and Elizabeth Babb and Robert Meriman and my sister Note [Nott] as she may. Supervisors: Mr. Bartholomew Stiles, clerk, Mr. Roger Peirson, and Mr. John Talbot ... Written with my own hand the day and year above said. Proved at Beccles 10 November 1598.

(Archdeaconry Suffolk R37/10)

Children:

RICHARD, b ca. 1573; d.s.p. 1615, age 41

NICHOLAS, b 1575; m 1610 Rachel Young. In a deposition of 4 Oct. 1639 Nicholas Peck of North Cove, Suffolk, gentleman, aged about 63, indicates he was familiar with the handwriting of Richard Crampton.

1a ROBERT, b about 1580; m Ann Lawrence. Rev. Robert came to Hingham, Mass. 1638, serving as minister there. He returned to England in 1641, leaving behind in the New World only dau. Anne Peck, who m Major John Mason.

MARGARET, b perhaps ca. 1582

MARTHA, b perhaps ca. 1584

1b JOSEPH, bapt. Beccles 30 April 1587; d Rehoboth, Mass. 23 Dec. 1663; m 1, Hingham, Norfolk, England 21 May 1617 Rebecca Clark, who d there Oct. 1637. He came to Hingham, Mass. with his brother, Rev. Robert Peck in 1638.

SAMUEL, b about 1589; d about 1619; a grocer of Ipswich, Suffolk, England, Samuel "traveled beyond the seas" about 1611. He is surely the Samuel Peck who witnessed the will of his mother's 1st cousin John Parkhurst, dated 29 March 1610.

Drawn by Charles C. Pyne — For Brayley's History of Surrey — Engraved by M.J. Starling

Chapel of Saint John the Baptist
Saint Mary's Church, Guildford

Ref.: Peck Genealogy; N.E.H.G.S.: 91:282-6, 355-363; 92:71 & 68:373-4

4

ROBERT PECK was probably born by 1508, probably near Beccles, Suffolk, as his presumed great grandfather was of Beccles at the time of his will in 1504.

John Leek of Beccles bequeathed land bought of Marsh to his "neve" (grandson) Robert Peck in his will dated 6 September 1529. This land is later bequeathed by Robert Peck in his will.

A suit of Drawer vs. Peck around 1630 concerns the legacies of Robert Peck and Katherine (Leek) Drawer from John Leek. Robert Peck was of Beccles at the time of the suit.

Around 1535 Robert Peck married as his first wife ... Norton, a daughter of Robert Norton of Halesworth, Suffolk, 8 miles from Beccles.

About 1540 Robert Peck married for his second wife Joan Waters, daughter of John and Margaret Waters of Beccles. The will of Joan Waters, dated 28 May 1547, mentions his daughter Joan Peck with her husband Robert and her children John, Robert and Margaret. Joan Peck "the younger" also mentioned has been supposed to be the step-daughter of Joan (Waters) Peck. If not, perhaps Robert Peck's mother was still living, and was also named Joan. (See the several articles in the N.E.H.G.S. Register per references below for a more extensive treatment of the Peck family.)

31 October 1556 - the will of ROBERT PECK of Beccles, co. Suffolk, England ... My body to be buried in the churchyard of Beccles, near unto the grave of Joan, my wife. To every one of my household servants 12d. To John Peck, my son, my messuage wherein I dwell and my tenement "late Mayster Rede" and the two meadows lying next the meadow in the tenor of Mathew Prynte and my little garden "late Philippe Doddes," my close "sometyme Helyn Churches," my "fryttlell as the further Wynde Myll late Richard Tyde," and three acres of land "late William Marshes," upon condition that he shall pay - to Thomas Pecke, my son, and to my three daughters Margaret, Olyve, and Anne. To Robard Pecke, my son, my other two meadows in Barstun (?Barsham) "late Churchmans" and the meadows late "Doctor Rede sometyme Baldewyns," my close at Ingate church, one acre of land "late Tyde at Ingatefelds," and the "three roode acres called Bells acre." To Thomas Pecke, my son, my two tenements I

purchased of John Walter and my tenter yard. To my daughters Margaret, Olyve, and Anne, to each £6.13s.4d. To every one of John Water's and William Water's children 4d. To every one of my godchildren 4d.

Executors: Richard Crampton and Thomas Hagas. Supervisors: John Waters and Robert Bradley. My little "pyctell called Caves pyctell" lying in Ingate shall be sold. To Joan Meriman, my daughter, a gown and a petticoat that were her mother's and the "worser paire of Corall beads." Witnesses: Sir John Gymbyn, Robert Tower, Robert Grene, Thomas Goodwyn, and John Waters. Proved 20 November 1556. (Ipswich Probate Registry R17/435)

Child of Robert and ____ (Norton) Peck:

JOAN, born say 1535; m about 1556 Richard Merriman

Children of Robert and Joan (Waters) Peck:

JOHN, b say 1542; d s.p. before 16 Feb. 1573/4
2 ROBERT, b say 1544
MARGARET, b say 1546; d s.p. before 16 Feb. 1573/4
OLIVE, m before 16 Feb. 1573/4, Richard Nott
ANNE, unm. 16 Feb. 1573/4; believed to have d.s.p.
THOMAS, apparently d.s.p. after 16 Feb. 1573/4 when his will was dated

The will of THOMAS PECKE of Beccles ... intending to travel into foreign countries. To be buried where it shall please God to call me. To Richard Pecke, my nephew (son of Robert Pecke, my brother) ... two tenements ... in Beccles, next unto a street called Balligate ... Olive, wife of Richard Note and Anne Pecke, my sister(s)... Executors: brother Robert Pecke ... said, Richard, my nephew ... Witnesses: Richard Crampton, Simeon Smythe. Proved 1580 (R28/253)

Ref.: Ackley-Bosworth Ancestry; N.E.H.G.S.: 89:333-9, 91:282-6

6

NICHOLAS BABBS, probably born about 1515 married probably about 1539, Helen Parkhurst, the daughter of George Parkhurst (See the Parkhurst Line).

The surname Babbs is also spelled Bab, Babb, or Babbe. Nicholas Babbs is first heard of in 1539 when he appears on a list of "Harnes Appoynted within the Towne of Guldeford". In June 1541, he was elected, along with one other, as Constable. On 16 June 1542, he and another were elected Flesh and Fish Tasters. On 3 November 1544, he served on the jury in the case of Campion and Compton versus Hamond. On 27 April 1545, Nicholas Babbs is on the list of approved men, indicating that he had earlier served as Bailiff. The same year, Nicholas is mentioned as an Affeerer. The Oxford English Dictionary gives examples of the term from 1467 to 1768. An Affeerer is basically an official who assesses fines which are not already standardly fixed. Nicholas was elected Bailiff again on 5 October 1545, and the same year he is listed as a Fishmonger for the whole of Lent, though his name is struck through, and he was apparently assessed 6p. for the privilege. On a tax list of 2 May 1546, Nicholas is listed under Saint Mary's Parish and was assessed 5p. for goods and 2s. for lands and tenements.

The only land record found for Nicholas is in 1550:

> Nicholas Babbe, plaintiff, vs. Henry Alby, gentleman, and Elizabeth his wife, and Christopher Parkeherste, son and heir of George Parkeherste, deforciants ... A messuage, 42 acres of land and 8 acres of pasture in Guldeford, Stoke next Guldeford and Merrowe - Octove of Hilary (Surrey Fines, No. 620)

Nicholas Babbs was buried at Saint Mary's, Guildford on 4 October 1550. He was called Mayor of Guildford in the record. His widow married secondly at Saint Mary's, Guildford on 18 April 1551, Thomas Beckingham.

The messuage in the 1550 land record above is certainly one of the three messuages passed on in 1558 (a messuage was a dwelling house with adjoining lands and outbuildings).

Thomas Coxe, Thomas Russell, William Coxe and Thomas Churcher, plaintiffs, vs. Thomas Bekyngham and Helen, his wife, and Richard Dawe, don and heir of Nicholas Dawe, deforciants ... 3 messuages, 2 barns, 3 gardens, 60 acres of land, 3 acres of meadow, 10 acres of pasture and 2 acres of woods in Guldeford, Stoke next Guldeford, a Merowe and Shalford - Morrow of Candlemas.

(Surrey Fines, No. 931)

The family attended the church of Saint Mary's in Guildford, which is still standing on Quarry Street there. It is Guildford's oldest church, containing elements erected from the 11th to the 15th centuries. The tower dates from the mid-eleventh century, showing Saxon stonework.

Helen was mentioned in her brother's will of 1573/4. She and her family were probably then living in county Suffolk.

Children:

RICHARD, prob. b about 1540; prob. the father of Joane and Elizabeth Babbs who were mentioned in Robert Peck's will of 1592/3

HENRY, bapt. St. Mary's 18 Aug. 1543, son of Nicholas Babbs; buried there 29 Aug. 1543

MARGARET, bapt. 27 Feb. 1544/5, dau. of Nicholas Babbs; m Richard Crampton. Richard was register and collector to the Archdeacon of Suffolk as early as 1553, continuing until his death, when his wife Margaret and then Robert Peck took over. Richard Crampton executed one Peck will and witnessed another. The will of Richard Crampton in 1580 mentions brothers-in-law Richard and Nicholas Babbs

3 HELEN, bapt. at St. Mary's 15 Sept. 1546; m Robert Peck, son of Robert and Joan (Waters) Peck

NICHOLAS, bapt. St. Mary's 9 Nov. 1549; Nicholas was witness on 10 Nov. 1590 to a deed from William Brook of Combs, Suffolk to Edmund Denny, ancestor of Samuel & Daniel Denny who emigrated to N.E. in the early 1700's. Nicholas is also mentioned in the wills of his relatives John Parkhurst and Richard Crampton

EDWARD, bapt. St. Mary's 16 Feb. 1550/01, over 4 months after his father was buried

Ref.: Guildford Parish Registers; Guildford Borough records; Surrey Feet of Fines; Colonial Homes, Vol. 9, pages 48, 49, 55; N.E.H.G.R.: 68:374, 89:338, 91:283, 92:71-3, Denny Genealogy, 1944

WILLIAM PHIPPEN of Wedmore, Somersetshire, lived in that part of the parish known as Burrow. There were several Phippen families living in various parts of this rather extended parish during the early part of the 17th century. William was a favorite name among them and it is impossible to sort them out, so incomplete are the records. This particular William Phippen mentioned in his will a brother, Joseph, living in Ireland. This undoubtedly was the Joseph Phippen who married Elynor Marten on 2 August 1603 at Wedmore, and had baptized there four children:

Christopher, baptized 17 August 1603
Isabella, baptized 5 December 1604
Joseph, baptized 12 October 1606
George, baptized 16 March, buried 24th, 1610/11

Joseph, of whom there is no further record in Wedmore, was probably several years older than William.

John Phippen, who married Dorothy Thorne on 10 June 1616, may have been another brother.

William's wife, Judith, was buried 10 December 1637. William Phippen was buried 5 October 1647 at Wedmore, as was his wife.

William Phippen was, according to his will, a baker. His only known children are those named in his will, an abstract of which follows.

In the name of God Amen, I **William Phipping** [of] Wedmore in the County of Somerset, Baker, being sick in body but thanks be to God of perfect memory, do make this my last will and testament in manner and form as following. That is to say, first I yield and bequeath my soul into the hands of Almighty God my creator and redeemer. Item, I give unto my daughter Joane x^s. Item, I give unto my daughter Francis x^s. Item, I give to my daughter Elizabeth xiij pounds which remains from Richard Page. Item, I give to my daughter Elizabeth xij pounds which remains from my brother Joseph Phipping upon bond. Item, I give to my daughter Elizabeth seven and forty shillings which I lent to my brother Joseph Phipping in Ireland. Item, I give to Elizabeth my daughter six pounds from Richard Numan upon bond. Item, I give to my daughter Elizabeth twenty shillings and two pair of stockings of two threads of worsted and one of yarn from the hands of Ellinor Andrewes, widow. Item, I give to my daughter Elizabeth xvj^s from William Peacocke of olom in the parish of Bitton in the County of Gloucestershire. Item, I make my daughter Elizabeth

whole executrix of this my last will and testament. I do appoint Richard Page and Richard Browne overseers. Of this money it shall be put out to use for the maintenance of my daughter Elizabeth and her children. Item, I give to the two overseers a groat apiece. Item, I give to my daughter Elizabeth seven shillings which remains from John Swease of Corblock in the parish of Wedmore. In witness whereof I have hereunto set my hand and seal the xxij day of September in the year of our lord 1647. The mark of William Phipping. Witness to the same Richard Webb, William Addams, Thomas Webb.
Item, I do make over the estate of the house at Wedmore to my son in law John Addams till the return of my daughter Judah out of New England. Proved at London 9 September 1650.
(Reference: Prerogative Court of Canterbury - Pembroke 186)

Children, probably all born at Wedmore:

JUDITH, b about 1619; went to N.E. in 1635; m 1, James Hayward; 1 ch.; m 2, 10 Jan. 1643/4, William Simonds; 12 ch.; she d 3 Jan. 1689/90
ELIZABETH, b about 1625/6; prob. the dau. who m John Adams; she had ch. by 1647
FRANCES, bapt. 10 Feb. 1627/8, "dau. of William"
JOAN, bapt. 9 Jan. 1630/31, "dau. of William Phippen of Burgo"

CHURCH OF SAINT MARY, WEDMORE

Ref.: Parish Register of Wedmore; P.C.C. Wills

HENRY PINDER was born in England, probably about 1580, and died in February 1661 at Ipswich, Massachusetts. He married first, on 22 May 1614 at the Church of Saint Mary the Great in Cambridge, England, Mary Rogers. She was born about 1582, and died in New England between March 1647 and 1655. He married secondly before 1655, Elizabeth (——) Andrews, the widow of Robert Andrews. She was born probably about 1590 and died at Ipswich on 29 May 1671. Henry Pinder is first mentioned in New England in 1636 but he surely came over before 1635 when his wife and children crossed.

No further record can be found in England on Henry Pinder or Mary Rogers.

"xiij Aprilis 1635 ... In the Susan & Ellen, Edward Payne Mr for New England Theis pties hereunder expressed have brought Certificate from the Minister & Justices of their Conformitie & That they are no subsedy men.

		Mary Pynder 53	
Francis Pynder	20	Marie Pynder	17
Joanna Pinder	14	Anna Pynder	12
Katherine Pinder	10	Jo: Pynder	8

In 1636, on the list of debts owed the estate of John Dillingham is £6.12s. by Goodman Pinder.

Robert Andrews, husband of Henry's second wife, left a will in which he mentioned the two sons of Humphrey Griffin. Altho not so stated in the will, Griffin was his son-in-law. Humphrey and Elizabeth (Andrews) Griffin had a daughter Elizabeth who married Edward Deare. The following deed proves that the widow of Robert Andrews was the mother of Elizabeth (Andrews) Griffin and that she married Henry Pinder.

31 July 1662 "I Elizabeth Pinder widdow formarly promysed to give unto my Grandchild Elizabeth Deare the full summ of Twenty pounds I doe now pforme this my promise and free gift. And doe now Confirme unto my Grandchildren Edward Deare and his wife and their heires one Cow, and alsoe eight acres of marsh ... which was sometime goodman Howes", Witnesses: Elizabeth Giffin [should be Griffin], Robert Lord, marshall (3:3)

Humphrey Griffin sold some land to Simon Tompson on 9 February 1655, and Elizabeth Pindar, for 40s. paid yearly, the same day relinquished all her rights in the land. It was evidently some of the land of Robert Andrews. This shows that Elizabeth had married Henry Pindar before that date. She was presented in Court in March 1647 as Goodwife Andrews for reviling her son-in-law, Humphrey Griffin, so she had not yet married Henry Pindar. In March 1647, Goody Pindar was a witness in a case, hence Mary, Henry's first wife, was still living.

Altho Henry Pinder lived in Ipswich from 1636 to 1661, about twenty years, there are few mentions of him in any sort of records. About 1653, with Thomas Rowell, he contracted to build a bridge, but it was not finished and the town appointed Robert Lord to sue them, which he did. (Essex Court Files 1:319)

> 25 January 1657 "I Henry Pinder of Ipswich .... carpenter in consideration of full satisfaction to me ... paid ... sell ... unto Twiford West of the same town ... cordwinder one commonage belonging to my house wherein I dwell", signed by mark. Witnesses: Rose Whipple, James Chute (*Essex County Deed 1:211*)

This is the only land record of his. Henry Pinder left no will and apparently no administration was taken on his or his widow's estates.

Children, born in England:

FRANCES, bapt. 6 Aug. 1615 at St. Mary the Great in Cambridge; she possibly m Robert Burnham

MARY, bapt. 14 Sept. 1617 at St. Mary the Great; m 21 March 1642/3 at Gloucester, Solomon Martin, b about 1619; 2 ch.; d 9 Feb. 1647/8; he m 2, 18 June 1648, Alice (____) Varnum of Ipswich; he was prob. lost at sea in 1655

JOANNA, b 1621, aged 14 in 1635; m 14 Nov. 1643 Valentine Rowell; 9 ch.; he d 17 May 1662; she m 2, 18 Sept. 1670, William Sargent; m 3, 26 Oct. 1676, Richard Currier; she d in Oct. 1690 ae about 69

ANNA, bapt. 13 Jan. 1622/3 at St. Andrew the Great (Hannah in bapt. rec.); aged 12 in 1635 list

KATHERNE, bapt. 23 Jan. 1624/5 at St. Andrew the Great, Cambridge; living in 1635, aged 10

JOHN, b early 1627; m about 1655, Elizabeth Wilson, dau. of Theophilus; d after 1699/70

> Joseph Fowler was fined for striking John Pinder on the Sabbath Day. Witnesses: Good. Pinder, Goodman Pritchet, John Anable and Ri: Bets.

PHEBE, bapt. 19 April 1629; prob. d before 1635

Ref.: Parish Registers; Essex County Quarterly Court Files; The Planters of the Commonwealth, by Charles E. Banks, 1961

JOHN RAMSDELL was among the first settlers of Lynn, Massachusetts, apparently arriving at Boston in the summer of 1630 with the Winthrop Fleet and going shortly to Lynn. He was a servant, that is employee, of Captain Nathaniel Turner and was probably unmarried when he emigrated. He was born about 1602. All this is deduced from a deposition he made on 30 June 1657, in which he stated that he was aged 55, that 25 years ago when he was a servant of Captain Turner, his master and other inhabitants of Lynn, before it was a town, fenced in Nahant, and that by reason of these householder's fencing, they had put their cattle there without molestation all these years.

Just where in England John Ramsdell came from is unknown. Ramsdell, Ramsdale and Ramsden seem to be variations of the same name, *dale* or *dell* being a small valley clearing and *den* roughly meaning the same. The name is found in several counties of England with a large concentration at Halifax, Yorkshire. There is a place called Ramsden in Oxfordshire.

The parentage of John Ramsdell's wife, Priscilla, is also a mystery. It is worth noting, as a possible clue, however, that he named a son Aquilla, a rare given name. At nearby Hampton, New Hampshire, there was an Aquilla Chase from Cornwall, England. He had a daughter named Priscilla. Could there be a connection?

John Ramsdell appears often in the court records as a juryman, witness, etc. He never was in trouble, was apparently a peaceful and quiet man. On 25 June 1650, he was sworn in as one of two constables of Lynn, his only public office. In June 1660, he was in court for taking John Mansfield's yoke of oxen to the pound. Mansfield thought it unwarranted. Apparently the dispute arose over whether the road from which they were taken was a public road or a path thru a common field. At that time, much of the farm land was held in a common field tenure. The matter was finally turned over for settlement to three local farmers who knew the land.

In June 1673, John Ramsdell gave testimony concerning the road to Marblehead from Lynn, which he had been familiar with for 42 years.

In the court records are several references to John Ramsdell's land "in the neck", a part of Lynn, and also to *Ramsdell's Corner* in Lynn.

In 1675, John Ramsdell made the following agreement with his son Aquilla, thereby providing for care in his old age and settling his estate.

Priscilla Ramsdell died 23 January 1675/6 and John Ramsdell died 27 October 1688, aged 86 according to a Bible record.

> 12 April 1675 - agreed between John Ramsdell, senior, of Lynn, county of Essex, husbandman, & Aquilla Ramsdell being ye natural son of ye sd John Ramsdell, of same town ... sd John Ramsdell for & in consideration of his own, also of his wife's inability to carry on & manage their affairs for their comfortable livelyhood ... by reason of age, hath with ye consent of his now wife in reference to her surrendering up of her thirds ... give to Aquilla his son to have possession at ye death of ye sd John Ramsdell & his wife, they being natural parents of ye sd Aquilla, all my house lot and housing upon it & orchard, the whole being six acres more or less, abutting easterly on ye marsh ... northerly with ye county highway ... also three acres more or less in ye same neck of land ... also three acres of fresh meadow ... also three acres of fresh meadow lying northwesterly from ye town ... also three acres of salt marsh ground lying above the bridge ... also two acres in the salt marsh in ye first division in Rumley marsh, being part of his three acre lot, he reserving one acre of it for himself ... also one acre of marsh bounded easterly with ye mill creek... unto ye said Aquilla ... after the death of his sd father & mother ... will manage all their business ... bring in one half of the hay, corn and other fruits ... to keep houses and fences in good repair ... all their firewood to their door ... the old orchard ... two of the trees in it for his & his now wife's use ... & also one acre of corn land near the barn, which ye sd Aquilla doth promise to plow it, to carry dung to it & to carry in the corn of it ... engage to afford unto his sd father & mother Christian burial & within two years next after both their deaths, to pay unto his brother Isaac Ramsdell ten pounds & within two years after that to pay to his brother John Ramsdell five pounds and so successively to pay each of his natural sisters one pound apiece, paying y eldest first ... if any die, then to their children ... Signed by marks of John Ramsdell & Aquilla Ramsdell. Confirmed 21 April 1677. (Essex County Deeds 5:64)

Children, born at Lynn:

PRISCILLA, prob. who m 7 May 1662 at Concord, James Adams, one of Cromwell's Scot prisoners (Ramesden in m record); 8 ch.; he worked with both John Gifford's & Daniel Salmon's teams carting for the Saugus Iron Works. In 1656, he sued Samuel Bennett for taking away his cart & wheels, & Nicholas Pinnion for debt. In 1658, he was a member of Scots Charitable Soc.; he d 3 Dec. 1707, she & 7 ch. surviving

HANNAH, prob. who m 11 Dec. 1662 at Concord, John Mason (Ramesden in m record), also apparently one of the Scot prisoners. In 1658, he was a member of the Scots Charitable Soc.; had a son John b 1664 at Concord; he d 10 March 1666/7 at Concord; she was prob. living 1675

ISAAC, prob. b 1635-45; m 12 July 1666 at Lynn, Eleanor, dau. of John & Ann Vinton, b in May 1648; ch.: Isaac b at Concord 1667 - d 1741/2, John b Concord 1670 - d 1676/7, Jonathan b Concord 1672 - d 1743, Dorcas d 1676, Nathaniel b 1677 at Lynn - d 1748, John b 1679/80 - d 1725, Joseph b 1682 - d 1756, Sarah b 1685, Eleanor b 1688. Isaac & wife on 15 Aug. 1713 sold a 10 acre lot, formerly his father's

JOHN, prob. b 1638-43; m 31 May 1671, Elizabeth Perkins, dau. of Rev. Wm. & Elizabeth (Wootton) Perkins of Topsfield, b 18 June 1643; 6 ch.; he d 23 Feb. 1714/15, she surviving

AQUILLA, m 1, Hannah ______ who d 10 Nov. 1688; m 2, Lydia per deed 11:220 of 1691; ch.: Jonathan b 1672 - d.y., Nathaniel b 1673 - d 1745, Aquilla b & d 1675/6, John b 1678, Jonathan b & d 1679, Hannah b 1680, Jonathan b 1683 - d 1684/5, Samuel b 1684, Priscilla b 1687, Benjamin b 1689/90, Moses b 1692/3, Elizabeth b 1696, prob. also Joseph of Lynn who was killed at Casco Bay 1690 by Indians (he would be the eldest); Aquilla served in King Phillip's War

ELIZABETH, m 12 Aug. 1674 at Malden, John Shaw; his 1st wife Hannah d 8 April 1674; he was a tailor

JONATHAN, b 31 March 1657; d in Aug. 1658

Ref.: The Essex County Quarterly Court Files; Essex County Deeds; Savage; Soldiers in King Phillip's War, by Bodge; V.R.

Old Tunnel Meeting House, Lynn, 1682

ESDRAS READE (*Esdras*) of the parish of Saint Mary Overies, Southwark, Surrey, England, married on 18 October 1621, Elizabeth Watson of the parish of Saint Michael's, Crooked Lane, London, where the marriage took place. This parish was later merged with Saint Magnus Martyr. Southwark is on the south side of the Thames River and is now a part of greater London.

In 1633, a suit was brought by Esdras Reade, tailor, of London, against his uncle, John Reade, husbandman, of Sutton Mallet, parish of Moorlinch, Somersetshire, from which record it was learned that Esdras was the son of Esdras Reade (who died about 1611) and his wife, Bathsheba (who died about 1630), and that the elder Esdras was the son of the widow Agnes Reade, living in Sutton Mallet in 1583. The registers of baptisms, marriages and burials of the parish of Saint Mary Overies, now called Saint Savior's, in Southwork, Surrey (1621-1638), have 6 baptisms and 6 burials for this family, altho the burial records state no relationships. In the case of the baptisms, the occupation of Esdras was given as tailor in 5 cases, brewer in the 6th.

On 10 October 1629, Elizabeth Reade was buried, probably having died in childbirth as was so often the case then. A little over a year later, on 22 February1630/31 at Saint Katherine by-the-Tower, Esdras Reade remarried to Sarah Dickinsson. About seven years later, they sailed for America.

The first record of Esdras Reade in New England is on 24 December 1638 - "Esdras Reade, a Taylor, is this day allowed to bee an Inhabitant and to have a great lot at Muddy River for 4 heads". Muddy River was then part of Boston and in 1705 became the town of Brookline. For some reason he was dissatisfied and within a few weeks he moved on to Salem, where on 25 February 1638/9 he was admitted an inhabitant. He lived in that part of Salem which later became Wenham. He received a ten acre grant there 21 January 1639/40 as an addition to an earlier one of ten acres, another 10 acres on 23 January 1642/3, and on 4 December 1643, 2 acres near the meeting house.

On 10 May 1640, Esdras Reade was admitted as a member of the Salem Church and on 31 May he had two children baptized. These were undoubtedly Bethia and Obadiah. On 7 February 1640/41, Sarah Reade was admitted a member of the church. He was made a freeman 2 June 1641.

In 1644 Esdras Reade, with other members of the Salem church including the pastor, the Reverend John Fiske, founded the town of Wenham, which was called before its incorporation, Enon, meaning "much water". He was a leading citizen of the town and was the first deacon of the Wenham Church, altho a probationary one, final confirmation being overlooked for many years. He represented the town at the General Court in 1648 and 1651.

In September 1654, propositions were made to the Reverend John Fiske and his church in Wenham to move to Chelmsford and join with other settlers from Concord and Woburn. Fiske and a number of the church members met at Chelmsford and looked over the prospects. Being satisfied, they made arrangements for the move. Then, for some unknown reason, the plans collapsed and lay dormant for a few months, only to be revived the next year. About 13 November 1655 there met at Chelmsford, Reverend Fiske and seven of the Wenham settlers plus several from Woburn and Concord. All were received into the fellowship of the church.

At the first town meeting at Chelmsford, held 22 November 1655, Esdras Reade was elected one of a committee "to officiate in ordering the publick affaires".

A deposition of 29 December 1657 says he was then 57, which would place his birth about 1600.

Three years later, he was again on the move, for in 1658 he was in Boston for the second time. In 1660 is found at Chelmsford, "John Webb is admitted to purchase all the rights and privileges granted by the town of Chelmsford to Esdras Reade."

On 4 August 1661, he and his wife Sarah joined the Second Church of Boston.

Nine years later he was living in Woburn, probably with his daughter Bethia Johnson, for in a deed of sale of land in 1670 he calls himself, "Esdras Reade, Taylor of Woburn". But by the next year he was back in Boston for the third time according to another deed, and must have lived there until his death in 1680.

He probably lived at what is now the corner of Salem and Prince Streets. He sold this estate 12 January 1673/4 to Samuel Brackenbury, physician, for £132. The deed gives the location as "at the intersection of a street that leads from the Second Meeting House in Boston towards Century Haven and a lane that leads from the said Street towards Winnissimmet Ferry Place".

He died 27 July 1680, aged 85, and was buried in the Copp's Hill Burial Ground of Boston. With him lies his wife, Sarah.

He died intestate and his small estate was administered by his son Obadiah. Te inventory of the estate, now gone from the probate files of Suffolk County, shows that he was engaged at his trade for there were in it the tools of the tailor's trade. Sarah died in March or May 16--, aged 70, her part of the double gravestone now broken and part missing.

Children, the first six baptized at Saint Mary Overie; the last two at Salem, Massachusetts.

ELIZABETH, bapt. 29 Aug. 1622; prob. the child, father unnamed, buried 15 Feb. 1622/3

SARAH, bapt. 8 Jan. 1623/4; prob. the child, father unnamed, buried 17 Sept. 1624

PHILIP, bapt. 25 July 1625; prob. the infant, father unnamed, buried 26 Dec. 1626

REBECCA, bapt. 27 Sept. 1627, father's occupation given as brewer; m 26 June 1656 at Concord, Joseph Parkhurst, both of Chelmsford

------

JONATHAN, bapt. 22 Dec. 1631; prob. the infant, father unnamed, buried 27 Dec. 1631

JONATHAN, bapt. 13 Aug. 1635; prob. the infant, father unnamed, buried 18 Aug. 1635

BETHIA, b about 1637-8, bapt. 31 May 1640; m at Woburn 28 April 1657, John Johnson, son of Capt. Edward & Susan (Munter) Johnson, bapt. 10 May 1635; 7 ch.; she d 2 Dec. 1717 at Canterbury, Conn. He d about 1720 (see#808)

OBADIAH, b about 1639-40, bapt. 31 May 1640; m 19 Aug. 1664, Ann, dau. of Thomas & Elizabeth Swift, b 14 Nov. 1647; 9 ch.; she d 13 Sept. 1680; he m 2, about 1682, Elizabeth, dau. of Thomas & Mary (Biscoe) Broughton, b 15 Jan. 1645/6 at Watertown; she d 26 Feb. 1712/13 ae 67 at Boston; he d 19 Feb. 1721/2 in 82nd year at Boston; he was a housewright

*

Note: A James Reade also had a son, Philip, bapt. in the same parish. Was James a brother to Esdras?

Ref.: The American Genealogist, Vol. 28; V.R.; History of the Reed Family, by J.W. Reed, 1861; Savage; Suffolk County Probate 1156; The Notebook of the Reverend John Fiske 1644-1675, edited by Robert G. Pope, published by Essex Institute, 1974

2

EDWARD RIDDLESDALE (*John, Henry, Jasper*) was probably born about 1592 in Assington, Suffolk. About 1619, he and his wife Mary were married, presumably in some nearby parish. Edward was buried 9 February 1630/31 at Assington, but of "Bures" Saint Mary according to the burial record. Presumably, he was buried at Assington to be near other members of his family. Mary remarried 27 June 1632 at Assington to John Wyatt, who was born about 1594. It was a second marriage for him also. His first wife, nee Martha Sheldrake, daughter of John and Joan Sheldrake, was baptized at Assington on 8 February 1596/7, and was buried on 16 March 1631/2. There is no record of any children by his marriage to Martha. Shortly after Mary's remarriage, she and John Wyatt left for New England and settled in Ipswich, Masachusetts, as did her sister-in-law, Susan (Riddlesdale) French. Altho John Wyatt referred to his *daughters* Mary, Sarah and Dorcas in his will, it appears that they were actually step-daughters, and that he never had any children of his own.

Goodman Wyatt owned land in Ipswich in 1638 and was listed as a proprietor in that town in 1639. He also had a share in Plum Island in 1664. In 1641, he and John West bought a cow which promptly died. They took the matter to court, for John Satchwell and Humphrey Griffin were appointed to view a "dead cow at Jo. Wyatt's" in March 1642. He was made a freeman in November 1645 and he served on trial juries in 1646, 50 and 55, and on the grand jury in 1647 and 1660. In 1647, he was a witness to the oral will of Luke Heard, his son-in-law. In September 1650, John Wyatt was excused from ordinary military training, to pay 5 shillings yearly for the use of the company. Again in 1659 and in 1664 he was released from training and to pay 2 shillings and 6 pence per year. In September 1665, he sued Enoch Greenleaf for £10 of debt for a pair of steers to have been paid for in wheat, malt and Indian corn at Wyatt's home in Ipswich. Wyatt won.

Their grandson, John Kimball, apparently lived with them as is seen from the following.

John Wyatt died in December 1665.

23 November 1665 - the will of John Wyatt of Ipswich ... weak in body ... to wife during term of her natural life £6 per annum in merchantable wheat, malt and Indian corn ... the use of room we now live in with the cellar under it and the upper rooms over it, and the use of the bedstead in the said room for her natural life, also I give her all her household goods that are remaining which are contained in an inventory annexed to the will, to be at her disposing ... also £5 per annum for three years to be paid in country pay at the current price. But in case she needs it sooner, then to be paid according to necessity. Moreover she shall have the use of all my household goods together with my grandchild John Kimball ... while he abides in the house ... if wife cannot live comfortably in the house with him then she shall have liberty to choose another place of being in the town, and he shall supply her with wood and pay her room. I give unto my three daughters, Mary, Sarah and Dorcas 5s apiece ... unto John Kemball my grandchild my dwelling house and all the ground belonging to it and all my meadow ground together with my Cattle and husbandry implements, provided he carry himself respectfully towards my wife, and in case he shall not, then I give unto my said grandchild £10 and so not to have to do with any part of my estate besides ... Loving friend Mr. Theophilus Wilson my sole executor ... and he to have 40s. ... my loving friends Mr. Robert Paine and Willm White the overseers.

An Inventory of all or the most part of the household goods and Chattels that Mary Wyatt, now wife unto John Wyatt of Ipswich, brought or delivered into her husband's possession at the time of her marriage - her apparell, a feather bed, a feather bolster & a pillow, a flockbed and a bolster, a green rug & three blankets, a pair of valance and three curtains, a pair of sheets and one pair of pillowbiers, two trunks and a great chest and great broad box, three platters one long and two broad ones, a great pewter candlestick and a little one, a great pewter salt, two pewter basins, a great one and a lesser one, two pewter great pint pots and two lessor pots, a pewter bedpan, one porringer and spoons and other small pewter saucers & plates, two iron pots a great & a little one, an iron kettle, a warming pan and a brass frying pan, a pestal and a mortar, a pair of andirons, two brass skillets, a 3 pint and a two pint one, a brass ladle and a brass scummer, a pair of pot hooks and a pair of pot hangers, a chafing dish. Proved 15 January 1665/6. (Essex County Will: 30736)

An Inventory of the Lands, cattles & estate of John Wiate, lately deceased, taken the 26th of December 1665

	£ s. d.
the dwelling house, barne & ground about it both homestead & pasture	60.00.0
a six acre lott in the comon field	25.00.0
a p'sell of marsh in the hundreds	12.00.0
a paire of oxen	13.00.0
three cowes	13.00.0
one steere & 2 calves	4.00.0
a mare	6.00.0
3 shotes	2.00.0
in Indian corne	5. 5.0
in Inglish corne	2. 5.0
in pewter & spoones	1. 0.0
a latten callender, driping pan, lamp & grate	0. 6.0
3 old kettells & a brass pott & little skillett	1.16.0
in pork & befe	1.15.0
powdering tub, keelers, beere vessells, churne & other small things	1.10.0
two bowles, 3 trayes & cheesmottes & dishes	0. 5.0
turnaps	0. 3.0
in butter & pork suite	0. 5.6

nyne pound cotten woole	0. 9.0
a trundle bed, wheele, a pair of cardes & old tub	0.10.0
3 peacks of malt	0. 3.4
ould bags	0. 3.6
a bedstead & 3 curtaines & fether bolster, a pillow, old coverlett & 3 blanketts & old tike	3. 4.0
his weareing Apparell	6. 0.0
five paire of sheetes	3. 6.8
three shirts	1. 1.0
4 small table cloths & towells & napkins	1. 1.0
2 paire of old pillow beeres	0. 4.0
6 caps & 5 bands	0.10.0
an old chest & cubbard & old box	0.16.0
a muskett	0.12.0
a little table, 3 chaires, salt box & salt	0. 8.0
in earthen ware	0. 4.4
fire pan, tongs, tramell & pothookes	0. 8.6
scales, waites, 2 pailes & other small things	0. 7.0
a grediron & cliver	0. 3.6
axes, beotle rings, wedges & other tooles	0.16.0
an old saddle, fetters, cart rope	0.10.0
4 hookes for to make ropes	0. 5.0
an old lennen wheele	0. 2.6
an old meale tub & 2 sives	0. 2.6
a trundle bed, flock bed, bolster & pillow	1.10.0
2 old sithes & one snath	0. 6.0
a plow & chaine & sled	1. 5.0
a cart wheeles, 2 yokes & tumbrell	3.10.0
a fann & a cushan	0. 7.0
Sum Totals	177.19.4
Debts dew from the estate about	21. 0.0
Cleare estate	£156.19.0

Mary remarried to James Barker of Rowley, 22 May 1666. His wife, Grace, had died 27 December 1665.

In 1667, John Kimball pledged his inheritance against his obligations to his grandmother as this deed shows.

25 March 1667 - I John Kimball of Ipswich, junior, husbandman sell unto Theophilus Willson of the same town, yeoman my now dwelling house and houselot and pasture, with outhouses, fences and all other appurtenances with a six acre lot ... and nineteen acres of marsh ... being all the houses and lands given & bequeathed to me the said John Kimball by my grandfather John Wiate, late of Ipswich, deceased ... the condition of this bargain & sale is such that if the above said John Kimball ... pay ... unto the abovesaid Theophilus Willson six pounds per annum in merchantable wheat, malt and Indian corn ... for the use ... of Mary the late wife of John Wiate of Ipswich during the term of the late natural life of the said Mary ... then this bargain ... to be void ... Signed John Kimball. Witnesses: William White, Samuel Graves. (Ipswich Deeds3:41)

On 16 March 1677/8, John Barker of Rowley sued John Kimball for not paying him 48 cords of firewood which was due to his wife, "formerly called Mary Wiate, grandmother to said Kimball," according to an agreement signed 15 January

1665 that John Kimball should bring to his grandmother's house four good cords of wood each year during her life in consideration of what his grandfather John Wiate enjoined him to do by will. Cordwood was worth about 5 shillings per cord then in Rowley. Probably young Kimball was reluctant to furnish firewood for the benefit of Barker who meant nothing to him. Barker died and was buried at Rowley on 7 September 1678. Mary Barker died 10 April 1683.

3 September 1678 - The will of James Barker of Rowley in New England ... born in Stragewell in Low Suffolk in Old England ... weak of body ... to my beloved wife Mary I give the things she brought with her when I married her & the use of the room we live in, with firewood ready cut for the fire from time to time, her rent at Ipswich & twenty shillings yearly for life, to be paid by my son Burzillai in work or as she shall see need to call for it, not money, & if any agreement appear of our Contract at marriage, that it be fulfilled equally by my executors ... Bequests to eldest child Burzillai, daughter Grace, sons James, Nathaniel ... daughter Eunice Watson.

Children:

EDWARD, bapt. 23 April 1620 at Assington; no further record of him

MARY, bapt. 29 Jan. 1621/2 at Assington. She must be the Mary who m about 1640, Henry Kimball, bapt. 12 Aug. 1615 at Rattlesden, Suffolk, son of Richard & Ursula (Scott) Kimball; 13 ch.; she d 12 Aug. 1672 at Wenham; he m 2, Elizabeth (Gilbert) Rayner; he d about May 1676

SARAH, bapt. 16 Nov. 1623 at Assington; m 1, about 1642, Luke Heard, who d 1647; 3 ch.; she m 2, Joseph Bixby, son of George & Anna (Cole) Bixby; 9 ch.; he d 19 April 1701; she d 3 June 1703, "a widow of 84 years", which has to be an exageration of her age.

DORCAS, perhaps the Dorcas Riddlesdale bapt. 18 June 1629 at Bures Saint Mary, tho the record says "dau. of Henry". This must be an error in the record. There was indeed a Henry Riddlesdale alias Loker living there, but he died in Feb. 1630/31, testate, naming his other known children (for whom no baptisms have been found) but naming no daughter Dorcas. Thus, if Henry had a dau. Dorcas, she must have d in infancy, and then another unrecorded Dorcas, dau. of Edward, was born. More likely, this Dorcas was attributed to the wrong father, there being some confusion with the two Riddlesdale families in the parish. A Dorcas Riddlesdale appears in the Ipswich Quarterly Court Records as a witness in March 1647, but there is no further record of her. She was the only Riddlesdale in N.E. records. She must be the daughter (i.e.step-daughter) that John Wyatt bequeathed to.

REBECCA, bapt. 5 Dec. 1630 at Bures Saint Mary. There being no further record of her, she must have d.y., perhaps in N.E.

Ref.: The Pillsbury Ancestry, by Holman; V.R.; Essex County Quarterly Court Files 1:112, 6:442

4

JOHN RIDDLESDALE (*Henry, Jasper*) was baptized 26 September 1557 at Boxford, Suffolk. John and his wife Dorcas were married about 1583, probably in Assington. The Assington parish register does not start until 1598 and there are no surviving Bishop's Transcripts for 1583, hence the deduction. Also, their last child was baptized in Assington and their children married there.

On 3 January 1613/14, John and Dorcas Riddlesdale sold a 10 acre close, two others of 5 acres and one of 2 acres to John Gryme the elder of Assington and his wife Faith for £120. All were pasture and lying in Assington. On the same day, Dorcas Riddlesdale released her interest in land leased in June 1555 by John and Robert Gurdon for 500 years to John Vigorus the younger, clothier of Langham, Essex. (Gurdon papers at Ipswich - HD22/1/4). John Vigorus was perhaps Dorcas's grandfather.

Dorcas was buried 24 September 1624 at Assington. John Riddlesdale was buried there 4 June 1629, but the burial record says that he was of "Bures". He was probably living with one of his children when he died, but was buried next to his wife back in Assington. Bures Saint Mary and Assington are adjacent parishes and Boxford is adjacent to Assington on the northeast.

Children:

SUSAN, bapt. 20 April 1584 at Boxford, "dau. of John Riddlesdale & Dorcas his wife"; m 5 Sept. 1608 at Assington, Thomas French, son of Jacob & Susan (Warren) French, bapt. 11 Oct. 1584 at Bures St. Mary. They went to N.E. where they settled in Ipswich, Mass.; 9 ch.; he d late 1639; she d in Aug. 1658 at Ipswich

RICHARD, prob b about 1586; buried 6 Nov. 1610 at Assington; admin. of his estate was granted 28 Feb. 1610/11 to his sisters Susan and Joan both of whose husbands were named in the admin. records. He was apparently unm. He must have been born by 1589 to have had an estate to admin.

THOMAS, mentioned in the will of his grandfather Henry Riddlesdale 1591; no further record of him

JOAN, prob b about 1590; m 11 Oct. 1610 at Assington, Richard Mather, a double wedding with her sister Dorcas. There is a good possibility that Joan & Dorcas were twins.

DORCAS, prob. b about 1590; m 11 Oct. 1610 at Assington, Thomas Dynes, a yeoman of Assington. She was buried 15 Dec. 1610 at Assington. Admin. of her estate was granted to her sisters Susan and Joan at same time as for her brother Richard. No ch.

2 EDWARD, prob. b about 1592; m Mary ______ & had 3 ch. bapt. at Assington: Edward 23 April 1620, Mary 29 Jan. 1621/2, Sarah 16 Nov. 1623, & 1 ch. at Bures St. Mary, Rebecca 5 Dec. 1630. He was buried 9 Feb. 1630/31 at Assington, but of "Bures". Presumably he was buried in Assington to be with other members of his family. Mary m 2, 27 June 1632 at Assington, John Wyatt, who was b about 1594, a 2nd m for both. They went to N.E. & settled in Ipswich, Mass. John Wyatt in his will named 3 daus.: Mary, Sarah & Dorcas. The 3 girls were actually his step-daus. Edward & Rebecca prob. died young, as there is no further record of them. As for Dorcas, she was apparently the one bapt. 18 June 1629 at Bures Saint Mary, tho the reord says "dau. of Henry". This is an error as Henry had no dau. Dorcas - apparently confusion between Henry and Edward. There was a Dorcas Riddlesdale who appears in the Ipswich Quarterly Court Records as a witness in March 1647, then no more of her

JOHN, b perhaps in 1594-98 at Assington; buried 10 Dec. 1602 at Assington, "son of John Riddlesdale"

SARAH, bapt. 2 March 1599/1600 at Assington, "dau. of John & Dorcas"; m 30 May 1620 at Assington, Mark Gryme, who was a legatee of John Gryme, senior, of Bures St. Mary, in his will of 1638

SAINT MARY'S CHURCH, BURES, SUFFOLK

Ref.: Parish Registers; Probate Records at Bury Saint Edmunds; N.E.H.G.S. - 143:213-220

8

HENRY RIDDLESDALE (*Jasper*) was probably the eldest son of Jasper and Elizabeth Ridsdale (or Riddlesdale) of Boxford, Suffolk. He was probably born about 1520-1528, presumably in Boxford. The parish register of Boxford starts in 1557, so there is no record of his marriage. His wife's name was Joan, according to the baptismal records of his last three children.

In 1555, Henry Rydysdale was paid 6d. by the churchwardens of Boxford for carriage of a load of wood. He helped to organize a church ale* in 1560, was a churchwarden himself in 1562. He was assessed at £10 in 1568.

Henry was buried on 25 June 1591 at Boxford. Joan survived him. An abstract of his will follows.

> 20 June 1591 - the will of HENRY RIDSDALE of Boxford, yeoman ... sick in body ... to John Ridsdale my son £14 to be paid within six months next after the end & completion of my lease which I have in the house where I now dwell called Coddenham Hall ... to Robert Ridsdale my son all my corn both wheat & mixtoland as it now standeth ... to Henry Ridsdale my son £60 ... to Richard Ridsdale my son £60 ... to John Stansbye my daughter's son £10 at age 21 ... to Richard Ridsdale my son's son £4 at age 21, but if he die, then said £4 to go to his brother Thomas Ridsdale at age 21 ... to the poor of Boxford 10s ... to Agnes Church, widow, 10s ... residue to Joan Ridsdale my wife, she to be sole executrix. Signed by mark. Witnesses: John Winterflod, William Brand, Symon Smyth, John Higham. Proved 9 December 1591. (Ref.: R2/42/127 & W1/48/110)

Children, baptized at Boxford:

ROBERT, was perhaps b 1554-5; he was mentioned in his father's will of 1591

4 JOHN, bapt. 26 Sept. 1557, "son of Henry"; m Dorcas ——— about 1583; 9 ch.; moved from Boxford to Assington; she was buried 24 Sept. 1624, he 4 June 1629, both at Assington, tho his burial record says he was of Bures St. Mary, the adjacent parish. He was prob. living with one of his children.

THOMAS, bapt. 2 June 1560, "son of Henry"; m 1 Sept. 1584 at Boxford, Susan Bronde, dau. of John, bapt. 23 Jan. 1560/61; ch.: Richard bp. 27 June 1589, prob b posth.; Thomas was buried 7 Feb. 1588/9; she m 2, 30 Jan. 1593/4, Richard Wendall

*A money-making social gathering involving the provision of food, drink, and entertainment.

JOAN, bapt. 23 Oct. 1562, "dau. of Henry"; m 30 Aug. 1582 at Boxford, Richard Walton, son of Richard, bapt. 8 April 1561. In their m rec., both fathers were named; ch.: Richard bp. 8 March 1582/3 - bur. 2 June 1583, Richard bp. 2 Sept. 1584, William bp. 2 Feb. 1585/6, Joan bp. 27 April 1588

JULYAN, bapt. 10 Dec. 1564, "son (sic) of Henry & Joan"; she m 13 June 1587, John Stanbye; they had a son John by 1591

HENRY, bapt. 6 March 1566/7, "son of Henry & Joan"; m 5 Sept. 1592 at Boxford, Bridget Smythe, dau. of Symond & Alice Smythe, bapt. 20 April 1572; ch.: Henry bapt. 27 June 1594

RICHARD, bapt. 13 Aug. 1570, "son of Henry & Joan"; m 17 Sept. 1593 at Groton, Rose Brand; he d intestate early 1610 (there are no entries of any kind in 1610 in the Boxford parish register); his widow Rose was granted admin. of his estate 5 June 1610. Theirs was a double wedding with John Clark & Joan Riddlesdale, relationship unknown.

The mark of Henry Riddlesdale from his will

BOXFORD.
Early 14th century North Porch constructed of wood.

Ref.: Parish Registers; Probate Records at Bury Saint Edmunds

16

JASPER RIDDLESDALE (or Rydysdale) of Boxford, county Suffolk, England, husbandman, was probably born about 1490. His wife was named Elizabeth.

Jasper Rydysdale, husbandman, was a churchwarden of Boxford 1542-3 and 1547-8. During the period 1540 to 1550, he was paid various sums for loads of straw, clay, gravel and carriage of lead to the church (2d. in 1547). These must have been for repair of church property, the lead certainly for the church roof. He helped to organize a church ale* in 1544. In 1548, he bought a blue linen cloth from the church for 2s. He also received rent money from the church for the church house - 1d. in 1544. He rented a house at Hagmer from the church for 12s.

Jasper had sisters Agnes, Christine Egle and Margery Skott. Jasper died toward the end of August 1552. Elizabeth made her will shortly after his death and died the next year herself. Abstracts of their wills follow.

29 August 1552 - the will of JASPER RYDYSDALE of Boxford, county Suffolk, husbandman ... to each of my daughters, namely Grace, Elizabeth, Jane and Amy £4 apiece to be paid by the hands of Elizabeth my wife and Henry my son, save that 4s.10d. which shall be paid of the debts that her husband Richard Keble owes me ... to Thomas my son my house & land with appurtenances called Dove's lying in a street of Boxford called Hagmer tye, the same Thomas my son paying to Richard & John his brothers £20, £10 apiece of good and lawful money, 33s.4d. apiece every year, that is £3.6s.8d. to both till the sum of £20 be fully paid ... the first payment within the first year after he enter and take possession of the same house & land ... money to be held by executors until they reach age 21 ... houses & land in Polstead called Osmonds to Elizabeth my wife for life, then to son William ... Elizabeth my wife and Henry my son to have my farm in Boxford, Henry paying to Robert my son his brother £10 within one year after he enter the place ... Elizabeth my wife & Henry my son to have all my corn, hay, horses, sheep, cattle ... Thomas Rydysdale and Henry Rydysdale my sons and Thomas Ryvett, parson of Boxford,to be supervisors & each to have 20s. ... Alice Bygg my kinswoman to have 3 yards of my red cloth ... to every godchild 4d. ... to the poor men's box of Boxford 3s.4d. ... I forgive Peter my son the 5 marks that he owes me ... I forgive my sister Agnes 13s. that she owes me ... to my 2 sisters Christine Egle and Margery Skott, to each of them 6s.4d. ... to Thomas Ryddsdale the son of Peter Rydysdale 2 sheep ... to Peter my son £3.6s.8d. to be paid him by Thomas Rydysdale and Henry Rydysdale my executors. Witnesses: Peter Fenne and Jafrey Purdy of Boxford, and Thomas Revett, parson of the same town, John Bonde of Polstead and Thomas Tomson of Boxford. Proved 15 September 1552. (Ref.: R2/31/61 & W1/13/46)

30 October 1552 - the will of ELIZABETH RYDYSDALE of Boxford, county Suffolk, widow ... to be buried in the church yard of Boxford ... to forty of the poorest houses in Boxford 6d. apiece ... to my son Thomas Rydysdale £4 within 1 year next

*A money-making social gathering involving the provision of food, drink, and entertainment.

after my decease ... to my son Peter Redisdale £4 within 2 years ... to Grace my daughter £3 in 3 years ... to Elizabeth my daughter £3 in 4 years ... to Jane my daughter £3 in 5 years ... to Amy my daughter £3 in 5 years ... to Robert Rydysdale my son £6 & a calf in 6 years ... to my son Richard Rydesdale £6 & a calf in 7 years ... to John Rydesdale my son £6 & a calf in 8 years ... to my son William Rydysdale £6 & a calf in 9 years ... if either Robert, Richard, John or William die before age 21 ... to be equally divided ... to Joan my daughter my best gown & my tawny damask sleeves ... to Elizabeth my daughter my best red peticoat & my best red cap ... to Grace my daughter my second gown & my second broad black hat ... unto Thomas my son my best kirtle ... unto my sister Rose Benet my red kirtle ... unto Amy my daughter my second red peticoat ... unto Peter my son my second white cap & my best black silk sleeves ... unto Harry my son my best silk hat & my best whgite cap ... unto mother Agnes sometime my beax my old red cap ... unto Thomas Frost's wife my russet peticoat ... residue to Harry Rydysdale my son, he to be sole executor ... supervisors to be Thomas Ryvet my son in law ... and for performance of this my last will ... said Harry Rydysdale to stand bound by his bill obligatory unto the foresaid Thomas Ryvet & Thomas Osborn of Boxford in the sum of £70 within 21 days next after my decease. Witnesses: Thomas Ryvet, Anthony Tompson, Rob't Pattey Wylliam Hall and Wylliam Rudland. Proved 13 April 1553. (Ref.: R2/31/77 & W1/13/54)

Children, presumably all born at Boxford:

8 HENRY, possibly the eldest & b about 1518-20; m Joan _____ ; 7 known ch.; he was buried 15 June 1591 at Boxford; Joan survived him

THOMAS, prob. b about 1522; perhaps he was the one who m Joan _____ & d before 1567 when a widow Joan Riddlesdale m 5 Oct. 1567 at Boxford, Launcelott Mayor, a widower

ROBERT

PETER, paid "farme", i.e. rent of 6s. in 1547 to the Boxford church. He was m with a son Thomas by 1552. No further record of him.

GRACE, was prob. the dau. who m Richard Keble before Aug. 1552

ELIZABETH, was perhaps the dau. who m Thomas Ryvet, perhaps about Sept. 1552

JANE, She & Amy were perhaps twins as they were both to receive their legacies at the same time according to their mother's will, otherwise, all the other children's legacies were scheduled a year apart

AMY

RICHARD, b after 1532 as he was under 21 in 1552

JOHN, b perhaps about 1536; m 29 Nov. 1562 at Boxford, Elizabeth Patten; apparently moved to Groton where he had bapt.: Henry (parents not named) 18 March 1564/5 - Bur. 17 Feb. 1565/6, Mary ("dau. of John") 13 Sept. 1567, Thomas ("son of John & Elizabeth") 8 Jan. 1569/70, perhaps Richard & Jasper also; John was buried 5 Dec. 1614 at Groton.

WILLIAM, prob. youngest child. His mother left him £6 and a calf to be delivered to him within 9 years after her death, per her 1552 will. He m Joan Johnson 2 Nov. 1561 at Polstead, the next parish

Ref.: Parish Registers; Probate Records at Bury Saint Edmunds; Boxford Churchwardens' Accounts 1530-1561, edited by Peter Northeast, Suffolk Records Society, Vol. XXIII; N.E.H.G.S. - 143:213-220

LOKER alias RIDDLESDALE

Contributed by Douglas Richardson of Tucson, Arizona

2

HENRY LOKER *alias RIDDLESDALE* (*Robert, John, Robert*) was baptized 7 February 1576/7 at Bures Saint Mary, Suffolk, as Henry Locar, parents not named. He married, probably about 1608, Elizabeth _____. They may have been married in a nearby parish, or perhaps in Bures Saint Mary between 1602 and 1609, for which period there are no marriage records there.

Perhaps Elizabeth was a sister of Bridget, wife of John Parmenter of Bures Saint Mary, later of New England. The Lokers and Parmenters both came to New England and settled in Sudbury. Two pairs of sisters named Bridget and Elizabeth were baptized at Bures Saint Mary at the right time. John Simpson had Bridget baptized in 1585/6 and Elizabeth in 1588. William Perry had Elizabeth baptized in 1586/7 and Bridget in 1593.

Henry Loker *alias* Riddlesdale was a glover. He was to be apprenticed according to his mother's will of 1592/3. As had his parents before him, he lived in that part of Bures Saint Mary which lies south of the River Stour and is Essex county, tho the parish church lies north of the river in Suffolk county. Apparently he dropped the name Riddlesdale and settled on Loker which had been an alias for several generations. His widow and children used only Loker after emigrating to New England. Henry Loker was buried 25 February 1630/31 at Bures Saint Mary. His will, dated three days before, follows.

> 22 February 1630/31 - the will of HENRIE LOKER of Bures Saint Mary, county Essex, glover ... to be buried in the churchyard ... to wife Elizabeth all household goods for life, but if she remarries, my eldest son Henry is to have my great brass kettle with a little table standing in the parlour, and my son John is to have the long table in the hall and the best barrell ... to daughter Bridget a flockbed, a coverlet, a blanket,

a bolster, 1 pair of sheets and a deal hutch ... to my younger daughter Ann the best cupboard, 1 of the biggest barrels and a little barrel. If my wife remains single, she shall have the use of these goods during her life ... From my stock I give my wife Elizabeth £12, my son Henry £12, and my son John £10, ... to daughter bridget £5 and 20s. due from John Matthews of Bures, shoemaker ... to younger daughter Anne £5, said sums to be paid to daughters at marriage or death of wife ... wife Elizabeth and two sons to use stock jointly, but if either son should marry and depart or leave by discontent, then he to have only half of what he is bequeathed otherwise. Wife Elizabeth & eldest son Henry sole executors. Witnesses: John Isaack, Jeffrie Hust, John Parmiter. Proved 15 April 1631. (R2/56/16 & W1/87/20)

Henry's widow, Elizabeth, and her four children went to New England in 1639 and settled in Sudbury. There she died on 18 May 1648.

John Parmiter, who witnessed Henry's will, is identical with the John Parmenter who also settled in Sudbury in 1639.

Children, probably all born at Bures Saint Mary:

HENRY, b prob. before 1610 as he was named as co-executor of his father's 1631 will; m 24 March 1647 at Sudbury, Hannah (__) Brewer, widow of John Brewer of Cambridge; ch.: Elizabeth who m 29 May 1667, Jacob Moore. In 1678 Henry Loker deeded his entire estate for love to his son & dau. Jacob & Elizabeth Moore. He d 14 Oct. 1688 at Sudbury.

JOHN, m about 1650, Mary Draper; ch.: John, Mary (posthumous) b 28 Sept. 1653 at Sudbury - m 14 Nov. 1672 at Lancaster, Jonas Prescott. He d 18 June 1653 at Sudbury, testate (Middlesex Probate 14283). (See Newton Genealogy p. 17-18 for a full transcript of the will.)

BRIDGET, elder dau.; m 1, by 1646, Robert Davis who was b 1608, d at Sudbury 19 July 1655; m 2, 26 Dec. 1655, as his 2nd wife, Thomas King; ch. by husband Robert Davis: Sarah b 10 April 1646. She & her 1st husband were named in her brother John's will. She d at Marlborough 11 March 1685

ANNE/HANNAH, m 9 Aug. 1636 at Bures St. Mary, Suffolk, Richard Newton; 9 ch.; she d 5 Dec. 1697 at Marlborough, Mass.; he d there 24 Aug. 1701 "almost a hundred years old". (See Newton Genealogy, by Ermina Newton Leonard, 1915 and T.A.G. 55:86-7 for more on this family.)

Ref.: Parish Registers; Probate Records at Bury Saint Edmunds; T.A.G. 55; N.E.H.G.S. 143:325-331

4

ROBERT RIDDLESDALE (*John, Robert*) of Bures Saint Mary, Suffolk, had a wife, Lucy, who was presumably the mother of all his children. They probably married about 1562-3. For reasons unknown, this family for several generations had gone with dual identity, that is, they had used both Riddlesdale and Loker as a surname. The baptisms and other records of the family usually record both names, sometimes one or the other. Robert Riddlesdale, alias Loker, was buried at Bures Saint Mary on 1 July 1585. Lucy Loker was buried on 3 February 1592/3. An abstract of her will follows.

> 1 February 1592/3 - the will of LUCIE RIDDLESDALE alias Loker of the hamlet of Bures St. Marie in Essex, widow ... nuncupative, that is to say by word of mouth ... goods and chattels first to the discharging of her debts, the apparreling of a child of hers called Henry which was to be put forth to be an apprentice ... the rest to be equally divided amongst all her children and her son Daniel to have the first and best part ... said Daniel to be executor. Witnessed by John Colman, minister there, and Mary Goslinge. Proved 3 April 1593. Inventory £9.17.6.
>
> (Ref.: W1/50/108 at Bury St. Edmunds Record Office)

Altho her will was proved at Sudbury, Suffolk, they apparently lived south of the River Stour in the part of the parish which lies in Essex.

Children, baptized at Bures Saint Mary:

DANIEL, bapt. 12 Dec. 1563, "son of Robert Lokyer"; m 17 Feb. 1594/5 at Bures, Mary George; they had a son John bapt. 25 April 1595 & living in 1638 in Bures

JOAN, bapt. 6 Jan. 1565/6, "dau. of Robert Ridesdale"; m 3 Oct. 1590, John Willsonne; he was buried 21 Oct. 1591; she m 2, 2 May 1592, Thomas Stere, a wid. with ch. whose wife Ann Stere was bur. 13 Jan. 1591/2 at Bures; ch. bapt. at Bures: Abigail 18 March 1592/3, William 13 June 1596, Jerome 14 May 1601, John 4 Dec. 1603. Thomas Stere d shortly before 9 July 1606 when Joan was granted admin. of his estate.

JOHN, bapt. 16 Aug. 1568, "son of Robert Loker alias Ridsdale"

ROBERT, bapt. 10 Feb. 1571/2 as Rideldale, parents not named

WILLIAM, bapt. 31 March 1575 as Locar, parents not named

2 HENRY, bapt. 7 Feb. 1576/7 as Locar, parents not named; m Elizabeth ______; ch.: Henry, Bridget, John, Ann. Henry was buried 25 Feb. 1630/31 at Bures St. Mary. His widow & ch. all went to N.E., settled in Sudbury where the widow Elizabeth Loker died 18 May 1648. Henry was a glover, i.e. glove maker. His will follows.

22 February 1630/31 - the will of Henrie Loker of Bures Saint Mary, county Essex, glover ... to be buried in the churchyard ... to wife Elizabeth £12 and all household stuff for life, but if she remarry, then certain things [enumerated] to eldest son Henry, son John, daughter Bridget and youngest dau. Ann ... to son Henry £12 ... to younger son John £10, to daughter Bridget £5 and 20s. due from John Matthews of Bures, shoemaker ... to younger dau. Anne £5, said sums to be paid to daughters at marriage or death of wife ... wife Elizabeth & two sons to use stock jointly, but if either son should marry and depart or leave by discontent, then he to have only half of what he is bequeathed otherwise. Wife Elizabeth & eldest son Henry sole executors. Witnesses: John Isaack, Jefferie Hust, John Parmiter. Proved 15 April 1631.

(Ref.: Archdeaconry of Sudbury Will, Colman 16)

SAINT EDMUND'S CHURCH, ASSINGTON

Ref.: Parish Registers; Probate Records at Bury Saint Edmunds, at Chelmsford; Newton Genealogy, by Ermina Newton Leonard; N.E.H.G.S. - 143:325-331

8

JOHN RIDSDALE (*Robert*) alias Locar/Loker, of Bures Saint Mary, Essex, was very likely the eldest son, by a first marriage, of Robert Ridsdale of Halstead which is about six miles southwest of Bures. The fact that they used these two alternate surnames certainly indicates that they were of the same immediate clan.

John Ridsdale's wife was named Joan. They apparently lived in that part of Bures which lies south of the River Stour and is in the county of Essex. John Ridsdale was buried in the churchyard of Bures 2 July 1552. His will, obviously an oral one, was written up and dated ten days after his burial. Joan survived him. An abstract of his will follows. In it, he bequeathed his shop gear to his son Robert, indicating that he plied some trade, as well as being a farmer. Joan was buried at Bures Saint Mary 30 April 1561.

> 12 July 1552 - The will of JOHN RYDSDALLE aka Locar of the hamlet of Bures, county of Essex... to be buried in the churchyard of Bures... to Robert Rydsdalle aka Locar my son all my shop gear.. to Wylliam Rydsdalle aka Locar my son 2 sheep & 2 lambs gaying at Payton Hall... to Allise Rydsdalle aka Locar my daughter 1 sheep & 1 lamb... to Annys Rydsdalle aka Locar my daughter 1 sheep & 1 lamb... to Lorrance Rydsdalle aka Locar 1 sheep & 1 lamb... to Joan Rydsdalle aka Locar my wife all the rest of my goods... she and son Robert to be executors. Witnesses: George Darby, vicar, & John Po____, William Peachy, et al. Proved 15 September 1552.
>
> (Archdeaconry of Sudbury Wills, W1/12/22)

Children, probably all born at Bures Saint Mary, Essex:

4 ROBERT, prob. b 1533-40; m Lucy _____ about 1562-3; 6 ch.; he was buried 1 July 1585, Lucy 3 Feb. 1592/3, both at Bures; she left a will

WILLIAM, named in his father's will of 1552; no further record of him

ALICE, unmarried in 1552

ANNE, unmarried in 1552

LAWRENCE, certainly a son, tho no relationship was given in the will of 1552. He received the same legacy as Alice & Anne. Surely the scribe merely overlooked stating that he was a son. Lawrence Loker m 16 July 1570 at Nayland, Margaret Maull.

Ref.: Probate Records at Chelmsford, at Bury Saint Edmunds; Parish Registers; N.E.H.G.S. - 143:325-331

16

ROBERT REDYSDALE, also known as Loker, is the earliest identifiable member of this family. He lived in Halstead, Essex, but was perhaps born in Borley, which is 8 miles to the north. This is deduced from his having made a bequest to the church there, and the fact that he owned property there. He was probably born about 1460 to 1475.

The surname seems to have evolved into Ridsdale and finally to Riddlesdale. Many other variations are found in the early records. It is obviously a place name, but just where the place is remains unknown. It probably started as Reed-dale, or had that meaning. How or why the alias Loker came about is a mystery, but it helps to identify this particular Riddlesdale clan. Some of his descendants went to New England where they finally discarded the Riddlesdale and went by Loker alone.

The wife Robert named in his will was Joan. She was probably a second wife and the mother of the children he named. That he had an earlier wife and grown children by that marriage is suggested by his repeated reference to his son *young* John. This implies an elder son John. When a man had two sons of the same name, it usually meant two different mothers. Of these two sons named John, the elder was probably the one who moved to Bures Saint Mary, the younger son remaining in Halstead on the land his father bequeathed to him.

Robert died presumably in January 1527/8 at Halstead shortly after making his will. His wife Joan survived him.

> 10 January 1527/8 - the will of ROBERT REDYSDALE alias Loker of Halstead, diocese of London ... to be buried in the churchyard ... to the church of Borsley 12d. ... to Joan my wife my tenement in Halstead which I bought of John Bantoft and my copy lands called Eastfield for life, then to young John my son ... to said John five quarters of barley priced at 20s. ... to the said John 26s. which I lent to the king, and a cow ... 16s. to be paid to priests, clerks & poor folk on my burial day ... to the making of the vestry 6s. 8d. ... to the guild of Jesus 16d. ... 10s. for a trental to be sung for me and my friends in the Grey Friars of Colchester the next 3 Fridays after my decease ... my executors to give every Friday 5d. to five poor folk in the town of Halstead for one year ...

to Thomas my son my house and lands at Borsley, he to pay yearly to Joan my wife 6s.8d. for life, paying also to young John my son 6s.8d. yearly for 5 years ... if he die without issue, then to young John my son and he to pay to Joan my wife 6s.8d. a year ... to Thomas my son a cow & 5 seam of barley the price thereof 20s. at the next harvest ... to every one of my other children a seam of barley ... to every godchild 4d. ... to Thomas Gregory 6s.8d. ... to Joan Gregory 6s.8d. at their marriage, each to be the heir of the other, but if both die then to my wife Joan the said 13s.4d. ... to the mending of the highway from the church of Halstead 6s.8d. ... Residue to wife Joan, she to be sole executrix, son John to be supervisor with his mother, he to have for his labor 6s.8d. ...Witnesses: Sir Stephen Chamberlyn one of the priests of the college, John Hevard, Thomas By, John Bye, etc.

(Ref.: 9BW31, Essex Record Office)

Children, probably all born at Halstead, Essex:

8 JOHN, alias Loker. Settled in Bures Saint Mary; m Joan ________; 5 ch. named in his will; buried 2 July 1552

DAUGHTER, prob., who m ________ Gregory & had the 2 ch. Thomas & Joan, by 1527, to whom was bequeathed 6s.8d. at their marriage

OTHER CHILDREN, bequeathed to by their father, but not named

THOMAS, named in his father's will by which he received a house & land in Borley

JOHN, called "young John"; he had 2 daus. & 2 sons, both named John; he m Alice ________; he d 1571 at Halstead. His will:

8 September 1571 - the will of John RIDSDALE alias LOKER of Halstead, husbandman ... sick and diseased in body ... to Alice my wife three milk beasts except my brown bullock, 6 of my best sheep, 1 wennel, sufficient stover for the cattle until Crouchmas*, 3 store pigs, 3 seams of bread corn, 3 seams of drink corn whereof 2 to be dredge corn** and the other in barley, and 2 beds in my chamber ... Mr. Penyngton the vicar of Acton oweth 18s. whereof my wife to have one half and John my eldest the other half ... wife to have the painted cloths, she paying Elizabeth Grene my daughter 12d. ... to my wife the third part of my household stuff ... if she at any time claim the third of my land given to my two sons, such goods to be equally divided between the two sons ... to John Ridsdale the elder my son my croft called Little Bradfield in Halstead nigh unto Boxe Mill .. to him certain timber that I have on Thomas Hunwick's ground or else the money I sold it for to Burnitt, and a table that I have at George Browne's or 6s., one of my milk beasts, a pair of new cart wheels at Horne's, the cupboard in the chamber, and the money of the 2 trees which Thomas Hunwicke sold to me and then sold to another ... to John Ridsdale the younger my son my messuage in Halstead wherein Robert Barons now dwells and my croft called East Field in Halstead ... to the wife of the said John the younger one seam of barley & to his children one brown bullock ... to the five children of my eldest son each a lamb; he hath 12s. to buy them ... to John Ridsdale my eldest son's child my best kettle, my wife to have it for her use, using it well, until he hath served his prenticehood ... to Elizabeth Grene my daughter a bed at George Browne's and a seam of dredge corn ... to her eldest

son 1 wennel ... to Mary Rise my daughter a seam of dredge corn, a wennel, and an unbound kettle with a latten bottom ... to Mary her daughter a wennel ... to two other children of the said Elizabeth Grene two shillings ... to two other children of my daughter Rise 2s. ... to Robert Barons a half year's rent of his house ... to my kinsman John Loker of Stisted 3s.4d. whereof he oweth me 12d. ... to my godchildren 4d. apiece ... I owe John my son the younger £4.10.4. ...residue to my two sons, they to be executors ... goodman Digby the elder supervisor. Witnesses: John Dygby, George Sexten, John Baker the elder, Richard Baker. Proved 22 November 1571.

(Ref.: Essex Record Office, 198 MR 3)

*Feast of the Invention of the Cross, 3 May
**Dredge Corn: a mixture of grains, especially of oats and barley

SAINT ANDREW'S CHURCH, HALSTEAD
(as being restored, 1849)

Ref.: Wills at Chelmsford, Essex, at Bury Saint Edmunds, Suffolk; Parish Registers

JOSEPH ROBINSON was among the early inhabitants of Salem, Massachusetts, where he and his wife, Dorothy, became the parents of at least one child. He undoubtedly was born in England and came to America with his parents. There were several Robinsons among the early Salem settlers, including the widow, Anne Robinson.

Joseph Robinson was in court in Salem in 1641, versus Charles Glover, George Wathen, and Richard Graves over a matter of trepass. At Salem as early as 1637 was William Robinson and his wife, Isabell. Perhaps he was a brother of Joseph. William had six children born at Salem from 1637 to 1654, and another and eldest son, Joseph, not recorded. The preference for the name Joseph suggests that these Robinsons were related. There is an old list of Salem land holders of 25 December 1637. On it is a Mrs. Robinson, two persons in the household. The unnamed second person could be this Joseph Robinson, a son not yet married to Dorothy. She was presumably a daughter of some early Salem family.

Joseph Robinson died, and on 4 February 1647/8 at Salem, she and Edmund Faulkner were joined in marriage by John Winthrop. He was one of only four at Andover to command the title of *Mr.* Immediately after the marriage, they went to Andover where they spent the rest of their lives. Their marriage was recorded at Andover; the first one recorded on the town books. He is 9th on a list of Andover settlers listed in the order that they came to town, probably about 1644 or earlier. Dorothy (Robinson) Faulkner died on 2 December 1668 at Andover. Edmund died 18 January 1686/7, having made his will 9 September 1684, "of a sound mind & memory, though sick and weak of body, ...". He bequeathed to and named his two sons, Francis and John, and his two daughters, Mary and Hannah. "I have excepted one pillow & pillobere out of my household stuff, which I give to my son in law Joseph Robinson, being willing, would my estate have reacht it, to have manifest my love toward him in a larger manner". Thus, we clearly establish that Joseph Robinson was a son of Dorothy by her first husband (Son in law was commonly used to mean stepson as we use it today).

In the Essex County Court Records (52:113) is a deposition by Thomas Fiske senior of Wenham, made 29 March 1692. He says that thirty years before, he "bought a parcel of land of Mr. Faulkner of Andover which land he said he had by his marriage with Joseph Robison's widow". The land was in Wenham but the evidence of title was so lacking that Faulkner returned the money and 40 shillings more. This document established the identity of Dorothy's first husband.

Edmund Faulkner's home was burned by Indians on 19 April 1676. He apparently then built the home which now still stands in Andover.

Children:

JOSEPH, b about 1645, prob. at Salem; m 30 May 1671, Phebe Dane, dau. of Rev. Francis Dane; 5 ch.; d 15 June 1719, Andover

----- Faulkner Children -----

MARY, b about 1649; m 30 May 1671, Joseph Marble at Andover; sev. ch.

FRANCIS, b May 1651 (per Savage), prob. b at Andover; m 12 Oct. 1675, Abigail Dane, dau. of Rev. Francis; he d 19 Sept. 1732 "in his 81st year"; she d 5 Feb. 1729/30; 7 or more ch. at Andover

JOHN, b 16 May 1654 at Andover; m 19 Oct. 1682, Sarah Abbott, dau. of George; he d 17 Dec. 1706; she d 6 Nov. 1723; 8 or more ch.

HANNAH, b 8 May 1658 at Andover; m 24 May 1689, Pascoe Chubb. They and their family were killed by Indians 22 Feb. 1697/8 (or Tuesday, the 23rd) in retaliation for his cruelty and treachery to the Indians two years before when he was Capt. of Pemaquid Fort

Ref.: Essex Probate File # 9305; Savage; V.R.

THE ROWELL ANCESTRY
Contributed by
William Haslet Jones

2

VALENTINE ROWELL (*Thomas, Valentine*) was baptized on 22 June 1622 at Mancetter, Warwickshire, England, the son of Thomas and Margaret (Milner) Rowell. He apparently came to New England as a very young man, for on 14 November 1643 at Salisbury, Massachusetts, the earliest record of him in America, he and Joanna Pinder were married. She was born in England in 1621, the daughter of Henry and Mary (Rogers) Pinder of Cambridge.

Valentine, along with his father who seems to have come with him to New England, took the oath of fidelity in 1646, was a townsman and was taxed in Salisbury in 1650. One of the first settlers of that part that later became Amesbury, he received land there from 1654 to 1662. There are a number of his deeds in the old Norfolk County Records from 1647 on (Deeds 1:110, 119, 127, 138, 142, 145, 148).

23 October 1647 - Tho: Bradbury of Salisbury, planter, conveyed to Valentine Rowell, 6 acres of meadow, formerly Mr. John Hodges, bounded by Thomas Dumer and Anthony Colby. Witnesses: Sam. Winsley, Tho. Rowell. Ackn. in Ct. 10:2:1660

12 April 1654 - Daniel Ladd of Haverhill conveyed to Valentine Rowell of Salisbury 4 acres of planting land with commonage at Salisbury-old-town, bounded by John Clough, Willi. Allin, swamp and highway. Witnesses: Richard Littlehale, Roger Lanckton.

April 1661 - Valentine Rowell of Salisbury, planter, for pine boards, conveyed to William Osgood of Salisbury, millwright, a right of commanage in Salisbury I bought of Daniel Lad.

5 April 1661 - Richard Currier of Salisbury, planter, conveyed to Valentine Rowell of Salisbury, planter, 2 acres of upland in Salisbury, on west side of Pawwaus river, bounded by John Weed, John Bayly, deceased, and highway.

5 April 1661 - John Bayly of Nuberie, husbandman, for the deed that follows, conveyed to Valentine Rowell of Salisbury, planter, 3 acres of meadow in Salisbury, bounded by Richard Currier, town creek and a little creek running up by Vinson's rocks.

4 April 1662 - Valentine Rowell of Salisbury, carpenter, conveyed to Henry Blesdale of Salisbury, tailor, one half of ye upper end of my lot of upland on west side of Pawwaus river in Salisbury, bounded by Edward Goe, Phillip Challis, etc. .... Witnesses: Tho: Bradbury, Samuel Hall. Acknowledged, wife Joanna released dower, in court at Salisbury 8 April 1662

5 April 1661 - Valentine Rowell of Salisbury, planter, for the above deed, conveyed to John Bayly of Nuberie, husbandman, 6 acres of meadow in Salisbury, bounded by Tho: Dumer (now of said Bayly) and Anthony Colby towards ye ferry.

12 April 1661 - Thomas Barnard of ye new town of Salisbury, for £5.15s conveyed to William Barnes, Richard Currier and Valentine Rowell, inhabitants of the same town, in behalf of ye new town, 10 acres of upland in said new town late in the possession of Isaac Buswell, near the mill. Witnesses: Wymond Bradbury, Samuel Hall. The above grantees conveyed the said land to Joseph Peasley same day.

5 March 1661/2 - Valentine Rowell of Salisbury, planter, conveyed to John Clough of Salisbury, house carpenter, 4 acres of planting land in Salisbury, bounded by Willi Allin, highway to mill, grantee, etc. Witnesses: Tho: Bradbury, Jane Bradbury Acknowledged in court by grantor and his wife Joanna.

9 April 1662 - Valentine Rowell exchanged my lot of sweepage, bounded by Mr. Winsley and goodman Dickison, at ye beach, with Jarret Haddon for William Huntington's lot of Higgledee pigledee meadow at fox island, bounded by Valentine Rowell and Phillip Challis. Witnesses: Anthony Somerby, John Bayly. Acknowledged by grantor, his wife releasing dower, in court at Salisbury 8 April 1662

Valentine Rowell died at Salisbury on 17 May 1662, just 38 days after making this last deed by which he exchanged a Sweepage lot with Jarret Haddon. On 14 October 1662, administration of his estate was granted to his widow, Joane. Lieutenant Challis and Richard Currier were ordered to make distribution of his estate to the widow and children, she to have half of it.

Joan remarried on 18 September 1670 to William Sargent, and thirdly, on 26 October 1676 at Amesbury, to Richard Currier.

Margery, the widowed step-mother of Valentine Rowell, did not obey the court order regarding her step-son Valentine's heirs. His widow Joanna, having remarried to William Sargent, they sued for the inheritance. The suit was against

Christopher Osgood, son of Margery by her first husband. William Chandler testified that Margery Coleman (she had remarried for a third time to Thomas Coleman) was at his home in Newbury when, the widow of Valentine Rowell hearing of it, came and demanded of her mother-in-law the £7 due. Margery answered that she had disposed of all her estate to her son Christopher, and he was to pay her debts, and that Chandler had the proof. Thomas Rowell, Valentine's eldest son, also had tried to collect the legacy from Christopher Osgood, but without success. The Sargents won the case and the children finally received their father's share of his father's estate.

In 1725, the estate of Valentine Rowell was still unsettled. Valentine Rowell, a grandson of the same name, in spite of the wishes of his cousins, renounced his right and Philip Rowell was appointed administrator of the estate of his grandfather, Valentine Rowell, late of Almsbury, he giving bonds with John Challis and Joseph Currier on the twelveth of February 1725. This long delay in the settlement of his estate was due to the deaths of him and his children at an early age.

Children, born in Salisbury, Massachusetts:

THOMAS, b 7 Sept. 1644; m 8 Sept. 1670, Sarah Barnes; 5 ch.; d 1684; she m 2, about 1685, John Harvey; m 3, about 1712, Daniel Hoyt
JOHN, b 1645/6; d 12 Sept. 1649
PHILIP, b 8 March 1647/8; m 5 Jan. 1670/71, Sarah Morell; 8 ch.; killed 7 July 1690 by Indians; she m 2, 31 July 1695, Onesiphorus Page; she m 3, 29 May 1708, Daniel Merrill
MARY, b 31 Jan. 1649/50; m 18 Sept. 1673, Thomas Freame; 6 ch.
SARAH, b 16 Nov. 1651; m 26 Oct. 1676, Thomas Harvey, son of Wm.; 6 ch.; she was alive in 1716
HANNAH, b Jan. 1653; m 1, 16 Sept. 1674, Thomas Colby, son of Anthony; 5 ch.; m 2, about 1691, Henry Blaisdell; d 9 Aug. 1707
JOHN, b 15 Nov. 1655; d 18 Feb. 1655/6
ELIZABETH, b 10 Aug. 1657; (One of these died
MARGARITE, b 8 Sept. 1659 before Sept. 1662)

Ref.: The Pillsbury Ancestry, by Holman; Old Families of Salisbury and Amesbury, by Hoyt; Essex County Probate 1:401; Essex County Quarterly Court Files 5:20

A South View of Manceter Church.

4

THOMAS ROWELL (*Valentine*) was baptized at Mancetter, Warwickshire, on 17 March 1594/5. He married first at Mancetter, 12 October 1615, Margaret Milner, who probably died at or soon after the birth of their son Samuel in 1636. On 5 October 1637 at Mancetter, he remarried to Jane Baghes, unless this was the marriage of another Thomas Rowell.

About 1639 or 1640, he emigrated to New England and settled in Salisbury, where he received land in 1640, 41 and 42. In December 1641, William Holdred sued Thomas Rowell. He and his son Valentine took the oath of fidelity in 1646. In 1648, Richard Currier and Thomas Rowell were sued by Samuel Winsley. In 1648/9, Thomas was fined for being in John Bourne's house during the "ordinances of a lecture day" (i.e. drinking on Sunday in an unlicensed place). In April 1649, being legally disabled, he was freed from all military training, he to pay 3 shillings yearly to the company of Salisbury.

> April 1649 - Ordered that Tho. Rowell of Salisbury, having used all proper means to fetch over his wife from old England, and she being disenabled by sickness to come at present, shall not be constrained to go over to her at once, only he is to use what means he possibly can to get her over.

In June 1649, Robert Lemon charged him with defamation, but then defaulted on the case.

He was a commoner and was taxed in 1650 in Salisbury.

His wife died about this time, for in 1650-51, he married for a third time to Mrs. Margaret (Fowler) Osgood, the daughter of Philip and Mary (Winsley) Fowler. She married first at Marlborough, Wiltshire, 28 June 1636, Christopher Osgood, who died in 1650. She married thirdly, before 1670, Thomas Coleman of Newbury and Nantucket. She married fourthly, about 1682, Thomas Osborne of Nantucket.

At the time of his marriage to Margaret, the following antenuptial agreement was drawn up.

"Know all men by these p^{r}sents Y^{t} I Thomas Rowell of Salisbury doe hereby covenant & make this agreem^{t} Concerning Margeret Ossgoods the widdow of Christopher Ossgoods of Ipswich whome god willing I intend to make my Lawful wife & now being in perfect health sense & memory Doe bind my selfe To the p^{r}misses Following: Videliz^{t}: As I take her to be my loving wife

I firstly take her issue being two sonnes & two daughters to be my one to endeavor to bring them up as a Father ought to doe: & Furthermorell bind myselfe that the said Margeret Shall quietly owne & posesse the halfe of my Estate which I shall be posessed with all, when it shall please god to change my life deliver the part or portion of goods which I shall have with her paying to the said issue their several portions Mentioned in there Fathers will acoording to the appointed times out of the said estate which I shall enjoy with her. In wittness whereof I have here Set my hand the 24th of February 1650

The Marke Ր of Thomas Rowell"

In the P^{r}sense of Phillip ffowler P marke

Essex County Probate

Christopher Osgood, in his will dated 19 April 1650, gave to his son Christopher, eldest daughter Mary, and daughters Abigail, Elizabeth and Deborah. The following February, Thomas Rowell adopted two sons and two daughters, so it is clear that Margery must have born a son after he made his will.* Two of the daughters married or died before February 1650/51.

Thomas Rowell moved to Ipswich in 1652. In November of the next year, he and Henry Pinder, his son's father-in-law, were sued by the town of Ipswich for not finishing a prison house. In or about 1654, he moved to Andover as the following deeds indicate.

"These witnesse that I the said Tho: Rowell of Ipswich Carpenter hath sold to the said Richard Ormsbie of Salisbury a Comonage which did beong to ye said houselott that did belong to the Lott he Sould to William Allin:

Witness William Brown Thomas X Rowell
Witness Vallentine X Rowell

Old Norfolk County Deeds, 1:100

"I Thomas Rowell of Andover ... Carpenter for ... fourteen pounds ... sell unto Lieut Robert Pike of Salisbury ... All my farme in ... Salisbury, 5 Apr. 1654" Witnesses: John Eaton, Robert Lord "I Margery Rowell doe give my Consent to my husbands bargain"

recorded in Essex County Deeds, 9:271, in 1694

In the court held in September 1654, Thomas was fined for taking tobacco out of doors and near a house. His wife was admonished for cruelty.

* Thomas, per Ipswich deed 4:406

In September 1656, Thomas Rowell, in behalf of his stepdaughter, Abigail Osgood, sued Frances Leach for having slandered her by saying she was with child. The charge was withdrawn.

19 February 1656 - Articles of agreement between Alexander Knight and Thomas Rowell and Robert Collings, all of Ipswich: farm let and lease of all of Knight's land in Ipswich, except two acres and his house lot, also two oxen, two plows, cart, sled, yokes and chains, for seven years, for sixteen pounds, and corn and hay sufficient in the judgment of Richard Kemball and John Gage for the wintering of three cows; also to plow the two acres and his house lot twice a year, and to bring him his fire wood; also to carry him a load or two of clay if he need it. Witnessed by Robert Lord & William Norton. Mr. Payne's land mentioned. Bond by Rowell and Collings. (Essex County Quarterly Court Files)

Thomas Rowell died at Andover on 8 May 1662, intestate. Administration of his estate was granted on 30 September 1662 to Margery, his widow, and his inventory was valued at £123.3s. According to the contract before the marriage, the widow was to have half the estate. The court ordered £29.10s. to be paid to Jacob Rowell, his son. To his grandchildren, children of his son Valentine Rowell, £7, that is, 40s. to the eldest son and 20s. each to the other five children. Jacob Rowell was to receive his portion at the age of 21, and the widow was to have liberty to pay the £7 to the grandchildren (Essex County Probate 1:395, as printed).

Inventory taken July 16, 1662 by John Osgood, Richard Barker and John Lovejoy.

	£	s	d
the house and barn and shop - - - - - - - - - - - -	24.		
a parcel of land by the house, fenced and sowed - -	40.		
3 acres of land near the house unfenced - - - - - -	3.		
~~a parcel of land further in the woods unfenced and all sold but five acres to Christopher Osgood but not yet assured unto him, all which valued at~~	~~12.10~~.		
meadow ground - - - - - - - - - - - - - - - - - -	12.		
2 Oxen £14, 2 Cows £10 - - - - - - - - - - - - -	24.		
a mare £8, 2 calves £1, 4 sheep, 3 lambs £2.1 -	11.	1.	
7 swine £5.10, 3 stookes of bees £1.10 - - - - - -	7.		
6 bushels wheat, 4 bushels Indian corn - - - - - -	2.	2.	
1 feather bed and bolster and 2 pillows and rug - -	6.		
1 flock bed and bolster and rug, 2 blankets - - - -	3.		
3 pair of sheets £1.10s., 3 pair of pillowbiers 10s.	2.		
wearing apparel - - - - - - - - - - - - - - - - - -	2.10.		

1 cupboard 10s., 3 chests £1, 1 box 5 s. - - - - -	1.15.
3 iron pots, 1 posnet, 1 skillet - - - - - - - - - -	1. 4.
1 brass kettle, 1 skimmer, 1 brass mortar - - - -	1.
pewter, 2 platters, 1 basin, 1 chamber pot - - - -	6.
2 beer bowls, 2 saucers, 1 porringer, 1 candlestick	3.
1 smoothing iron, 1 lamp - - - - - - - - - - - -	5.
1 warming pan, 1 frying pan, 1 spit - - - - - - -	5.
fire pan, tongs, tramell and chafin dish - - - - -	6.
carpenters tools - - - - - - - - - - - - - - - - -	1. 6.
3 gowns £1.10s., 1 sword and belt 7s. - - - - - -	1.17.
1 mattock, 1 pick, 2 axes, 3 wedges, 4 beetle rings	14.
1 chain, 1 coulter, 1 yoke, 1 plow, 1 sled - - - -	15.
2 spinning wheels, 4 chairs, 4 cushions - - - - -	10.
wooden vessels, 2 barrels, 1 keller, 2 powdering tubs	8.
1 tub with trays, pails, sieves and other old vessels	10.
earthen vessels, 2 pair of cards, 2 sickles - - - -	6.
Debts due to him: Mr. Dane - - - - - - - - - - - -	3.17. 6.
John Lovejoy owes - - - - - -	3.00. 2.
Steven Osgood - - - - - - - -	7. 6.
George Abbot, Senior - - - - -	2. 6.
Robert Collins of Ipswich - - - -	5.
William Avery, Ipswich - - - -	11.
Robert Kensman, Ipswich - - -	2. 6.
Total - - - - - - - - - - - - -	156.10. 2.

Debts he owes: Mr. Horen	£19. 12. 3.
Mr. John Geedmey	11.
Phillep Whorten, Boston	3.
Samuel Williams, Salem	1.
Mr. Robert Payne	1.10
Mr. John Appleton	1.
John Whipple	1.
Will Buckley	14.
Total - - - - - - - - - - - - - - -	£28. 7. 3.

Allowed in Ipswich court Sept. 30, 1662

Since this inventory was made there is lost three swine and a sheep. In debts appears about twenty shillings.

Income £156.10s. 2d.; debts £28. 7s. 3d.; cattle dead £5.; take out her estate £50; remain £73; her half £36.10s.; remain £36.10s.; to her child £25.10s.; to his 6 grandchildren, the eldest £2, ye rest £1.7s.

Additional inventory of the estate of Tho. Rowell brought in June 28, 1681 by his son Jacob Rowell and to whom administrat.

Jacob Rowell made choice of George Norton for his guardian, and the court on 31 March 1674 allowed it. In 1676, George Norton petitioned the court, stating "that his apprentice ran away from him about 2 years and a quarter before his time according to indenture, and having an estate valued at £29, besides some household stuff due to him next May, and petitioner fearing that there might be some fraudulent conveyance of it", he asked possession of the estate as guardian of Jacob Rowell.

George Norton, guardian to Jacob Rowell, was granted 28:9:1676, power to take into his hands said Rowell's estate which was ordered to him on 30:7:1662, at Ipswich court.

He gave bonds 24 November 1676 with Thomas and Samuel Hart of Ipswich as surities, receiving the estate.

Whereas George Norton of "Southfield in Hamsheer in the Massachusetts Collony" was appointed guardian to Jacob Rowell of Elizabeth Towne in New Jersey and he approving of the same, acquits the said George Norton of what estate of mine he had in his hands and of all debts and demands, in court held 28:4m:1681 ...

(Essex County Probate Records)

On 28 June 1681, Jacob Rowell brought in additional inventory and petitioned to reopen the estate. Margery was then living in Nantucket outside the jurisdiction of the court, so Jacob, the only surviving son, was appointed administrator.

Petition of Jacob Rowell. "That whereas ye father of yor Honors humble petitioner died intestate in ye year 1662 and administraion of his estate was granted to my mother and ye estate then mentioned disposed of by ye Honoured County Court at Ipswich according to an agreement made betwixt my sd father & mother before marriage which was just & equall as things were then represented to ye Hond Court my self being then hardly out of my infancie, and my mother not soe much taking notice of my future right ing her childrens psent profet, I humbly Conceive things was not soe fairly represented to yt Honord Court as ought to have been done, for the inventory then given was false, there being above six score acres of Land not inventoried, some meadow & other things, alsoe 50 li taken out of my fathers estate in Consideration of wt my mother had when he married her though I cannot understand she had half soe much with her, upon these and other Considerations, I have just cause to think that ye abovesd Hond Court at Ipswich did not dsipose of sd estate as they would have done, had they been rightly informed my humble request to this Hond. Court is that they would be pleased to revise ye premises, & take care of ye only child of a deceased father that he may have his due of his fathers estate, and that others may not goe away with it, to whome it Can not of right belong" --

The additional inventory which was filed was:

100 acres of farmland in the great division in Andover	£100
25 acres of upland on the Indian Plain being the 3rd div	£ 30
Meadow on ye west side of Shawshin River in 4 parcels	£ 30
5 acres of meadow which was ye last division of meadow	£ 15
7 acres & ½ of upland, which was ye swamp division	£ 7
Total	£182

Since, according to the decree of the court in 1662, Jacob was to receive his portion at 21, and since George Norton said his inheritance would be due him in May 1677, it is evident that he was born in May, 1656.

Thomas Rowell, when he came from England, brought his son, Valentine Rowell, and by his third marriage, to an obviously much younger wife, had the son Jacob who was born after his half brother had been married for about ten years. When the child was grown, he objected to the portion he had been given and reopened the case of his father's estate. The eldest son, Valentine, died within a few days of his father.

Children, by Margaret, baptized at Mancetter:

ALICE, bapt. 27 Feb. 1619/20; m 7 Oct. 1641, William Lakin

SARAH, bapt. 25 April 1621; m 16 July 1654, John Barton, a feltmaker

2 VALENTINE, bapt. 22 June 1622; m 14 Nov. 1643 at Salisbury, Mass., Joanna Pinder, dau. of Henry & Mary (Rogers) Pinder; 9 ch.; he d 17 May 1662; she m 2, William Sargeant; she m 3, Richard Currier; she d in Oct. 1690 aged 69-70

THOMAS, bapt. 1 Aug. 1624; perhaps d.y.

WILLIAM, bapt. 30 April 1629; buried 13 April 1652

JOSEPH, bapt. 26 Dec. 1630; perhaps the Joseph who m at Mancetter, July 1650, Elizabeth Pemmington, had a son Joseph bapt. 5 Aug. 1653; he & son prob. d before 1662

SAMUEL, bapt. 29 Dec. 1636; apparently d.y.

----Children by second wife, Jane----

[THOM?]AS, "son of Thomas & Jane", bapt. 6 June 1638; Did he m Frances, have ch. 1657, 1663?

----R, "son of Thomas & Jane", bapt. 12 May 1640

CHILD [torn], bapt. prob. 6 Dec. 1646 [paternity?]

----Child by 3rd wife, Margery (Fowler)(Osgood)----

JACOB, b in May 1656, prob. at Andover; m 1, 29 April 1690, Mary Younglove b 17 March 1667, d 15 May 1691; m 2, 21 Sept. 1691, Elizabeth Wardwell, b 15 Dec. 1666, dau. of Elihu & Elizabeth (Wade) Wardwell; 4 ch.; res. Elizabethtown, N.J. 1674, 1681, returned to Ipswich by 1690. 29 March 1692 he was convicted of paternity of widow Gamage's ch., ordered to pay her 20s., plus 2s.6d. per week

Ref.: The Pillsbury Ancestry, by Holman; Probate Records, Essex County Court Files, as published; Old Families of Salisbury & Amesbury, by Hoyt; N.E.H.G.S.-138; Vital Records; Parish Registers

8

VALENTINE ROWELL was born probably 1565 - 1570. On 12 January 1591/2 at Mancetter, Warwickshire, he married Elizabeth Hampton. Probably she was the daughter of John and Elizabeth Hampton. This John Hampton was a baker and was buried on 21 August 1591, Elizabeth on 28 March 1588, both at Mancetter. The village of Atherstone in the parish of Mancetter, their home, is about ten miles north of Coventry, astride the old Roman road known as Watling Street. At the time Valentine lived there, it was a center for the manufacture of felt hats.

Valentine was buried at Atherstone on 13 September 1613. Elizabeth was buried there on 14 February 1647/8.

At the time of his death, his estate was valued at £23.9.6. Apparently he left no will, but the record of the administration of his estate survives, as does the inventory. A translation of the Latin text follows.

> At the Lichfield Court the 20th day of October in the year 1613 Amen. Administration of the estate of Valentine Rowell deceased, who lived in Atherston. Elizabeth his widow was given the sworn oath, etc.
>
> A trust was established to provide for the children, Thomas Rowell, William Rowell, Alice Rowell, Elizabeth Rowell, Francis Rowell and Anne Rowell, created to pay at full age to the descendants of the deceased. Administration of the estate, until further notice, is by Elizabeth his widow. Descendants' payments to be withheld till full age, etc.

Children, baptized at Mancetter, Warwickshire:

SON, prob. b Oct. - Nov. 1592; buried 4 Nov. 1592

4 THOMAS, bapt. 17 March 1594/5; m 1, at Mancetter, 12 Oct. 1615, Margaret Milner; 7 ch.; m 2, 5 Oct. 1637, Jane Baghes; 3?ch.; m 3, 1650/51 Margaret (Fowler) Osgood. He d 8 May 1662 at Andover, Mass.

WILLIAM, bapt. 8 June 1597; m had ch.: Sarah buried 25 July 1635, John buried 8 Aug. 1642. He was named in 1664 Hearth Tax Roll at Atherstone. He was buried 8 May 1671

ALICE

ELIZABETH, bapt. 29 Sept. 1605; m 8 Feb. 1629, William Hall

FRANCES, bapt. 12 April 1608

ANNE, bapt. 18 April 1613; buried 29 Aug. 1624

An inventory of all the goods of Valyntyne Rowell of Atherstone, late deceased, taken by John Roz, Francis Power, Thomas Hamton, Will'm Grewe

In the hall

1 table and frame and 2 forms, 3 chairs,
1 cupboard, 2 shelves, 1 cradle - - - - - - - - 13s.4d.
19 pieces of pewter, 3 salt sellers, 3 candlesticks 13s.4d.
1 brass pot, 4 kettles, 1 posnet - - - - - - - - - 23s.4d.
2 benches, 2 pails, 1 churn, 1 stean, 1 piggin,
1 can, 1 dozen of trenchers, 6 dishes, 1 meal,
with other implements - - - - - - - - - - - - - 4s.
1 andiron, fire shovel and tongs, the pot *hangells*,
a pair of bellows - - - - - - - - - - - - - - - - 2s.
1 painted cloth, 1 brooch, 1 board cloth, 8 reeves
of onions with all other implements - - - - - - 2s.6d.

In the spence

1 kimnel, 1 barrel, 1 loom, 1 frying pan, 1 meal
sieve with other implements - - - - - - - - 5s.

In the parlor

2 bed steads, 2 covers, 3 boxes, 1 shelf, 2 pillows,
1 twilly, 3 coverlets, 1 wool bed, 1 bolster - 30s.
For his apparel - 30s.
6 pair of sheets, 1 board cloth, 2 pillow beres,
2 twillies - 20s.
3 painted cloths, 1 crock with cheeses in it, 1 pot
of butter, and all other implements - - - - - - 13s.4d.

In the chamber

2 bed steads, 2 painted cloths, 6 fleeces of wool 8s.
hay and corn - 50s.
3 pitchforks, 2 bills, a little wheel, with all
other implements - - - - - - - - - - - - - - - - 3s.

In the shop

His tools - 20s.
1 new cart wheel, a *clove* stock with other
implements - 8s.

In the workhouse

All his timber - - - - - - - - - - - - - - - - - - - £5.
1 cow, 1 calf - 50s.
14 sheep - 30s.
1 grindstone, 1 scythe, and hemp, with other
implements - - - - - - - - - - - - - - - - - - - 5s.
1 store pig - 3s.4d.
A total his debts owing him

A total his debts owing him

Catell of Atherstone - - - - - - - - - - - - - - - 22s.

Sum is £23. 9s.6d.

John ☐ Roz
William Grewe Thomas Hamton 20 October 1613
Francis Power

Ref.: N.E.H.G.S. - 138:128; P.C.C. Wills; Parish Registers

2

RICHARD SAWTELL (*John, John*) was baptized 7 April 1611 at Aller, Somersetshire, the son of John and Agnes (Pittard) Sawtell.

Richard Sawtell of Watertown, Massachusetts first appears in New England records 25 July 1636 as a proprietor of Watertown when he received a grant of 25 acres, it being Lot 8, the 4th division. He was apparently unmarried when he emigrated, for in February 1636/7, he was granted a one acre homestead lot, the allocation being at the rate of one acre per person in each family. He had a brother, Thomas, also in New England. Thomas was admitted freeman in 1649 and died in Boston in 1651, childless and apparently unmarried. In his will of 14 May 1651, proved 18 September, he referred to his brother Richard and a brother and sister Kenrick of Muddy River (Suffolk County Probate # 111). This would presumably be John and Ann Kenrick. Ann died 15 November 1656.

Richard Sawtell lived for about 25 years at Watertown and there all his children were born. Then, about 1662, he and his family all moved to the new plantation of Groton, where he was a proprietor with a 20 acre right and was chosen the first town clerk there for 1662-4.

On April 4, 1671, he petitioned the Middlesex Court to be excused from further military training. Since military service was required of all able bodied men to the age of 60, he presumably had reached that age. This fits in perfectly with the baptismal date for Richard Sawtell of Aller.

King Philip's War broke out in 1675 and on 13 March 1675/6, Groton was attacked and burned. His house was one of the five garrison houses in the town (History of Middlesex County). The inhabitants deemed it necessary to abandon the town at this time and he returned to Watertown and remained there the rest of his life, as did several of his children. On 4 November 1689, he was chosen a selectman of Watertown.

His wife, named Elizabeth, was probably a daughter of one of the early Watertown settlers, but which one is unknown. Richard Kimball had a daughter, Elizabeth, of marriageable age and was living in Watertown at the time.

She was still living when her father died, but who she married is unknown. However, there were at least two other Watertown men who married Elizabeths about that time, but there is no clue as to which of these was Elizabeth Kimball, if any.

In 1670 or 71, Richard Sawtell and his wife took into their home the illegitimate child of Zechariah Smith, deceased. In 1672, he went to court against Thomas, John and Joseph Smith to collect for the child's keep out of the estate of the boy's father, and charged them with illegally administering the estate. He won £10.

On 16 May 1692, Richard Sawtell wrote his own will. In this will he provided for his wife Elizabeth, mentioned son Obadiah of Groton, son Enoch of Watertown, daughters Bethia, Hannah Winn, Ruth Hewes, son John, son Jonathan, deceased, son Zechariah's children, and daughter Starling's children. His lands were at Watertown except for his 20 acre right in Groton. He died 21 August 1694, "an aged man". Elizabeth died 18 October 1694 and son Enoch was granted administration of the estate. His signature on his will is reproduced below.

Richard
Sawtell

A Henry Sawtell was a patentee of Flushing, New York in 1665 and was a freeholder of Newton, Long Island, New York, 4 December 1666. Any relationship to Richard of Watertown is unknown.

Children, probably all born at Watertown:

ELIZABETH, b 1 May 1638 at Watertown; m ____ Sterling, undoubtedly Daniel who was at the Groton garrison 1675-6. She was d by 1692 per her father's will. A Daniel Sterling, prob. their son, was taxed as a single person at Litle Cambridge 1688 and d 1690 in the disastrous expedition to Quebec.

JONATHAN, b 24 Aug. 1639 at Watertown; original proprietor of Groton where he m 3 July 1665, Mary Tarbell, dau. of Thomas; 5 girls, a son Jonathan who apparently d soon after his father; a selectman 1688-90; she d 26 April 1676 at Watertown; he d 6 July 1690 at Groton

MARY, b 19 Nov. 1640 at Watertown; m 19 April 1664 at Charlestown Joseph Johnson; d 22 March 1664/5; no ch.

HANNAH, b 10 Dec. 1642 at Watertown; m 13 July 1665, Increase Winn, son of Edward & Joanna of Woburn; 9 ch.; he was b 1641, d 14 Dec. 1690; she d 18 Feb. 1723 at Woburn

ZACHARIAH, b 26 July 1644 or 5 at Watertown (b rec. reads 1643 but this conflicts with Hannah); original proprietor of Groton; m 1, 13 April 1668 at Malden or 1669 at Charlestown (both rec.), Elizabeth Harris, dau. of John; 4 ch.: Zachariah b 1668-7(?), d 1737, Elizabeth b 1671; Anna b 1673/4, Mary b 1676 (?). He m 2, Anna Parker, dau. of Joseph & Margaret of Chelmsford, and had: prob. Esther, Margaret 1688. He d 1688-91; she was still a widow 1726 at Fairfield, Conn. with her dau. Margaret Wooster. He served in King Philip's War

BETHIA, b about 1647; m at Watertown 27 Jan. 1701/2, John Green; d 12 Oct. 1714 "in ye 68th year of her age" - g.s. at Watertown

OBADIAH, b about 1649; m Hannah Lawrence; 12 ch.; d 20 March 1740/41 "in 92nd year"

RUTH, b about 1651; m 9 March 1676/7, John Hewes, prob. son of John, b about 1653, a weaver of Watertown; 4 ch.; she d 15 Dec. 1721 ae 68. In Oct. 1671 she was sentenced to 15 stripes for fornication

RICHARD, served in King Philip's War at the Billerica garrison 20 Dec. 1675, also April and July 1676. He d 9 Aug. 1676 "according to England" - Watertown town records

JOHN, mentioned in father's will of 1692; m Elizabeth Post, dau. of Thomas of Cambridge whose will mentions him and a grandson John Satell. He, wife and ch. all d by 1700 when his brothers and sisters sold off his property.

ENOCH, weaver of Watertown; m Susannah Randall, dau. of John; 4 daus.; 1 son Richard; in King Philip's War; d 1 March 1741/2 at Watertown. Will signed Nov. 1737.

Ref.: Bond's Watertown; Groton Historical Series, Green; N.E.H.G.S. - 4:286, 46:149; Savage; Middlesex Probates #19950, 19965, 19951, etc.; Soldiers in King Philip's War, Bodge; Sterling Genealogy; History of Cambridge, Paige; C.C. Sawtell manuscript

In the name of God Amen I Richard Sawtell being not sick in boddy but in perfect memory considering ye certainty of my death and the uncertainty of ye time thereof, I doe therefore make this my last will & Testament for ye desposing of myself & y^t little of ye world which God hath given me. And first of all when my naturall life shall be ended I commit my body to ye dust from whence it was taken & my spirit to God y^t gave it in hope of a blessed and glorious Resurrection of my body to partake with my soule of Life everlasting through ye free grace of God in Christ Jesus Amen --- And for my worldly goods, if my beloved and Loving wife Elizabeth Sawtell doth (by gods providence) survive me, Then I bequeath unto her all my Lands & housing in Watertown & ye appertinances of ye Land during her life, And also all my lands in Groton with ye appertinances thereof during her Life and all my movable estate (whether without doares or within doares) of what denomination soever I give her to dispose of when shee will by sale or any other way as shee pleases --- And my will & exspectation is that my son Obadia shall improve the said Lands at Groton And y^t my son Enoch Sawtell shall improve the said Lands at Watertown. ---- And my will is that both of them each one for what of the said land he improves shall (eyther quarterly or yearly) pay unto his mother for ye use of ye said Lands so much as themselves shall agree upon. But if they cannot agree, Then what others which shee may choose shall agree upon & appoynt: and if ye benefit or incom of ye said Lands will not be enough for her comfortable provision for for foode Raiment phissick and atendance at all times when shee needs or any thing els that she doth or may need tho it be not here named -- Then my will further is y^t my abovesaid sons shall add unto the incom of ye said Lands by way of supply & not suffer their Aged tender & loving mother to want any thing that may make her life comfortable the little time shee may be here amongst them -- Whereof if they fail & suffer their mother to want what they may and in duty ought to supply her with --- Then by vertue hereof I give her full power & authority to desier two or three of her friends whome shee shall judge meete who shall be ye overseers of my will and shall by vertue hereof (she shee desiring & consenting) have full power & authoryty to assist in the sale of any of ye said lands for her comfortable supply & support or shee may herself if shee soe sees cause dispose of any of ye said Lands by sale or otherwise as shee sees best for her supply & support: And after ye death of my beloved wife I bequeath unto my son Enoch Sawtell all my the said Lands in Watertown & ye appertinances thereof, excepting only somuch of the Lands as perhaps is sould for his mothers support as aforesaid. I bequeath also my housing to him. But my desire & will is that my daughter Bethia Sawtell shall have her being in my house if they can live quietly & lovingly together lest shee will & can provide better for her self. And unto my son Obadia Sawtell I bequeath all the said Lands in Groton & ye appertananances thereof excepting only so much as perhaps is sould for his mothers support as is above said. And my will also is that he shall pay pay my Legacies as followeth, Namely to my son John Sawtell & to my daughters Bethia Sawtell Hanna Win & Ruth Hues to each of them ten pounds in mony if he be able or in that w^t is equivalent to mony as for my son Jonathan deceased I did for him in his life time what I judged meet (and more too) But yet unto his children I bequeath the moity of one shilling apece. And to my son Zacariahs children & to my daughter Starlings the moity of one shilling apeece if they desire it or to any other that can justly claim any of mine estate. All these legacies my will is yt they shall be payd by my son Obadia above said within the compas of six yeares after ye decease of my Loving wife his mother or sooner if he can But if it shall please God that I shall survive my wife, Then within the compas of six yeares after my decease this my will shall be performed & confirmed to every person conserned therein in every particular as is above in ye severall lines expressed excepting only my movables estate conserning wt my will is that it shall be devided among my children to every one a like share by valuation by such as may be called thereunto. And if my son Obadia should by Gods providence be totally & forever be be dispossest & disinherited of ye said Lands in Groton by the Enimy Indians or others, whereby he is disenabled to pay the said Legacies then what he hath not payd of them shall be nullified & voyd ffor ye performance of this my will according to the true intent & scope hereof, I appoynt & authorise my sons Enoch & Obadia Sawtell execors And for ye confirmation hereof I have hereunto set my hand & seale May 16 1692. May ye sixteenth one thousand six hundred ninety two.

Tht this is the will of the Testator & yt ye word execors enterlined wt should have been - - - - - executors was enterlined before ye sealing hereof is witnessed by us

John Warrin

The marke 0 of Stephen Randall

(The will was proved at Charlestown September 24, 1694)

In Watertown September the 14-1694

An Inventory of the estate of Richard Sautle Dasaced taken and aprised by us the subscribers as foloweth

his waring aparell - - - - - - - -	£ 01-15-00
a parsell of books - - - - - - - -	00-12-00
two guns and one sword - - - - - - -	02-00-00
in the bed roome-one fether bed, two fether pillows, one boulster, one rug, an ould blanket, two sheets, one bed stad all together - - - - - - -	04-10-00
four ould chests with sum other ould lumber -	00-12-00
in the chamber two flock beds, one pair of shets, six ould blankets, one ould rug, two pillows all togither	02-16-00
five shets, nine pilow bers, six napkens, two table cloths	01-15-00
ten yards of new coten cloth and seven yards of coten and wolin cloth -	01-17-00
a small parsell of coten and wol yarn - - -	00-14-00
three Yorn pots, one ould Bras ketell, two paier of pof poot hooks on tramel, one morter	01-10-00
two spineng whels, two poudring tubs, two bere vesells with sum other ould woodn ware all togither	01-00-00
one ould mare and one coult - - - - - -	01-10-00
one dwelling hous with twenty five acrers of land ajoyning - - - - - - - - -	50-00-00
seven acers and hallf of land lying at part of sd town - - -	15-00-00
a farm containing wildrnes land	02-00-00
a twenty acers right in Groaten lands - - - -	60-00-00
totall	147-11-00

Phillip Shattuck
William Shattuck
Samuell Randall

THE
PARISH
CHURCH
OF
ALLER

4

JOHN SAWTELL (*John*) of the parish of Aller in Somersetshire, was probably born about 1570 to 1575. On 9 October 1599 at Aller, John Sawtell *alias* Dolman, married Agnes Pittard. There is no known explanation for the use of this alias which his father also used. Sometimes the use of an alias is an indication of an illegitimacy in the ancestry.

John Sawtell was buried at Aller on 20 December 1622, and Agnes the next day, the 21st. What sort of epidemic took both parents only a day apart?

Thomas Gerard's *A Particular Description of Somerset* written in 1633 says of Aller:

> Aler we now call it, I thinke not from Aler or Alder trees because I have not seen many there; more probable I thinke named from the river which our forefathers, the Saxons, called Rhe, and well with it brookes that name, for whosoever seeth it in winter time will rather deeme it a broad river or Arme of the Sea than land.
>
> The Earles of Huntington not long sithence owners of it, who had at it an ancient Castlelike House highly seated in a low place, for it stands on the pitch of a high round mount, being no larger than to receive that house, the church, and the parsonage house.
>
> As for the parish, it lyes scattering a farr off on the sides of the neighboring hills, whence in winter they are forced to come to church in boats, and in them also carry their dead corpses to burial.
>
> Fro thence the river Parrett hasteth to meet Tone which it joineth at Antony ...

The arms traditionally ascribed to the Sawtell family are:

> *Argent, on a bend embattled, counter embattled, gules, between two cocks proper, a snake bowed or.*

The Sawtells in the early seventeenth century and before seem to have been simple yeoman farmers and as such, probably rarely, if ever, used a coat of arms. These probably came into occasional use well into the eighteenth century and later. Still, the arms had to have been designed and adopted at some time and it may well have been earlier. No arms for the Sawtells has ever been recorded in the Herald's College.

Children, born and baptized at Aller:

JOHN, b about 1600; m Katherine_____ ; had ch.: Thomasine bapt. 2 July 1629 at Aller - m 1 Aug. 1656 Thomas Adams

DOROTHY, bapt. 19 June 1602

ROBERT, bapt. 26 Feb. 1603/4; buried 5 Nov. 1605

HENRY, bapt. 4 Jan. 1605/6; buried 5 Jan. 1605/6

ELIZABETH, bapt. 19 Dec. 1606; buried 16 July 1609

2 RICHARD, bapt. 7 April 1611; went to N.E., settled in Watertown; m Elizabeth _____ ; 11 ch.; he d 6 July 1694; she d 18 Oct. 1694

ANN, m John Kenrick; went to N.E.; d 15 Nov. 1656; res. Muddy River, i.e. Brookline

THOMAS, went to N.E.; d 1651 in Boston; unm.; his will 14 May 1651, proved 18 Sept. refers to his brother Richard & sister Kenrick of Muddy River (Suffolk County Probate #111)

ELIZABETH, bapt. 15 April 1621

Ref.: Clement C. Sawtell manuscript; Langport and Its Church, by David M. Rose, 1911; Notes & Queries for Somerset & Dorset, March 1960, August 1956; Somerset Parish Registers: Marriages, Vol. I, W.P.W. Phillimore; Dwelly's Parish Records, Vol. XV

8

JOHN SAWTELL of Aller, Somersetshire, is the earliest Sawtell that can be identified as an ancestor. He was probably born about 1525 to 1535, presumably at Aller. His wife was named Agnes. He also used the alias Dolman, as his will indicates. There is no known explanation for the use of this alias, which his children also used. Sometimes the use of an alias is an indication of an illegitimacy in the ancestry. It could hardly have been for purposes of hiding a true identity when used so openly.

John Sawtell of Drayton, whose will was proved in 1549, was described as *alias* Dolman. He was certainly related to the above John and might have been his father. Drayton is a mere five miles from Aller.

John Sawtell made his will 20 May 1591 and died shortly thereafter. An abstract follows.

The name Sawtell seems to have originated in Somersetshire. The district they commonly inhabited was the triangle between Taunton, Somerton and Bridgewater. Here the name is found in ancient records back to the early 1500s. Richard, John and Robert Sawtell are listed in the Lay Subsidy Roll for 1524 in Curry Rivel, Somerset. Robert Sawtell of Langport Westover was Baliff in 29 Henry VIII (1537).

The Exchequer Lay Subsidy return for 1327 under Curry Rivel lists no persons named Sawtell. It does, however, list several Christian names followed by place identifications, such as atte wode, atte broke, and atte well. This was the beginning of such surnames as Atwood, Atbrook, and Atwell, which names, in most cases, evolved into Woods, Brooks, and Wells. Among these listings was a *Thoma atte Hele*, i.e. *Thomas at Hele.* Mr. Clement C. Sawtell of Lincoln, Massachusetts, suggested that this might be the origin of the Sawtell family; that sometime between 1327 and 1524, the spelling changed, first to *Thomas Sattel* and then to *Thomas Sawtell,* this being the origin of the Somerset surname of Sawtell. Hele was a hamlet or part of Cury Rivel, and is possibly the present Heale, where the first trace of the Somerset Sawtell family is found.

The fact that the name is not found in England before 1500 seems to preclude a Norman origin unless it is a variation of Sortell. Humphrey de Sartillei, who lived in Boxgrove in 1180, is said to have come from the Canton of Sartilly in Normandy, and on settling in Sussex, became one of the four Elder Knights of the Honor of Arundel under Henry II. Some of his descendants changed the spelling to Sortell. The will of Adam le Sotel of London was proved in 1298. Robert le Sotel of Bedfordshire was Baliff in 1273. The name Sautel appears among the French Huguenots in Ireland in the 1600s, and is found in France at an early date and even now. There are also definite Anglo-Saxon possibilities. Probably the name in its various forms has several separate origins.

20 May 1591 - the will of JOHN SAWTELL *alias* DOLMAN of Aller, county Somerset ... to be buried in the churchyard of Aller ... to the church 12d. ... to my son William Dolman my wain and new wheels, with band and all tackling belonging to the plough ... to my son John Dolman four acres of meadow lying by the Mastbrookes Drove and after his decease to William Dolman my son, and after his decease to Adrian Masters ... to my daughter Joan £10 ... to Adrian Masters one heiffer of one year old ... to my daughter Joan's children one ewe lamb apiece ... to my daughter Lucy's children one cow which is called Hurye, to be delivered when she has calved, my son William to have the use of the same for the children until they all come to age ... to son William Dolman £10 ... to my daughter Joan £10 more to be paid at her mother's decease ... to my son John Dolman £10 to be paid at his mother's decease ... to my son-in-law Robert Masters one bay mare colt of two years age ... residue to Agnes Dolman my wife, whom I make sole executrix. Proved 26 August 1591 by Agnes Sawtell alias Dolman, relict and executrix. Inventory £84.6.8.

(Lambeth Will 440 a Whitgift)

Children, presumably all born at Aller:

JOAN, prob. b about 1560; m 31 Oct. 1584, Robert Masters, Vicar of Aller; she had ch. by 1591

LUCY, m & had ch. by 1591

WILLIAM, prob. b about 1565; m 31 Jan. 1592/3, Alice Bennett; had ch.: Audrey bapt. & buried 18 Oct. 1598, Thomas bapt. 2 Feb. 1599/1600, Edmund bapt. 31 July 1602 - m 12 April 1627 Joan Frye - d testate, Marmaduke bapt. 16 Feb. 1605/6; Alice Sawtell alias Dolman buried 20 Jan. 1622/3. William d testate 1637 (P.C.C. 19 Lee)

4 JOHN, b prob. about 1570-75; m 9 Oct. 1599, Agnes Pittard; 9 known ch.; buried 20 Dec. 1622, Agnes buried 21 Dec. 1622

2

ABRAHAM SHAW (*Thomas, Thomas*) was born about 1590 in or near Northowram, Halifax, county York, England. He and his brother Jonas, whose fate is unknown, were the only sons of his father. They probably inherited an interest in coal and iron making facilities which his great grandfather mentioned in his will. In any event, Abraham had such interests as we learn from other sources.

On 24 June 1616 at Northowram, Abraham Shaw married Bridget Best, the daughter of Henry Best of Ovenden. She was baptized on 9 April 1592.

On 7 August 1633, Abraham Shaw signed an agreement with John Farrar of Ewood. The Farrar family had been involved with coal mining for fifty years in the area, ever since Henry Farrar of Ewood in 1582 received a grant from the Crown of all the coal owned by the Lord of the Manor of Wakefield in Northowram. The following is an abstract of the agreement:

> Abraham Shaw shall peaceably make soughs and pits and dig mines for searching and digging and getting coals until all the coals be gotten within any place or places in the wastes and commons of the greaveships of Hipperholme and Sowerby, where the grant made from one Tusser to Henry Farrar, Esquire, late of the Elwood, may permit.
>
> The said Abraham Shaw shall begin his work before Easter next ensuing, and bear all charges in wymbles and workmen, also all such further costs as shall be spent in sowing or sinking the first pit to be made in any part of the greaveships, and shall drive every sough which he shall take in hand till the level first begun shall withal be spent, and till he come to take the last waterhead, and after attaining the last waterhead, upon a true and just account to be made and given by him to John Farrar, the said Abraham Shaw shall take up and have allowance of the fourth part of the said charges (except of boring with wimbles for searching for coal) out of the half profit accruing to John Farrar forth of the premises, which one half of the profit is to be paid to John Farrar by Abraham Shaw as soon as there shall be any sale or profit made of any coals there, either in soughing, sinking, or driving the waterhead, at any month end upon demand during the continuance of the term, and then the whole charges of sinking any more pits, or opening any old pits formerly made to get coals within the compass of that ground so soughed, or where there is no need of soughing, and all the charges of tools, props, and stoops, driving of the waterhead, and other dead work that may come by fall-

ing in of the earth, as wanting of vent, shall be equally borne betwixt the said parties, and that all Banksmen for the several places or pits shall be chosen by consent of both parties.

That the said Abraham Shaw shall hire all workmen, and pay them their Godspennies only of his proper cost, and look to all works taken in hand, keep them afoot continually within a month's space, or else lose all his right to all such mines as be neglected (unless want of sale minister some impediment). The said Abraham Shaw shall bear all charges of sinking, soughing, and driving both head and level, of all such pits where no profit shall be made that will countervail all charge, and shall divide equally all profit with John Farrar, at all mines after coal be found, till they be all gotten, within so much of the wastes of Hipperholme as do reach from Sugden Head in Northowram to one gate called Stryndgate occupied by the said Abraham Shaw, or in any part of the Scholecote Brow (except one half year only for getting coals in his own lands, or the Scholecote Brow lying now common).

The said John Farrar shall yearly have to his own use 300 horse loads of coals, paying for the getting thereof, and also be pit free in any pits now intended to be mean between the said parties.

John Farrar may employ other persons to get the coals leased if the said Abraham Shaw refuse to bore, sink, and do his best endeavour, to get coals in any such places, upon a month's notice.

Seven months later, on 20 March 1633/4, Abraham Shaw of Scholecote Brow in Northowram, made an agreement with John Booth of Northowram, whereby Booth granted to Shaw power to dig, mine, make and sough pits for getting coals within any lands and tenement land at Dirtcar in Northowram, then in the tenure of John Booth and George Booth his father, for so long as coal might be found in the land. Shaw was to deliver gratis at the pithill to Booth two horse loads of coal weekly, from the time the first coal should be gotten, and he was also to pay a yearly rent of £10, either at the rate of 4s. per week or 16s. every month end, "A fortnight's space in the month of December, while there be no coals usually got, yearly excepted". The rent was to be increased to 5s. per week if Shaw sunk any new pits in the Dirtcar lands. He was to rail off his pit roads three yards and a half broad, and was not at any time to get coals, or make soughs up to or near any other man's coals, to loose or enable anyone else to get coals by means of the pits and soughs so made. Shaw was not to charge more than 2½ d. per horse load for the coals. All the pits were to be filled in when discontinued. If it were found difficult to dry the coals, however, or some other cause made it unprofitable to work the mines, the agreement was to be cancelled.

It is interesting to note that the colliers' Christmas holiday seems to have lasted a fortnight.

By means of these two agreements, Abraham Shaw obtained control of most of the coal on the slope of the hill forming the western boundary of Northowram, down to the Ovenden Brook, and on this hillside, the outcrops of all three beds of coal are to be found. Dirtcar, now Dirk Carr, an old farmhouse at the top of Range Bank, leading to the old Bradford Road, and Scholecote Brow below Catherine Slack, appear to be the two places where Shaw sank his pits and carried on his mining operations. Of his pits at Scholecote Brow, we have no details. The shaft was probably sunk in his own land, from which he would also work the manorial coal. At Dirtcar, the shaft was probably sunk in the wasteland, this being the first shaft to be sunk, mentioned in the agreement with Farrar, and the Dirtcar lease would be worked from this shaft. The agreement with Farrar, which looks at first sight as though it were a partnership agreement, is really a lease, with the rent varying according to the profit made. As a partnership agreement, the conditions would seem harsh, seeing that Shaw had to bear all the costs of searching, sinking, etc., and all losses made in working, but as a lease the terms were really more favorable than with a fixed rent, as he would not have to pay if no profit was made. John Farrar does not appear to have continued the mining operations commenced by his father Henry Farrar, as he leased the whole of his manorial coal to Abraham Shaw. As the latter had full control of the working of the pits, it would be interesting to know what kind of balance sheets he produced for Farrar's inspection. No doubt the profits were modest. The mention of the payment of Godspennies or hiring money to the miners shows that the miners were working on piece rates.

The same day, Farrar signed a bond for £100 to Shaw to guarantee his part of the bargain. On 10 May 1634 Abraham Shaw gave a £100 bond to George Denton, a chandler of

Halifax. On 5 June 1635 Shaw made a £100 bond to Joseph Lister of Netherbrea, the last record of him in England.

As the starting of these pits would entail a fair investment, Shaw appears to have obtained a financial backing from Abraham Sunderland of High Sunderland, and Michael Bairstow of Upper Range Farm, a member of the family who worked the tannery at North Bridge. These two took security on Shaw's leases, and a portion of them was assigned to George Denton of Halifax, who in 1637, "In consideration of the sum of £20, granted to John Lister of Overbrea, all and every such part and parcel of all and singular the Cole myne and Cole mynes lying betwixt one bridge leading into Halifax on the south part, and one place called the North Bank on the north parte, within the township of Northowram, which he had by grant of Abraham Sunderland, John Booth, Abraham Shaw, and Michael Bairstow". This pit was evidently the one sunk by Shaw to work the Dirtcar coal, lying on the north side of Range Bank, from North Bridge to the Bradford Old Road. John Lister must at a somewhat later date have acquired from Abraham Shaw the manorial coal adjoining and extending as far north as Pule Nick.

In 1651 these minerals were in the hands of John Lister of Overbrea and George Croyser of Southowram, and on 14 February of that year they sold for £33 to Thomas Lister of Shipden Hall the coal and mines between North Bridge and Pule Slack in Northowram, which they held from Abraham Sunderland, John Booth, Michael Bairstow, Abraham Shaw, Joseph Lister of Nethbrea, and George Denton of Halifax. All the tools, instruments and implements in use at the pits in Halifax (Range Bank) for getting coals there were assigned along with the mines. By this time, the pit sunk by Abraham Shaw and acquired by John Lister must have been worked out.

Perhaps Abraham Shaw ran into financial troubles and sold out or gave up, but about the winter of 1635-6, he must have ended his coal mining venture, leaving for New England where he appeared in the spring of 1636. He settled in Watertown, Massachusetts, where he is on the list of earliest proprietors, receiving 70 acres in the allotment of 25 July

1636 and 10 acres on 28 February 1636/7. His house and goods were all burned in October 1636, after which he moved to Dedham, where he received a 12 acre grant that year. Fires started easily in thatched roofs.

Abraham Shaw was made freeman on 9 March 1636/7. On 2 November 1637, the same year:

> Abraham Shawe is graunted haulfe of the benefit of coles and yron stone, wch shalbee found in any comon ground wch is in the countryes disposeing.

He was a constable of Dedham in 1638. About the end of 1638, he died, for Thomas Lechford, on page 329 of his notebook wrote:

> Abraham Shawe, sometime of Hallifax in the county of Yorke Clothier & late of Dedham in N.E. planter made his last will & testament about November 1638 & thereby made Joseph Shawe his eldest sonne & Nicholas Biram his sonne in lawe his executors & dyed leaving £100 and divers other dutyes in the hands of severall persons they gave a letter of attorney to Mr. Best of Hallifax aforesaid Clothier to receive the same and all profitts of Colemines whosoever & the same Colemines to sell &c.

> The last will & Testament of Abraham Shawe deceased.
>
> Memorandum that if it please Almyghtye God to take me to his mercye by death, That it is my minde & will that my estate be disposed of as followeth (that is to say) I bequeathe to my sonne John & Martha Shawe, being infants, ten powends betweene them, also betweene the aforesd Martha & Marye I leave as much quicke goods twelve powends as may be thought fitt; further, that Joseph and John shall have my lott att Dedham equally to be devided between them. Also, that all the rest of my estate whatsoever be devided, proportionate, betwene all my children. Witnesses: Nicholas Biram, Joseph Shawe.
>
> These psons were ordered to make an Inventorye of the estate by the help & advice of Mr. Edward Allen.

In 1639, Nicholas Byram and Joseph Shaw petitioned for permission to sell some of his land. It was granted. They were given administration of the estate on 29 October 1640.

Children, baptized in Northowram, Halifax, England:

SUSANNA, bapt. 24 March 1616/17; m Nicholas Byram

JOSEPH, bapt. 14 March 1618/19; m Mary ____ ; 3 & more ch.; he d 13 Dec. 1653 per Boston rec.

GRACE, bapt. 15 Aug. 1621; m before 1650, Wm. Richards of Weymouth; 5 ch.; survived husband 1682; not named in father's will of 1638

MARTHA, bapt. 1 Dec. 1623; buried 31 March 1625

MARIA (Mary), bapt. 18 June 1626; adm. to church of Charlestown on 1 July 1645; m about 1652, John Bicknell of Weymouth; 3 ch.; d 25 March 1658

JOHN, bapt. 16 Feb. 1628/9; buried 12 April 1629

JOHN, bapt. 23 May 1630; m about 1630, Alice Phillips; 11 ch.; he d 16 Sept. 1704 at Weymouth

MARTHA, bapt. 6 Jan. 1632/3

Ref.: N.E.H.G.S.: -2, 48, 49, 106; T.A.G. -57:85; Suffolk County Probates, Misc. Docket; The Halifax Coalfields, by W.B. Trigg, pub. 1931 in The Halifax Antiquarian Society Journal

4

THOMAS SHAW (*Thomas*) of Halifax, county York, England, was baptized there on 30 January 1562/3. He married on 3 August 1584, Agnes Smith, and by her had two children who both died in infancy. Agnes was buried 14 April 1588, "the wife of Thomas Shaw of Northowram", no name otherwise given. Thomas remarried on 16 December 1589 to Elizabeth Longbotham, who was baptized on 13 October 1560, and was the daughter of Brian and Alice (Mawd) Longbotham. Thomas Shaw died in January 1599/1600, leaving a will, an abstract of which follows. Elizabeth then remarried to Richard Moore, by whom she had three more children. Richard Moore died in 1624, and on 15 July of that year, administration of his estate was granted to Elizabeth, his widow and relict. The inventory came to under £40.

10 January 1599/1600 - the will of Thomas Shaw of Northowram, parish of Halifax, county of York, sick in body ... to be buried in the churchyard of Halifax ... debts to be paid, one third of goods to wife Elizabeth, two thirds to daughters Sarah, Susan, Martha Shaw and such child as wife may have conceived, and also to them £3 yearly out of my messuage or tenement whereon I now dwell for next ten years towards their support and education during their minorities, after which ten years my eldest son and heir Abraham Shaw shall for the next ten years pay unto my said three daughters and such child as my wife may have conceived £3 for the augmentation and enlargement of their portions, always provided wife Elizabeth to enjoy and possess to her use all my whole messuage and tenement during the ten years educating my children, if she so long live and be unmarried. And the tuition and educating of my said children to wit, Abraham Shaw, Jonas Shaw, Sara, Susan and Martha Shaw etc. I commit to said Elizabeth during their minorities, she to be sole executrix. Friend John Bairestow of Brormhirste, John Crowder of Ovenden, William Illingworth of Illingworth, Henry Beste of Haldesworth and John Longbothome to be supervisors, they all witnessing the will. Proved 15 May 1600. (Ref.: 28/118)

Children, probably all born in or near Halifax:

THOMAS, bapt. 25 April 1585; buried 16 Nov. 1587

JOHN, bapt. 7 Aug. 1586; d.y.; possibly he was the one rec. as Thomas Shaw, buried 20 Nov. 1586, his name thus confused with his father's

-----Children by Elizabeth-----

2 ABRAHAM, b about 1590; m 24 June 1616 at Northowram, Bridget Best, dau. of Henry Best, one of the supervisors of his father's estate; she was bapt. 9 April 1592; 8 ch.; he went to N.E. where he d in 1638

SARAH, bapt. 9 April 1592; d about April 1616, testate. Her will follows:

> 1616 - the will nuncupative of Sara Shawe late of Northowrome spinstred deceased. Memorandum that the daie and year abovesaid Sara Shawe being sicke in body but of perfecte memorie did make her last will and testament in manner following. She gave unto Abraham Shawe her brother eight pounds. Item, to Susan Shawe her sister fower pounds. Item to Jonas Shawe her brother fortie shillings. Item, to Martha Shawe her sister nyne pounds. Item, to John Moore, Joseph Moore and Grace Moore to evry of them twenty shillings. The residue of her goods not given she gave unto her mother wife of Richard Moore whom she made executrix of her last will and testament. Witnesses hereof Michell Tailor and Samuell Longbotham. Proved 17 April 1616. (Ref.: 34:11)

SUSAN, b about 1594; living i 1616

JONAS, b about 1596; m & had ch.; his wife buried 9 Dec. 1633; his will dated 25 April 1638 was proved in Feb. 1642

MARTHA, b about 1598; living in 1616

-----Children by Richard Moore-----

JOHN, b about 1601; living in 1616

JOSEPH, b about 1603; living in 1616

GRACE, b about 1605; living in 1616

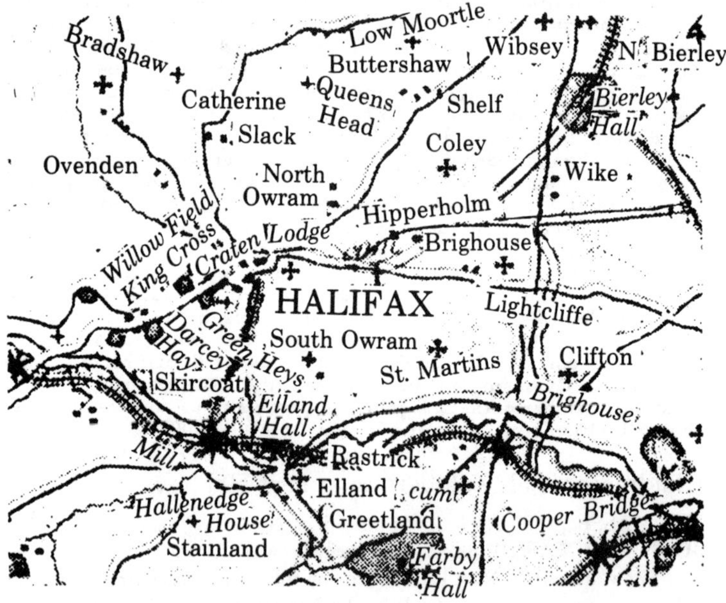

Ref.: Halifax Parish Registers as pub. by Yorkshire Archaeological Society, Vols. 36-45; Yorkshire Probates; T.A.G. 57:85-7

6

HENRY BEST of Holdsworth in the township of Ovenden, parish of Halifax, Yorkshire, was probably the grandson of Richard Best, who was buried on 8 November 1551 and *Johanna* (i.e. Joan or Jane), "nuper relict of Richard" Best, who was buried there on 6 June 1544.

Henry Best married on 23 December 1577 in Halifax parish, Grace Boithes, who was baptized on 16 July 1557, and was the daughter of John Boithes of Halifax. A John Boithes and Isabella Swift were married there on 3 June 1548. Grace apparently died before 1627/8 when Henry made his will, mentioning no wife. His will follows in full, the spelling modernized. Some of the legatees were probably sons-in-law.

the 9th of March 1627

Memorandum that I Henry Best of Houldsworth in the township of Ovenden do make this my last will and testament in manner and form following. First, I give and bequeath to Abraham Shawe forty pounds; also, I give to Robert Swayne eighteen pounds; also, I give to three children of Michael Firbher my grandchildren six pounds; also, I give to Marie Best twenty shillings; also, I give to Henry Best my grand child my bed with all that belongeth to it; also, I give to Michael Best my son Abraham Shaw and Robert Swayne all my apparel; also, I give to John Ilingworth twelve pence; also, to Anne Brooke 7 pence; also, I give to Anne Wilson twelve pence; also eight pounds I leave to bring me forth, and if any remain, I give it to my grandchild Henry Best, and I make Abraham Shawe my executor. Signed by mark. Witnesses: Tho. Lovjoy, John Ilingworthe, Michael Best; Proved August 1628 (Ref.: Pontefract D)

Children, baptized at Ovenden:

MARY, bapt. 14 Aug. 1586; possibly the Marie named in her father's will; if so, unm.

JOHN, bapt. 10 March 1587/8; he prob. d before 1628 & was prob. the father of Henry named in the above will

3 BRIDGET, bapt. 9 April 1592; m 24 June 1616 at Northowram, Yorkshire, Abraham Shaw, son of Thomas & Elizabeth (Longbotham) Shaw, b about 1590; 8 ch.; went to N.E.; he d late 1638, she earlier 1638, she earlier

DAUGHTER, m Michael Furber, had 3 ch. & seems to have d before her father's 1627 will

MICHAEL, prob., altho wording of the will makes it unsure; there was a contemporary Michael Best, son of Richard & Maud Best

DAUGHTER, prob., who m Robert Swayne named in will of Henry Best

8

THOMAS SHAW of Halifax, county York, was born probably a little before 1538 when the parish registers commence. He married on 4 October 1562, Sybil Mason, the daughter of Thomas and Jenet Mason of Halifax. She was baptized there on 3 February 1539/40. Thomas was buried on 14 March 1574/5 and administration of his estate was granted on 15 September following to John Pattyson of Yarm. John and William Mawd were bondsmen. Sybil remarried on 10 September 1576 to John Appleyard of Halifax, a widower. He was buried on 3 February 1586/7. She married a third time to John Mychell on 4 February 1588/9 at Halifax. He also was a widower, his wife having been buried on 8 October 1588.

Children, all baptized at Halifax:

4 THOMAS, bapt. 30 Jan. 1562/3; m 1, 3 Aug. 1584, Agnes Smith; she was buried 14 April 1588; 2 ch.; he m 2, 16 Dec. 1589, Elizabeth Longbotham, dau. of Brian & Alice (Mawd) Longbotham, bapt. 13 Oct. 1560; he d in Jan. 1599/1600; 5 ch.; she m 2, Richard Moore who d in 1624; 3 ch.; she survived him

ANN, bapt. 10 March 1564/5; m 16 Dec. 1589 at Halifax, John Strange, a double wedding with Thomas

GRACE, bapt. 13 Feb. 1567/8; buried 5 Jan. 1587/8

SYBIL, bapt. 30 Sept. 1571; buried 15 July 1572

SYBIL, bapt. 6 July 1573

Child of John Appleyard:

ALICE, bapt. 6 March 1579/80

Ref.: Yorkshire Probate Records; Halifax Parish Registers I, II; N.E.H.G.S. -106:50-52

10

BRIAN LONGBOTHAM of Northowram, Halifax parish, county York, England, was probably born about 1520 or so. Either he or another of the same name married on 25 January 1544/5, Agnes Crowther at Halifax. One child is recorded for them. She must have died, altho there is no burial record for her. Next, he married Alice Speght on 11 June 1553. An Annes Longbotham of Halifax was buried on 13 February 1557/8. This must have been his wife, as Agnes, Alice and Annis were more or less synonymous at that time.

On 15 January 1558/9, Brian Longbotham married Alice Mawd. Six children by her are recorded. She was buried on 12 January 1671/2, "the wife of Brian Longbotham". When he died has not been determined.

He probably had brothers Edward, Robert and Thomas.

Children:

BRIAN, "son of Brian Longbotham & Agnes Crowther", bapt. 18 Sept. 1544

RICHARD, bapt. 29 Oct. 1559, "son of Brian L. of Northowram"; prob. d in infancy

5 ELIZABETH, bapt. 13 Oct. 1560, "dau. of Brian L. of Northowram"; m 16 Dec. 1589, Thomas Shaw, son of Thomas & Sybil (Mason) Shaw, bapt. 30 Jan. 1561/2; he d in Jan. 1599/1600; 5 ch.; she m 2, Richard Moore who d 1624; 3 ch. by him; she survived Richard

EDWARD, bapt. 6 Sept. 1652, "son of Brian L. of Northowram"; buried 27 July 1572

LAWRENCE, bapt. 10 March 1564/5, "son of Brian L. of Shibden" (which is Northowram)

JOHN, bapt. 20 July 1567, "son of Brian L. of Northowram"

MARIE, bapt. 22 Oct. 1569, "dau. of Brian L. of Northowram"

Ref.: Halifax Parish Registers, pub. by Yorkshire Archaeological Society, Vols. 36-45; Probates of Yorkshire

18

THOMAS MASON of Halifax, England was born probably about 1500-1505. He apparently was in the iron smelting business, for in his will he left his "iron chimney" and his "smithy" gear to his two sons. His wife's name was Jenet.

On 11 February 1549/50 Annes Mason, mother of Thomas Mason of Halifax, was buried. She may, however, have been the mother of a different Thomas Mason, whose wife Annes was buried on 14 April 1563.

Thomas Mason died and was buried on 4 August 1551.

On 13 February 1552/3 at Halifax, Jenet Mason married Nicholas Webster. This was probably Thomas's widow. Nicholas Webster was buried on 22 March 1572/3. Jenet, wife of Nicholas Webster of Halifax, was buried on 23 March 1573/4. Altho the register calls her wife, rather than widow, this was probably the same Jenet.

4 August 1551 - the will of THOMAS MASON of Halifax, county of York ... to be buried in the churchyard at Halifax ... to James Mason my eldest son 2 parts of all my smithy gear, one horse and my iron chimney ... residue to Jenet Mason, my wife, Agnes, Elizabeth, Margaret, Alice, Sibell, Isabell and Margerie Mason my daughters, whom I make and ordain my full and lawful executors ... to William Mason my youngest son the third part of all my smithy gear. Witnesses: John Hardie, James Bawmforthe, John Wilkynson. Proved 6 October 1551. (Ref.: 13:783)

Children, all baptized at Halifax:

JAMES, "eldest son" in father's will; a James Mason was buried 8 Aug. 1551. Him?

AGNES, b prob. about 1530; m 4 Dec. 1553, William Paulden

ELIZABETH, living in 1551

JOAN, buried 18 July 1547

ISABELL, living in 1551

MARGERIE, m 4 May 1556, Richard Bentley

9 SYBIL, bapt. 3 Feb. 1539/40; m 4 Oct. 1562, Thomas Shaw who was buried 14 March 1574/5; 5 ch.; she m 2, 10 Sept. 1576, John Appleyard; 1 ch.; he was buried 3 Feb. 1586/7; she m 3, 4 Feb. 1588/9, John Mychell

ALICE, bapt. 8 Oct. 1542

WILLIAM, "youngest son", bapt. 31 July 1544; m 15 July 1566, Jenett Gibson; she d 10 July 1580; his dau. Margaret d 15 March 1580/81

CHILD, prob. b 1546; d shortly after; no rec. of

MARGARET, bapt. 23 Oct. 1548; buried 16 Sept. 1566

Ref.: Halifax Registers; Probates of Yorkshire

2

BAPTISTE SMEDLEY (*Francis*) was baptized 31 July 1609 in Saint Chad's Church at Wilne in the parish of Sawley, Derbyshire. He and his brother John, four years his junior, both came to New England and settled in Concord where he first appears on record in 1639. Possibly their father came with them, altho there is no record of him in America. Baptiste left no record of a family with him during his first few years in New England. He was made a freedman on 29 May 1644 and the next year, on 27 March 1645, he married Katherine Shorthose, the widow of Robert Shorthose. She had three children by her first marriage, but little is known of them.

Robert Shorthose was living in Charlestown as early as 1634, and there is much in the records about his land holdings there, and also about his troubles in court (for "swearing by the blood of God", etc). He must have died between 1640 and 1645.

Baptiste Smedley had ten lots with a total of 186 acres in Concord, according to a list of land holders.

On 7 August 1675, five days after his only son was killed by Indians in the battle of Brookfield, he made his will and died on the 16th following, "aged about 68". Actually, he was 66. Six months later, his son-in-law was also killed by Indians. Katherine died 22 November 1679. His will and inventory follow.

August. 7. 1675. I Baptists Smedly of Concord in New England aged ab[t] sixty eight yeare being weak in body, but well composed in my understanding do here order my last will: my body I committ unto the Earth my soul I commend unto my good God through Jesus Christ; my temporall estate I dispose off as followeth I give unto my Grandchild Samuel Smedly sixtye acres & five more or less, when he comes to the age of twenty one years at batesman pond & Four acres of Meadow in y[e] fiftye acre meadow & four acres of Meadow in James Bloods second division, and one acre & a half neer Browns spruce swamp, at these severall parcells be they more or less I give unto him when he comes to the age abovsd. I give to my grandchild Mary Smedly when shee comes to the age of sixteen years fifteen pounds to be paid in Corn at Concord at priceyn as it goes to the Country Rate, or in Cattle prized by indifferent men chosen. I give unto my grandchild Hannah Smedly fifteen pounds to be paid as her sister Maryes: I give unto my daughter in law Hannah Smedly twenty shillings, to be paid in Corne as it goes to the Country Rate within six months after my decease. I give unto my son in law Isaac Shepard his wife & children hazard lott being twenty five acres more or less & my house lott with all ye rest of my Estate of housing lands or whatsoever is mine; furthermore I give unto them my Grandchild Jabesh Rutter 'till he come of age of twenty one years: I give unto them the benefitt or Improvemt of what I have given my grandchild Samuel Smedly till he come to age above written: I give unto my grandchild Jabesh Rutter ten pounds to be paid when he comes to the age of twenty one years in corne as it then shall go to the country rate or in cattle prized by indifferent men chosen: The sd Isaac Shepard or his assigns upon consideration of wt is here given him & his & is willing to maynteyne me Baptist Smedly & my wife during or naturall life in this world with all things needfull for our condition & what our severall Charges shall be as also all the Legacyes here given & all just debts due from me to pay all which sd Isaac Shepard I do here now make my true & lawfull Executor the day & year aboves.

witnesses:
William Buttricke
Thomas Heald

his
Baptist Smedly
mark

his
Isaac Shephard
mark

Indorsed

What is given to the wife & children of Saml Smedly decd in this will is beside & above what his father Baptist Smedly gave unto the sd Samuel his son at his marriage

by me John Smedly

Proved 27 October 1675

An Inventory of the Estate of Baptis Smedly of Concord who departed this world the 16th of August 1675 --

Impri wearing aparil	01-10-00
one bed and Bolster one pellow one blanket	01-06-00
one Bed sted one Chest	00-08-06
Iron 13s Brass 11s-06d.	01-04-06
Lumber	00-11-00
2 oxen 2 Cows 2 steers	22-00-00
one Spade one Swoard	00-10-00
housen Barnes and Cow houses	20-00-00

one hous lot 7 acers 3 and a ½ Broke up	16-00-00
hasards lot with all within the fences	100-00-00
Being Twenty Six acers more or les	
nine acers and a ½ of medowish woods	17-00-00
sixty ffive acers of upland	20-00-00
Twenty acers in the Twenty score	03-00-00
ffourteen acers of wildernes land	04-00-00
his grand child Jabish Rutor	08-00-00
	215-19-00

The Debts do Robert Meriam	0-18-00
To John Smedly Senor	7-11-05
To Isaac Sheapard	36-07-06
To widow Cuteler	00-12-07
To ffinorall Charges	00-12-00
This estate was prized by us	46-01-06

Thomas Browne
Samuel Blood

The last item in the inventory of the estate is somewhat of a puzzle. It is the grandchild Jabish Rutor, valued at £8. Apparently, Baptist had yet another daughter who married either John or Thomas Rutter. She must have died and left the grandson Jabish, who was living with Baptist. His will indicates that Jabish was under 21. The £8 value must have been the value of the child's services as an indentured servant until he became of age. The two Rutter brothers were sons of John and Elizabeth (Plimpton) Rutter. John was born at Sudbury on 7 or 9 February 1645/6 and Thomas was born there 5 April 1650. John married 12 March 1688/9, the widow Hannah (Pendleton) Bush when he was aged 44 and had a son. Thomas married 15 October 1689, Jemima Stanhope and had six children. Either of these Rutter men could have had a first wife, the unnamed daughter of Baptist and Katherine Smedly.

Katheine had a niece, Rachel (----)(Starr) Hicks, who wrote in a letter dated 5 September 1666 from Hempstead, Long Island to her agent in Charlestown, Richard Russell, that she wished to sell the Starr house in Charlestown and to:

> "lett my Aunt Smedly have the refusal of it, for if shee will give anything likely I had rather shee had it than another, yet I must look that I do not wrong myselfe in underselling it."

Children (Shorthose):

REBECCA, prob. b about 1635; "Rebecca Shorthose alias Shadow, with the consent of her mother and friends" was bound as a servant girl for 7 years from 23 Nov. 1650 to William Tay of Boston, later of Billerica

JOHN, born 13 Sept. 1637 at Charlestown. "John Shadoes ye son of Katherine his mother," d 14 Aug. 1695 at Concord. Prob. crippled or retarded which would explain this record & his apparently being unm.

ELIZABETH, b 7 Sept. 1640 at Charlestown; prob. d.y.

----- Smedly Children -----

SAMUEL, b 27 March 1646; m 11 July 1667, Hannah Wheeler; 4 ch.; Hannah b 9 July - d 2 Aug. 1668, Hannah b 28 July 1669, Mary b 18 Jan. 1671/2, Samuel b 28 Feb. 1673/4; he was killed 2 Aug. 1675 at Brookfield while with Capt. Wheeler, being one of the 8 who fell at the first firing in the ambush at the swamp. She m 2, 8 Nov. 1676, Samuel Parry

MARY, b 7 June 1648; m 1, 10 Dec. 1667, at Concord, Isaac Shepard, son of Ralph & Thanklord Shepard, b about 1644; he was killed by Indians 12 Feb. 1675/6; 3 ch.; she m 2, 9 Jan. 1676/7, Nathaniel Jewell; 3 ch.; moved to Plainfield.

DAUGHTER, prob. b 1650; m John or Thomas Rutter, son of John & Elizabeth (Plimpton) Rutter of Sudbury; 1 son; she d before 1675;

Ref.: Middlesex Probate File 20541; Concord V.R., Town Records; N.E.H.G.R. - 89:374; Middlesex Court Files; Genealogies and Estates of Charlestown 2:864

4

FRANCIS SMEDLEY was probably born in or near Wilne or Draycott in the parish of Sawley, Derbyshire. His wife's name was Ellen. Since no marriage is found for them in Wilne where their children were baptized, presumably they were married elsewhere, probably in her home parish church. Ellen was buried at Wilne on 15 April 1638. There is no record of the burial of Francis. Since their sons Baptist and John emigrated to New England about this time — they appeared in Concord the next year — it is quite possible that Francis went to America with them. If so, there is no record of him, and being then an old man, he must have died within a few years.

Children, baptized at Wilne:

ANN, ("An Smethley, dau. of Francis"), bapt. on 23 March 1601/2
CHILD, another perhaps, b about 1604 of whom no record is found
ELLEN, bapt. 2 Feb. 1605/6 ("dau. of Francis Smedley of Draycott")
BAPTIST, bapt. 5 Sept. 1608; apparently d.y.
2 BAPTIST, bapt. 31 July 1609 ("son of Francis Smedlie"); he went to Concord in N.E. in 1639; m 27 March 1645, Katherine, widow of Robert Shorthose; 3 known ch.; he d 16 Aug. 1675, "aged about 68".
RICHARD, bapt. 2 April 1611 ("son of Francis of Draycott")
JOHN, bapt. 20 April 1613 ("son of Francis of Draycott"); he also went to Concord in N.E.; had a son John, prob. others. He was senior selectman of Concord in 1680

Ref.: Parish Registers; Savage; Concord Vital Records; Probate Records of Derbyshire

SAINT CHAD'S CHURCH, WILNE, DERBYSHIRE

ROBERT SMITH came to New England in 1638, brought over as an apprenticed servant, along with many other such boys, by a Mr. Whittingham. These boys came from around Boston, Lincolnshire, from which they were brought to London and put up there at Whittingham's expense from May 1st to June 24th, at which time they must have set sail for America. Robert Smith was probably about 12 at the time and indentured for about ten years, as were several other boys. Thus, he was born about 1626.

There arrived in Boston during the summer of 1638, twenty ships with about 3,000 colonists. Only a few of these ships are known by name. Upon their arrival in Boston, the boys were sold as indentured servants for the length of their terms to older colonists, the proceeds of the sales covering costs and hopefully a profit for Whittingham. The passage cost £5 per person, other expenses were about £3 more, and the boys were sold for £15 or £16 each, depending on their age and appearance. All this was set forth in testimony made to the Ipswich Court held 27 March 1655 at which time Robert Smith was one of those testifying on the matter of the length of term of one of his fellow passengers, Richard Coy.

Robert Smith must have been sold to some Ipswich resident and there grew to maturity. He first appears on record in October 1651, when he was allowed charges by the court on some legal matter with Thomas King, which Robert won.

About 1655, he married Mary French, daughter of Thomas and Mary French of Ipswich. She was baptized on 2 March 1633/4 at Boston. In March 1656 he and Mary were fined for incontinency before marriage.

In March 1659 Robert Smith, "aged about 33", deposed that he lived with Simon Tuttle's mother about eight or nine years before. Mrs. Tuttle was the wife of John Tuttle of Ipswich. This would have been after he was through with his service but still a single man.

About the summer of 1656, according to an account of Mrs. Tuttle which is in the court file, Robert Smith worked for her, felling trees and drawing them out of the swamp with his team of two oxen, one day mending the orchard fence, one day thatching. Robert, aged 33, verified the account on 28 January 1659/60.

From all this and the affiars of John Tuttle, who eventually moved to Ireland, we can deduce that Robert Smith probably was indentured to him and continued working for him after his time was up and for a year or so after he married.

About the time of his marriage or shortly thereafter, he moved to Topsfield Village where he owned 208 acres. Little is known of his life except that he did follow the trade of tailor as well as farmer, as did the members of his wife's family. Topsfield Village later became Boxford.

In 1680 Robert Smith took the oath of allegiance. In 1684, Robert's wife, whose name is not given, was a member of the church in Topsfield in full communion.

In 1687, Robert Smith "an Old decrepit man & son" were taxed 4s.6d. on 1 head, 1 house, 12 acres, 2 oxen, 1 horse, 2 cows, 2 calves and 3 swine. He was about 61, the son probably was Ephraim, then of age.

On 30 August 1693 he died, leaving the following will. Samuel was appointed administrator with the consent of his mother and brothers.

From the will, we learn of an age old family problem — a rebelious, selfish son, and on the other hand, another son dutiful and unselfish.

WILL OF ROBERT SMITH
7 AUGUST 1693

This is the last will and testament of me Robert Smith of Boxford in the county of Essex, in the name of God, Amen. I being in perfect memory although sick in body, do in the first place bequeath my body to the dust to be decently buried and my soul to my blessed lord and saviour Jesus Christ.

And for the estate the lord hath been pleased to give me, I do dispose amongst my children as followeth, viz.-

Primis - I do give to my son Samuel Smith all my first division which is four score acres and it is to be made up a hundred acres, that is to say, as they go to Cole pit neck. And Nathaniel Smith being unable to provide for himself, I do appoint my son Samuel to take the whole care of him both for clothing, meat, drink, washing and housing, finding for him both in sickness and health for his natural life.

2. I give to my son Ephraim Smith sixty acres of land as it is herein bounded be it more or less: beginning at a rock and ---- by the south side of Long Hill that is a boundmark between Mist. --'s land and mine and from that rock upon a straight line running westward to Corporal Thomas Andrews' stickey meadow and also the north side of this last line lying between Mist. Thomas Baker's land and Corporal Thomas Andrews' land up to a white oak tree to belong to Ephraim Smith and to his heirs and assigns forever.
3. I give to my son Jacob Smith fifty acres of land be it more or less as it is herein bounded, lying between Samuel Smith's land as it is above bounded and Ephraim Smith as he is above bounded and Corporal Thomas Andrews' land, Samuel Smith lying on the south east and Ephraim Smith lying on north or northwest and Corporal Thomas Andrews lying on the south and southwest, and all that is within this bounds I give to Jacob Smith and his heirs and assigns forever.
4. In consideration that my son Thomas Smith did leave me as soon as he was able to do anything and went and lived with his grandfather French and never came to me to help me in my old age, with what I have already given him, I do for---- order six pounds to be given to him in cattle within two years after my decease.
5. I give to my daughter Mary Townes and to my daughter Phebe Townes and to my daughter Emy Townes and to my daughter Mariah Smith all my movable estate within doors to be equally divided between them at the death of me and my wife. My true meaning is that what any of my daughters have already had shall be accounted and if any has her share already, then they shall have no share of what do remain to be divided, for my will is that my daughters shall be equal in that estate with what they have had, and if there is [any one that?] do fail to their share, then they shall have the ---------------- that my daughter Mariah Smith shall have as good a share [for herself?] as any of my daughters that are already married.
6. I do will my son Samuel Smith ---------------- [me] and my wife during our natural lives, he to -------- [and pro]vide all things fit for us so long as we do live, and --- his so doing, all the land above bounded to him to remain ----- and his heirs and assigns forever, and all my stock to remain to the disposing of my executor.
7. I do appoint my loving wife Mary Smith and my son Samuel Smith to be my sole executors to this my last will and I do give them full power to see this my last will fulfilled in every particular as is above said. Also, they have full power granted to them by me that if they stand in need of help to ashoate any whom they please to help them and what they shall do or cause to be done shall be binding and stand in force.
8. I do appoint my executors to pay all my lawful debts as witness my hand and seal this seventh day of August one thousand six

hundred ninety and three and in the fifth year of the reign pf our soverign Lord and Lady, William & Mary, King and Queen of England, Scotland, France and Ireland, defender of the faith.
Signed, sealed & delivered in the presence of us:

John Gould — Robert his o mark Smith

John French, senior

Proved 26 September 1693 at Newbury by
Capt. John Gould & John French, senior

3 October 1693 at Salem, the executors therein named appeared and renounced their executorship to the within will.
Also, Mary Smith, widow, and Thomas Smith and Ephraim Smith, the two eldest brothers, disclaimed their right of administration and pray that it may be granted to Samuel Smith the third son of the deceased within mentioned.

A True Inventory of ye Estate of Robert Smith of Boxford County of Essex in New England who departed this life ye thirtieth of August 1693-

	£ s d
ye houeseing and land at	150.00.00
4 oxen at £12, two cowes at £4	16. .
2 heifers at £3, 8 sheep at 40s, 3 hogs at 10s ea	6.10.
3 pigs at 4s ea, cart & plow & chain & tackling for oxen 30s	2. 2.
a mortising ax, 3 wedges, one bettle ring . .	6.3
1 musket 18s, 1 rapier 10s	1. 8.
1 bed and bedsteed and furniture to ye bed . .	5.
1 other bed with a blanket, one with sheets & two pillows	1.16.
one blanket & a pair of sheets and a bolster .	1. 5.
3 putter platter and a frying pan	8.
wooden ware 3s, more wooden ware 2s. 6d. .	5.6
4 iron potts £2. 10s, 1 pail, two chains 7s. 6d. .	2.17.6
1 table, one chest, one box, one meal trough . .	1. 7.
2 pr pott hooks	2.
The total is	£ 189.07.03

Mary Smith, the widow, went to live with son Samuel about a year after her husband's death, and lived with him for the next twenty-five years as the following document shows. She must have died during the winter of 1719-20, for on 16 February Thomas sold his rights in the estate to his three brothers. In 1726, three deeds were recorded by which the four daughters and their three living husbands quit their rights in the estate to Ephraim and Jacob, being paid off. Ephraim, Samuel and Jacob agreed to a division of the land — about 200 acres, each taking title to about what they were already occupying, with some minor adjustments.

We the subscriber being Desired by Sam^{ll} Smith, Son of and administrator on the Estate of Robart Smith of Boxford desced to asist him In his bill of charg for maintaining his mother and his brother Nathaniell Smith, his mother being upward of sixty years of age att his father's dath and his brother being uncapabell of taking care of himself all his days and his brother contined with him for the space of twenty four years and then departed this Life and the above Samuell Smith toock the care of him the tarme of twenty fower years and his mother livied with him after his father dath twenty five years and he toock ye care of her also . . and in our happurhnion we think it may be worth six pound pur year for the keeping his brother Nathaniell Smith twenty years and for the Last four years ten pound pur years . . . and for the maintaines of his mother for the space of twenty six years taking one year with another eight pound per year.

Benjamin Bixby
John Gould
Jacob Dorman
Phabe Gould

Topsfield June 3:1720

(Reference: Essex File 25729)

Children, born in Topsfield, except the first two:

THOMAS, b about 1657 in Ipswich; he m Martha Knowlton; in a deposition of 23 Sept. 1697 he & wife Martha were both aged 40. On 16 Feb. 1719/20 Thomas Smith, innholder of Ipswich, quitclaimed for £20 his rights in his parents estate to brothers Ephraim, Samuel & Jacob of Boxford; 8 ch.; he d testate 25 Feb. 1725/6 at Ipswich; she d 4 Feb. 1728/9

MARY, b 28 Oct. 1658 at Ipswich; m 2 Feb. 1680/1, John Towne, son of Jacob & Catherine (Symonds) Towne, b 2 April 1658; 10 ch.; moved to Framingham about 1700, in Charlestown 1708, to Oxford 1713; he d 1740 at Topsfield

PHEBE, b 26 Aug. 1661 at Topsfield; m 24 June 1684, Jacob Towne, brother of John, b 13 Feb. 1659/60; 10 ch.; he d 4 Oct. 1741; she d 14 Jan. 1740/41

EPHRAIM, b 29 Oct. 1663; m 6 Sept. 1694, Mary, dau. of John & Eliz. (Perkins) Ramsdell, b 27 Jan. 1674/5 at Topsfield; 8 ch. rec.; he d 1732

SAMUEL, b 26 Jan. 1665/6; he m & had ch. bapt. at Topsfield: Samuel July 1706, Elizabeth Nov. or Dec. 1708, twins John & Mercy 15 April 1711, Margaret 3 June 1713, Priscilla 2 Oct. 1715, Rebecca 2 May 1718

AMYE, b 16 Aug. 1668; m 10 Aug. 1687, Joseph, son of Edmund & Mary (Browning) Towne, b 2 Sept. 1661; 7 ch.; res. Topsfield where he d about 1777; she d 22 Feb. 1756 ae 87

SARAH, b 25 June 1670; d 28 Aug. 1673

NATHANIEL, b 7 Sept. 1672; prob. retarded

JACOB, b 26 Jan. 1674; m Rebecca, dau. of Samuel & Elizabeth (Andrews) Symonds of Boxford, b 31 May 1679; 7 ch.; his will 8 Dec. 1748, pr. 7 March 1750/51, bequeathed his lands in Boxford & Topsfield, cooper's tools, warlike accoutrements, gun; a carpenter

MARIAH, b 18 Dec. 1677; m 11 Feb. 1700/01, Peter, son of Peter & Frances Shumway, b 6 June 1678; 10 ch.; she d 17 Jan. 1738/9; he m 2, 1739/40, Mary Dana; 1714 settled in Oxford

Ref.: Ancestry and Posterity of Joseph Smith & Emma Hale; N.E.H.G.S.-55; V.R.; Essex County Quarterly Court Files, as published

SAMUEL SMITH was probably born about 1575-1580 in England. Possibly he and his wife are the Smiths, with two children, who came in the Winthrop Fleet in 1630 from Buxhall, Suffolk. According to Lewis, the historian of Lynn, Samuel Smith was among the settlers of Lynn in 1634 and lived at Swampscot. If so, he moved on to Salem, where he was among the proprietors and received 150 acres in the initial distribution dated 1636. Then, on 25 December 1637, he received one acre in the distribution of the marsh meadow lands. There were six members in his family, according to the notation before his name on the list. He next appears in Salem on 23 April 1638 when he was granted 200 acres in that part of Salem which was called Enon and was later set off as the town of Wenham. This grant was along the southeasterly side of Main Street. Upon this tract he built a house where he lived until his death in the autumn of 1642. This was the second grant of land in Enon. This 200 acres was in exchange for his original 150 acre grant which was voided.

The spring of 1638 was so cold that the seed corn rotted in the ground and planting had to be repeated. The first day of June was a typical June day, with bright sunshine and a gentle west wind. In the middle of the afternoon, the earth began to tremble, the houses shook, and many chimneys toppled. Half an hour later, a second but milder tremor occurred. This was the greatest earthquake of that century.

At the court held at Salem on 31 March 1640, Samuel Smith charged James Smith, senior, with theft, his wife Mary Smith with suspicion of felony. Both Samuel and his son testified against them. Their son, James junior, confessed to having taken a little piece of tobacco in their house when Goodman White lived there, and two quarts of meal and about a half pound of suet, and also a piece of cheese. Both father and son were fined for the theft. John White was to be paid for the goods stolen from him.

By order of the General Court, a road from Rowley to Ipswich and from Ipswich to Salem was laid out by a committee and recorded on 1 May 1640. The road ran along the east side of Mr. Smith's house, and from thence over the old planters meadow, etc.

The earliest town records of Wenham are lost. In preparation for the township, Samuel Smith and John Fiske, on whose land the first meeting house was probably built, each gave ten acres of their land to the new town that it might be divided into house lots on which the new settlers could build and live, constituting a little hamlet, the center of which was where the public buildings now stand. The land was divided into two acre lots. The first of the town records is devoted to this. It reads as follows:

The 2 day of ye first month 1642

There is given unto Wenham Twenty acres of ground being laid out of eyther side of ye meeting house. Ten acres given by Mr Smith out of his fearme & laid out by him begining wth the bounds of ye upper end of Phinehas Fiske Lott & soe to ye swampe; & the other Ten acres given by Mr John ffiske being laid out Joyneing to it on ye other sd of ye meeting house:

It is ordered & Agreed upon at this or meeting yt such as have any ground graunted of that wch is given to ye Towne wch lyes about ye meetinge house, such shall Come & live upon it themselves, & if not to lay it downe to ye plantation, & if any shall build upon it &c. & after remove themselves & make sale of the same it is ordered that the Plantation shall have the first pfare & give there Answere in a short time before they make sale of it to any other.

On 16 November 1640 Samuel Smith sold a house and eighteen acres of land plus about 2 acres of meadow to John Fairfield. Then, on 7 April 1641, John Fairfield traded his property to Thomas Smith, Samuel's son, for a like 18 acres and a house. This property Samuel Smith had bought of William Fiske who had before got it from one James Smith, who may have been a relation to Samuel, altho just how is not known. Abstracts of these deeds follow, as well as some depositions made years later for a dispute over the titles to the property or such.

16 November 1640 - Deed, Samuell Smyth to John Fairefeild, for £27.10s ...a certayne dwelling house & cowhouse situate in Salem a little off the great pond late in the possession of James Smith, purchased of him by William Fiske & sold by the sayd Willaim Fiske unto Samuel Smith aforesayd, together with the appurtenances to the sayd houses, with eighteen Acres of upland lying from the house nie east downe to the meadowes & aboute 2 pole & a halfe on this side the dwelling house with free egresse and regresse to the spring - abutting & certayne parcell of medow nie about 2 Acres by compute abutting upon the foresayd upland westward & upon John White's land eastward. Witnesses: John Fiske and William Fiske.

17 December 1640 - James Smith acquitted and discharged John Fairfild of all demands for a house and ground bought of him by Mr. Joh. Fiske. Witness: William Browne.

7 April 1641 - Agreement between John Fairfeld and Thomas Smyth to chang each with other for 18 Ackers of Land with A house upon each 18 ackers: & the housan to be both alike & what difference theare shall be in goodnes betwene them shall be allowed unto him that two men shall cast it: & for soe much Land as is broken up in the said John Fairfelds ground the other ptie is to break up as much as y[e] other psell of Land before y[e] next winter & alsoe to allow him soe much fencing stufe againe & lickwise dung for y[e] manuring of y[e] land & for y[e] meadowe that did belong to Jeames Smith Along y[e] River the said Joh fairfeld is to have & y[e] medowe ground that did belong unto Samewell Smith the said Thomas Smith is to have & for y[e] Confirming hearof both pties have sett to thear hands this psent day Above written.

June 1661 - Sarah Rumball, aged about seventy years, deposed that her son, Thomas Smith, sold this house and land to Robert Hase, and that said Smith enjoyed it several years peaceably and quietly. Sworn in Court

28 June 1661 - Danell Rumball, blacksmith, of Salem, aged about sixty-two years, deposed that: "About y[t] time that I wass a sutter to the widow Smith y[t] is now my wiff Thomas Smith her sonn did dwell in a house situatt nere y[e] housse y[t] was mr Smiths which houss and land y[e] Aforsad Thomas mad Salle off to Robert Haws Now dwelling at Roxbery my hand being to y[e] deed as A wittness".

26 June 1661 - Richard Coye, aged about thirty-five years, deposed that the eighteen acres of land was owned by Mr. Samuell Smith, who sold it to John Fayerfield, and it was part of the farm that the town of Salem gave the said Smith in Wenham. Also that Richard Hutten said that Walter Fayerfield should not have it unless he could recover it by law.

Samuel Smith made his will on 5 October 1642 and died soon after. He was probably already sick and dying when he made the will. His widow, Sarah, survived him and remarried the next year to Daniel Rumball, a blacksmith born about 1599. Sarah was born about 1591 and was almost certainly a second wife to Samuel Smith and perhaps not the mother of his younger children. That he had a prenuptual contract with Sarah, referred to in his will, is an almost certain indication of this. Still, Sarah called Thomas Smith her son in 1661 and her husband, Daniel Rumball, at the same time also spoke of Thomas being her son. It is possible that they meant stepson.

Daniel Rumball had his homestead at the northern end of the square in Salem between Elm and Walnut Streets, on the southern side of Essex Street, now included in Hawthorne Boulevard. Sarah was still living as his wife in 1675. His daughter Alice (by a former wife) married William Curtis. Daniel Rumball died in or soon after 1682 when he was well over eighty years of age.He was dead by November 1684 when his estate was mentioned. Sarah, who was about eight years older than Daniel, probably died earlier.

THE WILL OF SAMUEL SMITH OF WENHAM

this 5th of ocktober: 1642:

This my last will and teastament of Samewell Smith of Enon being in perfect memorey first I will and bequeath unto my wife Sarah Smith my farme in Enon with all the housen upon it as allsoe all the frutes upon it as corne hemp and the like: for har owne proper use for the tearme of har lif upon consideration that she shall discharg me of that promise upon maridge: which is unto my sunn: William Browne fiftie pounds: as allsoe that she shall give unto his two children William and John Browne £20 between ym: all which shall be paid by my exequetors hearafter named: my will further is to give unto Sarah my wif all my Cattell nowe upon the farme young and owld as neat bests horse bests and swine in full consideration of that hundred pounds that I stand bound unto har by A bond obligatore in lue of A former Joynter payabell after my dissease which shall be parformed by my Exsequetors as allsoe further my will is that my farme with all the medowe and upland belongine thearunto my sunn Thomas Smith shall have it to himself and his heairs for ever upon this consideration that he shall pay unto his sister mare if then living fiftie pownds in thre years after the entrie of it that is to say sixteene pounds and A mark A yeare and for the parformance hearof he is to lay in good securetye unto the Exsequetors if the lord take her away by death this payment is to be made unto the Children of the aforesaid William Browne and Thomas Smith that then shall be living Equally devided among them further my will is that if my sunn: Thomas shall die without issue that my land and housen upon it shall com to my daughter mare and har heaires forever: and after har to William Browne and his heaires for ever all wich debtes and legasies and other parformances are to be parformed by my two Exsequetors which I have Apointed which is my Loving wife and my trustie sun William Browne: & my will further is that if Sarah my wif shall marey that then the first gift of my farme shall stand voyd and my will is that she shall then resigne it up into my other exequetors hand with A Just accounte of all those goods and whatsoever belong to the manadgine of the farme & profit except that hundred pounds which har due which is to be paide har in Cattell by the Judgment of men: and all my houshould stufe within dores whatsoever it be I give to my wife: and my will is that my excequetor William Browne and my sunn Thomas Smith to Joyne with him to leat the farme: or improve it to the best advantage for the good of my daughter mare and to be accounted with and provided for by my excequetor William Browne in that particquler: Item with this consideration that if my wif marey that then the farme is to be leat as above said untill thear be gathered for my ------- A portion -------- A hundred and fiftie pounds to be paid unto the excequetor William Browne and he to pay that hundred & fiftie pounds at har day of maredg & if har mother leave har then the excequetor William Browne to se ye bringing of har up. allsoe my sunn Thomas Smith is to be Aquitted of that fiftie pound he stand ingadged to pay unto har: and all the overplush of A hundred and fiftie pounds if the lord give longer life unto my wif Arising out of ye farme is to be left in my sun browns hand and improved to the best use and after har dissease to be equally parted betwixt my daughter mare and all the grand children I shall have then living further my will is that my sunn Thomas Smith whome I feare not: will be truly faithfull to me shall be thearfore my Suprevisor of this my last will: witnes this present day above.

Samwell Smyth (seal)

Witness: Richard (his S mark) Pettingall
William Sawyer

Proved 27: 10: 1642. Wit: J^no. Thorndike, who deposed that he had his senses: Georg Emerey, that "he had a fitt of a feaver ye day before and the vapors in his stomake caused paine in his head, and did cause sleep troubld sleep & ye Last day till toward 2 of the Clock was very sensible". Mr. J^no. Fiske, Mrs. Fisk, and the two witnesses to the will, Richard Pettingell and William Sawyer, also deposed. (Salem Quarterly Court Rec.)

Inventory taken 18: 9: 1642, by Lawrence Leach, Jefferie Massey and Will. Howard:

	£ s d
Dwelling house, barn, etc.	40.00.0
farm of 234 acres, 33 broken up, 177 in common and 24 meadow	99. 8.0
6 calves	7.00.0
3 heffers	10.10.0
4 oxen	24.00.0
mear and coult	20.10.0
2 young stears	9.00.0
7 cowes	36.10.0
9 swine	14.00.0
Inglish and indian Corne	28.00.0
hempe	2.10.0
hay, etc.	12. 6.0
carte, plow, harrow, etc.	3.15.0
silver beacker, and 2 spounes	2.15.0
peauter, brasse, Iron potts	8. 5.0
2 muskitts, 1 birding pese & 1 pr. bandeleres	1.10.0
sword and belt	12.0
in cellar	3.10.0
corne & hemp sed	3.10.0
severall towles	1.16.0
bed, boulster & blanckits	2.00.0
bed & bedstead	4. 2.0

bed in chamber	12.0
bed, blanckits 7 Ceverlet	7. 8.0
another	9. 3.6
bed teek	2.00.0
bed, bedstead & furniture	4.14.0
wearing aparell of his	7. 6.0
A 11 Cushings	2.15.0
one carpitt	15.0
Cobbard Clothes	1.00.0
3 Chists & A whele	1.00.0
napkins & bord lining	4.18.0
pillow bears	3.00.0
sheets	7.16.0
bookes	15.0
wood worke, viz., 1 tabell & standard, warming pann & stooles	3. 3.0
1 grinstone, a brake, tuter & Iron Rake . . .	[? 3.14.8]
Total . . .	£395. 9.2
Goods not seen by appraisers but reported to them: Hand carte 5s, 2 towe comes 5s, a small cowe hide 8s . .	18.0
the boyes time Prised at three pownds intending the boyes Covenant to be performed as it is in the indenter .	3.00.0

Children:

SARAH, m William Browne; 8 ch. recorded: William b 1639, John b 1641 - d 1669, Samuel b 1644 - drowned ae 11, Joseph - a preacher who d 1678, Benjamin 1648, Sarah 1649 - m 1665 Thomas Deane, Mary b 1655/6 - m Wait Winthrop & d 1690, James b 1658 - d.y.; Sarah d 10 Feb. 1667/8; he d 20 Jan. 1687/8, testate; res. Ipswich

MARY, named in her father's will of 1642, then unm., prob. about 18, so b about 1624.

THOMAS, prob. b 1610 - 18; named as supervisor of his father's will:

> 15 July 1640 - Tho: Smith desireth a peece of upland Joyning to his meddow about 12 acres that soe hee may make use of the townes former grant.
>
> (Salem Town Records)
>
> 17 December 1640 - James Smith acquitted and discharged John Fairfild of all demands for a house and ground bought of him by Mr. John Fiske. Witness: William Browne.
>
> 7 April 1641 - Agrement between John Fairfeld and Thomas Smyth to chang with each other for 18 Ackers of Land with A house upon each 18 ackers: & the housan to be both alike & what difference theare shall be in goodness betwene them shall be allowed unto him that two men shall cast it: & for soe much Land as is broken up in the said John Fairfelds ground the other ptie is to break up as much as ye other psell of Land before ye next winter & alsoe to allow him soe much fencing stufe againe & lickwise dung for ye manuring of ye land & for ye meadowe that did belong to Jeames Smith Along ye River the said John fairfeld is to have & ye medowe ground that did belong unto Samewell Smith the said Thomas Smith is to have & for ye Confirming hearof both pties have sett to theare hands this psent day Above written.

In June 1641, Thomas Smith sued Christopher Foster and Daniel King for debt. In January following, Robert Isbell sued him, probably for debt. In December 1642, Thomas Smith and eleven others were charged in court with keeping their cattle in the common corn fields, and all but one of them were fined for it. These were Salem men.

In the fall of 1642, his father died and left him his farm in Wenham.

Some time after this, Thomas Smith moved to Gloucester, for on 11 June 1644, then of Gloucester, he sold to Robert Hawes of Wenham the Wenham property which he had inherited from is father. The following deed and deposition tell the story.

11 June 1644 - Indenture, between Thomas Smyth of Gloster and Robert Hawes of Wenham, said Smyth, for £31.15s, sold to said Hawes his house, cowhouse and twenty acres of land adjoining the house and thirty acres more near the great swamp, butting upon John Whit on one side and Phineas Fisk on the other, also six acres of meadow lying in the great meadow, all the said land lying in the town of Wenham. Witnesses: Danl Roumbel, Sarey (her mark) Roumble and William Dudbridg.

June 1661 - Mathew Edwards, aged about 29 years, deposed that the house now in possession of Richard Coye, which was late John Fairefield's, was built by Thomas Smith, as he said, upon an exchange, & also two akres of land lying before the house or betwixt the orchard and the highway were part of eighteen acres of land exchanged by Thomas Smith and Jno. Fairefield. More land was also laid out by Mr. Smith to deponent's uncle, John Fairefield, which he said was the rest of the land exchanged between himself and said Smith, and all of this land was afterward taken away by Ipswich at the running of the line, except two acres. Sworn in Court.

At the court held in Salem on 10 July 1644, Thomas Smith sued Robert Hawes, apparently over this sale. Perhaps he had not been paid in full.

At the court of July 1645, William Vinson and Thomas Smith of Gloucester were appointed as attorneys to represent Henry Glass, an apprentice boy, who had been sold by his master, Henry Phelps, to Nicholas Phelps (Henry's brother) to transport him beyond seas.

In July 1647, Phillip Cromwell, a man separated from his wife and child in England, was charged with spending too much time with the wife of Thomas Smith and three other wives, all of whom were at the house of Theophilus Downing of Salem one day when he was away. The other three wives were summoned to the next court, but Thomas's wife was not mentioned further.

In December 1647, Lancelott Grainger sued Thomas Smith of Ipswich. It appears that Thomas Smith's home, originally in Salem, then set off as the new town of Wenham, was later put into Ipswich when the town boundary line was settled.

Ref.: History of Salem, Mass., by Perley, 1926; Records and Files of the Quarterly Courts of Essex County, Mass.; Savage; Essex County Probate Records; Vital Records

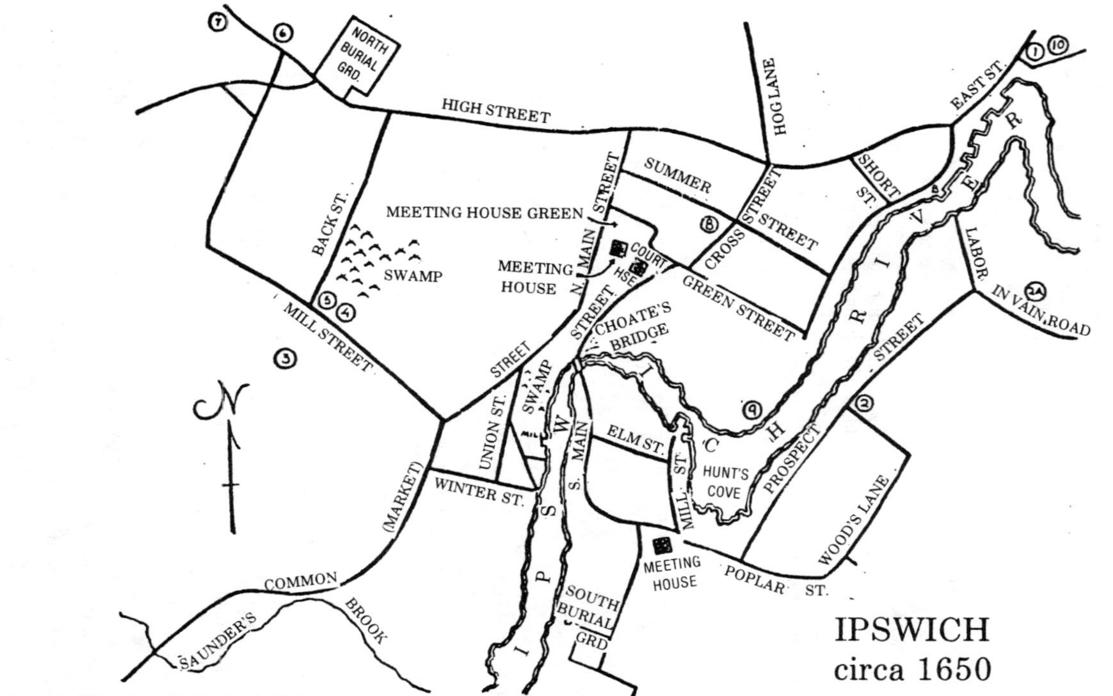

A. Stacy's Wharf B. Perkin's Wharf 2a. John Perkins bought land here 1. John Perkins, Sr. 2. John Dane 3. John Cogswell
4. Simon Stacy 5. William Warner 6. Alexander Knight 7. Simon Tuttle 8. John Dane (near R. Muzzy) 9. John Tuttle 10. John Perkins, jr.

THOMAS SMITH of Ipswich, Massachusetts, appears first on the record at the town meeting in Ipswich on 9 April 1639, when he was granted a one acre house lot there:

> Granted to Thomas Smith a house lot one acre to the street called West End, having a house lot granted to John Cooly south east, common near the common fence gate northwest. 9th 2 mo. 1639.
>
> William Whitred of Ipswich, carpenter, sold to Thomas Smith of Ipswich, shoemaker, a house and half-an-acre lot, bounded by William Purlers, having been granted to William Simmons, and by him sold to grantor, the house having been built by William Symmons. Entered 1 June 1639

There were several other Smiths in Ipswich at an early date, but any realtionship to Thomas is unknown. Also, there was a Thomas Smith in Lynn, later Salem, and then Gloucester at about the same time, as well as another Thomas in Newbury. The Salem man's property, or at least some of it, appears to have been near the Ipswich line and there may be some confusion between these two. However, Thomas of Lynn was made freeman in 1633, but Thomas of Ipswich did not gain the right to vote until 1650. This seems to show that there were two distinct Thomas Smiths, and not one moving around. Otherwise, there is no clear overlapping of the meager records to separate them.

In December 1647 Lancelott Grainger sued Thomas Smith of Ipswich.

Bartholomew Heath sued Thomas Smith for debt on 28 March 1648 at the Ipswich Quarterly Court.

In March 1648/9, Thomas Smith was on the trial jury at Ipswich and again in September 1650. At this later time he was made freeman.

Walter Tibbot, in his will of 1651, mentions a meadow he had bought of Thomas Smith. Tibbot was of Gloucester but had property in Ipswich.

> 15 September 1652 - Thomas Smith of Ipswich sold to Robert Lord of same town all my six acres of land granted my by the town of Ipswich, situated in Ipswich within the common field on the north side the river, having the land of the late James Hows and now in possession of the said Lord toward the northwest, land of William Marchant toward the southeast, land of Theoph-

ilus Willson toward the northeast and the common fence toward the southwest. Acknowledged by said Thomas Smith & Johana his wife yielded up her dower on 16 April 1670. (Ipswich deed 3:148)

Thomas Smith's house was mentioned in 1653 as a boundary in Ipswich in the north end of town and southeast of Theophilus Shatswell's house.

In March 1655 Joannah, wife of Thomas Smith, testified concerning a deathbed will of widow Alice Ward of Ipswich.

In the summer of 1655 Nathaniel Stow and Henry Kimball of Ipswich suffered damage to their corn when about 50 head of cattle belonging to various neighbors and kept in the common pasture next to their cornfields, broke thru the fence. Two of Thomas Smith's steers were among the herd. Some of the depositions follow.

Henry Kimball deposed that he saw Mr. Smith's steer in Nathanill Stowse corn and as he went to get him out he leaped over the five rail fence of Alicksander Knight's.

Samewell Younglove witnessed that he helped to bring fifty head of cattle out of Henry Kimball's and Nathaniel Stowe's corn, four of Richard Shatswell's, three of old Kimball's, two of goodman Marchant's, three of Goodwife Coolis, one steer of Mr. Smith's; and, also, he saw one post down and two lenghts of rails there. He saw some of the cattle go in there and the tracks of others.

William Dello deposed that there were two oxen of Tho. Smith's, two steers of Richard Setchwell's, and two cows of William Marchant's in Nathaniel Stow's corn two days before the general training at Ipswich.

Robert Lord, jr., deposed that he saw one steer of Thomas Smith's in Nathaniel Stow's corn and two cows of John Newman's, at four several times.

William Parker deposed that he saw cattle of Richard Shatchwell, John Numan, Thomas Smith, Rich. Kemball, Aron Pengrye and William Marchant in Henry Kimball's corn.

Thomas Smith was on the grand jury that sat at Ipswich on 30 September 1656, the trial jury of 30 March 1658, and again on the grand jury on 30 September 1662.

In 1664, he had a share of Plum Island.

At the court held on 27 March 1666 at Ipswich Thomas Smith was released from training but was to pay a bushel of Indian corn per annum to the company. This would suggest that he had reached the age of 60 that year and thus was born about 1606, or else he was just too feeble to serve. Then, in September 1672, he was released henceforth from training without any payment. Perhaps he was then age 60 and was born about 1612?

In January 1669/70 he sold his house to James Sayer (i.e. Sawyer) with an arrangement for the future comfort of himself and his wife, Joan, as the following two deeds indicate. It is interesting to note in these deeds the reference to the thatched roof of his home and daubing, which implies some sort of frame filled with wattle and daub.

21 January 1669/70 - Thomas Smith of Ipswich, shoemaker, for £42.10s in hand paid or secured to be paid, sold to James Sayer of Ipswich all my dwelling house, out houses, yards, gardens & ground about it, containing by estimation 1½ acres, situated in Ipswich at the northwest end, having the house and land of the widow Marchant & Henry Ossborne toward the northwest, land of Aron Pengry toward the southeast, one end abutting upon the street toward the southwest, the other end abutting upon planting ground on the hill, provided always that said Thomas Smith doth reserve liberty for himself & his wife to live in the said house in that end next Aron Pengry's ground and to make use of the cellar under the room and of the barn & yard, and liberty of the fire of the said James as a common fire for them both (the said James to provide and maintain the same), as also reserves half the herbage or commonage for his cattle and all this during the natural lifetime of me the said Thomas Smith and Joanah my wife. Acknowledged by said Thomas Smith and at same time Johana his wife yielded up her dower on 16 April 1670. (Ipswich deed 3:149-150)

21 January 1669/70 - James Sayer of Ipswich deeded back the above property to Thomas Smith, the deed, however, to be void if said Sayer performed the following obligations: Pay to said Thomas Smith the £42.10s at rate of £7 per year in wheat, malt, rye & Indian corn in case he require it, 20s in wheat, 20s in malt, the rest in rye & Indian corn, excepting the first year in regard of his building an end to the house, said Thomas to keep that end of the house reserved in tenantable repair for thatching & daubing during the life of him and Johana his wife, but Thomas hath liberty to leave the said £42.10s or part of it in the hands of said James until his death, in which case said James shall have a year to pay it unto those the said Thomas shall appoint, in corn and cattle at current prices; James to provide and maintain a common fire, and in case they desire to keep a private fire in their own room, James to provide them wood, Thomas to pay for cutting it and carting it home; James shall maintain the biggest part of the common fence next to Aron Pengry's land, Thomas that part next widow Marchant; Thomas to have half the herbage or commonage for his cattle, with use of the barn & barn yard, and if said Thomas shall remove while he liveth, he or his wife hath liberty to take away the house he makes use of as a barn. Acknowledged by said James & his wife Martha who yielded up her dower, 16 April 1670. (Ipswich deed 3:150-151)

The arrangement with James Sawyer did not work out, for on 31 May 1671 he sold the same home lot and house to Aaron Pengry his next-door neighbor for the same price, on credit, and on the same conditions, that is, that he and his wife Joan should have the right to remain in the half of the house next to Pengry's land. This, too, was a short lived bargain, for on 9 March 1676/7 he sold the property outright, again on credit, to Thomas Dow. Then, in 1679 he sold the last of his land in Ipswich as the following deeds show.

9 March 1676/7 - Thomas Smith of Ipswich, shoemaker, for £30 to me secured to be paid by Thomas Dow of Ipswich, sold to Dow all my house lot in Ipswich, having land of Caleb Kimball on the east, Robert Day on the south, the common on the west, High Street on the north, containing about $1\frac{1}{2}$ acres. Acknowledged 29 March 1677. (Ipswich deed 4:83)

28 June 1679 - Thomas Smith of Ipswich, shoemaker, sold to Benedict Pulsipher of Ipswich, all that my division lot of marsh at Plumb Island being a single share in the second range of lots, No. 60, being near unto Swamp Island, etc. (Ipswich deed 4:335)

In July 1677 he served on a jury of inquest into the death of Joseph Lord of Ipswich, who was killed while felling a tree about 2½ miles from the meeting house.

In the Quarterly Court of May 1680 and of November 1680, respectively, are found:

Thomas Smith, sr., and his wife being aged and impotent and unable to help and provide for themselves, said Smith came into court and gave up to the selectmen of Ipswich the following estate: three cows and one yearling, three acres of land at Muddy river, a bill of three pounds, six shillings of Pulsifer's and fifteen pounds due from Thomas Dow, about eleven pounds due him from Aron Pengry, sr., and all his household goods, etc., provided the town maintain them as long as they live.

Capt. Shuball Walker, one of the selectmen of Bradford, presented a writing to the court in behalf of the town under the hands of the selectmen of Ipswich, informing the court that Mr. Thomas Smith and his wife of Ipswich had come into their town contrary to order, and having warned the persons who entertained them not to do it, likewise to said Smith to depart, yet they abide in the town still and liable to be a charge to the said town, court ordered that the caution be entered.

This was routine legal procedure to keep the financial responsibility with the town of Ipswich and off the taxpayers of Bradford. The following bargain was made with the selectmen of Ipswich:

November 18, 1680 Richard and Benjamin Kimball of Bradford did covenant to and with the selectmen of Ipswich that they would take Thomas Smith and his wife to Bradford to the house of Mary Kimball the widow of Thomas Kimball and provide their meate, drink, washing, lodging, clothes and attendance with all things necessary for persons in such a condition for the space of one year beginning at the date hereof, the price for a year to be £25

December 8, 1681 agreed with Richard Kimball of Bradford to allow unto him further keeping and providing for his grandfather Thomas Smith for the year ensuing £13

Thomas Smith apparently died at Bradford in the winter of 1681/2, his wife having died earlier.

Richard Kemball presenting an Inventory of ye Estate of Thomas Smith disceased: whereunto he hath given oath to the truth thereof & If more be found, he will add the same Pour of Administration to sd Estate Is granted unto the sd Mary & Richard Kemball In court held at Ipswich 28 of March 1682

This is a true Inventory of the Estate of Mr Thomas Smith of Ipswich Deceased Aprised

	£ s d
Item bed & bedding	3-15-0
It one piece of carsay & searg	1-12-0
It pudder	0- 8-0
It scellets & pots	0-11-0
It one trammell & friingpan	0- 3-6
It one Table & chist	0- 6-0
It one axe	0- 3-6
It one saw	0- 6-0
Debts Due to the Estate in Thomas Dow his hands	11- 0-0
in Pulsifer hands	3- 0-0
in Aaron Pengrave his hands	2- 6-0
	24- 1-0
Debts Due from the Estate to Mr Rogers	4- 0-0
or therabouts	
To John Appleton	1- 8-0
Debt more to Richard Kimball	1-17-0
To Nath Russ	0- 5-0
& for buriall apparrel	2- 0-0
These perticulars above written was	9-10-0

Aprised by us Richard Hall
Samuell Hazeltine March 29th 1682

Children:

MARY, b prob. about 1635, prob. in England; m Thomas Kimball, son of Richard & Ursula (Scott) Kimball of Ipswich, b about 1633 at Rattlesden, Suffolk, England; 10 ch.; he was killed by Indians on the night of 2-3 May 1676; she m 2, 17 May 1682 at Ipswich, Thomas Knowlton; she d 20 Nov. 1688 at Ipswich

SARAH, possibly a dau. b 1641-2; she m 18 Nov. 1664 at Ipswich, Samuel Lomas, b 7 June 1639 - g.s. at Ipswich, d 24 Feb. 1720/21 ae 80

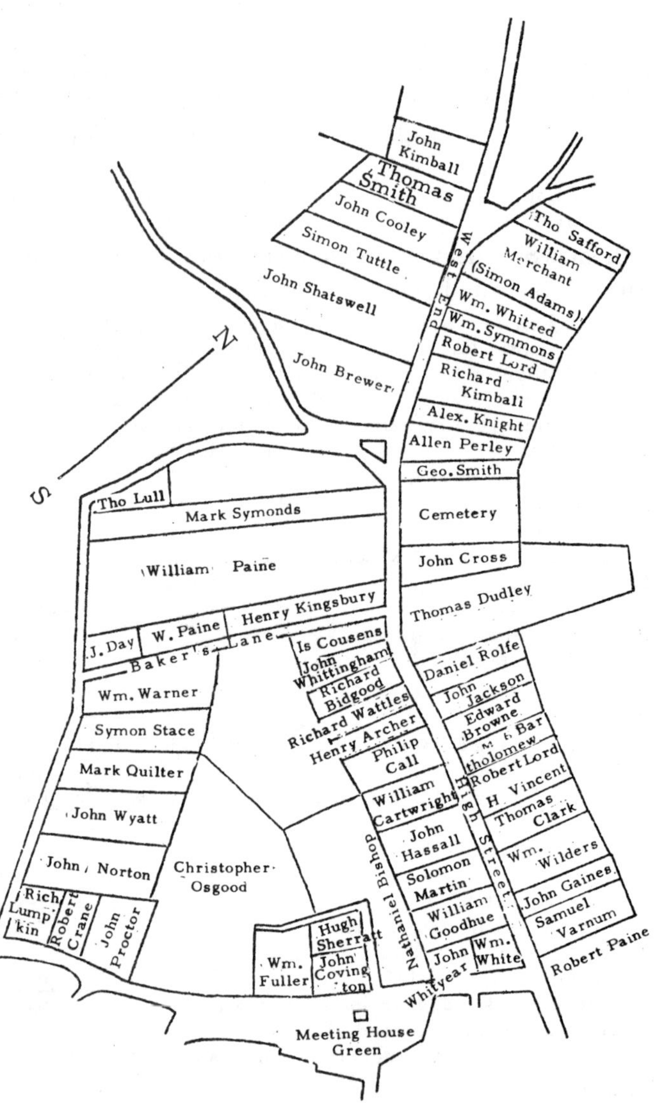

IPSWICH VILLAGE HOUSE LOTS

Ref.: History of Salem, Mass., by Perley, 1926; Records and Files of the Quarterly Courts of Essex County, Mass.; Savage; Essex County Probate Records; Vital Records

WILLIAM SMITH was probably the son of William Smith who appears briefly on the early records of Ipswich, Massachusetts. The elder William Smith made his mark as a witness to an assignment of William Ivory's interest in a mare to George Kesar on 26 April 1648. In December 1661, John Parmenter submitted a bill of 30s. for searching for William Smith. This may have been the elder William, possibly the younger man, but no other details are given.

There were several other Smiths in Ipswich, one of which was his brother, for years later he had a nephew nearby. William Smith probably was one of several brothers altho it is impossible to sort out the many Smiths who settled in New England at the time. There was another William Smith at this time living in nearby Salem. He was a sawyer, and was repeatedly in difficulties from excessive drinking.

William Smith was born about 1632, according to the following deposition made at the Ipswich Court in 1658*.

> William Smith, aged about twenty-six years, deposed that when he hired Richard Shatwell's land of Richard Kimball, about six years ago, old Goodman Scot showed him the bound stakes, which were in the hollow near the east end of the birch swamp and also next to Hutley's lot, etc. Sworn in Ipswich court 28 Sept. 1658.

Thus, about 1652 when he was about 20, he rented a piece of land and did some farming. He probably cropped this parcel only the one season and then went on to a more ambitious enterprise as is indicated by the following lease which was filed with the county court.

> Agreement of Robert [his mark] Wallis and William Smyth, both of Ipswich, with William Goodhue of Ipswich, to hire the latter's farm, and to break up twelve acres of ground, crosscut it and harrow it; also a six acre lot of meadow beyond Gravelly Brook, also a parcel of meadow in the thick woods at the upper end, Mr. Vincent having a parcel at the lower end. Said Goodhue was to build them a house thirty feet long with two chimneys, and a barn forty feet long with a leanto at one end twenty feet wide, and to provide them with four bullocks of

*There is another deposition, made 23 November 1674 at Salem, in which William Smith, aged about forty years, deposed. This would place his birth about 1634, but 1632 seems more likely.

four years each for which said Wallis and Smith were to fence in the farm for the first year's rent and afterward to pay £20 yearly for fourteen years from the time of their occupancy, March 1, 1653. The bullocks were to be appraised when they received them, and if Wallis and Smith paid the price of the cattle at the end of seven years they were to have four pounds each. The tenants were to keep the housing and fence in good repair and to pay the rent yearly at William Goodhue's house in town in wheat and barley or corn or pork. Goodhue was further to let them a common right that he bought belonging to a house in Hog lane now in possession of Jefferye Snelling. Witness: John [his mark] Johnson

In spite of the long lease, plans must have changed. For one thing, Robert Wallis died.

William Smith first appears on record in a deposition dated 25 March 1651 at Ipswich, regarding a slander case against Joseph Muzzey/Mussey.

> William Smith deposed that he heard Joseph Mussy say in Master Appleton's barn that John Broadstreet desired him to combine with him and to lie in wait at Muddy River to knock Goodman Crose off his horse and to knock him on the head, and said John would run away with his horse; and that said John had four bastards at Rode Iland, and he should go there ere long and should know them by their bangell ears, just like himself.

In the court held at Ipswich in March 1654/55, William Smith was discharged of his presentment. Just what the charge was is not stated.

On 25 November 1656, he and five others signed a bond for the appearance of Zerobabell Phillips to answer a charge of breaking into the house of Isaac Cummings. Phillips apparently failed to appear, and the bond was forfeited.

On 6 July 1657, William Smith and Rebecca Keyes were married, according to the Topsfield records. She was the daughter of Robert and Sarah Keyes, and was born at Watertown 17 March 1637/8 but was of Ipswich at the time of their marriage. About this time they settled in Topsfield and lived there the rest of their lives.

In the summer of 1660, he was deputized on the spot by the Constable of Topsfield, Daniel Clark, to assist in quelling a brawl which erupted at Clark's place. Clark, in addition to being the Constable, ran a tavern, but he had no license and freely sold to Indians. As a result of the brawl, Clark and the two young men were jailed and fined. William Smith signed a deposition (autograph) regarding this brawl in September, 1660. The fact that he could sign his name would seem to clearly distinguish him from the elder William Smith who is supposed to have been his father and who signed by mark in 1648.

In December 1661, there was an allocation of rights in some public land and he was on the list of commoners. On 7 March 1664/5, the land was meted out in three classes according to the amount of ministerial taxes paid. He was in the small group. About this time, the common field system of tenure which was used in parts of England was falling into disfavor by the colonists, who much preferred outright individual ownership. In 1678 the common lands were lotted out to the individuals, ending the common field system.

In June 1666, he was appointed Corporal in the militia, a rank he held the rest of his life.

He owed Thomas Dorman 20s. according to Dorman's will dated 24 April 1670.

On 2 February 1673/4, William Smith deposed that one hog which was taken in Mr. Ashby's corn, etc.

On 23 November 1674, William Smith and John Morall deposed that in 1670, before the Indian corn harvest, they saw John Gould deliver one bullock to Thomas Bishop, sr., at Ipswich, the price of which was £8 and it was put into Bishop's cow house.

In 1674 the iron works at Rowley Village was destroyed by fire and a lawsuit followed between the owners and the hired managers. William Smith testified to a conversation he had heard in July 1674, when at John Gould's house with some of the owners. He also testified to having been at the ironworks, of the disputes over the operation of the works, the hiring of men, etc.

In March 1676/7 at the Ipswich Court, a fine of 15s. against William Smith was remitted. Other details are not given.

In 1679, William Smith pledged £1 to support a new minister for Topsfield and the same year he was excused from further military training.

At the March 1679/80 town meeting, he was appointed Constable for the ensuing year. In 1682, he was a tythingman. In January 1682/3, he was granted a license to run the ordinary and was chosen Constable again; likewise the next year.

Running an ordinary, however, had its problems, especially on training days, which often became more festive than military. Apparently sometime in September 1685, a brawl erupted in his home, which was also the tavern, and in April 1686, a warrant was issued for Rebecca to appear in court as a witness.

> 20 April 1686 - Warrant for the appearance of Thomas Dearman, Timothy Dearman, Ensign John Peabody, Jacob Foster and Rebecca Smith, wife of Wm. Smith, and Elisha Perkins, all of Topsfield, as witnesses against Samuel Smith and Thomas Ellithrop of Rowley concerning fighting with William Woodberry and John Allen at William Smith's house, Topsfield, sometime the past summer.

On 10 May 1682, Joanna Smith, whose relationship to William, if any, is unknown, petitioned the court for leniency. She had been sentenced to be whipped for fornication. Later the punishment was remitted upon payment of a fine.

> *"compassion upon an unworthy poor wrech y[t] hath deserved the rigour and extremity of the law. I am in some measure sensible of my great sin in provoking God, the eyes of a jealous God, and humbly beg your prayers and the prayers of the people of god for mee. I am young, besides my naturall wicked inclination, being subject to the temptations of the adversarye, and his wicked suggestions. Poor wretch that I am, I have dishonored God, disgraced myself, and my poor friends, I humbly lye at the feet of your mercy", etc.*

The court records show that Job Smith, aged 19, deposed that he was at the house of his brother John Smith on the night that Joanna Smith charged his brother William Smith with uncivil carriages, etc. William Smith was bound to answer the charges, his uncle William Smith and Simon Stace being sureties for his appearance.

From all this we learn that William Smith had nephews William, John, and Job. These three nephews were probably sons of John Smith of Ipswich who died intestate in 1672, leaving a widow, Elizabeth. He is known to have had the following children:

JOHN, b 29 Oct. 1654; m 13 Nov. 1678, at Ipswich, Elizabeth Smith, dau. of George & Mary Smith
ELIZABETH, took the church covenant 1674; she m 30 March 1682 at Ipswich, William Chapman
WILLIAM, b 28 April 1659
THOMAS, b 7 June 1661
JOB, perhaps, b 1663 (aged 19 in 1682)
MORIAH, b 28 Feb. 1664/5
RUTH, b 8 Oct. 1666
PRUDENCE, b 11 June 1671
MARY, (twin), b 11 June 1671; d spinster, 1739

In April 1686, Rebecca Smith, wife of William Smith, was stated in a deposition as being aged about 47.

William Smith also served on juries and his name appears on several matters of the town. At the town meeting of Topsfield held 1 March 1691/2, the following resolution was recorded.

> At the desire of William Smith in the behalfe of his mother and his brother Joseph The Towne doth aquit and discharge them of the parsenag aquiting them from all ingagments in the leace and takes it in to thare poseation as it is now in being only the widdow Smith hath the libborty of the hous and orchard till mickelmas nex for sweping the meeting hous if she seese cause to stay so long but in case the Towne sees cause to improve one end of the house then the said widdow is to have the leborty of but one end of the hous as above said. Voted

From these few lines, we learn that William Smith was dead, his widow and son Joseph were apparently living in the parsonage under a lease from the town, and that by mutual agreement the lease was cancelled, except that she and Joseph could continue on in the house and have the use of the orchard until next Michaelmas (29 September 1692) in exchange for sweeping the meeting house, etc. Apparently there was no minister occupying it at the time.

Joseph appears once on the record as a witness with his father in 1685. After the above mention of his name, he appears no more on record. He must have been competent to be a witness, but was perhaps somehow handicapped.

Rebecca remarried 29 March 1693 at Topsfield to Daniel Killum of Wenham. She died on 7 September 1696 in Wenham and Daniel died there 21 March 1699/1700. She is incorrectly called Mary in the death record.

Children, recorded at Topsfield:

WILLIAM, b 17 July 1658; m Martha ____ ; ch.: Penelope 1687 - d.y., Rebecca - d.y., Martha 1691, William 1694; pound keeper 1695, fence viewer, surveyor of highways, hayward 1703; "very sick", made will 15 Nov., pr. 26 Dec. 1715, named wife Martha & the 2 ch.; Inv. £186.5s.; res. Boxford; she m 2, int. 15 June 1717, at Andover, Capt. John Barker who d 3 Jan. 1722/3 ae 78 - g.s. at Boxford

29 February 1687/8 - Joseph Estyes of Topsfield for £60 sold to William Smith, junior of Topsfield, 30 acres in Topsfield, including a house.
(Essex County Deed 8:43)

About 2 February 1691/2 - William Smith living in Topsfield, county of Essex, gave a mortgage deed to Lieutenant Thomas Baker of same town against two acres of upland and mowing land near his home, which he had bought of Joseph Eastey and which was near Billingates Hill, for a £26 loan to be paid back in five years in good young neat cattle under 7 years old, bulls excepted, and with interest of 13 shillings a year yearly in wheat, malt and Indian corn.
(Essex County Deeds 11:254)

15 December 1697 - Lieutenant Thomas Baker of Topsfield, yeoman, and William Smith of the same town, carpenter, for £51.4s. sold to Joseph Capen, clerk, with consent of our wives, land in Topsfield, being about 30 acres of upland, swamp and meadow, together with a dwelling house and a naked small frame designed also for a dwelling house, which land and house was formerly Joseph Easties of Topsfield, which ye said Smith bought of ye said Eastie, and which was near Billingsgate Hill. (Essex County Deeds 13:43)

REBECCA, b 3 March 1662/3; prob. d.y.

JOSEPH, b 28 June 1665; living 1692 at home; he was prob. physically handicapped

BENJAMIN, b 5 Jan. 1667/8; a Benjamin Smith of Salem m 22 Oct. 1700 at Salem, Sarah Peabody of Boxford, the m recorded at Salem & Topsfield; they had a son b at Boxford 7 Oct. 1701, John, bapt. 21 June 1702 at Topsfield (prob. the same ch.), Benjamin, Rebecca, Sarah & Stephen all bapt. 28 Sept. 1712 at Topsfield

SOLOMON, b 3 March 1669/70; prob. d.s.p. young

SAMUEL, b 6 April 1672; m 1, 16 Jan. 1694/5 at Topsfield, Phoebe Dow; m 2, 25 Jan. 1707/8, Rebecca Curtis, dau. of John; 12 ch. His land was referred to in 1698; d 12 July 1748, testate; she d 13 March 1753

SARAH, b 10 July 1674; m 1 or 2 Feb. 1691/2, Jonathan Bixby of Boxford, son of Joseph & Sarah (Riddlesdale) Bixby

SON, b 20 March 1677/8; apparently d.y.

MARY, b 3 July 1680

Ref.: Essex County Quarterly Court Files; V.R.; Town Records of Boxford; Topsfield Historical Society Collections; Probate Files

The Ancestry of

JOHN SPOFFORD & ELIZABETH SCOTT

Compiled by

John Brooks Threlfall

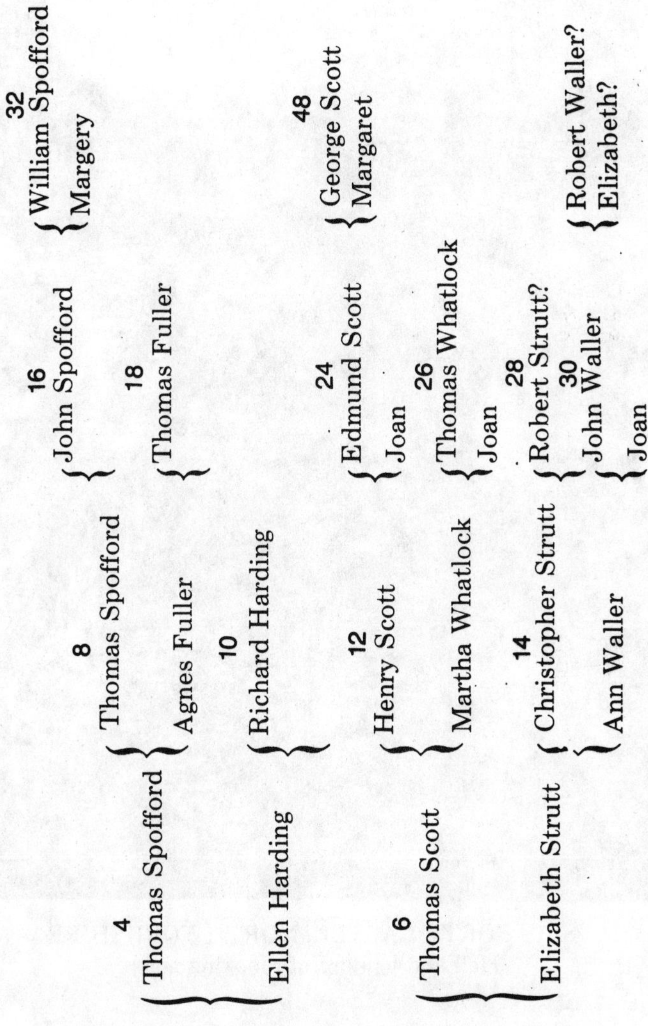

2 John Spofford + Elizabeth Scott

SPUFFORTH CASTLE, NORTH YORKSHIRE
Hall and Undercroft, looking north

Ref.: Parish Registers; Probate Records at Bedford

2

JOHN SPOFFORD (*Thomas, Thomas, John*) was baptized 21 April 1611 at Toddington, Bedfordshire. (He deposed as being about 50 in March 1661/2). He came to New England and settled in Rowley, Massachusetts where he had a 1½ acre house lot on Bradford Street in 1643. His name appears on the first division of home lots when he received this lot. He also was granted land in the fresh meadows, salt meadows, the tillage lands, the Merimac lands, and shares in the ox pasture, cow pasture and calf pasture. He lived for 30 years in Rowley and in 1669 moved to Spofford Hill in the west part of town where he was without doubt the first settler in that part now called Georgetown. He took this farm on a lease. For the first five years he was to pay as rent 300 feet of white oak plank, after that £10 each year - one half in English corn or Indian corn, and the other half in "fat cattel or leane". This lease was assigned over to his sons, John and Samuel, on 16 March 1676, and the rent was reduced to £8, and to be wholly remitted "during the time of the Indian Wars". The lease was extended for 60 years; then the land reverted back to the town.

John Spofford married Elizabeth Scott of Ipswich. She was the daughter of Thomas and Elizabeth (Strutt) Scott and was baptized at Rattlesden, Suffolk, England, on 18 November 1623, and was 23 at the time of the marriage.

He signed his will by mark on 7 October 1678 and it was proved 6 November following. His wife survived him and died 10 February 1691/2 at Bradford.

The name Spofford or Spofforth comes from the village of that name which lies 15 miles west of York.

John Spofford was about 35 when he married. This is about 10 years beyond the usual age. It suggests that he might have been married earlier, but there is no evidence of such a marriage. Also, he seems to have arrived in Massachusetts when he was about 30 or so. What was he doing from age 25 to 30 and where?

7 October 1678 - the will of JOHN SPOFFORD, Sr. of Rowley

... as for my dear and loving wife I give her the lease of the house and land of Mrs. Prudence Cottons also I give to her all the household stuff to be at her dispose excepting the arms and amunition also I give her two cows and one calf also four sheep I give to her and my son Francis to be equally divided betwixt them and I give to my wife one young horse also to have the use of four acres of land at ye farm during her life. Furthermore, I will that my son Francis his portion be at my wife's dispose till he come to the age of twenty one years if she live so long, for that end that he may be helpful to her to carry on her husbandry work. Item: that which I give to my son Francis is the two young oxen, one mare and the cart and all the furniture belonging to husbandry, also one yearling calf, these to be at my wife's dispose till he be at the age abovesaid, and then these things or the worth of them to be faithfully paid to him. Also, I give to him the small gun and the rapier, also four acres of land towards great meadow and what may befall by vertue of any town grants.

Item I give to my son John two steers coming three year old and the long fowling piece and one half of the lease of the farm altogether with twenty pound stocke I formerly gave him. Item I give to my son Thomas my village land and the gray horse and two sheep and one spring hog and one two year old heifer and the great musket. Item I give to my son Samuel the other half of the lease of the farm and two young steers, one that comes 3 years old and one that comes two years old, one spring hog with about ten pound stock I have already given him. Item I give to my daughter Elizabeth one two year old heifer and two sheep. Item I give to my daughter Mary one cow and one calf and two sheep. Item I give to my daughter Sarah one cow and one calf and two sheep. Also I appoint my loving wife and my son Thomas to be joynt executors of this my last will and my children's portions to be paid at their marriage or at twenty one years of age and if any die before, their portions to be divided amongst the rest. In witness hereof: I set my hand and seal October 7, 1678.

John (his X mark) Spofard

Witnesses: John Johnson, Phillip Nellson

[Written in the margin]
Whereas here is two cows and calf and four sheep mentioned, the four sheep only is to be divided between her and Francis. This twenty and ten pound that is given to John and Samuel, they have owned that they have formerly received.
Proved in Ipswich court 6 November 1678 by the witnesses.

Inventory of the Estate of John Spofford, Senior, of Rowley, taken 23 Oct. 1678 by John Johnson and Thomas Patch:

£20 in John Spofford, jr's. hands, £10 in Samuel's hand ..	£ 30.00.0
money	10.0
wearing cloaths	8.12.0
one bed and furniture belonginge to it	5. 0.0
another bed	3. 5.0
linnen	2. 0.0
a peece of home made cloath	4. 0.0
one fowlinge peece	2. 0.0
one muskett	1. 5.0
in brass	2.12.0
two Iron pots, one skillet,two friinge pans, two saws	2.10.0
other small things	1. 0.0
tubs, chairs, and other woodden things	2. 6.0
A trap, coslet and other things	1. 9.0
Books and other small things	2.10.0
Butter and cheese	2. 0.0
seaven Barrills of syder	4. 4.0
thre Barrills of small syder	1. 4.0
two oxen given in the will to Francis	11. 0.0
a mare given him	2.10.0
to him in cart and wheels	2.15.0
to him in a tumbrell and wheels	1. 0.0
to him in chains, yoakes, spanshakkells and one old share and boult	1. 6.0
to him a new plow	15.0
to him in axes, hows, and other things belonging to husbandry	1. 5.0
more in husbandry things to him in two saws and other tools	1. 0.0
to him two sheeps	10.0
to him four Acres of Lands and thre siths	4.11.0
to him a small gun and a rapier	2. 5.0
wedges given to him and old Iron	5.0
two horses	9. 0.0
four two yeare old cattell and vantage	10. 0.0
thre yearlings and vantage and four Calves	8.10.0
fourtene shepe, four swine and five pigs	11. 4.0
the village Land	30. 0.0
one musquet and Rapier	10.10.0
cotten wooll, sheepe wooll and other things	5.16.0
Indian corne and English corne	15. 0.0
Eightene loade of hay	13.10.0
five cows	17.10.0
Total	£228. 9.0

Debts oweing from the Estate:

the rent for the land this yeare	7. 0.0
to marchant Waînright	5.14.7
Sammuell Graves the hatter	13.0
John Wainright	8.5
Deacon Goodhew	2.8
Caleb Bointon the Smith	10.0
Edward Hazon	5.6
George Killborne	9.4
Doctor Bennit	32.0
Mr. Darby	10.0
Total	£16. 4.0

Attested by Elizabeth Spaford executrix of her husband's estate

Children, all born at Rowley:

ELIZABETH, b 14 Feb. 1646/7; m 24 April 1672, Alexander Sessions of Andover; 7 ch.; he d 26 Feb. 1688/9; she m 2, 18 July 1694, Richard Carrier whose wife had been hung as a witch; 2 more ch.; she m 3, —— Low, for Elizabeth Low of Andover, widow, in April 1724 conveyed land in Rowley which belonged to her father, John Spofford, deceased, & also her interest in her bro. Francis Spofford's estate (53:137, 66:53)

JOHN, b 24 Dec. 1648; m 9 March 1675/6, Sarah Wheeler; 8 ch.; he d at Bradford 22 April 1697 & she m 2, 12 June 1701, Caleb Hopkinson; she d 24 Oct. 1732 ae 80 per g.s. at Groveland

THOMAS, b 4 Jan. 1650/51; m 22 Sept. 1668, Abigail Haggett, dau. of Henry; she d before 1677; he m 2, 23 May 1686 at Rowley, Mary Leighton, dau. of Richard; no ch.; he d 20 July 1706. In Nov. 1671 he & Ezekiel Sayer were sentenced to be whipped or pay a fine for misdemeanors in the night while on watch. They had run a cart into a brook, strung a rope across a road which tripped a boy on horseback, and put a cartwheel before someones door - (Essex County Quarterly Court Files 4:441)

SAMUEL, b 31 Jan. 1652/3; m 5 Dec. 1675, Sarah, dau. of Thomas Burpee or Birkbee; 11 ch.; she d 18 Nov. 1729 in her 69th year - g.s. at Bradford; he d 1 Jan. 1742/3 - g.s. at Georgetown

HANNAH, b 1 April 1655; m at Newbury 20 May 1680, John Mitchell; 4 ch.; she d 24 April 1689; he m 2, 15 Nov. 1697, Constance Mooers (Morse?)

MARY, b 1 Nov. 1656; m ____ Hunnewell; no ch.; d before 1719; they held property in Westchester, N.Y.

SARAH, b 15 Jan. 1658/9; buried 15 Feb. 1660/61

SARAH, b 24 March 1661/2; d 14 Feb. 1713/14; m 19 Sept. 1682, Richard Kimball, son of Thomas & Mary (Smith) Kimball; 9 ch.

FRANCIS, b 24 Sept. 1665; d before 1719; no ch.

Ref.: Spofford Genealogy; N.E.H.G.S. - 9:318; V.R.

4

THOMAS SPUFFORD (*Thomas, John, William*) was baptized on 13 August 1565 at Toddington, Belfordshire. He married Anne Waindright on 31 October 1591. Anne was buried on 19 October 1605, leaving two small daughters. Six weeks later, on 30 November 1605, he remarried to Ellen Harding, daughter of Richard, baptized 20 January 1582/3 in Toddington. There is no burial record in Toddington for either him or Ellen, nor did they leave wills that can be found. This suggests that they lived out their old age with a child, perhaps in another parish, and that their estate had been distributed before they died.

Children, baptized at Toddington:

ANNE (or Agnes), bapt. 6 Jan. 1595/6; m 2 Feb. 1625/6 at Chalgrave, Francis White (there is a possibility that the correct m rec. for her is that of Ann S. who m Thomas Gurney 8 Feb. 1629/30 at Toddington); she was named in the will of her grandfather George Wainewright 1620/21, and her grandmother Anne Wainewright in 1622.

SARAH, bapt. 5 July 1601; she was also named in the will of her grandfather George Wainewright, but not in the will of her grandmother

---

THOMAS, bapt. 16 Oct. 1608; living 1612 per will of his grandfather, Thomas Spufford

2 JOHN, bapt. 21 April 1611; went to N.E. in 1638; m Elizabeth Scott, dau. of Thomas & Elizabeth, bapt. 18 Nov. 1623 at Rattlesden, Suffolk

GEORGE, bapt. 23 Oct. 1614

FRANCIS, bapt. 18 May 1617

ELIZABETH, bapt. 24 Dec. 1620

Ref.: Parish Registers; Probate Records at Bedford

BEDFORDSHIRE
REFERENCE to the HUNDREDS
1 Stodden
2 Willey
3 Barford
4 Biggleswade
5 Wixamtree
6 Redbornstoke
7 Clifton
8 Flitt
9 Manshead
The Figures prefixed to the Towns denote the distance from London
NORTHAMPTON SH.
HUNTINGDON SH.
BUCKINGHAM SH.
CAMB.
HERTFORD SH.
Kimbolton
63
HIGHAM FERRERS
63
S.t Neots
56
BEDFORD
50
Potton
48
Biggleswade
45
Shefford
41
Ampthill
45
Woburn
42
Fenny Stratford
45
Leighton Buzzard
41
Toddington
Dunstable
33
Luton
31
Hitchin
34
from Kettering
from Northampton
from Newport Pagnel
from Aylesbury
to Peterborough
to Huntingdon
to Wisbeach
to London
to S.t Albans
Icknield Way
R. Ouse
English Miles
1 2 3 4 5 6
40′
35′
20′ Longitude West 15′ from Greenwich

6

THOMAS SCOTT (*Henry, Edmund*) was baptized on 26 February 1594/5 at Rattlesden, Suffolk, England. There on 20 July 1620 he married Elizabeth, daughter of Christopher and Anne (Waller) Strutt. She was baptized on 16 May 1594. With their three children, his mother and sister Ursula Kimball's family, they left for New England in 1634 in the *Elizabeth*, which sailed from Ipswich on the last day of April and arrived at Boston in July. They settled in Ipswich, Massachusetts, where he was granted a house lot in 1635.

Thomas Scott took the freeman's oath on 4 March 1634/5. He was Selectman of Ipswich in 1636/7, constable in 1651, served on grand juries in 1645, 48 and 51, and on trial juries in 1647, 49 and 53. The town of Ipswich sued him for debt in 1646. He was one of Major Denison's subscribers in 1648. He was a glover by trade.

Governor Winthrop tells of one Scott and Eliot of Ipswich who "were lost in their way home and wandered up and down six days and eat nothing. At lenght they were found by an Indian, being almost senseless from want of rest". Such were the hazards of early seventeenth century New England.

Thomas Scott made his will on 8 March 1653/4 and died shortly afterwards. The will was proved the 28th following.

This 8th of march 1653/54 I Thomas Scott of Ipswich in Essex in Newengland doe appoint this my last will and Testament as followeth Impr. I doe give to my Daughter Elizabeth Twenty & five pounds to her & her heires to be paid the one halfe with in halfe a yeare after my deceace the other halfe with in a yeare after my decease to her & her heires.
Item I doe give to my daughter Abigaille Twenty & five pounds to be paid to her & her heires, the one halfe to be paid with in one yeare after my decease the other halfe to be paid with in a yeare & halfe after my decease
Item I doe give to my daughter Hannah Twenty & five pounds to her & her heires to be paid when she is Twenty & one yeares of age, & if shee doe marry before shee be of the age of Twenty & one yeares, The one halfe of it shall be paid at the day of marriage & the other halfe at the age of twenty and one yeares.
Item I doe give to my daughter Sarah Twenty & five pounds to be paid to her & her heires when she is Twenty & one yeares of age & if shee doe marry before shee bee of the age of Twenty & one yeares, one halfe shall be paid at the day of her marryage and the other halfe at her age of Twenty and one yeares.
Item I doe give to my daughter Mary Twenty and five pounds. To be paid to her & her heires, when shee is of the age of Twenty & one yeares. & if shee doe marry before shee bee Twenty and one yeares

of Age, the one halfe shall be payd at the day of her marryage & the other halfe at her Age of Twenty & one yeares. And I intend that my daughter mary shall bee maintained out of my estate soe as the executors shall see meete with her labour.
Item I doe give to my son Thomas Scot all my Estate ungiven: and doe appoint my Brother Richard Kembell and Thomas Rowlinson sen[r] and Edmund Bridges executors of this my last will & testament and doe appoint them to be paid whatsoever charges they shall be at out of my estate and hereunto I doe set my hand.

Witnessed by:
Daniel Warner — Tho. Scott
Will Adams, Jun[r]

Copy of will, Ipswich Deeds, vol. 1, *leaf* 163.

(The will was proved 28 March 1654)

Inventory taken 17 March 1653/4 by John Whipple and Theophilus Wilson

	£	s	d
In the parlor, one bedsted wth a feather bed, two feather bolsters, two pillows with a flock bed, two blankets, a rug, five curtaines and valants	8	15	04
two chests, one broad box, one Chaire with one old chest with two locks and a warming pan		15	10
a Coverled		12	
4 yards quarter and halfe of Canvis at 22d p yard		8	
2 peeces of Cotten Cloth containing 4 yards and a halfe at 3s p yard		13	6
4 yards of Cotten Cloth at 2s. 6d. p yard		10	
2 yards of white Cloth		5	
2 yards halfe a quarter of Carsy at 3s. 6d. p yard		7	
2 yards quarter and halfe of red Cotten at 2s. 6d p yard		5	10
a yard and halfe of Carsy		6	
a yard and halfe and halfe quarter of serge		6	6
a table Cloth		7	
2 small table clothes		3	4
a peice of locram, 3 yards		4	6
3 paire of sheetes		18	
5 napkins		3	4
4 pillow beers		6	
2 shirts		10	
2 towells		1	
a locke with 2 paire of Joynts		2	
36 lb. of pewter in the hall at one shilling p lb.	1	16	
one kettle weighing 17 lbs.		7	8
a kettle, 2 posnits & a Scumer weighing 11 lbs. 3q		10	
a kettle weighing 16 lbs.		10	
a brasse morter weighing 4 lbs. 1q		2	
a chamber pot		1	6
an Iron skillet		4	
an Iron kettle		5	
2 Iron potts weighing 53 lbs. and a halfe		15	
a trevet		6	
a smoothing Iron		1	
21 lbs. of Iron things		8	9
a frying pan		2	6
a paire of bellowes, a brush with other implements		6	8
6 ocamy spoones		2	4
old Iron		9	
2 plowshares		2	6
wedges		2	
3 pailes, an old kettle and a spade		5	

3 bookes		12	2
a hamer, a paire of pincers and an ax		4	
Two muskets, a sword and a paire of bandeleers with a long fowling peece	1	10	
500 & a halfe of nailes		4	
3 bells, a hacksaw, a framing saw, a handsaw & a paire of sheers		14	
9 old tubs		10	
porke	1	11	
a halfe headed bedsted, a pillow with a paire of blankets and a small bed	1	3	
12 Caskes		6	
a fan, 3 sickles, 2 sithes with other implements		7	
in wearing Clothes	8	3	10
in money	2	15	6
14 yards and a halfe of Cotten Cloth	2	3	6
girt webb		1	4
foure skins with a peece of match		9	
lead 7 lbs.		1	2
a flitch of bacon weighing 26 lbs. and a halfe		10	10
a gowne		15	
caps and bands with a paire of stockings		8	
wheate, 36 bushels and a pecke	9	1	3
55 bushels, 3 peckes of malt	13	18	9
a brasse frying pan		3	6
Indian Corne, 34 bushels	5	2	
Cattle in the hands of John West with tackling for plow and Cart	52		
in the hands of John davis	5		
Cattle in the hand of Robert Roberts	15		
Cattle at home and swine	33	5	
a beast in the hand of John Spofford	6		
in debts	4	18	
a house, a barne and land	129		
a grinstone		5	
Total	£ 318	19	11

10 May 1661 - Richard Kimball and Edmund Bridges acknowledged the receipt from Mr. Ezekiel Rogers of £25, the legacy given to Sarah Scott by her father. *Essex Co. Quarterly Court Files, vol. 9, leaf 48.*

23 April 1663 - Mary Scott certified to the receipt of £25 from Ezekiel Rogers of Ipswich which was the legacy left her by her father. *Essex Co. Quarterly Court Files, vol. 9, leaves 49, 50.*

29 September 1663 - Acquittances were brought in by Richard Kimball and Edmund Bridges, executors of the will of Thomas Scott, under the hands of the legatees, that is, the children of Scott, of the receipts of their several legacies. The executors were discharged 1 October 1663 - Haniell Bosworth certified that he received £25 from Richard Kimball and Edmund Bridges, which was a legacy given to his wife Abigail by her father, Thomas Scott.

Ipswich Quarterly Court Records, vol. 1, page 123.

Children:

HENRY, bapt. 27 Feb. 1621/2 at Brent Eleigh; d.y.

3 ELIZABETH, bapt. in Rattlesden 18 Nov. 1623; m John Spofford of Rowley; 9 ch.

ABIGAIL, bapt. at Rattlesden 5 March 1625/6; m Haniell Bosworth, b about 1615, d about 1683, leaving a widow & 2 daus.

THOMAS, bapt. at Rattlesden 15 June 1628; m Margaret Hubbard, dau. of Wm., sister of Rev. Wm. of Ipswich, author of *A History of N.E.* He d at Ipswich 6 Sept. 1657; she m 2, Ezekiel Rogers & d his widow in Boston 1678; 3 ch.; following records:

He, Joseph Fowler, Thomas Cook and two sons of Richard Kimball (John & Thomas) were presented in court at Ipswich 13 November 1649 and admonished for "going into the woods, shouting and singing, taking fire and liquors with them, all being at unseasonable time in the night, and occasioning their wives and some others to go out and search therein". His punishment was to learn Mr. Norton's catechism before the next court which he failed to do. He was of Stamford, Conn. in 1654 when he deeded to Richard Kimball and Edmund Bridges, his father's executors, all his father's real and personal property, to be divided according to the will. Kimball sold the land, a 50 acre grant in Ipswich, to Twyford West 31 January 1654/5.

Administration on the estate of Thomas Scott was granted to his wife Margaret on 29 September 1657. It was small, with no real estate, and was insolvent. Thomas Patch and Abigail Bosworth on 25 September 1683 petitioned for administration on the estate of their brother Thomas Scott, deceased.

Margaret Rogers made her will in Boston on 22 June 1678. Her estate in Ipswich was bound to make good £200 to her children and, when it was cleared of that obligation, £40 from it was to be given to her son and daughter Snelling's two children. Her estate in Boston was to be divided among her children. The estate of her son Thomas Scott of which she was executrix she left to her own executrix to be disposed of in accordance with Thomas's will. Executors: her daughter Martha Rogers & Capt. John Whipple. Overseers: Daniel Stone, Daniel Turel, sr., Thomas Cheevers. Both executors declined the trust on 17 Sept. 1678, but Capt. Whipple accepted administration the same day. After his death, Mrs. Martha Rogers was appointed on 6 Feb. 1683. The Boston property was worth £143, that at Ipswich £226

On 6 January 1694/5 William Rogers addressed a petition to the Probate Court saying: "Thomas Scott my Grandfather dyed in Ipswich about thirty and eight yers agoe... he left my Grandmother with onely two Children viz margerett Scott my mother and thomas Scott ... my sd uncle thomas Scott went into old England and dyed ther ... when I was about four yers old my mother dyed and in a short time after my Grandmother about sixten yers agoe ... my sd Grandfather dyed seazed of agood Considerable estat in land in Ipswich.. I am the onely surviving person descended from my sd Grandfather and now I come to the age of twenty one yers doe humly Crave that your Honnour will Grant administration to me of the estat of my sd Grandfather hath not bien leagally disposed of."

BENJAMIN, bapt. at Rattlesden 3 Feb. 1630/31; buried there 30 Aug. 1633

HANNAH, unm. in 1653/4; later m Edmund Lockwood of Stamford, Conn.

SARAH, unm. but alive in 1661

MARY, m after 1663, Thomas Patch, son of Nicholas of Wenham; 8 ch.; she d 26 Sept. 1723 ae above 80

Ref.: The Ancestry of Phebe Tilton; Probates

8

THOMAS SPUFFORD (*John, William*) was baptized on 10 December 1541 at Toddington, Bedfordshire, the son of John Spufford. On 23 November 1561, he married Agnes Fuller, daughter of Thomas Fuller. She was baptized on 26 December 1540 at Toddington. Agnes was buried 12 July 1587. He remarried to Anne Smith, a widow with children of her own. Thomas was buried 28 April 1612, and Anne was buried on 29 July 1617. Both left wills, abstracts of which follow.

26 April 1612 - the will of THOMAS SPUFFORD the elder of Todington, county of Bedford, sick on body ... to the poor 5s., toward the repairing of the parish church 5s. ... to my son Thomas Spufford 20s. within six months after me decease ... to said Thomas's two sons an ewe pugg apiece to be chosen out of my sheep flock by Thomas Fuller the elder and Cornelius White ... to son Henry Spufford three sheep and 20s. in six months ... to said Henry's children one pugg apiece ... to my son Nicholas Spufford my red heifer within 21 months ... to my son William Spufford my black heifer in six months ... to my son John Spufford's children 5s. apiece ... son John shall have the lease of the house wherein I now dwelleth ... to my daughter Joan Lawrence 10s. and to each of her children 6s.8d. in six months ... to Henry Davys and John Davys 5s. apiece and to each of my daughter Fysher's three younger children 5s. apiece in six months ... to Joan Pendret's two children one sheep apiece in one month ... to Anne Fysher 10s. and one sheep ... to my goddaughter Anne Smith, wife of Henry Smith of Little Brickhill my red cow and to each of her children one sheep apiece ... to Henry Ansell my servant 6s. ... to every one of my godchildren 12d. apiece ... residue to Anne my wife whom I make my sole executrix ... above named Thomas Fuller and Cornelius White to be overseers. Witnesses: Thomas Fuller, senior, Cornelius White, neighbor hereof, John Cocks, John Presker. (Ref.: ABP/W-1612/76)

26 July 1617 - the will of ANNE SPUFFORD of Todington, county Bedford, widow, sick in body ... to the poor of Todington 5s. ... to John Davye my grandchild £3 within 5 years next after my decease ... to my grandchild Anne Davye 40s. at age 18 ... to daughter Margaret Hunt one silver spoon ... to Anne Fysher my grandchild my best benchboard at John Pratt's, one pair of sheets, my best coverlet, my great kettle, my bedsted in the loft or upper chamber, all money due me by John Slaughter and Thomas Anthonie ... to Henry Fysher my grandchild 40s ... to William Fysher my grandchild & Elizabeth Fysher his sister

30s. each to be paid unto them by Henry Smith, tanner, being money which he oweth me ... to goddaughter Anne Smith, daughter of my son Henry Smith, tanner, one year's use of the £3 ... to the above named William Fysher and Elizabeth one ewe and a lamb ... to my daughter Joan Pendrett £3 ... to Mary Pendrett her daughter 40s. and to Edward Pendrett her son the like sum of 40s. within 4 years ... to said Mary 2 pair of sheets and two pewter platters ... to my daughter Anne Smith my best feather bed, one boulster, one blankett, two pairs of sheets & one silver spoon ... to William Smith her son 40s. in one year ... to daughter Elizabeth Spufford my stone pot hooped with silver, my bedstead in the parlor, a boulster and my salting trough ... to John Spufford my grandchild, son of my said daughter Elizabeth, my cow, and to every one of my said daughter Elizabeth's other children 20s. apiece ... to my son in law, viz. to Henry Spufford, 10s. ... to Nicholas Spufford one sheep ... to Agnes Hawse one lamb ...executors to pay to Cornelius White 24s. ... residue to my son in law John Spufford, he to be executor. Witnesses: William Fysher, Joan Cooke, Cornelius White, Thomas Vincent. (Ref.: ABP/W 1621/220)

Children, baptized at Toddington:

4 THOMAS, bapt. 13 Aug. 1565; m 31 Oct. 1591, Anne Waindright; 2 ch.; she was buried 19 Oct. 1605; he m 2, 30 Nov. 1605, Ellen Harding, dau. of Richard, bapt. 20 Jan. 1582/3 at Toddington; 5 ch.

JOHN, bapt. 17 Feb. 1566/7; m in June 1598, Elizabeth D---; ch.: John bapt. 1599, Thomas bapt. 1601, Richard bapt. 1604, Elizabeth buried 1606/7, Anne bapt. 1608, George bapt. 1610, Robert bapt. 1614, Francis bapt. 1617, Henry bapt. 1620, Elizaabeth bapt. & buried 1622, Jane bapt. 1623. Elizabeth, w of John, was buried 1 Oct. 1626; John m Isabel England 5 April 1627; he was buried 5 June 1635

JOAN, bapt. 26 Oct. 1569; m ——— Lawrence by 1612, had some ch.

HENRY, prob. b about 1571; had 3 ch. by 1612

ROBERT, bapt. 7 March 1573/4; apparently d.y.

NICHOLAS, prob. b about 1576-7; m 30 June 1611, Ellen Wright; ch.: Nicholas bapt. 1612/13, Matthew bapt. 1615

WILLIAM, bapt. 27 May 1579; still living 1612

AGNES, bapt. 1 Nov. 1581; buried 27 June 1606

ELIZABETH, buried 28 March 1583

Ref.: Parish Registers; Probate Records at Bedford

12

HENRY SCOTT (*Edmund, George*) was baptized on 1 November 1560 at Bradfield Saint George, Suffolk, England. He married at Rattlesden on 25 July 1594, Martha Whatlock, daughter of Thomas and Joan Whatlock. Martha was baptized on 18 July 1568 at Rattlesden. Henry was buried on 24 December 1624 at Rattlesden.

Robert Whatlock of Rattlesden, Martha's brother, made his will on 20 September 1622 and in it referred to his Scott relatives. He apparently was unmarried.

An abstract of Henry Scott's will follows.

24 September 1623 - the will of HENRY SCOTT of Rattlesden, Suffolk, yeoman ... to my wife Martha the house wherein I dwell &c. during term of her natural life; after that to my son Roger Skott and to his heirs forever ... to Abigail Kemball my grandchild forty shillings at her age of one and twenty years ... to my grandchild Henry Kemball twenty shillings at age of one and twenty and the same sum each to grandchildren Elizabeth and Richard Kemball at same age. To son Thomas Skott five pounds within one year after my decease. To Mr Peter Devereux, minister of Rattlesden, ten shillings. Wife Martha to be executrix. Proved 10 January 1624/5 (Ref.: Bury Wills - Pearle, L:117)

Ten years after her husband's death, Martha Scott set sail for America with her son Thomas Scott and her daughter Ursula Kimball and ten grandchildren of all ages, from a boy of 18 to a baby of one. They all embarked on the *Elizabeth* of Ipswich, on the last day of April 1634, the adults all having taken the oath of allegiance at the Ipswich Customs House before sailing. Margaret Scott's age is given on the list as 60, altho she was actually 66. The Scotts and Kimballs settled in Ipswich after a short stay in the Boston area where, presumably, Martha Scott died. There is no record of her death.

Children, baptized at Rattlesden:

6 THOMAS, bapt. 26 Feb. 1594/5; m 20 July 1620, Elizabeth Strutt; 7 ch.; he d in March 1653/4

URSULA, bapt. 14 Feb. 1597/8; m Richard Kimball; 11 ch.; she d about 1660

ROGER, bapt. 15 Nov. 1604; m 26 Feb. 1627/8, Sarah Grimwood; 5 ch. bapt. at Rattlesden: Susan 6 June 1632, Roger 26 May 1633, Sarah 4 March 1635/6, Abigail 26 Nov. 1637, and John 20 March 1639/40. A Roger Skot who took the oath of allegiance in 1678 was perhaps the son b in 1633 and followed his uncle to Ipswich, Mass. Roger d after 1652

THE CHURCH OF SAINT GEORGE
BRADFIELD, SUFFOLK

Ref.: The Ancestry of Phebe Tilton, by Walter Goodwin Davis, 1947; Parish Registers; Probate Records of Bury St. Edmunds

14

CHRISTOPHER STRUTT was born probably about 1560 to 1562. On 14 July 1590 at Rattlesden in the county of Suffolk, he married Anne Waller. She was the daughter of John Waller, and was baptized on 8 February 1561/2 at Rattlesden. Anne was buried 22 July 1611. Shortly thereafter, Christopher Strutt remarried to Susan, who bore him one child.

Christopher Strutt was probably the son of Robert Strutt the elder of Rattlesden, who was buried there on 4 August 1599. Perhaps the Agnes Strutt who was buried there on 5 September 1583 was Robert's wife. Of the several Strutts in the Rattlesden records at that time, probably the following were the children of the above Robert, and therefore Christopher was their brother: Susan, who married John Pearle on 24 July 1593 and was buried on 1 September 1595; Robert, who married on 20 June 1591 Susan Baker and had several children; William, who married Alice, had children and was buried on 20 January 1604/5; and Ottiwell, who married Susan Waller on 5 October 1585 and had as children Anne in 1586, Mark in 1588/9 (who died in 1595/6) and Susan in 1591. Ottiwell died in 1592.

Christopher Strutt was buried on 16 February 1627/8 at Rattlesden. He was living in Buxhall when he made his will. Buxhall is next to Rattlesden on the east. An abstract of his will follows.

27 March 1627 - the will of **CHRISTOPHER STRUTT** of Buxhall, county Suffolk, yeoman...weak in body...to be buried in the church or churchyard of Buxhall...40s. for the poor in the place where I am buried...to Susan Strutt my wife my tenement in Buxhall wherein I now dwell, with all the land, meadow and pasture thereunto belonging for life...to Grace Strutt my daughter all that tenement wherein John Munson now dwelleth situate in Rattlesden, together with the orchard...to Benjamin Strutt my son all those my lands, meadow & pasture in Rattlesden at age 21...executors to receive rent from same for payment of debts and educating of said son until he comes of age and if need require to sell three or four acres...to Susan Lockwood the wife of John Lockwood £10 to be paid by son Benjamin within two years after he reaches 21...to Grace Strutt my daughter £20 to be paid by son Benjamin, £10 of it within four years after he comes

to age 21, and the other £10 within six years...to Elizabeth Scott the wife of Thomas Scott 12d. to be paid by son Benjamin within three years after he is age 21 in full satisfaction of her childs portion... to Benjamin Strutt my son my tenement in Buxhall wherein I now dwell after the decease of Susan my wife...if Benjamin die before age 21, then his tenement to Susan Lockwood...to Grace Strutt my daughter my meadow and pasture in Rattlesden if my son Benjamin die before age 21 without heirs of his body...to Benjamin one of my best featherbeds & one cupboard...to Grace Strutt my daughter one featherbed.. residue to Susan my wife & Richard Raynesham whom Iordain joint executors. Signed by mark. Witnesses: Bryan Parker, clerk, & Robert Strutt. Proved 9 April 1628. (Ref.: Mason:133 or R2/54/133)

Children, baptized at Rattlesden:

INFANTS, 2, presumably twins, unbapt., buried 2 Feb. 1592/3

7 ELIZABETH, bapt. 16 May 1594; m 20 July 1620, Thomas Scott, son of Henry & Martha (Whatlock) Scott of Rattlesden; 7 ch.; they went to N.E.; he d 1653/4

SUSAN, bapt. 30 Nov. 1596; m 19 Sept. 1620 at Rattlesden, John Lockwood, perhaps the son of Thomas of Wetheringsett & bapt. 23 Oct. 1592; 8 ch. bapt. at Rattlesden: Susan 25 Nov. 1621, John 17 Aug. 1623-buried 18 Aug. 1635, Thomas 25 Dec. 1625, William 1 April 1627, Anne 31 Jan. 1629/30, Elizabeth 21 April 1633, Mary 27 March 1636, Sarah 3 Feb. 1638/9

GRACE, bapt. 25 Nov. 1621; unm. in 1627

ANN, prob. b Dec. or Jan. 1603/4; buried 3 Jan. 1603/4

BENJAMIN, bapt. 21 March 1615/16; m 21 Oct. 1639 at Bradfield Combust, Mary Lumlie, presumably one of 3 Marys bapt. at Great Waldingfield 1615-18

Ref.: Parish Registers; Probates at Bury St. Edmunds

16

JOHN SPUFFORD (*William*) of Toddington, Bedfordshire, was born probably about 1510, presumably at Toddington. Other than the records of baptisms of his children, there is no other record of him. He left no will, which suggests that he died suddenly, probably 1553 to 1558, that is, after the baptism of his last known child and before the burial records start.

Children, baptized at Toddington:

ANNE, prob., who m Mark Etheridge, 22 Nov. 1562 at Toddington
8 THOMAS, bapt. 10 Dec. 1541; m 23 Nov. 1561, Agnes Fuller, dau. of Thomas, bapt. 26 Dec. 1540; 9 ch.
WILLIAM, prob., bapt. 10 April 1546, parents not named
ROBERT, prob., bapt. 20 May 1548, parents not named
JOHN, bapt. 4 May 1550
RICHARD, bapt. 7 Aug. 1552

CHURCH OF SAINT GEORGE OF ENGLAND, TODDINGTON, BEDFORDSHIRE

Ref.: Parish Registers; Probate Records at Bedford

CARRIER'S WAGON UNLOADING AT TODDINGTON

18

THOMAS FULLER of Toddington, Bedfordshire, husbandman, died about 1573, testate, his wife having died earlier. There are no burial records between 1559 and 1581, so dates of their deaths are unknown.

10 May 1573 - the will of **THOMAS FULLER** of Todington, in county Bedford, husbandman, to be buried in the churchyard ... to Ralph Fuller my second son my house & all my freehold land, etc. in Harlington ... to John Fuller my third son all my freehold land, etc. in Todington in tail to my two daughters Anis Spofford the wife of Thomas Spofford and Margaret Anthony the wife of Thomas Anthony ... to Ralph Fuller my son 3 steer bullocks, my bay horse & my ---and colt ... to John Fuller my third son 3 steer bullocks & my trotting horse & my foal colt, £10 which he shall receive of my son Thomas Fuller of Todington ... Ralph and John Fuller my sons to have all my grain but son John to have 5 quarters of barley more than Ralph ... son John to have all grain growing in Todington, and to Thomas Spofford the elder, each of them a pewter platter, to his 2 daughters 2 kettles ... to Thomas Anthony the elder a pewter platter and to my son Thomas Fuller's daughter a pewter platter, to Anis Spofford and Margaret Anthony a fosser with all the linen that is in it ... to each godchild 4d. ... to Thomas Wyse my boy dwelling with me 5s., to Robert Wyngdyght that dwelleth with my son Thomas Fuller 5s., to John Fuller my son my standing bedstead ... Ralph Fuller and John Fuller shall keep and bring up one Alice Fuller to age 21, then to pay her out of my house and lands in Harlington 40s. at day of her marriage. Residue to two sons, they to be executors ... Thomas Anthony and Thomas Spofford to be overseers, they each to have 5s. Witnesses: Thomas Spofford, Thomas Anthony, John ----, John Fuller, Ralph Fuller, Thomas Fuller.

(ABP/W 1573/118)

Children, born at Toddington:

9 AGNES, bapt. 26 Dec. 1540; she must have been several months old, as the bapt. of Thomas followed only 8½ months later. She m 23 Nov. 1561, Thomas Spofford, son of John, bapt. 10 Dec. 1541; 9 ch.; she was buried 12 July 1587; he m 2, widow Anne Smith; he was buried 28 April 1612, Anne in 1617

THOMAS, bapt. 8 Sept. 1541; died in infancy

MARGARET, prob. b about 1543-4; m 11 Dec. 1565, Thomas Anthony; ch.: Thomas bapt. 1572, Jane bapt. 1578, Richard bapt. 1586

THOMAS, bapt. 12 April 1546, parents not named; m 14 Oct. 1568, Joan Worsley; ch.: Margaret bapt. 1570, John buried 1601/2; Jane, wife of Thomas buried 7 Jan. 1607/8

RALPH, bapt. 23 Sept. 1548; 2nd son per father's will; ch.: William bapt. 1581/2, Elizabeth bapt. 1586, Thomas bapt. 1595, Mary bapt. 1598

JOHN, b prob. 1550, "3rd son"; ch.: William bapt. 1578, John bapt. 1582, Margaret buried 1594/5, Thomas bapt. 1587, Elizabeth 1589/90. John Fuller was buried 2 May 1610

Ref.: Parish Registers; Probate Records at Bedford

24

EDMUND SCOTT (*George*) was born probably about 1525-1530 in Bradfield Saint George, Suffolk, and was the son of George Skott who died in 1547. Edmund's wife was named Joan. She was buried 15 May 1615 at Rattlesden, "an old woman". He was buried there 14 August 1621, aged "about ninety-seven years". His age was probably exaggerated as was so often the case.

Edmund Scott and his wife apparently moved from Bradfield to Rattlesden about 1566, for their children born after that date were baptized there. He appears in the records of Rattlesden in 1569 as a Questman, which is a parish officer. From 1588 to 1589, he was a church warden and in 1593 he was a collector. In 1611 Edmund Scott, Sr. again served as a collector.

Children:

EDMUND, b about 1558; m 16 Sept. 1583 at Rattlesden, Agnes Losse; ch. bapt. at Rattlesden: Edmund 18 Oct. 1586 - buried 30 June 1615 "a yonge man, ye son of Edmund ye younger"; Jonas 20 Oct. 1588, Nicholas 25 Sept. 1591, George 28 Dec. 1594, Robert 25 May 1597. Edmund was buried 14 July 1642 at Rattlesden

12 HENRY, bapt. 1 Nov. 1560 at Bradfield St. George (parents not named but this must be Edmund's son); m at Rattlesden 25 July 1594, Martha Whatlock, dau. of Thomas & Joan, bapt. 18 July 1568; he was buried 24 Dec. 1624; 3 ch.; she went to N.E. with her ch.

ANN, prob. b 1562; buried 28 July 1564 at Bradfield St. George, "daughter of Edmund and Joan"

MARY, bapt. 2 Aug. 1565, "dau. of Edmund & Joan"

DINAH, bapt. 18 June 1567 at Rattlesden; m 8 Jan. 1587/8, John Ransome; had Priscilla bapt. 2 June 1588

ANNE, bapt. 21 Aug. 1569 at Rattlesden; she was perhaps the Anne Skotte who m John Stockdale 17 Jan. 1602/3 at Buxhall & had 7 ch. bapt. at Rattlesden 1605-21, the 7th one 5½ years after the 6th one, suggesting it was older than an infant and thus the mother not so old at the end of her child bearing as to preclude her being this Anne. She & some of her ch. were named in the 1637 will of widow Mary Smith who was prob. her sister

ROSE, bapt. 15 Sept. 1571; buried 19 Sept. 1571

GEORGE, bapt. 31 Jan. 1573/4 at Rattlesden, no parents named

NICHOLAS, bapt. 13 June 1576; m 7 April 1603, Anne Batman; had a son Nicholas bapt. 22 Jan. 1603/4, buried 29 Nov. 1606. An Anne Scott was buried 4 March 1637/8 at Rattlesden

Ref.: Parish Registers; Bishop's Transcripts

THOMAS WHATLOCK was born probably between 1520 and 1530. Joan Whatlock, who married Bartholomew Orvis on 19 July 1562 at Rattlesden, was probably his sister. He lived and died in Rattlesden and was buried there 25 January 1608/9, "a very old man". An abstract of his will follows.

17 May 1607 - the will of THOMAS WHATLOCK of Rattlesden, knacker ... all household stuff to Joan Whatlock my wife ... to Henry Skott £6 to be paid at Michaelmas after my wife's decease ... to Martha my daughter £6 likewise ... to Thomas Skott the son of Henry Skott £6 at age 21 ... to Roger Skott the son of Henry £6 likewise ... to Ursula Skott the daughter of Henry £6 likewise ... these children in tail to each other ... £4.4 per year to wife for life ... the residue to my sons Roger and Robert Whatlock, they to be executors. Witnesses: John Moore, John Bowker and William Samon. Proved 30 January 1608/9. (Ref.: Strutt - 217)

His wife Joan was buried at Rattlesden on 14 March 1610/11, "ye Relict of Thomas Whatlock".

Children, born in Rattlesden:

ROGER, bapt. 15 May 1561; he evidently d.s.p. as he left property to his brother Robert

ROBERT, bapt. 20 July 1564; buried 28 Sept. 1622 at Rattlesden, "an ancient man"; m 1, 4 July 1591 at Rattlesden, Mary Bartholomew who was buried on 29 Sept. 1606; m 2, 25 June 1607, Ann Davy; m 3, Rachel who was buried 19 June 1621. He evidently left no ch. His will is abstracted as follows.

20 September 1622 - the will of ROBERT WHATLOCKE of Rattlesden, Suffolk, Knacker ... all houses and lands to Thomas Skotte my kinsman, of Rattlesden, glover ... to Martha Scott, my sister, £3 ... to Ursula Kemball, my kinswoman, £3 ... to Ellen Usher, my kinswoman, £2 ... to Andrew Bartholomew 20s. ... to Andrew Fordham of Rattlesden 20s. ... to Elizabeth Bell £15 and she to dwell in my house where Prudence Webb liveth (she remaining a maid) and also to have a bedstead, bedding, kettle of red brass, great posnett, etc. ... to widow Fordham, to Roger Scott, kinsman, at age 21 ... my brother Roger Whatlocke left me a house in Norfolk, I leave the same to Thomas Scott ... to poor of Rattlesden 40s. ... to Prudence Webb 5s. to Peter Devereau, minister of Rattlesden, 10s. ... Thomas Scott to be sole executor. Witnesses: Peter Devereau, George Salter, Henry Skotte. Proved by executor 8 October 1622 at Ipswich. (Ref.: Bradstreet 10:125)

13 MARTHA, bapt. 18 July 1568; m 25 July 1594, Henry Scott at Rattlesden; 3 ch.; Henry was buried at Rattlesden 24 Dec. 1624

ANNE, bapt. 21 Aug. 1569; prob. d before 1622

DOROTHY, bapt. 6 July 1572; buried 3 Nov. 1574

Ref.: Parish Registers; Wills at Bury St. Edmunds

30

JOHN WALLER (*Robert?*) was probably born about 1533-1535. All his known children were baptized at Rattlesden, Suffolk, in which records he was named as their father. His wife, Joan, was identified only in the record for their son John, baptized in 1567.

John Waller was probably the son of Robert Waller the elder of Rattlesden who died testate in late 1553. Robert made his will on 2 October 1553 and it was proved on 12 December 1553. In it, he named his wife Elizabeth, bequeathed a cow to his daughter Joan, and to each of his nine children gave 40 shillings, to be paid at age 22. One of these nine children may well have been John.

John Waller was buried at Rattlesden on 28 March 1593. His widow, Joan, was buried there on 29 July 1601.

12 March 1592/3 - the will of JOHN WALLER of Rattlesden, yeoman...to the poor 13s.4d...to my son John all freehold lands in Rattlesden & Woollpit.. to Anne Strutt my daughter & her executor £10 in one year..to Suzan Strutt my daughter £10 in two years...to John my son £10 in three years...to Elizabeth Lafflinge my daughter the use of £10 & after her decease to her children...to grandchildren at age 21 or marriage: Elizabeth Lafflynge £10, Thomas Lafflynge £10, Anne Strutt £4, Suzanne, Anne & Mark Strutt £3 each, John Waller £4, Suzan Waller £3, Elizabeth Waller £4..to John, Suzan, Anne & Elizabeth my children 20s. each... to son John all my copyhold lands, tenements, etc. in Wollpitt... copyhold tenement late purchased of William Nunn to Elizabeth my daughter and her husband Thomas Laffelyn for term of her life, then to my son John...to son William £10... residue to Joan my wife. Wife and son John executors. Witnesses: Roger Thomas & John Jackson. Proved 21 May 1593. (Norfolk Consistory Court Wills - 12 Clearke, MF 69)

Children, all baptized at Rattlesden:

SON, apparently, who d before 1592/3 leaving 3 ch.: John, Susan & Elizabeth. Of these, Susan m Thomas Goodrich 29 July 1607 at Rattlesden

ELIZABETH, b perhaps 1557-60; m 28 Aug. 1580, Thomas Lawghlinge; 3 ch. recorded

15 ANNE, bapt. 8 Feb. 1561/2; m 14 July 1590, Christopher Strutt; 6 ch. recorded; she was buried 22 July 1611; he m 2, Susan _____ ; he was buried 16 Feb. 1627/8

SUSAN, b prob. about 1564; m 5 Oct. 1585, Ottiwell Strutt at Rattlesden; he d 1592 testate; she survived

JOHN, bapt. 30 Aug. 1565; buried same day

JOHN, bapt. 27 April 1567; m Elizabeth ——— ; ch.: Margaret bapt. 16 May 1592 - buried 13 Jan. 1607/8, Anne bapt. 1 May 1594, John bapt. 3 Oct. 1596, Susan bapt. 22 Feb. - buried 24 Feb. 1598/9, Sara bapt. 24 Feb. 1600/01, Susan bapt. 12 Oct. 1603, Faith bapt. 18 Sept. 1609 - buried 3 Oct. John Waller, "single", m widow Agnes Denny of Combes 22 Oct. 1611 & had Robert bapt. 25 April 1613. Was this the same John Waller?

HENRY, bapt. 2 Oct. 1569; apparently d.y. as not in father's will

ROBERT, b prob. 1571-75; buried 21 Aug. 1585

WILLIAM, b prob. 1571-75; he had a dau. Susan bapt. 26 Dec. 1611 at Rattlesden

THE CHURCH OF SAINT NICHOLAS
RATTLESDEN, SUFFOLK

Ref.: Parish Register at Rattlesden; Probate Records at Bury St. Edmunds

WILLIAM SPUFFORD of Toddington, Bedfordshire, was born probably about 1470-1480. His wife was named Margery. No doubt sick and expecting to die, he made his will on 16 May 1534 and died shortly thereafter. An abstract of his will follows. He had a brother John.

The name Spufford/Spofford/Spofforth is a place name derived from Spofforth parish in North Yorkshire. The name means *ford by the Spaw.* It is mentioned in the Domesday Book, where it is called *Spawford.* In this parish, the famous de Percy family were feudal barons for two centuries until towards the close of the thirteenth century, the direct male Percy line became extinct. The present branch of the family descends from the marriage of Lady Agnes de Percy, sole inheritor of the vast family estates, and Josceline de Louvain, Duke of Brabant, a direct descendant of Charlemagne. The marriage was arranged on the condition that the bridegroom take the name of Percy. In this parish are the ruins of the Percy's ancestral castle, actually more of a fortified manor house than a great fortress such as other barons erected.

16 May 1534 - the will of WILLIAM SPUFFORD of Todington... to be buried in the churchyard of Saint George the Martyr of Todington ... to the mother church of Lincoln 2d., for tythes forgotten 2d. ... to Saint Anthony's light a pound of wax ... to Sir Roger for prayers 20d. ... to Joan Spufford my daughter 10 sheep ... to Elizabeth Layne my kinswoman a ewe and a lamb ... to Symon my son 10 sheep ... to Margery my wife my house and my land that I bought of Alice Grant, in tail to son Symon, then to son John, then to daughter Jane ... as long as son Symon is under age estate to be in custody of Symon Cowan and John Dawson his godfathers ... a trental to be sung at the altar of Saint Katherine in the church of Todington for my soul & my father's and mother's ... to son Symon a brown heifer, in tail to daughter Joan ... to son John 2 colts ... to John Spufford my brother 2 kyne ... to Margery my wife the copy of my house that I dwell in for five years, paying to John Spufford my son £10 and also 2 steers and 2 heifers, then the house to son John, in tail to son Symon, then to daughter Jane. Residue to wife Margery whom I make sole executrix. Thomas Cowke to be overseer. Witnesses: William Dawson, curate, Thomas Cowke, Symond Laweh, John Dawson, et al. Proved 1 June 1534. (R4 f 6d)

Children:

JOAN, b perhaps about 1508 as apparently of age in 1534

16 JOHN, b about 1510 as apparently of age in 1534; prob. 6 ch. or more

SYMON, b 1514-1530, prob., as under age in 1534

48

GEORGE SCOTT of Bradfield Saint George was probably born about 1495, presumably in Bradfield. He was perhaps a grandson of Adam Scott of Bradfield who died testate in March 1474/5, leaving his estate to George Scott and Benedict Freg---, probably a son and married daughter.

Robert Scott of Bradfield who died testate in March 1558/9 was probably a brother to George. Robert in his will mentioned a brother Thomas Scott, wife Idonye, 4 children: George, James, Joan, Agnes, and George Hunt, his brother-in-law.

George Scott died in late 1547 leaving a wife named Margaret, three sons and an unmarried daughter. An abstract of his will follows.

> 2 October 1547 - the will of George Scott of Bradfield Saint George, county Suffolk...to be buried in the churchyard of Bradfield...to the high altar 5s...to Margaret my wife £40 and ten milk neat and my two copies [land held of the lord] for her life and all household stuff. And after her decease Edmund my son to have the best copy and George my son the next...to each of them 10 marks and two milk neat...to Isabell Scott my daughter 20 marks and two milk neat...to Nicholas Scott my son my house in Hegsted after the decease of my mother, and twenty combes of barley, 5 combes of wheat and 5 combes of rye...to my mother one combe of mystlyn and one combe of barley...to each of my son Nicholas's children 5 combes of barley and a milk cow payable at age 21 or marriage...to each godchild two bushels of barley...to every servant taking wages one combe of barley and to every one not taking wages two bushels...to William Wyatt my blue coat...to Nicholas Scott my best marble coat...to Thomas Swanton my sleaved russett coat and my ---- coat and one combe of rye...at day of my burial £4 for charity, at thirty days another £4...Margaret my wife and Nicholas my son to be executors...my master Sir Thomas Jermyn to be supervisor. Witnesses Richard ----, priest, James Chapman and Robert Scott. Proved 10 February 1547/8. (Ref.: P.C.C. - F.2 - Populwell)

Children:

NICHOLAS, prob. eldest; m Isabell ________; 8 ch.: George, bp. 25 Dec. 1547, Robert, bp. 15 Sept. 1550, John, bp. 16 May 1554, Anne bp. 6 Oct. 1555, Thomas, Edmund, Margaret, Alice. Nicholas d testate 1563, naming wife & sons Robert, Thomas, Edmund - all under 25, & daus. Margaret, Alice, Anne - all under 24; so, sons George & John must have d.y. A George Scott was bur. 30 Aug. 1562, perhaps that son. Res. of Bradfield Saint Clare. An abstract of his will:

27 May 1563 - the will of Nicholas Skotte of Bradfield Saint Clare...to be buried in the churchyard...to Isabell my wife my lease of Byrds with other lands belonging to the manor of Saint Clare's Hall, for life, then to son Robert, in tail to son Thomas, then to son Edmund, then to daughter Margaret, then to daughter Alice, then to daughter Anne...wife Isabell to have all household stuff and cattle and to pay 4 marks apiece to each of the three daughters within 2 years of their reaching age 24, to pay to each of the three sons 4 marks at age 25, to each of my brother's children 20s apiece. And if the said *Nicholas's* children some live and some depart this present life...my right worshipful master Sir Ambrose Jermin, knight, to be my supervisor...witnesses: Henry Ballie, Thomas Alvis & George Skotte. Proved 23 July 1563. (Ref.: Woode 164)

24 EDMUND, prob. b 1525-30; m Joan ________; 9 ch.; she was bur. 15 May 1615 at Rattlesden; he was bur. 14 Aug. 1621, "aged about 97"

GEORGE, prob. b 1525-30; m Amy ________; (he may have had an earlier m 13 Oct. 1560 to Elizabeth Baker at Bradfield St. George, or was this the m of Robert's son?). An abstract of his will:

24 Aug. 1579 - the will of George Skot of Bradfield Saint George...to son John 20s. within 6 months...to daughter Dorothy £3 at marriage or age 24...to son Bennett £3 at age 23...to daughter Bridget £3 at marriage or age 24...to daughter Agnes £3 at marriage or age 24...to son George £3 at age 21...to wife Amy all movables and household stuff for life, she to be executrix, and she to pay to son Richard 20s. yearly starting at his age 20 as long as she lives...after decease of Amy, Richard to pay to eldest child, John, £3 within 2 years, to daughter Dorothy £3. Proved 28 February 1579/80. (Ref.: Browne 80)

ISABELL, unmarried in 1547

Ref.: Parish Registers; Probate Records at Bury Saint Edmunds; Prerogative Court of Canterbury wills

1

JOHN STANYAN *(Anthony)* was born 16 July 1642 at Boston and baptized there in the First Church on the 24th. He grew up in Exeter and Hampton Falls, New Hampshire where his father was a pioneer settler. In the Essex County Court files:

> John Stanyan, aged about eighteen years, testified as to bringing up the colt for Goodman Greane, which the later had bought of his father, etc. - sworn 22:1:1659/60.

On 17 December 1663 at Salisbury, Massachusetts, he married Mary Bradbury. She was the daughter of Thomas and Mary (Perkins) Bradbury and was born 17 March 1642/3 at Salisbury. They lived and died on his father's homestead in Hampton Falls, New Hampshire.

Several times he was in court suing Edward Colcord over matters of debt. He also appears on the court records over dealings with Henry Bennett who in 1677 attached his house for the non-payment of a debt to be paid in pine boards. Bennett was an uncle by marriage to John Stanyan's wife. From all this, it seems apparent that John Stanyan was operating a saw mill as had his father, and had numerous dealings in the trade.

In April 1674, he and twelve other men were convicted for holding a Quaker meeting and were admonished. Later, a warrant was issued against them for the court fees. He apparently had a lifelong sympathy for the Quaker cause, for years later, on 19 February 1711, he made the motion to have some of the common lands set off to them for a parsonage. He had the reputation among his contemporaries of being a very good man. John Stanyan was a selectman in 1692, 1699, 1701 and 1709 and a representative in 1705.

In 1694, Joseph Emmons had a shoemaker's shop at the Stanyan place.

His daughter Anne died about 1703 leaving five small children. Their father was a mariner, away much of the time, so the children were placed in foster homes by John Stanyan. In 1710, he petitioned the legislature for a guardianship so that the children might be apprenticed.

> province of Newhampshire } to ye worshipful her mages^{s} Justises now siting in sessions this 7th of March 1709/10
>
> may it ples youer worships it so falls out that youer humble petishoner has five gran children lefft which hee has bin forced to

tak car of his daughter the wiff of one Thomas Sellee children she being ded & sd Selle gon out of the country about seven years & no estat wherewith to maintain sd children (being three boys & too garls) & has provided good places for them but the partys where they are and fearfull that when they groo up may by Ese advice Atemp to go from them, there being no indenture on them. Therefore pray that youer worships ples to order & appoynt Ether my self or sum other persons whom your worships shall Judg most fit to bind sd children to thos persons that have taken care of them. So prays youer worships humbel poteshoner.

John Stanyan

John Stanyan died 27 September 1718 in the 79th year of his age per town record, 26 September, age 79 according to his gravestone in the old Quaker cemetery now in Seabrook. Actually, he was 76. On 20 November 1718 Mary, widow of John Stanyan, was admitted to the church of Hampton Falls. This suggests that she had for most of her life deferred to his preference for the Quakers, but upon his death returned to the Congregational church which she preferred.

She died 29 May 1724 at Salisbury (Old Norfolk County Court Book), perhaps while visiting.

13 February 1717/18 - I John Stanyan of Hampton, New Hampshire, being ancient & weak in body...to my beloved wife Mary the one half of my Dwelling house, (viz) the New End together with the East End of the old house with one half of all my buildings, one half of my orchard & Garden...other half to son Jacob...lands on both sides of Fall Rivers to Jacob, 2 oxen, 3 cows, 2 swine, 6 sheep and all household goods to wife Mary, except one bed to granddaughter Anne, daughter of son James to whom a cow if she lives with her grandmother...to daughter Mary, wife of Theophilus Smith 30 acres in Exeter where they live and £25...to son James the westerly half of house lot and other parcels, and one third of my tools, lands to remain in the Stanyan family after decease of James...to daughter Mehitable £25 and one quarter of lands at the New Plantation, and my silver tankard...to daughter Elizabeth £25, my great brass kettle... household goods to be divided among three daughters after wife dies...to son Jacob my homestead, being other half of home lot, and other parcels, these lands to remain after his death to his male heirs...to son Jacob all livestock except the above which is to wife as long as she lives, then to Jacob...to Jacob one third of all tools, half of money and debts due me, other half to wife Mary... to grandson John Silley several lots and one third of my tools...to grandson John Stanyan, son of James 40 acres...half the income of the estate to grandson John Sylley if he looks after his grandmother...wife Mary and son James and son Jacob to be executors.

Children, born at Hampton Falls, New Hampshire:

MARY, b 22 Oct. 1664; m Theophilus, son of Nicholas & Mary (Shatswell) Smith, b 14 Feb. 1667/8, d March 1737; 5 ch. per his will; she was not in husband's will, so prob. dead.

JAMES, b 26 June 1667; m Anne Hussey, dau. of John & Rebecca (Perkins) Hussey, b in May 1669; 2 sons, 9 daus.; he d testate about 1743;she was living in 1749; he was a Quaker in 1701.

JACOB, b 11 Jan. 1669/70; verdict on his untimely death filed 6 Dec. 1681.

JOSEPH, b 5 Dec. 1672; not mentioned in father's will, so probably died young.

MEHITABLE, b 1 Jan. 1675/6; m John Robinson, son of Jonathan & Sarah Robinson, b 7 Sept. 1671 at Exeter; 8 ch.; d about 1755 testate; she survived him.

ANN, b 17 Feb. 1677/8; m 2 July 1697 Thomas Sealy; 6 ch.; she was d by 7 March 1709/10 when her father deposed that he had 5 gr. ch. to care for, ch. of his dau., wife of Thomas Cille, she dead, he gone out of the country; he was a sea captain, d aged at son's home in Nottingham.

ELIZABETH, prob. b 1680; m at Salisbury 6 Jan. 1697/8, Jeremiah Stevens, the son of John & Joanna (Thorn) Stevens, b 6 Oct. 1675; 10 ch., she d 1 July 1737; he d 24 Nov. 1759.

JACOB, b 31 March 1683; m 29 Oct. 1704, Dorothy ____________; 9 ch.; she d 16 Nov. 1723; m 2, Lydia __________; 1 ch.; he d about 1764.

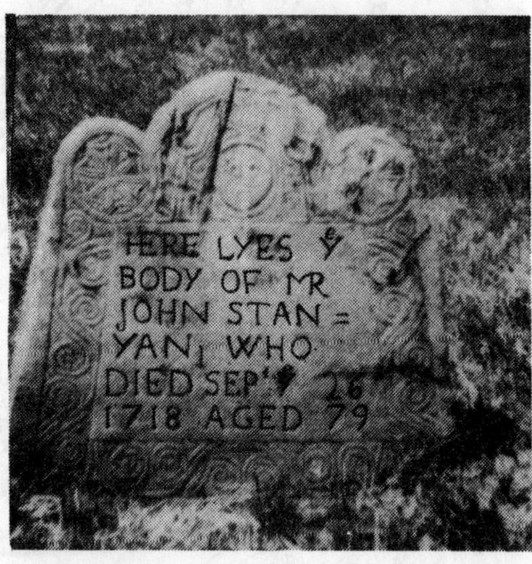

Ref.: History of Hampton Falls - Volumes I & II; Genealogical Dictionary of Maine & N.H., by Noyes, Libby, Davis; Court Files

province of
Northampshir

to ye worshipfull her magties Justises —
now sitting in sessions this 7th of march 1709/10

may it pleas youer worships it so falls out that youer humble petitioner has five gran children left which hee has bin — forced to tak care of his daughter the wif of one Thomas Seller children she ~~[illegible]~~ being ded & ye sd fello gon out of the Cuntry a bout seven years / & no estat whare with to main tain sd children (being three boys & two garls) & hee — provided good plases for them but the parish where they are, are fearfull that when they groo up may be [illegible] [illegible] Altering to go from them, there being no Indenture on them therfore prays that youer worships pleas to — order & Appoint Either my self or sum other person whom youer worships shall judge most fit to bind sd — children to thos persons that have taken care of them — so prays youer worships humboll petitioner —

John Hanger —

2

ANTHONY STANYAN sailed from London, England on the *Planter* about 6 April 1635 and arrived at Boston on 7 June. He was on the passenger list as age 24, a glover. He was probably about 28 as subsequent depositions of his indicate. No family accompanied him so he probably married after his arrival in Boston where he first lived. Where he came from in England is unknown. The name Stanyan originates from the village of Stanian in Northamptonshire.

Anthony Stanyan soon moved to Exeter, New Hampshire where he shared in the first division of land which was authorized in December, 1639.

He was usually designated as *Mr.,* a title reserved for the most respectable and able.

His first wife, whose name was Mary, was in Boston when their son John was born on 16 July 1642. Her parents probably lived there. On 17 May, 1644, he took the freeman's oath at Piscataqua Court. In 1646, he deposed that he was in Salem in December, 1644, at Mr. Clerk's farm. On 14 May 1645, he was appointed "to end small business at Exeter", and again on 6 May 1646. This was equivalent to Justice of the Peace. In November 1645, he was sworn in as constable at Exeter.

In September 1646, he pleaded guilt in court to striking John Busley and was fined. A year later he was in court on a charge of trespass, but the jury found the case too complicated to decide and referred it back to court.

On 26 May 1647, he was chosen town clerk of Exeter and the same day was appointed to lay out the road from Haverhill to Exeter.

On 28 March 1648, he had John Smart Sr. of Exeter in court for abusing him (assault) while he performed his duties as constable. In September he was again in court on a trespass charge.

He moved to Hampton in 1648 and the next year, on 25 March 1649, he was chosen one of the selectmen and again in 1662, 1668 and 1676. At Hampton, he received the fourth largest share of land, apparently being one of the leaders in the enterprise. It amounted to 27 acres, 135 poles. He settled on *The Hill* in what is now Hampton Falls.

He served a number of times on trial juries and in 1650 on the grand jury. In October 1650, he and two others were chosen to "end small causes" for Hampton. He and his wife had seats in the meeting house assigned to them in 1650. The same year he drew a share in the ox common.

In April 1652 Mr. Edward Gyllman acknowledged judgement to Mr. Anthony Stanian and to pay him 12,500 merchantable inch boards within one month. In 1653, he was chosen commissioner of the rates. The same year he was chosen to examine the merits of the case of Maurice Hobbs against the town and was in 1654 chosen one of the agents to manage the same on the part of the town. In October 1654, he sued Edward Colcord for debt of 3,000 boards. On 27 November 1654 he bought a one third interest in a mill.

He had two known children by his first wife. She died probably in 1655, and on 1 January 1655/6 at Salisbury he remarried to Anne, widow of William Partridge of Salisbury. On 11 June 1659 he secured to her children the payment of a legacy left to them by their grandfather, John Partridge of Olney, Buckinghamshire, England.

On 19 December 1656 he and two others were chosen "to seek out help for the ministry".

The following deeds apply to him.

6 January 1657/8 - Anthony Stanian of Hampton, planter, and his wife Anne, for £20, etc. conveyed to Mr. Tho. Bradbury and John Stevens, Sr., both of Salisbury, 36 acres of upland, being 3 ten acre lots and one 6 acre lot formerly purchased by William Partridg of Salisbury, deceased, the former husband of said Anne, the land being in Salisbury, and bounded by Merrimack river, common, John Bayly, Sr., deceased, and line laid out by Anthony Colby and Jarrett Haddon, near the path. Witnesses: Robert Pike and Judeth Bradbury.

(Old Norfolk County Deeds)

11 June 1659 - Anthony Stanian of Hampton and his wife Ann, conveyed to John Partridg of Boston, seaman, for £36, which sum was due to grantee for legacies given him by his grandfather John Partridg and his father Willi. Partridg, deceased, and for £13 to be paid to Hannah Partridg at 21 years of age, and for £13 to Elizabeth Partridg at 21 years of age, a house formerly of Willi. Partridg, late of Salisbury, deceased, and land in Salisbury, viz: 4 acres adjoining the house, 4 acres of meadow in the great meadows, 7 acres in the bareberrie meadows, and 8 acres of Higledee pigledee marsh towards Hampton,

at Hall's farm, and some beach sweepage. Also, the grantee gives grantor a certain lien on the property. Witnesses: Tho. Bradbury and Judeth Bradbury. (Old Norfolk County Deeds)

3 July 1661 - Anthony Stanian of Hampton, for £70, conveyed to Robert Downer of Nuberie, a house and 32 acres of land in Salisbury, viz: 4 acres adjoining the house, 4 acres in great meadow, 7 acres in bareberry meadows, 8 acres of salt marsh in first division of higgledee pigledee towards Hampton, 4 acres of salt marsh near Mr. Hall's farm, and sweepage at the beach towards Hampton (all of the lands and house being formerly of William Partridg, deceased). Witnesses: Anthony Sumersbie and John Browne. Acknowledged, and Anthony Stanian's wife Ann surrendered dower, in court at Hampton 8 October 1661. (Old Norfolk County Deed)

8 April 1662 - Tho. Carter of Salisbury, planter, for 25s. conveyed to Anthony Stanian of Hampton, yeoman, my interest in the farm that Salisbury bought of Sam. Hall, gentleman, and rights belonging to it except 2 acres of meadow formerly granted to me within the bounds of said farm. Witnesses: Geroge Broughton, Sam. Hall and Tho. Bradbury, jr. Acknowledged by grantor, his wife releasing dower, in court at Salisbury 8 April 1662 (Old Norfolk County Deeds)

On 9 June 1663 he was the only one who dissented to the laying out of 4,000 acres west of Hampton bounds. On 20 June 1665 he was chosen to exchange the town's land with Nathaniel Weare. On 18 July 1665 he was a constable. On 12 October 1665 he was chosen to lay out the farm of Mr. Cotton at Hogpen Plain. On 12 July 1667 he was licensed to keep the oridinary. In 1668 he dissented to the admission of John Lock as an inhabitant. On 12 April 1669 he dissented to bringing a suit against Henry Green. On 14 December 1669 he dissented to the giving of 40 acres to each of those who settled in the new plantation and also dissented in the vote to lay out the waste lands. On 3 March 1670 he received a grant of 160 acres. In 1670 he dissented to Andrew Wiggin's taking forty pines from the commons and the same year was chosen to prosecute James Rice for cutting timber. In 1671 he dissented to the confirmation of Mr. Cotton's farm at Hogpen Plain. He was a representative in 1654 and 1680.

Anthony Stanyan died before 21 February 1688/9, when his estate was appraised at £45.18.2. He had deeded all his real estate to his son John before he died. Anne Stanyan died 10 July 1689.

A True and Just Inventory of the Estatt of Mr Antony Stanyan of Hampton in the Province off New Hampshir Deceased Apprised by us whose Names are here underwritten this 21 of ffeb 1688/9

	lb s d
Inprimus One old Fether Bed and Bolster An old Rugg and Blanket	03-00-00
One Old Bedsted and Chayer Table and Cubberd and Tow Old Cheste	01-00-00
More an Old Cubberd	00-06-08
One Trammell and 2 Old Hooks	00-05-00
A Paier of Tongs 2 Bowls of Skells	00-05-00
One Old Spitt and a Spade	00-03-00
Weringe Cloaths	03-00-00
To 2 Oxen	12-00-00
To Three Cowes	12-00-00
To 2 Tow Yeare Olds	04-00-00
To 1 yearlinge	01-05-00
To 1 Bull 3 yeare Old	03-00-00
To 12 Sheepe	04-04-00
To One Sett of hopps for a Cart	00-06-00
To 3 Boxes for Wheels	00-04-06
To 3 Chaines	00-16-00
To 1 Paier of hookes	00-01-06
To 1 Pichforke	00-01-06
	45-18-02

Nath[ll] Weare
Joseph Smith

Children:

1 JOHN, b 16 July 1642 at Boston; m 17 Dec. 1663, Mary Bradbury, dau. of dau. of Thomas & Mary (Perkins) Bradbury, b 17 March 1642/3; 8 ch.; he d 27 Sept. 1718

MARY, m 10 Jan. 1665/6 Capt. John Pickering of Portsmouth; 5 ch.; living in 1710; he d 10 April 1721

THE HAMPTON FALLS HILL SETTLEMENT
SCALE: About 1000 Feet to the Inch.

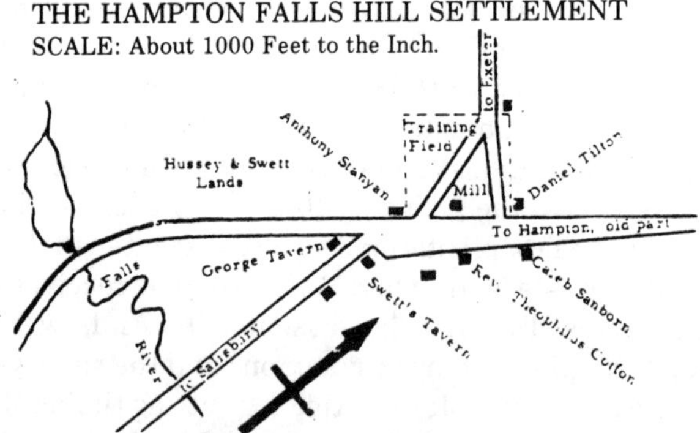

Ref.: History of Hampton Falls, Volumes I & II; Lechford's Notebook; Savage; Genealogical Dictionary of Maine and New Hampshire, by Noyes, Libby, Davis; Water's Gleanings 1:224; Essex County Quarterly Court Files; Essex Antiquarian, Volumes 1-13 by Sidney Perley; New Hampshire Court Files

The Ancestry of
MARY BARKER, wife of ISAAC STEARNS
Compiled By
John Brooks Threlfall

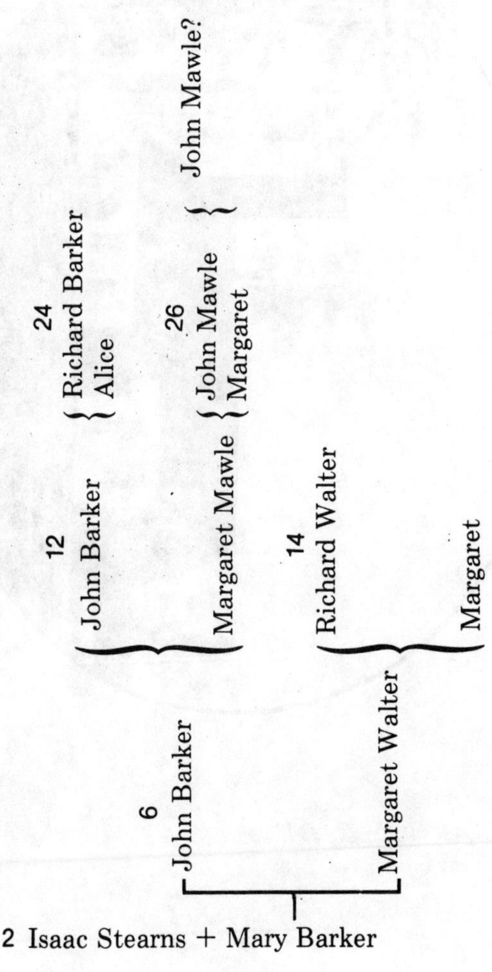

2 Isaac Stearns + Mary Barker

THE CHURCH OF SAINT MARY, HIGHAM, SUFFOLK

Reproduced from *Ecclesiastical Antiquities of the County of Suffolk*, 1818, by Isaac Johnson — courtesy of the County Record Office, Suffolk, England

ISAAC STEARNS of Higham, Suffolk, was born about 1590. On 20 May 1622 at Stoke Nayland, the adjacent parish, he married Mary Barker of Nayland. She was the daughter of John and Margaret (Walter) Barker of Nayland. Mary's father, John Barker, was buried 10 March 1616/17 at Nayland and shortly thereafter her mother, the widow Margaret, remarried to one Munnings of Gaines Colne, now known as Colne Engaine, which is about 10 miles to the west and across the Stour River into Essex. This is learned from the records of Thomas Lechford:

Isaacke Sterne of Watertown, planter, sometime of Stoke Nayland, Suffolk, tayler, & Mary his wife, daughter of John Barker late of Stoke, Nayland, clothier, deceased, makes a letter of attorney to Thomas Gilson of Sudbury, Suffolk, baker, to receive & recover of & from ——. Munnings of Gaynes Colne, Essex, yeoman, £5 due unto her by some bond or agreement made by the s[d] ——— Munnings before or after his marriage with Margaret Barker, mother of s[d] Mary

(Lechford's Notebook)

Isaac Stearns probably came to New England in the Winthrop Fleet. On the morning of 8 April 1630, the first five ships set sail from Yarmouth, Isle of Wight, and arrived at Salem on the 12th of June. The other six ships of the Winthrop Fleet sailed in May and arrived in July, bringing altogether about 700 passengers. Not being satisfied with the prospects of Salem, the colonists soon moved on to Charlestown and thence to Watertown where they settled. Isaac Stearns settled near Mount Auburn. In 1642, his homelot was bounded on the north by the land of John Warren, on the west by the highway, on the south by the land of John Biscoe, and on the east by Pequusett Meadow, a part of which meadow he owned. In the distribution of the estate of his son Samuel in 1724, this homelot "where his grandfather had lived", was assigned to the eldest son Nathaniel. Probably all the families of the name Stearns in the United States are descended from three early immigrants, viz. Isaac or Charles, who settled in Watertown, or Nathaniel, who settled in Dedham. Isaac, in his will, calls Charles "my kinsman". Probably Nathaniel was also related.

Isaac Stearns was admitted a freeman on 18 May 1631, and he was a selectman for several years.

On 4 December 1638, Isaac Stearns and John Page were fined 5 shillings "for turning the way about" (i.e. changing the highway). In 1647, he and Briscoe were appointed by the selectmen "to consider how the bridge over the river shall be built, and to agree with the workmen for doing it, according to their best discretion." This was the first mention of a bridge over the CharlesRiver in Watertown.

Isaac Stearns died 19 June 1671, leaving a widow Mary, who died 23 April 1677.

His will, dated five days before his death, and with his autograph signature, is extant in the Middlesex Probate office. Isaac Sternes

I, Isaac Sternes, of Watertown, in the County of Middlesex, being sick in body, but through the goodness of God in sound memory, do declare this to be my last Will and Testament, in the manner and form as followeth:

Imp.-ffirst, I return my spirit into the hands of God that gave it, and my body to the earth from whence it was taken.

2dly.-My will is, that Mary, my beloved wife, should enjoy my whole estate, for her maintainance, so long as she shall remain a widow; but if my said wife shall marry again, then my will is that she should enjoy only what the law intended and provided for in the law titled dowers.

3dly.-I give and bequeath to my grandchildren, the children of my sonne John Sternes, fower score pounds [which] being added to what my son had formerly, will be a double portion with the rest of my children.

4thly.-I give unto my son Isaac Sternes, seventy pounds, which being added to what he have had already, will be his proportion according to the rest of my children.

5thly.-I give to my son, Samuel Sternes, seventy pounds, which being added to what I formerly gave him will be his proportion with the rest of my children.

6thly.-I give to my grandchildren, the children of my daughter Mary, deceased, five and thirty pounds; my grandchild, Isaac Lernot, to have ten pounds of the said 35 pounds -- the remainder, which will be twenty-five pounds, to be equally divided to the rest; which said thirty-five pounds being added to what I formerly gave my daughter, Mary Lernot, will be an equal proportion with the rest of my children.

7thly.-I give to my daughter Sarah Stone, forty pounds, which being added to what she formerly had, will be her proportion.

8thly.-I give to my daughter Elizabeth Manning twenty pounds, which being added to what I formerly gave her, will be her proportion; further, my will is, that the said twenty pounds given to my daughter Elizabeth aforesaid, be secured for the good and benefit of the children.

9thly.-I give and bequeath to my daughter Abigail Morss, five acres of meadow, lying and being at Samuel's farm, to enjoy and possess for her and her heirs forever; and my will is, that my daughter Abigail Morss, may take the said five acres of meadow next to Samuel's meadow, or next to Capt. Mason's; and besides the meadow, I give to my said daughter Abigail, forty pounds, all which being added to what she have had formerly, will be her proportion.

10thly.-My will is, that my kinsman Charles Sternes, shall have ten pounds of my estate. Further, my will is, that my whole estate remain whole and unbroken for comfort and maintainance of my beloved wife, as said above, so long as she doth remain a widow — save only the five acres of meadow given to my daughter Abigail, which she is to enjoy presently.

ffurther. I nominate and appoint my beloved sons. Isaac Sternes and Samuel Sternes, executors, to this my last Will and Testament, and have hereunto set my hand, this fourteenth day of June, one thousand six hundred and seventy-one, in presence of.

Before subscribing, my will is, that when those several legacies are paid out according to my Will within mentioned, then my will is, that the remainder of my estate shall be equally divided among my children then living, and so subscribe the day aforesaid by putting to my hand in presence of.

William Bond, Sen'r
John Biscoe, Sen'r

The appraisal of his estate indicates he was comparatively affluent for his time, considering that he had previously given respectable portions to each of his seven living children. It included 14 parcels of land of 467 acres total, plus stock, farming utensils, provisions and household goods.

A true Inventory of the lands, goods and chattels of Isaac Sterne's Sen'r., taken the 28th. of the 4th. 1671, who deceased the 16th. of the 4th, 1671, prized and taken by us, whose names are here underwritten:

Housen and homestall of twelve acres of land	£100 00
Four acres of upland and two acres of meadow	18 00
Eight acres of upland	26 00
Six acres of meadow	30 00
Three acres of marsh	15 00
Fourscore acres of upland	60 00
Twelve acres of upland	5 00
Nine acres of upland	12 00
Sixty acres of upland	15 00
Fifteen acres of upland	8 00
Foure acres of meadow land	8 00
Twenty-five acres of meadowland	60 00
One hundred and ninety acres of meadow land	40 00
Two hundred and five acres of meadow land	10 00
Two Horses	10 00
Foure oxen	16 00
Six cowes	18 00
Two heffers	4 00
Three yearlings	3 00
Seven sheep and five lambs	4 00
Wearing clothes, linning and wooling	4 00
Beding and tabell linning	4 10
New Cloath	4 10
Swine, to the value of	4 00
Beding and bedstead in the parlor	4 10
Cubboard, stooles and table	3 00
Beding and bedstead in the hall	3 00
One moose skin	10
One old bed and other lumber in the old chamber	1 00
Sheep's wool	08
Two old chests, two spinning wheels, a chese press, and other lumber in ye low chamber	1 00
Beame and scales, waites and measures	1 00
One payer of quarnes and other lumber in th quarne house	10
Brass putter and iron and other utensils in the chimne	6 10
Beer barrels, pondering tubbs and other small utensils	1 00

Corne and mealle	1 00
Mault and pease	2 10
Lumber in the parlor chamber	10
Two bags of hopes	3 00
Cart, plow, chains and other husbandry instruments	3 00
Salt, meall and ches, other provisions	3 00
Corne growing in the ground	6 00
Tobacco in the rowle and leafe	06 08
Two muskets, one fowling piece, one sword	2 00
To one cart rope	05
To sacks and hay in the barns	15
Not footed in original. I make	£524 04 08

William Bond, Sen'r
John Biscoe, Sen'r
Henry Freeman

That this is a true coppie of ye originall attested in Oct. 1671, and y^n put upon Record, and burned in ye fireing of ye court house, is sworn by Isaac sternes and Samuel Sternes, 1, 8, 72, in open court, at Cambridge.

Children:

JOHN, bapt. 20 April 1623 at Higham, next to Nayland

MARY, bapt. 6 Jan. 1625/6 at Nayland; m 1, 9 July 1646 at Woburn, Mass., Isaac Learned, only son of William; 6 ch.; he d at Chelmsford 27 Nov. or 4 Dec. 1657; she m 2, 9 June 1662, John Burge of Weymouth; she d before 21 Dec. 1663, the date of the inventory of her estate

ANNA, (or Hannah), bapt. 5 Oct. 1628 at Nayland; m 25 Dec. 1650 at Watertown, Mass., Henry Freeman, son of Samuel & Appia Freeman; no ch.; she was buried 17 June 1656; he m 2, 27 Nov. 1656, Mary Sherman; he d 12 Nov. 1672

JOHN, b perhaps 1630-31, or perhaps the child bapt. in 1623; one of the first settlers of Billerica; he m 1653, Sarah Mixer, only dau. of Isaac & Sarah Mixer of Watertown; she d 14 June 1656; he m 2, 20 Dec. 1656, Mary Lathrop of Barnstable; he d 5 March 1668 at Billerica

ISAAC, b 6 Jan. 1632/3 at Watertown; m 24 June 1660, Sarah Beers, dau. of Richard & Elizabeth; 6 ch.; he d 29 Aug. 1676; she m 2, Sgt. Thomas Wheeler of Concord; she d 21 Jan. 1723/4

SARAH, b 22 Sept. 1635 at Watertown; m 7 June 1655, Deac. Samuel Stone of Cambridge, son of Gregory & Lydia; 8 ch.; she d 4 Oct. 1700; he m 2, Abigail (Carter)(Fowle) Walker, wid. of Samuel Walker; he d 27 Sept. 1715 ae about 80

SAMUEL, b 24 April 1638; m 1 Feb. 1662/3, Hannah Manning, dau. of Wm. & Dorothy, b 21 June 1642; 10 ch.; d 3 Aug. 1683; she d 26 Feb. 1723/4

ELIZABETH, b about 1640; m 13 April 1664, Samuel Manning, brother of Hannah; 2 sons; she d 24 June 1671 at Billerica; he m 2, Abiah Wright; he d 22 Feb. 1710/11 ae 67 - g.s.

ABIGAIL, prob. b 1642; m 27 April 1666, dea. John Morse, son of Joseph & Esther (Pierce) Morse, b 28 Feb. 1638/9; 9 ch.; she d 16 Oct. 1690; he m 2, Sarah ——; he d 23 July 1702

Ref.: Genealogy of Isaac Stearnes, by Van Wagenen; Lechford's Notebook in N.E.H.G.R. 40:269; Bond's History of Watertown; Town Records; Parish Registers

6

JOHN BARKER (*John, Richard*) was baptized 30 April 1563 at Nayland, "son of John Barker". On 29 June 1585 at Stoke Nayland, he married Margaret Walter who was baptized 8 September 1564 at Nayland, the daughter of Richard and Margaret Walter. On 10 March 1616/17 at Nayland, John Barker, "householder", was buried. Margaret remarried to ______ Munnings of Colne Engaine, Essex, who was living in 1640.

Children, baptized at Nayland:

JOHN, bapt. & buried 22 June 1586 at Nayland, "son of John Barker junior"

MARGARET, bapt. 31 March 1588

CHILD, perhaps, b about 1590?

JOHN, bapt. 28 Dec. 1591, "son of John" prob. d.y.

THOMAS, bapt. 29 Jan. 1592/3, "son of John"; a Thomas Barker, householder, was buried 26 May 1622 - he or his uncle? William, his son, buried 8 Sept. 1622

RICHARD, bapt. 15 July 1595, "son of John"; Richard Barker, single, was buried 28 June 1614 - he or his uncle?

SAMUEL, bapt. 14 March 1597/8; buried 11 May 1600, "son of John"

3 MARY, b about 1600; m Isaac Stearns of Higham by Nayland, 20 May 1622 at Stoke Nayland; 9 ch.; went to N.E. about 1630, prob. with the Winthrop Fleet; he d 19 June 1671; she d 23 April 1677

ANNE, bapt. 4 March 1601/2, "dau of John"

CHILD, perhaps, b about 1604?

JOHN, bapt. 22 April 1606, "son of John"

Ref.: Parish Registers; Probate Records at Bury Saint Edmunds

Aspall
Kenton
Saxtead
Monk Soham
Earl Soham
DEBENHAM
Ashfield
Thorpe
O
Gipping
Old Newton
Stow Upland
Mickfield
F
E
Drinkstone
Shelland
Onehouse
Rattlesden
Gipping
STOWMARKET
Stonham Parva
Pettaugh
Framsden
Kettleburgh
Monewden
Letheringham
Buxhall
Combs
Creeting
Felsham
Little Finborough
NEEDHAM MARKET
Battisford
Barking
Cosbeck
Coddenham
Ash Bocking
Otley
Charsfield
Dallinghoo
Debach
Bredfield
Brettenham
Cockfield
Thorp Morieux
Ringshall
Wattisham
Darmsden
Hemingstone
Swilland
Clopton
Burgh
Boulge
Hitcham
Kettlebaston
Gt. Bricett
Willisham
Baylcham
Blakenham Magna
Nettlestead
Barham
Henley
Witnesham
Grundisburgh
Hasketon
BILDESTON
Brent Eleigh
Monks Eleigh
Naughton
Nedging
Chelsworth
Offton
Somersham
Claydon
Akenham
Tuddenham
Westerfield
Culpho
Playford
Little Waldingfield
Milden
Semer
Elmsett
Flowton
Whatfield
Burstall
Sproughton
Bramford
Rushmere
Kesgrave
Lindsey
Kersey
Aldham
Hintlesham
IPSWICH
Foxhall
Waldringfield
Brightwell
Edwardstone
Groton
HADLEIGH
Washbrook
Copdock
Belstead
Bucklesham
Newbourn
Hemly
Newton
Boxford
Layham
Chattisham
Wherstead
Nacton
Levington
Kirton
Falkenham
Little Cornard
Assington
Polstead
Shelley
Little Wenham
Raydon
Freston
Woolverstone
Chelmondiston
Stoke
Gt. Capel
Wenham
Holton St. Mary
Tattingstone
Holbrook
Shotley
Walton
NAYLAND
Higham
Langham
Stratford St. Mary
East Bergholt
Brantham
Stutton
Harkstead
Erwarton
Boxted
Wormingford
Little Horkesley
Great Horkesley
MANNINGTREE
Mistley Thorn
Wrabness
Ramsey
Bradfield
HARWICH
Dover Court
River Stour
Ardleigh
Weeks or Wix
Little Oakley
West Bergholt
Fordham
Little Bromley
Great Oakley
Gt. Bromley
Elmstead
Greenstead
Lit. Bentley
Beaumont cum Moze
Aldham
COLCHESTER
Stanway
Copford
Tendring
Wivenhoe
Frating
Gt. Bentley
Weeley
Thorpe le Soken
Kirby le Soken
WALTON
Alresford
Thorrington
Donyland
Fingringhoe
Abberton
Langenhoe
Gt. Holland
Lt. Clacton
Brightlingsea
Frinton
Gt. Clacton
Lit. Holland
Osyth
St. Clich
Peldon
Gt. Wigborough
Lit. Wigborough
Layer Marney
Layer Breton
Messing
Tolleshunt Knights
Virley
Salcott
E. Mersea
W. Mersea
Tolleshunt Darcy
Tolleshunt Major
Tollesbury
Goldhanger
BLACKWATER RIVER
Bradwell
Tillingham
Steeple
St. Lawrence
Scale of Miles
0 1 2 3 4 5 10 15 20 25

12

JOHN BARKER (*Richard*) of Nayland, Suffolk, England, was born about 1540. On 26 May 1562 at Nayland, he and Margaret Maull of Nayland were married. He was a cloth maker. On 22 October 1588, John Barker the elder, "a householder", was buried at Nayland. Margaret Barker, "widow", was buried 11 January 1589/90 at Nayland. Both of them left wills.

24 June 1587 - the will of JOHN BARKER of Nayland, Suffolk, clothier ... to wife Margaret my house which I now dwell in and my house where William Harvye now dwells and my house where Robert Webbe now dwells, etc. for life and afterwards to my son Richard and his heirs forever ... to her my house which I bought of Mr. Horne of London and my house and ground where John Knope now dwells, etc. for one year and then to my son John ... Other houses and lands disposed of ... my son Thomas ... my son William ... daughters Dorothy and Alice Barker ... daughters Anne and Joice Barker ... daughter Katherine Beriffe ... to son Legate ... cousin John Leache ... Margaret Fenner ... cousin William Killmache ... cousin Thomas Koppine at age 21 ... Dorothy Prestone ... Provision made for good bringing up of Richard, Thomas and William Barker, my three younger sons, and of Dorothy, Alice, Anne and Joice Barker, my four youngest daughters ... wife Margaret to be executrix and John Beriffe my son-in-law and John Barker my son to be supervisors. Witnesses: William Fisher senior and William Fisher junior. Proved 10 December 1588.

(Ref.: P.C.C. Leicester 14)

24 December 1589 - the will of MARGARET BARKER of Nayland, Suffolk ... to be buried in the churchyard of Nayland ... to my brother James Mawle of Nayland ... my children ... their late father John Barker my husband ... John Barker of Nayland my son ... messuage, croft and garden sometimes William Hornes and Thomas Hornes, grocers of London, situate in the village of Nayland ... to my son Richard Barker a legacy bequeathed him by his father ... Messuage, etc. and lands lying in Wethermounteford *alias* Wormingford and Mount Bures, Essex ... to my son Thomas Barker a legacy from his father ... a deed of Christian Turnour of Colchester, Essex, widow ... messuage, etc. in Lammarsche and Much Henny, Essex ... to my daughter Alice Barker ... to the rest of my daughters ... to John Gent, yeoman, of Walton on the Naves [Naze] in the Sooke, Essex, messuage and land in Much Horskley, Essex (upon certain conditions) ... to my daughter Margaret Legatt ... to Thomas Legat of Sutton in Hornchurch, Essex, gentleman, a messuage, etc. there ... to my grandchild Jane Legate ... to my grandchild Margaret Barker ... to Margaret

Fenner ... to my grandchild John Berriffe ... to the three children of my brother James Mawle, James and Anne [*sic*] ... to the two children of my brother John Mawle, John and Robert ... to the two children of my brother George Mawle, John and Margaret ... to the children of my brother Richard Barker at marriage or age 21 ... to my sons Richard, Thomas and William £3 each, which was their grandmother Mawle's gift ... to my brother James Mawle's wife. ... to John Bowes and Margaret his wife ... to my cousin Kynwellmarshe his wife ... to the wife of William Fisher of Buers ... to my cousin Leache ... for executors Mr. Thomas Waldegrave of Buers in Essex, esquire, and John Beriffe of Brightelingsey, my son-in-law, and for supervisors Mr. Wynterflood of Ason [Assington] and William Fisher of Buers. Thomas Winterflood was one of the witnesses. Proved 7 February 1589/90.

(Ref.: P.C.C. Drury 10)

Children, all baptized at Nayland; all recorded as "son/dau. of John Barker":

6 JOHN, bapt. 30 April 1563 at Nayland, "son of John Barker"; m 28 June 1585 at Stoke Nayland, Margaret Walter, dau. of Richard & Margaret, b about 1565; he was buried 10 March 1616/17; she m 2, —— Munnings of Colne, Essex

MARGARET, bapt. 28 Oct. 1565, "dau. of John Barker"; m Thomas Legate before 1587; had a dau. Jane, etc.; res. Sutton in Hornchurch, Essex; he d 1622. See P.C.C. will Savile 66

KATHERINE, bapt. 17 May 1568; m John Beriffe of Brightlingsea, Essex, before 1587; had a son John, etc.

ALICE, bapt. 9 Oct. 1570; buried 4 Nov. 1570

DOROTHY, bapt. 20 Oct. 1572

RICHARD, bapt. 24 April 1575

THOMAS, bapt. 14 Sept. 1578, "son of Thomas"; this must be an error as there was no Thomas Barker having ch. at Nayland then, & the facts otherwise fit the son of John

ALICE, bapt. 14 Aug. 1580

ANNE, bapt. 28 Oct. 1582; m 18 Aug. 1608 at Nayland Robert Turner if same person

WILLIAM, bapt. 19 Oct. 1585

JOYCE, bapt. 31 March 1588

Ref.: Parish Registers; Probate Records at Bury Saint Edmunds

14

RICHARD WALTER of Nayland, Suffolk, England, a beer brewer, was probably born 1520-1535. He apparently first married Elizabeth ——, who as "wife of Richard Walter" was buried 13 December 1562 at Nayland. In 1563, he remarried to Margaret ——, who was probably born 1530-1540. He apparently had a sister who married John Winterflood, and thus the Thomas Winterflood he bequeathed to would have been a nephew. Peter Walter, who was underage, was probably another nephew. Since he did not name Peter's father, nor his "brother" John Winterflood's wife, the brother and sister were probably then dead. Also, he named no other relatives, so one can reasonably assume that he singled out these two because they had lost a parent.

Richard Walter, being sick, made his will 17 May 1569. He, "a householder", was buried 4 June 1569 at Nayland. His wife was pregnant at the time of his death. The child was a boy whom she named John as we learn from the will of Margaret Maull, who died in 1586. (See No. 6410). Her bequeathing to the three Walter children suggests a relationship. While Margaret Walter was then married to Margaret Maull's grandson, John Barker, there must have been a closer relationship for her to have included the two brothers. Perhaps Margaret Maull was nee Walter, and these three recipients of her kindness were a grand niece and two grand nephews.

17 May 1569 - the will of Richard Walter of Nayland, county Suffolk, beer brewer ... sick in body ... to Margaret my wife for her life all my capital messuage, houses, buildings, stables, yards and garden where I do now dwell, then to Richard my son, in tail to Margaret my daughter, then in tail to the child my wife is now withall, then to Thomas Wynterflood the son of John Wynterflood of Assington ... to the said Margaret my wife for her life all that my messuage, etc. now in the occupence of me the said Richard Walter and of one James Smythe, then to Margaret my daughter, in tail to son Richard, then to child unborn, then to the same Thomas Wynterflood ... to wife Margaret etc. .... two tenements in Nayland now held by Thomas Sterlinge and John Hylle, and Long Croft in Stoke now in the occupancy of John Smythe ... after her death to the unborn child, in

tail to Richard my son, then to daughter Margaret, then to said Thomas Wynterflood ... to Richard my son £20, one silver salt and one goblet of silver weighing together 9 ounces to be delivered to him at age 21 ... to said daughter Margaret £10, my best maser and five silver spoons at age twenty ... to unborn child £10 at age twenty ... to the poor of Nayland 30s. ... to Peter Walter 10s. at age 21 ... residue to wife Margaret ... Executors to be wife Margaret and my brother John Winterflood. Witnesses: Thomas Ive, Thomas Blithe and John Smythe. Proved 11 May 1570. (Ref.: IC 500/2/34/16)

Children, baptized at Nayland:

7 MARGARET, bapt. 8 Sept. 1564; m 28 June 1585 at Stoke by Nayland, John Barker of Nayland; 8 ch.; he was buried 19 June 1617 at Nayland. She m 2, ——— Munnings of Colne Engaine, Essex.

RICHARD, bapt. 16 Sept. 1567; living 1586; perhaps the Richard Walter of Sudbury who d 1592, intestate, leaving a widow named Agnes; inv. 31s. 10d.

JOHN, bapt. 1 July 1569, a posthumous son; living 1586

Ref.: Probate Records at Bury Saint Edmunds; Consistory Court of Norwich Wills; Parish Registers

RICHARD BARKER of Nayland, Suffolk, England, was probably born about 1505-1510. From his will, we learn that he was a prosperous property owner and that he held a lease on a mill in nearby Wormingford, Essex. He had several brothers and a sister Ellen, to each of whom he left 20 shillings. Alice, wife of Richard Barker, was buried at Nayland 27 December 1560 and Richard Barker, "householder", was buried 27 July 1561. Thomas Barker, who had a daughter Katherine baptized 18 September 1559 at Nayland and William Barker whose daughter Elizabeth was buried 15 June 1560, were probably his brothers.

23 July 1561 - the will of RICHARD BARKER of Nayland, county Suffolk ... to be buried in the sanctuary of Nayland ... to my son John Barker my messuage the which I now dwell in and all my fields called Pound's Fields and one pasture called Potter's Fen and the pightell to the said fen belonging ... and all my lease and term of years of such lands as I hold by indenture of master Rosse, being in Nayland and Horkesley in county Essex ... and £100 in money ... and my lease in Wormingford mill which I hold of the demise of the right worshipful master William Waldegrave until Richard comes to age 21 when he shall have half of the said lease ... to Richard Barker my son all my lands and tenements in Wormingford called Bowden's ... to Thomas Barker my son my tenement called the Pery and my fields on the back side and one parcel of meadow called Newland's meadow and the parcel called Mothertopp's, containing 7 acres, and my tenement with the appurtenances that James Solle dwelleth in, late George Abbe's, all in Nayland ... to Katherine Barker my daughter my tenement in Bures ... to Margaret Barker my daughter my tenement in Nayland that James Knoppey dwelleth in and a parcel called Lange containing 2 acres ... to Elizabeth Barker my daughter my tenement in Nayland now in the tenure of Thomas Blyth ... to John Barker my son 2 acres of meadow in Lewes meadow in Nayland ... to Margaret my daughter 4 acres out of my land called Holleland in Nayland ... to Elizabeth Barker my daughter 4 acres out of the said land called Holeland ... Residue of Hollelands to Thomas Barker my son ... to Richard Barker my son 100 marks ... to Thomas Barker my son 100 marks ... to Margaret Barker and Elizabeth Barker my daughters £30 each and 3 milk kine each, twelve months after my decease ... to Agnes Howlet my servant one cow and 40s. ... to Alice Bricman my servant one cow and 40s. ... to Thomas Barker my son 2 milk beasts and one feather bed ... to daughters Margaret and Elizabeth one feather bed each ... all my brass, pewter, copper and laten shall be equally divided between John, Thomas and Richard Barker my sons and Margaret and Elizabeth my daughters ... to every servant not afore bequeathed to 6s.8d. apiece ... to Richard Risbie 20s. ... to every one of my brothers

20s. ... to John Barker my kinsman of Colchester 40s. ... to my sister Ellen 20s. and one flock bed ... Residue to John Barker and Richard Barker my sons, they to be executors. Supervisors to be John Malle and Thomas Rose, each to have £6.8s.4d. for their pains ... said Thomas Rose to have the government of Thomas Barker my son as well of his lands and tenements until he reaches 21. Witnesses: John Gentt senior, Thomas Harrison, John Garod, William Lyne, William Kinwelmarsh, Thomas Blith, John Grute. Proved 21 October 1561.

(Ref.: P.C.C. 32 Loftes)

Children, probably all born at Nayland:

12 JOHN, prob. b 1535-38 as he was of age in 1561; eldest son; m 26 May 1562 at Nayland, Margaret Maull; he was a clothier; buried 22 Oct. 1588; she d end of Dec. 1589; both testate; 10 ch.

KATHERINE, prob. b 1537-40; unm. 1561; no further record in Nayland

MARGARET, perhaps b 1539-43; m 25 Oct. 1562 at Nayland, Anthony Speede; he d testate (1 Nov. 1591 - 23 Nov. 1591) naming wife Margerye & ch.: Joshua, John, Benjamin & Hanna, all under 21; this suggests that Margaret died childless & he rem. Sometimes Margaret & Margerie were interchanged at that time.

RICHARD, prob. b 1541-43, 2nd son & underage in 1561; m 26 June 1569 at Nayland, Dorothy Abbes, prob. the dau. of George Abbes who d testate 1554 leaving wife Elizabeth, his mother & some ch.under 18. Ch.: Dorothy bp. 17 Nov. 1572 - bur. 1 Dec. 1572, Richard, bp. 8 March 1573/4; his wife Dorothy was buried 3 Nov. 1574; he m 2, Mary Woodgate, dau. of Stephen of E. Bergholt; ch.: Margaret bp. 29 Jan. 1582/3, Mary bp. 16 Sept. 1594 who was their only surv. ch.; he d 7 Nov. 1594 per I.P.M.; she m 2, Henry Bright & had 8 more ch.; she m 3, William Cole, was living 1618

ELIZABETH, perhaps b about 1540-44; m 5 Oct. 1563 at Nayland, John Coppyn a widower; 3 ch. bp.: Richard 11 Feb. 1564/5, Elizabeth 16 Dec. 1566, Thomas 1 March 1567/8; she m 2, 23 Dec. 1571, George Preston; ch. bp.: Dorothy 12 April 1573, Susan 28 Feb. 1574/5

THOMAS, perhaps b about 1545-50; he must have been the youngest child, as his father assigned him to the guardianship of Thomas Rose, the only child so provided for; he left Nayland, as there is no further record of him there; he m Anne ______

27 February 1584/5 - the will of THOMAS BARKER of Colchester, Essex, clothier ... lands and tenements in Nayland and Stoke by Nayland, Suffolk, to wife Anne for life ... to son John at 21 ... to sons Richard and Thomas at 21 ... to child wherewith my wife is now pregnant. Servant Robert Cooke ... Edmund Seborne and Thomas Foster. Kinswoman Elizabeth Coppins. Sister Elizabeth Preston and her husband ... Kinsman George Preston ... to Richard Coppinge who dwelleth with Hawkins ... to cousin Thomas Coppinge ... to the widow Briant ... to cousin Dorothy Preston. Wife Anne to be executrix and friends Mr. John Pye and Richard Symnell supervisors. Proved 5 May 1585

(Ref.: P.C.C. Brudenell 19)

Ref.: Prerogative Court of Canterbury Wills; Probate Records at Bury Saint Edmunds; Parish Registers;

26

JOHN MAWLE (*John?*) of Stoke Nayland, Suffolk, England, was probably born about 1510-1515 and was probably the son of John Mawle, senior, who was buried at Stoke Nayland on 5 February 1560/61, aged 72. Christine, "wife of John Maull", who was buried 9 May following, could have been the widow of the recently deceased John, or the wife of the younger man. In any event, the wife who survived John Mawle and died in 1586 was named Margaret.

John Mawle was a prosperous clothier with considerable property in and around Nayland and across the Stour River in Essex County. She was possibly nee Abbes as is suggested by her will, in which case she was the daughter of George Abbes of Stoke Nayland who died testate in 1554, mentioning children under the age of 18 but not naming them. George Abbes also mentioned his sister-in-law, Elizabeth Abbes, and her children who were also under 18.

The Thomas Mawle mentioned toward the end of John's will was perhaps a brother. There had been Mawles living in Hornchurch, Essex, for several generations and so it is fairly sure that John descended from these.

John Mawle and his wife both left wills, abstracts of which follow. John died late in 1579 and Margaret in 1586.

12 September 1556 - the will of ROBERT MALLE of Hornchurch, county Essex, yeoman, sick in body ... to be buried in the church of Hornchurch at the west end of the stone that lieth over Mr. Richard Fowler ... to the high altar 12d. ... to my son Thomas 6s.8d., to my son George Malle 6s.8d. ... residue of goods & cattle to Alice my wife and William Malle my son, they to be executors ... son William to pay to his son Robert Malle £6.13s.4d. out of portion of same William at day of his marriage ... son John to be discharged of all debts he oweth me ... to be overseers my four sons George Malle, John Malle, Thomas Malle and Robert Malle, each to have 3s.4d. for his pains ... to George my son my best gown, to William my son my second gown. Witnesses: John Owtred & William Drywood. (Reference: 6ER8)

5 September 1579 - the will of JOHN MAWLE of Nayland, clothier ... sick in body ... to wife Margaret all my capital messuage in Nayland wherein I do now dwell, for life, one little hog yard now in the management of John Barker ... after her death to son James Mawle, but if said James decease before Margaret his wife, then

to said Margaret his wife £5 per year for life ... to my wife Margaret my tenement wherein John Knoppe now dwelleth in Nayland which I purchased of Mr. Ford, for life, then to son Robert...to wife all my copyhold lands called Noches which I hold by copy of court roll of Mr. Rivett of his manor of Nether Marsh in Stoke, one messuage over against the fulling mill wherein one William Kendwellmarsh now dwelleth and another tenement wherein one John Godderitcht now inhabiteth, in Nayland ... after death of Margaret to son George ... to wife Margaret all properties in Monte Bures and Whether Muntforde *alias* Wormingford in county Essex, now in the manor court of John London and Christopher Underwood, then after her death to son John ... to wife all rights in lands, pastures, etc. in House croft, Much Fayer field and Bulmers in Nayland which I had of the grant of Sir Thomas Danby, knight ... to son James all leases, interests, etc. in Wilger land pattens, he to pay son John £5 yearly ... other land which was granted by Sir Thomas Danby to go to son John, he to deliver to wife Margaret 20 loads of wood per year ... to son George all interests, leases, etc. in Wormingford mills which I hold by indenture with John Barker my son-in-law of the grant of Sir William Waldegrave, knight ... to wife Margaret £100, to son John £100, to son George 100 marks and all shears, etc. for occupation of shearman ... to wife Margaret all moveables of household stuff ... to Mills £4, to Richard Fell 20s., to Ned Swanne 20s., to Thomas Finar 10s. to T--- Long 10s., to Margaret Smith 10s., to Alice Turner 10s., to Tom Green 5s., to Hough Edwards 5s., to the poor of Nayland £4, to each child of my daughter Barker £10 at age 16, to John Mawle the son of George my son the reversion of my lands in Thorpe, Essex after the decease of Thomas Mawle and Joan his now wife ... residue to son James whom I appoint executor. Witnesses: John Winterflod, Thomas Nicholson, clerk, Robert Chamber, John Barker. Proved 26 January 1579/80. (Reference: P.C.C. 3 Arundell)

3 December 1586 - the will of MARGARET MAULL of Nayland next Stoke, Suffolk, widow...sick of body...to be buried in the church of Nayland...to James Maull the younger son of James Maull my son all my capital messuage or tenement wherein I now dwell, with the tenement my son George Maull dwells in & the other tenement thereto adjoining which I late purchased of Giles Fyrmon...to the said James Maull my son's son all my several indentures of lease in those lands called Horscroft & Much Fayrefilde..to Anne Maull daughter of my son James my indenture of lease of Kingsfylde which my late husband had ... if either James or Anne die before age 21 or marriage, the survivor to be the heir, if both die, then to their father James Maull ... to George Maull my son my indenture in lands called Bullmers in

Nayland ... to James Maull the younger the great bed in the parlor with the trundlebed whereupon I now lie, the cupboard, great table, chairs, stools, benches, lyverye table & cloake cubborde, cloth hanging, candlestick, cobirons, fire shovel, tonges & the window curtains, one of my silver goblets with all my ambries, boones, berestalls in the buttrey, kitchen & milkhouse, the cheesepress therein with the rest of the lumber in the said house ... unto Anne Maull the daughter of my son James Maull the bed in my maid's chamber with the furniture to it and the great press in the said chamber, the round table & both the great hutches in the chief gessing chamber ... executor to have use of, to lease, etc. lands until said James Maull the younger & Anne Maull his sister come of age or marry ... to John Maull my son one of my best silver goblets, conditionally that he deliver to my executor the half dozen silver spoons I lent him, the best bed in the gessing chamber with the furniture, the tables & carpet in the little parlor with the forms and stools to them belonging and a half dozen of my best cushions, the least of my two greatest copper kettles ... to Robert Maull my son the second bed called the low bed in the chief gessing chamber, one of my best goblets & six of my second sort of silver spoons ... to George Maull my son the best bed in the second gessing chamber with the furniture to it & the tables & table cloth, forms, chairs, stools & cubbords in the hall & all my brewing vessels, boulting tuns, hutches, tubs and beer vessels in the backhouse, ?eldinghe house & buttery ... my silver salt with the cover to it and six of my second sort of cushions ... to Margarett Barker my daughter my great danske chest in the parlor with my apparel that is in it with all the linen in the hutch at the great bed, she to distribute amongst her daughters, and the hutch I give unto Katherine her daughter ... to the children of my son George two of my silver spoons apiece ... to every of the children of my daughter Barker unmarried one of my silver spoons apiece ... unto Richard Walter, John Walter and Margaret Barker their sister one of my silver spoons apiece ... to every one of the children of my son John Maull one of my silver spoons apiece ... to Margarett Abbes otherwise Skarlett my kinswoman 40s. ... to Anne Abbes otherwise Leache her sister 40s. ... all my corn, cattle & debts owing to me shall go toward the payment of a bond I stand bound unto John Wynterflood of Assington, gentleman, for the payment of £30 which I have long since given to Anne Maull my grandchild ... residue to be divided into three parts, one part going to James & Anne the children of son James Maull, the second part to George Maull my son, the third part to Robert & John Maull my two sons ... to Elizabeth Barker one of the beds ... to Margarett Fener 40s. whereof my husband owed her 20s. & another of the beds in the men's chamber ... executor to be John Gente of Walton, county Essex, supervisor to be John Winterflood of Assington, gentleman. Witnesses: John Barker the elder, Thomas Legate & Edward Swayne. Proved 11 February 1586/7. (Reference: Bright 92=R2/40/92)

Children, probably all born at Nayland:

13 MARGARET, bapt. ; m 26 May 1562 at Nayland, John Barker; 10 ch.; she d late Dec. 1589 or Jan.; he was buried 22 Oct. 1588

JAMES, m Margaret ____; had ch.: James, Anne, others; he d intestate 1608

JOHN, had ch.: John, Robert,

GEORGE, shearman, had ch.: Grace bapt. 9 Oct. 1562, Elizabeth, Judith, John. b before 1579, Margaret b 1579-89

ROBERT, living 1586, but perhaps d before 1589 or s.p.

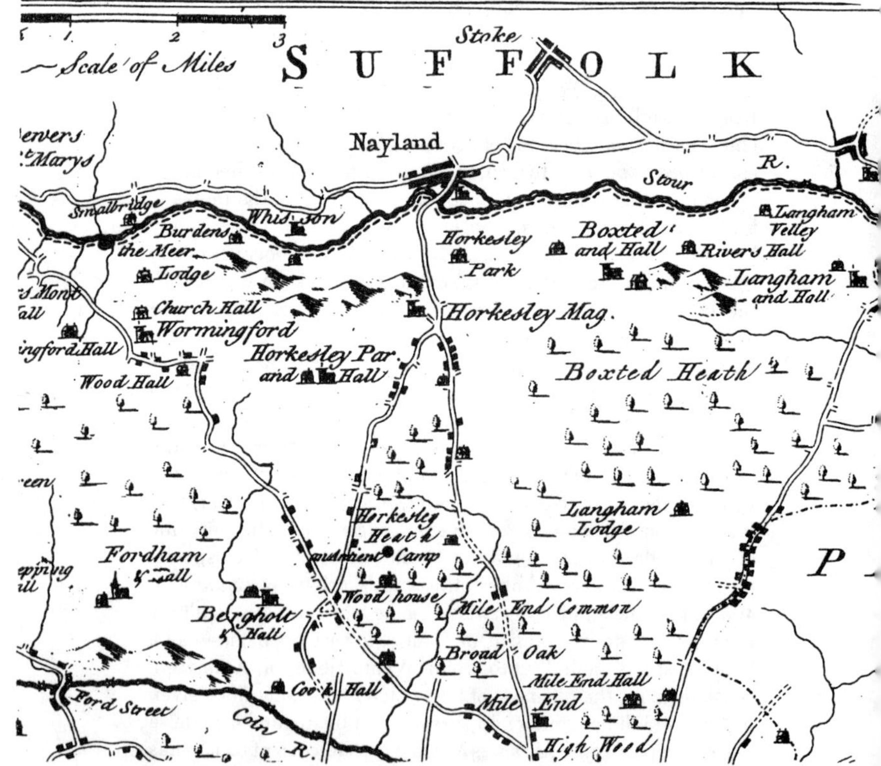

Ref.: Parish Registers; Probate Records at Bury Saint Edmunds

2

GREGORY STONE (*David, Simon, David, Simon, John, Walter, William*) was born in the parish of Great Bromley, Essex, England, and was baptized there on 19 April 1592. He married first, on 20 July 1617 at Nayland, Margaret Garrard, the daughter of Thomas and Christian (Frende) Garrard. She was baptized at Nayland on 5 December 1597 and was buried there on 4 August 1626. He married secondly, about 1627, perhaps at Dedham, Essex, England, Mrs. Lydia Cooper. By her first husband she had two children, John and Lydia.

After his marriage, he lived in Nayland until emigrating to America in 1635. Surely it was his Puritan faith that caused him to leave England for a home in the wilderness of New England. In the Diocesan Registry at Norwich is preserved the visitation of the Arch-deaconry of Sudbury (western Suffolk) for 1629. The following parishoners of Nayland were then presented for refusing to kneel to receive communion: John Warren (#806), John Firmyn, Christopher Scarlett, John Kent and Gregory Stone. A few years later, all these nonconformists, except possibly Scarlett, were in New England. Gregory's brother Simon came to New England in 1635 in the ship *Increase* but the ship in which Gregory arrived is unknown. These brothers first settled in Watertown where they received several parcels of land. He was admitted freeman on 25 May 1636. On 6 February 1636/7, he was granted land in Cambridge and on 21 September 1637 he bought from Roger Harlakenden a house and five acres in Cambridge and about that time moved to Cambridge, then called Newtowne. On 30 September 1639 he sold his Watertown lands. By grant and purchase he later acquired over 400 acres, particularly in Cambridge Farms (now Lexington and Lincoln), where his sons David and Samuel later settled.

On 6 September 1638 he was one of three Representatives from Cambridge to the General Court. This seems to have been his only public office altho he was continually on committees of town affairs. He and his wife were among the signers of a certificate in behalf of Winifred Holman, accused of witchcraft, stating that they "never knew anything in her life concerning witchery."

Gregory Stone of Cambridge, aged about sixty-seven years, deposed that November last he had a black mare colt in the pound, and Joseph Cooke of Cambridge claimed it. It had no mark, but the same day it had a slit given it on the top of one ear and a shred on the middle of the ear cut off, and the pound keeper told deponent that Mr. Cook did it, and Stone brought away the colt. Cooke followed him to his house and told him that he made it. Sworn, 18:7:1658, before Richard Russell, commissioner of Charlestown. Copy.

In 1664 he and three other Cambridge men presented to the General Court a memorial signed by them and about 140 others, protesting against the then proposed government of New England by a Royal Commission, as an arbitrary government in which they were not represented, and contrary to the intent of the original Patent of the Colony. He was a deacon of his church for at least 30 years until his death.

On 22 November 1672, he wrote his will and died a week later on 30 November, aged 80. His widow died on 24 June 1674. They were both buried in the old Cambridge cemetery.

In the name of God, - Amen. I Gregory Stone of Cambridge in New England, being through the Lord's favor of sound Judgment and memory, do make & ordeine my last will & testam[t] in manner following, viz., my imortall soul I do freely resigne into the arms & mercyes of God my maker, Jesus Christ my only redeemer, and to the holy spirit, to carry mee on & lead mee forever, my body to be decently interred at the discrcion of my Xian friends. And for outward state I do dispose thereof as followeth, i. e.

To my daughter Elizab. Potter I do give ten pounds to be p[d] within halfe a years after my decease. To my grandchild Lidea Fiske I do give two acres of land lying in Westfield between y[e] lands of Jn[o] Holmes & Thomas Oakes, to enjoy it as soone as it shall be free of y[e] corne sowne before my decease. To my grandchild Jn[o] Stone sonne of David Stone, I do give my little cow called mode, & my little young colt, or five pounds, provided he live with my wife one year after my decease, & do her faithful service according to his best ability, during which time my wife, shall find him his meat, drink, and cloathing, & at the end of the year deliver him the above named cow & colt. To my dearly beloved wife Lidea Stone, I do leave my dwelling house & lands thereunto adjoyneing, & Pastures, corne lands, meadows, & wood lands, and all the appurtenances thereof, as also my household goods & other moveable estate not above bequeathed (excepting only my wearing cloathes to Jn[o] Stone & David Stone my sonnes). And it is my will that my wife shall enjoy the whole during her life, provided always if shee do marry againe, then at her marriage shee shall resigne the houses &

lands adjoining with the appurtenances to those of my children to whom I shall bequeath the same, and while she enjoys them it is my will that the houses & lands shall in all respects be kept in good repayre, by her, and so left when shee shall leave them. And to my three sonnes, John Stone, Daniel Stone & David Stone, I do bequeath my dwelling house, barne, & lands adjoyneing, being by estimation fifteen acres more or less, also the wood lotts, & priviledges of the comons belonging thereunto, & fifty acres of land liing at my farme, being the half p[t] of one hundred acres y[t] I had there; the other fifty acres I dispose of to my sonnes Samuel Stone & Joseph Meriam. And some addition made mee by the Towne between it and my farme by Isaac Sternes, w[ch] 2 parcells I do order to my sonne David Stone for ten pounds toward his share, and this he shall enjoy imediately after my decease. Also I do give to my said three sonnes the Tables, formes, bedsteads, & copper that are in the dwelling house. And it is my will y[t] when my said sonnes shall come to possess the abovs[d] houses & lands, whether at my wife's death or marriage, w[c]h shall first happen, my will is that it shall be in the liberty of my sonne John Stone to possess the whole, he paying to his other brothers thirty pounds apeece, i. e., to Daniel thirty pounds, & to David twenty pounds, the ten pounds above mentioned being by mee appoynted to make up the thirty. Or if he my sonne John like not so to do, then I do order that they Joyntly sell y[e] whole, & divide y[e] pay, to Jn[o] the one halfe p[t] & to my sonnes Daniel & David the other halfe. And the remainder of my estate in lands, cattell, chattels, moveables, debts, moneys, or w[t]ever, after my deare wife's decease, I do give and bequeath y[e] same to my three youngest children, to be equally divided between them, viz[t] to Elizab. Potter, Samuel Stone, & Sarah Meriam. And I do ordeyne my sonnes John Stone and Samuel Stone, Executors of this my last will & testam , to whome I do comitt the care for their deare mother, my wife. And in testimony that this is my last will, (renouncing all former wills by mee made) I do hereunto put my hand & seale, this 22th of Novemb[r] 1672.

Mem. before the divission be made as above, I do give & bequeath to Jn Cooper ten pounds, & to Lidea Fiske ten pounds, and the remainder to be divided as above is declared.

Sealed & d. d.
In pesence off us
Thomas Danforth sen[r]
Edward Hall
Solomon Prentiss

Gregory
Stone (seal)

Taken upon Oath by all the witnesses subscribed-14.10. 1672
Cambridge december the 13 1672

An Inventory of the Estate of deacon gregory stone whoe departed this life November the 30 apprised by wee whose names are heere to subskribed.

his wearing apparill	£ s d
It shirts bands and handcherifs and Caps . . .	00-13-00
A gray sute a payer of Red drawers . . .	00-18-00
A murry Coate	00-16-00
A tany Coate	00-12-00
A blacke Coate	00-08-00
A serge Cloake	00-10-00

A gray lined Jackit gray	00-06-00
A gray Jackit	00-05-00
A black serge Jackit	00-02-00
An olde Cloth Jackit	00-01-00
A blue payer of brechis and drawers . . .	00-02-00
A Red wastcoate	00-01-06
A gray wastcoate	00-01-06
A mans hoode	00-01-06
A new payer of gloves	00-01-08
A payer of old gloves	00-01-00
A payer of mittins	00-01-00
A payer of moose leather gloves	00-02-00
two payer of stockins	00-03-06
A blacke hat and band	00-04-00
two old hats	00-04-00
three payer of shooes	00-05-00
A payer of bootes	00-02-06
	06-02-08
In the parlor	
A feather bed bolster and two pillowes and pillow beeres	02-13-00
A flocke bed	01-00-00
A payer of Curtains and vallance	00-05-00
A payer of Cotton sheetes	00-15-00
A Coverlit and blancit	00-05-00
A green Rug 24[s] and blancit 9[s]	01-13-00
A flock bed A feather bolster and A pillow and pillow beere .	01-05-00
A payer of sheetes	00-03-00
two blancits	00-12-00
A Coverlit	00-16-00
fower gray Cushins	00-08-00
two feather Cushins	00-01-06
fower Cushins	00-02-00
five Chayers	00-04-00
A winescot Cubard	00-11-00
A winescot Chest	00-10-00
two boxis one more box	00-04-00
fower yards of gray Carsey	01-00-00
A payer of koboyrns and tongs	00-14-00
A warming pan	00-07-00
three baskets and A brush	00-03-06
lining yarne	00-04-00
A looking glas and A grate	00-04-00
A deske	00-01-00
[Farm stock]	
A gray mare and Colt	03-00-00
an old mare and Colt	01-10-00
A hefer 2 yeere olde	02-00-00
A young Cow	03-00-00
one blacke Cow	03-05-00
A Red Cow	03-05-00
A brooken horned Cow	03-00-00
A small hefer	01-10-00
two oxen	11-00-00

two swine A fatting	01-05-00
five swine	02-15-00
twenty five sheepe	12-10-00
	38-00-00
In the hall Chamber	
A Rug and blancit	00-19-00
A payer of Cotten sheetes	00-10-00
two pillowes and beeres	00-10-00
one feather bed and bolster	02-08-00
An olde blancit	00-02-00
teere flax	00-10-00
hose yarne	00-04-00
blue woolle	00-01-04
Cotten wooll	00-11-00
sheepes wooll	01-10-00
lames wooll	00-11-00
fower baskets and A box	00-02-06
A payer of stockards	00-09-00
fower aggors	00-02-00
	08-09-10
In the parlor Chamber	
A mingell Coulered Rug	00-08-00
A bl[ancit] 9^S a payer of sheets 9^S	00-18-00
A bede and bolster	00-10-00
A saddell	00-[10-00]
A panill and wantly [sic] bottom	00-02-06
ould Carte Ropes	00-04-00
Indian Corne	05-06-08
A bee hive 2^s A bage and hops and malt 4^s	00-06-00
sackes and sackin	00-03-06
one $\frac{1}{4}$ parte of A flaxe Combe	00-02-00
pease beanes and A bage	00-03-00
	08-13-08
[In the barn?]	
A beetill and weedgis	00-08-00
3 axis	00-05-06
4 sipths 2^s horselocke and fetters 4^s	00-06-00
A bill hooke 2^s A trowill 1^s	00-03-00
A payer of hookes and Ringe	00-02-00
two bayles for payles	00-01-00
A bolt and shackill 1^s 6^d A hand sawe 2^s	00-03-06
two hammers and A shave	00-02-00
A brande oyrn and A file	00-01-06
A cisell and pincers	00-01-00
A A Coulnter 2 boxis and A bolt	00-05-00
olde oxen [sic]	00-04-06
two pichforks	00-02-06
Color trase and whipletre Chaine	00-03-06
2 ladders 1^s and olde fan 1^s	00-02-00
Rye and wheate	01-04-00
pease 2^s 8^d barly 1^s 4^d	03-12-00
	07-07-00

A dung forke spade and shovell	00-05-00
A whele barrow	00-03-00
A Carte and wheeles	01-00-00
two plowes 13^{s} plowe Chaine and hookes 5^{s} .	00-18-00
A yooke staple and Ringe	00-01-06
A gardin how	00-01-00
	02-08-06
In the buttry	
Two wheeles and A Reele	00-06-00
A Churne 2^{s} 6^{d} scales and weights 2^{s} 6^{d} . .	00-05-00
Cheese fats 2^{s} two payer of Cards 18^{d} . .	00-03-06
trayes and bowles	00-02-00
A Keeler and Coule	00-05-00
4 tubs 3^{s} A Chese pres 3^{s}	00-06-00
two sives 3^{s}	00-03-00
a driping pan A speete and Racks . . .	00-12-00
A gridoyrn and frieing pan	00-05-00
three brase kettells	02-02-06
two brase skillits	00-05-00
A basting ladell and scumer	00-02-00
Rye and Indian meale	00-18-08
	05-17-12
In the Celler	
12 bushells of Apples	00-12-00
tubs 4^{s} beefe and A powdering tub 1^{l} 5^{s} 6^{d} .	01-09-06
beere vesells 12^{s} in Cheese 2^{l} 2^{s} . . .	02-14-00
meshing tub powdering tub	00-07-00
two bushells of wheate	00-08-00
beefe tallow 3^{s} A butter tub and lanthorn 4^{s} .	00-07-00
bowills 7^{s} butter and 2 butter pots 8^{s} . .	00-15-00
two stone bottills 1^{s} a bushell of salt 3^{s} .	00-04-00
Earthen ware 1^{s}	00-01-00
	06-17-06
In the hall	
two sickells 1^{s} 6^{d} A croskut saw 6^{s} . . .	00-07-06
an oyrn for A driping pan	00-02-00
A tramill 3^{s} A tosting oyrn 1^{s}	00-04-00
firpan and tongs	00-02-00
A payer of Coboyrns	00-08-00
A bible 4^{s} and psalme booke 1^{s} . . .	00-05-00
three printed bookes	00-02-00
two oyrn pots and hookes 8^{s} 3 payles 3^{s} . .	00-11-00
wooden dishis 1^{s} Earthen ware 18^{d} . . .	00-02-06
17 peuter dishis great and small . . .	02-00-00
two peuter basons 5^{s} 3 poringers 3^{s}6^{d} . .	00-08-06
three peuter pots and A beaker	00-09-00
16 spoones 2^{s}6^{d} A tunill 6^{d}	00-03-00
two peuter Candlsticks	00-03-00
a pecke and A double hooke	00-02-00
two salt sellers A wine Cup and A saucer .	00-03-06
two peuter Chamber pots and A culinder . .	00-06-00
30 trenchers 1^{s} 6^{d} A Chafing dish 1^{s} 6^{d} . .	00-03-00
A payer of sheers 6^{d}	00-00-06
A fouling peice 1^{l} A muskit firelock 12^{s} .	01-12-00

A muskit sword and bandilers	00-14-00
six Cheesis 4^s6^d two payer of sheetes 1^l5^s .	01-09-06
A payer of Cotten sheetes	00-15-00
A payer of sheetes 10^s three sheetes 5^s . .	00-15-00
A pillow beere 1^s 12 napkins 6^s . . .	00-07-00
two fine pillow beeres	00-11-00
A payer of sheetes	00-11-00
five table Clothes 17^s six towells 3^s . .	01-00-00
	14-00-00
A laced Cubard Cloth	00-12-00
A fine towill	00-03-00
	00-15-00
A table and forme	00-07-00
A table and two formes	01-04-00
the dwelling house barne and orchyard and land adjoining, being 15 akeres more or les with the wood lots and towne Rites	140-00-00
two akers of plow land In the west field . .	05-00-00
fifteene akers of pastur land In the west field .	37-00-00
two akers and A halfe of plow land in the west field	06-05-00
an Aker and halfe of land In the great swampe .	01-00-00
In monyes in the house	02-10-00
In poultry	00-08-00

Tho. ffox x his marke
ffr. Moore
Walter Hasting

Jn° Stone & Samuel Stone Execut[rs] being Sworne do say that this is a true Inventory, & if any more appeare they ad the the same hereto.

Befor Dan[ll] Gookin Assis[t]
& Thomas Danforth R.

Children, born at Nayland, Suffolk, England:

JOHN, bapt. 31 July 1618; m 1639, Ann Roger; 10 ch.; he d 5 May 1683 ae 64; she survived him

DANIEL, bapt. 10 Aug. 1620; m Mary ——— ; 7 ch.; a physician, he moved to Boston; she d 8 Aug. 1658; he d 20 March 1686/7

DAVID, bapt. 22 Sept. 1622; m 1, Elizabeth ——— ; 1 son d.y.; m 2, Dorcas ——— ; 6 ch.; he d 16 Jan. 1703/4; she d 13 July 1704; a cooper; res. Cambridge Farms

ELIZABETH, bapt. 3 Oct. 1624; buried 6 Aug. 1626 at Nayland

-----by second wife, Lydia-----

ELIZABETH, bapt. 6 March 1628/9; m about 1652, Anthony Potter of Ipswich; 7 ch.; she d at Ipswich 10 March 1712 ae 83 - g.s.

SAMUEL, bapt. 20 Feb. 1630/31; m 7 June 1655, Sarah, b 22 Sept. 1635, dau. of Isaac Stearns of Watertown; 8 ch.; she d 26 Oct. 1700; he m 2, Abigail (Carter)(Fowle) Walker of Woburn, widow of Lt. James Fowle & Deacon Samuel Walker; he d 27 Sept. 1715; she d 11 May 1718

SARAH, bapt. 8 Feb. 1632/3; m at Concord 12 July 1653, Joseph Merriam jr.; 9 ch.; he d 20 April 1677 ae 47 - g.s.; she d 8 April 1704

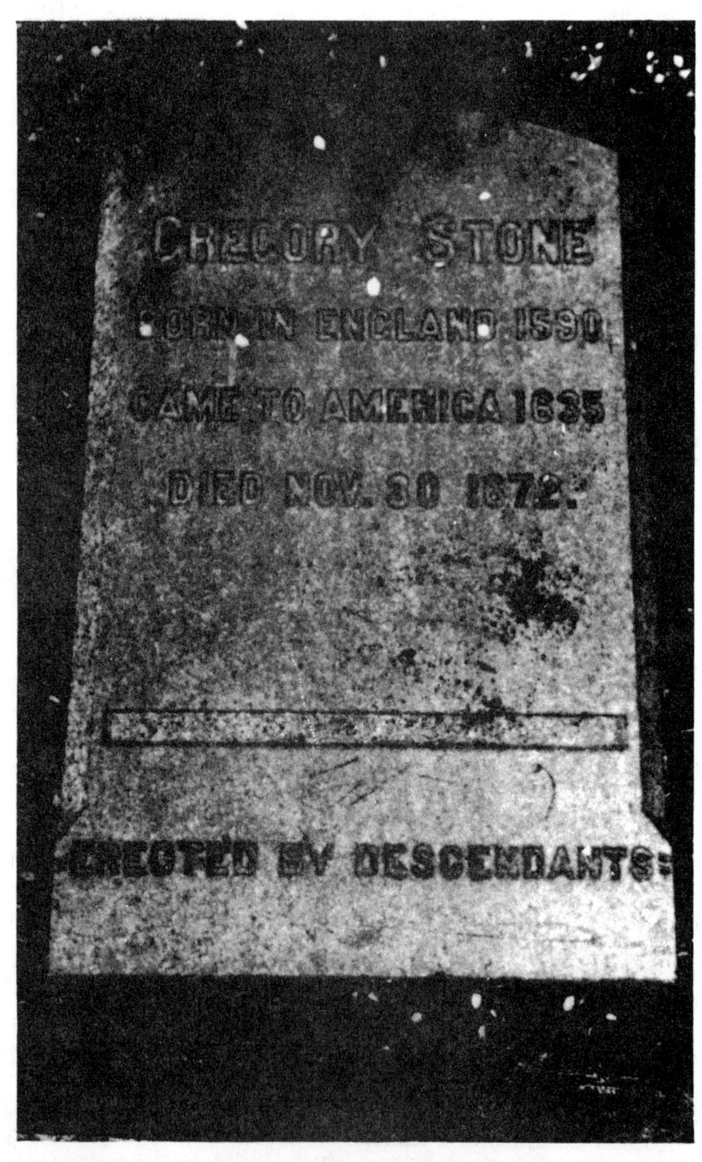

Ref.: Gregory Stone Genealogy; Middlesex Probate 21596; V.R.; Savage; History of Cambridge, by Lucius R. Page, 1877; Parish Registers; Essex County Quarterly Files

6

THOMAS GARRARD ((*John*) was baptized 14 March 1561/2 at Nayland, Suffolk, England. Thomas married 10 June 1591 at Nayland, Christian Frende. She must have died and he remarried to Sarah _____, for Sarah, late wife of Thomas Garrard, deceased, was buried 31 January 1626/7.

Children, all baptized at Nayland:

CHILD, perhaps, b early 1592 and bapt. in another parish from which the mother came?

MARY, bapt. 26 Dec. 1593; buried 22 April 1594

THOMAS, bapt. 21 Dec. 1595; buried 27 June 1597 (the surname in the burial record is not clear - "Garad"?)

3 MARGARET, bapt. 5 Dec. 1597; m 20 July 1617, Gregory Stone, son of David & Ursula (_____) Stone; he was bapt. 19 April 1592 at Great Bromley, Essex; 4 ch.; she was buried 4 Aug. 1626 at Nayland; he m 2, Mrs. Lydia Cooper and went to N.E. in 1635; he d 30 Nov. 1672, aged 80; Lydia d 24 June 1674; both buried old Cambridge cemetery

CHILDREN: perhaps 2 or 3 born 1599 to 1603 altho there is no record of them in the Nayland parish register

KATHERINE, bapt. 1 Jan. 1604/5

The Church of Saint James Nayland, Suffolk

Ref.: Gregory Stone Genealogy; Parish Registers

SAINT GEORGE'S CHURCH, GREAT BROMLEY, ESSEX
Gregory Stone was baptized in this church.

12

JOHN GARRARD (*John?*) was probably the son of John Garrard who was buried 22 March 1577 at Nayland, Suffolk. John's wife was apparently named Jane, for in the Nayland parish register is recorded the burial on 26 January 1598/9 of Jane, wife of John Garrard, householder. John Garrard "the elder" was buried there 29 November 1601. No will has ever been found. The fact that he was designated "the elder" implies that a younger John Garrard was then living in or near Nayland. In this case, the chronology and limited information available seems to indicate that the younger John Garrard was a brother, not a son. This younger John made his will 6 September 1617 and it was proved 20 January 1617/18. He named his son John, his grandson John (by his son John), his youngest son Edward whom he named to be executor, daughters Katherine and Margaret, and son John's wife (but not by name). He left money for the poor of Nayland and Bures Saint Mary, the next parish, and referred to lands in Wyston and Assington. The younger John's son John apparently was the John Garrard who married Margaret Christopher 9 November 1581 at Bures Saint Mary. Her surname is not at all clear in the register. There is an x abbreviation which usually means Christ, and then a superscript which might be *er*. This younger John had nine recorded grandchildren by his son John, of which four were then alive and of these, grandson John was aged 20 and the youngest. Edward Garrard, a householder, who was buried at Nayland 28 April 1612, was probably a brother of these two Johns.

Children, baptized at Nayland:

WILLIAM, bapt. 24 June 1560; buried 23 Sept. 1564

6 THOMAS, bapt. 14 March 1561/2; m 10 June 1591, Christian Frende. He m 2, Sarah ——— who was bur. 31 Jan. 1626/7; he d earlier

GEORGE, bapt. 14 March 1561/2, apparently a twin to Thomas; m ———; ch.: Mary bapt. 24 Jan. 1601/2, Dorothy bapt. 5 Jan. 1603/4, Joan bapt. 27 April 1609. He was buried 20 Jan. 1609/10, "a householder".

NICHOLAS, prob. b about 1564-8; m Frances ———; ch.: Rebecca bapt. 27 feb. 1592/3, Ann bapt. 3 July 1595, William bapt. 21 Feb. 1599/60. He was buried 16 May 1617. She died testate 1634

16 July 1634 - the will of Frances Garrard of Nayland, county Suffolk, widow, sick in body ... to Rebecca Smith my daughter £4 ... to my daughter Ann Barber 40s ... to my grandchild Jeremy Barber 40s ... to my grandchild Joseph Smith 10s ... to Sarah Smith my grandchild 10s .. to my two grandchildren Rebecca Barber and Ann Barber 10s each ... to Jeremy Barber the long table in my chamber to Sara Smith my great chest now standing at my bed's feet ... house in Nayland to be sold within one year and the money to be distributed as aforesaid ... residue to my son William Garrard except 10s. to be paid to my executor and 30s. to my grandchild Rebecca Smith ... kinsman Edward Houlton to be executor. Witnesses: George Pratt, Paul Wood. Signed by mark. Proved 10 September 1634 (Ref.: W1/94/117 & R2/58/68)

MARGARET, buried 2 Nov. 1573, "dau. of John Garrard"

SAINT JAMES'S CHURCH, NAYLAND, SUFFOLK

Reproduced from *Ecclesiastical Antiquities of the County of Suffolk*, 1818, by Isaac Johnson — courtesy of the County Record Office, Suffolk, England

Ref.: Parish Register of Nayland; Probate Records at Bury Saint Edmunds

WILLIAM STRAW first appears in Amesbury, Massachusetts about 1683 when he married Mehetable, probably the daughter of John and Frances Hoyt. Where he came from is a mystery. Possibly he came from Virginia or Barbados, where the name is found in early records. He may have had his origins with the Straw family that lived in and around Glemsford, Suffolk, England in the sixteenth and seventeenth centuries. There was a William Straw living in Glemsford in 1638. Here the family also used the *alias* Lawrence. This leads one to suspect a connection with these Glemsford Straws, for William Straw named his youngest son Lawrence.

Mehetable died about 1688-91, and about 1691, William Straw remarried to Margaret ______ . William Straw made his will on 23 May 1709, and it was proved on 2 October 1712. On 31 May 1709, he deeded land to John Challis. He was a tailor, farmer and a sargeant.

> I William Straw of Almsbury in y^e^ County of Essex, in her Majest^s^ province of y^e^ Massachusets bay in New England Taylor - being through the goodness of God of perfect memory & understanding, Do make this my last will & Testament in forme & manner following. Imprimis I commend my spirit to God who gave it, & my body to ye dust from whence it was taken in full assurance y^t^ I shall receive it again at ye gener^ll^ Resurrection - Nextly what worldly goods & estate God hath been pleased to bless me withall I dispose of as followeth: viz:- I Give & bequeath unto my eldest son William Straw all my housing & land, & a payr of two year old steers, & my largest Iron Kettle To have & to hold to himself his Heirs & Assigns for ever. He ye s^d^ William Straw paying or causing to be payd out of ye premises all my just debts & funerall charges. And ye sum of Eight pounds to my son John Straw And ye sum of twenty shillings to my Daughter Dorothy Trell relict of John Trell dec^d^ or to their respective Heirs or Assigns at my now dwelling place in Almsbury in mony or other good pay to their Satisfaction at price as it is worth in mony within ye space of seven years next after my decease wch I give & bequeath to each of them as their full portion out of my estate always provided that this my bequest unto my s^d^ son William Straw be not so interpreted or Improved as in ye least to Infringe upon ye Thirds or legal right of Dowrie of Margaret my now wife wch I leave & commend unto her own dispose & Improvement during ye term of her natural life - - - - - - - - - - - - - - - - - -
> It I Give & bequeath all ye rest of my estate of what sort soever it be unto my s^d^ Wife Margaret & my sons Samuel Straw & Lawrence Straw in equal proportion or to their Heirs or Assigns respectively as their full portion out of my estate - -
> ffinally I make constitute & ordaine my s^d^ eldest son William Straw sole Execut^r^ to this my Last will & Testament - - - -
> And in Confirmac̃ of ye premises I have hereunto subscribed my Hand & Seal ye Twenty third day of May In ye Eighth year of ye Reign of our Sovern Lady Anne by ye Grace of God of

Great Brittain France & Ireld Queen Defender of ye Faith Annoq Dom One Thousd seven hundred & Nine

Signd Seald & published to be his last Will & Testament in ye presence of us

Joseph Hoyt
Jacob Bagly
Theophilus Iersson (?)

William Straw

An Inventory of the Estate of Sargent Willm Straw

	£ s d
his waring clothes	3-00-0
an Iorn pott and 2 kittells	1-04-0
Lumbor housallstof	1-00-0
sheeps wool	0-10-0
a hous Land barn and outhut	81-00-0
plow bridl	0-06-0
10 sheep	3-00-0
2 -2 year old steers	3-00-0
a mare and collt	4-00-0
2 calves	1-00-0
hay In the barn	2-00-0
3 swin	2-05-0
chest and beding	3-00-0
	105- 5-0

James Ring Jnu
William Straw

Sworn p Execrs - Novr. 3. 1712

Children, born at Amesbury:

DOROTHY, b about 1684; m 1, 30 July 1707 at Concord, John Trull, prob. the son of John & Sarah (French) Trull of Billerica, b 13 July 1669, & a widower with 2 ch., his wife having d 3 Jan. 1698/9. She was a widow in 1709; m 2, int. 9 Dec. 1710, Luke Wells, b 19 March 1673/4, son of Rev. Thomas & Mary (Perkins) Wells; 3 sons; she d 29 Sept. 1715 at Amesbury; Dorothy Straw filed intention of m 21 Nov. 1706 to Stephen Merrill, but apparently they didn't marry

WILLIAM, b 22 May 1686; m 13 July 1713 at Amesbury, Lydia Purington of Salisbury; 9 ch.

JOHN, b 1 July 1688 at Amesbury, "2nd son"; m 20 or 30 April 1710 at Amesbury, Lydia Sargent; d Nov. 1750 at kingston, N.H.; 8 ch.

----by second wife, Margaret----

SAMUEL, b 13 Aug. 1692 at Amesbury; m 12 Dec. 1717 at Amesbury, Elizabeth Diamond, dau. of Israel & Abigail (Prowse) Diamond, b 7 May 1697; 9 ch.; S. Hampton 1745, Kingston 1759

LAWRENCE, b 31 May 1699 at Amesbury; m 3 June 1725 at Amesbury, Abiel Jewell (or Abigail), b 7 Nov. 1702, dau. of John & Hannah (Prowse) Jewell; 9 ch. b at Amesbury; S. Hampton 1756; Kingston 1757; d 1762; will signed by mark.

*A William Straw, son of Bernard & Dorcas Straw, was baptized on 1 January 1662/3 at St. Katherine by the Tower, London.

A William Straw, son of William & Mary, was baptized 14 January 1649 at St. Dunstan's in Stepney, London.

Ref.: Essex County Probate 26817; Vital Records

DUNCAN STUART, the name sometimes spelled as Stewart, first appears on record at Ipswich, Massachusetts in 1654 when at the Quarterly Court held in March of that year:

> Duncan Stewartt and An Winchest were sentenced to be whipped for fornication, the man that afternoon and the woman when she should be called out by the magistrates, after she was delivered. Together they were to bring up the child and pay the charges.

Ann Winchest was a servant, that is, an employee. In 1652, her master was John Cogswell who, with the consent of the court, assigned her to Cornelius Waldo in September of that year. In September of 1653 Ann deposed regarding a statement by her mistress Waldo. Ann must have come to New England as an indentured servant girl, probably an orphan, a few years earlier, for there is no record of this surname in New England other than for her. It is a rare place name. It appears once in the index of Oxfordshire probate records for George Winchurst, gentleman, of Culham, 1690.

Duncan Stewart and Ann Winchurst must have been married in 1654. There is no more record of her under her maiden name and Duncan's wife was named Ann.

As for Duncan Stuart, he was probably one of the Scot prisoners taken at the Battle of Dunbar on 3 June 1650 by Cromwell's forces. Many of these unfortunate men were shipped off as indentured servants and sold to the colonists for an arbitrary term of servitude. His name is not on the list of similar prisoners shipped over after the battle of Worcester exactly one year later, altho admittedly there are a few illegible names on the list. Most of these latter prisoners were sold for terms of up to ten years. The fact that Duncan Stuart seems to have gained his liberty and married in a much shorter time suggests that he was among the earlier unrecorded group, that is, those men taken at Dunbar.

Duncan Stuart had a house lot in Ipswich in 1656. About 1659 he and his family moved to Newbury. Here he was chosen as a fence-viewer on 22 March 1685/6, and also a tithing-man. His name is on the Newbury tax list of August 1688. Shortly thereafter he moved to Rowley where his name appears on the records for the first time in 1689. He apparently first considered moving to Scarboro, Maine, where he bought 100 acres at Blue Point from Timothy Collins in December 1680. He was taxed there in 1681, but apparently never lived there. He sold the property to Francis Wainwright in 1708. He was assessed £2 on the Rowley tax list of 1691. In an Essex county deed in 1698 he is called "laborer". He was aged about 75 according to a deposition of 1698 in the Suffolk County Court File (SJC 3784). He was living on 16 March 1702/3 "northwest of Rye Plain Bridge and Long Hill" when the minister's rates were abated. A deed of 1704 describes him as "late of Newbury, but now of Rowley". Of two deeds he acknowledged in 1708, he was called *Planter* in one and *Husbandman* in the other.

Duncan Stuart died 30 August 1717, "Aged tis tho't abot 100 yrs". According to his statement made in 1698, he would have been 94, and thus would have been born about 1623 and would have been about 27 at the time of the Battle of Dunbar. Ann died at Rowley 9 July 1729.

Children:

CHILD, b 1654, must have d.y.

KATHERINE, b 8 June 1658 at Ipswich; prob. m Paul Wentworth before 1681; 13 ch. bapt. at Rowley; he deposed in April 1739 as age 79

MARTHA, b 4 April 1659; perhaps m John Wentworth by 28 Aug. 1679; he was in Canton Mass. by 1704, of Boston 1716; Martha was of Boston 1709; 6 or more ch.

CHARLES, b 5 June 1661; prob. d.y. as no further record of him

ELIZABETH, b 2 Nov. 1662; m Sylvanus Wentworth, 7 Nov. 16__; a dau. Elizabeth b 27 Aug. 1689 at Rowley

JAMES, b 8 Oct. 1664; m Elizabeth ____ ; ch.: James 29 July 1688, Charles 16 Jan. 1689/90, Edward, Elizabeth

JOHN, b about 1666-7; m Elizabeth ____ ; ch.: Elizabeth b 11 Dec. 1689; his wife d 20 Dec. 1689

HENRY, b 1 May 1669 at Newbury

SAMUEL, b about 1671 at Newbury; m 30 Jan. 1700/01 at Wells, Me., Dorcas Baston; he was a carpenter & innholder; 8 ch. all b at Wells: Samuel 1704, Joseph 1706, John 1709, Zebulon 1713, Jeremiah 1716, Dorcas 1718, Amos 1722 - d.y., Amos 1724; Dorcas was a widow & school mistress in March 1752

HANNAH, b about 1673; m Colin Fraser

EBENEZER, b about 1676; m Elizabeth ____ who d 12 April 1749 ae "about 72" at Newbury; he d 30 April 1749 ae "about 73" testate; ch.: Ann bapt. 6 April 1712, Charles bapt. 1 June 1718

Ref.: Essex County Quarterly Court Files; History of Newbury, by Currier, by Coffin; Early Settlers of Rowley, Mass., by Blodgette & Jewett; Savage; Vital Records; Genealogical Dictionary of Maine & New Hampshire, by Noyes, Libby, Davis

THAKE

Hertfordshire, England

Contributed by William Haslet Jones, Villa Park, Illinois. Joanna Thake married Samuel Richardson in England. They and their two children emigrated to Massachusetts about 1636. The Thake family resided in Barkway, Hertfordshire.

2

WILLIAM THAKE (*Richard, John, John, John*) was baptized 11 August 1571 at Barley Parish, county Hertfordshire. He was married on 4 January 1597/8 to Joan Wood, the daughter of   Wood of the adjacent parish of Therfield. She was baptized in Therfield on 27 September 1574 and was buried at Barkway on 14 May 1621 (see the Wood Family for her ancestry).

William Thake was buried 25 October 1630 at Barkway. An abstract of his will follows.

> 25 September 1630 - the will of WILLIAM THAKE - of Nuthampstead in the parish of Barkway, Malster ... sick in body ... I give to the poor of Nuthampstead 5s, I give to Annis Rugbye my daughter 5s, I give to William Thake my son my leaden diskerne, etc. to the said William my executor hereafter named, I give to Stephen Thake my son £6, I give to Joan Thake my daughter £20, I give to Winifred Thake my daughter £20, I give to Mary Thake my daughter £20, I give to Fortune Thake my daughter £20 ... at age 21 ... residue to my son William Thake & he to be my sole executor. Witnesses: Andrew Duxford, Symon Heris. (Essex 50BW64)

Children:

ANNYS, m .... Rugbye

WILLIAM, bapt. 11 Feb. 1598; m 27 June 1630 Grace Duxford (related to Duxfords at Westmill), dau. of Andrew & Agnes Duxford. Had: William bapt. 30 Nov. 1634, John bapt. 20 Aug. 1637, Andrew bapt. 10 April 1640, and Stephen

JOHN, bapt. 20 May 1606; buried 5 Jan. 1606/7

1 JOANNA, bapt. 2 Feb. 1606/7; m 18 Oct. 1632 Samuel Richardson

WINIFRED, bapt. 28 Dec. 1609; alive 1630

MARY, bapt. 29 March 1612; m 10 Oct. 1633, William Madle

ROBERT, bapt. 9 Oct. 1614; buried 5 March 1622/3

FORTUNE, bapt. 2 Nov. 1617; m 18 Oct. 1638 John Cottise; had: John bapt. 1640 and Marie bapt. 1646. Fortune was buried 1652

(See WYMAN-RICHARDSON Lineage)

Ref.: Hertfordshire Parish Records; Essex Wills

4

RICHARD THAKE (*John, John, John*) was born about 1550 at the parish of Clavering, county Essex. He was buried at Barkway on 15 May 1589. His wife's name was Margaret. She was buried 1 October 1600. The family resided at the village of Nuthampstead, within the parish of Barkway. An abstract of his will follows.

> 5 May 1589 - the will of RICHARD THAKE - of Nuthampsted in the parish of Barkway, and my body to be buried in the churchyard of Barkway, I give to the poor of Nuthampsted 5s, I give to Margaret my wife 30s to be paid yearly by William my son, I give to Margaret my daughter £10, I give to Joan my daughter £10, I give to Will'm my son one acre of free land lying in little w'wick. Residue of all my stuff to Margaret my wife, and I ordain Margaret my wife and Will'm my son executors, Thos. Canon to be overseer. Wit. Thos. Canon, John X'len, Will'm Kepford. Proved 10 January 1589/90. (Essex 258BW37)

Children:

MARGARET, bapt. 7 Aug. 1569 at Barley; m 27 July 1592 Anthony Pigram at Brent Pelham

2 WILLIAM, bapt. 11 Aug. 1571 at Barley; m 4 Jan. 1597/8 Joan Wood

ANNIS, buried 13 Feb. 1574/5 at Barkway

JOAN, bapt. 20 Feb. 1575/6; m 23 Oct. 1596 John Morris

STEPHEN, m 15 July 1591 at Barley, Margaret Patten

JOHN, m widow Sprak, 15 Oct. 1612; he was buried 6 March 1648; she was buried 19 Feb. 1664/5; had: Mary bapt. 1614, d 1620/21

RICHARD, m ____ ; had: Richard bapt. 1616 & Mary bapt. 1618

Ref.: Hertfordshire Parish Records; Essex Wills

8

JOHN THAKE (*John, John*) was born about 1525 probably at the parish of Clavering, county Essex. He was a malster (brewer) by trade. His will names his wife Agnes and his four sons. He died in the spring of 1568.

> 30 May 1568 - the will of JOHN THAKE the elder of Clavering, malster, and my body to be buried in the church yard of Clavering ... I give to John Thake my son two obligations due me ... I give to William my son one cow ... I give to Richard my son 20s, ... I give to Steven Thake my son £10 delivered at the day of his marriage, the residue of all my goods I give to Agnes my wife whom I ordain executrix. Witnesses: Willm Holgle, the elder; George Daye, the younger; Willm Dellowe; Edward Brooke & Robert Bathe. Proved 22 June 1568. (Essex, 148BW37)

Children:

JOHN, alive in 1568; eldest son

WILLIAM, b about 1548; m 1, 16 Oct. 1569 Grace Wende at Barley. She d 1582; he m 2, 2 May 1584, Agnes Meriton; had: Agnes bapt. 1574, Joane bapt. 1570, Richard bapt. 1577, Edward d 1580, William bapt. 1580 - d 1630, Ann bapt. & d 1581, Ann bapt. 1582, Thomas bapt. 1583, Grace bapt. 1586 Elizabeth bapt. 1587

4 RICHARD, alive 1568

STEVEN, m ____ ; had: Stephen bapt. 1572, John bapt. 1575

AGNES, m 5 July 1555, Thomas Jypps

KATHERINE, m 3 March 1562, Stephen Gippes

GEORGE, m 10 April 1559, Joan Godfrey

THE PARISH CHURCH, CLAVERING, ESSEX

Ref.: Hertfordshire Parish Records; Essex Wills

16

JOHN THAKE (*John*) probably was born about 1490 at Clavering. In 1533, he and John Hager bought 6 acres of [arable] land, 3 acres of meadow, and 5 acres of pasture in Great Chishill, Essex, for £40. In 1535, he and John Mosse bought a messuage, 14 acres of [arable] land, 1 acre of meadow, and 2 acres of pasture in Clavering, Essex for 40 marks, (Essex Feet of Fines). His wife may have been the widow Joan Thake who left a will in 1547. Her will is dated 9 November 1547 and was proved 14 January 1547/8 (Essex 122CR3). She gave most of her property to her brother, Richard Hager, and his family.

Children:

8 JOHN

JOAN, named in 1547 will

32

JOHN THAKE was born perhaps in 1465 at Clavering. John was married twice. From his will, we learn the names of his wives, Katherine and Agnes. Both preceeded him in death. His will is dated 3 April 1504

> 3 April 1504 - the will of JOHN THAKE of Clavering ... my body to be buried in the church of Clavering by the image of the blessed Virgin Mary ... to the high alter 3s4d. ... I bequeath to John Jr. my son all my goods, lands & tenements etc, ... to celebrate the souls of Katherine and Agnes my late wives ... I ordain the said John my executor. Witnesses: William Thake, John Byrlyng, George Canan, John Vawdy
>
> (Essex 96CR2)

Children:

16 JOHN Jr.

Ref.: Hertfordshire Parish Records; Essex Wills

ALEXANDER THOMPSON was born and grew up in Scotland. According to various depositions, he was born sometime between 1627 and 1631.

On 3 September 1650 Oliver Cromwell defeated the Royalists at Dunbar and took ten thousand Scots prisoner. Three thousand had fallen, fighting hopelessly to the last. Cromwell lost twenty men. After this battle there was a year of military jockeying for position, with Charles II avoiding a battle and gradually marching southward towards London, hoping to reinforce his army.

A year to the day after Dunbar, the young King decided to cross swords once more with Cromwell at Worcester. The same results ensued. Cromwell decscribed it as "the crowning mercy of the Lord," as nightfall found the enemy in flight, and Charles a fugitive, disguised as a cook.

Cromwell's forces again had taken numbers of prisoners whose fate had to be determined. Within two days of the battle, the Council at London ordered that all the officers taken with the Earl of Derby and every tenth private soldier should be put on trial for rebellion. This naturally meant that every officer and tenth soldier would pay the supreme penalty. There is a tradition among the descendants of one of these prisoners that when the lines were drawn for picking out every tenth soldier, he counted down the rows and found that he would probably be one of those selected for trial. Breaking rank, he took the desperate chance of escape or being shot. A mounted officer pursued and wounded him, and his life was spared. Further consideration was given to the disposition of these captives and they were finally marched to London under guard and herded to Tothill Field at the Artillery Grounds, about a half mile west of Parliament House. On September 16, it was proposed that a thousand of these prisoners be sent to Bristol for shipment to New England, but there is no record that this was done. Such Scottish ministers as were prisoners were to be exported, one to every two hundred men, but these clergymen were to be free from compulsory service.

As a result of various proposals, an unknown number, perhaps three hundred, were selected for transportation to New England. Becx and Company of London, who had interests in the Lynn iron works, sawmills, and other businesses in New England, had trafficed in the prisoners of Dunbar the year before. They were again interested in the prisoner labor potentials, and the ship *John and Sarah* was chartered to bring them to Boston. The master of this ship was John Greene of Charlestown, a merchant who owned lands in Maine, was a dealer in lumber, and had interests in sawmills in Durham and Newmarket in New Hampshire. The identity of this ship, probably a New England vessel, is not certain. A ship of 39 tons of this name was sold here in 1648 to Robert Allen of Norwich and Nicholas Davison of London, but it is difficult to think of this small craft as the one which brought the prisones over, although Davison was a resident of Charlestown at one time and had intimate business connections in New England.

All arrangements having been made, the cosigners, Becx, Rich and Greene, gave the following instructions to the master of the transport.

London, this 11th: of November 1651

Capt. Jno. Greene - Wee whose names are under written freighters of your shipe the John & Sara doe Order you forthwith as winde & weather shall permit to sett saile for Boston in New England & there deliver our Orders and Servants to Tho: Kemble of Charles Towne to be disposed of by him according to orders wee have sent him in that behalfe & wee desire yow to advise with the said Kemble about all that may conserne that whole Intended voiage using your Indeavors with the said Kemble for the speediest lading your shipp from New Eng. to the barbadoes with provisions and such other things as are in N. E. fitt for the west Indies where yow are to deliver them to mr. Charles Rich to be disposed of by him for the Joinct accont of the freighters & so to be Retourned home in a stocke undivided thus desiring your care & Industrie in dispatch and speed of the voiage wishing yow a happy & safe Retourne wee Remaine your loving friends.

Signatum et Recognitum
in pncia: Jo: Nottock notar Publ:
13 May, 1652

John Becx
Robt Rich
Will Greene

Captain Greene probably left the Downes on 8 December and with the usual time to make the trip, arrived in Boston certainly before 24 February following, and landed 272 of those taken on board at London. The usual toll of scurvey must have taken about ten percent of the total number.

This second consignment of human cargo found a wider distribution among the towns of Massachusetts and nearby provinces, as news of the first had whetted the greed of those who failed to procure cheap labor the year before. They were sold as before to planters and mill owners throughout the colonies in this section for terms of six to eight years of labor. The arrangement had the sanction of John Cotton and that was enough to deaden the New England Puritan conscience. More of these prisoners were sent to the southern colonies and to the West Indies than were to New England, but the morality was the same.

Evidently, the prisoners were sold at Boston, and those destined for the Lynn iron works were marched from Boston to Lynn, a trip that took two days with one death along the way.

Among the men listed on the manifest of the *John and Sarah* was Alexander Thompson. He was sold to Robert Starkweather, formerly of Roxbury, who sold his interests there about this time and moved to Ipswich.

Although it is not supposed that there was any general abuse of these prisoners, euphemistically called Apprentices, inevitably this bondage resulted in complaints, and on 23 May 1655 several of them petitioned the General Court of the Massachusetts Bay Colony for their freedom, but their request was denied.

The first record of Alexander Thompson in New England is eight years later in November 1659 when Daniel Black, a fellow prisoner of the Battle of Worcester, sued him for a debt of wheat and malt and a hat. Both no doubt had their liberty by that time.

On 19 September 1662 he married Deliverance Haggett, daughter of Henry and Elizabeth Haggett of nearby Wenham and formerly of Ipswich.

In June 1667 his age was given as about 40, which places his birth about 1627. At the court of September 1667 John Clerke sued Alexander "Tompson" and his wife for slander and obtained a verdict. The slander charge arose from a complaint, dated 17 August 1667, of Alexander Thompson and wife Deliverance against John Clerke of Wenham: "She said that on July 18, Clerke came into her house with her husband to light their pipes of tobacco, and after her husband had gone to reaping, Clerke smoked awhile and going to the end of the house called to her husband to come in and smoke. He answered that he would when they had carried another end. Clerke came back and tried to kiss her, but having her child in her arms, the child cried out", etc. On 20 August, upon further testimony of Hannah Welsh, John Clerke was bound to good behavior and Thompson was bound to prosecute and Hannah Welsh and Henry Haggett were to appear as witnesses. Robert Colbourne, aged about sixty years, deposed that Clerke asked Thompson's wife why she raised such false reports of him, etc. Apparently the slander verdict was the result of the charges being made and not being followed up with prosecution and proof. The witness, Henry Haggett, was either her father or her brother. Hannah Welsh was her sister. Deliverance, like her parents, was apparently prone to quarrelling.

In November 1674 Alexander Thompson, aged about forty-six years, deposed that he had "loaned Lt. Nath. Brown a pair of sheep shears at the last shearing time and said that Brown returned another pair, which he claimed were the same which he put in the bottom of his bag of wool before the men went from home. Later, his brother John brought back the right shears and the deponent took others home to Nathaniel, both their wives being present with them."

Alexander Bravand (1613 - 1678) in his will provided that four of his fellow Scots, one of whom was Alexander Thompson, should receive some of his goods.

On 17 April 1679, Alexander Thompson, aged about forty-eight years, deposed that when he lived with his master Starkweather about twenty-seven years ago, "this meadow was then called John White's meadow, and the very ditch which was now broken down was then full of cocks of hay in White's day." In November 1679, he gave testimony on the extent of damages done by hogs rooting in a meadow.

In March 1680, Daniel Davison complained that when he went to Lumass's house to complain of the damage his swine had done to his corn, Lumass called him a Scotch rogue, and told him to get out of his ground or he would knock him down, he having a ten pound rock in his hand.

Alexander Thompson heard Lumass at Graves's house calling Davison a limb of the devil, saying that all Scotchmen were hypocrites and devils.

On 3 November 1683 Alexander Thompson of Ipswich bought from the widow Hubbard of Ipswich for £59, a piece of land of about ten acres lying on the east side of Perry's Brook. The deed was not recorded until 29 May 1728.

He made his will on 21 November 1693 and it was probated in April 1696. He died 17 December 1695 and he was survived by his wife. His will reads:

> "I Alexander Tomson of Ipswich ... Being at this time Crasey of Body but in perfect understanding and deposing memory ..."

He left everything to his wife for life or as long as she remained a widow, then two thirds of the land and housing to his son David, the other third of the land to son John. This indicates that David was the eldest son who was getting the customary double share. David and John were to pay £5 to each of the other children. His widow was to be sole executrix. He signed the will by mark.

Children, probably all born at Ipswich:

DAVID, b 19 May 1664; m Mary ——— before 1693; 7 ch.: Mary 1694, David 1696, John 1698/9, Hannah 1700, Jacob 1703, Martha 1704/5 - d.y., Mercy 1706. He d early 1706; in 1697 he served in military for which his son John received land in New Ipswich, N.H., 1735. She m 2, 22 June 1717 James Patch

MARY, prob. b about 1666; unm. 1729 when she admininstered her brother Alexander's estate

ELIZABETH, prob. b about 1668; an Elizabeth Thompson m James Johnson of Greenland, New Hampshire; int. 25 Sept. 1708

JOHN, b about 1670; aged 13 per deposition of Feb. 1683/4 (41:37); "of Ipswich" 1707 and 23 Nov. 1723 when he gave to/received from John Thorne deeds for the 4 acres he inherited; no rec. of a family, no estate

HANNAH, prob. b about 1672; m Stephen England of Newbury

WILLIAM, prob. b about 1674; named in father's will of 1693; no further rec. found

ALEXANDER, prob. b about 1676; m 3 Aug. 1699 at Ipswich, Mary, widow of ____ Snell (Snelling?); a fisherman; his estate administered by sister Mary Thompson 1729; 4 daus.: Mary, Eliza, Hannah, Sarah. He signed a note 16 April 1729, so d soon after

HENRY, prob. b about 1678; mentioned in father'a will of 1693 but no more record of him; no deeds

SARAH, b about 1680; m 3 Jan. 1704/5, Joseph Ingalls at Chebacco; he d 1724; 5 ch.

MATTHEW, prob. b about 1682; m Catherine ____ about 1710 in Stratham, N.H. and d there 23 March 1754 ("Old Mr. Mathew Thompson died" - T.R.)

Ref.: Early Inhabitants of Ipswich, Hammatt; Essex Quarterly Court Records; Probate 27481; Deeds 42:50 - 51, 50:162; N.E.H.G.S. - 1:378; Published V.R.

RICHARD THORLEY (Tharly, Thurla, Thurlow, etc.) settled in Rowley, Massachusetts, sometime before April 1640 when his daughter Lydia was born there. With him was his wife Jane and at least three children. Just where in England they came from is unknown. He was one of the original proprietors and in 1643 had a two acre house lot on Weathersfield Street, "bounded on the west side by Mr. Edward Carlton's house lot and on the south end by the street". At various times he received other allotments from the town, about nine in all, and a total of about 27 acres of meadow and marsh land.

He was made a freeman 28 March 1648, was on the trial jury in 1651, the grand jury in 1653. In 1651 he sold his property in Rowley to Captain John Johnson and moved to Newbury where he bought another farm.

> 1 December 1651 - Mathew Chaffey of Boston, shipwright, and Sarah his wife, convey to Richard Thorley, for £155, a farm in Newbury containing 400 acres, bounded from the mouth of Cart Creek and extending thence easterly ten score rods and abutting on the river to the south, thence on a line north and by west sixteen score rods up into the country unto two birchen trees, marked, standing upon a bank of rocks, thence on a straight line westerly ten score rods to a tree standing upon a mound or a hill, thence by a straight line east by south to the mouth of said creek again. (Essex Deeds, 1 Ipswich: 100).

In 1653 he had a grant of land from the colony. He took it upon himself to build a bridge over the Newbury River (now called Parker River) so that the General Court in 1654 voted:

> Richard Thorlay, having built a bridge, at his own cost, over Newbury River, hath liberty to take 2d for every horse, cow, oxe, or any other great cattle, as also one half peny a peece for every hogg, sheep, or goat, that shall pass over the s[d] bridge, as long as he shall well and sufficiently repayre and mayntayne the same, provided that passengers shall be free.

This was the first toll bridge in America.

In 1660 it was ordered that a road be laid out from the meeting house at the north end of Newbury to Rowley. After heated arguments over location, it was finally decided to run it by way of Thorley's bridge, at which time defects in the bridge were mentioned, lack of railings.

At the court meeting 26 March 1661, Richard Thorley was released from ordinary training; he had to pay 8 shillings annually to the use of the company. Service being required until age 60, this suggests that he was born about 1601.

He had a servant named James Parks who died 24 June 1664.

He was one of the Newbury men who signed a petition to the General Court in behalf of Lieutenant Robert Pike who had been censured for a statement he had made. He sided with Mr. Woodman in the dispute against Mr. Parker, the minister, in 1670-71, and was eventually fined 4 nobles for the matter (equal to £1.6.8).

On 27 January 1669 he gave part of his farm to his son Thomas, in case of his death it to go to his son Francis. His wife joined him in the deed.

She died 19 March 1683/4 and he died 10 November 1685.

Children:

FRANCIS, b 1630-32 in England; m 5 Feb. 1654/5 at Newbury, Ann Morse, prob. dau. of Anthony; 9 ch.; he d 26 Nov. 1703 "ae 73"; aged about 45 in 1677 deposition. Court rec. shows: Rose Whitlock v Francis Tharley for unjust molestation. Released each other from any "lyes or bonds concerning marriage". It must have been some sort of breach-of-promise suit. Date was prob. 1653.

MARY, prob. b about 1635-36; m 20 Nov. 1653 at Newbury, John Woolcott, prob. son of John; 9 ch.; he d 30 Sept. 1690 at Springfield, Mass.; she survived him.

THOMAS, born 1635 in England; m 13 April 1670 at Newbury, Judith March, prob. dau. of Hugh; 7 ch.; aged 35 per 1670 deposition. He killed 7 wolves in Newbury, sued the town for the bounty, was paid £14. Judith was fined for serving liquor to some Indians on the Lord's Day in her home; she d 11 July 1689; he d 23 June 1713 "aged 82".

LYDIA, b 1 April 1640; m 20 Oct. 1661, Nathaniel Wells, m 2, Nathaniel Emerson.

MARTHA, b about 1642; m 27 Nov. 1662, Lt. John Dresser; she d 29 June 1700.

JOHN, b 19 July 1644 at Rowley; d 4 July 1659; his death rec. is only rec. of him; was no doubt a son of Richard.

Ref.: Savage; Pope's Pioneers of Mass.; Essex County Quarterly Court Files; V.R.

2

JOHN WARREN (*John, John, Robert*) was baptized on 1 August 1585 at Nayland, Suffolk, England, the son of John and Elizabeth (Scarlett) Warren. In the summer of 1630, at the age of 45, he, his wife Margaret, and their four children joined the Winthrop Fleet and sailed for America. There were about 700 who came in eleven ships and arrived in June and July. The first five vessels landed at Salem on June 13th and following days.

John Warren settled in Watertown on Lexington Street, near Waverly. On 18 May 1631, he was admitted freeman. In 1635, he and Abraham Browne were appointed to lay out all highways and to see that they were repaired. He was a selectman in 1640. His homestead lot of 12 acres was bounded west by the highway, east by William Hammond, north by John Biscoe, and south by Isaac Stearns. He also owned in 1642 seven other lots amounting to about 266 acres. In October 1651, he and Thomas Arnold were each fined 20 shillings for an offense against the laws concerning baptism. On 14 March 1658/9, he was warned for not attending public worship, but "old Warren is not to be found in town". On 4 April 1654, he was fined for neglect of public worship £3.10s. (14 Sabbaths missed at 5 shillings each). On 17 May 1661, the houses of "old Warren and goodman Hammond" were ordered "to be searched for Quakers". His dissenting religious views were apparently like those of Nathaniel Biscoe, Senior, who returned from Watertown to England and Thomas Arnold who moved to Providence. They were perhaps Baptists.

His wife, Margaret, died 6 November 1662 and he died 13 December 1667, aged 82. His will was made a few days before he died. He signed by mark, apparently too feeble to do otherwise.

30 November 1667 - I John Warren of Watertown... being aged & weak in body ... to my son Daniel Warren the p'cell of land that he now lives on, being about the quantity of 16 acres ... to my sons John Warren & my son Daniel Warren my dividend and all my remote meadow with another p'cell of remote land

cald by the name of Farm land .... to Daniel my best flock bed with my green rug that lyeth upon my bed and two of my four pewter platters ... & to my daughter in law Mary Warren wife to my son Daniel one pewter porenger ... to my daughter Mary Bagulow a p'cell of remote land of 16 acres .... already in her possession .... to my daughter Mary Bagulow 1 small pewter dish .... to my daughter Elizabeth Knape 13 acres of plow land .. in the further plaine in Watertown ... and one iron spit which she hath already in her possession & further .... A booke cald *the plaine man's pathway to heaven* ... to Daniel Warren son to my son Daniel Warren one of my cows .. to my grandchild Mary Bagulow a bind box that was my wife's ... to Michall Bloyse daughter to Richard Bloyse deceased [his son's step-daughter] one pewter plate ... to each of my grandchildren 2 shillings & 6 pence ... remainder to my beloved son John Warren, he to be sole executor. Signed by mark. Proved 17 December 1667

The inventory of the goods and chattells of John Warren Senior late deceased of Watertowne the 13: day of December: 1667:

one tenament of housein and ten accres of upland and three accres of medow - - - - - - - - - - - - - - -	60-00-00
Sixteene accers of wast land - - - - - - - - - - -	08-00-00
Sixty accers of divident land - - - - - - - - - - -	15-00-00
thereteene accers of meddow - - - - - - - - - - -	10-00-00
Farme land one hundred and fifty accers - - - - - -	30-00-00
Wearing clothes wollen and lining sheets and pillow beers	08-00-00
Three cows - - - - - - - - - - - - - - - -	10-00-00
in the parlor a beedsteed Sattall curtains and fether bed three fether pillows one fether bolster one flock bed tow blankets one Rug - - - - - - - - - - - - - -	08-00-00
Three chests one box one standing cubord one warming pan one pare of silver waits and all other lumber - - - -	04-00-00
one silver spoon tow bibels and other books - - - - -	01-10-00
one tine pan and pewter - - - - - - - - - - - - -	02-00-00
Three kettells two skillets tow pots - - - - - - -	02-10-00
one --ater one pare of cob irons Tongs with other iron things - - - - - - - - - - - - - - - -	01-10-00
Table chaires and stooles one paire of Bellowes one friing pan with other lumber in the hall - - - - -	01-02-00
of husbanding irons and tools - - - - - - - - - -	01-15-00
of things in the leanetow - - - - - - - - - - - -	00-02-00
in the chamber one flock bed and bolster tow blankets one bedsteed and tubs - - - - - - - -	02-00-00
one musket one sword one halbert one brase hook - -	00-15-00
things in the cellar tow beere barrells tow chests with other lumber - - - - - - - - - - - - - - - -	01-00-00

Taken by us the: 16: of December (1667:)

John Coollidge
Henrie Bright
Henry Freeman

John Warren

Children, all baptized at Nayland, Suffolk, England:

SUSAN, bapt. 14 April 1612

MARY, bapt. 23 April 1615; buried 17 Dec. 1622

ELIZABETH, bapt. 25 June 1619; buried 25 Nov. 1622

SARAH, bapt. 20 April 1620; buried 7 Sept. 1621

JOHN, bapt. 12 May 1622; m 11 July 1667, Micael Bloys, widow of Richard & dau. of Robert Jennison; 7 ch.; he d Jan.-Feb. 1702/3; she d 14 July 1713, both at Watertown

MARY, bapt. 12 Sept. 1624; m 30 Oct. 1642, John Bigelow, son of Randall, bapt. 16 Feb. 1616/17 at Wrentham, Suffolk; 13 ch.; she d 19 Oct. 1691; he m 2, 2 Oct. 1694, Sarah Bemis; he d 14 July 1703 at Watertown

DANIEL, bapt. 25 Feb. 1626/7; m 10 Dec. 1650, Mary Barron, dau. of Ellis & Grace Barron; 9 ch.; she d 13 Feb. 1715/16

ELIZABETH, bapt. 21 July 1629; m about 1654, James Knapp, son of William, b about 1627; 2 ch.; she was one of the bewitched persons mentioned by Cotton Mather

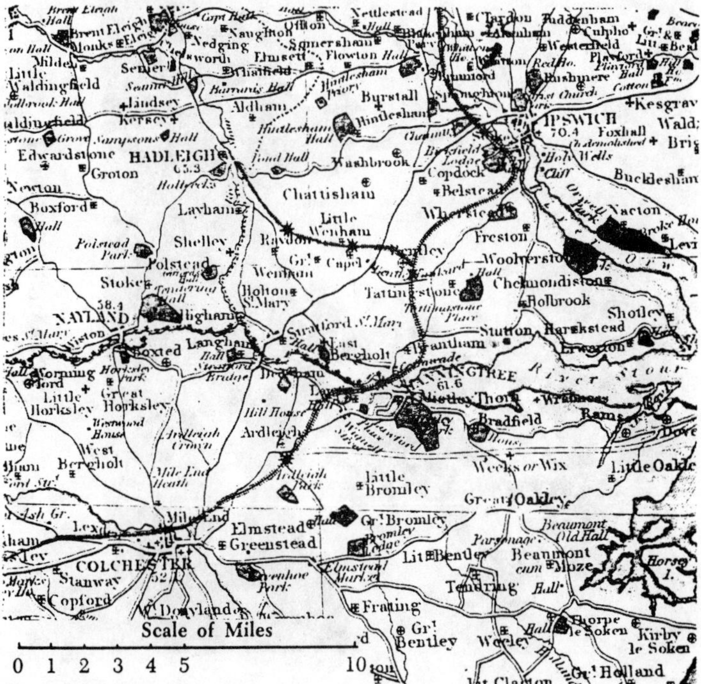

Ref.: Bond's Genealogies and History of Watertown; Middlesex Probate 23862; Watertown Records; Parish Registers

SAINT JAMES'S CHURCH, NAYLAND, SUFFOLK

4

JOHN WARREN (*John, Robert*) was born about 1555, and was a cardmaker of Nayland. A card was a metal comb or wire brush used for combing flax or wool. John Warren married first, on 4 October 1584 at Nayland, Elizabeth Scarlett, the daughter of John and Mary Scarlett, baptized 30 August 1561. She was buried 27 March 1603. He married secondly, Rose ______, who was buried 11 August 1610, and thirdly, on 23 April 1611, Rose Riddlesdale. She was the widow of Richard Riddlesdale and nee Rose Brand of Boxford.

John Warren was taxed 16 pence on his land in the subsidy (tax) of 8 James I (1611).

He made his will on 27 March 1613 and died within a few months. An abstract of the will follows. He was presumably buried in the churchyard of Nayland as he requested.

> 27 March 1613 - the will of JOHN WAREN of Nayland in the County of Suffolk, cardmaker. To be buried in the parish churchyard of Nayland. To wife Rose £20, the household goods and plate she brought with her, my tenement where William Bawlden dwells, during her life, and during her widowhood the parlor and chamber in my now dwelling house. To son John and his lawful issue my mansion house where I now dwell, with the barn, stable and garden lying in Fen Street, excepting the aforesaid two rooms. To daughter Mary and her lawful issue, after the decease of my wife, my said tenement in Fen Street where William Baulden dwells, and in default of such issue to my son John, he to pay 40s. apiece to all my children then living. To sons Isaac, Nathaniel, Amos, and daughter Elizabeth, £10 apiece. To sons Joshua and Thomas £10 each at twenty-one. My plate to be divided equally between my wife and son John, and my household goods to be equally divided among my wife and all my children. To the poor people of Nayland 20s. All the residue of my goods unbequeathed I give to my son John, whom I make my executor. [Signed] John Warrene. Witnesses: William Foorth, John Walter, and Edward Collinges. Proved 4 November 1613 by John Warren, son of the testator and the executor named in the will. (P.C.C., Capell, 98)

Rose returned to Boxford and there married for her third husband, Richard Grymes, on 20 November 1617.

Children, baptized at Nayland:

2 JOHN, bapt. 1 Aug. 1585; m Margaret ______; 7 ch,; went to N.E. with the Winthrop Fleet in 1630, settled in Watertown; she d 6 Nov. 1662; he d 13 Dec. 1667

DANIEL, bapt. 13 Nov. 1586; buried 13 Feb. 1596/7

ISAAC, bapt. 28 Jan. 1587/8; living 1613

NATHANIEL, bapt. 7 Sept. 1589; m 12 Sept. 1618 at Nayland, Mary Gonne; ch.: Nathaniel bapt. 6 June 1619 - d 1682, Mary bapt. 4 march 1620/21, Thomas bapt. 4 May 1623; he was buried 17 Jan. 1624/5

AMOS, bapt. 14 March 1590/91; living 1613

ELIZABETH, b perhaps 1592-3; living 1613

JOSHUA, bapt. 2 April 1594; living 1613

JOSEPH, bapt. 19 Dec. 1596 (*sic*); buried 22 July 1596 (*sic*)

MARY, bapt. 22 March 1598/9; living 1613

THOMAS, bapt. 22 Feb. 1600/01; m 15 Jan. 1638/9 at Nayland, Mary Rancke, both single persons; ch.: Samuel bapt. 24 Nov. 1639

THE CHURCH OF SAINT JAMES, NAYLAND, SUFFOLK

Ref.: N.E.H.G.S. - 64; Parish Registers; Probate Records at Bury Saint Edmunds

8

JOHN WARREN (*Robert*) was born about 1525, and lived in Nayland, Suffolk, England. His estate in Nayland was called *Corlie* or *Curlie.* His first wife is unknown but he married secondly, 5 September 1563, Agnes (or Anne) Howlet who was buried 25 November 1567. He probably married thirdly, at Great Horkesley on 30 January 1568/9, Margaret Firmety, previously the wife of one Cole. She was buried 19 April 1576. John Warren made his will 21 April 1576 and it was proved 5 June following. He made his brothers, James and William, executors. He was buried on 23 April 1576. An abstract of his will follows.

21 April 1576 - The will of John Warren of Nayland nexte Stoke in the County of Suffolk, husbandman . . . To John Warren my eldest son and to the heirs of his body lawfully begotten my house that I now dwell in with the lands, woods and pastures thereunto belonging with the appertenances lying in the parish of Nayland, known by the name of Curlie, being by copy of court roll of Sir Thomas Danby, knight, Lord of the Manor, which I now deliver by surrender to John Prentise and Robert Patton to the use of my eldest son John, on condition that he pay £20 out of the said house and lands to my second son John Warren . . . If he die without living issue then to my second son John and the heirs of his body, and if the said John my myddle son die without living issue then to son Richarde Warren and to his heires lawfully begotten . . . For lack of such heirs to daughter Anne Warren and her heirs . . . To son John the Elder my farm implements, and to him and his brothers John the middle and Richard and his sister Anne the household goods, pewter, brass and livestock..... To Agnes Coole, my wife's daughter, all the appurtenances that did belong to my wife that last was... To John Cole, my wife's son, a chafing dish and a laten candlestick... To twelve of the poorest people of Nayland 12d to be divided among them. All the residue of my goods and chattels, debts paid and my expenses discharged, to be equally divided among my four children and my two brothers James and William Warren whom I make executors, and I give them five loads of wood lying felled on my ground for their pains . . . I make John Prentise supervisor and I give him 12d ..... Witnesses: John Prentise, Robert Patten, Anthonye Speed and James Warren. Proved 5 June 1576 by the executors named, William Warren in his own person and James Warren in the person of said William.
(Archdeaconry of Sudbury at Bury St. Edmunds, Wroo, 142)

The true inventories indented and made the 25 daye of Aprell Anno Domini 1576 of all the moveable goodes and cattelles of John Warren of Naylande in the countie of Suffolk husbondmann late diceacid seene and prised by the discresion of John Prentise, John Melles, Thomas Mells and Thomas Warren with others.

In Primis the haull		
Item ann oulde counter table and two fourmes	2s	
one long plonke table with 2 trestelles		16d
one almerie and one coupe		12d
thre chayers one chayer stoole one olde joyned stoole and 2 playne stooles		12d
one olde table stoole and one litle forme		4d
4 olde peces of stayned clothes		4d
3 trammelles one gridiron one fire pann one payer of tonges one old Iron pele	3s	
The Chamber		
one couboarde		20d
one playne bedsteadle one fetharbed one flockbed one fethar trammson 2 fethar pillowes one payer of blanketes one litle olde red coveringe	6s	8d
one litell bedsteadle and one flockbed lyenge thareon one payer of blanketes on shorte tramsonn one flocke pillow & one olde striped coveringe	4s	
one shipp cheste and hutches and two litell fourmes	5s	
4 litell stayned clothes 2 shelves one washinge skepp with a batteldar and a Roulinge pinn		20d
Item of the naprye		
one olde payer of sheetes and one fine sheets one pillowbeere one olde table clothe 2 shurtes and one towell	2s	6d
Item of his apparrell to his bodie		
2 jurkines one olde blacke coate 2 payer of hosen and a felte hat	3s	4d
Ann uppar chamber		
a playne bedsteadle with a flock bed thareon one tramsam one flocke pillow one blanket one Dornacle coveringe	3s	4d
2 olde stayned clothes one warbill one pitcheforke 2 elme bowes 8 shaftes one quarter staffe one olde sworde		12d
4 bowshells of maulte	5s	

The Butrie

4 bras kettells greate and small one bras cauderon one bras pann with ears one strayner & one skyllet pann		13s	4d
2 braspottes one litell one and one summwat bigger		2s	6d
3 latten chafinge dishes and fyve latten candellstickes one latton ladle 2 scummers and one latton pott		6s	8d
17 peces of pewtar small ad greate & 3 pewtar saultes		6s	8d
3 spittes one Iron dropping pan one aundron of Iron one frieng pan one bread grate & 2 payer of sheers		8s	
half a dozen of trenchers 4 trene spoones & a half a dozen of trene dishes			2d

The mylke house

3 trowes one olde footed table 2 earthen pannes one mylk boull 3 chese moates 2 chese liddes one charne & one creme pot			16d
one payr of mustarde quarnes one shelve one syne one payer of butter scoles one cragg one olde tub one ale pot one mylke payle & one chese pres			16d

The carte house

one oulde tumbrell with a payer of shood wheeles one plowe 2 shares one coultar 2 plowgh cheenes a foote towe a speneshackell with a pynn a plowe eare a dowble hooke 3 nayles & 2 carte cloutes		5s	
a payer of Iron harrowes fyve Iron wedges 3 sythes a payer of malte quarnes a spade a mattock 2 hookes 2 pese meekes 2 fannes 2 pullinge sowes with sertaine olde Iron		6s	8d

The yardes & feldes

2 shootes		4s	
sertayne wood unmade to the quantitie of 5 loades more or les		5s	
2 bestes	£2	13s	4d
one bullock of 2 yeers olde		13s	4d
one yeerlinge		10s	
one wennell		3s	4d
half an acre of wheate on the grounde		10s	

Somme tottallis is £9 13s 11d

Item of debt that was oweing the saide John Warren when he departed.
Item one Nicholas Hawes of Shellie ought him 13s 4d.

Item of debtes that John Warren ought when he departed.

to James Warren of Wiston	3s	4d
to Thomas Hinsam of Nayland	3s	4d
to Gorge Allin of Wiston	2s	8d
to Henrie Adkinson of Naylande	2s	6d

Summe is 12s 2d

Children, by his first wife:

JOHN, b about 1550, "the elder" of Corlie; buried 22 May 1583, "a householder"

4 JOHN, b about 1555; m 4 Oct. 1584 at Nayland, Elizabeth Scarlett, dau. of John & Mary, bapt. 30 Aug. 1561; 10 ch.; she was buried 27 March 1603; m 2, Rose —— who was buried 11 Aug. 1610; m 3, 23 April 1611, Rose Riddlesdale, widow of Richard & nee Rose Brand of Boxford. He d testate 1613

RICHARD, buried 30 Sept. 1612, "a householder"

Child, by second wife:

AGNES/ANNE, bapt. 8 Oct. 1564; living in 1576

Child, by third wife:

MARGARET, b about 1569-71; buried 15 April 1571

Ref.: N.E.H.G.S. -64; Parish Registers; Wills at Bury Saint Edmunds

10

JOHN SCARLETT of Nayland, Suffolk, England was born probably about 1525-1530. On 26 January 1554/5 at Layham, Suffolk, was recorded the marriage of John Scarlett and Margaret Martin. Layham is about five miles northeast of Nayland. Since there are no further records of them in Layham, they probably moved to Nayland shortly after their marriage. John Scarlett probably grew up in Nayland where the parish register starts in 1558. Margaret Martin probably was from Layham where the register starts in 1538. There were several Martin families in Layham at that time and several Margaret Martins marrying about that time, so it is impossible to discover her exact relationship to these other Martins. Margaret must have died between 1555 and 1558 before the Nayland register starts, and then he remarried, for when he died he left a widow named Emma.

On 11 May 1560 at Nayland was buried Em[ma] Smithe, servant to John Scarlett.

No John Scarlett was listed in the 1568 Subsidy (tax) list, which indicates that he paid no tax, hence had negligible assets.

John Scarlett was buried 11 November 1571 at Nayland. The same day administration of his estate was granted to his widow, Em[ma] (A5/1/242). She, "Em Skarlet", remarried 13 September 1574 at Nayland to Thomas Parish.

Children:

JOHN, prob. b about 1555 at Nayland; m about 1577, Mary ____; 7 ch.: Ann prob. b about 1577 - m John Bond before 1640 when *Ann Bond alias Scarlett wife of John Bond & sister of Mary Scarlett was granted admin. of Mary's estate,* Susan bapt. 8 Sept. 1579, Mary who d unm. & was buried 2 Sept. 1640 "an ancient maid", Christopher who prob. had a son Thomas, Dorothy buried 15 June 1585, George who d between 1614 & 1624 & left 2 ch., Frances who m about 1612-14 Daniel Cole & had 2 ch. & prob. d by 1624. John was buried 19 Sept. 1614; Mary was buried 30 Nov. 1625. Abstracts of their wills follow:

5 September 1614 - the will of JOHN SCARLETT of Nayland, county of Suffolk, mercer, being sick in body ... to be buried where it shall please God to take me out of this miserable world ... to the poor of Nayland 20s. ... to him who shall preach my funeral sermon 10s. ... to Mary my daughter £30 ... to my son George £15 to be paid at Our Lady Day come three years ... to Thomas Scarlett my grandchild £10 to be paid to him at age 16 ... my daughter Frances Coole should have the £15 paid according to an obligation which I entered to Daniel Coole my son in law upon condition that George Coole father to the said Daniel Coole do affirm unto Frances Coole my daughter all that copyhold land, which the said George promised before diverse witnesses upon condition of the said marriage and payment of a certain sum of money ... to my daughter Coole one of the best pewter platters ... to Mary my wife and Christopher my son all residue unbequeathed, they paying my debts, they to be executors. Signed by mark. Witnesses: Dorothy Moore, Gregory Franklin, Thomas Blythe. Proved 29 November 1614 at London by Christopher Scarlett his son and Mary Scarlett his widow. (P.C.C. will 108 Lawe = 11/124, f. 348)

26 August 1624 - the will of MARY SCARLETT of Nayland, county Suffolk, widow ... fullness of years ... to my son Christopher Scarlett 20s. ... to Mary Scarlett my daughter £20 and a long list of household goods ... to the 2 children of my daughter Ann 20s. each, same to 2 children of my son George deceased ... to daughter Ann £3 ... to Thomas Scarlett my grandchild £7 and some household goods ... to Mary Cole my grandchild one gilt silver spoon and one gold ring and unto Frances Cole my grandchild one fair silver spoon ... residue between said daughter Mary and grandson Thomas Scarlett. Executors to be loving friend William Forth of Ipswich, gentleman, and Daniel Coale my son in law. Witnesses: Dorothy Moore & William Gatteward. Proved 9 March 1625/6. (R2/53/421 & W1/81/207)

ALICE, perhaps b 1557; Alice, "dau. to John", was buried 2 March 1560/61 at Nayland

JOAN, bapt. 16 May 1559, "dau. to John"; no further record found

5 ELIZABETH, bapt. 30 Aug. 1561; m 4 Oct. 1584, John Warren, son of John; 10 ch.; she was buried 27 March 1602/3; he m 2, Rose ——— who was buried 11 Aug. 1610; m 3, 23 April 1611, Rose Riddlesdale, widow of Richard of Boxford & nee Brand; he d testate 1613; Rose m 3, 20 Nov. 1617 at Boxford, Richard Grymes

JAMES, bapt. 11 Jan. 1563/4, "son to John"; no further record found

RICHARD, b perhaps 1566; buried 20 Dec. 1579, "son to John"

THOMAS, bapt. 29 Sept. 1568; buried 11 Sept. 1579, "son to John"

FRANCES, b prob. 1570-71; buried 17 Oct. 1580, "dau. to John"

Ref.: Parish Registers; Probate Records at Bury Saint Edmunds; Prerogative Court of Canterbury Wills; Suffolk Green Books No. XII

16

ROBERT WARREN was born perhaps about 1485 and had a wife, Margaret. His will, dated 29 October 1544, is abstracted as follows:

> 29 October 1544 - the will of ROBARTE WARREN, aged and sick in body. To be buried in the churchyard of our lady at Wyston [Wissington]. To the high altar there 12d. To wife Margarett the house I dwell in now which I did purchase of the widow Payne, with all the lands, groves, woods, meadows, and pastures unto the same belonging, as I myself hold it by copy of court roll of the manor of Alpheley Hall, during the term of her life, and after her death to James my son and his heirs, and if he die before his mother then to his next brother and to his heirs lawfully begotten, and so from one brother to another. My milch beasts and oxen to be sold and the money used to pay debts, and the residue to my wife. To my son James a white bullock. To son Lawrence and to daughter Anne 20s. each after the decease of their mother. To son Thomas three horses, harness, a cart, plough, etc. All the wheat being in Hawkyns barn to be divided equally between my wife and son Thomas, he to pay my son William 20s. out of my land called Wyston Prestney at twenty years of age. Residue of all goods to wife Margarett, with an hundred of wood out of Wyston Prestney, and I make her my whole executrix. Mr. James Abbe of Nayland, supervisor. Witnesses: Henrye Lorkyn, Willm. Plampyn of Wyston, and Thomas Gostlynge of Grotton, and others. Proved 22 February 1544/5 by the executrix
>
> (Archdeaconry of Sudbury [Bury St. Edmunds,], Longe, 489)

Strangely, in his will he did not mention his son, John, unless the copy at Bury Saint Edmunds is imperfect. This son John, however, is mentioned in the will of his brother Thomas in 1559.

In the Subsidy return for Suffolk in 1327, there is listed Walter Waryn of Nayland, taxed for 3 shillings, which represented one twentieth of the value of his moveables. There were several others named Warren in other towns of Suffolk. Walter, however, being the only one in Nayland, was presumably the ancestor of Robert.

In the Subsidy of 1524, Robert Waryn of Wyston was down for a tax of four pence on £1 of wages. Also on the Wyston list was a John Waryn taxed 3s. on goods valued at £6. John, who was the second wealthiest man on the Wyston list, was probably the father of Robert.

Probably Thomas Warren, also of Wiston, who left a will dated 1558, was Robert's brother.

Children:

JAMES, b about 1515(?); he d 1594; his will:

1 May 1594 - the will of JAMES WARREN of Wissington, yeoman, sick in body ... to wife Annys houses and lands with appurtenances wherein I now dwell for her life ..to William Warren my eldest son after her decease, conditionally that he pay £30 to the rest of the children as follows: To George Warren my youngest son £10 of which 50s. within one year after decease of wife Annys, then £5 within the next year, and 50s. the next year ... to Margaret Warren my daughter £5 of which 50s. by the end of the fourth year after decease of wife Annys and another 50s. the next year following ... to Elizabeth Warren my daughter £5 of which 50s. within the sixth year after decease of wife Annys and 50s. the next year ... to Richard Warren my son £10 of which £3.6.8 within the eighth year after decease of wife Annys and same in each of the next two years ... to wife Annys all bedsteads and bedding thereto belonging, all brass & pewter ... to son William my cupboard & my chest after decease of wife ... to son George my best coat ... residue to wife & William Warren my son whom I make my executors .... Witnesses: Richard Colman, William Clarke, and John Durfall. Signed by mark. Proved 9 July 1594 (R2/42/514)

LAWRENCE

THOMAS, b about 1520(?); he had several ch. by his wife, Marian, who apparently was a widow when he m her; she later m William Harrison

13 March 1559/60 - the will of THOMAS WARREN of Stoke Nayland in the County of Suffolk and diocese of Norwich, yeoman ... to be buried within the sanctuary of Stoke Nayland ... to my wife Marian for life my house that I now dwell in called Morris with all lands belonging thereto, toward the maintenance of her living and the honest and good bringing up of her children and mine. After her decease the same to my son Edward Warren and heirs lawfully begotten, and for lack of such heirs the same to my son Simon and his heirs. To wife Marian for life Harkingbeene and all the land that belongeth thereto, that is a hole Bayliship, and my copy grove called wyssten pressen and my free land called Derelye, and a parcel of grove called little wessen pressen; all these lands on her decease to descend to my son Simon and his heirs lawful begotten, and for lack of such issue to my son Edward and his heirs lawfully begotten. To my three daughters, Jane Warren, Agnes Warren, and Ann Warren, £3.6.8d. apiece at twenty-one or day of marriage. To sons Simonde Warren and Edmund [*sic*] Warren 40s apiece at twenty-one. To brother John Warren, to James Warren, William Warren, Laurence Warren, and

Ann Lorkin, 3s.4d. apiece. To godsons Thomas Lorkin and William Podmare a lamb apiece. To Thomas Holton, godson, a lamb and 3s.4d. To godson Thomas Warren, son of Robert Warren 20d. To godson John Warren, son of John Warren, 3s.4d. To wife Marian all goods and chattels moveable and unmoveable unbequeathed, and I make her the sole executrix to pay and receive my debts. She shall bestow 30s. at my burial. Supervisor Edward Holton, and for his pains 13s.4d. Witnesses: John Prentise, Willm Plampen the elder, Willm Plampen the younger, Thomas Spakeman, and John Ley, with others. Proved 20 March 1559/60 by the executrix named in the will.

(Suffolk Wills at Bury Saint Edmunds, Sparrow, 85)

ANN, m _____ Lorkin

8 JOHN, b about 1520; not mentioned in his father's will; 6 ch.; d 1576

WILLIAM, under age in 1544; ch.: Faith bapt. 13 May 1665, Robert bapt. 7 May 1570, William buried 29 March 1572, William buried 27 Aug. 1574; a William Warren, householder, was buried 4 June 1576, but this may be another man, as "William Warren in his own person and James Warren in the person of said William" proved their brother John's will the next day, 5 June. Possibly this probate notation confused the two brothers and it was James who proved the will. A William Warren d 1600/01, testate, possibly this man.

A DOOR IN THE CHURCH
WISSINGTON, SUFFOLK

Ref.: N.E.H.G.S.-64; Parish Registers; Probate Records at Bury Saint Edmunds

THE PARISH CHURCH OF SAINT MARY AT WISSINGTON, SUFFOLK

GEORGE WHEELER (Thomas) was baptized 23 March 1605/6 at Cranfield, Bedfordshire, England, the son of Thomas Wheeler.

It is apparent from the Cranfield records that there were two contemporary adult Thomas Wheelers living there at the beginning of the seventeenth century, and by 1613 three George Wheelers had been baptized. The George of this monograph was apparently the son of Thomas Wheeler of "the Town End" who disappears from the parish register after the baptism of his last child in 1614. Thomas "of the blakehouse" who died in 1634/5 left a will in which he named his many children, but no son George, hence this George had to have been the son of Thomas of "the Town End".

On 8 June 1630 at Cranfield, George Wheeler and Catherine Pin (or Penn or Pinge?) were married. When his second child was baptized, he was living at Wharley End in Cranfield.

With wife Catherine and three children, accompanied by several other related families of Cranfield, he left for New England and settled in Concord, Massachusetts, where he appears in the first town records of 1638 and every year thereafter until 1684 when he died. Perhaps he was there as early as 1636 when the town was first settled. He was a leader in the town business and held many positions of trust, serving on substantially every committee of consequence. He was a substantial landowner. His house lot alone consisted of eleven acres, and he owned lands at Brook Meadow, Fairhaven Meadow, by Flint's Pond, by Walden Pond, on the White Pond Plain, on the Sudbury line, etc. He and Timothy Wheeler owned considerably property jointly, and together they owned most of the real estate left by Reverend Peter Bulkeley.

His daughters, Sarah, Mary and Ruth, were married in a triple wedding at Concord.

His wife Catherine died on 2 January 1684/5 and three weeks later, on 28 January, he made his will. He signed by mark. Since his will was probated 2 July 1687, he probably died in May or June 1687. An abstract of his will follows.

He bequeathed to his two sons, Thomas and John, but Thomas died a few months before he did, so son John was the only surviving son. He bequeathed to the children of his son William, deceased, to his daughter Fox's children (she was also deceased), and to his four daughters: Elizabeth Fletcher,Sarah Dudley, Ruth Hartwell and Hannah Fletcher.

28 January 1684/5 - the will of GEORGE WHEELER, Sr. of Concord, county Middlesex, Massachusetts Colony ... being in a *compident* measure of memory & understanding ... my whole estate shall stand engaged & be responsible for my comfortable maintenance in all respects during the turn of my life ... to my two sons Thomas Wheeler and John Wheeler my mansion dwelling house, barns, cowhouses and orchards ... down to John Scotchford's house, I give to my son Thomas & that part of my lot lying between Joshua Wheeler & John Scotchford, I give to my son John ... to my two sons Thomas & John my six acres bought of Gershom Bulkeley, also my twenty eight acres of woodland lying in the north quarter over the river ... to the children of my son William deceased £66.7s. in equal right of property, only my will is that my meadow at Brook Meadow on both sides of the brook, excepting that part I give to my son Thomas as also my one acre in ash swamp at Fairhaven ... to be disposed of to my son Willliam's children ... Also, the two acres & a half of meadow joining to my son William's pasture, it is not my son William's ... to my son Thomas my piece of meadow at Brook Meadow joining to John Wheeler's meadow ... three acres more or less ..to my son John two acres & a half of meadow in spring meadow ... to my two sons Thomas & John my meadow in the meadow called the great meadow ... to my son John my fourteen acres at the south field on the east side of the country way against Comye's house, also two acres in muddy meadow swamp ... to sons Thomas & John my forty four acres north of Walden pond ... to son Thomas fourteen acres ... adjoining to Nathaniel & John Billings ... to my son John six acres joining to Daniel Dane southeast from Mount Taber ... to sons Thomas & John my eight acres joining to Mr. Flint's pond ... to my son John my four acres in John Mille's pasture joining to the south river ... to sons Thomas & John out of my moveable estate £5 apiece ... to son Thomas £10 ... to my daughter Fox's children £6 ... to my four daughters: Elizabeth Fletcher, Sarah Dudley, Ruth Hartwell & Hannah Fletcher £15 apiece in country pay ... I will & reserve to myself ... begin in the year 1682 on to the day of my death ... to sons Thomas & John seven acres lying in the corner near Watertown Line ... no legacy shall be required until two years after my death ... two sons Thomas & John Wheeler the executors. Signed by mark. Witnesses: Samuel Meriam, Jonathan Hubard and John Scotchford. Proved 2 July 1687. Administration granted to John Wheeler, son and surviving executor.

(Middlesex Probate Records 10:2)

Children:

WILLIAM, bapt. 24 July 1631 at Cranfield; m Hannah Buse 30 Oct. 1659 at Concord; 8 ch.; d 31 Nov. 1683

THOMAS, bapt. 14 Aug. 1633 at Cranfield, "son of George Wheeler of Wharley End"; m 10 Oct. 1657 at Concord, Hannah Harwood; d 16 Dec. 1686; 11 ch.; estate of £285

ELIZABETH, bapt. 3 Jan. 1635/6 at Cranfield; m 11 Oct. 1656 at Concord, Francis Fletcher; d 14 June 1704 at Concord; 8 ch.

SARAH, b Concord 30 March 1640; m 26 Oct. 1665, Francis Dudley; 7 ch.; d 12 Dec. 1713

JOHN, b Concord 19 March 1643; m 25 March 1663, Sarah Larkin; 9 ch.; d 27 Sept. 1713

MARY, b Concord 6 Sept. 1645; m 26 Oct. 1665, Eliphalet Fox; d 24 Feb. 1678/9; 8 or 9 ch.

RUTH, b prob. about 1647; m 26 Oct. 1665, Samuel Hartwell; d 19 Dec. 1713; 11 ch.

HANNAH, b prob. after 1649 at Concord; m 5 July 1673 (? torn) at Chelmsford, Samuel Fletcher, son of William, who was b about 1652-3; 9 ch.; d 11 Dec. 1697

THE PARISH CHURCH OF CRANFIELD, BEDFORDSHIRE

Ref.: Suffolk Probate 1580; Amer. Genealogist 12, 14, 27 and 28; Cranfield Parish Register

4a

THOMAS WHEELER (*Henry?, John, Thomas*) of Cranfield, Bedfordshire, was probably born about 1567 to 1577. That he was closely related to the many other Wheelers of Cranfield seems beyond doubt. Records which can be specifically identified with him are unknown, except for the baptisms of his children. About 1600, several Wheeler men were living in Cranfield who were married and having children. There were two Thomases, four Johns and three Richards. That there were two distinct Thomas Wheelers is apparent from the records of baptisms of their children. There was a child just about every year for over twenty years, and a few just too close together to be by one mother. This Thomas Wheeler had five children recorded in the baptismal register. There may have been earlier children of whom there is no record, because the register prior to 1600 no longer exists. If so, they probably died young; otherwise one might find later on a record of their marriage or some other record.

Thomas or his wife must have died about 1614-15, for their last recorded child was baptized in 1614. He left no will and there is no clue as to the identitiy of his wife or when either died. Perhaps he was buried on either 2 or 8 October 1643, on each of which dates a Thomas Wheeler was buried at Cranfield. On the other hand, would he have been left behind when his sons went off to New England?

Bedfordshire is a rural area with no large cities. Along its western border and about midway north and south are the parishes of Marston Mortaine and Cranfield. Families named Wheeler lived in these parishes as early as the fifteenth century. A John Wheeler of Marston Mortaine made his will on 24 November 1500. It was proved on 12 December 1500. In it, he bequeathed to his daughters Anne and Syscell a cow each, to his daughter Jane a pot, to his daughter Joan a pan, to Anne a possnet, several bushels of barley for various church bequests, and the residue of his estate to his brother Richard Wheeler and to Robert Dogett. He was perhaps the ancestor of this Thomas Wheeler.

Children, baptized at Cranfield, Bedfordshire:

THOMAS, bapt. 20 Nov. 1603; he was in Lynn, Mass. in 1635, was a constable; he was apparently the Thomas Wheeler who later went to Stonington, Conn. & d 6 March 1686 ae 84 - g.s.; m Mary ____ ; 3 ch.

2 GEORGE, bapt. 23 March 1605/6; m 8 June 1630 at Cranfield, Catherine Pin (i.e. Penn?); A Henry Penn m Catherine Hull 24 May 1612 at Newport Pagnell, which is about 5 miles west of Cranfield. Perhaps Catherine who m George Wheeler was their daughter; 10 ch.; she d 2 Jan. 1684/5; he d about May or June 1687 at Concord, Mass.

JOHN, bapt. 23 Oct. 1608; buried 27 Dec. 1611

ELIZABETH, bapt. 27 Feb. 1610/11

RICHARD, bapt. 13 June 1614, "son of Thomas Wheeler of the Towne end"; possibly he was the Richard Wheeler of Lancaster, Mass., tho there is no evidence for it

THE FIFTEENTH CENTURY FONT
IN THE CHURCH OF CRANFIELD, BEDFORDSHIRE

Ref.: The American Genealogist 12, 14, 27, 28; Parish Registers; Bedfordshire Probate Records; Concord V.R.; Unpublished Studies of Lt. Col. Raymond D. Wheeler

8a

HENRY WHEELER (*John, Thomas*) was probably born about 1535 to 1540, perhaps at Cranfield, Bedfordshire, where he died in 1577. His wife's name was Isabel. An abstract of his will follows.

> 9 July 1577 - the will of HENRY WHELER of Cranfield ... to be buried in the churchyard of Cranfield ... all my land to my wife until my son John comes to the age of 23 ... to Thomas my son 20s. a year during the term of 10 years ... to Alice my daughter £4 after the 10 years, 4 pair of sheets, 4 pillowberes and a table cloth ... to the poor man's box 12d. ... to the reparation of the bells 12d. ... to the highways 12d. ... I do owe unto Annes Doo £6.13.4. ... I do owe to Robert Sturme £5 ... residue to Isabel my wife whom I make my sole executrix ... Overseers John Sugar, William Johnson, James Becley. I do appoint Thomas Sugare, Thomas Stevenson to be overseers of the children's stock that they may have it. Proved 11 October 1577.
>
> (Bedfordshire Will ABP /W 1577/52)

Children, probably all born at Cranfield:

JOHN, b about 1565, as he was aged 40 in 1605 when he made a statement about the will of Robert Vaux, which he witnessed by mark as "John Wheler of Dorstwell" in Bedfordshire (Will 1606/57). He was buried at Cranfield 18 Oct. 1645 "Jn. Wheeler of Doswell"); ch.: John bapt. 29 Aug. 1602 - buried 9 Aug. 1604, Ruth bapt. 10 May 1606 - buried 21 Oct. 1606, Martha bapt. 25 Nov. 1608, John bapt. 25 Feb. 1610/11 - buried 3 March 1610/11, Catherine bapt. 25 Feb. 1610/11 - buried 26 Feb. 1610/11, Daniel bapt. 9 Jan. 1613/14 - buried 22 July 1636

4 THOMAS, b perhaps 1567 - 1577; 5 ch. recorded

ALICE, b perhaps 1569 - 1577

Ref.: Probate Records at Bedford; Unpublished Studies of Lt. Col. Raymond D. Wheeler; Parish Registers

2b

THOMAS WHEELER (*Thomas, John?*) was born about 1590 at Cranfield, Bedfordshire, the "eldest son". There he grew up. On 5 May 1613 at Cranfield, he and Ann Halsey were married. This was a double wedding with Robert Halsey and Ann Wheeler. Presumably it was a case of a brother and sister marring a sister and brother. Unfortunately, the relationships are not yet proved. About 1636-7, along with his brothers and at least two sisters, he emigrated to New England and settled in Concord, Massachusetts. From the Roll of Arrears of Payment of Ship Money, 1637, county Bedford (a tax list): "Thomas Wheeler gone into New England, 01-05-00". He was made a freeman of the colony on 17 April 1637.

Within a few years, many Concord families were attracted to Fairfield, Connecticut. There Thomas Wheeler and his two youngest brothers and other Concord families migrated in the summer of 1644, led by the Reverend John Jones. Fairfield had been settled in 1639 by a few familes from Windsor, Connecticut, and other places under the leadership of Roger Ludlow. The Jones party swelled the population of Fairfield, but Concord lost "a 7th or 8th part of the Towne" and "many more resolved to goe after them, so that many houses in the Towne stand voyde of Inhabitants and more are likely to be".

It is said that he was the first settler at Black Rock and that he built a stone house or fort having a plank roof on which he mounted two four-pounders, one pointing toward the mouth of the harbor, the other toward an Indian fort situated at the head of the harbor, now known by the name Old Fort, which at times was defended by 200 Indians and served as their refuge in the numerous wars with rival tribes from further inland. His home lot at Pequonnock of 2½ acres, recorded in January 1649, was bounded on the northeast with the home-lot of Thomas Wheeler, junior, on the northwest by James Bennett's, on the southeast by John Evart's and on the southwest by the highway.

Thomas Wheeler made his will on 16 January 1653/4 and the inventory was made on 23 August 1654. He provided generously for his wife Ann, and to his "eldest son Thomas" who lived in Concord, he gave his home-lot and all land, divided or undivided, in Concord. To his daughter Sarah, wife of Thomas Sherwood, he gave 10 shillings, and to her son Thomas a colt. To his four grandchildren (Mary, James, Thomas and John Bennet, children of his daughter Hannah, then dead) and to James Bennet who had married his daughter in 1639, he gave 10 shillings each. To his son John, his sole executor, he left all his estate in Fairfield, reserving to his wife Ann the right to his house and lands left for her use at Greenlea. He made Lieutenant Thomas Wheeler (who was his youngest brother), Robert Lockwood and Andrew Ward overseers of his will. His widow, Ann, died in Fairfield in 1659, her will dated 21 August and her inventory dated 20 October following. She bequeathed to her eldest son Thomas and his wife and children, to the children of her daughter Hannah (mentioning Sarah and Hannah Bennet by name), to grandchild Sarah Sherwood and Annis Sherwood "wife of my son-in-law". She gave her best hat to Rebecca Turney, and to Ann Squire a petticoat. An illegible part of the will may have mentioned her son John.

Children, baptized at Cranfield, Bedfordshire:

ANN, bapt. 30 Jan. 1613/14, "dau. of Thomas Wheler, Jun."; buried 16 July 1615

ALICE, bapt. 15 June 1616, "dau. of Thomas Wheler of Warley"; m 16 Oct. 1634, John Billington, son of George, bapt. 14 Feb. 1612/13; ch.: Mary bapt. 14 Feb. 1635/6, Elizabeth bapt. 12 May 1638, John bapt. 25 Dec. 1640, George bapt. 11 Dec. 1642, Thomas bapt. 20 Sept. 1645, Susan bapt. 15 Aug. 1647, Ann bapt. 16 April 1649. They remained in England. He was buried there 26 Sept. 1671

ANN, bapt. 15 Feb. 1617/18; m about 1639, James Bennett; ch. bapt. at Concord: Hannah 1 June 1640, Thomas 10 Oct. 1640; moved to Fairfield, Conn. about 1644 with her father; 2 more ch. recorded at Fairfield, plus more ch.; she m 2, Joseph Middlebrook who d about Nov. 1686. Ann d before 1654, leaving 4 ch.

THOMAS, bapt. 9 April 1620; m 1, Sarah Merriam, dau. of Joseph & Sarah (Goldstone) Merriam; 10 ch.; m 2, Sarah (Beers) Stearns; 2 ch.; he d 24 Dec. 1704; "eldest son" per his mother's will

ELIZABETH, bapt. 4 Nov. 1622, "dau. of Thomas Wheler of Warley"; prob. d.y.

JOHN, bapt. 27 Feb. 1624/5; m 1, Judith Turney, dau. of Benjamin; m 2, about 1673, Elizabeth Rowland; he settled in Fairfield with his father; freeman 1669; he was granted 100 acres by the Gen. Ct., was deputy from the town several times; he had 14 ch. of which 13 survived him & whose ages were given in the distribution of his estate in 1690: Judith 29, John 26, Elizabeth 23, Thomas 21, Mary 19, Rebecca 18, Joseph 16, Hannah 14, Abigail 10, Obediah 8, Anne 6, Jonathan 3, Davis 1. His estate totaled £1656.4s.6d.

SARAH, bapt. 10 Aug. 1628; m Thomas Sherwood, Jr.; had a son Thomas who was named in her father's will, also a dau. Sarah; he m 2, Ann Turney; m 3, Elizabeth (____) Cable; m 4, Sarah (Hide) Coley

Note: There were 5 more children of Thomas Wheelers baptized at Cranfield: Mary 17 Feb. 1627/8 "dau. of Thomas", Susan 4 April 1630 "dau. of T.W. tenant to ye Lordship", Sarah 20 June 1630 of T.W."of ye Woode", Mary 24 Feb. 1635/6, Elizabeth 7 Jan. 1637/8 of T.W. "joiner". Obviously there were several Thomas Wheelers. Certainly Elizabeth's father was one who remained behind in England. After these there were no more children of any Thomas Wheeler at Cranfield for the next 30 years.

THE NORMAN DOORWAY, OF THE CRANFIELD CHURCH

Ref.: T.A.G. 12, 14, 27, 28; Cranfield Parish Register; History of Fairfield, by Elizabeth H. Schenck, 1889; Unpublished Studies of Lt. Col. Raymond D. Wheeler

4 b

THOMAS WHEELER (*John?*) was born about 1560-65, probably at Cranfield, Bedfordshire, where he lived and died. He was probably the son of John Wheeler of Cranfield who made his will 9 February 1566/7 and died shortly thereafter. In his will, he named his wife Alice and two minor children, Thomas and John. An abstract of his will follows. The fact that he left only these two children, both minors, suggests that they were quite young and only the first of what might have been a much larger family, had he lived. Conceivably, of course, these two sons might have been nearing maturity and the sole survivors of a larger number. However, the first possibility seems more probable. The naming pattern of Thomas's children suggests that his father was John. Strangely, however, he named no daughter Alice, nor did he name one Rebecca after his wife, so the naming pattern for the sons is not much evidence.

> 9 February 1566/7 - the will of JOHN WHEELER of Cranfield, county Bedford, husbandman, sick of body ... to be buried in the churchyard of Cranfield ...to the church of Lincoln 2d. ... for tythes forgotten 12d. ... to the bells 12d. ... to the poor men's box 8d. ... to the highways 3s.4d. ... to the poor within the parish 6s.8d. ... to Robert Tatham a yearling bullock ... to Annes my servant 2 couples of ewes & lambs ... to Matthew Vauxe a red heifer ... whereas the church by my office oweth me 20d, I do forgive the same ... I will & give all my copy hold land within Cranfield as by surrender thereof made into the hands of Robert Styrmy ... to the use of Thomas Wheler my son ... and he to enter to the same at age 21, paying out of the same to John my son when he cometh to the age of 21 years £10 & within 8 years next after the same payment another £10 to the same John ... residue to Alice my wife, she to be sole executrix ... supervisor to be Robert Styrmy & he to have for his pains 20d. Witnesses: William Baker, William Wheler, jun. & Richard Mowse. (Bedfordshire Wills 1567/89)

Thomas Wheeler made his will on 7 December 1627, added a codicil to it on 18 June 1633, and died about 10 February 1634/5, for he was buried on the 11th. The burial record calls him "Thomas Wheler of the blakehouse". Since his will clearly indicates two living sons named Thomas, and his children were born over a period of about thirty years, it is clear that he had at least two wives. His last wife, named in his will, was Rebecca. She was last recorded as living in her daughter Abiah's will of 10 April 1637. Within a year or two, Rebecca and the children all left for New England. This can be deduced, as many of the children were underage at the time, and surely would not have gone to New England without their mother. However, no record of her in New England has been found, so she apparently did not live long after. Thomas's will follows, certain parts crossed out just as in the original document.

In the name of God amen the seaventh day of december in the yeare of our lord god one thousand Sixe hundred Twenty and Seaven I Thomas Wheler sen of Cranfield in the County of Bedf. yeoman weake in bodie but of good and pfecte remembrance Gods holie name be praised doe make and ordayne this my last will and testament in manner and forme followinge That is to say ffirst I give and bequeath my soule unto allmightie god my Creator hoping assuredly through the merittes of Jesus Christ to be made ptaker of life everlastinge And my bodie to the Earth whereof it is made Item I give and bequeath unto Rebecca my wife (for and during the terme of her life if she keepe herself a widow) all that Capitall messuage or tenement with the apptenances lying and being in the Towne end of Cranfield aforesaid wch I lately purchased of John Vause Esquire And after the decease of the said Rebecca my wife or day of her marriage with any pson whatsoever I give and bequeath the said Capital messuage or tenemente with all houses edifices buildings yards and gardens groundes comons pfitts andapptenances thereto belonging to Joseph Wheler my sonne and his heirs for ever uppon theese condicons followinge vizt that he the said Joseph my sonne shall well and truly pay or cause to be payd out of my said messuage and pmisses the full sume of Thirtye pounds of lawfull money of England to my executor or executrix hereafter named or to such other pson or psons as my said executor or executrix shall nominate and appoynte of debts where I owe And also pay or cause to be payd out of my said Messuage with the apputenances unto Thomas Wheler my youngest son the full sume of Twenty poundes of lawfull money of England wch sumes of Thirty poundes ~~and twenty poundes~~ are to be payd by the said Joseph ~~when he cometh to the full age of one and twenty~~ years within one yeare after my decease And for the better payment of the said sumes by him the said Joseph I have surrendered to his use Twelve acres of Coppie hold land Provided allwaies and my will and minde absolutly is that if the said Joseph my sonne or his assigns doe not pay the said sumes of Thirty and twenty poundes in such maner and forme at such dayes and to such pson or psons as afore is expressed then the gift and bequest of the said Messuage or tenement with the apptenances shalbe voyd and of none effect to all intents and purposes whatsoever And I give and bequeath the said Messuage wth the apptenances comons and pfitts whatsoever to the said Thomas Wheler my yongest sonne and his heires for ever and for default of such issue the remaynder thereof to

Efraim Wheler my sonne and his heirs for ever aniething herein to the contrarie hereof in anie wise notwithstanding Item I give and bequeath to Thomas Wheler of Warley my eldest sonne the sume of Twelve pence Item I give to Priscila Cockes my daughter twelve pence Item I give to John Wheler my sonne twelvepence Item I give to Elizabeth Bread my daughter twelve pence Item I give to Suzana Wheler my daughter ~~one ewe lame a table and fframe atandinge in the plor at Borne end house~~ Item I give to Abiah Wheler my daughter ~~one whyte weaninge calfe and~~ Two table clootes Item I give to Marie Wheler my daughter one standinge bedsted and Two Table Clootes Item I give to the said Joseph my sonne one fframe scovell standing in the yard at my messuage at the towne end the old carte and ould wheeles and a dung carte Item I give to the said Efraim Wheler my sonne one frame scovell at the ould Barne and ffower principallpostes for a house And all the longe timber under the little scovelles in the close yard at Borne end ~~and one weaning calfe~~ And my will is that Thomas Tomkins shall lawfully convey and assure That ffrehold I bought of him to the said Efraim my sonne and his heires for ever Item I give to the said Thomas Wheler my youngest son ~~one pott one Tegg~~ and five pounds of lawful money of England to be payd to him by my executor and executrix at the age of 24 years ~~Item I give to Allin Broad my sonne in law one carte Bodie lying behinde the stoles in the ould barne and 2 broad ristes~~ Item I give and bequeath to the said Rebecka my wife all my movable goodes wthin my two dwelling houses at Borne end and the towne end (unbequeathed) and two heffers the one a red the other a little browne one and one ewe sheepe And also my will is that Timothie Wheler my sonne shall have halfe of my messuage closes lands and medowes at Borne end aforesaid and half the benefitt and pfitt thereof for Thre yeares next after my decease (for an ease or helpe towards the payment of my debts) All the rest of my goods and cattelles as well reales as psonales unbequeathed I give and bequeath to the said Timothie my sonne whome I make my full and sole executor of this my last will and testament And if he the said Timothie refuse to be executor of this my will then I make Rebecka my wife executrix of this my last will and I doe hereby utterly revoke and annull in deed and in law all former willes testaments legaces bequestes and executors by me formerly made And lastly my will is that the legacy of xx£ shallbe payd by the said Joseph to the said Thomas my youngest sonne out of my said messuage with the appurtenances when he cometh to the age of xxi years In witness whereof I the said Thomas Wheler the elder have to this my last will and testament sett my hand and seale the day and yeare first above written

(signed)
Thomas Wheler the elder

Postscrip the 18 daie of June 1633. Itm I give and bequeath unto Efraim Wheeler my sonne one little pshtle late Tomas Tomkins containing one rood and halfe with the apurtenances to the heires and assignes of the said Efraim for ever

(signed)
Thomas Wheler the elder

Signed and delivered in the psence of Tho: Arnald, Richard Arnald, Thomas Baker. No Inventory
Probate 24 February 1634 granted to the executors named at the Archdeaconry Court of Bedford.

Autograph of
Thomas Wheler the elder
from his will, 1627.

Children, baptized at Cranfield, Bedfordshire:

2 THOMAS, b about 1590, "eldest son"; m 5 May 1613 at Cranfield, Ann Halsey; they settled in Concord, Mass. & then to Fairfield, Conn. where he d in 1654, she in 1659

PRISCILLA, b about 1592; m 17 June 1612 at Cranfield, Stephen Cocks of Stagsden, a nearby parish; ch.: Susanna bapt. 10 Sept. 1615, Ann/Agnes bapt. 27 Oct. 1616 - buried 11 March 1625/6, John bapt. 30 Jan. 1619/20 - buried 1 Feb. 1619/20. She was buried at Stagsden 25 Nov. 1627

ANN, perhaps, who m 5 May 1613 at Cranfield, Robert Halsey; no further record of them in Cranfield; if a dau., she must have d before her father's will as he didn't mention her

JOHN, b perhaps about 1596; he was alive in 1627 per his father's will

DEBORAH, b perhaps 1598-1600; buried 30 March 1600, "Deborah Wheler dau. of Thos. Wheler", perhaps this Thomas

ELIZABETH, bapt. 18 July 1602, "dau. of Thomas Wheler of Wharley"; m 14 Nov. 1622 at Pulloxhill, Bedfordshire, which is 10 miles SE of Cranfield, Allen Breed, son of John & Agnes (Pratchett) Breed. He was b about 1600 at Westoning, Bedfordshire. They settled in Lynn, Mass.; ch.: Allen bapt. 27 Jan. 1630/31, Elizabeth bapt. 23 May 1632 - d.y., Elizabeth bapt. 26 Dec. 1634, John b about 1638; she d & he m 2, 28 March 1656, Elizabeth Knight; he d 17 March 1690/91

TIMOTHY, bapt. 28 Dec. 1604; m 1, at Cranfield 30 April 1632, Susan Knight, prob. dau. of John Knight & bapt. at Cranfield 21 Sept. 1606; she or a 2nd wife "Jane" d at Concord 12 Feb. 1642/3; he m last, Mary Brooks, dau. of Thomas & Grace Brooks of Concord. He d at Concord 30 July 1687 aged "about 86" - g.s., but actually aged 82; called Captain; ch.: Deborah bapt. 12 April 1637, Sarah b 22 June 1640, Mary b 3 Oct. 1657 - d 6 Oct. 1660, Elizabeth b 6 Oct. 1661, Rebecca b about 1666

SUSAN, bapt. 31 May 1607; m 20 Jan. 1633/4 at Cranfield, Obadiah Wheeler of Cranfield, son of John & Elizabeth, bapt. 5 Dec. 1609; ch.: Joshua bapt. 15 Sept. 1637, John b 27 Jan. 1640/1 - d.y., Ruth b 23 April 1642 - prob. d.y., Son b 25-d 29 Nov. 1643, Samuel b 22 Feb. 1644/5, Susanna b 17 March 1648/9. She d at Concord 24 March 1648/9. He m 2, had 3 more ch. He d 27 Oct. 1671 at Concord

JOSEPH, bapt. 18 Feb. 1609/10; m 1, Elizabeth ——— who was buried 19 July 1642 at Concord; ch.: Ephraim b 14 April 1640 - buried 19 July 1642, Joseph b 1 Dec. 1641 - buried 18 July 1642. He m 2, Sarah Merriam, widow of Joseph & dau. of John & Frances (Jefferie) Goldstone; ch.: Mary b 20 Sept. 1643, Rebecca b 6 Sept. 1645. He m 3, Frances (Watson)(Wheeler)(Cook) Greene, widow of Isaac Wheeler of Charlestown, Richard Cook, then of Thomas Greene of Malden. He was called Lieutenant. He was alive in 1681, aged 71

ABIAH, bapt. 17 Jan. 1612/13; buried 18 April 1637 at Cranfield

10 April 1637 - the will of ABYA WHEELER of Cranfield in the county of Bedford, spinster, being weak of body ... to be buried in the churchyard of Cranfield ... unto Ephraim Wheeler my brother one acre of arable land with the appurtenances lying on a furlong called Waker furlong in Perrie field, late the land of Henry Taylore ... unto Tymothie Wheeler my brother 40s. ... unto Elizabeth Bread my sister 10s. ... unto Susan Wheeler my sister 40s. ... to Agnes Underwood 40s. ... the aforesaid sums all to be paid within five years by my brother Ephraim ... all my good whatsoever I do give and bequeath unto Rebecka Wheeler my loving mother whom I do make sole executrix. Signed by mark. Witnesses: Thomas Baker, Obadiah Wheeler. Proved 25 May 1637 (Bedfordshire Wills 1637/110)

MARY, bapt. 20 Oct. 1615, "dau. of Thomas Wheler of Bornend; she ("Alice" *sic*) m 16 Oct. 1634 at Cranfield, John Billington, son of George, bapt. 14 Feb. 1612/13; a dau. Mary b & d 1636; she ("Mary" in rec.) was buried 19 April 1636, 4 days after her baby; he m 2, 2 June 1637, Mary Bright

EPHRAIM, bapt. 16 March 1618/19; freeman at Concord 1639; m Ann Turney; moved to Fairfield, Conn. 1644; ch.: Isaac b 23 Dec. 1642 at Concord, Mary, Ruth, Hannah, Rebecca, Judith, Abigail, Samuel b about 1658, Timothy b about 1660, Ephraim. He d at Fairfield, Conn. 1670?

THOMAS, bapt. 8 Dec. 1621, "youngest son" per his father's will; m Ruth Wood, dau. of William; 7 known ch.; settled in Concord, thence to Fairfield, returned to Concord where he d 10 Dec. 1676; apparently in Marlborough, Mass. 1664-70; Lt., Capt. in King Philip's War, was wounded in battle at Manameset near Brookfield in Aug. 1675 when he & his men, against the advice of their Indian allies, advanced along a trail between a hill & a swamp & were caught in an ambush. His son Thomas, Jr., altho severely wounded, rescued him. He wrote an account of the battle which has been widely referred to.

HENRY WHITFIELD (*Thomas, Robert, Robert, Myles, etc.*) was probably born at Mortlake, Surrey, a suburb of London where his parents had a home. Supposedly he was born about the summer of 1590, according to various investigations and known school and college requirements. His father was Thomas Whitfield, a prominent London lawyer. His mother was Mildred Fortune Manning of Greenwich, Kent. His father naturally hoped he would become a lawyer and gave him a liberal education. He first attended Winchester College (school) and then on 19 June 1610, at the age of 19, entered New College, Oxford. While there, he met and became a lifelong friend of George Fenwick, later a leader of the settlement of Saybrook, Connecticut. Upon graduation, Henry Whitfield began the study of law at the Inns of Court, but soon changed to the ministry, being encouraged by such eminent ministers of his day as Dr. Stanton, Mr. Byfield, and others.

In 1617, already a clergyman, he and his father entered into the following contract with his bride-to-be and her father. He was shortly thereafter married.

Indenture tripartite made 20 September, 15 James I (1617) between Thomas Whitfeld of Mortlake, county Surrey, esquire, and Henry Whitfeld of Okelye in the same county, clerk, on the first part; Thomas Sheafe of Wickham, county Barks., Doctor of Divinity and Dorothy Sheafe, spinster, his daughter, on the second part; Thomas Woodwarde of Lyncolns Inne, county Middlesex, esquire, Richard Kinge of Lyncolns Inne, esquire, Thomas Rashleigh of the Strande, London, gentleman, and David Rawsoune of St. Gregoryes, London, woollen draper, on the third part, being the settlement previous to the marriage of the said Henry Whitfeld and Dorothy Sheafe; in consideration of £400, her marriage portion, the said Thomas Whitfeld and Henry Whitfeld covenant to levy a fine and suffer recovery of their messuage and 100 ac. of fresh marsh in Bexhill, called Wrenhams, and also of their closes of pasture and fresh marsh, called Jesus marshe in Aylsham *alias* Haylsham, the said recovery to enure, as to the said messuage and 70 ac. of fresh marsh land in Bexhill to the use of the said Henry Whitfeld and Dorothy Sheafe, and the heirs of the said Henry Whitfeld, and as to the other 30 ac. of fresh marsh called Wrenhams and the lands called Jesus marshe to the use of the said Henry Whitfeld, his heirs and assigns. Seal & Signatures of *Thomas Whytfeld* and *Henry Whitfeld*. (Ref.: Sussex Archaeological Society, Vol. 37, p 46)

Dorothy's father, Thomas Sheafe, was a clergyman, a native of Cranbrook, Kent, and was a Canon of Saint George's Chapel, Windsor, and Rector of the church at Welford, Berkshire. In these surroundings Dorothy Sheafe was reared.

About the time of his marriage, Henry Whitfield was appointed Rector of the church of Saint Margaret at Ockley, Surrey, no doubt thru the office of his sister-in-law's father, Sir Edward Culpepper. Sir Edward was lord of the manor of Ockley and held the advowson of the church, that is, the right to appoint the rector.

Henry Whitfield enjoyed a life of comfort and some wealth. His father, who died in 1629, left and had given him a fair estate. For twenty years he enjoyed the quiet gracious life of an English vicar among the rolling meadows and dales of Surrey. He also preached thruout the surrounding countryside whenever possible.

During the reign of Charles I, in the early 17th century, the Church of England began its persecution of dissidents within the church. Separatists and Puritans alike were censured and some had to flee England. Henry Whitfield was not among the dissidents at first. He conformed to the faith during most of his term as vicar at Ockley, while maintaining personal friendships with such persecuted non-conformists as Mr. Cotton, Mr. Hooker, Mr. Goodwin and Mr. Nye, who were often sheltered under his roof. Eventually, their influence persuaded him to non-conformist views and he himself was called before the High Commission Court of Archbishop William Laud and he was censured. In 1638, Henry Whitfield resigned his position as pastor at Ockley and sold his personal estate.

Indenture made 1 February, 14 Charles I (1638/9), by which Henry Whitfield of Ockley, county Surrey, clerk, and Dorothy Whitfield, his wife, and Thomas Whitfield of Worth, esquire, son and heir of John Whitfield, late of Worth, esquire, deceased, sell to Edward Godman of Westminston, gentleman, for £2,000, the messuage or dwelling house and fresh marsh, containing 100 ac. in Bexhill, called Wrenhams. Seals & Signatures of *Hry Whitfeld, Dorothe Whitfeld, Tho: Whitfeld.* (ibid. 37:49)

Chirograph of a fine levied at Westminster in three weeks from Michaelmas, 15 James I (1639), between Thomas Woodward, esquire, and Richard Kyng, esquire, querist, and Thomas Whitfeld, esquire, and **Henry Whitfeld**, clerk, deforciants, by which the deforciants remise and quitclaim one messuage, 20 acres of pasture and 140 acres of fresh marsh in Boxhill and Aylsham *alias* Haylsham, to the said Thomas Woodward and Richard Kyng and the heirs of Thomas [Latin] (ibid)

The next year, he and his family emigrated to New England. With him came twenty-four families of young people (he was 49 at the time). Most were farmers of Surrey, Kent and Sussex.

During the long voyage across the Atlantic, Whitfield drew up an agreement which was signed by all the heads of the accompanying families. It has come down to us as the Guilford Covenant. The original is lost, but a clerk's copy survives.

The Reverend John Davenport, a friend of Whitfield's, had emigrated and founded the New Haven Colony. Whitfield's college friend George Fenwick, now Colonel Fenwick, had helped found the Saybrook Colony in 1635. It was natural then that Henry Whitfield should aim for the shores of what is now Connecticut. They landed first at Quinnipiac, or what now is New Haven, where they were welcomed by Davenport and the settlers there. After some consultation with Davenport and Colonel Fenwick (who had accompanied Whitfield from England where he had been on a visit) it was agreed that Whitfield would found a settlement about halfway between the two existing ones. Either by land or sea, Whitfield's group reached the site of what is now Guilford, and in September 1639, purchased land from the Menuncatuck Indians (see deed). With them, too, came the "little red cattle" given them by Lady Fenwick of Saybrook, said to have been some of the first cattle brought to New England.

Arriving in Menuncatuck late in the season, the colonists probably only got started on the home of Henry Whitfield, closing in enough to give them shelter for the first winter. These colonists were not familiar with the advantages of wood construction and so this house was constructed of native stone. The style is like that found north of London rather than in Surrey. Perhaps William Leete of Cambridge, a natural and aggressive leader, was the planner and master builder. The stone was from a ledge about a quarter mile east of the house. Tradition says that Indians were employed to haul it on hand-barrows. The mortar was made of yellow clay and crushed oyster shells. The walls are two feet thick and the timbers are hand hewn oak. The inside partitions were of pine planks. It is now a museum and the oldest extant house in the original thirteen states. It was restored in 1939.

In this house Henry Whitfield, his wife and seven of their nine children settled down and lived for eleven years. In the fall of 1650, having made known his plans to return to England, he set sail, leaving his wife and most of his children behind. The whole town accompanied him to the water side, "with a spring tide of tears because they should see his face no more". Just why he returned, and without his wife, is unknown. In any event, after a roundabout trip by way of Boston, he reached England about the time Cromwell was made Lord Protector and the Puritans were secure in power. He settled in Winchester where he lived seven more years and died in September 1657. He was buried on the 17th in Winchester Cathedral. He left a nuncupative (oral) will and by it left all to the disposal of his wife Dorothy, according to the statement of Nathaniel and Mary Whitfield. Dorothy was granted administration 29 January 1657/8. An abstract of his will follows.

Memorandum that on or about the seventeenth day of September One Thousand six hundred fifty seven or thereabouts HENRY WHITFEILD of the City of Winchester in the County of Southtõn Clerke with an intent to make his will and dispose of his estate, being of good and disposing memory and understanding, did utter, nuncupate and declare his last Will & Testam^{t} in manner and forme following, or the lyke in effect, viz., I doe give and bequeath all my estate whatsoever unto my wife to bee disposed of by her to and amongst my children as shee shall see cause. In testimony whereof wee the Witnesses p^{r}esent when the said dec̃ed uttered the same words or the lyke in effect have hereunto sett our hands. Nath: Whitfeild, Mary Whitfeild.

Letters of Administration issued forth 29 January 1657 unto Dorothy Whitfeild widow, the relict and universal legatory named in the will of Henry Whitfeild late of Winchester in the County of Southampton deceased to administer the goods etc. of the said deceased. (Prerog. Court of Canterbury Wills, Wootton 17)

The earliest known print of the Henry Whitfield House as it appeared in the *Ladies Repository Magazine*, Volume 23, 1863.

14 August 1655

Henry Whitfield to Henry Scobell, Esquire, Clerk of the Council of State, about augmenting the income of Presbyterian and Independent Preachers, and recommending a German in his neighborhood as a fit person to partake of such an augmentation. (Note, it was about this time that Cromwell had projected some specious proposals of reconciliation between the Presbyterians and Independents. See Echard, p. 719 b)

Sir:

I Received your Letter, in the Day I make Answere to it. I was glad to see the Breathings of your Spirit in this Way, wherein you may doe our Lord much Service.

The Truth is, the Want of Meanes doth very much hinder the Gatheringe of Churches in the Nation. I suppose much more might have binn donn, if such a Course might have binn taken.

We are not so happy in this Countie, as to reckon many Churches gathered, especially in the purest Way. Here be diverse godly Men that are Presbyterians, that have gathered some Churches in a hopeful Way, & some are now gatheringe. The Time you set me for the Returne of Answere is so short, that I have not Time to make any Inquirie in the Countrie. But I shall doe it with all the Care & Speed I can; & give you a farther Account of your Letter.

Here is neere unto us a German Stranger, a godly Man, that was driven out of his Countrie many Yeeres since for his Religion, who came into England, & hath binn a Preacher for about eighteen Years. Hee is a good Scholler, & painfull in his Place. Hee hath a Livinge (as they call it) of £xl per annum, with an Augmentation of £x per annum. Hee hath a Wife, & ten Children. His Wife is great with the eleventh, All little, & at home with him. This Man, having but a small Parish, is nowe gatheringe together the godly minded of his Parish, & resolving to enter into a Church Way according to Christ. His Straits are great, by Reason of his great Charge. I should desire that this Man's Condition might bee taken into Consideration, if it might sute with what you intend. Surely some small yeerly Allowance would much refresh the Bowels of him and his Family, and would much incourage him in his Worke begunn. But I shall leave it with you, & your selfe to the Guidance of our Lord Christ, in all your Purposes & Endeavours for his Praise, in whom I rest.

Aug. xiv. M,DC,LV

To the much honoured Mr. Henry Scobell, at his House at Westminster, in the old Abby-Yard, present these. Post paid.

(This Letter was published by Francis Peck, London, 1732, in his DESIDERATA CURIOSA, XIII:8)

LETTER OF HENRY WHITFIELD TO DR. STOUGHTON

(Note reference to harassment of non-conformists by agents of Archbishop Laud)

Sir

I would intreat a favr from you being it is wth us as you knowe, and how wee shall bee enquired into, and especially the Archbpps visitation beinge presently after Ester in or Diocess and I am at this time destitute of a Curate my sute unto you is that if you knowe of a youngue man who were now loose and at liberty to come downe unto mee for I would not draw any out of any setled place my owne standinge beinge very uncertaine yet I thinke I may through gods mercy abide as I am till ye end of sumer which I account a great time and a large favor if it may bee soe. hee is to doe nothinge for mee but read prayer and officiate in that kind helpe in ye administration of ye Sacrament or the like because preachinge is now at a great rate; hee shall have after 20l p annu for the time hee is to stay with mee and hee is to live in a gentlemans family in my parish wher hee shall bee conveniently provided for since my owne house is full. If you can helpe mee you may send to Mr Stone in Catteaton Street not far from you wher the bearer lives who will give directions of his cumming unto mee. I should bee glad to have a line from you on Friday by or carrier to knowe what you could doe. I would also gladly heare how it goes wth yor selfe about the Booke for I heard you were like to bee questioned. Thus not doubting of yor love desiringe mutual prayers I rest

March 2. 1634

Yor loving frend to his power

Hry Whitfield

Sir

I would intreat a favor from you being it is wth us as you knowe, and how wee shall bee enquired into, and especially the Archbpps visitation beinge presently after Ester in or Diocess and I am at this time destitute of a Curate my sute unto you is that if you knowe of a youngue man who were now loose and at liberty to come downe unto mee for I would not draw any out of any setled place my owne standinge beinge very uncertaine yet I thinke I may through gods mercy abide as I am till ye end of sumer which I account a great time and a large favor if it may be soe.

hee is to doe nothinge for mee but read prayer and officiate in that kind helpe in ye administration of ye Sacrament or the like because preachinge is now at a greate rate. hee shall have after 20l p anna for the time hee is to stay with mee and hee is to live in a gentlemans family in my parish wher hee shall bee conveniently provided for sinc my owne house is full. If you can helpe mee you may send to Mr Stone in Cateaten street not far from you wher this bearer lives who will give directions of his cuming unto mee. I should bee glad to have a line from you on Friday by or carrier to knowe what you could doe. I would alsoe gladly heare how it goes wth yor selfe about the Booke for I heard you were like to bee questioned. Thus not doubting of yor love desiringe or mutual prayers I rest.

March 2. 1634

Yor lovinge frende
to his power
Hry̅ Whitfeld

Dorothy Whitfield continued to live in the stone house on its commanding knoll long after her husband's departure. Three of the daughters were married in New England; the other children lived with her, but Mary and Nathaniel were with their father when he died, so they must have returned to England prior to 1657. What became of son Thomas and the youngest child Rebecca is unknown. Probably they died young. In 1659, Dorothy Whitfield returned to England and lived there until her death in 1669.

Henry Whitfield wrote several pieces, of which were published the following:

Some Helps to Stirre up Christian Duties (3rd edition, 1636)
The Light Appearing More and More Towards the Perfect Day, or a Farther Discovery of the Present State of the Indians in New England Concerning the Progresse of the Gospel Among them (London, 1651)
Strength out of Weakness (London, 1652)

These last told of the spread of the gospel among the Indians.

Mather wrote of Henry Whitfield that from childhood thru his entire life, he was a pious and prayerful person.

See THE ANCESTRY OF REVEREND HENRY WHITFIELD AND HIS WIFE DOROTHY SHEAFE, by John B. Threlfall, 1989, privately printed, for further information on this family.

Children, born and baptized at Ockley, Surrey:

DOROTHY, bapt. 25 March 1619; m Samuel Desborough, b Nov. 1619, son of James of Elltisley, Cambridgeshire; they returned to England with her father; she d late 1654 of smallpox; 1 known ch., Sarah, b 1649

SARAH, bapt. 1 Nov. 1620; m 1641 Rev. John Higginson of Salem & Guilford, son of Francis & Ann (Herbert), b 6 Aug. 1616; 7 ch.; she d 8 July 1675; he d 9 Dec. 1708 ae 92

ABIGAIL, bapt. 1 Sept. 1622; m Rev. James Fitch of Saybrook & Norwich, b 22 Dec. 1622 at Bocking, Essex, Eng.; 6 ch.; she d 9 Sept. 1659; he m 2, Priscilla Mason; he d 18 Nov. 1702 at Lebanon, Conn. to where he moved

THOMAS, bapt. 28 Dec. 1624; prob. d.y.

JOHN, bapt. 11 Feb. 1626/7; came to Guilford with parents, returned to England; prob. he was one who m Elizabeth Waldish, only dau. of Alexander who d testate 1665 as:

27 November 1662 - the will of Alexander Weldish of Bread in Sussex, gen[t]...wife's son Thomas Freebody...my three grandchildren Dorothy Whitfeild, Elizabeth Whitfeild and Jane Whitfeild, daughters of mine only daughter Elizabeth Whitfeild, at days of marriage or ages of one and twenty... Books wherein my wife's name is written by my son Whitfeild ...Daughter Elizabeth Whitfeild sole executrix and Thomas Lake of Gowtherst in Kent Esq. overseer. Son John Whitfeld...George Weldish...Children of Dorothy Lenham late of Gowtherst deceased, widow...The children of my sister Dorothy Hermon deceased....Wife (name not given) Proved 5 February 1665/6 (P.C.C., Mico - 37)

NATHANIEL, bapt. 28 June 1629; retuned to Eng. about 1665; living 1685 when he admin. estate of his nephew, Francis Higginson of London

Mense Aprilis Anno Dñi 1685. Decimo die em[t] Comõ Nathanieli Whitfeild avunculo et priñcili creditori Francisci Higginson nuꝑ ꝑõae sc̃i Olavi Hartstreete London caelibis defti he'ntis etc. ad adstrand bona, iura et cred dc̃i defti. (Administration Act Book 1685, L. 45)

MARY, bapt. 4 March 1631/2; living in 1657

HENRY, bapt. 9 March 1633/4; buried at Ockley 28 Feb. 1634/5

REBECCA, bapt. 20 Dec. 1635; no more known

Ref.: N.E.H.G.S.-51,52,53; Mass. Hist. Coll. 3rd Series, IV; N.Y. Gen. & Biogr. Rec. 43:94; Magnalia Christi, by Cotton Mather; The Henry Whitfield House, 1970; Drake's American Biography; History of Guilford, by Steiner, by Smith; P.C.C. Probates; Annals of the American Pulpit, by Sprague

St. Margaret's Church in Ockley, Surrey, England looks today very much as it did in 1638 when Rev. Whitfield resigned his ministry there and led a band of emigrants to the shores of New England to found the town of Guilford, Connecticut.

2

THOMAS WISWELL (*Ralph, John* probably) was baptized 20 September 1601 at Warrington, Lancashire. He and his twin brother John both came to New England and settled in Dorchester as early as 1635. He was early made a freeman, was a proprietor of Dorchester and, with his wife Elizabeth, was a member of the church about 1636. He was a selectman of Dorchester in 1644, '45, and '52. On 5 June 1664 he was dismissed from the Dorchester church for the beginning of a new church at Cambridge Village (now Newton) and was chosen as ruling elder there. On 25 September 1657, he deeded his houses and lands in Dorchester to his son Enoch, who was about to marry.

Thomas Wiswell married first, it is said, Elizabeth Burbage of Great Packington, Warwickshire. She was the mother of all his children and died between 1665 and 1669. Secondly, he married Isabell (Muston) Farmer, sister of the Reverend Thomas Muston of Wykin and afterwards of Brinklow in England. She was the widow of John Farmer of Anseley, Warwickshire.

Thomas Wiswell was excused from military training on 6 October 1663, but had to pay 5 shillings per year to the military company. He was 62.

He died on 6 December 1683, aged 82, and she died on 21 May 1686 at her son's home in Billerica.

This is an Inventory of the Estate of Elder Thomas Wiswall of Cambr village who decead. 6 December 1683 Apprized by us the subscribers.

His wearing cloaths both linnen & woollen	006 07 00
In the lower Lodging Room	
A featherbed, a feather bolster, 2 feather pillows a straw bed & Rug, a blankett & bedstead with curtains altogether	005 00 00
4 pr of old sheets, 4 pillowbeers	001 15 00
2 Table cloaths, 11 napkins, 4 Towells	001 00 00
a Table, a form, 6 joynd stools, a little Table	001 05 00
A great chair, 2 small chairs, 6 cushions	000 08 00
A chest, 2 Trunks, a warming pan	000 15 00
A small cupboard, 4 bibles, 4 Psalm books, 6 other small books	001 08 00
2 old brushes a little looking glass	000 02 00

In ye chamb over ye lodging Room

A featherbed, a feather bolster, a Red Rug, 2 blanketts, with curtains vallaince, bedstead	008 00 00
Another featherbed, a feather bolster, old Rug & coverlet, one blankett, an old bedstead	003 10 00
A Chest, 4 pound of cotton, 3 pound of flax, a small pr cell of yarn, a doz. & ½ of Trenchers	000 16 00
In the chamber over the fire Room	
A small flockbed with ye furniture to it.	000 12 00
Abt 20 bush. Indian corn in ye ears, abt. 3 bush of Rye, abt. a bush & ½ of Malt	002 12 00
In the barne	
Abt. 20 bush. Indian Corn in ye ears, abt. 12 bush. of unthreshed Rye, about 10 bush. of oats in ye straw	04 00 00
In the Cellar	
Abt. a barrell & ½ of Salt beef, 25 cheeses, 8 barrell of Cyder with ye barrells, abt. 6 pound of Rough suit, 3 earthen vessells	005 01 00
In the com̃on fire Room	
A small Table, a meal Trough	000 10 00
10 pewter platters	003 00 00
6 pewter porrings 16 spoons	000 06 00
A pewter flaggon, a drinking pott	000 10 00
2 drinking cups, 3 Salts, a little bottle, a candlestick, 2 chamb potts, 2 other dishes of pewter	00 16 00
5 brass kettles, a brass pan, a skillett, a chafing dish, a mortar & pestle, a frying pan	02 10 00
3 tinning pans pans, 4 pails, a wooden bowl	000 08 00
An Iron pot & potthooks a trammell, a fire shovell & Tongs 3 sieves	000 12 00
6 cows in good condition	015 00 00
3 cows very old	005 00 00
3 heifers coming 3 yeers old & a bull	007 10 00
3 calvs comiming a yeer old	002 10 00
3 mares yt are grown fitt for use	005 00 00
3 mares coming 3 yeers old	003 15 00
1 mare colt coming 2 yeers old	001 00 00
9 Swine	008 10 00
An Old Anvill 2 hammers	002 05 00
Irons for a Cart	000 14 00
A cross cutt saw, a hand saw	000 05 00
2 pitches or craws of Iron	000 08 00
one Axe, a broad hough, 2 beetlerings, 3 wedges, a short chaine, a plow chaine, 2 Augers	000 17 06
A prcell of old Iron	000 10 00
A hand vice, a sicle, a small beam, 4 small weights	000 03 06
Arms & Ammunition	001 10 00
2 old wheels & other lumber	000 05 00

2 old hogsheads, a tub, 2 trays, 2 milk bowls 2 small bear barrells	000 08 00
An old bridle & saddle, a pannell	000 10 00
A churne, 2 sacks, a grid Iron	000 05 00
A dwelling house & barn with a small orchard to it & about two hundred & seven acres of upland & meadow w:r of yr is about six acres of ye land yt is broak up	220 00 00
Abt a yeer & half service in a man servant	008 00 00
A p'rcell of stone fence abt ye aforesd land	007 00 00
The Irons to the pump	000 05 00

Apprised the 14. Decemb 1683
by us
Thomas Prentice
James Trowbridge
William Bond

Decemb: 18. 83
Sworne in Court of Noah Wiswall & Ebenezar Wiswall Adams

Jonathan Remmington Clericus

Children:

ENOCH, b about 1633 in England; m 25 Nov. 1657 Elizabeth Oliver, dau. of John & Elizabeth (Newgate) Oliver; 12 ch.; d 28 Nov. 1706 ae 73; a tanner; res. Dorchester; she d 31 May 1712

ESTHER, b about 1635; m 16 May 1655, William Johnson, son of Edward & Susan (Munter) Johnson of Woburn; 9 ch.; he d 22 May 1704; she d 27 Dec. 1707

ICHABOD, perhaps; he entered Harvard 1654, was 1st minister at Duxbury in 1676; m Priscilla Peabody, dau. of William; 7 ch.; he d 23 July 1700; she d 3 June 1724 ae 71

NOAH, bapt. 30 Dec. 1638 at Dorchester; m at Newton 10 or 16 Dec. 1664, Theodosia Jackson, dau. of John & Margaret; 9 ch.; killed by Indians at Wheelwrights Pond, N.H. 6 July 1690

MARY, according to Savage

EBENEZER, b 8 March 1641/2, bapt. 9 June 1650; m 26 March 1685, Sarah (Payson) Foster, wid. of Elisha & dau. of Giles Payson; no ch.; he d 21 June 1691; she d 22 Aug. 1714; res. Newton

SARAH, bapt. 19 March 1642/3; m Nathaniel, son of George Holmes of Roxbury, b 1 Feb. 1639/40; she d before 27 March 1667 when he m 2, Patience Topliff; he d 12 Feb. 1712/13

ELIZABETH, bapt. 15 April 1649

BENJAMIN, perhaps, bapt. 15 April 1649

THOMAS, bapt. 9 June 1650

HENRY, perhaps, bapt. 9 June 1650

Ref.: Wiswall Genealogy; V.R.; Pope's Pioneers of Massachusetts; Savage; N.E.H.G.S. -126:298

Heywood.

WARRINGTON CHURCH, LANCASHIRE

4

RALPH WISWELL (*John,* probably), a locksmith, was born about 1570 according to the Inquisition Post Mortem taken on the estate of his brother Thomas in 1619 at which time, Ralph was the next heir, aged 49 and more. At the time of his death he resided in the town of Haydock which is part of the parish of Winwick, Lancashire, and is about 6 miles north of Warrington, where his children were baptized. In the Winwick Parish Register are the following records. Probably Ralph was the child baptized in 1569.

Child of John Wiswell, baptized 11 November 1565
Child of John Wiswell, baptized 14 April 1569
Child of John Wiswell, baptized 4 December 1571
Child of John Wiswell, baptized 7 October 1573
Child of John Wiswell, baptized 19 April 1576
Jane Wiswell, baptized 28 October 1577
Elizabeth Wiswell, baptized 2 January 1579/80
John Wiswell, baptized 24 January 1582/3

John Wiswell & Jane Barowe, married 11 February 1602/3

Thomas, son of John Wiswell, baptized 12 December 1605
Robert, son of John Wiswell, baptized 23 October 1608

John Wiswell, buried 30 December 1608

Wiswell is a place name deriving from the village of that name in the parish of Whalley, Lancashire. It means Wiswell, well being a spring, but what Wis means is lost to history. Wiswell is about 30 miles northeast of Haydock.

Ralph Wiswell had a brother Thomas who lived in nearby Ormskirk and died on 10 April 1619, leaving no family. Ralph was the next heir as the Inquisition stated. An abstract follows.

INQUISITION taken at Preston, 7 September, 17 James [1619] before Edward Rigby, Esquire, Escheator, after the death of Thomas Wiswall, by the oath of the same Jurors, who say that Thomas Wiswall was seised in fee of 1 messuage and 2 acres of land, meadow and pasture, in Ormeskirke, which are held of William, Earl of Derby, in free socage by fealty and 18d. rent, as of his manor of Ormeskirke, and are worth per ann. (clear) 6s. 8d.

Thomas Wiswall died 10 April last past [1619], and Ralph Wiswall, his brother and next heir, is aged at the time of taking this Inquisition 49 years and more. (Lancashire Inquisitions, p. 137, pub. by Record Society)

Thomas married Alice Pickett on 20 October 1592 at Ormskirk, where she died in April 1618. She was buried in the church there on 12 April. Thomas was buried in the high chancell on 11 April 1619. Thomas had an illegitimate son, Edward, baptized on 7 March 1588/9 at Ormskirk, but the child must have died and he apparently had no children by his wife Alce.

In addition, Ralph had a sister, Anne who was apparently unmarried in 1632. She is mentioned in the inventory of his estate. James Wiswell, who died testate in 1603 leaving a widow, Elizabeth, may have been another brother. He named a sister Elizabeth, children of his sister, and children of Ralph Wiswell, altho he did not state the relationship of Ralph. An abstract of his will follows.

> 19 April 1603 - the will of James Wiswell of Wavertree in the parish of Childwall, county Lancaster, yeoman, being visited with sickness ...to be buried in the parish church of Childwall ...wife Elizabeth, son William ...unto such child or children as shall be born unto me hereafter either by this my wife or any other, but if none, then that third to my sister's children, viz. Margaret Houghe, Edward Merser, Thomas Merser, Alice Merser, all the daughters of William Dwaryhouse, all the children of William Diconson, Jane Merser, all the natural children of William Wright, Margerie Mosocke, and Margaret Mossock, saving that I doe give unto the children of Rauffe Wiswall soe much as one of my said sister's children shall have for their porcon out of the said third part. Another third part to various bequests including to James Diconson, Edward Merser £10 which his brother John doth owe to me, etc. ..unto Jane Merser...any remainder of this third to wife and son William ..to sister Elizabeth (Lancashire Wills pr. at Chester)

Ralph Wiswell died early in 1631/2, for the inventory of his estate was taken on 13 March following.

Note that in the following Inventory of Ralph's estate, among the listed creditors was his son John. Then there was listed Thomas, first noted as another son, then changed to read as his brother. This must be an error, for his brother Thomas was clearly dead. Later Ralph's sister was noted originally as sister of "the said John and Thomas Wiswell", and was then crossed out and corrected to read "sister of Ralph". Clearly the scribe was confused and John and Thomas were Ralph's sons, Anne probably his sister, or possibly a daughter.

A true and wise Inventorie of all the goodes, Cattell and Chattells of Raphe Wiswall late of Haidock in the Countie of Lancaster, Locksmith, deceased, taken and apryzed by Richard Worthington of Pemberton, yeoman, Richard Gerard of Windle in the said Countie, Locksmith, Richard Moulton of Brild in the said Countie, Shoemaker, and Thomas Lasleden of Ashton in the said Countie, yeoman, the xiijth day of March Anno regni dn̄i nr̄i Caroli dei gracia Anglia, Scotie, ffrancie et Hibernie, Regs fidei Defensor &c septimo Anno gr dn̄i, 1631

	£ s d
one Steedie or Anvyle	1-10-0
one paire of Bellowes	0- 6-5
in hammers and pinchers	0- 2-4
two Troughes & one grindleston	0- 2-0
two vysses	0- 4-0
two paire of Tongues, one Crachin, & a poker	0- 0-8
in Lockstocks	0- 2-0
one Ladder, three Spades, a fewe Bords and other implements	0- 6-0
in Chaines for horse Treasses 55li weight	0-18-4
in Dore Bandes 147li weight	1-20-5
other iron ware of severall sorte 120li weight	1- 5-0
in Iron ware of severall kynde 50li weight	0- 4-2
in Cressitts, Bakespittles & other Iron ware weighing 40li	0-11-9
in fflanders Tooles, vidht Chissells, ffyles and plaine Bitts	0-10-0
in Hang Locks & plate Locks	0-15-8
eight paire of Cards	0- 4-4
foure dozen and an halfe of hooks at 3s the dozen	0-13-6
in Bands of severall sorte & other odde Iron ware weighing 59li	1-12-8
in Chafeing dishes and frying pannes	0- 5-6
fyve Latchells	0- 3-4
sixe Scythes	0- 4-0
in hand sawes	0- 3-4
in newe Birmingham ware	0- 7-11
in ould Locks of dyvers sorts and ould keyes	0- 1-8
seaven stocke Locks	0- 5-2
more in Locks of severall sorte	0- 7-6
in Chest Locks	0- 6-4
in Saddlers ware and other things more	0- 2-0
in Gimblett Bitts & wimble Bitts, paireing knyves Shoomakers pinchers & shapeing knyves	0- 4-6
in Tinfoile & Crab locks & other things	0- 5-9
in horse locks, Can locks & horse Combes	0-12-0
in Arrowe heads & girdles	0- 5-9
in Chissells & setting sticks	0- 3-6
in Tainter hooks, one Beame knyffe and three paire of Sheares	0- 2-1
one dozen of Cupbord locks	0- 5-9
in testeing pricks, basteing ladles, Dogge Cooples and Chaines	0- 4-0
two paire of Ballance & other implemts	0- 4-0
in ould Carpenters Tooles	0- 1-6
in Birmingham Cest locks for the insyde	0- 4-0

in Birmingham Cupbord locks, dore locks & smoothing Irons - - - - - - - - - - -	0-18-0
in Steele spurres and Stirrop Irons - - - - -	0- 6-4
in lead waights - - - - - - - - - - - -	0-15-0
in Brass waights, the Ballances & Beame - - -	0- 4-0
one Chest & dyvers other ould things - - - -	0- 4-4
one Presse, two Bedstidds & one grate wth other implem^{ts} in the Chamber over the Smithie in Warrington - - - - - - - -	1- 6-8
in keyes, ffyle and unfyled wth some other things -	0- 4-0
in ffyles - - - - - - - - - - - - -	0- 3-4
one Trowell - - - - - - - - - - - -	0-00-2
in ould Chissells, Locks, and severall ould things -	0- 7-0
one Vysse - - - - - - - - - - - - -	0- 5-0
in stocks for locks being foureteene score in number	1- 0-0
in Hammers - - - - - - - - - - - -	0- 2-4
23.3^{li} pounds of Iron - - - - - - - - - -	0-16-7
more in iron 24^{li} at 2^{d} the pound - - - - - -	0- 4-0
one Tinne pan weighing 4^{li} - - - - - - -	0- 6-4
in Brasse 3^{li} - - - - - - - - - - -	0- 2-0
in Tooles, spole shaves, Chessells & other thinges -	0- 2-4
for an ould Brydle, ropes & mittons - - - - -	0- 1-6
one Cutting Axe, An Hatchett & Aginnett - - -	0- 2-0
one Hacke & a little Sawe - - - - - - - -	0- 1-4
two spades - - - - - - - - - - - -	0- 0-8
one Wheele Barrowe - - - - - - - - - -	0- 1-4
in lead 2^{li} weight - - - - - - - - - -	0- 0-2
one Vysse - - - - - - - - - - - - -	0- 4-6
in Timber - - - - - - - - - - - - -	0- 3-0
one harrowe wth bordes & other things - - - - -	0- 7-6
in Hay - - - - - - - - - - - - - -	0-10-0
in wheate - - - - - - - - - - - - -	7-10-0
one ould Cowe - - - - - - - - - - - -	2- 0-0
in Ashler stones - - - - - - - - - - -	0- 2-0
one locke, brasse keyes and other things - - -	0- 7-6
one little steele Bowe & some other odd things - -	0- 5-0
A little binding peece wth a Case for ye same - -	0- 4-6
in Moulds, Scrue plates & pinnes - - - - - -	0-13-0
one ould Culiner & a Sword & a Dagger - - -	0- 4-0
in Spitts & Iron ware aboute the fyre - - - - -	0- 5-6
one paire of Bellowes - - - - - - - - -	0- 0-6
in salt pitre & an ould Chafeing dishe - - - - -	0- 0-8
in Chaires, stooles & Cushions - - - - - -	0- 3-0
two Tubbes & a washing Tressee - - - - - -	0- 3-0
in pott brasse 26^{li} weight - - - - - - -	0-10-10
in pan brasse 28^{li} - - - - - - - - - -	0-17-0
two smoothing Irons - - - - - - - - - -	0- 3-4
in Pewter - - - - - - - - - - - - -	0-14-0
two brasse Candlesticks - - - - - - - - -	0- 1-8
for Trenchers & platters - - - - - - - - -	0- 0-9
one ould Cupbord - - - - - - - - - - -	0- 3-4
one Morter & a pestell - - - - - - - - -	0- 2-6
in Stanes, pitchforks & one Bill - - - - - -	0- 3-0
one Byble wth some other fewe books - - - - -	0-20-0

two Measures - - - - - - - - - - -	0- 7-0
three Chests - - - - - - - - - - -	0-13-4
in Trine ware - - - - - - - - - - -	0- 8-2
in Sacks & poakes - - - - - - - - -	0- 2-8
more in Pewter - - - - - - - - - -	0-18-0
one Bowe and a Pistoll - - - - - - - -	0- 6-8
in Bedding of all sorts except sheets - - - - -	4- 0-0
two Bedstidds - - - - - - - - - -	0-10-0
one pewter Dish - - - - - - - - - -	0- 4-0
one featherbedd Ticke & a Boulster - - - - -	0-12-0
in linnen clothes - - - - - - - - -	1- 0-0
three Coffers & one Boxe - - - - - - -	0-10-0
the apparrell of the dead - - - - - - -	2- 0-0

More goodes belonging to the decedent at Maudsley w^th^in the said Countie as followeth:

for ould Iron - - - - - - - - - - -	0- 4-0
in Iron & worke loomes of dyvers sorts - - -	1-11-0
for an ould packett Cart, saddle, tresses & a paire of Bellowes - - - - - - - - - -	0- 7-0
for one Harrowe - - - - - - - - - -	0- 3-0
for a vysse - - - - - - - - - - -	0- 2-0
for timber in the open Chamber - - - - - -	1-12-8
for timber in the little Chamber - - - - - -	1- 4-9
for two Chests & a Boxe - - - - - - - -	0- 7-0
for a paire of Weighes - - - - - - - -	0- 3-4
for Timber & grindlestone & other things in the Chamber belowe - - - - - - -	0- 6-8
one Cupbord & a Tubbe - - - - - - - -	0-13-0
three Bedds - - - - - - - - - - -	1- 5-0
for two Chests & two Bords - - - - - - -	0-12-0
for a grate, lyme, patches & a Chaire w^th^in the house	0-11-10
for timber w^th^out the house - - - - - - -	0-12-0
for timber & two dozen of stocks for locks in the Sheeppen	1- 9-0
one plowe & a slead - - - - - - - - -	0- 2-0
for Timber in the little house - - - - - - -	1- 0-0
oweing by one Thomas Tristram a Scythsmith to the said Raphe Wiswall as hath since the death of the said Raphe beene confessed by the said Thomas Tristram - - - - - - - - - -	4- 0-0

Sum total omniu' bono' deb' Radi Wiswall defunct - - - - Lxvij li xv s ix d

Debts Claimed and demaunded by dyvers p'sons to bee due and oweing unto them by the said Raphe Wiswall as followeth:

	£ s d
by Thomas Eccleston of Maudley, yeoman - - -	20- 0-0
by Elizabeth Porter of Bispham, Widdowe - - -	10- 0-0
by William Burscowe of Leigh, Husbandman - -	12- 6-0
by Humphrey Peetterson of Wooln'hampton, loryman	1- 7-6
awarded by the meadiacon of mr Mort & mr fflood to bee paid to **John Wiswall** sonne of the said Raphe Wiswall deceased - - - - - - - - - -	5- 0-0
by George Barrowes of Newton - - - - - -	0- 0-9
by Thomas Wiswall ~~another sonne~~ brother of the said Raphe -	1- 2-0

by Anne ~~Worthington~~ Wiswall naturall sister of the said ~~John and Thomas~~ Raph Wiswall - - - - 0-15-0

by Isabell Richardson of Warrington - - - - 3- 0-0

by George Morris of Ashton, Bandsmith - - - 0- 4-6

by Mathew Turton of Ashton, Dawber - - - - 0- 0-6

by Thomas Massie of Warrington, Clothier - - 0- 7-6

Sum total debit Liiij^{li} vi^{s} ix^{d} 54- 6-9

Soe remaining clearely all the said debts last before mencõned being distcharged out of the whole goods the some of - - xiij^{li} ix^{s} 0

Children, baptized at Warrington:

JOHN, son of Ralph, bapt. 20 Sept. 1601; he & his brother Thomas went to N.E.; he d 16 Aug. 1687

2 THOMAS, son of Ralph, bapt. 20 Sept. 1601; he d 6 Dec. 1683 per record ae 80 which must be off by 2 years if the same person; 10 ch.

CHURCH OF SAINT MARY & ALL SAINTS
WHALLEY, LANCASHIRE

Ref.: Lancashire Parish Registers as published; Lancashire Probate Files at Preston; Lancashire Inquisitions, published by Record Society

2

FRANCIS WYMAN (*Thomas, Thomas, Thomas*) was born about 1595, supposedly in Barkway, Hertfordshire, possibly in a nearby parish. He was the son of Thomas and Joan (Chrishall) Wyman (or Wymant) of Barkway.

On 2 May 1617, Francis Wyman married Elizabeth Richardson of West Mill, Hertfordshire. West Mill is about 5 miles south of Barkway. She was the daughter of Thomas and Katherine (Duxford) Richardson and was baptized at West Mill 13 June 1593. She was buried 22 June 1630 at West Mill. Apparently, Francis Wyman remained a widower for the next eleven years, raising his three sons. Then, with his eldest son aged 23 and the two younger sons, Francis and John off to New England, he remarried on 29 June 1641 at Welwyn, which is 10 miles southwest of West Mill, Elizabeth Cable. Fifteen years later, on 12 July 1656, "the wife of Francis Wyman of West Mill Green was buried." Apparently he remarried shortly thereafter, for his will indicates that he left a widow named Jane. Francis Wyman was buried at West Mill on 19 September 1658. An abstract of his follows.

The Tithing Book of West Mill records:

> 1617. Francis Wyman of Reyners Croft paith tiths
> 1618. Francis Wyman at Brook End paid tiths.

Many more such entries follow. Brook End is about one mile west of the West Mill church and West Mill Green is about one half mile to the west of Brook End. Braughing, where son Thomas found a wife, is about two miles southeast of West Mill.

The Wymans were probably of the same family as the Wymonds, Wymants, etc.

Saint Mary's Church in West Mill where Francis Wyman was first married and in which churchyard he was buried, was built in the 13th century.

15 September 1658 - The will of Francis Wyman of the parish of Westmill in the county of Hertford, husbandman ... I do give and bequeath unto Jane my wife the full sum of ten shillings of lawful English money to be paid unto her by mine executor presently after my burial. Item, I do give and bequeath unto my two sons Francis Wyman and John Wyman w[ch] are beyond sea ten pounds apiece of lawful English money to be paid unto them by mine executor if they be in want and come over to demand the same. I do give and bequeath unto my sister Susan Huit, widow, the full sum of forty shillings of lawful English money to be likewise paid to her by mine executor within one whole year next coming after my decease. Item, I do give and bequeath unto Thomas Wyman my son all that my messuage or tenement wherein I now dwell with all the other buildings, housen and outhousing thereunto belonging, and all my lands, orchard, garden and yards, with all and singular their appurtenances whatsoever, to him and his heirs forever. All the rest of my goods &c. to my said son Thomas, whom I appoint executor. Proved 14 February 1658/9.

((Reference: Pell - 116)

Children, all baptized at the West Mill church:

THOMAS, bapt. 5 April 1618; m 5 or 6 March 1653 at Braughing, Ann Godfrey; had Thomas b & d 1654, Thomas bapt. 1655, Francis bapt. 1660, Henry bapt. 1667/8, William bapt. 1670; he was buried 31 March 1677, testate (Essex 24MW8)

FRANCIS, bapt. 24 Feb. 1619/20; emigrated to N.E. 1640; tanner, farmer; m 1, 30 Dec. 1644, Judith Pierce of Woburn; no ch.; m 2, 2 Oct. 1650, Abigail, dau. of William & Mabel Reed of Woburn; 12 ch.; he d 28 Nov. 1699 "aged about 82" - g.s.; his house built about 1666 on outskirts of Woburn, now part of Burlington, still stands; he left a will

JOHN, bapt. 3 Feb. 1621/2; emigrated to N.E.; m 5 Nov. 1644, Sarah Nutt, dau. of Miles & Sarah (Branson) Nutt; he d 9 May 1684; 10 ch.; she m 2, 25 Aug. 1684, Thomas Fuller; she d 24 May 1688

RICHARD, bapt. 14 March 1623/4; buried 27 March 1645 at Braughing

ELIZABETH, bapt. 26 March 1626; m 23 May 1659, William Wall

WILLIAM, bapt. 31 Aug. 1628; buried 18 July 1630

GEORGE, perhaps, whose will dated 1693 at Braughing (Essex 37MR8)

Ref.: The Wymans, by Horace Wyman, 1897; Parish Registers; V.R.; Savage; N.E.H.G.S. - 3:38, 50:45; Essex County, England, Wills; Prerogative Court of Canterbury Wills; History of Woburn

4

THOMAS WYMANT (*Thomas, Thomas*) was born about 1565-70, probably at Barkway, Hertfordshire. There on 8 November 1593, he married Joan Cressal, i.e. Chrishall. Her surname is derived from the parish of Chrishall in Essex just five miles to the northeast of Barkway. He may be the Thomas Wymant, widower, who married 13 March 1632 at Saint Albans, Jane Thorington (or Thornton), a widow of Saint Peter's parish. He left no will.

Thomas was probably the son of an earlier Thomas Wymant of Barkway who married there 17 September 1562, Ellen Brand. This senior Thomas and Ellen (Brand) Wymant were parents of a son William who had a daughter, Ann, baptized in 1599. The senior Thomas was in turn probably the son of a still earlier Thomas Wymant, born about 1515, and probably the father of Henry, baptized 4 March 1542/3 at Barkway, of Richard who had a daughter, Katherine, of Ciceley who married 30 November 1559 Robert Gue of Ardeley, and of Thomas as deduced. Thus, there were apparently three generations of Thomases.

Children, probable:

2 FRANCIS, b perhaps 1592, perhaps bapt. elsewhere than Barkway; m 2 May 1617 at West Mill, Hert., Elizabeth Richardson, dau. of Thomas & Katherine (Duxford) Richardson; 6 ch.; she was bapt. 13 Jan. 1593/4, buried 22 June 1630 at West Mill; he m 2, m 3; he was buried 19 Sept. 1658

EDWARD, bapt. 15 July 1600; m 23 July 1620 at Barkway, Alice Pertour; ch.: Francis, Martha bapt. 1626 - d 1646, Edward bapt. 1628, John bapt. 1633, Robert bapt. 1646

ELIZABETH, bapt. 24 Sept. 1602

SUSAN, bapt. 8 Feb. 1606/ ; m _____ Huitt (Hewett); named in will of Francis as sister & a widow

Ref.: Parish Registers; Probate Records

THE CHURCH OF SAINT MARY MAGDALENE
BARKWAY, HERTFORDSHIRE

6

THOMAS RICHARDSON was born about 1565-70. On 24 August 1590 at West Mill, Hertfordshire, he married Katherine Duxford of that parish. The marriage record states that he was of Standon, which is the next parish to the south. She was the daughter of Richard and Joan Duxford, and was born about 1565-70. They settled down in West Mill.

Katherine was buried 10 March 1630/31 at West Mill. Thomas was buried there 7 January 1633/4. An abstract of his will follows.

> 4 March 1630/31 - the will of Thomas Richardson of Westmill in the County of Herts, husbandman, being sick in bodye but of good an perfect memory..to Katherine my wife during the term of her natural life my little close of pasture called Little Hunnymeade containing half an acre, and after her decease to my son Samuel....to son John 40s. within 3 years after decease of me and Katherine my wife... to son James 12d... to son Thomas £ 3 to be paid within 5 years after decease of me and Kathyrine my now wife... to Katherine my wife all my movable goods for her life, then to son Samuel whom I do ordain my sole executor. Witnesses: Richard Baker, Philip Baker. Signed by mark. Proved 31 July 1634 at Hitchin by son Samuel Richardson. (Reference: Archdeaconry of Huntingdon Probate Registry)

Children, baptized at West Mill:

3 ELIZABETH, bapt. 13 Jan. 1593/4; m 2 May 1617 at West Mill, Francis Wyman; 6 ch. bapt. at West Mill; she was buried 22 June 1630; he m 2, 29 June 1641 at Welwyn, Elizabeth Cable; m 3, Jane _____ ; he was buried 19 Sept. 1658 at West Mill

JOHN, bapt. 7 Nov. 1596; living in 1630; perhaps he was the John Richardson in Watertown in 1630

JAMES, bapt. 6 April 1600; m Agnes _____ who d 1 Feb. 1632/3; ch.: James bapt. 15 Sept. 1629, Ann bapt. 1 Feb. 1632/3 - d 25 March 1632/3; res. Aspenden

SAMUEL, bapt. 22 Dec. 1604; m 18 Oct. 1632 at Great Hormead, Joane Thake, dau. of William & Joan (Wood) Thake of Barkway. She was bapt. 2 Feb. 1606/7; ch.: Samuel bapt. 26 Jan. 1633/4, Elizabeth bapt. 22 Nov. 1635. His name does not appear in the tythe book of West Mill after 1635. Against Over Green where he and his father lived, is written "none". After that date, he and his brother Thomas sailed for N.E., and on 1 July 1636 they were on a committee to lay out lots in Charlestown for hay. 8 more ch.b in Mass. He & his 2 brothers Ezekiel & Thomas founded the town of Woburn. He d 23 March 1657/8, intestate. Joan's will dated 20 June 1666 names her daus. Mary Mousall & Elizabeth, etc. **(See THAKE Lineage)**

EZEKIEL, bapt. 24 Sept. 1606; he was a planter in Charlestown in 1630. His departure previous to his father's will, perhaps against his father's wishes, may account for his not being named in the will. He prob. came with the Winthrop Fleet. He & his wife Susanna were members of the Charlestown church 27 Aug. 1630; he d testate at Woburn 21 Oct. 1647; brothers Samuel & Thomas named in his will; ch.: Theophilus b 1633, Phebe b 1632, Josiah b 1635, John b 1638 - d.y., Jonathan b 1640 - d.y., James b 1641, Ruth b 1643 - d in infancy. His will:

20 July 1647 - the willof EZEKIEL RICHARDSON - of Woburn ... wife Susanna & eldest son Theophilus to be executors ... to son Josiah £30 at age 21 ... to son James £30 ... to dau. Phebe £30. I discharge whatsoever demands have been between brother Samuel Richardson and myself ... to brother Thomas Richardson's son Thomas 10s. Overseers to be Edward Converse and John Mousell of Woburn ... 30s. apiece to them ... residue to executors, provided wife may peaceably enjoy her habitation in the house. Witnesses: Thomas Carter, scribe, Edward Converse, John Mousall. Proved 1 June 1648

MARGARET, bapt. 19 April 1607; prob. d.y.

THOMAS, bapt. 3 July 1608. His wife Mary joined Charlestown church 21 Feb. 1635/6, he joined 18 Feb. 1637/8; moved to Woburn; ch.: Mary b 1638, Sarah b 1640, Isaac b 1643, Thomas b 1645, Ruth b 1647, Phebe b 1649, Nathaniel b 1651. He d 28 Aug. 1651; she m 2, 26 Oct. 1655, Michael Bacon, sr.; she d 19 May 1670

CHURCH OF SAINT MARY THE VIRGIN,
WEST MILL, HERTFORDSHIRE

Ref.: N.E.H.G.S. - 57, 297-300; Ancestry of Sarah Hildreth, by Walter G. Davis; Parish Registers

14

RICHARD DUXFORD (*John*) seems to have been the first of the name to settle in Westmill, Hertfordshire. The name comes from Duxford in Cambridgeshire, which is 6 miles west of Linton and 16 miles NNE of Westmill. What little is known of him comes from his will and the parish register. His wife was Joan, and she was buried 24 September 1616. Richard was buried 23 April 1622, both in Westmill.

Since the earliest baptisms in the parish register of Westmill start in 1580, there is no certainty that his children were born there. Possibly they were baptized in another parish. An abstract of his will and his inventory follow.

23 March 1618 - the will of RICHARD DUXFORD of Westmill, Hertfordshire, husbandman... weak in body... to daughter Joan Darde my tenement with appurtenances and one half acre of ground whereon it standeth, namely the house wherein Francis Wyman now dwelleth.... to Agnes Duxford, Joan Duxford, William Duxford, Clement Duxford, Richard Duxford and Elizabeth Duxford my son William Duxford's children, to each of them 6s. 8d., the eldest within one year, the next eldest the nest year, the third eldest the third year, the three youngest at age 21, to be paid by my daughter Joan Darde out of the tenement.... to Katherine Richardson my daughter one messuage or tenement called Barwicke wherein she now dwelleth... to Agnes, Joan, William, Clement, Richard & Elizabeth Duxford my son William's children, to each of them 6s. 8d. to be paid by my daughter Katherine in same way as payments by daughter Joan.... to Elizabeth Wynan the wife of Francis Wyman one chamber at the east end of the tenement wherein I now lie if she fortune to be a widow, for as long as she remain a widow.... to Katherine Richardson my daughter one feather bed and bolster... rest of my movable goods unbequeathed to my daughters Joan Darde and Katherine Richardson, they to be executors. Signed by mark. Proved 2 July 1622 by the daughters. (Reference: 32HW34)

The Inventory of the goods and chattels of Richard Duxford late of Westmill in the county of Hertford, husbandman, deceased; praised by William Browne, Richard Baker, Robert Coningesbye and John Nuttinge the 27th day of April Anno dom. 1622.

one ould Cubbard, fower old Chests	6s.
one olde bedsted, one olde stole, three shelves wth other trash	4s.
three payer of old sheets wth other small lynan	.10s.
one olde feather bede, one boulsters, two olde pillowes	6s.8d.
one Coverlett, three blankets	.10s.
brass, Irore worke and peaulter	10s.2d.
two old tubes and other old wodden vessell . .	3s.4d.
one Cowe	46s.8d.
his apparell	6s.8d.
Some is	£5.3s.6d.

William Browne Richard Baker
Robt Coningesbye John (N) Nuttinge

Children:

NICHOLAS, perhaps, a laborer of Standon, who was convicted of horse stealing, sentenced to be hung. On 28 Nov. 1583 he broke into the close of Matthew Edwardes at Standon and stole a horse valued at 40s. On 28 Feb. 1583/4 he was transferred from the custody of the sheriffs of London to the Sheriff of Hertfordshire to stand trial at Hertford Assizes. His ultimate fate, after being found guilty, is not known, but he was prob. executed, as no more is heard of him

JOAN, b prob. 1560-65; m 20 Oct. 1583 at Westmill, John Darde of Munden; he prob. had a brother, William, who m Margery Hammond at Westmill in 1586

7 KATHERINE, b prob. 1565-70; m 25 Aug. 1590 at Westmill, Thomas Richardson; 7 ch.; she was buried 10 March 1631/2, he on 8 Jan. 1633/4

WILLIAM, b prob. 1565-74; m 9 June 1595 at Westmill, Alice Heminge; she prob. had a brother, Nicholas, who had ch. bapt. at Westmill & a sister, Margaret, who m there 1595 John Sell; 6 ch.: John bapt. 18 Jan. 1595/6, Agnes bapt. 25 June 1598, Richard, Joan, Clemence, Elizabeth. He was buried 12 Aug. 1612, Alice 4 April 1619. They lived at Brook End. Inv. of his estate was £10.9.10

1 April 1619 - the will of Alice Duxford of Westmill, county of Hertford, diocese of Lincoln, widow... weak of body ... to Richard Duxford my son one half acre of free land after my mother's decease, lying in a field called Whites field in a corner of the field called Danacres in the parish of Much Munden... to Agnes Duxford------ two pillowberes, to Joan Duxford my daughter one f[eatherbed?] ---------to Clement Duxford my daughter one flaxen ------------- to Elizabeth Duxford my daughter one flaxen tablecloth, one kettle ----- pewter platter & one hutch. All the rest of my goods unbequeathed ------to John Duxford* my son. Signed by mark. Witnessed by Robert Coningesbye, William Hammond and William Brown. Proved 20 April 1619 (--- = missing parts)

*His will 1636/7 (Reference: 32HW22)

Ref.: Parish Registers; Probate Records at Hertford and at Lincoln

28

JOHN DUXFORD of Ashwell, Hertfordshire, was probably born about 1510. His name, Duxford or Duxforth, derives from the village of Duxford in Cambridgeshire, which is 15 miles NEE of Ashwell. John Duxford was listed on the 1545 Subsidy (tax) Roll at Clothall, a parish 4½ miles south of Ashwell. Since neither a Parish Register nor Bishop's Transcipts for Ashwell before 1604 have survived, John's will is the only source of information on his family so far discovered. The tenor of his will suggests that his children were in their late teens or twenties. For some reason, he was concerned that his wife might need outside help in settling his estate.

That his son Richard was the same Richard who later appeared in Westmill seems fairly certain. The name Duxford was not common and the chronology fits. Westmill is a mere 10 miles to the southeast of Ashwell. An abstract of his will follows.

> 12 February 1557/8 - the will of JOHN DUXFORTH of Ashwell, county Hertford ... sick in body ... to be buried in the churchyard of Ashwell ... to goddaughter, James's wife, a swarm of bees ... to Dorothy my daughter a feather bed, bolster, cupbord, coverlet, 3 pairs of sheets, a table form, brass pot, kettle and 6 quarters of malt ... Richard my son to have 6 quarters of malt, 3 of them being his own ... James my son to have 5 marks for 3 years and then he to give it to his brother John, and he to receive it at the feast of All Saints next of John Brown ... Agnes my wife to have residue, she to be executrix. Sir William Wilson, curate of Ashwell, to be supervisor, desiring him to be so good to go to the ordinary with my wife to see this probated. If any man do stop, let or hinder her right, I will she complain to Mr. Byll whom I trust well will not suffer her to be oppressed. Witnesses: Sir William Wilson, curate, John Johnson, James Duxforth. Proved 26 April 1559 at Baldoke. Summary of Inventory .£7.8.1.
>
> (Ref.: Huntingdon Wills 7:221)

Children, probably all born at Ashwell:

JAMES, perhaps eldest; he was married by 1557/8, his wife being goddaughter to James's father.

DOROTHY,

14 RICHARD, prob. b 1535-40; settled in Westmill; m Joan ____; 3 known ch. who reached adulthood; Joan was buried 24 Sept. 1616; he was buried 23 April 1622, testate.

JOHN, surely the youngest of the three boys.

Ref.: Hertfordshire Wills at Huntingdon

CHURCH OF SAINT MARY THE VIRGIN,
WEST MILL, HERTFORDSHIRE

circa 1830

INDEX OF SURNAMES

CORRECTIONS AND ADDITIONAL NOTES

Re Lieut. John Andrews covered on pages 1-8, he may have been the John Andrews baptized 22 October 1620 at Woodton, Norfolk, son of William and Elizabeth (Sheldrake) Andrews. The parish registers tell the following re this family:

WILLIAM ANDREWS of Woodton, Norfolk, was born perhaps 1588-90, perhaps the son of Robert or Walter Andrews. William Andrews married 9 October 1617 at Beckingham, Elizabeth Sheldrake. He was buried 26 February 1623/4 at Woodton. There is no further record of the family in or near Woodton. She probably remarried a year or so after William's death, but there are several years of marriage records missing from 1624 on. All this suggests that she, with a second husband, and the children went to New England. Lieutenant John was too young to have likely gone alone.

Children:

WILLIAM, bapt. 10 Jan. 1618/19, "son of William & Elizabeth"
JOHN, bapt. 22 Oct. 1620, "son of William & Elizabeth"
RICHARD, bapt. 23 March 1622/3, "son of William & Elizabeth"
PRUDENCE, bapt. 20 June 1624, "dau. of William & Elizabeth; " She was probably a posthumous child, tho there was no mention in the baptismal record of her father being dead.

NOTE: The above is only a possibility. Readers should NOT take this as proven fact. There is reason to believe that Lieut. John came from Norfolk.

Herewith is a photo of the gravestone of Thomas Andrews, third son of Lieutenant John Andrews. It is located in the old cemetery at Essex, Mass. next to William's. The right node is broken off but the illustration has been reconstructed to the original appearance.

Page 43-44 — James Bigge's wife, Anne, may have been a sister of George and William Saxbie who were named as uncles in the will of John Scotchford. John Scotchford was referred to as "my brother Scotchford" in the will of John Bigge who died in 1605 (page 39). This John Scotchford may have been a half brother to John.

Page 59, re Bigge family. In an Inquisition Ad Quod Damnum of 33 Edward I (1305), File LIV:14, there is reference to Eylgar Bygge and Edith his wife re lands in Cranbrook and other parishes in Kent. He was probably an ancestor of Roger and all the other Bigges of that area.